Logic Programming

Logic Programming

Ehud Shapiro, editor

Koichi Furukawa, Fernando Pereira, and David H. D. Warren,
associate editors

The Art of Prolog: Advanced Programming Techniques, Leon
Sterling and Ehud Shapiro, 1986

*Logic Programming: Proceedings of the Fourth International
Conference,* edited by Jean-Louis Lassez, 1987 (Volumes 1 and 2)

Concurrent Prolog: Collected Papers, edited by Ehud Shapiro, 1987
(Volumes 1 and 2)

*Logic Programming: Proceedings of the Fifth International
Conference and Symposium,* edited by Robert A. Kowalski and
Kenneth A. Bowen, 1988 (Volumes 1 and 2)

Constraint Satisfaction in Logic Programming, Pascal Van
Hentenryck, 1989

Logic-Based Knowledge Representation, edited by Peter Jackson,
Hans Reichgelt, and Frank van Harmelen, 1989

Logic Programming: Proceedings of the Sixth International Conference, edited by Giorgio
Levi and Maurizio Martelli, 1989

Logic Programming

Proceedings of the Sixth International Conference

edited by
Giorgio Levi and Maurizio Martelli

The MIT Press
Cambridge, Massachusetts
London, England

This book was printed and bound in the United States of America

Library of Congress Cataloging-in-Publication Data

Logic Programming

    (MIT Press series in logic programming)
    "Papers presented at the Sixth International
Conference on Logic Programming, held in Lisbon,
Portugal, June 19-23, 1989"—CIP forword.
    1. Logic programming—Congresses. I. Levi, G.
(Giorgio), 1942–   II. Martelli, Maurizio. III. In-
ternational Conference on Logic Programming (6th : 1989 :
Lisbon, Portugal) IV. Title. V. Series.
QA76.63L64   1989   006.3   89-8295
ISBN 0-262-62065-0

Contents

Programme Committee

G. Levi	Univ. of Pisa, Pisa, Italy (Chairman)
K. R. Apt	CWI, Amsterdam, The Netherlands, and Univ. of Texas at Austin, Austin, TX, USA
M. Bruynooghe	Katholieke Universiteit Leuven, Heverlee, Belgium
T. Chikayama	ICOT,Tokyo, Japan
W.F. Clocksin	Univ. of Cambridge, Cambridge, UK
J. Conery	Univ.of Oregon, Eugene, OR, USA
M. Dincbas	ECRC, Munich, F.R. Germany
M.R. Genesereth	Stanford Univ., Palo Alto, CA, USA
M. Hermenegildo	MCC, Austin, TX, USA
C.J. Hogger	Imperial College, London ,UK
F. Kluzniak	Warszawa University, Warszawa, Poland
E.L. Lusk	Argonne National Laboratory, Argonne, IL, USA
M.J. Maher	IBM-T.J. Watson Research Center, NY, USA
J. Maluszynski	Univ.of Linköping, Linköping, Sweden, and Univ. of Utah, Salt Lake City, UT, USA
M. Martelli	CNUCE, Pisa, Italy
Y. Matsumoto	Kyoto Univ., Kyoto, Japan
F. G. McCabe	Imperial College, London, England
D. Miller	Univ. of Pennsylvania, Philadelphia, PA, USA
J. Minker	Univ. of Maryland, College Park, MD, USA
G. Mints	Estonian Academy of Science, Tallinn, USSR
L. Naish	Melbourne Univ., Melbourne, Australia
R. Overbeek	Argonne National Laboratory, Argonne, IL, USA
L. M. Pereira	Univ. Nova de Lisboa, Lisboa, Portugal
A. Porto	Univ. Nova de Lisboa, Lisboa, Portugal
T. C. Przymusinski	Univ. of Texas at El Paso, El Paso, TX, USA
Y. Sagiv	Hebrew University, Jerusalem, Israel
E. Y. Shapiro	Weizmann Institute of Science, Rehovot, Israel
O. Shmueli	Israel Institute of Technology, Haifa, Israel
C. Zaniolo	MCC, Austin, TX, USA

Foreword

This volume contains the papers presented at the Sixth International Conference on Logic Programming, held in Lisbon, Portugal, June 19-23, 1989. The previous meetings of the Conference were in Marseille (1982), Uppsala (1984), London (1986), Melbourne (1987), and Seattle (1988).

We received 150 submitted papers from countries all over the world. The Programme Committee met in Pisa, Italy, from February 24 to February 25. Most of the people in the Committee also attended an informal Logic Programming workshop on February 27, which was organized by GULP (the Italian Logic Programming Association).

Most of the submitted papers were of high quality and merit. A significant number of good quality papers could not be included in the program, as we could accommodate only 39 papers. In addition to the contributed papers, five speakers accepted our invitation to give a presentation: Jean-Louis Lassez (banquet speaker), Gilles Kahn, Paris Kanellakis, Jan-Willem Klop, and Teodor C. Przymusinski.

On behalf of the Programme Committee we would like to thank all the referees who contributed to the development of the program. Finally, but most importantly, we want to express our thanks to all those individuals who helped us organize the Conference.

Giorgio Levi and Maurizio Martelli, Pisa, Italy, March 1989.

Referees

Abramson H., Abreu S.P., Aggoun A., Alegria J.A.S., Ali K.A.M., Alkulaj L., Almgren J., Aparício J.A.M.N., Apt K.R., Azadegan S., Bacha H., Balsamo S., Barahona P., Barbuti R., Bellia M., Bezem M., Blair H., Bowen K.A., Brand P., Brazdil P., Brown M.A., Bruynooghe M., Bundy A., Butler R.M., Calejo M., Callebout A., Camarinha De Matos L., Carlsson M., Cavedon L., Chassin De Kergommeaux J., Chen W., Chikayama T., Chomicki J., Chu D., Ciepielewski A., Clark K.L., Clocksin W.F., Codish M., Comon H., Conery J., Cousineau G., Crammond J., Cunha J.C., Daels J., David G., Davison A., Debray S., Demoen B., De Schreye D., De Vries F.J., Dincbas M., Dorochevsky M., Drabent W., Elshiewy N.A., Feldman Y., Ferrari G., Ferreira C., Fiadeiro J.L., Filè G., Filgueiras M., Foster I., Francez N., Franzen T., Freeston M., Fujita H., Gaasterland T., Gallagher J., Genesereth M.R., Gerth R., Greene K.J., Gregory S., Gupta A., Haridi S., Hasegawa R., Hasida K., Hausman B., Hawley D., Hermenegildo M., Herold A., Hill P., Hogger C.J., Hughes K., Huntbach M., Ichiyoshi N., Janssens G., Jaffar J., Kahn K., Kale L., Karlsson R., Kesselman C., Kesten Y., Kimura Y., Kiyono M., Kleinmann A., Kliger S., Klop J.W., Kluzniak F., Kondo S., Kraus S., Kumar V., Kunen K., Kurokawa T., Lafont Y., Lam M., Lassez C., Lee A., Legatheaux Martins J., Legeard B., Levi G., Lin Y.J., Lin Y., Lindstrom G., Litcher A.M., Lloyd J.W., Lobo J., Longo G., Lopes G., Lusk E.L., Maher M.J., Maluszynski J., Mamede M., Mancarella P., Marriott K., Martelli M., Martini S., Matsuda H., Matsumoto Y., McCabe F.G., Meier M., Meyer D., Miller D., Mills J., Minker J., Mints G., Monteiro L., Mulkers A., Muthvkumar K., Naganuma J., Naish L., Nakajima K., Nakashima H., Nakazawa O., Nasr R., Nilsson M., Okumura A., Onai R., Overbeek R., Palamidessi C., Pedreschi D., Pereira F., Pereira L.M., Port G., Porto A., Przymusinski T.C., Rajasekar A., Ramkumar B., Reddy U., Ribeiro M.C., Rossi F., Sagiv Y., Sahlin D., Saint-Dizier P., Saraswat V., Sardu G., Sato H., Schultz J.W., Sernadas A., Shapiro E.Y., Shen K., Shimada Y., Shirai H., Shmueli O., Simonis H., Singh V., Sjöland T., Søndergaard H., Sterling L., Stevens R., Stuckey P., Subrahmanian V.S., Sugano H., Sugimura R., Szeredi P., Takahashi K., Takeuchi A.,Tamaki H., Tanaka H., Topor R.W., Trindade L., Turini F., Uehara K., Van Hentenryck P., Vieille L., Wada K., Wallace M., Warren D.H.D., Warren D.S., Weemeeuw P., Wolfson O., Xu J., Yang R., Yap R., Yardeni E., Yokota K., Yoshida K., Zachary J., Zaniolo C.

Abstract Interpretation and Implementation Issues

On the Efficiency of Optimising Shallow Backtracking in Compiled Prolog

Mats Carlsson

SICS, Swedish Institute of Computer Science
PO Box 1263
S-164 28 Kista, Sweden

Phone: +46—8—7521543
Net mail: matsc@sics.se

Abstract

The cost of backtracking has been identified as one of the bottlenecks in achieving peak performance in compiled Prolog programs. Much of the backtracking in Prolog programs is shallow, i.e. is caused by unification failures in the head of a clause when there are more alternatives for the same procedure, and so special treatment of this form of backtracking has been proposed as a significant optimisation. This paper describes a modified WAM which optimises shallow backtracking. Four different implementation approaches are compared. A number of benchmark results are presented, measuring the relative tradeoffs between compilation time, code size, and run time. The results show that the speedup gained by this optimisation can be significant.

1 Introduction

The distinction between two types of backtracking, a simple one which is amenable to optimisation, and a general one, was introduced in [8]. The simple type was called *shallow backtracking* and occurs when a head unification fails with more alternatives for the same procedure to try. The general case was called *deep backtracking*; it occurs when there are no more clauses of the current procedure to try when a head unification fails. If the machine state changes between a procedure call and a shallow failure can be minimised, then shallow backtracking can be implemented much more efficiently than deep backtracking.

We feel that there are many justifications to exploit an optimised mechanism for shallow backtracking in Prolog implementations. Firstly, the implementation of *if-then-else* where the *if* part consists of simple tests becomes more efficient, without complicating the compiler by introducing conditional jumps and the like, as in

```
Head :-
        ...
        (X<Y -> p(X, Y); q(X, Y)),
        ...
```

Secondly, in or-parallel Prolog implementations like Aurora [10], the relative cost of deep backtracking is higher than in sequential implementations. We expect that optimising shallow backtracking in Aurora will have a significant effect on performance. Finally, Tick showed [6] that shallow backtracking is the predominant form of nondeterministic Prolog execution.

The distinction between the two kinds of backtracking was built into PLM, the Prolog engine of Prolog-10. However, no such distinction is made in the later WAM, or "New Engine", for Prolog [9]. We assume herein that the reader is familiar with the WAM. To avoid ambiguities, we describe our WAM terminology in Section 2.

Proposals for incorporating shallow backtracking into the WAM have appeared in the literature, first in [6], for a detailed description see [3]. The key idea is that the *try* and *try_me_else* instructions only save a small part of the machine state, postponing completion of the choicepoint until a *neck* instruction is reached. This new instruction is inserted into the compiled code for each clause and is responsible for completing or updating a choicepoint where appropriate. It is placed at the earliest possible point in a clause where it can be determined that the head unification and any simple tests have succeeded. Consider, for example, the recursive clause of *append/3*:

```
append([X|L1], L2, [X|L3]) :-
        append(L1, L2, L3).
```

<u>standard WAM code</u>   <u>WAM code with neck instruction</u>

```
get_list A1                      get_list A1
unify_variable A4                unify_variable A4
unify_variable A1                unify_variable A5
get_list A3                      get_list A3
unify_value A4                   unify_value A4
unify_variable A3                neck
execute append/3                 unify_variable A3
                                 put_value A5,A1
                                 execute append/3
```

Thus before the *neck* instruction is reached, the arguments for the body goal cannot be set up. As this example shows, inserting the *neck* instruction impacted the register allocation so that an extra *put_value* instruction was needed. Thus the proposed method may incur a performance overhead which may outweigh a faster backtracking mechanism. This fact motivated Van Roy et.al. [7] to introduce multiple entrypoints into compiled clauses. In their scheme, a compiled clause *C* can have four entrypoints depending on

(i)   whether or not there are alternative clauses for *C*;
(ii)   whether or not a previous clause has created a choicepoint for this procedure.

The four entrypoints correspond to different compiled versions of the head of *C*, specialised for the combinations of conditions (i–ii). These code streams then merge into a single compiled version of the body of *C*. Obviously, if condition (i) is true, unification failure triggers shallow backtracking, otherwise it triggers deep backtracking. Multiple entrypoints have obvious drawbacks: increased code size and compilation time.

With the *neck* instruction, the cost of creating choicepoints is slightly higher than in the standard WAM due to the negative effects on register allocation and to the extra instruction decode. However, we observe that creating and restoring choicepoints are rather expensive operations anyway.

This report tries to compare the relative merits of four different approaches to implementing backtracking (DB, SB1, SB2, and SB3) with respect to compilation time, code size, and run time. The unit of compilation is a clause in all approaches:

DB.   This approach does not optimise shallow backtracking at all.
SB1.   This approach inserts a *neck* instruction into each clause. There is one code stream per clause.
SB2.   This approach generates two code streams for each clause: one with a *neck* instruction, used when there are alternatives for the current goal, and one without a *neck* instruction, used for determinate goals and for the last alternative in a list.
SB3.   This approach is a hybrid between SB1 and SB2: Approach SB1 is taken when the body is empty or consists of simple tests only; approach SB2 is taken for other clauses.

In the above approaches, the register allocation is only impaired in code streams containing *neck*. For approaches SB2 and SB3 it is arranged at compile time so that the indexing code refers to the correct code stream, to avoid a runtime decision.

2   WAM Terminology

The implementation strategies described above have all been implemented as modifications SICStus Prolog [2], a compiler-based system with a WAM emulator written in C. Strategy SB3 is the one normally used in SICStus Prolog. Its abstract machine is close to the standard WAM but differs in some respects. For example, the local stack is split into an environment stack and a choicepoint stack. This modification was first proposed in [5] to improve the locality of memory references. Other changes were made as prerequisites for optimising shallowing backtracking, as described in Section 4.

We use the following abbreviations for the principal WAM registers:

P	program pointer
CP	continuation program pointer
E	current environment
B	current choicepoint
TR	top of trail
H	top of heap
A1, *A2*, ..	argument registers

A *choicepoint* is a stack frame with the following fields. Note that the "previous choicepoint" field is replaced by the "top of environment stack" field, since the local stack is split:

P(B)	alternative program pointer
CP(B)	continuation program pointer
E(B)	current environment
A(B)	top of environment stack (shadowed by the *AB* register)
TR(B)	top of trail
H(B)	top of heap (shadowed by the *HB* register)
A1(B), *A2(B)*, ..	argument registers

An *environment* is a stack frame with the following fields:

CE(E)	continuation environment
CP(E)	contnuation program pointer
Y1(E), *Y2(E)*, ..	permanent variables

3. Shallow backtracking in the WAM

In this section we describe the changes in the compiler and abstract machine necessary for optimising shallow backtracking. The compiler is a pure clause compiler, i.e. it translates one Prolog clause at a time to WAM instructions. The only way in which the indexing code is affected by the changes is by the introduction of two entrypoints per clause, as described in Section 3.2.

The key idea of the optimisation is that the *try* and *try_me_else* instructions allocate space for a choicepoint but only fill in a couple of fields, postponing completion of the choicepoint until the *neck* instruction is reached. This new instruction is inserted into the compiled code for each clause and is responsible for completing or updating the choicepoint after a successful head unification with more alternatives to try.

3.1 Basic scheme

We now describe the simplest approach, SB1. To implement it, a new WAM register, *PB*, is introduced. *PB* holds a pointer to the next alternative clause for the current goal, or 0, if none exists. When head unification failure occurs, shallow backtracking is used if $PB \neq 0$, otherwise deep backtracking must be used. In the shallow case, the arguments and most control registers are guaranteed to be valid: all that needs to be done is to reset all trail entries between *TR(B)* and *TR*, and to restore the top of heap from *HB*. In the deep case, all arguments and control registers must be restored from the choicepoint.

The *try* and *try_me_else* instructions are modified to create a *partial* choicepoint. The only valid fields of a partial choicepoint are *TR(B)*, initialised to the current top of trail, and *P(B)*, initialised to zero. The WAM registers *AB*, *HB*, and *PB* are initialised to respectively the current top of environment stack, the current top of heap, and the alternative clause. The *retry* and *retry_me_else* instructions are modified to update *PB* rather than *P(B)*. The *trust* and *trust_me_else* instructions set *PB* to zero.

In the basic scheme, a *neck* instruction is inserted into all clauses. Its semantics is summarised by the following table:

PB=0	PB≠0, P(B)=0	PB≠0, P(B)≠0
noop	fill in choicepoint	set *P(B)* to *PB*
set *PB* to zero	set *PB* to zero	

Thus, the *neck* instruction does nothing if *PB* is zero. Executing a *neck* with *PB* nonzero and *P(B)* zero corresponds to the first successful head unification for the current goal with more alternatives to try. In this case, all remaining fields of the choicepoint are filled in, including *P(B)*, and *PB* is zeroed. Executing a *neck* with both *PB* and *P(B)* nonzero corresponds to a successful head unification after having backtracked to this choicepoint. *P(B)* is assigned the value of *PB*, and *PB* is zeroed. A *neck + cut* combination is recognised as a special case: the current choicepoint is flushed, *AB* and *HB* are reset to their previous values, and *PB* is zeroed.

The compiler is modified to insert a *neck* instruction before the first *cut* or body goal which the compiler cannot compile inline. The *neck* instruction is inserted into all clauses including the last clause of a procedure, as the clause compiler has no way of knowing whether yet another clause for the same procedure will appear later. The *neck* instruction affects the compiler's register allocation as the instruction copies the procedure's argument registers when it completes a partial choicepoint. As a result, the register allocation is often poorer than in the standard WAM, requiring more temporary variables and more moves. The extra moves occur if arguments for the first body goal cannot be placed in the correct argument register until after the *neck* instruction. Notice that for clauses where the body is empty or consists of simple tests only, no extra moves are ever needed, as simple tests may take their arguments in any registers.

3.2 Optimisations

The drawback of the simple approach is for deterministic cases having to execute a no-op *neck* instruction which also impairs the register allocation. This can be avoided by emitting two instruction streams per clause: one with a *neck* instruction and one without. We call this approach SB2. It is arranged at load time so that *try(_me_else)* and *retry(_me_else)* instructions use the code streams with *neck* and all other ways of entering a clause use the code streams without the *neck*. The implications for the abstract machine is that **PB** is always nonzero when the *neck* instruction is reached, and for the compiler and loader some extra complications to manage the two code streams per clause.

To conserve space, the code for the body is shared between the two streams. The instruction streams are actually laid out as a single sequence with two entrypoints, *NonDet* and *Det*, and a jump. *NonDet* is entered when there are more alternatives to try; *Det* is used for the last alternative and for determinate calls. The *NonDet* instruction stream contains a branch to the body code whereas the *Det* stream just continues into the body code, minimising overhead for deterministic cases. The general instruction stream outline is depicted below:

```
NonDet:   < head unification instructions >
          ...
          < simple tests >
          neck
          < moves >
          branch S
Det:      < head unification instructions >
          ...
          < simple tests >
          < moves >
S:        < body code >
```

The drawback of this approach is the code size overhead which is particularly serious for unit clause databases. To reduce the overhead, we introduce approach SB3 as using SB1 when there is very little to gain from duplicating code, and SB2 otherwise.

In approach SB3, we emit a single code stream, with a *neck* instruction, for clauses where the body consists of simple tests only, in particular for unit clauses. For all other clauses two code streams are emitted. This strategy is based on the observation that for clauses where there are no general body goals constraining the register allocator, no extra register transfers are ever introduced by the *neck* instruction. The main implication for the abstract machine is that the *neck* instruction again needs to check whether *PB* is zero.

4 Nonstandard WAM features

The SICS abstract machine differs in some respects, not only by optimising shallow backtracking, from the standard WAM. Some of the other changes are however crucial for the shallow backtracking mechanism:

4.1 One-level indexing
In the SICS abstract machine, clause indexing is done in one step when a compiled predicate is entered, even in situations with a mixture of clauses with variable and nonvariable first arguments. This indexing step singles out an applicable subset of clauses, and at most one choicepoint is created. Although not essential for the shallow backtracking mechanism, this modification increases its effectiveness as the number of alternatives per choicepoints increases. This technique is further discussed in [1].

4.2 Split environment pointer
Since an *allocate* instruction can occur before a *neck* instruction, it would seem that the *E* register has to be saved by *try(_me_else)* and restored when a shallow failure occurs. This is avoided in the SICS abstract machine by introducing the *E2* register which is used instead of the *E* register whenever a permanent variable is accessed. The motivation for this is both to improve shallow backtracking and to delay as long as possible filling in the control part of environments and updating *E*. In particular, *E* is never updated between the beginning of a clause and the *neck* instruction.

This modification is done by modifying the *proceed* instruction and splitting the *allocate* instruction into two parts: *preallocate*, placed before the first occurrence of a permanent variable, and *postallocate*, placed before the first *call* instruction:

```
preallocate:
      E2 = max(E+env_size(CP),A(B));

postallocate:
      CE(E2) = E;
      CP(E2) = CP;
      E = E2;

proceed:
      E2 = E;
      P = CP;
```

4.3 Preserving argument registers
With the shallow backtracking optimisation, the contents of the argument registers must not be altered prior to the *neck* instruction, as *neck* may copy these registers into a choicepoint after a number of unification steps. In the standard WAM, certain instructions (e.g. *get_value*, *unify_value*) are allowed to store the dereferenced result of the operation back into an argument register. However, this must be disallowed for shallow backtracking to work.

5 Performance evaluation

To study the effectiveness of optimising shallow backtracking, three performance aspects were studied: compilation time, code size, and execution time.

Strategy SB3 is currently implemented in SICStus Prolog. The other strategies were implemented by modifying parts of SICStus Prolog, carefully trying not to introduce any new overheads that would blur a comparison.

5.1 Benchmark programs
Four Prolog programs were studied. None of them can be considered a toy program. They were written by different people and likely represent different coding styles. The programs include two compilers which were expected to have very little nondeterminism. The other two programs were expected to contain a lot of nondeterminism. The programs were:

CHAT: an English language parser by F.C.N. Pereira and D.H.D. Warren, running a query that took 15.2 seconds. The size of CHAT is 2812 Prolog clauses.

PLM_COMPILER:
> the Berkeley Prolog compiler by Peter Van Roy, running a query that took 2.5 seconds. The program consists of 738 Prolog clauses.

PLWAM: the SICStus compiler by myself, compiling itself which took 250 seconds. The program contains 1147 Prolog clauses.

TP: a propositional theorem prover by Ross Overbeek, running a problem that took 47.7 seconds. The size of TP is 155 Prolog clauses.

In the size figures above, a disjunction $(P; Q; R)$ counts as three clauses. The timings were made using approach DB (not optimising shallow backtracking).

In order to measure the amount of potential shallow backtracking, we computed for each program the following dynamic properties:

P_f the fraction of deep failures to total failures, and

P_c the fraction of completed choicepoints to total number of *try*:s and *try_me_else*:s.

These figures for the benchmarks are summarised in the following table.

Table 1:   Available shallow nondeterminism.

	P_f	P_c	$(1/P_f)+(1/P_c)$
PLWAM:	.20	.26	8.85
CHAT:	.47	.28	5.70
TP:	.33	.27	6.70
PLM_COMPILER:	.23	.34	7.29

These figures confirm Tick's observation that shallow backtracking is the predominant form of nondeterministic Prolog execution. The $(1/P_f)+(1/P_c)$ figure indicates the availability of shallow nondeterminism in each program. The higher the figure, the better the expected runtime speedup yielded by the shallow backtracking optimisation.

5.2 Performance data

The timing and code size data are presented in three tables below. All data have been normalised with respect to strategy DB:

Table 2:   Compilation time.

	SB1	SB2	SB3
PLWAM:	.97	1.16	1.12
CHAT:	.98	1.18	1.05
TP:	.97	1.07	1.02
PLM_COMPILER:	.97	1.15	1.10

Table 3:   Code size.

	SB1	SB2	SB3
PLWAM:	1.01	1.15	1.10
CHAT:	1.01	1.20	1.05
TP:	1.01	1.09	1.05
PLM_COMPILER:	1.01	1.16	1.10

Table 4:   Execution time.

	SB1	SB2	SB3
PLWAM:	.92	.89	.90
CHAT:	.96	.93	.92
TP:	.85	.85	.85
PLM_COMPILER:	.93	.89	.90

5.3 Discussion

Several observations can be made about the performance data presented above. Firstly, there is surprisingly little variation between the four sample programs. This shows that there is a fair amount of exploitable "shallow nondeterminism" over a wide range of applications. Secondly, the results do not correlate perfectly with the dynamic properties computed in Section 5.1, but we do note that optimising shallow backtracking yielded the least speedup for CHAT, which was expected. Lastly, we found that much of the deep backtracking in TP could easily be made shallow by rearranging code, unfolding tests, etc. By applying these changes we increased the scope of the shallow backtracking optimisation, yielding a speedup factor of as much as 1.5 compared to the unchanged program under approach SB3.

The performance data is summarised in the following table of relative figures:

Table 5: Performance summary.

	DB	SB1	SB2	SB3
Compilation time:	1.0	≈.97	1.07–1.18	1.02–1.12
Code size:	1.0	≈1.01	1.09–1.20	1.05–1.10
Execution time:	1.0	.85–.96	.85–.93	.85–.92

As we can see from this table, strategies SB2 and SB3 offered the best runtime speedups (7% to 15%) for the sample programs. Strategy SB2 was not significantly faster for any of the programs, and as strategy SB3 is the more space economic of the two, it seems a sensible choice.

Strategy SB1 is attractive as it has very little compilation time and code size overhead. Although it did yield significant speedups for the sample programs, it can have a big run time overhead on examples like *append*, because register allocation is impaired in the deterministic case. In fact, strategy SB1 slowed down the well-known *naive reverse* benchmark, where *append* is the inner loop, by a factor of 1.29. This large factor is partly due to the way the SICStus compiler collapses certain WAM sequences into single byte codes: the *neck* instruction was inserted into such a sequence (see page 3), and the inner loop size grew from 4 to 7 byte codes. A native code implementation would probably not display this anomalous behaviour. In a native code implementation, strategy SB1 could be the best choice, especially since the need to keep the code size down is more urgent than in a bytecode implementation.

Meier reports only 3–4% slowdown of naive reverse.

6 Comparison with other work

Our implementation is much like Meier's. The main difference is that Meier introduces new WAM registers which are written by the *try* and *try_me_else* instructions, read when shallow backtracking occurs, and copied into a choicepoint by the *neck* instruction. No partial choicepoint is constructed. On hardware like the MC68020, however, the extra WAM registers would have to be stored in memory anyway because of shortage of machine registers. This was our motivation for building a partial choicepoint instead.

Meier's abstract machine always preserves the E register up to the first *call* instruction by maintaining the top of the environment stack in a register TE and using two sets of *unify* instructions: one for head unification which accesses permanent variables using TE, and another for the clause body which uses E. One set of *unify* instructions suffices for us.

The design of Van Roy et.al. uses up to four entrypoints per clause whereas ours uses at most two entrypoints. The scope of the shallow backtracking optimisation is somewhat restricted in their design, as head unification for "nondeterministic entries" is not allowed to bind variables.

Tateno et.al. [4] describe a design similar to ours but restricted to predicates in which all clauses but the last one have a cut before the first general body goal. Their design allows head unifications to bind variables and handles the trail specially for such bindings.

To the author's knowledge, all published speedup figures for optimised shallow backtracking have been for toy programs. We ran the same toy programs to see if the results could be reproduced. In all cases, the published figures were rather better than our results. For example, Meier uses the *memberchk* predicate as an example where shallow backtracking is extremely advantageous, and reports a 65% performance improvement. Using strategy SB3, we measured a speedup factor of 1.34 over strategy DB:

```
memberchk(X, [X|_]) :- !.
memberchk(X, [_|Xs]) :- memberchk(X, Xs).
```

Van Roy et.al. report a speedup factor of as much as 2.6 for the *min_list* predicate, listed below. Again using SB3 we measured a speedup of 1.22 over DB:

```
min_list([X], X).
min_list([X|L], M) :-
        min_list(L, Y),
        minimum(X, Y, M).

minimum(A, B, A) :- A<B, !.
minimum(A, B, B).
```

7 Conclusions

The main contribution of this paper is to present actual measurements of the effectiveness of optimising shallow backtracking in non-trivial Prolog programs, running on a highly optimised Prolog system. The measurements show that this optimisation is worthwhile over a wide range of applications, yielding a speedup of 7%–15%. We expect the optimisation to be more important for or-parallel implementations than for sequential ones. We showed that program transformation can significantly increase the scope of the optimisation.

Three approaches to this optimisation were presented, two of which involve generating two code streams for each compiled clause. We showed that if only a single code stream is generated, the overhead on deterministic programs can be intolerable if executed by a bytecode emulator. We expect that in a native code implementation, with its more urgent need to keep the code size down, the overhead on deterministic programs may be tolerable.

A great deal of extra analysis can be done in a procedure compiler, at the cost of increased compilation time, since a procedure compiler knows precisely which clauses may be used nondeterministically and which may not. Mode declarations provide further information in this respect.

Acknowledgements

The author is indebted to Carl Kesselman, Hiroshi Nakashima and the referees for their comments, which substantially improved the presentation.

This research would not have been possible without the support of my family.

References

[1] M. Carlsson, *Freeze, Indexing and Other Implementation Issues in the WAM*, Proc. Fourth International Conference on Logic Programming, pp. 40–58, Melbourne, May, 1987.

[2] M. Carlsson, J. Widén, *SICStus Prolog User's Manual*, SICS Research Report R88007B, October, 1988.

[3] M. Meier, *Shallow Backtracking in Prolog Programs*, ECRC Internal report, February, 1987.

[4] H. Tateno, H. Nakashima, S. Kondo, K. Nakajima, *Neck Cut Optimization: An Optimization technique for the Shallow Backtracking*, Internal report, Mitsubishi Electric Corporation and ICOT, 1989.

[5] E. Tick and D.H.D. Warren, *Towards a pipelined Prolog processor*, in Proc. International Symposium on Logic Programming, pp. 29–40, Atlantic City, February, 1984.

[6] E. Tick, *Studies in Prolog Architectures*, Technical Report No. CSL-TR-87-329, Stanford University, June 1987.

[7] P. Van Roy, B. Demoen, and Y.D. Willems, *Improving the execution speed of compiled Prolog with modes, clause selection, and determinacy*, Proc. TAPSOFT'87: Joint Conference on Theory and Practice of Software Development, pp. 111–125, Pisa, March 1987.

[8] D.H.D. Warren, *IMPLEMENTING PROLOG—compiling predicate logic programs*, D.A.I. Research Report 39, University of Edinburgh, May, 1977.

[9] D.H.D. Warren, *An Abstract Prolog Instruction Set* , SRI International #309, 1983.

[10] D.H.D. Warren et.al., *The Aurora Or-Parallel Prolog System*, in Proc. International Conference on Fifth Generation Computer Systems, Tokyo, 1988.

A Simple Code Improvement Scheme for Prolog

Saumya K. Debray

Department of Computer Science
The University of Arizona
Tucson, AZ 85721, USA

Abstract: The generation of efficient code for Prolog programs requires sophisticated code transformation and optimization systems. Much of the recent work in this area has focussed on high level transformations, typically at the source level. Unfortunately, such high level transformations suffer from the deficiency of being unable to address low level implementational details. This paper presents a simple code improvement scheme that can be used to complement high-level transformations for a variety of low level optimizations. Applications of this scheme are illustrated using three low level optimizations that reduce tag manipulation, environment allocation and redundant bounds checks.

1. Introduction

The generation of efficient code for Prolog programs requires sophisticated code transformation and optimization systems. Most of the recent work in this area has concentrated on high level transformations, typically at the source level [8,9]. Such high level transformations have the advantage of being relatively simple to formulate and prove correct. However, they suffer from the deficiency that low level implementational details are often simply not expressible at the source level. As a result, after all appplicable high level transformations have been carried out, the programmer still finds himself penalized by low level inefficiencies that he is unable to overcome. To rectify this, source level code improvement systems should be complemented by transformation and optimization systems working at a lower level.

This paper presents a simple code transformation scheme that can be used for a variety of low level optimizations. Like those described by Marien et al. [6], these optimizations are at the level of intermediate code, or virtual machine, instructions; they are somewhat higher level than the machine code level optimizations described by Turk [10]. The transformation scheme consists of a *hoisting* transformation on flow graphs, together with three generic transformations on basic blocks: *code introduction, code elimination,* and *code migration.* Code hoisting is a transformation that is generally applicable; specific optimization algorithms are obtained by specifying particular instruction sequences that may be introduced at or eliminated from a point, or moved from one point to another within a basic block, together with conditions under which this may be

---

This work was supported in part by the National Science Foundation under grant number CCR-8702939.

done. These generic transformations may also be augmented with local transformations that depend on the particular optimization under consideration. Because optimization-specific transformations are usually local to basic blocks, implementation and verification of optimizations is simplified. Applications of this scheme are illustrated using three low level optimizations: reduction of redundant tag manipulation operations, environment allocation and bounds checking. These techniques may also be applicable to other low level optimizations, e.g. those of Marien et al. [6].

The reader is assumed to be acquainted with the basic terminology of logic programming. The examples in the paper are based on a virtual machine model that resembles the Warren Abstract Machine [11] in many ways, especially in the parameter passing mechanism. However, the transformation scheme is not dependent on the WAM in any way, and applies equally to other machine models. Indeed, the transformations are not restricted to Prolog, and can be extended to other control strategies by appropriately defining the notions of "basic block" and "flow graph".

It is assumed that the predicates under consideration are *static*, i.e. any code for that predicate that can be executed at runtime is available for inspection by the compiler. This precludes predicates that can be modified at runtime via *assert* or *retract*, and predicates that contain dynamic goals of the form $call(X)$ where X is a variable. In this context, it should be noted that the code transformations discussed may require information about the program, e.g. the type of a variable or the contents of a register at a program point; this may require dataflow analysis, which has to take primitives like *assert/1* and *call/1* into account, and may impose restrictions on their use [4].

2. Basic Blocks and Flow Graphs in Prolog

The notions of "basic block" and "flow graph" are well known in traditional compiler theory. A *basic block* is a sequence of (intermediate code) instructions with a single entry point and single exit point: execution of a basic block can start only at its entry point; and control can leave a basic block only at its exit point. Thus, if control enters a basic block, each instruction in that block will be executed. A *flow graph* for a procedure is a directed graph whose nodes are the basic blocks of that procedure, where there is an edge from a node B_1 to a node B_2 if it is possible for control to enter B_2 immediately after it has left B_1. If there is an edge from B_1 to B_2 in a flow graph, then B_1 is said to be a *predecessor* of B_2, and B_2 is said to be a *successor* of B_1.

When dealing with logic programs, this definition of a basic block does not work quite as desired, because whereas most operations in traditional languages have only a single continuation (the "success continuation", which is usually the next instruction), operations in logic programming languages, e.g. at the WAM code level, typically have two continuations: the "success continuation" and the "failure continuation". As a result, dividing the WAM code for a Prolog program into basic blocks using the traditional definition typically results in a large number of trivial basic blocks, each containing a single WAM instruction. The resulting flow graph is large and messy, with much of the control flow structure of the original program obscured, and is not very amenable to compile-time optimization.

It is therefore necessary to change the notion of a "basic block" slightly for logic programs. We propose the following definition:

Definition: A *basic block* in a logic program is a maximal sequence of instructions **I** with the following properties:

(*i*)   **I** has a single entry point, i.e. execution can enter **I** only through its first instruction; and

(*ii*)   **I** has a single successful exit point: if control enters **I** and each instruction in **I** succeeds, then each instruction in **I** is executed exactly once. ♦

With this definition of basic blocks, execution can leave a basic block in two ways: via success, and by failure. If control flows from a block B_1 to a block B_2 via successful execution, the changes to variables and registers effected by B_1 are visible to B_2. However, if control flows from B_1 to B_2 via failure, then changes to the virtual machine state effected by B_1 will in general be invisible to B_2. This can be made explicit by using two kinds of edges in the flow graph: *success edges* and *failure edges*:

Definition: The flow graph of a clause is a directed graph whose nodes are the basic blocks of that clause. There is a success edge from a block B_1 to a block B_2 if control, upon leaving B_1 successfully, can go immediately to B_2. There is a failure edge from B_1 to B_2 if execution, on failing in B_1, can go immediately to B_2.

The flow graph for a predicate consists of the flow graphs for each of its clauses, together with an *entry node* that is distinct from the nodes in the flow graphs for the clauses. The edges of this flow graph are defined as follows:

(1)   there is a success edge from the entry node to the header node of the flow graph of the first clause of the predicate;

(2)   there is a failure edge from the header of the flow graph for a clause C_i to the header of the flow graph for a clause C_j if execution backtracks to C_j when C_i fails.

♦

Information flow during the execution of a predicate can be made more explicit by elaborating slightly on its flow graph: the result is a graph called its augmented flow graph.

Definition: An *augmented flow graph* for a predicate p is a directed graph G whose nodes are those for its flow graph, and whose edges are defined as follows:

(1)   if there is a success (failure) edge from B_1 to B_2 in the flow graph for p, then there is a success (failure) edge from B_1 to B_2 in G;

(2)   if there is a success edge from B_1 to B_2 and a failure edge from B_2 to B_3 in G, where $B_1 \neq B_3$, such that execution can succeed through B_1 into B_2 and then fail back into B_3, then there is a success edge from B_1 to B_3 in G. ♦

The reasoning behind the edges added in (2) is as follows: if execution can go successfully from B_1 to B_2 and then fail into B_3, then B_3 will in general see changes to the machine state effected by B_1 but not those effected by B_2. From the point of view of B_3, therefore, it is as if execution had succeeded through B_1 and gone immediately into B_3. This justifies adding a success edge from B_1 to B_3 in the augmented flow graph. The discussion that follows will generally concern itself only with augmented flow graphs, and hence not explicitly distinguish between ''flow graphs'' and ''augmented flow graphs''. Depending on the implementation, some changes to machine registers or flags effected by B_2 may be visible to B_3: these can be taken into account during the transformation using the failure edge from B_2 to B_3. An example of an augmented flow graph is given in Figure 1.

3. The Transformation Scheme

The transformation scheme consists of a pair of dual transformations on flow graphs called *code hoisting*, and three generic transformations on basic blocks: *code introduction*, *code elimination*, and *code migration*. The hoisting transformations are generally applicable to flow graphs that satisfy certain criteria. Particular code optimization algorithms are obtained by giving specific code introduction, code elimination and code migration sets, i.e. sets of instruction sequences, together with conditions under which an instruction sequence may be inserted at or deleted from a point within a basic block, or moved from one point in a block to another.

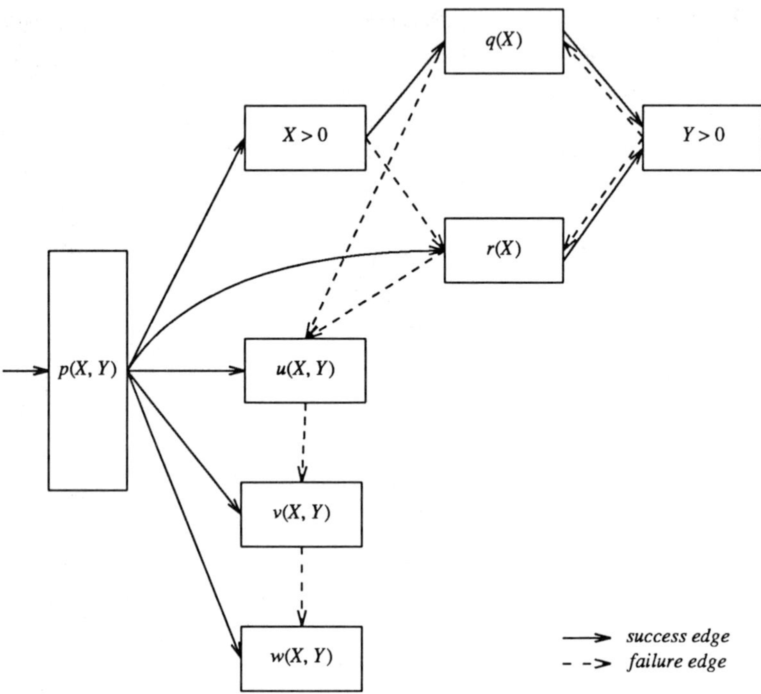

$p(X, Y) :\!- (X > 0 \rightarrow q(X) ; r(X)), Y > 0.$
$p(X, Y) :\!- u(X, Y) ; v(X, Y).$
$p(X, Y) :\!- w(X, Y).$

Figure 1: Example of an augmented flow graph for a predicate

3.1. Code Hoisting

Code hoisting consists of two dual transformations on flow graphs, called *upward* and *downward* code hoisting respectively.

3.1.1. Upward Code Hoisting

Upward code hoisting is defined as follows: let **A** and **B** be sets of basic blocks satisfying (*i*) for any $A \in$ **A**, if B is a successor of A then $B \in$ **B**; and (*ii*) for any $B \in$ **B**, if A is a predecessor of B then $A \in$ **A**. Let every block $B \in$ **B** start with a sequence of instructions S. Then, upward code hoisting deletes the instruction sequence S from the beginning of each block in **B**, and inserts it at the end of each block in **A** (if a block A in **A** ends in a transfer-of-control instruction I, then the sequence S is inserted immediately before I, as shown in the figure below). If any of the blocks in **B**, say B_k, is the initial block of the flow graph, then a new block A is created containing only the instruction sequence S, A is made the new initial block of the flow graph, and B_k is made the only successor of A.

To see when this transformation can be applied, consider a block B0 with two successors, B1 and B2. Let the instruction sequence in B0 before hoisting be T0 followed by a transfer-of-control instruction (which can be a conditional or unconditional jump, or an instruction that creates or manipulates a choice point, e.g. a *try*, *retry* or *trust* instruction). Let the instruction sequences in B1 and B2 be, respectively, S followed by T1 and S followed by T2. The relevant fragments of the flow graph before and after hoisting are

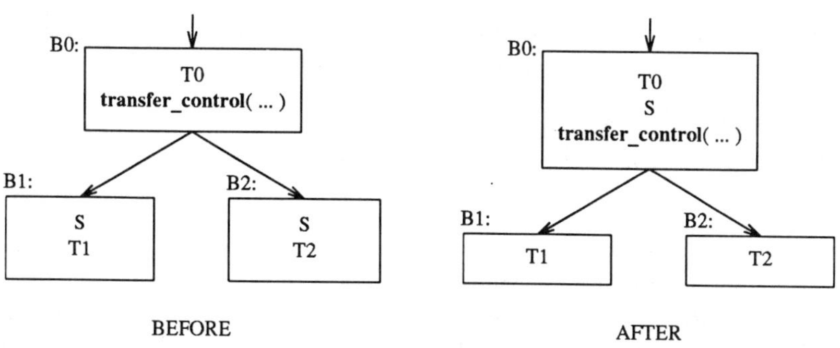

First, observe that in the flow graph before hoisting the instruction sequence, S is executed after the branch instruction in B0; after hoisting, however, S is executed before the branch instruction. It is necessary to ensure, therefore, that S does not define anything used in the conditional jump. The transfer-of-control instruction at the end of B0 may itself define registers or variables used in S, e.g. if the transfer of control is achieved by a *try*, *retry* or *trust* instruction. In general, therefore, it is necessary to ensure that hoisting does not disturb definition-use relationships between the blocks involved in the transformation.

While this condition ensures correct forward execution behavior, it does not guarantee proper execution upon backtracking. To see this, suppose that execution backtracks to B2 upon failure in B1. In the flow graph before hoisting, the instruction sequence executed, when B2 is entered upon backtracking from B1, is S followed by T2; however, after code hoisting, only T2 is executed when execution backtracks into B2. If

S defines any variable or register that is used in T2 but is not saved in the choice point for these execution paths and restored upon backtracking, then the transformation can result in incorrect execution. Also, if S has any externally visible side effects, e.g. through *assert, write*, etc., then the code before and after hoisting behave differently. To ensure correctness of backward execution, therefore, it is necessary to ensure that either (*i*) execution cannot backtrack from B1 to B2 (i.e. the two execution paths are mutually exclusive); or (*ii*) the instructions being hoisted do not have any externally visible side effects, and if they define any variable, register or flag that is subsequently used in the block they are hoisted from, then that variable, register or flag is restored from the choice point upon backtracking. A strong mutual exclusion condition is needed here, since execution cannot be permitted to fail back into B2 once it has entered B1. Thus, in this case it must be possible to determine exactly which execution path to try simply from the instruction sequence T0 in B0.

3.1.2. Downward Code Hoisting

This is the dual of upward code hoisting. Let **A** and **B** be sets of basic blocks satisfying (*i*) for any $B \in$ **B**, if A is a predecessor of B then $A \in$ **A**; and (*ii*) for any $A \in$ **A**, if B is a successor of A then $B \in$ **B**. Let every block in **A** end with a sequence of instructions S. Then, downward code hoisting deletes S from the end of each block in **A**, and inserts S at the beginning of each block in **B**.

The correctness conditions for downward code hoisting are analogous to those for upward hoisting. Its utility lies mainly in the the optimization to reduce the amount of redundant environment allocation, discussed in the next section, and in the reduction of redundant tag manipulation operations across procedure boundaries, discussed in [3].

3.2. Code Introduction

This transformation on basic blocks is specified by a set of pairs $\langle S, P \rangle$, called the *code introduction set*, where S is a sequence of instructions (or instruction schemas), and P is a condition. If $\langle S, P \rangle$ is in the code introduction set of an optimization, then at any point within a basic block where the condition P is satisfied, the instruction sequence S can be inserted without affecting the behavior of the program.

The primary purpose of code introduction is to allow code hoisting to be performed. This is illustrated in the applications discussed in the next section. The following points should be noted:

(1) The presence of a pair $\langle S, P \rangle$ in the code introduction set of an optimization means that whenever P is satisfied at a point within a basic block, S can be inserted at that point without affecting the behavior of the program. It is up to the designer of that optimization to ensure that this is indeed the case. However, because this is a local transformation, this can often be done by local reasoning. This simplifies the task of specifying and reasoning about such low level transformations significantly.

(2) In general, the code introduction set of an optimization specifies only when code *can* be introduced at a program point without altering the behavior of the program, not when it *should* be introduced. However, pragmatic considerations, e.g. cost criteria based on which the compiler may decide whether code introduction is worth performing at a particular program point, may also be incorporated into the condition associated with each code fragment in the code introduction set if desired.

3.3. Code Elimination

This is specified by a set of pairs called the *code elimination set*, which consists of a set of pairs $\langle S, P \rangle$, where S is a sequence of instructions (or instruction schemas), and P is a condition. If $\langle S, P \rangle$ is in the code elimination set of an optimization, then at any point within a basic block where the instruction sequence S occurs and the condition P is satisfied, S can be eliminated without affecting the behavior of the program.

While code elimination is conceptually the dual of code introduction, their functions are very different: code introduction is intended to make code hoisting possible; this hoisting is then intended to make code elimination possible; finally, the actual optimization is achieved by code elimination. In general, therefore, the code introduction set and code elimination set of an optimization are different. As with code introduction, it is usually the case that only a few instruction sequences need be considered for any particular optimization.

3.4. Code Migration

This is specified by a set of triples $\langle S_1, S_2, P \rangle$ called the *code migration set*, where S_1 and S_2 are sequences of instructions or instruction schemas that are permutations of each other, and P is a condition. If $\langle S_1, S_2, P \rangle$ is in the code migration set of an optimization, then at any point in a basic block where the instruction sequence S_1 is encountered and P is satisfied, S_1 can be replaced by S_2. Since S_1 and S_2 are permutations of each other, this specifies conditions under which specific instruction sequences can be moved from one point in a basic block to another. In most cases, the sequence being moved consists of a single instruction.

4. Applications to Code Optimization

This section describes three applications of the transformation scheme to low level code optimization.

4.1. Tag Manipulation Reduction

Objects that are passed around in Prolog implementations are typically associated with bit patterns, called *tags*, that indicate their types. Runtime operations often follow the pattern: (*i*) examine the tag bits of the operands to ensure that they are of the appropriate type(s); (*ii*) untag each operand; (*iii*) perform the operation; and (*iv*) tag the result. While one or more of these steps can be omitted for some operations by careful choice of the tagging scheme, some tag manipulation is necessary in general, and can, in many cases, lead to redundant tagging/untagging and type checking that can incur a significant penalty. Actually, some care is necessary if untagged objects are to be passed around, since operations such as unification and indexing may require tagged operands. The compiler therefore has to ensure that, while untagged objects are passed around and manipulated wherever possible, tags are correctly restored where necessary. Moreover, garbage collection and debugging in the presence of untagged objects require additional support in order to correctly identify untagged objects [3].

Two instructions are assumed for explicit tag manipulation. The instruction "**untag** u, t" checks that the object u has the tag t: if so, it removes the tag, converting u to its untagged form; otherwise, it fails. The instruction "**tag** u, t" adds the tag t to the object u, i.e. converts u to its t-tagged form. There are assumed to be a set of operations "**tagged_op(...)**" that operate on tagged objects and possibly yield a tagged object; and a set of operations "**untagged_op**(...)" that operate on untagged objects and possibly yield an untagged object. The code introduction transformation is given by the following: suppose it is known, at a program point, that an object u is of type t (this information must be obtained separately, e.g. via dataflow analysis), then the instruction sequence "**untag** u, t; **tag** u, t" may be introduced at that program point. Code elimination is given by the following: if the sequence of instructions "**tag** u, t; **untag** u, t" occurs at any point in a program, then it may be deleted. Code migration consists of moving **untag** instructions to the tops of their basic blocks, and **tag** instructions to the bottoms of their blocks. If an instruction "**untag** u, t" is being migrated across a sequence of instructions I in this process, then it is necessary to ensure that I does not contain any procedure calls, and does not define or use u; a similar comment applies to the migration of **tag** instructions.

The essential idea behind the transformation strategy is to first uncover tag manipulations, then identify pairs of **tag** and **untag** instructions that "cancel out". The transformation proceeds as folows:

(1)   make tag manipulations explicit by "unfolding" operations of the form **tagged_op**(...), i.e. replacing them by **untagged_op**(...) instructions preceded by explicit **untag** operations and followed by explicit **tag** operations;

(2)   use instruction migration within each basic block to move **untag** instructions to the top of the block and **tag** instructions to the bottom of the block;

(3)   repeatedly perform upward code hoisting to move **untag** instructions from basic blocks to their predecessors. This may require code introduction in some basic blocks. Considerations for such code introduction are discussed later.

(4)   use code elimination to eliminate pairs of **tag/untag** instructions that cancel out.

The transformation becomes interesting when there is more than one path in the flow graph being considered, where some paths require that an object u be tagged while other paths can (and may prefer to) have u untagged. A common example of this is in loops, e.g. in tail-recursive Prolog programs where the recursion itself may manipulate untagged objects, but where the termination of the recursion involves unifications that require tagged operands. In this case, it is necessary to restore tag bits just before the unification instructions are executed at the termination of recursion. A flow graph representing such a situation is given in Figure 2(a).

After unfolding the **tagged_op** instruction in block B2 of Figure 2(a) and performing code migration in B2, it is not possible to hoist the **untag** u, t instruction from B2 into B0, because there is no corresponding **untag** instruction in block B1. This is rectified by using code introduction to add a pair of **untag/tag** instructions into B1, and migrating the **untag** instruction to the top of B1. At this point, the **untag** u, t instruction can be hoisted from blocks B1 and B2 into B0 and migrated upward. Another upward hoisting step then yields the flow graph of Figure 2(b). At this point, code elimination gets rid of the **tag/untag** instruction pair in block B2. The resulting flow graph achieves exactly what was intended: the object u is untagged once at the entry to the loop, and then passed around the loop untagged. This avoids the cost of repeated removal and restoration of tags during iteration. However, at the end of the loop, just before an instruction that demands that u be tagged, its tag is restored.

A point to note is that the benefits of the transformation illustrated above are not limited to the conversion of a **tagged_op** instruction to an **untagged_op** instruction in block B2. For example, if the virtual machine under consideration supports two types of tests, one for tagged operands and another for untagged operands, then a "**tagged_test** u"

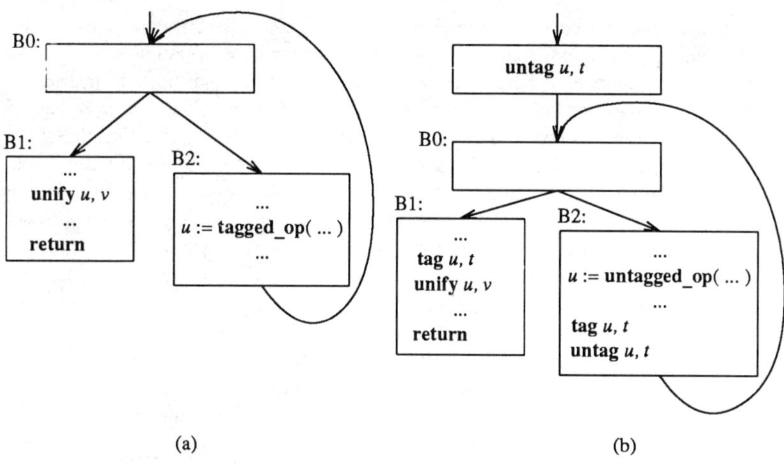

Figure 2

instruction in block B0 can be converted to an "**untagged_test** u" by this transformation. The loop is thus optimized to a point where the only tag manipulation on u appears at the very beginning, just before entry into the loop, and at the very end, at the exit from the loop. In between, operations on u in the body of the loop do not incur the penalty of repeatedly untagging and tagging it.

An important point to note is that all possible aliases of an object should have the same representation, tagged or untagged, at any particular point in a program. Aliases may be determined using dataflow analyses designed for this purpose (e.g. see [5]). Alternatively, since registers cannot have pointers to them, the optimization may be limited to objects resident in registers – the latter alternative, while simpler, is conservative and may fail to exploit the optimization to its fullest.

If untagged objects are passed around at runtime, it is necessary to ensure that they are not misinterpreted, e.g. during garbage collection or debugging. This can be done by storing additional information about the representation of local objects and registers in the symbol table entry for each predicate. The scheme, which is similar in many ways to a proposal by Appel for strongly typed polymorphic languages like ML [2], is discussed in more detail in [3].

4.2. Environment Allocation Reduction

When the execution of a procedure begins in a Prolog program, it may not always be necessary to allocate an environment for that procedure on the stack. In the WAM, for example, parameter passing is done through registers, and if a clause can be executed using only register operations, i.e. if no space is used on the runtime stack, then the clause can be executed without allocating an environment.

When dealing with clauses that contain complex control-flow connectives, it may be the case that some execution paths in the clause require the allocation of an environment while others do not. In such cases, the simplest code generation strategy is to allocate an environment at the entrance to the clause. However, this is suboptimal if the execution path chosen does not require environment allocation. In this case, some redundant environment allocations may be eliminated using our transformation scheme. The hoisting transformation used here is *downward code hoisting*, and the only instruction considered for downward hoisting is the **"allocate"** instruction. The code introduction transformation is not used here. The code elimination transformation specifies that if the sequence of instructions **"allocate; deallocate"** occurs at any point within a basic block, it may be eliminated. Code migration is used to move **allocate** instructions downward; the details are omitted for reasons of space. The transformation strategy is to use downward code hoisting and migration to move an **"allocate"** instruction down from the beginning of the clause. If it can be moved all the way down to a **"deallocate"** instruction, then the **allocate/deallocate** pair may be deleted using instruction elimination. Even if this is not possible, however, delaying environment allocation can be advantageous, since in the transformed code, unification may fail before the **"allocate"** instruction is encountered, saving some work. This may be especially useful in highly nondeterministic ''search''-type applications, where execution tends to fail relatively often.

The savings realized from just the reduction in environment allocation tend to be relatively small, because the bulk of the work in a program tends to be done along execution branches that require environment allocation (though on some programs, e.g. a non-tail-recursive factorial program and a program to test whether a term is ground, we observed speedups of over 10% from environment allocation reduction alone). The principal benefit of this transformation, in our experience, is that by delaying environment allocation, variables are kept in registers longer, enabling other optimizations, e.g. tag manipulation reduction, to be carried out more easily. An example application of this transformation is given as part of an example considered in the next section.

4.3. Bounds Check Reduction

The Prolog builtin *arg/3* can be used to access any specified argument of a compound term. In most implementations, this can be done in $O(1)$ time, and hence is commonly used in programs that manipulate arrays, records and trees. For example, a predicate that checks whether a term is ground might be written as

ground(X) :–
  nonvar(X), (*atomic*(X) $\rightarrow$ *true* ; (*functor*(X, _, N), *ground_args*(N, X))).

ground_args(N, X) :–
  N =:= 0 $\rightarrow$ *true* ; (*arg*(N, X, T), *ground*(T), N1 is N–1, *ground_args*(N1, X)).

However, a closer examination indicates that *arg/3* performs many more operations than are involved in indexed access to a structure in a conventional language, and hence is significantly more expensive: executing the goal *arg*(N, T, X) involves the following operations:

(1)   check the tag of T to ensure that it is bound to a constant or structure;

(2)   check the tag of N to ensure that is bound to an integer;

(3)   check that $N > 0$;

(4)   look up the symbol table to retrieve the arity A of T;

(5)   check that $N \leq A$;

(6)   compute the address of the $N^{th.}$ argument of T;

(7)   retrieve the $N^{th.}$ argument of T;

(8)   unify the $N^{th.}$ argument of T with X.

Many of these computations become redundant when successive arguments of a term are accessed in a loop, as in the *ground_args/2* example above. In this case, for example, operations (1) and (4) above are loop invariant computations, and can be moved out of the loop; and operation (2), and the tag manipulation implicit in operations (3) and (5), can be eliminated from the body of the loop using the transformation to reduce tag manipulation discussed earlier. However, this still leaves a significant amount of overhead in the task of accessing an argument of a term. This section considers how part of this overhead, namely part or all of the bounds checks, can be eliminated. In the *ground_args/2* predicate above, for example, it is easy to see that in any call

$$?\text{-} \ldots, ground\_args(N, T), \ldots$$

if N exceeds the arity of the term T, then this is detected right away, and the call fails; while if N does not exceed the arity of T, then this is verified in the first iteration, and since the value of the first argument of N decreases in subsequent iterations of the loop, further checking of the index against the upper bound is unnecessary.

This optimization can be handled as an instance of our transformation scheme. The expression "$t[i]$" denotes the $i^{th.}$ argument of the term referenced by t, retrieved without performing any bounds checking. Thus, a literal "$arg(I, T, X)$" is translated to the instruction sequence

$ub := arity(T)$
if $I > ub$ **then** *fail*
if $I < 1$ **then** *fail*
unify $X, T[I]$

where, for the sake of simplicity, the tag manipulation operations have been omitted. The code introduction transformation in this case is given by the following: if, at a point in a program, it can be guaranteed that the value of a variable x is a number N satisfying $N \geq LB$ for a known constant LB, then the instruction "**if** $x < LB$ **then** *fail*" can be inserted at that point without affecting the behavior of the program. Similarly, if it can be guaranteed that the value of x is a number N satisfying $N \leq UB$ for a known constant UB, then the instruction "**if** $x > UB$ **then** *fail*" can be inserted at that point without affecting the behavior of the program.

In this case, code elimination cannot be made based on purely local considerations. Code elimination for this optimization is given by the following: let p be the point immediately before the first instruction of the basic block B under consideration, and suppose that

(*i*)   every path consisting only of success edges, from the initial block of the flow graph to the point p, contains an instruction "**if** $x \ominus c$ **then** *fail*", where $\ominus$ is a relational operator and c is a constant, such that x is not redefined between that instruction and p; and

(*ii*) B contains an instruction $I :$ "**if** $y \ominus c$ **then** *fail*" at a point p, such that whenever "$y \ominus c$" is true at p, "$x \ominus c$" is true at the entrance to B.

Then, the instruction I can be deleted from B without affecting the behavior of the program.

While verifying this relationship between the expressions "$y \ominus c$" and "$x \ominus c$" may be difficult in general, simple special cases can be given that cover most commonly encountered situations. Two such special cases are: (*i*) $\ominus$ is '>' or '>=', and $x \geq y$; and (*ii*) $\ominus$ is '<' or '=<', and $x \leq y$. In either case, the relationship between x and y can usually be verified using classical flow analysis techniques to detect induction variables [1].

Code migration here is as follows: given a sequence of instructions S followed by an instruction

$$I \ : \ \textbf{if } x \ominus y \textbf{ then } \textit{fail}$$

where $\ominus$ is a relational operator, and S does not define x or y and does not contain any *call* instructions, I can be moved to the point immediately before S.†

The transformation proceeds in much the same way as in the case of tag stripping: code hoisting is performed, aided by code introduction where necessary, followed by code elimination. This is repeated until there is no change to the code. This can be illustrated by considering the *ground_args/2* example above. The flow graph before transformation is shown in Figure 3(a). First, the instruction "$ub := arity(X)$", which is a loop

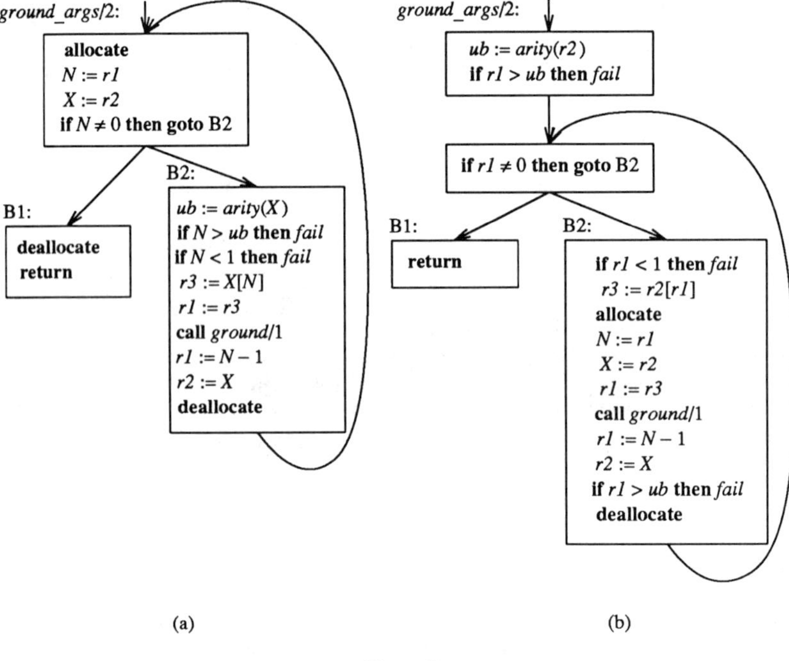

Figure 3

---

† This transformation does not, strictly speaking, preserve equivalence, since it can improve the behavior of programs containing errors.

invariant computation (since X is not redefined anywhere in the loop), is moved into the header of the loop. Next, the environment reduction transformation discussed in the previous section is performed: the **"allocate"** instruction is hoisted downward, followed by instruction migration and the elimination of an **allocate/deallocate** pair in block B1. Next, code introduction is performed to introduce the instruction "**if** $r1 > ub$ **then** *fail*" immediately before the **return** instruction in B1, followed by code hoisting into the block labelled *ground_args/2*. Another code hoisting step then yields the flow graph of Figure 3(b). Let p be the program point immediately before the first instruction of the block B2 in Figure 3(b). We observe that the definition of $r1$ that reaches the instruction "**if** $r1 >$ ub **then** *fail*" at the end of B2 is "$r1 := N - 1$", and the only definition of N that reaches this instruction is "$N := r1$", which implies that the value of $r1$ at the end of B2 is less than its value at the beginning of B2. The other condition for code elimination is also satisfied. This allows the bounds check at the very end of block B2 to be eliminated. In the resulting code, the bounds check against the upper bound is performed only once, at the entry to the loop.

5. Pragmatic Considerations

The paper so far has discussed a low level code transformation scheme that can be instantiated in different ways to obtain different kinds of specific low level optimizations. For the specific optimizations so obtained, it is usually the case that the code introduction and hoisting transformations follow specific patterns that are easy to identify. Such patterns may be taken advantage of to realize more efficient implementations of these optimization algorithms.

The optimizing transformations discussed perform code introduction and hoisting in the hopes of eventually realizing a code elimination step. One simple way to guide the transformation, therefore, is to ensure that code elimination will be possible before applying the transformation. This can be done using *reaching definitions* [1]. A definition d of a variable x is said to *reach* an instruction s if there exists an execution path from d to s along which there is no redefinition of x. Sets of reaching definitions can be obtained using classical dataflow analysis techniques [1]. Once these have been computed, a program point that is being considered for the introduction or hoisting of a sequence of instructions is tested to see whether the set of definitions that reach that point suggest that code elimination will eventually be possible. The transformations are carried out only if this is found to be the case. For example, in tag manipulation reduction, the flow graph is first tested to see if a "**tag** u t" instruction can reach an "**untag** u t" instruction along the back edge of a loop: if there is no such reaching definition, the transformation is not considered further at that point.

Another important consideration is the code introduction step, which opens up avenues for code hoisting and the eventual code elimination. This must be performed with some care in order to avoid slowing down the program by introducing code inside loops. Since the sole purpose of code introduction is to allow code hoisting to be carried out, it is necessary to define which basic blocks need to be taken into account when considering code hoisting from a block B. This is given by the *siblings* of B, defined as follows:

Definition: Given a basic block B, a basic block Q is a *sibling* of B if (*i*) there is a basic block P that is a predecessor of both B and Q; or (*ii*) there is a basic block R such that Q is a sibling of R and R is a sibling of B. ◆

It is not difficult to see that if the block B starts with a sequence of instructions S, then S can be hoisted from B into the predecessors of B only if every sibling of B starts with S. Let $sibs_Y(B)$ denote those siblings of B that also start with the instruction sequence S, and $sibs_N(B)$ denote those siblings of B that do not start with this sequence. In order to perform hoisting, it is necessary to introduce S at the beginning of each block in $sibs_N(B)$, by means of code introduction (provided that the preconditions for this are satisfied). Suppose that the code introduction transformation adds an instruction sequence S' at the beginning of each block in $sibs_N$. If the cost of the instruction sequence S is C, and that of $S'-S$ (the suffix of S' left over after hoisting S) is C', then code introduction should be performed only if there is a net savings realized, i.e. if

$$C * \sum_{P \in sibs_Y(B)} freq(P) \quad > \quad C' * \sum_{P \in sibs_N(B)} freq(P)$$

where $freq(B)$ is the expected frequency of execution of a basic block B. In general, of course, the estimation of execution frequencies is difficult. However, code of good quality can usually be generated by assuming "reasonable" values for the number of times the body of a loop is executed on the average, e.g. assuming that each loop is executed five or ten times on the average.

6. Experimental Results

Experiments were run on SB-Prolog to gauge the efficacy of the transformations discussed for reducing redundant tag manipulation and bounds checking. The only objects considered for tag stripping in our experiments were integers, and the additional instructions introduced to deal with untagged operands were those for arithmetic and relational operators. Only intra-procedural optimizations were carried out.

When testing the improvements resulting from tag manipulation reduction, we deliberately chose a set of programs that performed a great deal of integer tag manipulation: our objective was to see what sort of performance improvements might be obtained under favorable circumstances. The programs tested were the following: *factorial*, a tail recursive factorial program; *tr_fib*, a tail recursive program to compute fibonacci numbers; *fibonacci*, a linear recursive (but not tail recursive) program to compute fibonacci numbers; *nth_element*, a program to extract a specified element of a list (in our experiment, the last element of a list of 50 elements); and fourqueens. As the figures in Table 1 indicate, the performance improvements are quite encouraging. This suggests that even better performance gains are possible, by considering tag stripping for objects other than integers as well, using inter-procedural tag stripping, and compiling to native code.

Program	Iterations	pre-optimization	post-optimization	% Δ
factorial(10)	100000	27.12 secs	14.04 secs	48.2
tr_fib(40)	30000	34.97 secs	21.14 secs	39.5
nth_element	10000	21.24 secs	15.60 secs	26.6
fibonacci(40)	10000	24.72 secs	20.54 secs	16.9
fourqueens	1000	13.07 secs	12.02 secs	8.0

Table 1 : Experimental speedups due to tag manipulation reduction

The programs used to test improvements resulting from the reduction of redundant bounds checks were the following: *ground*, a program to test whether a term is ground; *subst*, a program that, given terms t_1, t_2 and t_3, returns the term obtained by substituting each occurrence of t_1 within t_2 by t_3; *subsumes*, a program to check whether one term subsumes another; *array_upd*, a program to update an element of a given array (tested with an array of size 256, organized as a balanced quadtree of depth 4); and *mat_mult*, a program to multiply two matrices (tested with two 50×50 matrices). The results of our experiments are given in Table 2. The improvements in this case are disappointingly small (Markstein et al. report that static elimination of bounds checks in imperative languages like PL/I can result in a 7-10% decrease in the number of instructions executed [7]). This is due at least in part to the overhead of byte code interpretation in SB-Prolog, and suboptimal use of hardware registers (compared to similar programs in Fortran or PL/I), which tend to swamp the improvements due to the elimination of redundant bounds checks; we expect better speedups from this optimization in systems that have smaller byte code interpretation overhead, or that compile to native code. Apart from the byte code interpretation overhead, the programs tested tend to do significant amounts of other operations, such as unification and procedure calls, which are absent in comparable programs in PL/I or Fortran: the overhead incurred in these operations also dilute the speedups measured from this optimization.

Finally, we tested the combined effects of all three optimizations – reduction of redundant tag manipulation, environment allocation and bounds checks. The results are given in Table 3.

7. Conclusions

Most of the research to date on improving the efficiency of Prolog programs has focussed on high-level transformations. However, these have the shortcoming that they cannot express low-level, implementational details, and hence cannot address low level optimizations. This paper describes a simple code improvement scheme that can be used for a variety of low level optimizations. Applications illustrated include the reduction of redundant tag manipulation operations; reduction of redundant environment allocation;

Program	Iterations	pre-optimization	post-optimization	% Δ
mat_mult	1	34.40 secs	33.72 secs	1.98
ground	100	42.97 secs	42.53 secs	1.0
array_upd	5000	32.27 secs	32.00 secs	0.8
subst	500	57.72 secs	57.43 secs	0.5
subsumes	50	47.33 secs	47.11 secs	0.4

Table 2: Experimental speedups due to bounds check reduction

Program	Iterations	pre-optimization	post-optimization	% Δ
mat_mult	1	34.40 secs	23.56 secs	31.5
ground	100	42.97 secs	31.02 secs	27.8
subst	500	57.72 secs	51.09 secs	11.5

Table 3: Speedups due to combined optimizations

and reduction of redundant bounds checking. Such a system can be a useful complement to high level code improvement transformations.

Acknowledgements

Comments by the anonymous referees contributed to numerous improvements in the paper.

References

1. A. V. Aho, R. Sethi and J. D. Ullman, *Compilers - Principles, Techniques and Tools*, Addison-Wesley, 1986.

2. A. Appel, Runtime Tags Aren't Necessary, Tech. Rep. CS-TR-142-88, Dept. of Computer Science, Princeton University, Princeton, NJ, Mar. 1988.

3. S. K. Debray and J. C. Peterson, Compile-time Tag Stripping, Unpublished manuscript, Dept. of Computer Science, The University of Arizona, Tucson, Nov. 1988.

4. S. K. Debray, Flow Analysis of Dynamic Logic Programs, *J. Logic Programming*, 1989 (to appear). (Preliminary version appeared in Proc. Fourth IEEE Symposium on Logic Programming, San Fransisco, CA, Sept. 1987).

5. G. Janssens and M. Bruynooghe, An Instance of Abstract Interpretation Integrating Type and Mode Inferencing, in *Proc. Fifth International Conference on Logic Programming*, Seattle, Aug. 1988, pp. 669-683. MIT Press.

6. A. Marien, G. Janssens, A. Mulkers and M. Bruynooghe, The Impact of Abstract Interpretation on Code Generation: an Experiment in Efficiency, in *Proc. Sixth International Conference on Logic Programming*, Lisbon, Portugal, June 1989. MIT Press.

7. V. Markstein, J. Cocke and P. Markstein, Optimization of Range Checking, in *Proc. ACM SIGPLAN '82 Symposium on Compiler Construction*, Boston, June 1982, pp. 114-119. SIGPLAN Notices vol. 17 no. 6..

8. H. Seki and K. Furukawa, Notes on Transformation Techniques for Generate and Test Logic Programs, in *Proc. Fourth IEEE Symposium on Logic Programming*, San Fransisco, CA, Sep. 1987, pp. 215-223.

9. H. Tamaki and T. Sato, Unfold/Fold Transformations of Logic Programs, in *Proc. 2nd. Logic Programming Conference*, Uppsala, Sweden, 1984.

10. A. K. Turk, Compiler Optimizations for the WAM, in *Proc. 3rd. International Conference on Logic Programming*, London, July 1986, 410-424. Springer-Verlag LNCS vol. 225.

11. D. H. D. Warren, An Abstract Prolog Instruction Set, Technical Note 309, SRI International, Menlo Park, CA, Oct. 1983.

The impact of abstract interpretation :
an experiment in code generation

André Mariën(1)   Gerda Janssens(2)   Anne Mulkers(2)
Maurice Bruynooghe(2)

1) BIM, Kwikstraat 4, 3078 Everberg, Belgium
2) K.U.Leuven, Department of Computer Science,
Celestijnenlaan 200A, 3030 Heverlee, Belgium

0. Abstract

In recent years a lot of work has been done on the abstract interpretation
of logic programs. One of the motivations is that the information
gathered allows the generation of more specific code which executes
faster. The purpose of this paper is to substantiate this claim. We have
done a number of experiments to assess the impact of knowledge about
modes, types, length of reference chains and opportunities for compile
time garbage collection on the speed of the generated code. To find out
about the limits of what is achievable, we have also measured the speed
of comparable C programs.

1. Introduction

Compared with the first implementation in 1972, current Prolog systems
are amazingly fast. Nowadays, Prolog is suited for the programming of
large industrial applications. The programmer is offered a system where
he has not to bother about the low level details of the machine.
Developing a compiler which generates code which is competitive, with
regard to space and time consumption, with compilers of imperative
languages is a challenging task. The work of David Warren on
compilation and on the Warren Abstract Machine [20] was of major
importance.   These techniques are the basis for commercially available
up-to-date Prolog systems [1] [17]. However a substantial gap with
imperative languages still remains. It is well known that the utilization
of mode information yields substantial improvements. Recently, a lot of
work has been done on abstract interpretation. One of the purposes is to
derive mode information automatically. But also the derivation of other
kinds of information has been suggested, including types and liveness
information [6].

This paper describes an experiment carried out to assess the impact on the resulting efficiency when using automatically derived extra information about modes, types, reference chain length and reusability of data structures. The reference chain length information is a new technique to deal more efficiently with dereferencing. An overview is given of our investigations concerning the use of this information and its influence on the speed of some algorithmic Prolog predicates.

Already the famous DEC-10 compiler used mode declarations to optimize the code. Mellish [13] was the first to consider automatic derivation of modes. Debray was the first to address properly the problem of dependencies between variables [9]. Nowadays, mode inferencing is often used to illustrate frameworks for abstract interpretation [14], [3].

In [2] types and modes are redundant information used to verify Prolog programs. The polymorphic type system in [16] makes static type checking possible based upon type declarations. Type inference systems are proposed in Mishra [15] and Zobel [22]. Yardeni and Shapiro [21] take a declarative approach when defining a well-typed program. All these type systems consider a type as a set of ground terms. A more procedural approach is taken in [4] where types possibly include non-ground terms which is claimed to be preferable for code generation. Somogyi [18] takes a different approach by adding tags containing mode information to the types. Touati and Despain [19] found that Prolog programs do not build long reference chains and that dereferencing is a very frequent operation and should be implemented with attention to performance. This motivates our extension of the type inference system with information about the length of reference chains. Compile time garbage collection is proposed in [6]. An alternative method for ground Prolog is described by Kluzniak [11]. The complexity of abstract interpretation has been studied in [12], and its speed for some simple cases in [10]. In [8] a method is given to detect mutually exclusive clauses based upon non unifiable ground arguments which can be used for sophisticated clause indexing.

2. Description of the additional information

The additional information is inferred by using the abstract interpretation framework proposed in [3] in which abstract substitutions are computed at a fixed number of program points : in each clause just after the head, between two calls in the body and after the last call. Note that a canonical form of the clauses is used : all head and call arguments are variables. The abstract substitution possibly differs from one point to another and this granularity is suited for code generation as is shown in the sequel. The abstract framework makes it possible to focus on the abstract domain. This explains the tendency to domains with more expressive power. The aspects of the abstract domains necessary to keep track of the dependencies between values of variables are not mentioned in this paper; only the aspects used for code generation are discussed. The three example programs used are naive reverse, tree insertion and the sum of all the elements of a list.

naive reverse :

```
append( _A1 , _A2 , _A3 ) :-          nrev( _A1 , _A2 ) :-
      _A1 = [],                             _A1 = [],
      _A2 = _A3 .                           _A2 = [] .
append( _A1 , _V , _A3 ) :-           nrev( _A1 , _L ) :-
      _A1 = [_X|_U],                        _A1 = [_X|_T],
      _A3 = [_X|_W],                        nrev( _T , _T1 ),
      append( _U , _V , _W ) .              _A2 = [_X],
                                            append( _T1 , _A2 , _L ) .
```

tree insertion :

```
insert(_E,_A2,_A3) :-        _A2 = [],
                            _A3 = t([],_E,[]).
insert(_E,_A2,_A3) :-        _A2 = t(_Left,_N,_Right),
                            _A3 = t(_NewLeft,_N,_Right),
                            _E =< _N,
                            insert(_E,_Left,_NewLeft) .
insert(_E,_A2,_A3) :-        _A2 = t(_Left,_N,_Right),
                            _A3 = t(_Left,_N,_NewRight),
                            _E > _N,
                            insert(_E,_Right,_NewRight) .
```

Remark : a second version for insert/3 was used in the tests. We will refer to this version as *insert_if* :

```
insert(_E,[],t([],_E,[])) .
insert(_E,t(_Left,_N,_Right),t(_NewLeft,_N,_NewRight)) :-
      ( _E =< _N ->
            _NewRight = _Right,
            insert(_E,_Left,_NewLeft)
      ;     _NewLeft = _Left,
            insert(_E,_Right,_NewRight)
      ) .
```

The reason for this is that it is easier for a compiler to generate code without backtracking for the second version. Both versions are timed as soon as modes are introduced .

sum of a list :

```
sumlist(_List,_Sum) :-
      sumlist(_List,_Sum,0) .
sumlist([],_Sum,_Sum) .
sunlist([_Number|_List],_Sum,_PartSum) :-
      _NewPartSum is _PartSum + _Number,
      sumlist(_List,_Sum,_NewPartSum) .
```

Note that this predicate is not written in normal form, as that is only necessary to explain the compile time garbage collection, which is irrelevant for this predicate.

2.1 Modes

Each variable is associated with its mode [3]. The possible modes are : f)ree if a variable is still unbound, g)round if the variable is completely ground and a)ny if no information is available. This corresponds to the DEC-10 modes - (f), + (g), ? (a) .

Given a query for *nrev/2* with mode *nrev(+,-)* the call-modes derived by abstract interpretation are :

```
  :-mode nrev(+,-) .
  :-mode append(+,+,-)
```

Given a query for *insert/3* with mode *insert(+,+,-)* the call-mode derived by abstract interpretation is :

```
  :-mode insert(+,+,-) .
```

Given a query for *sumlist/2* with mode *sumlist(+,-)* the call modes derived by abstract interpretation are :

```
  :-mode sumlist(+,-) .
  :-mode sumlist(+,-,+) .
```

First of all, mode information can be used to enhance clause indexing. In the predicates *nrev/2, append/3* and *sumlist/3* it is clear that because the first argument is ground, and it has a value with a different tag in both clauses, tag checking is sufficient to do the indexing, thereby eliminating the try_me_else and trust_me_else instructions. Also, the get_list instruction in their second clause can be deleted with a small change to the switch_on_term instruction. In *insert/3,* indexing uses the second argument. Further, it is assumed that the compiler will recognize the test in the second version in the if-then-else as a simple test which can be implemented without resorting to the creation of a choicepoint.

A second effect of modes is the optimization of all the unify instructions generated for arguments which are known to be input or ouput. The normal unify instructions can operate in two modes : read-mode or write-mode. The correct mode is now known at compile time and this eliminates run-time checking.

2.2 Types

A type in our type system describes a possibly infinite set of finite Prolog terms that need not to be ground. The mode information is in fact derived from the type information. The types must satisfy a number of restrictions described in [4]. From the perspective of code generation, it is important to mention that a type can be defined by different alternatives, but that the alternatives have different toplevel functors, so indexing on the main functor is adequate.

Given a query for *nrev/2* with specification :
   ?-nrev(List,Free) .
with *type List == nil | Int.List*, the call-types derived by abstract interpretation are :
   nrev(List,Free)
   append(List,List,Free)
Given a query for *insert/3* with specification :
   ?-insert(Int,Tree,Free)
with *type Tree == nil | t(Tree,Int,Tree)*, the call-type derived by abstract interpretation is :
   insert(Int,Tree,Free)
Given a query for *sumlist/2* with specification :
   ?-sumlist(List,Free) .
the call-types derived for sumlist/2, sumlist/3 and is/2 are :
   sumlist(List,Free)
   sumlist(List,Free,Int)
   is(Free,Int+Int)
In *all predicates* except sumlist/2 there is a switch_on_term to determine which of the two clauses should be executed. The indexing code first checks whether the tag is a list tag - or structure tag for insert/3 - and if not, the argument must be nil. There is no need to explicitly test the value for the constant nil. This way, the get_constant nil is removed from the code.

A major improvement can be made in *arithmetic*. In Prolog, a variable in an arithmetic expression may be instantiated to an integer, a real, or an arithmetic term. This requires a lot of runtime checking. When the type of a variable is known to be Int, the system needs only to make the distinction between a reference tag or an integer tag. Tagging and untagging is still done, as at other points in the program the current data structures may be used in places where more general types are derived.

2.3 Reference chain length

The abstract domain used to derive reference chain length information is an extension of the previous one (types) : we are not only interested in possible values, but also in an implementation related item : the reference chain length. The WAM is emulated using data structures based upon tagged references. When a variable gets instantiated, its cell contains a pointer to the location of the value, or, for basic types, the value itself. The exact mechanism is implementation dependent. It is possible to have long reference chains in Prolog, but most of the time a variable cell points straight to its value [19]. To keep track of the reference chain length, we use an upper and a lower bound, and use the notation lower..upper in the type descriptions. The lower bound can be used during dereferencing to reduce 'check and loop' to a chain of memory fetches, and the upper bound to detect undefined variables one iteration earlier. If upper and lower bound are the same, the exact length is known. A frequent case is upper bound equal to lower bound equal to zero. A good understanding of the execution mechanism of the particular implementation at hand is required.

Given a query for *nrev/2* with specification :

  ?-nrev(ConsList,Free) .

with *type ConsList == 0..0->(nil | .(0..0->Int, ConsList))* and *type RefConsList == 1..1->(nil | .(0..0->Int, ConsList))* the extended call-types derived by abstract interpretation are :

    nrev(ConsList,Free)
    append(ConsList,ConsList,Free)

Note:

If we look at the second clause of nrev/2 then, in BIM_Prolog, the type of _T1 just before calling append, is : RefConsList. However, if the abstract interpretation derives a non zero lower bound for the argument of a call, both lower and upper bound are reduced with the lower bound, giving a lower bound zero again. This information must be provided to code generation. This means that the put-instruction for _Tl must reduce the type from RefConsList to ConsList. Therefore the shown call-substitution for the first argument in append is ConsList.

Given a query for *insert/3* with specification :

    ?-insert(Int,Tree,Free)

with *type Tree == 0..0->(nil | t(Tree,0..0->Int,Tree))* the extended call-type derived by abstract interpretation is :

    insert (Int,Tree,Free)

Given a query for *sumlist/2* with specification :
      ?-sumlist(IntList,Free) .
with *type IntList == 0..0->(nil/.(0..0->Int,IntList))*
the extended call-types derived by abstract interpretation are :
      sumlist(IntList,Free)
      sumlist(IntList,Free,0..0->Int)

The obvious benefit of having reference chain lengths, is that for *all the predicates* shown here, dereferencing need not be done. This amplifies the effects of knowing the types.

2.4 Compile time garbage collection

Compile time garbage collection is a method to recognize at compile time where a structure can be reused instead of allocating a new one. This means the introduction of destructive assignment during Prolog execution. The derived information shows at which program points a structure becomes dead. This information can be used by the compiler to reuse the record if a structure needs to be created in the same clause after the point where the structure became dead. Liveness is determined for one branch of the or-tree. Therefore, the proposed system may require destructive assignment trailing. The analysis of liveness uses the information of the type inference system. It requires keeping track of alias-information.

The liveness information derived for the second clause of *append/3* in the nrev benchmark is :

```
append(_A1,_A2,_A3) :-
      _A1 = [_X|_L1],
      % at this point, A1 points to a dead structure
      % it can be reused for the list construction which follows
      _A3 = [_X|_L3],
      append(_L1,_A2,_L3) .
```

Note:
- We assume *type ConsList == 0..0->(nil | .(0..0->Int, ConsList))*.
- For nrev it is less obvious how one should do compile time garbage collection. In the tests no compile time gc was done for nrev. It will briefly be discussed how one could do it, using more complex techniques. In the tests the garbage collection will only be partial, but significant.

The liveness derived for the second clause of *insert/3* is :
insert(_A1,_A2,_A3) :-
        _A2 = t(_L,_V,_R),
        % at this point, A2 points to a dead structure in this branch
        % it can be reused for the term construction which follows
        _A3 = t(_NL,_V,_R),
        _A1 =< _V,
        insert(_A1,_L,_NL) .

Note:
- We assume type Tree == 0..0->(nil I t(Tree,0..0->Int,Tree)).
- The third clause is similar.
- When reusing the structure in the second clause, and trailing is
  required, then also the old value must be trailed !

For the test program *sumlist/2* there is no opportunity to do compile
time garbage collection, as no structures are created.

As for the optimizations, this requires a more elaborate explanation, as
it is not straightforward to see what can be done and how it can be
done. If there exists a term which becomes dead after unification, and in
the same chunk a new term must be constructed which needs lower or
equal space, the space of the first term can -partially- be used for that
new term. A chunk is defined as either a chunk-without-head or a head
immediately followed by a chunk-without-head. A chunk-without-head
is a number, possibly zero, of in-line calls followed by an out-of-line
call. In-line calls are calls which use only argument registers of the
WAM. The best results are obtained when a term with equal functor
must be constructed, and which has many arguments in common with
the dead term.

The proposed scheme is as follows :
- if there is a term which can be reused, save a reference to that term in
  a WAM temporary register before doing the unification

- before constructing the new term, set a register, D, to the saved
  structure. D is the destructive overwrite register.

- proceed in destruct mode :
    . if an argument is the same, generate a destr_unify_skip
    . if it is different, trail if needed (both value and cell address) and
      perform the unification as if it were write-mode but using D
      instead of H

A few typical cases in which this technique can be used :
. to construct the same functor :

```
foo(_A1h,_A2h) :-
      _A1h = t(A,B,C),
      % if at this point, the t/3 record pointed to by A1 is dead
      % it can be reused in the construction hereafter
      _A2h = t(A,U,C) .
```

. to construct a smaller functor :

```
foo(_A1h,_A2h) :-
      _A1h = t(A,B),
      % if at this point, the t/2 record pointed to by A1 is dead
      % it can be reused in the construction of t/1 hereafter
      _A2h = t(A) .
```

. to construct a functor in the first subgoal :

```
foo(_A1h) :-
      _A1h = t(A,B,C),
      % if at this point, the t/3 record pointed to by A1 is dead
      % it can be reused in the construction hereafter
      _A1g = t(A,U,C),
      foo(_A1g) .
```

The variables _A1h, _A2h and _A1g refer to the argument registers A1,A2 and A1 of the WAM.

2.4.1 append/3

After the unification _A1 = [_X|_L1], the list record is reusable. We need to construct the record [_X|_L3]. This one differs only in its second argument. Therefore, we must destructively change _L1 in _L3. The following code could be used :

```
          new code                    old code
GET_VAR          A1,X5
GET_LIST         A1          GET_LIST         A1
UNIF_XVAR        X4          UNIF_XVAR        X4
UNIF_XVAR        X1          UNIF_XVAR        X1
DEST_GET_LIST    A3,X5       GET_LIST         A3
DEST_UNIF_SKIP               UNIF_XVAL        X4
DEST_UNIF_XVAR   X3          UNIF_XVAR        X3
```

This adds two extra moves to the normal code, but reuses two heap cells. One cell need not be reconstructed. A very small time penalty will result. However, this modified predicate is capable of appending much longer lists without calling the garbage collector. This may save a considerable amount of time for real applications.
It is possible to fold the two get_lists into one. A further optimization

would be to use a dest_unif_skip instead of the dest_unif_xvar X3 instruction. This could probably be derived with the technique as proposed by [7] and used there to eliminate tag checking.

2.4.2 nrev/2

We did not change anything, as it is not one of the cases described above. This means too that only part of all created garbage is reused. Code migration would make it possible to use destructive assignment in this case too :

```
         new version                    old version
   nrev( _A1 , _L ) :-              nrev( _A1 , _L ) :-
        _A1 = [_H|_T],                  _A1 = [_H|_T],
        _X = [_H],
        nrev( _T , _T1 ),               nrev( _T , _T1 ),
                                        _A2 = [_H],
        append( _T1 , _X , _L ) .       append( _T1 , _A2 , _L ) .
```

After the unification _A1 = [_H|_T], we can reuse the list record for the construction of [_H]. _X will be in the environment instead of _H. This optimization was not included in the timing results.

2.4.3 insert/3

```
insert (_EL,_A2,_A3) :-
      _A2 = t(_L,_V,_R),
      % t (_L,_V,_R) can be reused after this unification
      % for the construction of t(_NL,_V,_R) in the next unification.
      % They differ in their first argument only.
      _A3 = t(_NL,_V,_R)
      _EL =< _V,
      insert (_EL,_L,_NL) .
```

The code to perform both unifications :

```
GET_XVAR              A2,X6
GET_STRUCT            A2,t/3
UNIF_XVAR            X2
UNIF_XVAR            X4
UNIF_XVAR            X5
DESTR_GET_STRUCT     A3,t/3,X6
DESTR_UNIF_XVAR      X3
DESTR_UNIF_VOID
DESTR_UNIF_VOID
```

We trade four heap pushes for a couple of moves, if no trailing is needed. The result is almost equal in time. The advantage is the reduced space overhead, if no trailing must be done.

3. C programs for the same problems

To have an idea of where we stand in current Prolog compiler construction as compared to procedural languages, the three programs were written in C.

Three versions were made for nrev/append :
. a version using no destructive assignment, **recursive** append
. a version using no destructive assignment, **iteration** for append
. a version using **destructive** assignment, iteration for append

Three versions are tested for insert :
. a version using no destructive assignment, **recursive** insert
. a version using no destructive assignment, **iteration** for insert
. a version using **destructive** assignment, iteration for insert

Only two versions are timed for sumlist :
. a version using no destructive assignment, **recursive** sumlist/3
. a version using no destructive assignment and written as a single procedure sumlist/2 with **iteration** for the code corresponding to sumlist/3

They were neither coded with readability in mind, nor with the biggest care for efficiency. We believe the typical C programmer will not produce faster code if not instructed to do the best he can.

4. Measurements and discussion

The measurement results are presented with relative figures. All measurements were done on a SUN 3/50, connected to a loaded network. A comparison with timings on a SUN 3/260 showed no significant differences in the relative values.

Table 1 gives an impression of achievable speedups. This table shows the big impact of knowing the modes. It should be noted that these speedups are the result of years of practical experience in using modes in BIM_Prolog. Types increase the speed of insert/3 and sumlist/2 considerably. This is due to the presence of calculations and the terms t/3 in insert/3 and the calculations in sumlist/2 . The speed of nrev/2 does not change that much. This is so because lists are represented with a special tag. The type test is thus implicit in the tag check.

Introducing length information is definitely a good idea. This may obsolete the need for special hardware dereferencing support. Finally, destructive assignment can be introduced to do compile time garbage collection, with no measurable time overhead.

	Normal	+modes	+types	+ length	+destruct
nrev	100	51	45	41	41
insert	100	72	54	41	42
insert_if	---	100(28)	58(16)	39(11)	38(11)
sumlist	100	85	44	31	--

Table 1 : Normalized timings of Prolog programs

The table entries for insert are for the insert with backtracking *insert* and the version without, *insert_if* (bottom line, in parenthesis the relative time with respect to normal case of the top line).

	recursive	iteration	destructive
nrev	100	27	18
insert	100	53	25
sumlist	100	46	--

Table 2 : Normalized timings of C programs

Table 2 shows the speedups for the C programs. Destructive assignment seems to be important for very high speeds. This should motivate further research in introducing compile time garbage collection in Prolog systems.

A positive conclusion : there is no order of magnitude difference in speed between a well readable and understandable Prolog predicate, and its obscure C brother.
It should be noted that improvements can be made in the Prolog versions. One further optimization was described for nrev/2 with destructive assignment. Another one is the recognition that the tail need not be set to undef before calling append in nrev/2 . A technique similar to [7] may be used.

nrev	prolog	normal 602	+modes 308	+types 274	+length 250	+destruct 248
	C	recursive 360	iteration 100	destructive 65		
insert	prolog	normal 1274 ---	+modes 925 368	+types 696 216	+length 533 146	+destruct 541 141
	C	recursive 186	iteration 100	destructive 46		
sumlist	prolog	normal 450	+modes 383	+types 200	+length 140	
	C	recursive 216	iteration 100			

Table 3 : Normalized timings

Table 3 allows a comparison between C and Prolog programs. As the normal (100%) version the non-destructive C version with iteration is used.

The difference with C is mainly due to two factors :
- in C no tags are used, because of (virtual) strong typing
- the C code has a better register allocation
This is because we used almost pure macro expansion, with no peephole optimizations.

5. Conclusion

Our results indicate that it is worthwhile to gather information by means of abstract interpretation. Using the information during code generation results in substantial speedups. It is encouraging that the speed difference with the C programs is less than a magnitude for such algorithmic programs where imperative languages are at their best. However, the speed difference is still substantial (100 - 250 for nrev, 100 - 146 for insert and 100-140 for sumlist, and twice as much for nrev and insert with destructive assignment). It is an indication that there is room for further optimization. One should note that the code we have tested can be obtained by straightforward extensions of current commercial Prolog compilers. Applying transformation and optimization techniques at low level as in recent work [7] would give further improvements. Especially, we hope this would allow to obtain speed ups in the case of destructive assignment comparable to those in the C version.

6. Acknowledgements

Maurice Bruynooghe is supported by the Belgian National Fund for Scientific Research, Gerda Janssens is supported by the contract OT/86/48, Anne Mulkers is supported by the contract RFO/AI/02

7. References

[1]   BIM_Prolog reference manual,
          B.I.M., B-3078, Everberg, Belgium.

[2]   Bruynooghe, M., Adding redundancy to obtain more reliable
          and more readable Prolog programs,
          Proc. First International Conference on Logic Programming,
          Marseille, 1982, pp. 129-133.

[3]   Bruynooghe, M., A practical framework for the abstract
          interpretation of logic programs,
          (to appear in the Journal of Logic Programming)

[4]   M. Bruynooghe, G. Janssens, An Instance of Abstract
          Interpretation Integrating Type and Mode Inferencing,
          Proc. Fifth International Conference and Symposium,
          ed. R. Kowalski and K. Bowen, 1988, pp. 669-683.

[5]   Bruynooghe, M., Mulkers, A., Muzumbu, K., Compile time
          garbage collection for Prolog,
          Draft, Dept. Comp. Science, K.U.Leuven, Belgium, 1988.

[6]   Bruynooghe, M., Janssens, G., Callebaut, A., Demoen, B.,
          Abstract interpretation : towards the global optimization
          of Prolog programs,
          Proc. 1987 Symposium on Logic Programming, IEEE Press, 1987,
          pp. 192 - 204.

[7]   Debray, S.K., A simple code improvement scheme for Prolog,
          Proc. Sixth International Conference on Logic Programming, 1989

[8]   Debray, S.K., Warren, D.S., Automatic Mode inference for Prolog
          programs,
          Proc. 1986 Symposium on Logic Programming,
          Salt Lake City, 1986, pp. 78-88.

[9]   Debray, S.K., Warren, D.S., Detection and Optimization of
          functional computations in Prolog,
          Proc. Third International Conference on Logic Programming,
          London, 1986, pp. 490-504.

[10]   Hermenegildo, M., Warren, R., Debray, S.,
          On the practicality of global flow analysis of logic programs,
          Proc. Fifth International Conference and Symposium on
          Logic Programming, MIT press, 1988, pp. 687 - 699.

[11]   Kluzniak, F.,
Compile time garbage collection for ground Prolog,
Proc. Fifth International Conference and Symposium on
Logic Programming, MIT press, 1988, pp. 1490 -1505.

[12]   Manilla, H., Ukkonen, E., Flow analysis of Prolog programs,
Proc. 1987 Symposium on Logic Programming, IEEE Press, 1987,
pp. 204 - 214.

[13]   Mellish, C.S., The Automatic Generation of Mode declarations
for Prolog programs,
DAI Research paper 163, Dept. of Artificial Intelligence,
University of Edinburgh, August 1981

[14]   Mellish, C.S., Abstract Interpretation of Prolog programs
Proc. Third International Conference on Logic Programming,
London,1986, pp. 463-476.

[15]   Mishra, P., Towards a theory of types in Prolog,
Proc. First Symposium on Logic Programming,
Atlantic City, 1984, pp. 289-298.

[16]   Mycroft, A., O'Keefe, R.A., A Polymorphic Type System
for Prolog,
Artificial Intelligence 23(1984) pp. 295-307.

[17]   Quintus Prolog reference manual

[18]   Somogyi, Z., A system of precise modes for logic programs,
Proc. Fourth Int. Conf. on Logic Programming,
Melbourne, 1987, pp. 769-787.

[19]   Touati, H., Despain, A., An empirical study of the
Warren Abstract Machine,
Proc. 1987 Symposium on Logic Programming,
San Francisco, 1987, pp. 114-124.

[20]   Warren, D.H.D., An Abstract Prolog Instruction Set,
technical Report, SRI international,
Artificial Intelligence Center, August 1983

[21]   Yardeni, E. and Shapiro, E., A type system for logic programs,
in Concurrent Prolog : collected papers, ed. E. Shapiro,
MIT Press Cambridge, 1987, pp. 211-244.

[22]   Zobel, J., Derivation of polymorphic types for Prolog programs,
Proc. Fourth International Conference on Logic Programming,
Melbourne, 1987, pp. 817-838.

Removal of Dereferencing and Trailing
in Prolog Compilation

Andrew Taylor

Basser Department of Computer Science
The University of Sydney
N. S. W. Australia 2006

andrewt@basser.oz.au

Abstract

This paper deals with the global data flow analysis of Prolog programs for
an optimizing compiler. There has been much recent work on global
analysis of Prolog programs using a technique called abstract interpretation.
This recent work has focused on automatically deriving mode information
for Prolog programs. We extend the abstract domains used for deriving
mode information to include information on two implementation artefacts:
choice-points and reference chains. We have implemented an analyser
using this abstract domain as part of a project to build an optimizing Prolog
compiler. We have obtained very promising preliminary results from this
analyser that suggest many instances of dereferencing and trailing operations can be removed from Prolog programs.

1. Introduction

Powerful features such as unification and backtracking make Prolog more
useful for many applications than conventional languages such as C.
Unfortunately such features can be expensive in time and space to provide
on a general purpose (Von Neumann) machine. One remedy is to build
hardware especially designed to execute Prolog e.g. [Dob87], [Tic84]. An
alternative approach is to employ sophisticated compiler technology to produce efficient code for conventional machines. We believe that such compiler technology combined with one of the crop of fast new RISC machines
can produce comparable execution speeds to special purpose hardware. We
believe the reference chain and choice-point analysis described in this paper
will be a key part of the compiler technology.

The Warren Abstract Machine (WAM) [War83] is widely known and the
basis of several Prolog implementations. We have assumed some basic
features of the WAM will be used, in particular, that a variable cell may
contain a reference to another variable, examining the contents of a variable
may require dereferencing an arbitrary length chain of references and when
a variable is bound its address is examined to see if it was created before
the last choice-point and, if so, its address is pushed on to the *trail* stack.

Programs compiled with existing Prolog compilers pay the price for the Prolog's powerful features even where they do not use them. This is because these implementations compile each predicate separately. In the absence of information about how a predicate will be called and how the predicates it calls behave, general and probably inefficient code must be produced. Consider the following program; *append* is always called with its first two arguments bound and its third argument unbound. There is no way to detect this from the definition of *append* alone. The same *append* predicate can be used in several ways. For instance it can be used to split a list by calling it with its first two arguments free and its third argument bound. Therefore a compiler that examines *append* in isolation is forced to produce code that implements all possibilities.

```
main :- append([1, 2], [3, 4], X), write(X), nl.

append([], L, L).
append([H|T], L, [H|Z]) :- append(T, L, Z).
```

Figure 1, is a schematic diagram of the code that a typical compiler will produce for the clause *append([], L, L)* in the above program. *A1*, *A2* and *A3* are the argument registers.

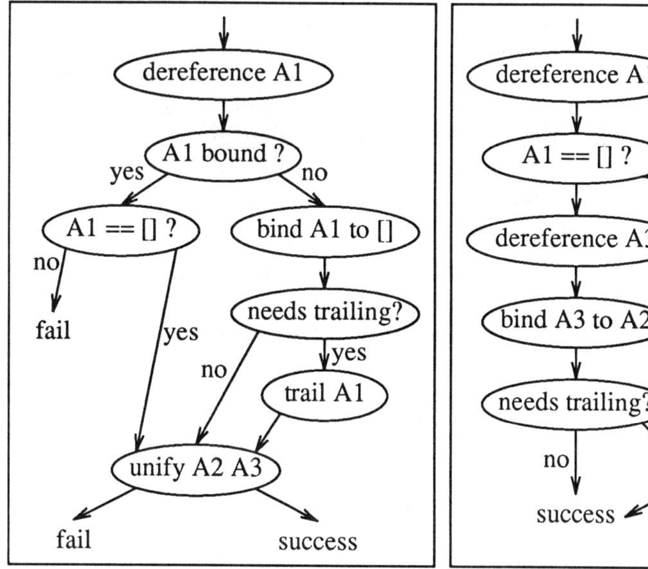

Figure 1: append([], L, L) - code #1   Figure 2: append([], L, L) - code #2

[War77] addressed the problem of unnecessarily general code by allowing the user the option of making mode declarations. These specify how a particular predicate's arguments will be instantiated when it is called.

The mode declaration

     :– mode append(+, +, –).

declares that *append* is always called with its first two arguments bound and its third argument unbound. A compiler employing this information could produce the code in figure 2. This code is no smaller but considerably faster than the code in figure 1 as it no longer tests if *A1* is bound and the expensive call to the general unify routine has been removed. Another advantage of mode declarations is that they provide useful documentation. However they have several disadvantages:

- They are extra work for the user. It is tedious supplying mode declarations for every predicate in the program.

- They can be a source of errors. An incorrect mode declaration accepted blindly by a compiler can result in incorrect and difficult to diagnose program behaviour. Ideally a call which violates a mode declaration should produce an exception. Unfortunately the cost of checking for such violations may negate the benefits of the mode declaration. A possible compromise is making such checking a compile-time option.

- They contain insufficient information. There is more information available in our previous example than that supplied by the mode declaration.

Examination of the program as a whole reveals that none of *append*'s arguments will ever need dereferencing and the binding of its third argument never needs trailing. This information would allow a compiler to produce the smaller and faster code in figure 3. It is pointless extending mode declarations to allow the user to specify such information; it is too complex, low-level and implementation dependent to be provided by the user.

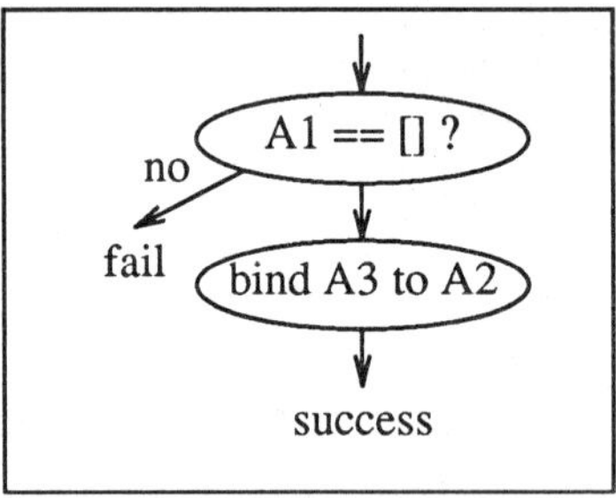

Figure 3: append([], L, L) - code #3

2. Global Analysis

It is difficult to justify general statements about Prolog programs because large Prolog programs are not yet in widespread use and both Prolog implementations and Prolog programming style are still evolving. However Mellish's suggestion in [Mel85] that large parts of real Prolog programs do not require general code is very plausible. Mellish suggested that a compiler can detect this via static global analysis. There has been much work since on global analysis: [Deb86], [Bru87], [Bru87a], [Deb87], [Klu87], [Man87], [Zob87], [War88]. An elegant technique named abstract interpretation [Cou77] is the basis of much of this recent work. Briefly, this involves symbolic execution of the program over an abstract domain. Recursion is handled by computing fixpoints. Suitable choice of the abstract domain allows interesting information to be gathered during this execution with termination and completeness of the execution guaranteed.

An example of an abstract domain is that used by Debray [Deb87] to compute mode information. Debray's domain contains five types {**d, nv, f, c, e**} where: **d** is the set of all terms, **nv** is the set of non-variable terms, **f** is the set of uninstantiated variables, **c** is the set of all ground terms and **e** is the empty set. These types combined with a denotation to indicate aliasing between variables make up Debray's abstract domain. Aliasing is important in the following example:

$$\text{main} :- X = Y, X = 1, \text{write}(Y).$$

An abstract interpreter that ignored aliasing could incorrectly infer that the variable Y is unbound when *write* is called. Executing our earlier program over Debray's abstract domain would yield the same information for *append* as the mode declaration supplied and thus allow the same optimization without any action on the part of the user.

3. An Abstract Domain for Reference Chain and Choice-point Analysis

The abstract domain we have chosen is considerably more complex than Debray's. We differentiate between different categories of constants. We have added list and compound terms types. Most importantly we have allowed information on reference chains and choice-points to be denoted. This is our abstract domain:

nil - *ref*	**ground**(ref_1) - *ref*
atom - *ref*	**free**(*alias, trail*) - *ref*
integer - *ref*	**notvar**(*alias, trail*) - *ref*
float - *ref*	**unknown**(*alias, trail*) - *ref*
number - *ref*	**term**(*functor*($type_1, \ldots type_n$)) - *ref*
constant - *ref*	**list**(*type*, ref_1) - *ref*

The *ref* paired with each of the above types indicates the length of the chain which must be dereferenced to reach the object.

- **0** indicates no reference chain

- **1** indicates a reference chain of length 1

- **1-0** indicates a chain of length 0 or 1 (equals **0 + 1**)

- **?** indicates a chain of unknown length

The other types have the following meaning:

- **nil** - the atom "[]".

- **atom** - the set of all atoms.

- **integer** - the set of all integers.

- **float** - the set of all floating point number.

- **number** - **integer** + **float**

- **constant** - **atom** + **integer** + **float**

- **ground**(ref_1) - the set of all ground terms whose sub-term's reference chains are all of type ref_1.

- **free**(*alias, trail*) - the set of all uninstantiated variables which may only be aliased to the variables indicated by *alias* and, if *trail* is false, which have been created since the last choice-point.

- **notvar**(*alias, trail*) - the set of all non-variable terms which any variable which is a sub-term may only be aliased to the variables indicated by *alias* and, if *trail* is false, all such variables have been created since the last choice-point.

- **unknown**(*alias, trail*) - the set of all terms which any variable which is a sub-term may only be aliased to the variables indicated by *alias* and, if *trail* is false, all such variables have been created since the last choice-point.

- **term**(*functor*($type_1, \ldots type_n$) - the set of all terms of form *functor/n* whose arguments are in $type_1, \ldots type_n$, respectively.

- **list**(*type*, ref_1) - the set of all (flat) lists of 0 or more items belonging to *type* with the cdr reference chains all of type ref_1.

If the **list** and **term** types are allowed to be nested to an arbitrary depth then the abstract domain is infinite. This is undesirable because it makes termination hard to ensure. The problem is caused by rules such as this:

    a(X) :- a(f(X)).

We limit the nesting of types to keep the domain finite. A nesting depth limit of 4 seems to be adequate for most programs.

The **list** type is a compromise. Ideally we would prefer a domain that could represent arbitrary recursive types exactly so that, for example, the types for a program that implemented binary trees would be precise. Unfortunately this seemed difficult and perhaps not feasible to implement. One recursive type in particular, the list, pervades Prolog programs so we have provided an exact representation for it alone.

Although they may have a separate internal representation, strictly lists are not a separate data type in Prolog. List cells are really '.'/2 terms and the atom "[]" is used to terminate the list. The terms [1, 2] and '.'(1, '.'(2, [])) are equivalent. This gives an abstract interpreter a choice when abstracting a term to a type. For example, the term "[1]" can be abstracted to **list(integer - 0, 0) - 0** or **term('.'(integer - 0, nil - 0)) - 0**. Our implementation chooses, whenever possible, to abstract terms to **list** types.

We have chosen only to denote when two variables *may* be aliased. The abstract domain in [Bru87] also has a denotation to indicate that two variables *must* be aliased. This is more expensive to implement. In particular it means that occur-checking must be done. However it produces more precise information about some programs, for example those that involve difference lists, and so may be worthwhile. For this reason we are examining adding this to our abstract domain.

The domain in [Bru87] also allows last-use information to be collected on structures and lists. This yields an interesting class of optimizations involving the re-use of structures. We are currently trying to incorporate this into our abstract domain.

4. Abstract Execution

[Deb87a] contains an elegant description of abstract execution over the simpler {**d, nv, f, c, e**} domain. Proofs of soundness and completeness are given as well as an analysis of complexity. Abstract execution over our extended domain is much more messy and hence an exact description of abstract execution is beyond the scope of this paper. Proofs of correctness and completeness would be difficult because of the presence of implementation artefacts in the abstract domain. We have not presented an analysis of worst-case complexity of abstract execution because we feel that worst case behaviour will not occur in real programs and hence a worst-case result would only be of academic interest.

Analysis of the reference chains created during a program's execution requires intimate knowledge of the code that will be be produced for the program. The simplest optimizations can change the reference chains formed. Hence reference chain analysis is specific to a particular compiler. Worse still there is a catch-22 situation in that the code a compiler will produce may depend on the information from the reference chain analysis. It is possible a compiler will have to make two passes to take full advantage of reference chain analysis. Currently our analysis assumes that the program will be compiled by an extremely naive Prolog to WAM compiler.

During abstract execution it must be determined for each call to a predicate whether a choice-point will be left by that call. This is done using similar techniques to those used to infer functionality in [Deb86a]. This is a slightly stricter notion than determinacy. For example, the predicate below is determinate but it must leave a choice-point behind.

```
a :– write(hello).
a :– write(world), fail.
```

At present we do not examine the bodies of clauses for mutually-exclusive tests. So, for example, it is assumed that the following predicate leaves a choice-point.

```
a(X) :– X < 0, write(negative), nl.
a(X) :– X > 0, write(positive), nl.
```

5. Implementation of an Analyser

We have implemented a global dataflow analyser based on the abstract domain just described. The analyser is named *Prion*. It consists of over 3000 lines of SICStus Prolog [Sic87]. A complete description of *Prion*'s implementation is beyond the scope of this paper, however it can be found in [Tay89]. We will describe a few of the more important aspects of *Prion*'s implementation.

An important component of *Prion* is the extension table. This is where information is gathered during analysis. There is an entry in the table for each call of a different type that occurs during execution. Each entry also contains the result of the call. This information is used to allow fixpoint computation and to avoid repeated computation. Each entry also contains a boolean variable indicating whether a call of this type has already been executed in the current iteration. This allows termination to be ensured. Efficient access to, and modification of, this table is important. We have used SICStus Prolog's internal database predicates (*recorded/3*, *recorda/3*, etc.) which seem adequate for our purposes.

As in [War88] we have taken advantage of Prolog's *logical variable* to represent aliasing. Possible aliasing between two program variables is indicated by a Prolog variable in one type's representation being bound to a Prolog variable in the other type's representation. The instantiation of a program variable is propagated to all the program variables to which it may be aliased by binding this Prolog variable.

Calls to built-in predicates constitute 45-50% of all goals [Tou87]. It is important they be handled as precisely as possible. *Prion* classifies them into several types, namely:

- Predicates that neither instantiate their arguments nor yield information about them e.g *write*/1. These are ignored.

- Predicates that don't instantiate their arguments but do yield information about them e.g *atomic*/1. *Prion* looks up their output type in a table and *intersects* it with the call's inputs.

- Predicates that instantiate some of their arguments e.g *read*/1. *Prion* looks up their output type in a table and *unifies* it with the call's inputs.

- Predicates which can't be handled precisely by table look-up and are used frequently. These include *arg*/3, *'=..'*/2, *is*/2, *call*/1, *setof*/3 and *bagof*/3. They are handled by calls to special purpose routines.

For a variety of reasons the information *Prion* yields about a given program may be imprecise. The user can assist by providing input and output mode declarations for predicates. These declarations are intersected with the input and output types of the predicates during execution. Some consistency checking is done by warning the user if this intersection is an empty set. This almost certainly indicates an incorrect mode declaration. The syntax of the mode declarations is the same as that used to describe our abstract domain but without the aliasing, reference chain and choice-point denotations. Usually it will only be useful to add mode declarations for a fraction of the predicates in a given program. *Prion* can list predicates which are likely candidates for mode declarations.

6. Problems with Global Analysis

There are several potential problems with incorporating a global program analyser such as *Prion* into a Prolog compiler:

- It precludes incremental compilation. This is not a problem if the global analysis is optional as this allows incremental compilation during program development and global optimization for the final version. A global pass could also be used by a compiler for other optimizations such as inter-procedural register allocation.

- Predicates created or modified at run-time can not be analysed. Although some cases can be handled (see [Deb87a]) in general the effects of predicates such as *assert* and *retract* defy analysis. *Prion* requires the user to declare any predicates which may be modified at run-time. Most Prolog compilers require this anyway, it is little work for the user and provides useful program documentation.

- The predicate *call* can hide the flow of control. In general it is impossible to divine which predicate a call to *call* calls. However in many cases *call* is used to implement simple meta-predicates such as the predicate *debug* in the following program fragment.

    main :– debug(append([1], [2], L)).

    debug(X) :– write(enter), call(X), write(exit).

These can be handled in our abstract domain because the argument to *call* will be of type **term** and hence the predicate being called and the type of its arguments will be known. Alternatively many such uses of *call* could be removed by partial evaluation before global analysis. *Prion* requires programs containing other uses of *call* to declare the predicates that may be called. Hopefully this is not an onerous requirement.

- There may be an obstacle to using global analysis to optimize the most important predicates in a program. There is an adage that most programs spend 90% of their execution time in 10% of their code. This probably applies to Prolog programs too. It is likely that general-purpose predicates such as *member* and *append* will be included in this 10%. Unfortunately it is also likely these predicates will be called from many places in the program with several different types of arguments. As a result global analysis may not improve their code and hence may not produce much overall benefit.

A compiler could produce a different version of a predicate for each type of call to it. This could greatly increase code-size and, if so, is probably only practical if the compiler can be selective i.e. only produce extra code for important calls. Profiling data would certainly allow this and possibly heuristics, for example the depth of a call in the program's call-graph, would suffice.

7. Preliminary Results

The information from *Prion* can be used in many places by a Prolog compiler. The exact optimization benefits will not be known until we have a compiler utilizing this information. However to gain a preliminary assessment of the likely benefits we have implemented a simple compiler for the heads of clauses. This compiler has hooks to gather statistics on what information *Prion* yields for each occurrence of a list, structure or constant in the clause heads of a program. This is equivalent to gathering information in a WAM-based implementation on the operands of the *get_constant, get_nil, get_structure, get_list, unify_constant* and *unify_nil* instructions (in clause heads).

We have gathered statistics on four programs: *boyer*, from the Gabriel benchmarks, by Evan Tick; *browse*, from the Gabriel benchmarks, by Tep Dobry and Herve Touati; *read*, a version of the public domain parser by Richard O'Keefe and David H.D. Warren and on a version of *Prion* itself. We have also gathered statistics on the same version of *Prion* but with mode declarations added for 36 of its 246 predicates. The first three are also used as test programs in [War88].

Program	Lines	Predicates	Rules	Facts	Analysis Time
browse	102	16	27	5	4
boyer	399	25	72	63	9
read	634	44	92	17	256
prion	3198	246	526	312	2956
prion+modes	3198	246	526	312	938

Table 1: Test Programs: Analysis Times (in seconds)

The analysis was run on a SUN 3/280 using SICStus Prolog 0.6 #8. The analysis times for *read* and *prion* suggest *Prion* is currently too slow to form part of a Prolog compiler. In both cases most of the time is spent analysing one large set of mutually recursive predicates. The problem is that the complex abstract domain means more iterations are necessary to reach a fixpoint. We are hopeful that changing *Prion*'s handling of mutual recursion will solve the problem. Further improvement in speed could be obtained from a faster Prolog implementation which, of course, is the aim of this work.

[War88] describes an elegant technique called abstract compilation. This involves transforming the program to be analysed into a program which, when run, does the abstract execution. This can also be considered as partial evaluation of the abstract interpreter with respect to the program to be analysed. Rough profiling of our implementation suggests the level of abstract compilation suggested in [War88] is too shallow to produce significant benefits. The time spent in the interpretation which would be removed is insignificant. Deeper abstract compilation may produce more significant benefits.

Program	Total	Mode (%)		
		Bound	Free	?
browse	40	60	30	10
boyer	538	11	68	21
read	123	45	38	17
prion	1767	18	51	31
prion+modes	1767	39	51	10

Table 2: Test Programs: Mode Analysis

The second column (Total) contains the number of instances of constants, lists and structures in the program's clause heads. The next three columns summarise what was inferred about the mode of input arguments for these instances.

Program	Total	Reference Chain Length (%)			
		0	1	0-1	?
browse	40	65	20	0	15
boyer	538	48	19	0	33
read	123	60	22	0	8
prion	1767	46	21	2	31
prion+modes	1767	48	21	2	29

Table 3: Test Programs: Reference Chain Analysis

The second column (Total) contains the number of instances of constants, lists and structures in the program's clause heads. The next four columns summarise what was inferred about the dereferencing code needed for these instances.

The reference chain analysis was very successful. It would allow 70-90% of the branch-and-test loops needed for arbitrary dereferencing to be removed. The results tally with the dynamic data gathered in [Tou87]. This found 50-75% of chains dereferenced were of length 0 and almost all the rest were of length 1.

The mode analysis was similarly successful allowing, in 70-90% of cases, one of the unification alternatives to be removed.

Program	Predicates	C-Determinate	Bindings	No Trailing
browse	16	87%	16	50%
boyer	25	84%	365	66%
read	44	57%	118	35%
prion	246	75%	1236	51%
prion+modes	246	75%	1236	70%

Table 4: Test Programs: Choice-Point and Trailing Analysis

The third column (C-Determinate) contains the percentage of predicates that it was inferred would leave no choice-point behind. The fourth column (Bindings) contains the number of instances of binding code. This is all the cases where the input mode was not inferred to be bound. The last column contains the percentage of instances where it can be inferred than no trailing code is needed. Apart from *read*, which makes more extensive use of backtracking than the other programs, the results are pleasing. In the other programs 75-85% of the predicates can be inferred to leave no choice-point and as a result 50-70% of the trailing code can be removed. More trailing code could be removed by a more sophisticated compiler which, where possible, re-ordered code so that binding code was only reached when execution had committed to a particular rule.

8. Conclusions

The only conclusion that can be directly inferred from our results is that reference chain and choice-point analysis can dramatically reduce the amount of code a compiler need produce for clause heads. We are confident that this will be accompanied by a similar reduction in the execution time spent in clause heads. We are also confident that the same information will enable substantial optimization of the other parts of Prolog programs.

9. References

[Bru87] M. Bruynooghe, "A Framework for the Abstract Interpretation of Logic Programs", *Research report 62, Katholieke Universiteit*, Leuven.

[Bru87a] M Bruynooghe et al., "Abstract Interpretation: Towards the Global Optimization of Prolog Programs", *Proc. 4th IEEE Symp. on Logic Programming, San Francisco*, Sep. 1987.

[Cou77] P. Cousot and R. Cousot, "Abstract Interpretation: a Unified Lattice Model for Static Analysis of Programs by Construction of Fixed Points", *Conf. Rec. 4th ACM Symp. on Princ. of Programming Languages*, pp 78-88, 1977.

[Deb86] S. K. Debray and D. S. Warren, "Automatic Mode Inference for Prolog Programs", *Proc. 1986 Int. Symp. on Logic Programming*, Salt Lake City pp 78-88, Sept. 1986.

[Deb86a] S. K. Debray and D. S. Warren, "Detection and Optimization of Functional Computations", *3rd Int.l Conf. on Logic Programming*, London, July 1986.

[Deb87] S. K. Debray, "Static Inference of Modes and Data Dependencies in Logic Programs", Tech. Rep. 87-15, Dept of Computer Science, University of Arizona, Tucson, Mar. 1988.

[Deb87a] S. K. Debray, "Flow Analysis of a Simple Class of Dynamic Logic Programs", *Proc. 4th IEEE Symp. on Logic Programming*, San Francisco, Sep. 1987.

[Dob87] T. P. Dobry, "A High Performance Architecture for Prolog", Ph.D. Thesis, Computer Science Division, TR UCB/CS 87/352, University of California, Berkeley, April 1987.

[Klu87] F. Kluzniak, "Type Synthesis for Ground Prolog", *Proc. 4th Int. Conf. on Logic Programming*, Melbourne, May 1987.

[Man87] H. Mannila and E. Ukkonen, "Flow Analysis of Prolog Programs", *Proc. 4th IEEE Symp. on Logic Programming*, San Francisco, Sep. 1987.

[Mel85] C. S. Mellish "Some Global Optimizations For a Prolog Compiler", *J. Logic Programming*, Vol. 2(1), pp 43-66, 1987.

[Sic87] "SICStus Prolog Users Manual", Swedish Institute of Computer Science, Sweden, Sep. 1987.

[Tay88] A. Taylor, "Global Analysis of Prolog for Compilation", Technical Report, Basser Dept. of Computer Science, Sydney University, April 1989.

[Tic84] E. Tick and D.H.D. Warren, "Towards a Pipelined Prolog Processor", *International Symposium of Logic Programming*, pp 29-40, 1984.

[Tou87] H. Touati and A Despain, "An Empirical Study of The Warren Abstract Machine", *Proc. 4th IEEE Symp. on Logic Programming*, San Francisco, Sep. 1987.

[War77] D.H.D. Warren "Applied Logic - Its Use and Implementation as a Programming Tool", Ph.D. Thesis, Univ. Edinburgh, Scotland, 1977.

[War83] D.H.D. Warren "An Abstract Prolog Instruction Set", Technical Note 309, SRI International, Menlo Park, California, 1983.

[War88] R. Warren, M. Hermenegildo and S. K. Debray, "On the Practicality of Global Flow Analysis of Logic Programs", *International Conf. Symp. on Logic Programming*, Seattle, pp 684-699, Aug 1988.

[Zob87] J. Zobel, "Derivation of Polymorphic Types for Prolog Programs", *Proc. 4th Int. Conf. on Logic Programming*, Melbourne, May 1987.

AND-Parallel Execution Models

Non-deterministic Stream AND-Parallelism based on intelligent backtracking

Christian Codognet

L.I.E.N.S.
45 rue d'Ulm
75230 PARIS CEDEX 05
FRANCE

Philippe Codognet

LCR Thomson-CSF
B. P. 10
91401 ORSAY CEDEX
FRANCE

Abstract

IBISA (*Intelligent Backtracking In Stream And-parallelism*) is a new abstract parallel execution model for logic programs based on an unification graph intented to keep the history of bindings; this structure originated from previous work on sequential intelligent backtracking. Both accurate backtracking and efficient selective reset are hence performed. Stream parallelism is naturally induced, using a synchronization mechanism close to that of guarded languages. Conversely to most AND-Parallel models using forward control information for improving backtracking, IBISA uses a (more precise) information developed for backward control for forward execution. IBISA takes advantage from the formal framework and from the implementation-oriented simplifications already developed for sequential intelligent backtracking.

1 Introduction

In the last few years, research on parallel execution models for logic programming has become more and more on focus, and has sprouted in several (more or less) exclusive directions. The most important alternative is *parallel* logic programming versus parallel *logic* programming, that is either to have a parallel language, derived but distinct from the original logic programming paradigm (viz. guarded languages), or to retain this paradigm and get as much parallelism as possible within it (by means of AND and/or OR parallelism). This paper takes place in the (nearly) no man's land between the two fields (taking shots by both sides) and proposes to conciliate Stream AND-Parallelism, as used in guarded languages, and non-determinism. Our approach was initiated by previous work on sequential intelligent backtracking [Cod 88] and consists in using the accurate information on variable bindings obtained this way for controlling both forward and backward execution. Previous AND-Parallel models such as [Con 83] and its followers [Deg 84] [Her 86] [Lin 86, 88a & b] [Woo 86] [Con 87] [Win 87] [Som 88] have introduced dependency graphs among literals to control AND-Parallel forward execution, reusing them thereof to achieve a better backward execution. Along these lines, [Som 88] already copes with Stream AND-Parallelism, but at the expense of a rather complex mode declaration. IBISA departs from these approaches, and has for backbone the *Dynamic Conflict Graph (DCG)*, an unification graph which records for each binding the literal responsible of it. The DCG has been introduced by [Cox 81] [Mat 85] for an intelligent backtracking method, and then developed and formalized in [Cod 86, 88, 89a & b]. This structure is also (implicitly) present in [Per 82], where it is presented in a completely different way. Thanks to the DCG, it is possible to distinguish exactly which literals are responsible of an unification failure, making backward execution as precise as possible, both in the choice of backtrack point and selective reset, and even allowing simultaneous backward and forward execution. Selective reset is intented to avoid useless deduction/backtracking work by retaining, upon backtracking, parts of the deduction work irrelevant to the failure: it will hence use the same information on variables bindings as intelligent backtracking. In IBISA, selective reset is performed in a way different from [Win 87] or (the appendix C of) [Lin 88a] that calls for less overhead. It is worth noticing that the previously referred AND-Parallel models have used a structure developed to control forward execution for improving backward execution when IBISA does it backward (sic). Indeed the extra precision of the DCG makes room for Stream-AND Parallelism. A dynamic synchronization mechanism is naturally induced by the DCG, similar to that of guarded languages, relying then on a simple mode annotation. IBISA is hence a unification-oriented model as opposed to process-oriented models of the Conery family.

In this paper, IBISA is presented as an abstract parallel computation model and we will not explain management of parallel processes, scheduling and so on. The main idea is in fact to implement IBISA by modifying an existing Stream And-parallel implementation, e.g. that of a guarded language [Fos 87] [Sha 88].

Using the framework developed for a sequential intelligent backtracking method, the DIB (Depth-first Intelligent Backtracking [Cod 88]), IBISA inherits the formalization and proofs of correctness of the DCG as well as a simplified version of it efficiently implemented [Cod 89b]. Moreover IBISA can be seen as an instance of the General Intelligent Backtracking scheme of [Cod 89a] adapted to parallel execution, thus taking advantage of its proof of completeness.

Following this introduction, section 2 presents the basic notions of plan (proof tree), DCG (unification graph) and unification conflicts. Forward and backward execution mechanisms of IBISA are detailed in section 3, while section 4 adresses its completeness (w.r.t. an exhaustive computation) and section 5 deals with some implementation-oriented simplifications. A comparison with related work and a short conclusion end the paper.

2 Preliminaries

The reader is assumed to be already familiar with the classical notions of Logic Programming, see for instance [Llo 87]. A *logic program* is a pair $< S, G >$ where S is a sequence of definite clauses and G is a negative clause called a goal. A *sequential* execution of a program $< S, G >$ consists in applying a sequence of either *expansion* or *backtracking steps* to a couple $< P, D >$ where P is a *plan* for $< S, G >$, i.e. a (partial) proof-tree, and D is a graph representation of the corresponding m.g.u. called the *Dynamic Conflict Graph* associated to P. A *parallel* execution consists in applying several *expansion* or *backtracking* steps in parallel - one restriction in IBISA will be that two backtracking steps cannot be executed in parallel.

After briefly presenting the notions of plan and DCG, we will detail what information about variables bindings may be found in the DCG and how it is used upon unification conflicts. The reader will find in [Cod 88, 89a & b], a formal presentation of these notions and proofs of properties here simply stated.

2.1 Plan

A *plan* for a program $< S, G >$ is essentially a partial proof-tree representing the refutation of G using S, each node corresponding to a deduction step. It is hence a tree, i.e. a partial function from $\mathbf{N}^*$ (the set of words over natural numbers) to a set of labels, whose nodes are labelled by $< Up\text{-}literal,$ *Down-literal, Potentials, Alt, Reset* $>$ where *Up-literal* is the call literal of a deduction step and *Down-literal* is either Ω if the call is still to be satisfied or the head of the clause used; *Potentials* is the sequence of alternative clauses not yet tried; *Alt* is a set of intelligent backtrack points and *Reset* is a set of nodes to be reset in case of backtracking, as will be explained in section 3.2. A node of a plan is *open* if its down-literal is Ω, *closed* otherwise. A plan is *closed* if all its nodes are closed. A plan P defines a set of equations $\mathcal{E}_P$, containing, for each closed node n of P, the equation "*up-literal(n)=down-literal(n)*". A plan is *unifiable* if $\mathcal{E}_P$ has a finite solution, and is *complete* if it is closed and unifiable. A complete plan corresponds to a refutation of the goal.

2.2 Dynamic Conflict Graph

The plan contains the purely deductive part of the proof, and the Dynamic Conflict Graph (DCG) is used to record variables bindings, i.e. to represent the current substitution.

Consider the set of equations $\mathcal{E}_P$ defined by a plan P, the *Dynamic Conflict Graph associated to* $\mathcal{E}_P$, noted $\mathrm{DCG}(\mathcal{E}_P)$, is an oriented graph whose nodes are non-oriented graphs called *classes* representing terms sharing the same value. For a term t, $\bar{t}$ denotes the class containing it. Every edge e of a class is labelled by an integer i identifying a closed node of P or, equivalently, an equation of $\mathcal{E}_P$. Oriented arcs represent functional dependencies between a term and its subterms. They do not simply run from one class to another, but from a node inside a class to another one. An arc is thus labelled by a triple $< f(t_1, ..., t_n), t_i, i >$. In what follows, this is shown graphically by letting the arc run between the two concerned class elements, viz. in the next figure the arcs (f, Y) and (f, b). We will not detail here the construction of the DCG associated to a set of equations but simply give an example.

Example 1
Consider the following set of (numbered) equations :
$$\{(1 , p(X,a)=p(f(Y),Y)) , (2 , r(Y)=r(U)) , (3 , s(Z)=s(a)) , (4 , q(X)=q(f(b)))\}$$

The associated DCG is depicted in the following figure :

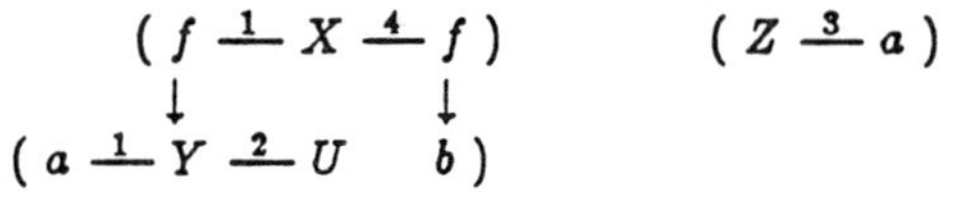

$$(f \xrightarrow{\ 1\ } X \xleftarrow{\ 4\ } f) \qquad (Z \xrightarrow{\ 3\ } a)$$
$$\downarrow \qquad\qquad\quad \downarrow$$
$$(a \xrightarrow{\ 1\ } Y \xrightarrow{\ 2\ } U \qquad b)$$

The unsolvability of this set of equations can be detected in the DCG as two different function symbols, namely a and b, are in the same class.

In the general case, let P be a plan and $\mathrm{DCG}(\mathcal{E}_P)$ its corresponding DCG. $\mathrm{DCG}(\mathcal{E}_P)$ contains a *clash* when some class contains two nodes with different function symbols at the root. It contains an *infinite term* when, considering only the oriented arcs of $\mathrm{DCG}(\mathcal{E}_P)$ and each class as a single node, one obtains a circular graph. $\square$

It is showned [Cod 89a] that $\mathcal{E}_P$ admits a finite solution iff $\mathrm{DCG}(\mathcal{E}_P)$ contains neither a clash nor an infinite term. Moreover, in this case, $\mathrm{DCG}(\mathcal{E}_P)$ represents the m.g.u. of $\mathcal{E}_P$: one can define a substitution on each class, as any class contains at most one function symbol, and compose them in a bottom-up fashion as the DCG has no cycle.

Besides representing the m.g.u. of a system of equations, the DCG gives precious information about the history of unification, which is called in [Por 88] the *source* of a derived equation. In the previous example, one can intuitively see that "a=b" is solely derived from equations 1 and 4.

2.3 Unification conflicts

To determine precisely the causes of unification failure, we first need to introduce the notion of *connection* between two terms of a class. A connection represents the complete history of the unification of two terms of a class c and is a generalized path that may contain not only edges of c but also edges of other classes if the two terms were unified through unification of terms they were part of. Instead of giving a complex formal definition, let us rather see the intuitive meaning of this notion by getting back to the previous example. The (unique) connection between a and b is :

$$a \xrightarrow{\;1\;} Y, \; f \xrightarrow{\;1\;} X, \; X \xrightarrow{\;4\;} f, \; b$$

In case of a clash it is then easy to compute, from a connection between the two terms with different function symbols at the root, the set of labels of the edges of the connection: this set is called the *conflict* corresponding to the clash and determine the equations of $\mathcal{E}_P$ responsible of the clash. Continuing the same example, the conflict corresponding to the clash is hence $\{1,4\}$.

One can similarily define a conflict corresponding to an infinite term. It is showned in [Cod 89a] that every conflict corresponding to a clash (resp. infinite term) of $\mathrm{DCG}(\mathcal{E}_P)$ is a non-unifiable subset of $\mathcal{E}_P$, and that, conversely, for any minimal non-unifiable subset M of $\mathcal{E}_P$ there is a clash or an infinite term of $\mathrm{DCG}(\mathcal{E}_P)$ s.t. M is a conflict corresponding to it. From now on, for the sake of simplicity, we will only treat the clash and put aside the infinite term.

3 IBISA

3.1 Forward component

Let us first describe the effects of a single expansion step on a plan before handling simultaneous ones, i.e. control forward execution.

Definition Let P be a non-complete unifiable plan and n an open node of P labeled by $< L, \Omega, < c_1, ..., c_n >, Alt, Reset >$ where $c_1 = H \leftarrow B_1, ..., B_m$. An *expansion step* on node n consists in changing the down-literal of n from Ω to H and giving this node m sons corresponding to $B_1, ..., B_m$; all these nodes are open, have empty Alt and $Reset$ sets and have their *initial potentials*, i.e. the set of all clauses whose head unifies with the up-literal. A corresponding DCG is constructed for $\mathcal{E}_P \cup \{L = H\}$. $\square$

In Prolog, control of forward execution is given by the order of the literals inside a clause and that of the clauses in the program. Dialects as Prolog II or μProlog provide primitives to explicitly *delay* the execution of some literal. A more direct and precise control mechanism has been introduced by IC-Prolog and the ancestor of guarded languages, Relationnal Language, leading to current Stream Parallel languages such as GHC, Concurrent Prolog or Parlog [Sha 88] that use *mode declaration* to specify a *synchronization* between literals of the resolvent (i.e. active processes). Mode annotations on the variables of literals, or simply on their arguments, specify which variables are *produced* (i.e. instanciable) by a literal and which ones are *consumed* (i.e uninstanciable). When unification leads a literal to instanciate a consumed variable, this literal is *suspended* until that variable is instanciated enough (by some other literal).

The same technique is used in IBISA and is achieved by using mutual exclusion on each class of the DCG : if several processes try to modify at the same time a single class of the DCG, only one of them ("producer" of some variable in the class) will be able to proceed while others ("consumers") will be suspended. Observe that this suspension mechanism is hence *dynamic* and takes place during the unification phase, conversely to other AND-Parallel models such as [Deg 84] or [Lin 88b] that (pessimistically) determine at the entry of a clause which body literals to suspend by using tests on the instanciations of variables. These models are therefore restricted to *dependant* AND-parallelism, prohibiting Stream AND-parallelism. Synchronization schemes by mode annotation have been developed for Parlog, GHC or Concurrent Prolog and can be used as well in IBISA. Abstract interpretation may also be used to produce an automatic mode declaration in a way similar to what has been done for Prolog programs.

We will here assume that some scheme is used to specify an annotation of the program, giving for each literal l of the program a set $Var_p(l)$ of produced (instanciable) variables and a set $Var_c(l)$ of consumed (non instanciable) variables. The synchronization mechanism can be stated as follows :

1. when a process l tries to instanciate a variable X in $Var_c(l)$, i.e. to introduce a non-variable term in $\overline{X}$ or one of its child class in the DCG, this process is suspended on that class.

2. when a process l instanciates a variable X in $Var_p(l)$, it "wakes up" the processes suspended on $\overline{X}$.

Note that several processes may have simultaneous access to the same class of the DCG if they are all consumers of variables in that class and it already contains a non-variable term, that is, multiple read is possible. This suspension mechanism can be easily implemented by modifying the algorithms of construction of the DCG [Cod 88].

Exemple 2

Consider the following program, where X? denotes a consumed variable as in Concurrent Prolog :

(1) p(f(T),c) ← s(T) .   (3) s(a) .
(2) q(c,U) ← ... .   (3') s(b) .
(2') q(d,U) ← ... .   (4) r(f(b)) .
and the goal : ← p(X,Y), q(Y?,Z), r(X?) .

Starting processes for literals *p*, *q* and *r* of the goal results in expanding *p* with clause (1) and suspending *q* and *r*, leading to the following plan:

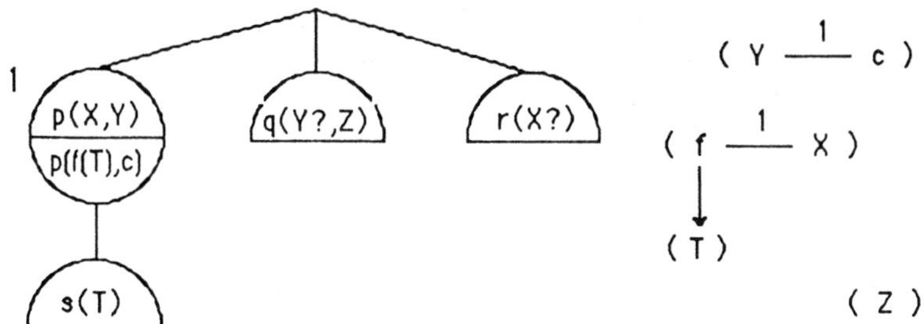

q and *s* can then be developed in parallel. Once the expansion of *s* is completed, *r* can start, concurrently with work in the subtree of *q*, leading to :

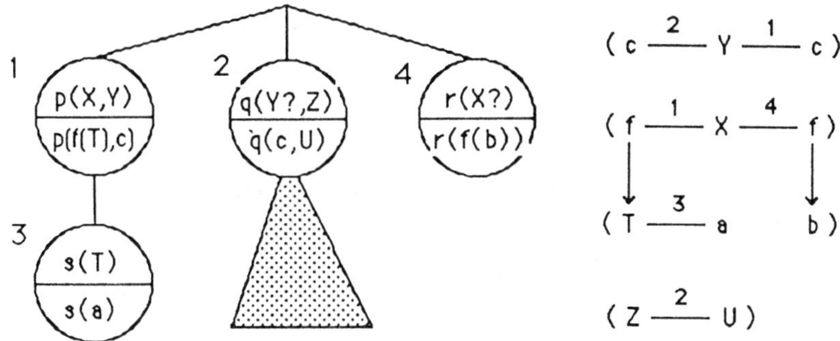

This DCG contains a clash with conflict $\{1,3,4\}$. Backtracking must now take place, but expansion can go on in the subtree of *q*. □

3.2 Backward component

Backward execution is invoked in case of failure and consists first in choosing a node to backtrack to and second in pruning the plan to perform a backtracking step.

In Prolog, backtracking always takes place to the maximal (w.r.t. the lexicographical order) node of the plan and the backtracking step is performed by reopening this node. A sequential intelligent backtracking method as the DIB will choose the maximal *intelligent backtrack point* computed by conflict analysis (i.e. the maximal element of a conflit) and perform a backtracking step by pruning any node of the plan superior to this node, for also using a depth-first left-to-rigth strategy. In IBISA, as in most sequential intelligent backtracking methods, a set containing *intelligent backtrack points* (i.e. nodes to backtrack to) is attached to each closed node of the plan. These sets, called *Alt* sets in IBISA and DIB, are similar to the set of rejected procedures of [Bru 84], B-lists of [Lin 87], Witness sets of [Win 87], Candidate sets of [Con 87] or R-sets of [Som 88].

When backtracking to a node n in IBISA, the part of the plan posterior to n is not systematically deleted but only selectively pruned, retaining thus deduction work irrelevant to the failure. This will be achieved by attaching to each closed node n a set *Reset(n)* telling the nodes to prune in case of backtracking to n: those nodes only have to be reset and their subtrees deleted.

3.2.1   Where to backtrack to ?

Whenever a clash occurs, IBISA first computes the conflict associated to it. It is useless, recall 2.3, to backtrack to a node that is not element of the conflict, thus the (intelligent) backtrack points will be the elements of the conflict. In case several conflicts happen at the same time, one can choose to consider backtrack points that solve all conflicts, see [Cox 87] or [Cod 89a], but this approach is intractable as shown in [Wol 86]. We choose in IBISA, as in the DIB, to solve only one conflict at a time and to treat simultaneous conflicts in a row.

Once a conflict is computed, some total order on its elements is needed to allow, by always backtracking to the maximal backtrack point, to enumerate correctly intelligent backtrack points. This order must be compatible with the partial order among nodes induced by the tree-structure of the plan, as one has to backtrack to a child node before considering its parent in the plan. One will take the *computation order* among nodes, i.e. the order in which expansion steps effectively take place (simultaneous steps may be ordered in any sense). In case of sequential intelligent backtracking methods, this computation order is the lexicographical order among nodes, because of the depth-first left-to-right strategy of those methods.

3.2.2   How to backtrack ?

Definition

Consider a plan P and a node n of P labeled by
$<up\text{-}literal(n), down\text{-}literal(n), potentials(n), Alt(n), Reset(n)>$.
A *backtracking step to n* produces a new plan as follows :
for any node $\alpha \in Reset(n)$, the subtree rooted in α is deleted and α is *reset*: its down literal is set to Ω and it is given its initial potentials. n is *reopened*, i.e. its down-literal is also set to Ω but its potentials are unchanged. A new corresponding DCG is obtained by removing all arcs and edges introduced

by the deleted equations. $\quad\square$

We will see in the next section how *Reset* sets are incrementally computed during backtracking, in a manner dual to *Alt* sets, and how to perform selective reset while retaining the completeness of the method. Intuitively, $Reset(n)$ contains any node m greater than n whose expansion has resulted in a clash involving n.
Note that this precise backtracking and reset mechanism makes sense in a Stream AND-parallel model designed to keep as much as possible the deduction work already done and to allow processes to work simultaneously to the failure analysis on parts of the plan irrelevant to that failure.

3.3   IBISA algorithm

• **while** the plan is unifiable and not complete expand in parallel the open nodes of the plan using the suspension mechanism described in section 3.1 .

  • **if** a clash occurs in a class c while developing a node n :

    – suspend any literal working on c

    – compute a conflict K corresponding to the clash

    – $Alt(n) := Alt(n) \cup K$

    – $(n', Alt(n'), Reset(n')) := Real\_BP(n, Alt(n), Reset(n))$

    – **if** $n' = root$ **then exit** *search space exhausted*
      else backtrack to n'

    – wake up literals suspended on c

  • **if** the plan is complete and unifiable
    then exit *solution*

Real_BP returns the node to which actually backtrack : a node with potential(s). It also collects in a dual manner *Alt* and *Reset* sets :

function *Real_BP*(n, *ALT*, *RESET*)
if n has a potential **or** $n = root$
then return $(n, ALT, RESET)$
else **let** m be the father of n in the plan
      let $n_1 = Max(ALT \cup \{m\})$
      return *Real_BP*$(n_1$, $Alt(n_1) - \{n\} \cup ALT$,
                  $Reset(n_1) \cup \{n\} \cup \{\alpha \in RESET \ / \ \alpha \notin$ subtree of $n\})$
end if
end *Real_BP*

For the sake of simplicity, this algorithm stops as the first solution is reached; it can easily be extended to give all solutions to a goal in the manner described in [Cod 88] : intelligent backtracking has to be inhibited on the part of the plan that has contributed to any solution.

4 Completeness of IBISA

4.1 The General Intelligent Backtracking scheme and IBISA

[Cod 89a] describes a General Intelligent Backtracking scheme that encompasses several existing methods. One of them, called the *parallel GIB*, was introduced by [Cox 81, Mat 85] and developed in [Cod 86]. In that method, once the conflict corresponding to a clash is computed, several plans are constructed, each one corresponding to one backtrack point, in which only the subtree rooted in that backtrack point is pruned. These plans are hence developed in parallel (read: independently).

Example 3
Consider the skeleton of plan P sketched below and suppose that DCG($\mathcal{E}_P$) is non-unifiable and contains a clash $\{i,j,k\}$.

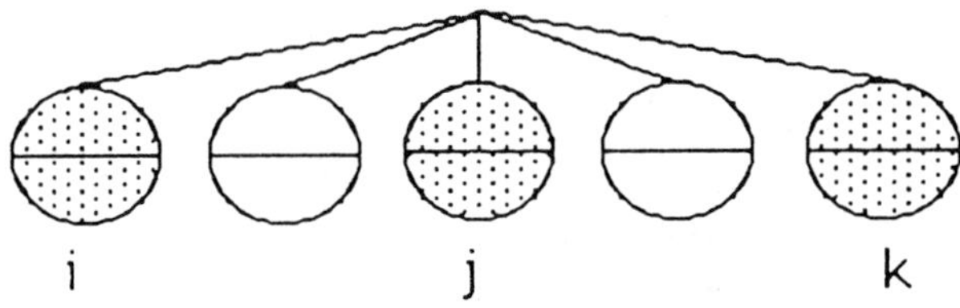

The parallel GIB will then generate three plans : P_i identical to P excepted that node i is reopened, and similarly P_j with j reopened, P_k with k reopened. Observe that these nodes are reopened and not reset, that is they do not recover their initial potentials.   □

In the same spirit, we want in IBISA to have a limited pruning in order to save previous deduction work as much as possible but we also want to have a single plan for the sake of implementation. This means that we always have a privileged backtrack point for resuming the computation, others being recorded, as in the DIB, in the *Alt* set of that node. In case of backtracking to a node n, reopening nodes in $Reset(n)$ is necessary in IBISA in order to simulate with a single plan the different plans that the general method would have produced at once and develop independently.
Going back to the previous exemple, IBISA will (from the same non-unifiable plan P) solely produce P_k and set $Alt(k)$ to $\{i,j\}$. In case of backtracking to k, when k has no potential left, IBISA will use $Alt(k)$ to perform a backtracking step to j, and put k in $Reset(j)$. The backtracking step to j hence

produces a plan P'_j identical to P_j excepted for k which is reset. From that plan, P_j can therefore obviously [1] be generated. In the subsequent computation, in case of backtracking to j and j has no potential left, IBISA will use $Alt(j)$ to backtrack to i and put j and $Reset(j)$ (containing k) in $Reset(i)$. This step produces then a plan P'_i with i reopened and j and k reset. Again P_i can be generated from P'_i.

A greater precision can be achieved in IBISA by using, as in the parallel GIB or the general method of [Bru 84], one Alt set associated to each *potential* of the node instead of a single Alt set for the whole node and one corresponding $Reset$ for each such potential. $Reset$ set would then contain couples $< node, potential >$ allowing to reset a node from a given potential and not from scratch.

Another computation is defined in [Cod 89a], the *sequential GIB*, that uses direct storage of whole plans in an unique set attached to each (potential of a) closed node. This method is closely related to the general method of [Bru 84]; let us briefly describe it by going back to example 3 : deduction is resumed with only one plan, say P_k, while P_i and P_j are put in $Alt(k)$. In case of backtracking to k and k has no more potential, the computation is switched to P_j (for example) and P_i put in $Alt(j)$ in P_i.

IBISA can be seen as an "economical" alternative to the direct storage of those whole plans thanks to the Alt and $Reset$ sets, both simply containing nodes of the plan. It is no surprise then that the completeness of IBISA w.r.t. an exhaustive computation relies on that of the sequential GIB.

4.2 Completeness

We will just sketch the main idea of the proof of completeness, details may be found in [Cod 89a & b].

We can associate to a parallel execution of a logic program $< S, G >$ by IBISA a sequential execution by using the computation order between expansion steps: this will be called the *IBISA computation* associated to $< S, G >$. It is a subsequence of the depth-first (left-to-right) exploration of a certain SLD-tree (not necessarily the OLD-tree as in Prolog). We will show the completeness of the IBISA computation w.r.t. the exhaustive computation, i.e. that IBISA does not skip any complete plan. This will be done via the sequential GIB computation that is showned complete w.r.t. the exhaustive one [Cod 89a].

Theorem 1 *Let A_1 and A_2 be the (possibly infinite) sequences of complete plans respectively produced by the exhaustive and the IBISA computations associated to a logic program $< S, G >$. Then A_1 is a prefix (strict or not) of A_2.*

---

[1] dubious readers are held over until the next section

The two computations differ only in case of deep backtracking, leading hence to a proof by induction on the number of backtracking steps performed by IBISA: the exhaustive computation either reaches the plan obtained by IBISA and the sequences of complete plans produced till then by the two computations are equal or it loops and will never produce any complete plan.

We would like to use now the completeness of the sequential GIB w.r.t. the exhaustive computation. However, the plan generated by IBISA after a deep backtracking step differs from that generated by the sequential GIB for the following two reasons.

(i) As it does not use the extra machinery associating *Alt* and *Reset* to each potential, recall the discussion in the previous section, IBISA has to do extra (useless) work to reach the right potential for each reset node. Remark that this may cause a loop (preventing the right potential to be reached) only if the exhaustive computation does loop as well. So completeness w.r.t. exhaustive computation is not concerned but completeness w.r.t. sequential GIB is impossible.

(ii) The plan generated by the sequential GIB exactly represents the state of computation at the time the clash was encountered (this is a plan the parallel GIB would have produced immediately after the clash). The corresponding IBISA plan however may contain nodes some potentials of which have been consumed in the meantime. For all those nodes, we apply the following fact $(\star)$, analogous to that of the DIB [Cod 88] and that of the sequential GIB [Cod 89a], which only relies on the correctness of conflicts and the way *Alt* sets are computed.

Fact $(\star)$ **:** Let P be a plan obtained in the IBISA computation associated to a logic program $< S, G >$. Let n be a node of P having at least one potential already consumed (i.e. that took part in a clash) such that no complete plan containing n has been already found. Then, there is no complete plan P' such that :

(i) P' coincides with P on $Alt(n)$, i.e. such that the up- and down-literals of those nodes and of their ancestors are identical in P' and P,

(ii) n is expanded in P' with a consumed potential. $\qquad\square$

This ensures that no complete plan have been skipped by IBISA (w.r.t. sequential GIB) and thus the completeness of IBISA (w.r.t. exhaustive computation).

5 Simplifying IBISA

The DCG is an interesting structure to precisely determine the causes of unification failures, but is too complex to implement efficiently. In order to implement the DIB, [Cod 88 & 89b] have introduced the sDIB, for *simplified DIB*, featuring the same (expansion/backtracking) algorithm as the DIB but a different data structure : the DCG has been replaced by a *simplified DCG (sDCG)*. The overhead of sDCG construction is reduced (w.r.t. DCG construction) : a class of the sDCG is no longer a non-oriented graph with labelled edges but an oriented one (representing exactly Prolog bindings) together with a *label*, that is a set containing the labels of all edges in the DCG class. The sDCG can be implemented by simply adding class labels to the term representation of a standard unification algorithm. Moreover, conflict computation is fastened as only involving unions of labels of classes instead of computations of paths inside those classes. The price to pay is a loss in accuracy as s-conflicts in the sDCG are supersets of corresponding conflicts in the DCG.

Here is an example of a transformation of a DCG class into a sDCG one :

$$X \xrightarrow{\ 1\ } Y \xrightarrow{\ 2\ } a \qquad\qquad X \longrightarrow Y \longrightarrow a - > \{3,2,1\}$$
$$\big|3 \qquad\qquad\qquad\qquad\qquad\qquad\qquad \uparrow$$
$$Z \qquad\qquad\qquad\qquad\qquad\qquad\qquad\quad Z$$

(a) DCG   **(b) sDCG**

Several important optimizations allow the sDCG to be implemented with only 20% overhead w.r.t. usual unification, see [Cod 88 89b] for a performance evaluation of the sDIB w.r.t. Prolog and other intelligent backtracking methods.

One of these optimizations is the lazy conflict computation that allows conflict analysis to take place only in case of deep backtracking while nothing is done in case of shallow backtracking. Lazy conflict computation, although designed for the sDIB, still holds for IBISA. We will here sketch how to adapt to IBISA others optimizations of the sDIB aiming at reducing class labels. Indeed, including every literal labelling an edge of a DCG class into the label of the corresponding sDCG class is not necessary. First consider an expansion step of a node n introducing a function symbol in a class already containing an identical one: it is shown in [Cod 89b] that recording n in the label of the sDCG class is unnecessary in the sDIB, thus n does not need to be backtracked upon. It is neither necessary to backtrack to n in IBISA, but, in case of deeper backtracking, n has to be reset. For this reason a label lab has to be divided in two parts: lab_{Alt}, identical to the sDIB label, and lab_{Reset}, containing nodes such as n. lab_{Alt} will be used to compute conflicts and Alt sets while both lab_{Alt} and lab_{Reset} will be considered for reset purposes.

Similarly, an expansion step of a node n introducing a new variable in a class, i.e. binding this variable for the first time, has not to be recorded in the sDIB. In IBISA the same holds, as neither backtracking to n nor resetting n in case of deeper backtracking is here necessary.

6 Comparison with related work

6.1 Parallelism

Original AND-parallel models such as [Con 83] and the improved versions of [Lin 86, Woo 86] use a dependency graph between all literals in the resolvent that is dynamically computed, thus allowing Stream AND-parallelism. However the overhead of recomputing the graph at each step prevents any efficient implementation and has led these authors to develop restricted versions [Con 87, Lin 88a & b] based on static dependency graphs inside a clause, as initiated by [Deg 84]. These models no more allow Stream AND-parallelism but only Restricted AND-parallelism. On the other hand, these schemes are easier to implement and may lead to reasonable implementations, see [Lin 88b].
The last model of the Conery family, [Som 88], copes with Stream-parallelism by using a special mode declaration scheme. This scheme is rather complex and obliges to statically specify the literal producer of each part of a compound term.

6.2 Backtracking

The dependency graph and failure analysis of AND-parallel models allow for some kind of intelligent backtracking, but less precise than that of IBISA. Particularly when using compound terms - a most frequent case - those mechanisms are unable to correctly determine intelligent backtrack points. Indeed, the information on variable bindings provided by dependency graphs is less precise than that of the DCG, especially to determine connections involving ancestor classes. This was already the case in the sequential method of [Lin 87], see [Cod 88 & 89a] for a comparison with the sDIB and DIB. Besides, using a dependency graph inside a clause only, as [Con 87, Lin 88b] do, prevents intelligent backtracking outside the clause boundary.
The mode annotation of [Som 88] allows his backtracking to get intelligently across this boundary, but not (because of its statical nature) to be as precise as that of IBISA when using compound terms.

6.3 Reset

Again, the selectivity of the reset relies on the information on variables bindings (and conflicts) and, again, the DCG is more precise than the dependency graph of AND-parallel models. [Lin 88a & b], for implementation

reasons, and [Som 88] perform no selective reset; others schemes as [Win 87, Con 87] or the appendix C of [Lin 88a] differ from IBISA as they do not maintain explicit *Reset* sets but compute on each backtracking step the literals to be reset. Roughly speaking, this is done by resetting, when backtracking to a node n, the nodes in (the smallest set solution of) :
$$R = \{ m \ / \ n \in Alt(m) \ \vee \ \exists m' \in R, m' \in Alt(m) \} .$$
Finally notice that [Win 87] maintains a distinct *Alt* set for each potential, as proposed in 4.1, thus increasing selectivity and overhead.

7 Conclusion

We have presented IBISA, a new abstract Stream AND-Parallel model based on a data structure (called the DCG), introduced for a sequential intelligent backtracking method (called the DIB), and giving complete information about the history of variable bindings. This information is more precise than that commonly used in AND-Parallel models, allowing for example accurate intelligent backtracking outside the clause boundary. IBISA also incorporates selective reset, both more precise, owing to the DCG, and more simple, by maintaining explicit *Reset* sets attached to each node and incrementally computed, than previous approaches. An implementation of IBISA, based on a simplified DCG (implemented with low overhead for the DIB) seems feasible by using guarded languages implementation techniques.

References

[Bru 84]   M. Bruynooghe and L. M. Pereira : "Deduction revision by Intelligent Backtracking", in Implementations of Prolog, J. A. Campbell (Ed.), Ellis Horwood 1984.

[Cod 86]   C. Codognet, P. Codognet and G. Filè : "A very intelligent backtracking method for Logic Programs", proc. ESOP 86, LNCS 213, Springer Verlag 1986.

[Cod 88]   C. Codognet, P. Codognet and G. Filè : "Yet Another Intelligent Backtracking Method", proc. 5th ICLP/SLP, Seattle 1988.

[Cod 89a]   C. Codognet : "Intelligent Backtracking in Logic Programming : a general framework", Ph.D. dissertation (in french), University of Paris VII, January 1989.

[Cod 89b]   P. Codognet : "Intelligent Backtracking in Logic Programming : from theory to implementation and application to parallelism", Ph.D. dissertation (in french), University of Bordeaux-I, January 1989.

[Con 83]   J. S. Conery : "The AND/OR Process Model for Parallel Execution of Logic Programs", Ph.D. Dissertation, Tech Rep 204, University of California, Irvine, 1983.

[Con 87]   J. S. Conery : "Implementing Backward Execution in nondeterministic AND-Parallel Systems", proc. 4th ICLP, Melbourne, MIT Press 1987.

[Cox 81]   P. T. Cox and T. Pietrzykowski : "Deduction plans : a basis for intelligent backtracking", IEEE PAMI vol. 3 (1981).

[Cox 87]   P. T. Cox : "On determining the causes of non-unifiability", Journal of Logic Programming, 1987.

[Deg 84]   D. De Groot : "Restricted And-Parallelism", proc. FGCS 84, ICOT 1984.

[Fos 87]   I. Foster and S. Taylor : "Flat Parlog : a basis for comparison", International Journal of Parallel Programming, Vol. 16 No 2, 1987.

[Her 86]   M. V. Hermenegildo and R. I. Nasr : "Efficient managing of Backtracking in AND-Parallelism" proc. 3rd ICLP, London, LNCS 225, Springer Verlag 1986.

[Kum 87]   V. Kumar and Y-J Lin : "An Intelligent Backtracking Scheme for Prolog", proc. 4th SLP, Salt Lake City, 1987.

[Lin 86]   Y-J. Lin, V. Kumar and C. Leung : "An Intelligent Backtracking Algorithm for Parallel Execution of Logic Programs", proc. 3rd ICLP, London, LNCS 225, Springer Verlag 1986.

[Lin 88a]   Y-J. Lin and V. Kumar : "An Execution Model for Exploiting AND-Parallelism in Logic Programs", New Generation Computing Vol. 5 No 4 (1988).

[Lin 88b]   Y-J. Lin and V. Kumar : "AND-Parallel execution of Logic Programs on Shared Memory Multiprocessor : A Summary of Results", proc. 5th ICLP/SLP, Seattle, MIT Press 1988.

[Llo 87]   J. W. Lloyd : "Foundations of Logic Programming", Springer Verlag, series in symbolic computation, 1987.

[Mat 85]   S. Matwin and T. Pietrzykowski : "Intelligent backtracking in plan-based deduction", IEEE PAMI vol. 7 (6), Nov. 1985.

[Per 82]   L. M. Pereira and A. Porto : "Selective backtracking", Logic Programming, K. Clark and S.A. Tarnlund (eds.) 1982.

[Por 88]   G. Port : "A simple approach to finding the cause of non-unifiability", proc. 5th ICLP/SLP, Seattle, MIT Press 1988.

[Sha 88]   E. Shapiro (Ed.) : "Concurrent Prolog", collected papers, MIT Press 1988.

[Som 88]   Z. Somogyi, K. Ramamohanarao and J. Vaghani : "A Backtracking Algorithm for the Stream AND-Parallel Execution of Logic Programs", Tech. Rep. 88/10, University of Melbourne, also in proc. 5th ICLP/SLP, Seattle, MIT Press 1988.

[Win 87]   W. Winsborough : "Semantically Transparent Reset for AND Parallel Interpreters based on the Origin of Failure", proc. 4th SLP, San Francisco, 1987.

[Wol 86]   D. A. Wolfram : "Intractable unifiability problems and backtracking", 3rd ICLP, LNCS 225, Springer Verlag 1986.

[Woo 86]   N-S. Woo and K-M. Choe : "Selecting the Backtrack Literal in the AND/OR Process Model", 3th SLP, Salt Lake City, 1986.

Complete and Efficient Methods for Supporting Side-effects in Independent/Restricted And-parallelism

K. Muthukumar
M. Hermenegildo

MCC and University of Texas at Austin, C.S. Dept.
Net Address: `muthu@cs.utexas.edu`, `herme@cs.utexas.edu`

Abstract

It has been shown that it is possible to exploit Independent/Restricted And-parallelism in logic programs while retaining the conventional "don't know" semantics of such programs. In particular, it is possible to parallelize pure Prolog programs while maintaining the semantics of the language. However, when builtin *side-effects* (such as write or assert) appear in the program, if an identical observable behaviour to that of sequential Prolog implementations is to be preserved, such side-effects have to be properly sequenced. Previously proposed solutions to this problem are either incomplete (lacking, for example, backtracking semantics) or they force sequentialization of significant portions of the execution graph which could otherwise run in parallel. In this paper a series of side-effect synchronization methods are proposed which incur lower overhead and allow more parallelism than those previously proposed. Most importantly, and unlike previous proposals, they have well-defined backward execution behaviour and require only a small modification to a given (And-parallel) Prolog implementation.

1   Introduction

It has been shown [7, 10] that it is possible to exploit Independent And-parallelism (where only sets of goals which do not share variables can be executed in parallel – [4], [3], [11], [2], [8], [12], [16], [17], ...) while retaining the conventional "don't know" semantics of such programs. In particular, it is possible to parallelize pure Prolog programs while maintaining the full syntax and semantics of the language. However, when builtin *side-effects* (such as write or assert) appear in the program, if an identical behaviour to that of sequential Prolog implementations is to be preserved, such side-effects have to be properly sequenced. For example, consider the following clause

```
p(X,Y) :- a(X), write(X), b(X,Y), write(Y).
```

and assume that X and Y are always bound to ground terms upon entry into p. In this case all subgoals in the body of p are independent and could in principle be executed in parallel.

However, because of the presence of side-effects, the four subgoals cannot be truly executed in parallel or in any arbitrary order if a behavior identical to that of a sequential execution is to be preserved: a(X) and b(X,Y) can be first executed in parallel while the execution of write(X) should be delayed until the execution of a(X) is over. This is necessary to avoid X being written in case a(X) fails. Similarly, the subgoal write(Y) should wait for the completion of execution of subgoals b(X,Y) and write(X). The same argument will hold if write(X) and write(Y) are replaced by subgoals a1(X) and b1(Y) which are 'side-effect procedures' (i.e. they contain a call to a side-effect within the subtree that they generate).

One simple solution, for example, chosen in PEPSys [16], is to separate the program into sequential and parallel modules, with side-effects only being allowed in sequential ones. This solution is correct although it can potentially force sequentialization of significant portions of the program which could otherwise run in parallel. Some other solutions have been proposed within the scope of Or-parallelism [6], generally based on a run-time exploration of the execution tree to the left of a given side-effect. A side-effect synchronization method along these lines is proposed as an alternative in [13].

If side-effects are allowed within parallel code and a behaviour of the program identical to that observable on a sequential implementation is to be preserved then a good solution appears to be to add some sort of synchronization code to the program. In [5], DeGroot proposed a solution along such lines, based on the use of "synchronization blocks." DeGroot's approach is (at least during forward execution) correct and achieves its objective. However, it also suffers from the following limitations:

- First, and most importantly, as mentioned by DeGroot, the model is incomplete because it has no backtracking semantics, i.e. it only solves the side-effect synchronization problem if no goal fails during the execution of the program.

- The method is based on the use of synchronization blocks, which are complex data structures that are external to the standard Prolog storage model. This complicates the implementation so that relatively significant modifications to the parallel abstract machine may be required.

- DeGroot's method is only applied to the case when all goals in the program are executed in parallel. The case where there is a mixture of sequential and parallel goals (and, more generally, the case where sets of goals can conditionally be executed either sequentially or in parallel) needs to be addressed.

- Also, in DeGroot's method all side-effects are synchronized by a single chain of synchronization blocks (semaphores). This limits parallelism unnecessarily.

- Finally, DeGroot's method doesn't make any provision for "parallel builtins."

In this paper we present a new solution to the side-effect synchronization problem (and we also mention two other alternatives). This solution is based on ideas similar to DeGroot's but solves all the shortcomings pointed out above.

The rest of the paper is organized as follows. Sections 2.1 and 2.2 introduce some annotation syntax and terminology. Section 2.3 then describes a desirable behavior of an And-parallel system in the presence of side-effects, and presents our technique for synchronizing side-effects in order to achieve such behaviour. Section 3 shows how the model operates during backtracking and describes the abstract machine modifications needed to implement such operation. Section 4 then describes some optimizations which reduce the number of semaphores needed and increase the attainable parallelism. Finally, section 5 presents two alternative implementation methods, and section 6 summarizes our conclusions.

2   A Backtrackable Method for Synchronizing Side-Effects

2.1   &-Prolog and the RAP-WAM Model: An Annotation for Parallelism

We believe that the techniques presented herein are applicable to most models based on Independent And-parallelism. However, for the sake of concreteness, the discussion will be presented in terms of the Independent/Restricted And-parallel (RAP-WAM) model [8, 9]. This model has its roots in DeGroot's seminal work on *Restricted And-Parallelism* [4]. RAP-WAM completes DeGroot's RAP by providing backward execution semantics to the model, improved graph expressions (&-Prolog's CGEs)[8],[1] and an efficient implementation model based on the Warren Abstract Machine (WAM) [14]. The RAP-WAM model is used in this paper not only for the sake of concreteness but also because of the convenience of its Prolog-compatible source language, &-Prolog, which makes it possible to discuss the side-effect synchronization techniques directly on the source program and to describe and implement the algorithms for adding side-effect synchronization code as a series of rewritings of the original Prolog program.

&-Prolog is basically Prolog, with the addition of the parallel conjunction operator "&" and a set of parallelism-related builtins, which includes several types of groundness and independence checks, and synchronization primitives.

---

[1]&-Prolog's CGEs offer Prolog syntax and permit conjunctive checks, thus overcoming the difficulty in expressing 'sufficient' conditions for independence with the expressions proposed by DeGroot: given "f(X,Y,Z):- g(X,Y), h(Y,Z)." the most natural annotation for this clause, that g and h can run in parallel if the terms in X and Z don't share variables and Y is bound to a ground term, can be expressed easily with CGEs ("f(X,Y,Z):- (indep(X,Z), ground(Y) => g(X,Y) & h(Y,Z)).") but is very difficult with DeGroot's expressions.

Parallel conditional execution graphs (which cause the execution of goals in parallel if certain conditions are met) can be constructed by combining these elements with the normal Prolog constructs, such as "->" (if-then-else). For syntactic convenience (and historical reasons), an additional construct is also provided: the Conditional Graph Expression (CGE). A CGE has the general form

$$(\ i\_cond \ \texttt{=>} \ goal_1 \ \texttt{\&} \ goal_2 \ \texttt{\&} \ \dots \ \texttt{\&} \ goal_N \ )$$

where the $goal_i$ are either normal Prolog goals or other CGEs, and i_cond is a condition which, if satisfied, guarantees the mutual independence of the $goal_i$s. The CGE can be viewed simply as syntactic sugar for

$$(\ i\_cond \ \texttt{->} \ goal_1 \ \texttt{\&} \ goal_2 \ \texttt{\&} \ \dots \ \texttt{\&} \ goal_N$$
$$; \ goal_1 \ , \ goal_2 \ , \ \dots \ , \ goal_N \ )$$

i.e., the operational meaning of the CGE is "check i_cond, if it succeeds execute the $goal_i$ in parallel, else execute them sequentially." The $goal_i$ can themselves be CGEs, i.e. CGEs can be nested in order to create more complex execution graphs. i_cond can in principle be any set of Prolog goals but is in general either true (an "unconditional CGE") or a conjunction of checks on the groundness or independence of variables appearing in the $goal_i$s. Thus, the following &-Prolog clause

```
p(X,Y) :- q(X,Y), r(X), s(X).
```

could perhaps be rewritten for parallel execution as

```
p(X,Y) :- (ground(X) => q(X,Y) & r(X) & s(X) ).
```

or, with the same meaning as the CGE above, as

```
p(X,Y) :- (ground(X) -> q(X,Y) & r(X) & s(X)
                      ; q(X,Y), r(X), s(X) ).
```

or, perhaps, and still within &-Prolog, as

```
p(X,Y) :- (ground(X) -> q(X,Y) & r(X) & s(X)
                      ; q(X,Y), (ground(X) -> r(X) & s(X)
                                             ; r(X), s(X) )).
```

In the current RAP-WAM system, the task of parallelizing a given program (performing rewritings of it such as those above) is in general performed automatically by the RAP-WAM compiler, based either on local (clause-level) analysis, or on a global, abstract interpretation-based analysis [15] that often makes run-time independence checks unnecessary. The full power of &-Prolog is, however, also available to the user for manual parallelization if so desired. For the purposes of this paper it will be assumed that the program is already annotated with CGEs. Also, it will be assumed that such CGEs are not nested. This can be done without loss of generality by assuming that nested CGEs are "pulled out" as separate clauses. Furthermore, for simplicity, only unconditional CGEs (i.e. where i_cond is true) will be used. The method, however, is just as valid for any &-Prolog clause, as shown in section 4.1.

2.2 Some Terminology

- A Prolog builtin predicate which has side-effects is called a *side-effect builtin (seb)*.

- Furthermore, these sebs are classified as *soft-sebs* and *hard-sebs*. Soft-sebs are those side-effects which do not affect the following computation (e.g *write*). Hard-sebs are those side-effects which alter the contents of the prolog database and hence *can* affect the following computation (e.g. *assert*).

- A clause that has at least one subgoal which is either a side-effect builtin or a side-effect procedure (*sep*) is called a *side-effect clause(sec)*. Furthermore, it is classified as a *hard-sec* if it has at least one subgoal which is a hard-seb or a hard-sep. Otherwise, it is classified as a *soft-sec*.

- A procedure that contains at least one side-effect clause is called a *side-effect procedure(sep)*. It is classified as a *hard-sep* if it contains at least one hard-sec. Otherwise, it is classified as a *soft-sep*.

- Procedures which are neither *sebs* or *seps* are classified as *pure* procedures.

2.3 Synchronizing Side-Effects with Semaphores

As mentioned before, one approach towards ensuring that the order of execution is preserved is to add some sort of synchronization code to the program. DeGroot's solution [5] is based on the use of "synchronization blocks." In DeGroot's description a synchronization block (*sb*) consists of two memory words: the first word (*sb.ecnt*) is used to maintain a count of goals involved in the synchronization, while the second word(*sb.signal*) is used for signaling the completion of a side-effect predicate. These synchronization blocks are presumably allocated from a special memory area devoted to this purpose. DeGroot also defines abstract operations which create and manage these blocks.

We will describe our method by making incremental modifications to DeGroot's.[2] The first step is to make use of normal Prolog objects to implement the synchronization blocks. Let us in principle define a "Synch-Block" as the Prolog structure (`Signal,Ecnt`). This is the same as DeGroot's synchronization blocks except that synch-blocks are standard *Prolog structures* containing *logical variables*. This helps in two ways:

- This method has the advantage that a small set of new Prolog builtins is all that is required to implement all synchronization operations. These are described later in this section. Also, semaphores are allocated from (and integrated into) the normal Prolog storage model. Finally, no

---

[2]In attention to the reader, the explanation will be however self-contained so that no prior knowledge of DeGroot's method is required.

```
:- foo.
foo :- s1 & s2.
s1 :- a & s3.
s2 :- b & s4 & c.
a :- d & e.
s3 :- f & sse & g.
b :- h.
s4 :- j & hse.
c :- k & l.
```

Figure 1: Example program with side-effects

change in the syntax of the language is required: annotation of a clause with semaphores can be performed as a rewriting of the clause.

- In addition, correct backtracking behaviour is guaranteed because the Synch-Blocks are integrated within the standard backtracking machinery. No additional program annotation is needed for implementing backtracking in the presence of side-effects. This is explained in section 3.

Now, let us analyze how synch-blocks are actually used. As explained in DeGroot [5], the variable Signal takes on the values yes and no and the variable Ecnt takes on values from the set of natural numbers. Informally speaking, Signal indicates whether a side-effect builtin has finished executing (yes or no) and Ecnt has the count of the number of "pure" subgoals that are yet to finish executing before a side-effect builtin can start executing.

We now show how the synch-block structure can be simplified. As a first step, let us focus on the values taken by Signal. We replace yes with the number 1 and no with the number 0. Next, we define a semaphore Sem equivalent to the synch-block (Signal,Ecnt) as follows:

$$\mathtt{Sem} = 2 * \mathtt{Ecnt} + \mathtt{Signal}$$

Observe that the values of Signal and Ecnt can be obtained from Sem as follows:

$$\mathtt{Signal} = \mathtt{Sem}\ \mathrm{mod}\ 2;\ \mathtt{Ecnt} = \mathtt{Sem}\ \mathrm{div}\ 2$$

So, essentially, the semaphore Sem carries the same information as the synch-block (Signal,Ecnt), but is simpler in structure, being a single logical variable.

To illustrate how semaphores can be used to synchronize side-effects, consider the example program in Figure 1. For the sake of clarity, all the CGEs have their i_conds equal to true and also, the predicates do not have any arguments. In this program, sse is a soft-seb and hse is a hard-seb. s1, s2, s3, s4 are side-effect procedures and a, b, c, d, e, f, g, h, j, k, l are 'pure' procedures.

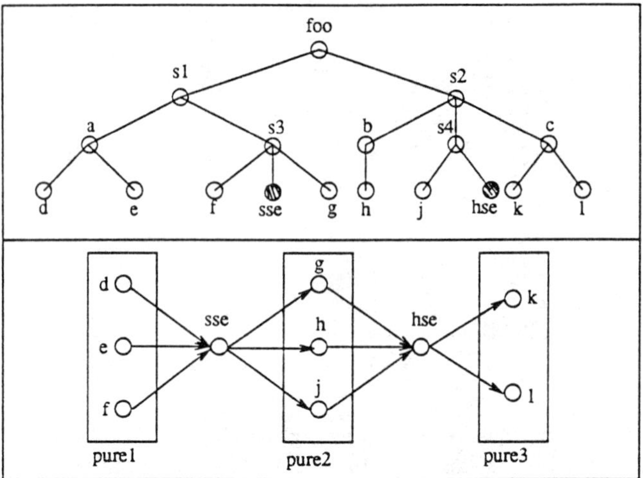

Figure 2: Execution tree and arrangement of segments

---

(1) Subgoals in *pure1* and *pure2* can together be executed in parallel.
(2) Subgoal *sse* can be started only after the subgoals in *pure1* have been executed.
(3) Similarly, subgoal *hse* can be started only after *sse* and the subgoals in *pure1* and *pure2* have been executed.
(4) Finally, since *hse* is a hard side-effect builtin, the subgoals in *pure3* have to wait for the completion of *hse*.

Figure 3: Conditions for proper execution of program in Figure 1

This program has an execution tree as shown in Figure 2. It can be seen that the leaves of this tree can be divided into alternating segments: pure1(d, e, f), then a soft side-effect builtin(sse), then pure2(g,h,j), then a hard side-effect builtin(hse) and finally, pure3(k,1). Figure 3 lists the conditions to be satisfied for the proper execution of the program.

To satisfy the conditions in Figure 3 and still attain maximum parallelism in the execution of this program, three semaphores Sem1, Sem2, Sem3 are added to it. (Informally, one can think of Sem1 as the semaphore for the subgoals in *pure1* and Sem2 as the semaphore for the subgoals in *pure2* and Sem3 as the semaphore for the subgoals in *pure3*).

When the program is started, Sem1 = 1. This is because *pure1* has no side-effect builtin to its "left" and so the subgoals in *pure1* can start executing immediately. But, since sse and hse, the side-effect builtins to the "left" of *pure2* and *pure3* respectively, are not yet finished, Sem2 and Sem3 start out with the value 2. This indicates that the side-effects sse and hse are not yet done.

Now, the values of the semaphores are changed as follows:

```
Sem1 := Sem1 + 3*2 (for the 3 subgoals in pure1)
Sem2 := Sem2 + 3*2 (for the 3 subgoals in pure2)
Sem3 := Sem3 + 2*2 (for the 2 subgoals in pure2)
```

The subgoals in pure segments wait for the values of the corresponding semaphores to become *odd* and then they start executing. The side-effect builtins wait for the corresponding semaphores to be equal to 1 and then they start executing. For example, the subgoals in the segment pure1 (i.e. d,e,f) wait on Sem1 being odd. Since this condition is true when the program is started, subgoals d,e,f immediately start executing in parallel. Note that none of the side-effect builtins (sse and hse) or the pure segments(*pure2, pure3*) can be executed at this time, because their waiting conditions are not satisfied. After each of the subgoals in *pure1* has been executed, Sem1 is decremented by 2, so that when all the 3 subgoals are done with their execution, Sem1 has the value 1. Now, the side-effect builtin sse which was waiting on (Sem1 = 1), starts executing and when it is done, decrements Sem2 by 2 and makes the value of Sem2 odd (by incrementing Sem2 by 1 if it is even and by doing nothing if it is already odd).This triggers the execution of the subgoals in the segment *pure2* which were waiting on Sem2 being odd. The same pattern of execution is repeated. In summary, the execution order of the subgoals in the leaves of Figure 2 follows the conditions in Figure 3. The conditions on which the various segments wait are illustrated in Figure 4.

Observe that even though condition 1 in Figure 3 states that subgoals in segments *pure1* and *pure2* can be executed in parallel (since sse is a soft side-effect builtin), in the execution sequence that we have described so far, *pure1* is first executed in parallel and then, *pure2* is executed in parallel. So, we have not achieved maximum potential parallelism in the execution of the subgoals. To realize this goal, all we have to do is to make Sem2 odd at the beginning. This triggers the parallel execution of the subgoals in *pure2* immediately.

Before we annotate this program with semaphores, we need to define certain operations on them. These operations are as follows:

```
wait_odd(Sem)  The current process waits on Sem being odd.
wait_one(Sem)  The current process waits on Sem = 1.
inc2(Sem,N)    Backtrackable, atomic increment: increments Sem by 2N.
dec2(Sem)      Backtrackable, atomic decrement: decrements Sem by 2.
make_odd(Sem)  Backtrackable, atomic operation:
               Increments Sem by 1 if it is even, else no-op.
```

All these operations have backtracking semantics, which are described in section 3. Figure 5 shows the program in Figure 1 annotated by semaphores.

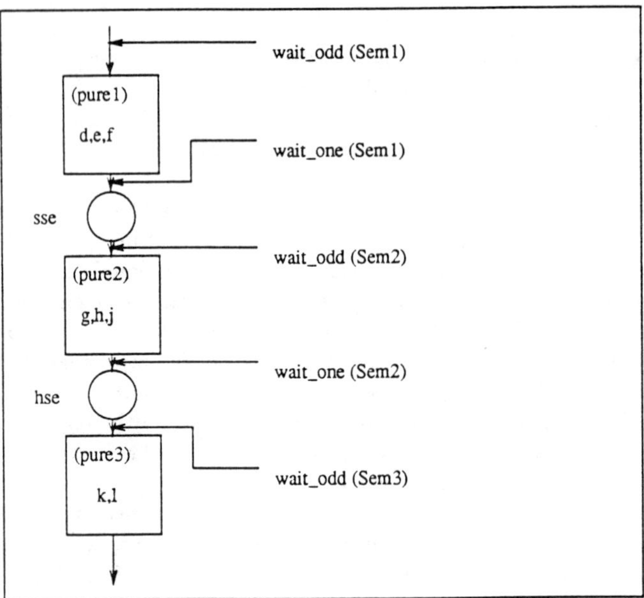

Figure 4: Synchronization between segments

3   Backtracking in the Presence of Side-Effects

In this section, we show how, in the model presented herein, backtracking can
still be supported while correctly sequencing the side-effects.

Consider the following program:

```
  :- s1.
s1 :- a, ( b & s2 & c ), d.
s2 :- e & hse & f.
```

Here, a,b,c,d,e,f are pure procedures and hse is a side-effect builtin. Thus,
s1, s2 are side-effect procedures. First, let's consider how backtracking
would proceed in the normal case, i.e. if hse were not a side-effect. We
assume in principle that the backtracking method presented in [10, 8] is used.
This method dictates that if after the CGE (b & s2 & c) is entered one
of b, s2 or c fails, then the other two goals will be "killed" and execution
will return to the next alternative of a ("inside" backtracking). If, however,
the CGE is exited successfully and d fails, the rightmost of b, s2, c with
alternatives will be found, redone, and execution will proceed in parallel again
with the rest of the goals in the CGE to the right of the one being redone.

Since, on the other hand, hse is a hard side effect and, therefore, s2 a
side-effect procedure, the program would be annotated as follows:

```
          :- Sem1 = 1, Sem2 = 2, s1(Sem1,Sem2).
s1(Sem1,Sem2) :- a, inc2(Sem1,1), inc2(Sem2,1),
```

```
:- Sem1 = 1, Sem3 = 2, foo(Sem1,Sem3).
foo(Sem1,Sem3):-Sem2 = 2,
                (s1(Sem1,Sem2) & s2(Sem2,Sem3)).
s1(Sem1,Sem2):- inc2(Sem1,1), make_odd(Sem2),
                ((wait_odd(Sem1),a,dec2(Sem1)) & s3(Sem1,Sem2)).
s2(Sem2,Sem3):- inc2(Sem2,1), inc2(Sem3,1),
                ((wait_odd(Sem2),b,dec2(Sem2)) & s4(Sem2,Sem3) &
                (wait_odd(Sem3),c,dec2(Sem3))).
a :- d & e.
s3(Sem1,Sem2):- inc2(Sem1,1), inc2(Sem2,1),
                ((wait_odd(Sem1),f,dec2(Sem1)) &
                (wait_one(Sem1),sse,dec2(Sem2),make_odd(Sem2)) &
                (wait_odd(Sem2),g,dec2(Sem2))).
b :- h.
s4(Sem2,Sem3):- inc2(Sem2,1),
                ((wait_odd(Sem2),j,dec2(Sem2)) &
                (wait_one(Sem2),hse,dec2(Sem3),make_odd(Sem3))).
c :- k & l.
```

Figure 5: Program annotated with semaphores

```
                ((wait_odd(Sem1),b,dec2(Sem1)) &
                 s2(Sem1,Sem2) &
                 (wait_odd(Sem2),c,dec2(Sem2))
                ),d.
s2(Sem1,Sem2) :- inc2(Sem1,1), inc2(Sem2,1),
                 ((wait_odd(Sem1),e,dec2(Sem1)) &
                 (wait_one(Sem1),hse,make_odd(Sem2),dec2(Sem2))
                 & (wait_odd(Sem2),f,dec2(Sem2))
                 ).
```

It is important to note that, as mentioned before, `dec2(Sem)`, `inc2(Sem, Int)` and `make_odd(Sem)` are "backtrackable" procedures, i.e., they undo the effects created by them on their parameters when they backtrack. The backtracking behavior of these procedures is described as follows:

`make_odd(Sem)` does nothing if Sem is already even,
                else atomically decrements Sem by 1 if Sem is odd.
`dec2(Sem)`   atomically increments Sem by 2.
`inc2(Sem,N)`   atomically decrements Sem by 2N.

Note that the backtracking behaviors of these procedures are the reverse of what they do in the forward direction, as it should be. Also note that no backtracking behavior needs to be described for the "waiting" procedures

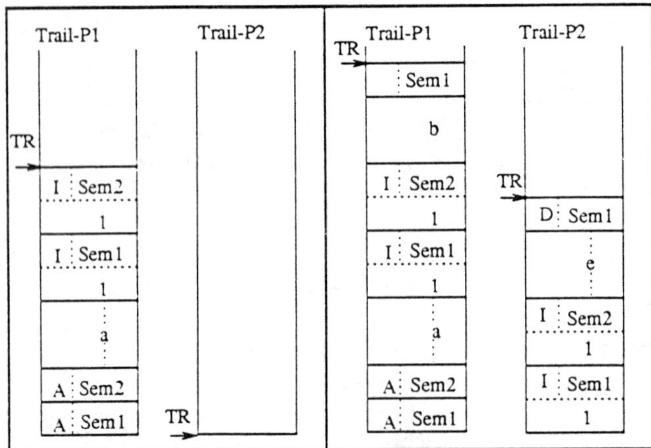

Figure 6: Implementation of Backtrackable Increment and Decrement

wait_odd and wait_one. One way of implementing this backtracking behaviour in a WAM-based, parallel abstract machine such as the RAP-WAM
[8] is by having each worker record in its trail the actions performed by it
on the semaphores, as shown in figure 6. This figure shows two snapshots
of the trail of two workers, one just before the CGE in s1 is entered, and
the other one while the execution of b and s2 is proceeding in parallel. Note
that this implementation is similar to that of setarg in SICStus Prolog [1],
but the *nature* of the action (i.e. increment, decrement, etc.) rather than
the previous value is saved. This is recorded as a tag for the trail entry (I -
increment, D - decrement, A - normal trail entry, etc.), the rest of the entry
being the address of the semaphore. This is important since increments and
decrements can occur in any order. A value – the amount of increment – is
saved, however, for the inc2 primitive. Also note that, depending on the optimizations implemented in the abstract machine, the variables that are used
as semaphores should be marked as permanent (or even moved to the heap)
to prevent possibly incorrect deallocation from last call- and other possible
optimizations.

Now we describe how backtracking is done in two cases viz., (1) when d
fails (case 1) and (2) when c fails (case 2).

- In **case 1**, assume that the subgoal e has unexplored alternatives, while
  hse, f, c do not. When d fails, alternatives for the subgoals in the
  CGE have to be explored and this is done with the subgoals being considered in the right-to-left order. Unwinding of the subgoal c leads to
  Sem2 = 3, with Sem1's value not being changed. Unwinding of the subgoal s2 leads to unwinding of the subgoals e, hse, f. This leads to
  Sem1 = 3 and Sem2 = 6. Now, the subgoals e, hse, f, c are all re-
  started in parallel and it is clear that parallelism is obtained, maintaining at the same time the sequential behavior necessary in the presence

of side-effects. If the CGE succeeds, the subgoal d can be tried again.

- In **case 2**, assume that the subgoal a has unexplored alternatives. Since c has failed, the CGE cannot succeed, so backtracking has to be done for all the subgoals in this CGE, i.e. for b, s2, c. Note, however, that b and s2 cannot be simply "killed" because in the sequential model s2 would have completed and produced its side-effect before c's failure. The idea again is to mimic the behaviour of the sequential model. A conservative modification of the "inside" backtracking actions which assures compatibility with the sequential model follows: if a goal fails, all goals to its right in the CGE are killed as before. Also, all goals to the left of the failing goal up to the previous side-effect goal are killed. The rest of the goals are allowed to continue to completion, after which they are all backtracked (including the side-effect goal, which may have other alternatives) by recursively applying the algorithm. It is clear from the backtracking behaviors of the synchronization procedures that after this is done, Sem1 and Sem2 are restored to their respective values of 1 and 2. Now a succeeds with an alternative binding for the variables and the CGE is reexecuted with the correct initial values for the semaphores.

Thus, backtracking in the presence of side-effects is relatively simple in this model. Nothing special is required because the semaphores are implemented as *logical variables*. Some optimizations can be made on this model. For example, in **case 1**, if the subgoal c has unexplored alternatives, no backtracking has to be done on Sem2 and also, the re-execution of the subgoal c need not be accompanied by any waiting or decrementing operation on Sem2. But implementing this optimization will require primitives in addition to the ones described in Hermenegildo [8].

4 Optimizations and Other Issues

4.1 When the *i_cond* is non-empty

Our previous discussion was limited to CGEs with i_cond = true. In this section, we show how a *conditional* CGE is annotated with semaphores. Consider the following clause:

```
s1 :- (i_cond => a & se1 & b & se2 & c).
```

a, b, c are pure procedures and se1 and se2 are side effect builtins. If se1 and se2 were not side-effect builtins, this clause would have been annotated as:

```
( i_cond -> a & se1 & b & se2 & c
          ; a , se1 , b , se2 , c )
```

The presence of side effects changes the annotation as follows:

```
s1(Sem1,Sem2) :-
```

```
( i_cond ->
            Sem3 = 2, inc2(Sem1,1),
            inc2(Sem2,1), inc2(Sem3,1),
            ( (wait_odd(Sem1),a,dec2(Sem1)) &
              (wait_one(Sem1),se1,make_odd(Sem3),dec2(Sem3)) &
              (wait_odd(Sem3),b,dec2(Sem3)) &
              (wait_one(Sem3),se2,make_odd(Sem2),dec2(Sem2)) &
              (wait_odd(Sem2),c,dec2(Sem2)) )
          ; a, se1, b, se2, c, dec2(Sem2), make_odd(Sem2) ).
```

Let us call the code that is executed if i_cond succeeds as `parallel code` and
the code that is executed if i_cond fails as `sequential code`. The following
points are worth noting:

- The `parallel code` needs the use of a new semaphore Sem3 (because of
  the two side-effects in the body), while the `sequential code` doesn't.

- While the `parallel code` has several synchronization primitives operating on the various semaphores, the `sequential code` operates only on
  Sem2 and this is just to signal that the side-effect builtin corresponding
  to Sem2 has been completed.

Several such optimizations can be used while annotating a given program with
semaphores.

4.2 When Side-Effects Don't Need to be Synchronized

Another observation which can be made is that sometimes the user doesn't
really care in which order side-effects are executed, i.e. the user doesn't need
the parallel system to produce identical results (and in the same order) to
those of sequential implementation. For this purposes we propose to include
a whole new set of "parallel built-in side-effect predicates," for which no
synchronization code is generated. For example, there would be a `p_write/1`
version of the standard `write/1` predicate, and similarly for other side-effect
built-ins. An example showing the use of the `p_format/3` predicate is shown
below. This predicate locks access to the stream that it is writing to but is
otherwise not synchronized with other builtins. Note that in the example,
since each do_x parallel goal identifies its output in the file, we don't care in
which order each of them writes into the file. The introduction of parallel side-
effects such as `p_format/3` allows for more parallelism (and less overhead due
to synchronization chores) that is attainable if the sequential Prolog semantics
is enforced.

```
p(X,FileName)      :-
        ( ground([X,FileName]) => do_a(X,FileName) &
                                   do_b(X,FileName) &
                                   do_c(X,FileName) ).
do_a(X,FileName) :-
```

```
        do_a_lot(X,Result),
        p_format('Result of a = %i',[Result],FileName).
do_b(X,FileName) :-
        do_b_lot(X,Result),
        p_format('Result of b = %i',[Result],FileName).
do_c(X,FileName) :-
        do_c_lot(X,Result),
        p_format('Result of c = %i',[Result],FileName).
```

4.3   Multiple Synchronization Chains

Sometimes, even if the standard Prolog behaviour is to be preserved, it turns
out that some aspects of the order in which side-effects are executed are not
observable and therefore the synchronization requirements can be relaxed.
Consider, for example, the case when parallel goals are writing to two different files: only the order of writing *within each file* needs to be preserved.
However, it is still required that the "pure" procedures preceding the side
effects be completed before the side effects are themselves executed. Consider
the following example:

```
s1(X,Y) :-  ( ground([X,Y]) => a(X) & write(file1,X) &
                                b(Y) & write(file2,Y) ).
```

Here, a(X), b(Y) are pure procedures. Since there are two side effects in this
CGE, we need three semaphores, Sem1, Sem2, Sem3. Normally Sem2 has the
initial value of 2. This forces write(File2,Y) to follow write(File1,X).
However, in this case, there is no need to sequentialize the two write statements since they write to *different* files. So, we can intialize Sem2 to 0. This
has the effect that it does not sequentialize the two write statements. This
is a very useful optimization especially if the write statements take a long
time to complete.

The following example further illustrates the point:

```
s1(X,Y) :- (ground(X) => foo(X) & a(X) & bar(Y) & b(X) ).
a(X) :- do_a_lot(X,Res1,Res2),
        write(Res1,file1), write(Res2,file1).
b(X) :- do_b_lot(X,Res1,Res2),
        write(Res1,file2), write(Res2,file2).
```

Other optimizations beyond those presented in sections 4.3 and 4.2 are
described in [13].

5   Two Alternative Methods Using Semaphores

In this section, we describe two different variations on the same idea of implementing semaphores. The first method's objective is to avoid introducing
semaphores as additional arguments for the side-effect predicates. The second
method encodes the information in synch-blocks in a different way from what
was described before. These methods and the associated program transformations are described in more detail in [13].

5.1 Method 1: Reducing the Argument-Passing Overhead

In section 2.3, semaphores were introduced as additional arguments for the side-effect predicates. This results in

- `compile time overhead` – additional work done in adding the semaphores as arguments to the side-effect predicates.

- `runtime overhead` – more arguments for the side-effect predicates imply a longer runtime for the program, even though they contribute nothing to the solution of the underlying problem.

In this method, semaphores are not introduced as additional arguments for the predicates, but are stored in a *global list data structure*, called the **semaphore list**. This scheme can be easily implemented in a shared memory parallel processor.

A separate chunk of memory is earmarked for the **semaphore list**. A program which has side-effect predicates is started with the **semaphore list** having two semaphores (in that order), Sem1 which has the value 1 and Sem2, which has the value 2. A side-effect predicate which is called in the body of a clause, has access to a pointer `Local Head`, which points to a semaphore in the **semaphore list**. The following "macros" are used in this method.

- `side_effect(Pred,P)` calls the side-effect procedure `Pred` after setting its `Local Head` to the pointer P. This points to the 'leftmost' semaphore for `Pred`.

- `pure(Pred,P)` – P points to a semaphore, say Sem. This procedure is defined as follows: `pure(Pred,P) :- wait_odd(Sem), Pred, dec2(Sem)`.

- `add_semaphores(N)` – creates N semaphores and inserts them in the **semaphore list**. If Sem1 is the semaphore pointed to by `Local Head` and the next semaphore in the **semaphore list** is Sem2, this procedure inserts N semaphores between Sem1 and Sem2.

As an example of how this method is used, consider the following clause:

```
s1 :- a & s2 & b & s3 & c.
```

`s1`, `s2` and `s3` are side-effect procedures and `a`, `b` and `c` are 'pure' procedures. This clause is annotated as follows:

```
s1 :-   add_semaphores(1),
        (  pure(a,1) &
           side_effect(s2,1) &
           pure(b,2) &
           side_effect(s3,2) &
           pure(c,3)
        ).
```

This method is attractive, although the use of additional global (heap) storage should be traded off with the reduction in procedure calling time.

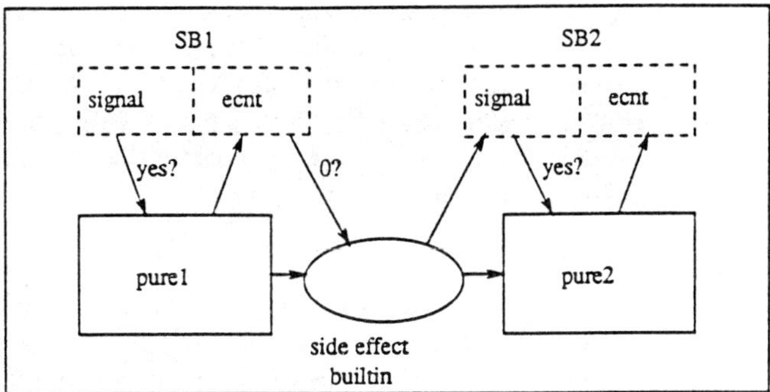

Figure 7: How Synchronization Blocks help achieve synchronization

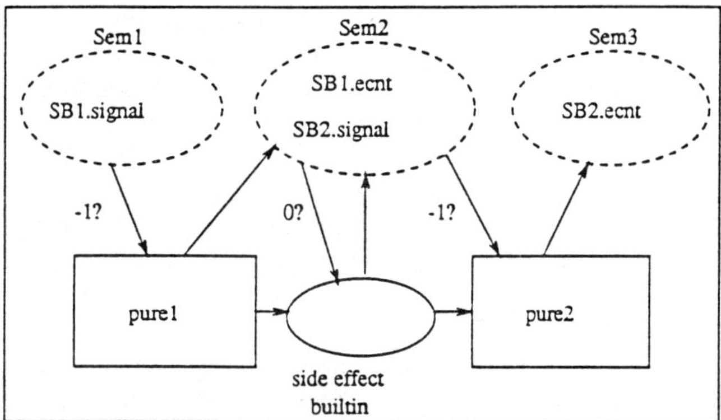

Figure 8: Construction of the semaphores in Method 2

5.2   Method 2: An Alternative Encoding for Synch-Blocks

Consider the side-effect builtin in Figure 7. This has one synch block(SB1) to its 'left' and another synch block(SB2) to its 'right'. Now, take the 'ecnt' record from SB1 and the 'signal' record from SB2 and put them together and encode them in one semaphore, say Sem2. This is done for all the side-effect builtins. The 'leftmost' semaphore, of course, will have only the 'signal' part of a synch block and the 'rightmost' semaphore will have only the 'ecnt' part of a synch block. Figure 8 shows the constructions of the semaphores for the program segments in Figure 7.

How is the information in SB1_ecnt and SB2_signal encoded into just one record in Sem2? This is done as follows: Before the execution of the program, Sem2 is created (with value = 0) and then incremented by the number of subgoals in *pure1*. After each 'pure' subgoal in *pure1* has finished executing, it decrements Sem2 by 1. Meanwhile, 'side-effect builtin' waits on (Sem2 = 0) for its execution. This will start executing once all the subgoals in *pure1* are done. Sem2 is decremented by 1 (thus making its value = -1), after the execution of the 'side-effect builtin' is completed. The subgoals in *pure2* which were waiting on (Sem2 = -1) now start executing in parallel. This method offers the advantage of conceptual (and implementation) simplicity, but requires more semaphores than that described in section 2.3. Also, in that method, it is possible to execute the subgoals in a pure segment immediately following a soft side effect builtin *in parallel,* even before that builtin has been executed. This cannot be done in method 2.

6 Conclusions

We have presented an efficient and complete method for implementing Independent/Restricted And-Parallelism in the presence of side effects. This method does not suffer from the drawbacks of previously proposed solutions, i.e (1) it supports backtracking, (2) it uses a simple data structure for semaphores and a compact set of primitives on the semaphores, (3) it allows more parallelism, (4) it deals with the case of having a mixture of parallel and sequential goals, and (5) since it implements semaphores as *logical variables,* it can be easily added to a parallel abstract machine-based system through only minor modifications. We have also presented two additional methods for implementing And-Parallelism in the presence of side effects. These methods, an additional and rather interesting method (based on keeping track of the execution graph), as well as the algorithms for detecting side-effect procedures and annotating them with semaphores are described in detail in [13].

7 Acknowledgements

The authors would like to thank the other members of the PAL group, Kevin Greene and Roger Nasr, for their comments on earlier drafts of this paper.

References

[1] M. Carlsson. Freeze, Indexing, and Other Implementation Issues in the Wam. In *4th Int. Conf. on Logic Prog.*, pages 40–58, Mit Press, May 1987.

[2] J.-H. Chang, A. M. Despain, and D. Degroot. And-Parallelism of Logic Programs Based on Static Data Dependency Analysis. In *Compcon Spring '85*, pages 218–225, February 1985.

[3] J. S. Conery. *The And/Or Process Model for Parallel Interpretation of Logic Programs.* PhD thesis, The University of California At Irvine, 1983. Technical Report 204.

[4] D. DeGroot. Restricted AND-Parallelism. In *International Conference on Fifth Generation Computer Systems*, pages 471–478, Tokyo, November 1984.

[5] D. DeGroot. Restricted AND-Parallelism and Side-Effects. In *International Symposium on Logic Programming*, pages 80–89, San Francisco, IEEE Computer Society, August 1987.

[6] B. Hausman, A. Ciepielewski, and A. Calderwood. Cut and Side-Effects in Or-Parallel Prolog. In *International Conference on Fifth Generation Computer Systems*, Tokyo, November 1988.

[7] M. Hermenegildo and F. Rossi. *On the Correctness and Efficiency of Independent And-Parallelism in Logic Programs.* Technical Report ACA-ST-032-89, Microelectronics and Computer Technology Corporation (MCC), Austin, TX 78759, January 1989.

[8] M. V. Hermenegildo. *An Abstract Machine Based Execution Model for Computer Architecture Design and Efficient Implementation of Logic Programs in Parallel.* PhD thesis, University of Texas at Austin, August 1986.

[9] M. V. Hermenegildo. An Abstract Machine for Restricted AND-parallel Execution of Logic Programs. In *Third International Conference on Logic Programming*, pages 25–40, Imperial College, Springer-Verlag, July 1986.

[10] M. V. Hermenegildo and R. I. Nasr. Efficient Management of Backtracking in AND-parallelism. In *Third International Conference on Logic Programming*, pages 40–55, Imperial College, Springer-Verlag, July 1986.

[11] L. Kale. Parallel Execution of Logic Programs: the REDUCE-OR Process Model. In *Fourth International Conference on Logic Programming*, pages 616–632, Melbourne, Australia, May 1987.

[12] Y.-J. Lin, V. Kumar, and C. Leung. An Intelligent Backtracking Algorithm for Parallel Execution of Logic Programs. In *Third International Conference on Logic Programming*, pages 55–69, Imperial College, Springer-Verlag, July 1986.

[13] K. Muthukumar and M. Hermenegildo. *Efficient Methods for Supporting Side Effects in Independent And-parallelism and Their Backtracking Semantics.* Technical Report ACA-ST-031-89, Microelectronics and Computer Technology Corporation (MCC), Austin, TX 78759, January 1989.

[14] D. H. D. Warren. *An Abstract Prolog Instruction Set.* Technical Report 309, Artificial Intelligence Center, SRI International, 333 Ravenswood Ave, Menlo Park CA 94025, 1983.

[15] R. Warren, M. Hermenegildo, and S. Debray. On the Practicality of Global Flow Analysis of Logic Programs. In *Fifth International Conference and Symposium on Logic Programming*, August 1988.

[16] H. Westphal and P. Robert. The PEPSys Model: Combining Backtracking, AND- and OR- Parallelism. In *Symp. of Logic Prog.*, pages 436–448, August 1987.

[17] W. Winsborough and A. Waern. Transparent and- parallelism in the presence of shared free variables. In *Fifth International Conference and Symposium on Logic Programming*, pages 749–764, 1988.

Applications

Test Generation using the Constraint Logic Programming Language CHIP

H. Simonis

European Computer-Industry Research Centre GmbH
Arabellastr. 17
D-8000 München 81
West Germany

1 Abstract

In this paper we present an application of the constraint logic programming language CHIP to the automatic test pattern generation for combinatorial circuits. CHIP allows a simple and declarative expression of this problem as a constraint satisfaction problem. Using a demon mechanism to propagate values as soon as possible we derive an efficient test generation program requiring only a fraction of the development effort necessary with conventional approaches. Example results on the ISCAS benchmark set (containing circuits with more than 1000 gates) are given which are comparable to specialized algorithms written in procedural languages.

2 Introduction

Recently, several papers have addressed the use of logic programming (Prolog) for test pattern generation [SA84] [Gup86] [Gul85] [VT87]. They have shown how to express the problem in Prolog in an easy and declarative way. Unfortunately the simple generate-and-test method used by the Prolog system for the generation of tests can only be applied for rather small circuits. Execution time will normally grow exponentially with the circuit size. Attempts to improve the performance by implementing a better strategy in Prolog lead to much more complicated programs [TG87]. No examples using circuits with more than 50 gates have been presented in any of these papers.

On the other hand, a wealth of specialized algorithms for generating tests in procedural languages has been developed (e.g. [Rot66]

[Goe81] [FS83] [ISC85] [STS87]). These programs are rather complex and difficult to understand or to modify, but very efficient. Tests can be generated for circuits having thousands of gates.

In this paper we present a test generation program that tries to combine the advantages of the two approaches. The problem is stated in a clear logical form but is solved in an efficient, demon-driven way. The test generation program is written in CHIP (Constraint Handling In Prolog), an extended Prolog language combining logic programming with constraint solving techniques [DVHS$^+$88b]. CHIP differs from Prolog by its 'active' use of constraints that enables it to avoid the combinatorial explosion. The order of execution for constraints is determined dynamically by solving them as soon as enough information is available.

CHIP has been used on a wide range of applications especially in Operations Research [DVHS$^+$88a] and circuit design [SD87b] [SD87a] [SND88]. Besides the demons described in this paper, CHIP provides facilities for boolean unification (symbolic solution of boolean equations), improved search procedures (eg forward checking) and a constraint solver for linear equations and inequations over integers and rationals [DVHS$^+$88b].

In the next section we give a short description of the test generation problem. We then show how circuits can be described in CHIP and explain the demon mechanism used to achieve a data-driven computation. We continue with an explanation of our test generation algorithm and show some experimental results on the ISCAS test generation benchmark set.

3   Automatic Test Pattern Generation

When an integrated circuit or a circuit board is produced, testing is performed to insure it is free from manufacturing errors. Since exhaustive testing of the device is impossible, a limited number of test patterns are applied to check for certain types of errors.

The fault model conventionally used assumes a single *stuck-at* fault on the logic gate level. A stuck-at error means that an input or output line of a gate is always set to one (stuck-at-1) or to zero (stuck-at-0). A test for a particular fault should show a different output for the correct and the faulty circuit. Note that it is not necessary to locate the fault. Therefore one pattern can test many different faults.

The test patterns are generated by a program (called *automatic test pattern generator*) given a circuit description and a specific fault model. Another type of program (called a *fault simulator*) is used to measure

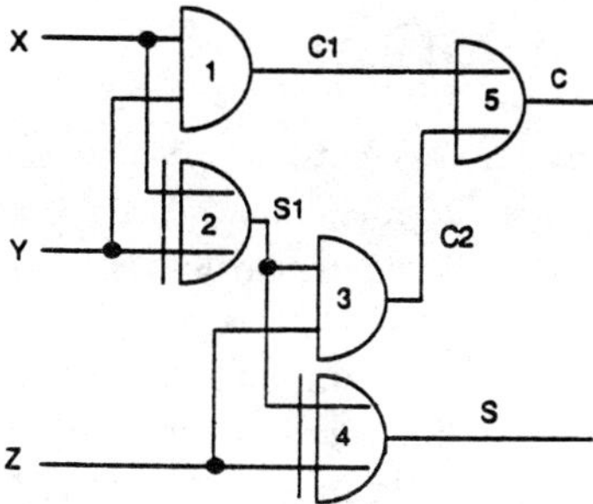

Figure 1: Full-adder Circuit Diagram

```
fa(M,N,X,Y,Z,S,C) :-
        and(M,[1|N],X,Y,C1),
        xor(M,[2|N],X,Y,S1),
        and(M,[3|N],Z,S1,C2),
        xor(M,[4|N],Z,S1,S),
        or(M,[5|N],C1,C2,C).
```

Figure 2: Full-adder Circuit Description

the fault coverage, the percentage of faults recognized by the test set.

Test generation algorithms usually work on combinatorial circuits only. Sequential circuits can be transformed into combinatorial parts using scan-path techniques [Wil86].

4 Circuit Description

Prolog can be considered as a very simple but also very powerful hardware description language. It supports in a natural way top-down development and mixing of various hierarchical levels of circuit description. In Prolog (and of course also in CHIP), a circuit can be specified by means of *clauses*, which describe components and modules, and *logical variables*, which describe connections between modules. Suppose we want to describe a full-adder (see figure 1). The CHIP clause describing this circuit is shown in figure 2 (variables begin with a capital letter, constants and predicate names are in lowercase). The definition of the basic elements 'and', 'xor' and 'or' can be given, for example, by a set of ground clauses (the truth-table definition) :

```
and(simul,N,0,0,0).
and(simul,N,0,1,0).
and(simul,N,1,0,0).
and(simul,N,1,1,1).
```

and the like for the others.

In this description, the first argument of a predicate contains the operation mode. This could be for example 'test' (for test generation), 'simul' (for circuit simulation) , 'time' (for delay time computation). It is used to distinguish between several user-defined operation modes. The second argument of a predicate is used to assign a unique identifier for each part (module or basic component) of the circuit. Thus a hierarchical naming convention can be easily implemented. The other arguments represent the inputs and the outputs of the components. Note that no distinction is necessary between inputs and outputs. Connections (wires) between components are represented by shared *logical variables*. Since fanout points are of special interest in test generation, it is possible to include them explicitly in the circuit description (see figure 3). This way connections are represented not by shared variables, but by predicates linking distinct variables. The module thus defined can now be used in other circuit descriptions. Parametrized libraries of modules can be generated using recursive descriptions. This kind of hierarchical description of circuits follows the style of logic programming in a top-down development. One can replace the description of a lower-level component without affecting the higher-level circuit definition. The use of this circuit description for simulation, formal verification, fault diagnosis etc is shown in [SD87a].

Similar ways of describing hardware in Prolog have been proposed by [SA84] [Gul85] [Esh85] [Gup86] [Clo87].

```
fa(M,N,X,Y,Z,S,C) :-
        fanout(M,[1|N],X,[X1,X2]),
        fanout(M,[2|N],Y,[Y1,Y2]),
        fanout(M,[3|N],Z,[Z1,Z2]),
        and(M,[4|N],X1,Y1,C1),
        xor(M,[5|N],X2,Y2,S1),
        fanout(M,[6|N],S1,[S11,S12]),
        and(M,[7|N],Z1,S11,C2),
        xor(M,[8|N],Z2,S12,S),
        or(M,[9|N],C1,C2,C).
```

Figure 3: Full-adder with Fanout-stems

5 Demons in CHIP

In the last section we saw a description of an and-gate via its truthtable.
Using this method in Prolog is very simple, but has some serious drawbacks. The components will always be computed in the order in which
they appear in the circuit description. If not all input-values for a gate
are known, the system will choose the first case in the table which unifies
with the arguments and assign arbitrary values to the free inputs. If a
wrong selection is made, the system has to backtrack to this choice. This
'generate-and-test' strategy normally requires exponential computation
time. It is therefore not applicable to larger circuits. A much better
performance can be expected using *demons* [Dav84] [SD87b]. Demons
provide a way to specify a data-driven behaviour. They consist of a
set of rules which describe how a constraint can be satisfied. A rule
specifies the condition under which it can be applied on the left hand
side and some action which solves the constraint on the right hand side.
Such a rule can for example be formulated as:

```
If the first input of an and-gate is zero
      then the output is also zero.
```

It is then written as:

```
and(0,X,Y):- Y = 0.
```

If a demon appears in the resolvent, it is checked whether it matches
with one of the rules. We use matching (one sided unification) which
will not bind any variables in the resolvent. As soon as one of the rules
can be applied, the demon constraint is solved by executing the right

```
?-demon and/3.

and(0,Y,Z):- Z = 0.
and(X,0,Z):- Z = 0.
and(1,Y,Z):- Y = Z.
and(X,1,Z):- X = Z.
and(X,Y,1):- X = 1, Y = 1.
```

Figure 4: Demon Definition 1

hand side of this rule. If no rule matches, the demon will be suspended until further instantiation of the variables in the literal. This mechanism is similar to the execution of guarded Horn clauses in GHC [Ued85].

In CHIP, demons can be defined with the *demon declaration*. We show here two different implementations of a and-gate demon. The first one (see figure 4) defines the behaviour of the gate using two signal values 0 and 1. Its behaviour can be deduced automatically from the truthtable. As soon as some input or the output is known, the constraint can be solved except for the case when the output is equal to zero. In this case we have to wait for some further instantiation.

For test generation we use a demon definition with the four signal values 0, 1, d and dnot (see figure 5). The value d denotes the value at the point under test, the value dnot stands for the negated d value. These additional values are introduced in order to trace the effect of the fault through the circuit. Some additional rules are necessary to cope with these signals. Rule 6 for example specifies that as soon as input one is set to d, the output will be set to d and the second input will be set to one (in order to propagate the d-value to an output). This demon corresponds directly to the implication procedure found in conventional test generation programs. The five logic values 0, 1, d, dnot and X (don't care) of [Rot66] also occur in the demon definition (with X being replaced by the uninstantiated logical variable).

6 Test Generation

We can now describe our test generation algorithm. We want to find a set of test patterns to detect all single *stuck-at-0 (s-a-0)* and *stuck-at-1 (s-a-1)* errors in combinatorial circuits. Since we want to distinguish between errors on different fanout branches, we have to introduce fanout points as described above into the circuit description. For efficiency, we

```
?-demon and/3.

and(0,Y,Z):- Z = 0.
and(X,0,Z):- Z = 0.
and(1,Y,Z):- Y = Z.
and(X,1,Z):- X = Z.
and(X,Y,1):- X = 1, Y = 1.
and(d,Y,Z):- Y = 1, Z = d.
and(X,d,Z):- X = 1, Z = d.
and(dnot,Y,Z):- Y = 1, Z = dnot.
and(X,dnot,Z):- X = 1, Z = dnot.
```

Figure 5: Demon Definition 2

can ignore s-a-1 errors at inputs of or/nor-gates, s-a-0 errors at inputs of and/nand-gates and all errors at inputs of not/driver-gates, since these faults are detected by the tests for the corresponding gate outputs.

To generate a test for a fault at a given gate, we have to solve two different subproblems. First we have to *control* the gate-output, i.e. we have to assign values to some of the primary inputs such that the value at the gate output is different from the assumed fault. We then have to make the fault *observable*, i.e. to find a path from the gate under test to some primary output where we can observe a difference between the correct and the faulty circuit.

Our approach takes the following form: suppose we want to test an and-gate for a stuck-at-0 fault. We assign a 'd' value to the output of the gate and the value 1 to its inputs. The system now automatically propagates these values towards the inputs and the outputs. If the 'd' value reaches the input of a gate, the other inputs will be set by the demons described above in a way to propagate the value. If the d value reaches a fanout-stem, we have to decide on which of the branches we want to propagate the 'd' or 'dnot' value. Since not all constraints will be solved at the end of the propagation, we need a *consistent labeling* assigning values to the remaining points.

We will illustrate the method on a small example. If we want to make a test for s-a-0 of gate number 7 in figure 3, we assign 'd' to its output C2 and '1' to its inputs Z1 and S11. The value 'd' at the input of gate 9 fires a rule for the or-gate setting the output to 'd' and the input C1 to '0'. The value '1' at the points Z1 and S11 is propagated via the fanout points 3 and 6 to the points Z, Z2, S1 and S12. The value '1' at

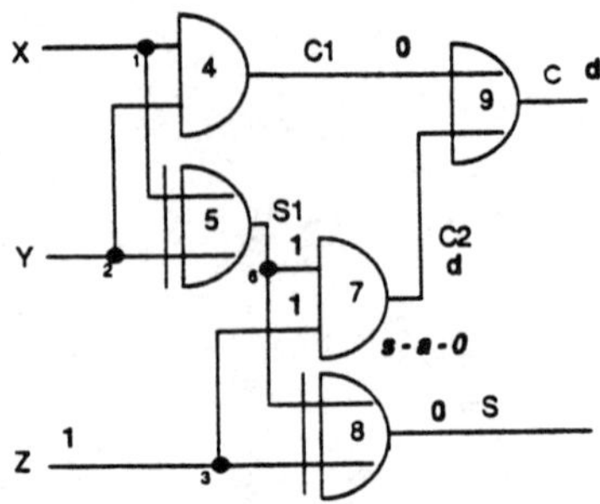

Figure 6: Full-adder Test Generation

the inputs Z2 and S12 of gate 8 fires a rule setting the output S to '1'.
Note that not all constraints are satisfied, unless we assign values to the
inputs X and Y. This will be achieved in a consistent labeling step. As
soon as we assign '0' to X , '1' will be assigned to Y. We obtain a test
pattern for gate 7 as '0','1','1'. The program for the test generation is
shown in figure 7. It uses the circuit description from figure 3 and the
demon definition from figure 5. For or- and xor-gates we use definitions
equivalent to the ones shown for the and-gate. The call and result for
the small example is

```
?- test([7],s_a_0,In,Out).
```

```
In  = [0,1,1]
Out = [0,d]
```

7   Experimental Results

We have used our program to generate tests for some of the benchmark
circuits of the 1985 ISCAS (IEEE Symposium on Circuits and Systems)
[ISC85]. The circuits are real-life examples used to compare procedural
test generation programs. Our results are shown in table 1.

Circuit	Gates	Faults	Coverage	Pattern	Time
d432	160	457	99.12	71	39
d499	202	684	98.83	73	84
d880	383	837	100.00	64	72
d1355	546	1500	99.26	102	143
d1908	880	1810	99.50	143	331
d2670	1193	2484	94.6	273	555

```
% test(+,+,-,-): generate test for output of
%                Gate at Fault s_a_0 or s_a_1
test(Gate,Fault,[X,Y,Z],[S,C]):-
        fa(test(Gate,Fault),[],X,Y,Z,S,C),
        labeling([X,Y,Z]).

% labeling(+): assign 0 or 1 to all inputs of the circuit
labeling([]).
labeling([0|T]):-
        labeling(T).
labeling([1|T]):-
        labeling(T).

and(test(Gate,s_a_0),Gate,1,1,d). % test for s_a_0
and(test(Gate,s_a_1),Gate,0,_,d). % two alternatives for
and(test(Gate,s_a_1),Gate,_,0,d). %     s_a_1
and(test(Gate,Fault),Gate1,In1,In2,Out):-
        Gate ~= Gate1,           % if not gate under test
        and(In1,In2,Out).        % then call demon
```

Figure 7: Test Generation Program

A fault coverage of 100 percent can not always be achieved since most circuits contain some redundant (untestable) gates. Execution times (in seconds) are given for the test generation (without fault simulation) on a SUN-3/280 running the CHIP interpreter. Both fault coverage and execution times are comparable to programs written in procedural languages.

The CHIP program is used only for generating the test pattern. The deterministic parallel fault simulation is done inside a C program, which is generated automatically from the CHIP circuit description.

The complete test generation program in CHIP requires 2 pages of CHIP code (excluding data).

8 Conclusion

In this paper we have presented an application of the constraint logic programming language CHIP to test generation for combinatorial circuits. We have developed a simple and declarative test generation algorithm based on a circuit description in logic. Demons, a data-driven extension of Prolog, allow an efficient execution of the program. The system thus combines the simplicity of logic programming with the speed of specialized programs. We have shown that the system can solve standard benchmarks in an acceptable time.

9 Acknowledgements

I would like to thank Mehmet Dincbas and the other members of the CHIP team for their help and many fruitful discussions.

References

[Clo87]   W.F. Clocksin. Logic Programming and Digital Circuit Analysis. *Journal of Logic Programming*, 4(1):59–82, 1987.

[Dav84]   R. Davis. Diagnostic Reasoning Based on Structure and Behavior. *Artificial Intelligence*, 24:347–410, 1984.

[DVHS+88a] M. Dincbas, P. Van Hentenryck, H. Simonis, A. Aggoun, and T. Graf. Applications of CHIP to Industrial and Engineering Problems. In *First International Conference on*

Industrial and Engineering Applications of Artificial Intelligence and Expert Systems, Tullahoma, Tennessee, USA, June 1988.

[DVHS+88b] M. Dincbas, P. Van Hentenryck, H. Simonis, A. Aggoun, T. Graf, and F. Berthier. The Constraint Logic Programming Language CHIP. In *Proc Fifth Generation Computer Systems 1988*, Tokyo, Japan, Nov 1988.

[Esh85] K. Eshghi. Application of Meta-Level Programming to Fault Finding in Logic Circuits. In *Logic Programming and its Applications*, pages 208–219. Ablex Publishing Corporation, 1985.

[FS83] H Fujiwara and T. Shimono. On the Acceleration of Test Generation Algorithms. *IEEE Trans Comp*, C-32(Dec):1137–1144, 1983.

[Goe81] P. Goel. An Implicit Enumeration Algorithm to Generate Tests for Combinational Logic Circuits. *IEEE Trans Comp*, C-30(Mar):215–222, 1981.

[Gul85] E. Gullichsen. Heuristic circuit simulation using PROLOG. *INTEGRATION, the VLSI Journal*, 3:283–318, 1985.

[Gup86] R. Gupta. Test-pattern Generation for VLSI circuits in a Prolog Environment. In *Proceedings of the Third International Conference on Logic Programming*, pages 528–535, London, July 1986.

[ISC85] ISCAS. Special Session on ATPG. In *Proc IEEE Symposium on Circuits and Systems*, July 1985.

[Rot66] J. Roth. Diagnosis of Automata Failure: A Calculus and a Method. *IBM Journal of Research and Development*, 10:278–291, 1966.

[SA84] D. Svanaes and E.J. Aas. Test Generation Through Logic Programming. *INTEGRATION, the VLSI Journal*, 2:49–67, 1984.

[SD87a] H. Simonis and M. Dincbas. Using an Extended Prolog for Digital Circuit Design. In *IEEE International Workshop on AI Applications to CAD Systems for Electronics*, pages 165–188, Munich, W.Germany, October 1987.

[SD87b]   H. Simonis and M. Dincbas. Using Logic Programming for Fault Diagnosis in Digital Circuits. In *German Workshop on Artificial Intelligence (GWAI-87)*, pages 139–148, Geseke, W.Germany, September 1987.

[SND88]   H. Simonis, H.N. Nguyen, and M. Dincbas. Verification of Digital Circuits Using CHIP. In *IFIP WG 10.2 International Working Conference on the Fusion of Hardware Design and Verification*, Glasgow, Scotland, July 1988.

[STS87]   M. Schulz, E. Trischler, and T. Sarfert. Socrates: A Highly Efficient Automatic Test Pattern Generation System. In *Proc Int Test Conference*, Washington D.C., Sept 1987.

[TG87]   Y. Tohma and K. Goto. Test Generation for Large-Scale Combinational Circuits by using Prolog. In *Proc 6th Conf Logic Programming*, Tokyo, Japan, June 1987.

[Ued85]   K. Ueda. Guarded horn clauses. Icot tech. report tr-103, Institute of New Generation Computer Technology, Tokyo, 1985.

[VT87]   P. Varma and Y. Tohma. Protean, A Knowledge Based Test Generator. In *Proc IEEE 1987 Custom Integrated Circuits Conference*, Portland Or, May 1987.

[Wil86]   T.W. Williams. *VLSI Testing, Advances in CAD for VLSI Vol. 5*. North-Holland, Amsterdam, Netherlands, 1986.

Solving Simple Substitution Ciphers in Andorra-I

Rong Yang
Department of Computer Science
University of Bristol, BS8 1TR, England

Abstract

A decoding system for simple substitution ciphers, called DSSA, is presented in this paper. DSSA is developed using a parallel logic programming system Andorra-I, which is based on the Andorra model, a logic programming computation model combining both *and-* and *or-* parallelism. Benefitting from the Andorra model, the DSSA system is very smart, efficient and flexible. The results have shown that it can save at least 70% of the reductions of a standard Prolog system.

The paper consists of four parts. Section 1 describes the background of decoding simple substitution ciphers and shows why the Andorra model is important for this application. Section 2 gives a brief introduction to the Andorra model and Andorra-I. Section 3 explains the main features of the DSSA system and its programs in detail. In Section 4, we discuss some results and further work.

1   Introduction

1.1   Simple Substitution Ciphers

Secret writing has a long history since ancient times. One of the simplest ways to encode a message is to replace each letter of the message by a substitute letter. This is called the simple substitution method. In this method, the key is a permutation of 26 letters (disregarding numbers and other characters). Therefore, to break a simple substitution cipher, there are 26! possibilities to try. However, there is no need to visit 26! possible nodes in the search tree, if one takes into account the frequency of letters, digrams and trigrams (sequences of letters), etc. For example, the most frequently used English letter is supposed to be 'e', so one can try to replace the letter which has the highest frequency in the cipher by 'e'. If it is a correct guess, the search space will be reduced to 25!.

Today, with the availability of computers, the simple substitution cipher is not regarded as a safe method by cryptologists. However, decoding this cipher is still a very interesting topic for researchers in Artificial Intelligence, since it is a typical and practical problem solving style subject. By investigating how to use computers to decode the simple substitution cipher efficiently, one may obtain some general methodologies for problem solving. There have been many efforts (for example, [1,6,8]) which were based on a sequential computation model. In this paper, we present a decoding system developed on an and- and or- parallel logic programming system Andorra-I [11,13]. The system is called DSSA (**D**ecoding **S**imple **S**ubstitution cipher in **A**ndorra-I), and is composed of less than 400 clauses (including a common word dictionary). The results have shown that it is a very efficient system because of its use of Andorra's control strategy. Moreover, it is flexible and allows us to easily introduce new kinds of search knowledge.

1.2   Why the Andorra Model

First, we give an example to show a cryptanalyst's approach to solving our problem. Assume a cipher is as follows:

UIF FOFNZ JT UXP NJMFT BXBZ JO UIF IPVTF OFYU UP

UIF CPPL TIPQ

where F is the most frequently used letter (8 times), P and U are next most frequent (6 times), etc. According to statistics results, we know 'e' is the most frequently used letter, 't' is the second, 'o','a' and 'n' are the third, etc. Therefore, a cryptanalyst may first guess that F might be 'e', and P might be 't'. After replacing F by 'e' and P by 't', the cipher text will be:

UIe eOeNZ JT UXt NJMeT BXBZ JO UIe ItVTe OeYU Ut

<u>UIe CttL TItQ</u>

Now, the cryptanalyst might easily spot that the last but one word of the cipher is '?tt?', which is very unlikely to match a real English word. That means P should not be 't'. The question is how can a computer program achieve this efficiently instead of scanning all the text after every substitution. In logic programming languages, a letter can be represented by a logical variable, so one letter can be replaced in one step, i.e. one unification. However, to check that a replacement does not create an illegal word could take a time proportional to the length of the cipher text if the system does not know where the words related to the replacement are.

Another important point can be shown by continuing to follow the above example. Assume the cryptanalyst tries to replace P by 'o' instead of 't', and to replace U by 't', then he gets:

<u>tIe eOeNZ JT tXo NJMeT BXBZ JO tIe IoVTe OeYt to</u>

<u>tIe CooL TIoQ</u>

Now, it is easy to find out that the word 'tXo' must be 'two', since according to his knowledge, he knows that this is the only match. Thus, X should be replaced by 'w'. After this replacement, he might find that 'BwBZ' should be 'away'. Replacing X,B and Z did not rely on the letter frequency analysis, but another strategy (we call it *determinate word mapping*). How can we easily write a program to be able to change search strategies intelligently like this?

Conventional Prolog is not suitable because of its fixed left-right depth-first strategy. Two solutions to achieve a dynamic controllable strategy are coroutining Prologs [9] and committed choice languages. However, both the existing coroutining mechanisms for Prolog and the suspension mechanisms for committed choice languages are controlled by explicit conditions on variable bindings; using these, it would be complicated to specify the desired control. Moreover, the committed choice languages cannot express *don't know* non-determinism.

The other important point is that illegal words must be detected, and determinate word mapping must be performed, before non-deterministically replacing a letter. This can efficiently reduce the search space, allowing us to recover from an illegal word (e.g. '?tt?') by undoing the most recent choice (P = t), i.e. chronological backtracking. Thus, we need a 'lazy' form of don't know non-determinism.

In summary, to solve our problem, we need to combine coroutining facility and 'lazy' don't know non-determinism. However, the ideal solution is a logic programming computation model which integrates both dependent and-parallelism and "lazy" or-parallelism. This is just what the Andorra model is.

2 The Andorra Model and Andorra-I

2.1 A Brief Introduction

The Andorra model is a parallel logic computation model which was first proposed by David Warren [11]. The model is designed to exploit both dependent and-parallelism and or-parallelism. The basic idea is that all the **determinate** goals, i.e. those which can be reduced determinately, are executed in and-parallel first. When determinate reduction cannot continue further, the leftmost Prolog goal will be selected to fork or-branches (making a choicepoint). Then, after one step of this non-deterministic reduction, deterministic reduction will start again on each or-branch, The execution between or-branches can be done in parallel similarly to the or-parallel Prolog system Aurora [10].

Two key features of the Andorra model are: (1) like P-Prolog [12], it uses a determinacy check as a synchronization mechanism; (2) unlike P-Prolog, it delays creation of or-branches until determinate reduction stops. Feature (1) allows us to exploit and-parallelism transparently from traditional Prolog programs without modification. Feature (2) brings two important advantages: avoiding unnecessary choice point creation and simplifying implementation. From the users' point of view, a language based on the Andorra model can be used either as Prolog or as a flat committed choice language. Furthermore, since the Andorra model integrates both and- and or- parallelism, it can execute a new style of parallel programs which cannot be expressed in either Prolog or committed choice languages. The DSSA system presented in this paper is one application which fully benefits from this new approach.

Andorra-I is a prototype implementation of the Andorra model, which is being developed on Sequent multiprocessors and on SUN workstations (as a uniprocessor version) [14]. It is an interpreter style system written in C. Currently, Andorra-I programs just use the Prolog syntax. Additionally, determinacy test code is provided for the predicates which may be determinate during execution. The test code

is described in detail in [13]. We assume that the test code will be
generated by compiler analysis with or without some user annotations;
[2,7] have given some results on this subject.

To give a general image of Andorra-I, an Andorra-I program called
`exclusive_list` is shown in Program 1, together with its determinacy
test code.

```
% exclusive_list(L): L is a list in which no pair of
% elements have same value.

exclusive_list([]).
exclusive_list([A|T]):- not_member(A,T),
                        exclusive_list(T).

% not_member(A,T): A is not a member of T.

not_member(_,[]).
not_member(X,[Y|T]):- not_equal(X,Y), not_member(X,T).

% exclusive_list(L) is determinate when L is not a
% variable.  Its det-test code is as follows:

det exclusive_list {              % if 1st arg is a variable,
    if_g_var_sus    exit 1 1      % suspend on it, otherwise,
    switch_on_list 1 L1 L2 fail % use 1st or 2nd clauses to
L1 commit  1                      % reduce the goal, or fail
L2 commit  2                      % according to whether it's
}                                 % a nil, list or other.
```

Program 1. exclusive_list

A goal `exclusive_list(L)` succeeds if and only if no pair of elements in L have same value. We can see that it is determinate as long as L is instantiated. In the determinacy test code of `exclusive_list`, the first instruction **if_g_var_sus** L G T dereferences the Gth argument of the goal, and tests whether the value is unbound. If it is unbound, suspend the current goal on this variable and go to L. Otherwise, put the value into the temporary register T and continue to the next instruction. **switch_on_list** T $L1$ $L2$ $L3$ will test the value in T and go to $L1$, $L2$ or $L3$ depending on whether the result is nil, a list or otherwise. **commit** N selects the Nth clause of the current procedure to reduce. The procedure **not_member** has the same determinacy test code as `exclusive_list` except that the second argument is tested instead of the first one. **not_equal** is an object level inequality which tests whether its arguments are the same and suspends when arguments are not ground.

Assume there is an initial goal

```
?- L = [X,Y,Z], multi_generator(L), exclusive_list(L).
```

where `multi_generator(L)` produces the solutions of L non-determinately. In this case, according to the Andorra model, `exclusive_list(L)` starts to run immediately after the unification L = [X,Y,Z]. It ends up suspending three test goals `not_equal(X,Y)`, `not_equal(X,Z)` and `not_equal(Y,Z)`. Then, `multi_generator(L)` is reduced, making a choicepoint (or forking an or-branch). As long as it produces bindings to any two of the variables in L, the corresponding `not_equal` goal can test them immediately.

2.2 A Useful Primitive in Andorra-I: Priority Declaration

In committed choice parallel programming, scheduling between runnable goals does not affect successful termination, because if any goal fails, all the computation must fail. However, in combining and- and or- parallelism, if the system can execute a failing goal first, a lot of unnecessary computation can be avoided.

For example, suppose we have two goals, `exclusive_list(L)` and `not_equal(X,2)`, which are suspended. Assume another goal binds L to [A,B,C|S] and X to 2. Then both goals become determinate at the same time. In this case, it is more efficient to execute `not_equal(2,2)` first if only one worker (processor) is available.

To help the system 'intelligently' pick a failing goal, like `not_equal(2,2)`, as soon as possible from a mass of woken goals, Andorra-I provides a simple mechanism to allow goals to be assigned two priority levels. High priority goals are always executed before low priority goals. The information of which goal has high priority can be declared by the user or obtained from an analysis system. For the above example, one could declare:

```
:- high_priority not_equal/2.
```

3 DSSA system

The target of the DSSA system is to decode a simple substitution cipher whose plaintext (the original message) is not on a specialized topic, and is comparatively long. To simplify the problem without loss of generality, the spaces in plaintexts appear in the cipher in the same positions (i.e. spaces are assumed to be uncoded), since the substitution of spaces can be easily found out by a frequency analysis of characters.

3.1 General Description of DSSA

Feature 1. Using a Small and Efficient Dictionary

Generally speaking, a cryptanalyst has to have very extensive knowledge of English. Similarly, breaking a cipher with computer assistance requires an electronic dictionary. Looking up a word or matching a likely word from such a big database is quite expensive. In the DSSA system, we only use a very small dictionary which currently contains about 200 - 300 of the most commonly used words. The idea is based on a statistics result that says if one knows the 15, 100, or 1000 most common words, one will be able to understand about 25%, 60%, or 85% (respectively) of text on average [3]. Therefore, we need only let the computer know the most common words, our program uses a counter to record how many words it could not match in its common word database. When the figure exceeds a certain amount, the substitutions tried so far are assumed incorrect. Then, the search on the current or-branch should be terminated. This method can be used not only in breaking simple substitution ciphers, but also in other decryption methods.

Feature 2. Automatically Changing Decryption Strategies

The usual method of breaking a simple substitution cipher is mainly based on:

1. a frequency analysis of letters, digrams, trigrams, etc.;

2. trying to match an incomplete word to a likely word;

3. checking if any illegal words, digrams and trigrams occur after a guess.

Currently, in DSSA, we use the following three strategies:

S1: replacing letters in the order of their frequency in the cipher by 'e', 't', 'n', 'o', 'a', and so on, i.e. the most common letters first;

S2: replacing letters by determinate word mapping (for example, if there is a word '?p' in the cipher, we can determine that '?' must be 'u').

S3: replacing letters by non-determinate word mapping (i.e. guessing).

Basically, the system starts to apply S1 first, then as more and more letters are replaced, S2 and S3 will be applied instead. In the DSSA system, there is no specific part of program written to control when and how to change the strategies between S1 and S2. This is actually controlled by the Andorra model, i.e. the policy of executing deterministic goals eagerly.

3.2   Details

DSSA comprises five main parts, as shown in Fig.1.

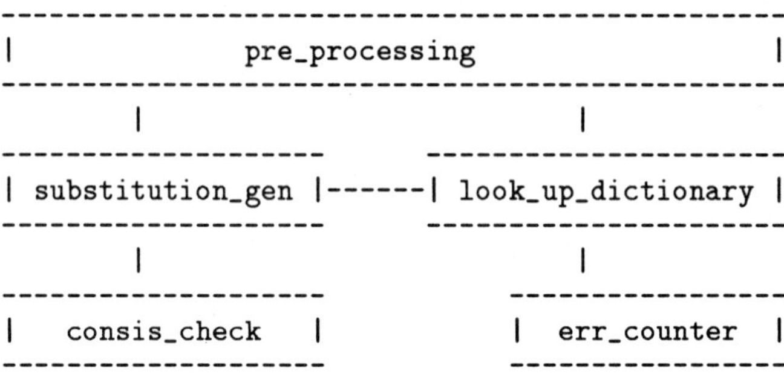

Fig. 1 The Structure of DSSA

The 'pre_processing' part reads the ciphertext and converts each distinct character in the cipher to a unique variable. These variables are collected into a list ordered by the frequency of the character in the cipher, the most frequent one at the front. This is named the FrequencyList.

'substitution_gen' is a generator of substitutions for characters in the cipher. Its program is called **permute_subset** shown in Program 2. There are two input lists: one is a ground list, an AlphabetList of all the letters ordered by their commonness; another is a variable list, the FrequencyList produced by the 'pre_processing' part. It works by incrementally generating a permutation of FrequencyList and binding each variable in the permuted list to the corresponding letter in AlphabetList. For example, **permute_subset([X,Y],[e,t,o])** will produce multiple solutions of **[X,Y]**: **[e,t],[e,o],[t,e],[t,o],[o,e]** and **[o,t]**. Optionally, instead of using the whole of FrequencyList, one can take just an initial sublist of FrequencyList (call it TopN), permute this and bind its variables to the most common letters. Obviously, the latter method cannot produce all the substitutions but it is possible to leave the remainder of them to the 'look_up_dictionary' part, i.e. using the strategy **S3** mentioned in the previous subsection. It will be more efficient if the cipher is reordered so that the words containing more high frequency letters appear before those containing fewer such letters, because then the search space can be reduced. This reordering is done by the 'pre_processing' part.

```
% permute_subset(FrequencyList, AlphabetList).

permute_subset([],_).
permute_subset([A|S],X):- select_and_delete(A,X,W),
                          permute_subset(S,W).

% note that select_and_delete is always non-determinate

select_and_delete(X,[X|Y],Y).
select_and_delete(A,[X|Z],[X|W]):-
                          select_and_delete(A,Z,W).
```

```
              Program 2. Substitution generator
```

The 'look_up_dictionary' part is in charge of scanning all the words in the cipher and looking up the common words dictionary. The program for scanning the cipher is called **look_up_dic(ReorderedCT, ErrMes)** and is shown in the Appendix. Here, **ReorderedCT** is input, the reordered version of the ciphertext, while **ErrMes** is output, a message stream linking **look_up_dic** to the 'err_counter' part.

The common words are divided into different groups according to their length, the corresponding predicates being **word1**, **word2**, **word3** and so on (shown in the Appendix). If a word cannot be found in the dictionary, an error message is sent to 'err_counter'. This is implemented by putting the following clause at the end of each **wordN**:

```
wordn(_,_,...,ErrMes):- send_err(ErrMes).
```

Since all words with one or two letters are included in this dictionary, procedures `word1` and `word2` do not need to send an error message; instead, they fail immediately if the word is missing from the dictionary.

It is interesting to look at the determinacy conditions of `wordN`. Take `word2(X,Y)` as an example, it will be determinate if any one of the following conditions holds:

(1). `X` is either c,f,j,...,z; (definitely fail)
(2). `Y` is either a,b,c,...,z; (definitely fail)
(3). `X` is d,g,h,n,t,s,w;
(4). `Y` is m,r,p;
(5). both `X` and `Y` are instantiated.

We can see that it would be quite difficult to express these kinds of condition using the suspension mechanism of existing coroutining Prologs or committed choice languages.

The 'consistency_check' part checks the consistency of the substitutions, i.e. it makes sure that no two different variables are replaced by the same letter. This is done by the `exclusive_list` program described in Section 2.2 (Program 1).

The 'err_counter' part receives the messages from 'look_up_dic' and counts them. When the count exceeds a certain amount, it fails (See `err_counter` in the Appendix).

To merge the **err** messages from individual goals (i.e. `wordN`), one can use a merge network. However, it is wasteful to use the merge network in this case, since every goal only needs to send one message. To avoid this, the procedure `send_err(M)` which is executed whenever an unknown word is found sends an **err** message to a stream M directly without passing through the merge network.

```
send_err(M):- test_var(M), !, M = [err|_].
send_err([_|M]):-  send_err(M).
```

            Program 3. send_err

In the above program, there is a special 'test_var' predicate which is used to locate the unbound variable at the tail of M and append the message to this tail. `test_var` can be regarded as a parallel version of **var**, similar to LOCKVAR proposed in [4]. The semantics of `test_var(X)` is similar to `var(X)` in the sense of testing whether `X` is unbound. The basic difference from `var(X)` is that `test_var(X)` locks `X` if `X` is unbound so that `X` can be guaranteed not to be instantiated by other goals. There are two restrictions on its use. First, `test_var(X)` can only appear in the 'guards' of clauses. Second, if `test_var(X)` is used in the 'guard', the output unification of `X`, i.e. `X = a_term`, must appear in the body. Actually, `test_var` can be treated as a low level primitive, i.e. not necessarily available to the users. The main reason of introducing `test_var` in Andorra-I is to provide a more efficient alternative to the output unification in the guard as used in [5].

So far, all the procedures of DSSA have been explained. In the Appendix, the full program of the DSSA is listed except the 'pre-processing' part. To simplify the problem, we omit the programs for 'pre_processing', but assume the results of pre-processing can be obtained by calling a procedure

```
init(CT, ReorderedCT, ME, AList, FList, TopN).
```

Three arguments, `CT` (Cipher Text), `ME` (Maximum Error count) and `AList` (Alphabet List) are input from the users. The others, `ReorderedCT` (Reordered Cipher Text), `FList` (Frequency List) and `TopN` (Top N of `FList`) are supposed to be produced by 'pre-processing'.

The top level goal is called `dssa`:

```
dssa:- init(CT, ReorderedCT, ME, AList, FList, TopN),
       permute_subset(TopN, AList),
       look_up_dic(ReorderedCT, ErrMes),
       exclusive_list(FList),
       err_counter(0, ME, ErrMes).
```

The execution flow of `dssa` is explained as follows. The goal `init` produces all the information first. Then `permute_subset`, `look_up_dic` and `exclusive_list` receive their input lists from `init`, and start to concurrently, because they are determinate. As shown in Program 2, a goal `permute_subset([A|B],X)` can be reduced deterministically to two subgoals `select_and_delete` and `permute_subset`, but these two new subgoals have to be suspended immediately. The other two goals, `look_up_dic` and `exclusive_list`, can be reduced continuously until their input lists are completely scanned. As a result of executing those two goals, all the goals for `not_equal`, `word1`, `word2`, `word3` and so on are suspended on their particular variables. Now the non-deterministic execution phase starts. The leftmost `select_and_delete` goal is reduced and a choice point is made. This reduction sends out a tentative substitution to other goals. Then, substitution may cause some suspended goals to wake up and execute immediately. Note that we can assign high priority to goals like `not_equal`. The shared variable `ErrMes` between `look_up_dic` and `err_counter` plays a role in communicating between these two goals. The `err_counter` goal is suspended initially waiting for messages on this input channel 'ErrMes'. When an 'err' message is received from the word mapping, `err_counter` will become determinate immediately. Then `err_counter` will be reduced one step, incrementing the counter by one. It will fail if the maximum error count is exceeded.

4 Some Results and Further Work

DSSA has been implemented on the SUN version of Andorra-I. Several examples have been solved in DSSA successfully. For example, the solution for the following ciphertext:

```
[T,F,O,E,' ',N,P,S,F,' ',N,P,O,F,Z,' ',U,P,' ',N,F,' ',
  O,F,Y,U,' ',N,F,F,U,J,O,H,' ',X,J,M,M,' ',C,F,' ',
  P,O,' ',G,S,J,E,B,Z,' ',B,U,' ',P,M,E,' ',Q,M,B,D,F]
```
is
```
[s,e,n,d,' ',m,o,r,e,' ',m,o,n,e,y,' ',t,o,' ',m,e,' ',
  n,e,x,t,' ',m,e,e,t,i,n,g,' ',w,i,l,l,' ',b,e,' ',
  o,n,' ',G,r,i,d,a,y,' ',a,t,' ',o,l,d,' ',p,l,a,c,e].
```

One interesting point is that no substitution is made for variable G. This is because G appears only once in one word in the cipher and that word (i.e. friday) is not included in our small dictionary. However, it has little effect on the understanding of the above plaintext. We believe that if a cipher has a longer text, the number of unsolved characters will be fewer.

To show how much efficiency can be gained by using Andorra-I, we ran the system without the determinism test code for the dictionary part. This means that the word mappings have to be tried in a simple left to right order, simulating the traditional Prolog behaviour. The result of testing the above example is that the modified version needs 2968 reductions with 326 backtracks, while the Andorra version only needs 951 reductions with 28 backtracks (a saving of about 70%).

As further work, DSSA will be improved by introducing more knowledge of English. The current system is still very weak in the sense that it relies only on the frequency of letters, and the dictionary. In fact, the analysis of frequency of sequences of letters can also play an important role in breaking simple substitution ciphers. For example, the statistics results tell us that the most frequently used trigram is supposed to be 'the'; the most frequently used final trigram is 'ing'; the most frequently used digram is 'th', and so on. Therefore, we are going to extend DSSA so that it can make guesses and discover illegal sequences of letters by using these kinds of knowledge. This extension can be achieved easily, since DSSA is written in a logic programming language. Any new knowledge can be simply inserted in the top level conjunction, as shown below.

```
extended_dssa:-
        init(CipherText, ReorderedCT, MaximumErr,
            AlphabetList, FrequencyList,
            TopN, DigramList, TrigramList),
        permute_subset(TopN, AlphabetList),
        look_up_dic(ReorderedCT, ErrMes),
        common_digram(DigramList),          %
        common_trigram(TrigramList),        %   extended parts
        illegal_trigram(TrigramList),       %
        ......                              %
        exclusive_list(FrequencyList),
        err_counter(0, MaximumErr, ErrMes).
```

Finally, from the point of view of language issues, the encouraging conclusion from developing the DSSA system is that languages based on the Andorra model will be more expressive and efficient than traditional Prolog.

Acknowledgements: The work is supported by the UK Science and Engineering Research Council. Many thanks are due to David Warren who gave the original idea and the direction of the work, also thanks due to Peter Szeredi, Steve Gregory, and Vítor S. Costa for their valuable discussions and help.

References

[1]   M. J. Carroll and S. Martin, October 1986. 'The Automated Cryptanalysis of Substitution Ciphers', *CRYPTOLOGIA*, vol. 10, No. 4 pp. 193-209

[2]   V. S. Costa, Jan. 1989. Personal communication.

[3] D. Crystal, 1988. 'The English Language', Penguin.

[4] S. Gregory, 1987. 'Parallel Logic Programming in PARLOG', Addison-Wesley.

[5] S. Kliger, E. Yardeni, K. Kahn and E.Y. Shapiro, Nov. 1988, 'The language FCP(|,:,?)', *Proc. of 3rd FGCS*.

[6] G. Nagy, S. Seth and K. Einspahr, 1988. 'Decoding Substitution Ciphers by Means of Word Matching with Applications to OCR', *IEEE Transactions on Pattern Analysis and Machine Intelligence*, 9(5), pp. 709-715.

[7] L. Naish and P. Brand, Jan. 1989. 'Determinacy analysis', The workshop of PEPMA project, Bristol University.

[8] S. Peleg and A. Rosenfeld, 1979. 'Breaking Substitution Ciphers Using a Relaxation Algorithm', *Comm. of the ACM*, 22, 598-605

[9] L. M. Pereira, 1982. 'Logic control with logic', *Proc. of 1st International Logic Programming Conference*.

[10] D. H. D. Warren *et al.*, E. Lusk *et al.*, S. Haridi *et al.* Nov. 1988. 'The Aurora Or-Parallel Prolog System', *Proc. of 3rd FGCS '88 Conference*.

[11] D.H.D. Warren, Feb. 1987. Personal communication.

[12] R. Yang and H. Aiso, July 1986. 'P-Prolog: A Parallel Logic Language Based on Exclusive Relation', *Proc. of 3rd International Logic Programming Conference*, pp. 255-269.

[13] R. Yang, September 1988. 'Programming in Andorra-I', Technical Report, Dept. of Computer Science, Bristol University.

[14] R. Yang, Nov. 1988. 'Implementation Notes on the Andorra Model', Technical Report, Dept. of Computer Science, Bristol University.

Appendix: The DSSA system

```
% the top level goal of DSSA

dssa:- init(CipherText, ReorderedCT, MaximumErr,
            AlphabetList, FrequencyList, TopN),
       permute_subset(TopN, AlphabetList),
       look_up_dic(ReorderedCT, ErrMes),
```

```prolog
        exclusive_list(FrequencyList),
        err_counter(0, MaximumErr, ErrMes).

% an example tested for this paper

init([T,F,O,E,' ',N,P,S,F,' ',N,P,O,F,Z,' ',U,P,' ',N,F,' ',
  O,F,Y,U,' ',N,F,F,U,J,O,H,' ',X,J,M,M,' ',C,F,' ',P,O,' ',
  G,S,J,E,B,Z,' ',B,U,' ',P,M,E,' ',Q,M,B,D,F],

 [N,F,' ',C,F,' ',P,O,' ',T,F,O,E,' ',O,F,Y,U,' ',N,P,S,F,
  ' ',N,P,O,F,Z,' ',U,P,' ',B,U,' ',P,M,E,' ',X,J,M,M,' ',
  Q,M,B,D,F,' ',G,S,J,E,B,Z,' ',N,F,F,U,J,O,H],

 1,

 [e,t,n,o,a,i,r],  % this list could be longer

 [F,P,O,U,N,M,J,B,E,S,Z,T,C,X,Q,D,G,H,Y],

 [F,P,O]).

% permute_subset(FrequencyList, AlphabetList)

permute_subset([],_).
permute_subset([A|S],X):- select_and_delete(A,X,W),
                          permute_subset(S,W).

select_and_delete(X,[X|Y],Y).
select_and_delete(A,[X|Z],[X|W]):- select_and_delete(A,Z,W).

% look_up_dic(Text, ErrMes)

look_up_dic([],E).
look_up_dic(S,E):- get_word(W,S,Rest), match(W,E),
        look_up_dic(Rest,E).

get_word(W, [], []).
get_word(W, [' '|Rest], Rest).
get_word([X|W], [X|T], Rest):- X \== ' '
        get_word(W, T, Rest).

match([],  _).
match([X1], _):- word1(X1).
match([X1,X2], _):- word2(X1,X2).
match([X1,X2,X3], ErrMess):- word3(X1,X2,X3,ErrMess).
```

```
    ...

% the common word dictionary

word1(a).       word2(g,o).     word2(o,f).
word1(i).       word2(h,e).     word2(o,n).
                word2(i,f).     word2(o,r).
word2(a,m).     word2(i,n).     word2(s,o).
word2(a,n).     word2(i,s).     word2(t,o).
word2(a,t).     word2(i,t).     word2(u,p).
word2(b,e).     word2(m,e).     word2(u,s).
word2(b,y).     word2(m,y).     word2(w,e).
word2(d,o).     word2(n,o).

word3(a,c,t, _). ... word3(_,_,_, E):- send_err(E).

word4(a,b,l,e, _). ... word4(_,_,_,_, E):- send_err(E).

word5(a,b,o,u,t, _). ... word5(_,_,_,_,_, E):- send_err(E).
    ...

% err_counter(Start, Maxmum, ErrMes)

err_counter(_, _, []).
err_counter(N, M, [err|T]):- N < M,  N1 is N+1,
        err_counter(N1, M, T).

% send_err(ErrMes)

send_err(M):- test_var(M), !, M = [err|_].
send_err([_|M]):-  send_err(M).

% exclusive_list(L): the elements in L are exclusive

exclusive_list([]).
exclusive_list([A|T]):- not_member(A,T),exclusive_list(T).

% not_member(A,T): A is not a member of T.

not_member(_,[]).
not_member(X,[Y|T]):- not_equal(X,Y), not_member(X,T).
```

Constraints

A Relevant Scheme for Prolog Extensions:
CLP(Conceptual Theory)

Henri Beringer*,   Franck Porcher

Electronique Serge Dassault

55, Quai Marcel Dassault

92214 Saint Cloud FRANCE

ABSTRACT

Numerous Prolog extensions have been proposed over the past few years. Upon further considerations with regard to the role of functional terms, we propound a general type of extension which covers up some major requirements in logic programming. We regard Prolog as a basic knowledge representation language and define our scheme as the addition of a **Conceptual Theory** to Prolog (yielding thus an instance of the **CPL** framework that we call CLP(C.T.)). This scheme allows to produce some logic programming languages that have the ability both to deal with complex representations of concepts (and their intended properties) and to handle full symbolic constraints (relations) about them. By this schemelight, some known Prolog extensions are easily described, compared and their limitations shown. Then, we describe Cosylog, a new language over this scheme, that oversteps these restrictions by offering a lot of interesting features. Efficiently implemented, we prove it as a positive stage towards more powerful CLP(C.T.) languages.

INTRODUCTION : the very role of functional terms

Prolog is often regarded as a theorem prover for first order logic restricted to definite clauses. All objects handled are identified either by constants or ground functional terms. Functional terms are built with Skolem functions introduced by the transformation of a general formula in a (some) definite clause(s) (while erasing existential quantifiers). For instance, the formula : $\forall X, \exists Y, p(X, Y) \wedge q(Y)$ is translated into two definite clauses: $p(X, f(X))$ and $q(f(X))$ where f is an **arbitrary** new Skolem function.

According to this view of Prolog, the *meaning* of a Skolem function is only defined by the set of clauses using it (hence deriving from the same initial formula). The ground functional terms are nothing else than **object identifiers** like Prolog constants.

The practical use of functional term is totally different. A particular structure is chosen to represent a particular kind of objects in a way which reflects as much as possible the properties of these objects. For instance, the *cons* operator (written here as a dot) is generally and implicitely chosen to refer to lists whose only first element and end of list are known.
Let us have the two following Horn clauses definig the predicate p :

$$p(X,cdr(L,X)).$$
$$p(X,cdr(L,*)) \leftarrow p(X,L).$$

---

*Now at :   Centre de recherche informatique de Montréal
1550 Bd de Maisonneuve Ouest, Bureau 1000
Montréal (Québec) Canada H3G1N2

Although *p* is operationally isomorphous to Prolog usual *member* predicate, its meaning isnot obvious because the *cdr* functional data structure used for lists encoding do not has been previously clarified. When adding a clause equivalent to :

$$add\_\_as\_\_first\_\_element(CAR,CDR,cdr(CDR,CAR))$$

we define the exact meaning of the *cdr* functional term and the predicate *p* can be easily read as

$$p(X,L) \leftarrow add\_\_as\_\_first\_\_element(X,*,L).$$
$$p(X,L) \leftarrow add\_\_as\_\_first\_\_element(*,CDR,L) \& p(X,CDR).$$

equivalent to *member* predicate with *cons* operator for lists encoding.

In other words, functional terms are used to directly encode some properties of the target world's objects. So, more than object identifiers, functional terms are **representations** of world's objects. A functional term is a collection of properties referring to a set of world objects which have these properties. Each Skolem function is given an intended interpretation by the programmer.

We define the *functional terms canonical interpretation* for Prolog as a mapping from their syntactical structure to the domain of rational trees. In this canonical interpretation, a functional term refers to some rational trees having the properties directly described by itssyntactical structure. For instance, the term $a(X, X ,b)$ is canonically interpreted as the set of trees having a as root and three daughters : the two first being equal and the third being the constant b.

Unification can be regarded as a process able to handle representations of sets of rational trees. When unifying the terms $T1$ and $T2$, Prolog produces a term $T3$ which describes the conjunction of the properties specified in $T1$ and in $T2$. So, in the canonical interpretation, $T3$ represents the intersection of the sets of rational trees represented by $T1$ and $T2$. Prolog is then able to check the compatibility of two representations considered as collections of properties of rational trees. Attractive aspects of Prolog are the declarative expression of object properties, and the fact that these properties are used as soon as possible to reduce the search space (in detecting incompatibility).

However, the canonical interpretation is seldom the intended one: functional terms often refer to objects other than rational trees. In such cases, terms are still used as representations but mappings between objects properties and terms structures are not always straightforward. This brings about some limitations in Prolog's ability to detect incompatibility between two representations:

1) Two equivalent but syntactically different representations of a same world object cannot be unified. Let us consider the two terms *set(a.b.c.nil)* and *set(c.b.a.nil)* to be both interpreted as the set $\{a, b, c\}$. Prolog will not be able to equate them.

2) On the other hand, Prolog may handle terms which are absurd according to the intended interpretation. If an interval of real numbers *[MIN,MAX]* is represented by *interval(MIN,MAX)*, we cannot easily prevent Prolog to accept such odd terms as *interval(3,0)* : this term could have been the result of the unification of the two following acceptable representations: *interval(3,X)*(an interval beginning at 3) and *interval(Y,0)* (an interval ending at 0).

These two examples illustrate classical problems encountered during Prolog programming. The programmer has to encode into the very structures of terms as much as possible of the object properties his program deals with in order to gain :

- easy access to information,
- independence from algorithmic considerations when "updating" or "testing" these properties (using simple unification),
- efficiency of the resulting program because an inconsistence between these properties is detected as soon as possible, reducing the search space.

Rather than requiring from the programmer a difficult and often imperfect coding of semantic properties in the structure of functional terms, we propose to offer him a more straightforward language to describe the intended properties. Such a representation language could be drawn from the existing knowledge representation systems. Indeed Prolog must be extended to deal with these representations and, in particular, to be able to check the compatibility of two representations (some kinds of user-defined knowledge can be used for this operation). These idea are at the root of the notion of **Conceptual Theory Scheme**. We briefly recall features of some known kinds of Prolog extension and describe this scheme afterwards.

1   DIFFERENT KINDS OF PROLOG EXTENSION

Intrinsic limitations of Prolog have been identified early and numerous works have been undertaken to overcome them. Some of them are concerned with control of the resolution algorithm [DINCBAS 84], but most try to extend the semantic of functional terms and fall into at least one of the two following theoretical frameworks.

1.1   Extension of equality

The numerous attempts to provide Prolog with "semantic" knowledge about functional terms use different ways to specify equalities between terms. Hence, they fall into the theoretical framework of *logic programming with equality* described in [JAFFAR et al 84]. An equality theory allows natural introduction in Prolog of :

> - functional evaluation [KORNFELD 83], [DINCBAS 86],
> - tree structures built with slot and value [McCORD 85], [BOYER 88]
> - explicit taxonomy between terms [MONTINI 87].

Hence, an equality theory is a powerful way to extend Prolog. However, it remains limited to simple rewriting system of functional terms. This entails some unpleasant features because no global coherence over the set of used terms can be ensured (only local compatibility between the two unified terms is checked). In particular, a pure equality theory does not allow the proper handling of named individuals: one cannot prevent an individual named *john* from being declared in one place as fair-haired and in another as dark-haired.

Furthermore, the general problem of term equivalence given an equality theory is undecidable. Though some interesting procedures have been exhibited for semi-decision in the general case [HULLOT 80] [FAGES 83] and for decision in the particular case of commutative and associative theories, algorithms for equation resolution modulo a congruence [DINCBAS 86] are generally inefficient, often incomplete and may never end.

1.2   Constraint Logic Programming

A more radical way to extend Prolog has been proposed in [JAFFAR LASSEZ 87]. The main idea is that Prolog unification may be regarded as a particular case of constraint resolution limited to equality constraints. Unification of two terms may be split into two operations: adding a new equality constraint to the existing ones and testing if the resulting equality system can still be satisfied. This change of definition opens the way for other types of constraints ($\neq$ and, in some semantic domains, order constraints) and for the definition of global coherence rules (not restricted to the scope of the two terms being unified). Moreover, the constraints resolution module can be divided in several sub-modules, each dealing with a specific semantic domain and using specific knowledge about it.

Many Prolog extensions such as Prolog II and Prolog III [COLMERAUER 87] are encompassed by this framework. The CLP($\mathbb{R}$) language handles equalities and inequalities between real numbers [HEINTZE 87], and CHIP [VAN HENTENRYCK 87] solves constraints on finite domains restricted terms, boolean terms and linear rational terms.

The kind of extension we put forward is a particular case of *Constraint Logic Programming*. But instead of several constraints satisfaction modules, each of them dealing with a specific semantic domain, we want to offer a general one which takes into account **user-defined** knowledge.

2   CONCEPTUAL THEORIES

It seems that the most imperious needs in artificial intelligence community are about general knowledge representation. So, adding capacity to Prolog on this subject seems quite interesting and can be based on the idea developed for the numerous knowledge representation systems. In other words, we propose to investigate a particular kind of CLP dealing with general *concepts*.

We intend to define a general *knowledge logic programing Scheme* in which the definition of a *knowledge programing language* could amount to a formal type characterization -the **Conceptual Theory**- of the knowledge it handles. Such new logic programming languages will be able to handle complex representations of concepts and their properties (written in a user-friendly *representation language*) as well as relations between them (such as equality). During computation, the current set of concepts, properties about them and relations between them has to be constantly consistent according to a given set of axioms and some user-defined knowledge (such as a type taxonomy). A **Conceptual Theory** is defined as the coupling of the three following elements (regarded as a subset of first order logic) :

1) **Conceptual description**: A set of n-ary predicates used to represent the *properties of the concepts* handled by the user program.

2) **Knowledge structure**: A set of n-ary predicates that allows to define *global additional knowledge* about concepts properties not taken into account with conceptual description (e.g. the *subtype* predicate used to set up a type taxonomy).

3) **Axiomatic** : A *set of axioms* over the two previous sets of predicates which is used by a concept properties consistence checking system while resolution phasis.

A *conceptual constraints logic programming language*, CLP(C.T) for short, is defined by the *conceptual theory* it uses and *conceptual representation language* it provides to the user (i.e. a syntax for conceptual description). To implement a CLP(C.T.), one has to achieve a **complete** and **efficient** constraints resolution module (more precisely a coherence checking algorithm).

Programming in a CLP(C.T.) language is twofold. Aside from the traditional list of clauses, the user determines properties about concepts and knowledge about them -the *conceptual model-*. This new part of logic programming is an interesting one because it is natural and purely declarative.

The choice of the conceptual theory is a difficult one. It has to be powerful enough to make the extension useful and simple enough to allow complete and efficient constraints satisfaction module to be defined. Each call to this module has to stay an elementary operation of the resulting language (which can be compared to unification). Then, a general knowledge representation system built with Prolog such as DLOG [GOEBEL 85] whose operations are incomplete and use complex resolution steps (which are time consuming) is not to be considered as a CLP(C.T.). On the other hand, CLP(C.T.) scheme is not relevant for the CIL language [MUKAI 85] which offers only syntactic facilities to deal with functional terms (as named functions).

3 SOME CONCEPTUAL THEORIES OF KNOWN PROLOG EXTENSIONS

In order to illustrate the CLP(C.T.) scheme, we point out the implicit conceptual theories of some typical Prolog extensions. This allows us to compare them easily. These languages will be regarded as dealing with concepts which are identified (explicitly or not) by a referent being either a variable (it is a generic concept) or a constant (it is then an individual concept). They all make use of at least one of the two following notions:

- **Relations** (or functions):
  - In most conceptual theories, it is possible to handle (binary) relations between concepts as part of their properties (not described by simple Prolog predicates). This allows easy access to concepts related to a known one (or in other words this provides Prolog with a powerful and user friendly data structure). Moreover, some simple constraints are easily enforced (for example, one can easily enforce that somebody has a unique father in using the relation *father* between son and father and defining this relation as *functional*). Up from now, we will use the 3-ary predicate *rel(C1,R,C2)*[*] to describe a relation R between the concepts *C1* and *C2*.

- **Types** (or features)
  - Unary predicates about concepts are very common in knowledge representation systems with the feature name(type, ...) as predicative symbol and the concept referent as only argument. With the aim to remain independent of the possibly features number, we have chosen to describe them with the binary predicate *isa(C,T)* where C is the concept having the type (or feature) T.
  - Types are often organized in a taxonomy which we will refer to as the predicate *T1* $\leq$ *T2* meaning *T1* is a subtype of *T2* (more specific than *T2*). Axioms about the taxonomy differ greatly from one system to another.

3.1 Functional structures in Prolog

Adding *functional structures* to Prolog seems very useful. Such extensions has been often defined and proved convenient for natural language processing [BOYER 88], [McCORD 85]. They can be regarded as simple CLP(C.T.). Here concepts are not explicitly referred to and are just presented as a new type of terms. However it is possible to interpret each node of a functional structure as a separate concept and each function as a relation between concepts. The conceptual theory of these languages is the following:

- **Conceptual description** : It is based over the following pair predicates:
  - *rel(C1,R,C2)*,
  - *isa(C,T)*.

  We will add the *isa* predicate to distinguish between *standard Prolog terms* (type *prolog*) which are interpreted as referents of concepts and new *functional structures* (type *fs*) whose referents are new Prolog variables. The usual Prolog equality rules applies to referents.

- **Knowledge structure** : None (possibly declaration of relations)

- **Axiomatic** : All relations are functional. A *functional structure* and a *standard Prolog term* cannot be equated :

  - $\forall C1, C2, C3, R, \quad rel(C1,R,C2) \wedge (rel(C1,R,C3) \supset C2 = C3$
  - $\forall C, \qquad isa(C,prolog) \supset not\ isa(C,fs)$

---

[*] Typographic remark : Up from now and throughout this paper, *italic classic font* will be used to describe Conceptual Theories and conceptual systems when modern font will be used only to describe original examples extracted from all following examinated languages.

If this extension is a simple one, it is very useful and Boyer offers a complete program which deals with it in a very efficient way (mostly during a compilation phase) [BOYER 88]. This work is likely to be reusable for more complex theories. One easy extension to this will be, in Cosylog, to use different kinds of relations . Hence multi-valued relations will be possible and some knowledge about relations will be taken into account.

A simple example of this extension, drawn out [BOYER 88], may be the resolution of the equality :

$$is\_number\_of(X, [agreement: [number: X]]) = is\_number\_of(plural, [cat: verb,\ agreement: Y])$$

In the above conceptual theory, this equality may be rewritten in herein conceptual system :

$$\left\{ \begin{array}{llll} is\_number\_of(X,C1) = is\_number\_of(plural,C3) \\ isa(C1,fs),\ isa(C2,fs), & isa(C3,fs), & isa(plural,prolog),\ isa(verb,prolog) \\ rel(C1,agreement,C2), & rel(C2,number,X), & rel(C3,cat,verb), & rel(C3,agreement,Y) \end{array} \right\}$$

Usual Prolog unification adds $\{X = plural, C1 = C3\}$, and the system becomes :

$$\left\{ \begin{array}{llll} isa(C1,fs), & isa(plural,prolog), & isa(C2,fs), & isa(verb,prolog) \\ rel(C1,agreement,C2), & rel(C2,number,plural), & rel(C1,cat,verb), & rel(C1,agreement,Y) \end{array} \right\}$$

The first axiomatic part axiom entails $C2 = Y$, then the system can be reduced to the following one

$$\left\{ \begin{array}{llll} isa(C1,fs), & isa(plural,prolog), & isa(verb,prolog), & isa(C2,fs), \\ rel(C1,agreement,C2), & rel(C2,number,plural), & rel(C1,cat,verb) \end{array} \right\}$$

corresponding to the term (in the Boyer' syntax)

$$is\_number\_of(plural, [cat: verb, agreement: [number: plural]])$$

3.2   Taxlog : types and taxonomy in Prolog

The idea of providing types and their associated taxonomy in logic programming is often encountered. It is a simple way to state some parts of knowledge which, when expressed directly in definite clauses, is not used by Prolog in an efficient way. These extensions can be easily analyzed as CLP(C.T.) languages. We will describe the conceptual theory of one of them : Taxlog [MONTINI 87].

The main specificity of Taxlog is to treat types (or *classes*) as concepts and then to allow types of types (or *metaclasses*). However, this capacity makes the definition of the compatability algorithm rather difficult. Then, in order to simplify this algorithm, the current implementation of Taxlog put strong constraints on the structure of the taxonomy : no multiple inheritance is allowed. This is too restrictive when faced with real problems. The resulting conceptual theory can be described in the following way:

- **Conceptual description** : It is based on the only predicate

    . $isa(C,T)$

    because concepts and types are not distinguished and are referred either by Prolog constants or variables. C must more be a variable ant T a declared type (which is also a concept).

- **Knowledge structure** : Before running a Taxlog program, the user must define **exhaustively** its taxonomy. Indeed, he requires the two predicates : $isa(C1,C2)$ ($C1$ is an instance of $C2$) and $C1 \leq C2$ ($C1$ is subclass of $C2$).

Axiomatic :

$\leq$ is an order:	$\forall\, C,\ C \leq C$	
	$\forall\, C1,C2,$	$C1 \leq C2 \wedge C2 \leq C1 \supset C2 = C1$
	$\forall\, C1,C2,C3$	$C1 \leq C2 \wedge C2 \leq C3 \supset C1 \leq C3$
Transitivity:	$\forall\, C1,C2,C3$	$isa(C1,C2) \wedge C2 \leq C3 \supset isa(C1,C3)$
Level distinction:	$\forall\, C1,C2,$	$isa(C1,C2) \supset\ not\ (\exists\ C3,\ C1 \leq C3\ \wedge$ $C2 \leq C3)$
No multiple inheritance:	$\forall\, C1,C2,C3$	$C1 \leq C2 \wedge C1 \leq C3 \supset C3 \leq C2 \vee C2 \leq C3$
	$\forall\, C1,C2,C3$	$isa(C1,C2) \wedge isa(C1,C3) \supset C3 \leq C2 \vee$ $C2 \leq C3$

In Taxlog, the contraints satisfaction module has to check that the *isa* relations stated by clauses result from the declared taxonomy. An exemple given by Montini may be reinterpreted in the following way. Let us have the declarations system (knowledge part) :

$$\{isa(doggy1, dog), isa(doggy2, dog), isa(dog, animal\_species)\}$$

and the unique clause :

$$contains(A, zoology\_book) : A\ isa\ animal\_species.$$

The goal contains(dog, zoology_book) succeeds because the set of properties *{ isa(dog, animal_species) }* results from the declarations. On the contrary, the goal contains(X, zoology_book) : X isa dog does not succeed because unification of this goal with the head of the only clause yields the system *{isa(X,dog), isa(X,animal_species)}* which is not consistent with declarations (the last axiom asks for a subtype relation "$\leq$" between *dog* and *animal_species*).

To conclude on Taxlog, let us say that if types of types may be useful (but not so important), constraints about the taxonomy are too strong. The fact that the complete taxonomy of concepts has to be known means that the extension of a type is fixed once and for all. It is often required to handle intensional types for which the exact extension is not known. Furthermore, multiple inheritance and concepts belonging to multiple classes is a traditional requirement of knowledge representation system. We will present with Cosylog a more flexible notion of type (giving up the types of types capacity).

3.3. Login : types and relations together

Merging the notions of types and relations, Login [AIT-KACI, NASR 86] is an specially interesting language. Every Prolog's functional term is regarded as a particular notation of a functional structure (called ψ-term) which supports named relations and types. In CLP(C.T.) words, in place of classical Prolog functional terms, Login offers unnamed typed concepts linked by functional relations. The taxonomy defined by the programmer has to be a complete lattice (whose lowest type is written " $\bot$ " and greatest type "$\top$"). Types are compatible only if they have one common subtype different from " $\bot$ ". The conceptual theory of Login may be described by:

- **Conceptual description** : It is based on the two predicates

  . $isa(C,T),$
  . $rel(C1,R,C2).$

Concepts are not named but some equalities may be enforced by *coreference links*. These coreference links are established with variables which, in our scheme, are simply regarded as concept referents. The two predicates *isa(C,T)* and *rel(C1,R,C2)* may be defined in conceptual description.

- **Knowledge structure** : With the predicate "$\leq$", the user defines a taxonomy of types which has to be a complete lattice (see below). Every Prolog constants belongs implicitly to the taxonomy.
- **Axiomatic** :

Functional relations:	$\forall\, C1,C2,C3,R,$	$rel(C1,R,C2) \wedge rel(C1,R,C3) \supset C2 = C3$
$\leq$ is an order:	$\forall\, T,$	$T \leq T$
	$\forall\, T1,T2$	$T1 \leq T2 \wedge T2 \leq T1 \supset T2 = T1$
	$\forall\, T1,T2,T3$	$T1 \leq T2 \wedge T2 \leq T3 \supset T1 \leq T3$
Complete lattice:	$\forall\, T,$	$T \leq \top \wedge \bot \leq T$
	$\forall\, T1,T2, \exists\, T3,$	$T3 \leq T1 \wedge T3 \leq T2 \wedge (\forall\, T4,\ T4 \leq T1 \wedge T4 \leq T2 \supset T4 \leq T3)$
No absurd concept:	$\forall\, C,$	$not\ isa(C,\bot)$
Transivity:	$\forall\, C,T1,T2$	$isa(C,T1) \wedge T1 \leq T2 \supset isa(C,T2)$
Type compatibility:	$\forall\, C,T1,T2$	$isa(C,T1) \wedge isa(C,T2) \supset \exists\, T3,\ T3 \leq T1 \wedge T3 \leq T2 \wedge isa(C,T3)$

Let us have the following taxonomy (extracted from [AIT-KACI, NASR 86]:

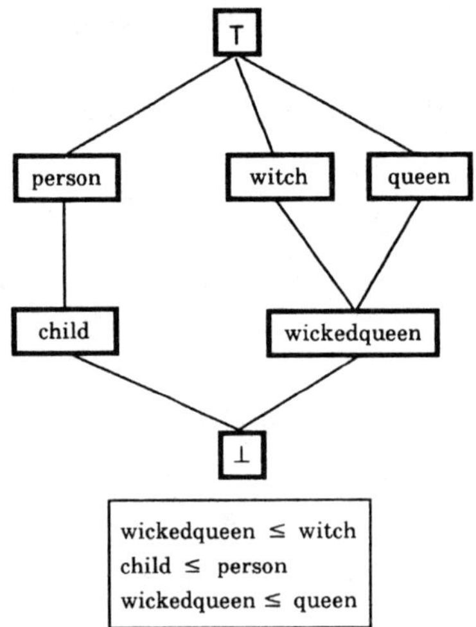

and the two following Login terms :

$$C1 = child(knows \Rightarrow Y:witch;\ likes \Rightarrow queen)$$
$$C2 = person(likes \Rightarrow X;\ knows \Rightarrow X)$$

with their corresponding conceptual system

$$S1 = \left\{ \begin{array}{lll} isa(C1,child), & isa(Y,witch), & isa(C3,queen) \\ rel(C1,knows,Y), & rel(C1,likes,C3) \end{array} \right\}$$

$$S2 = \left\{ isa(C2,person), \quad rel(C2,likes,X), \quad rel(C2,knows,X) \right\}$$

If we want to equate C1 and C2 (if C1 and C2 are unified), we have to check consistency of:

$$\{isa(C1,child), \quad isa(C1,person), \quad isa(Y,witch), \quad isa(C3,queen)$$
$$rel(C1,knows,Y), \quad rel(C1,knows,X), \quad rel(C1,likes,C3), \quad rel(C1,likes,Y)\}$$

From the axiom about relations (which are functions), the equalities $Y = X$ and $C3 = X$ are enforced, yielding the conceptual system:

$$\left\{ \begin{array}{llll} isa(C1,child), & isa(C1,person), & isa(X,witch), \\ isa(X,queen), & rel(C1,knows,X), & rel(C1,likes,X) \end{array} \right\}$$

Because of the last axiom, for each concept is added the greatest lower bound of the set of its types (it must not be $\perp$). So, the type *wickedqueen* is given to X and the resulting term (in a minimal form[*]) is:

$$child(knows \Rightarrow X: wickedqueen; \quad likes \Rightarrow X)$$

This language is rather powerful. The CLP(C.T.) scheme allows clear comparison of the mentioned extensions and let us draw the following "formula":

$$LOGIN = BOYER + (TAXLOG \text{ - metaclasses + multiple inheritance})$$

However, LOGIN has some limitations which are overcome in our language "Cosylog":

- The user may need relations which are not functions. This is easy to provide. The nature of each relation may be part of the user-defined knowledge.

- In many problems it would be convenient to refer to a concept by a name (this gives Prolog a kind of global variable capacity).

- When defining or extending the type taxonomy, the complete lattice property is difficult to preserve. Moreover, when independent points of view have to be mixed, many compound types are needed. For example, if the taxonomy contains the types *student* and *professor*, and also the types *french* and *english* the user has to define the types : *french-student, english-student, french-professor* and *english-professor* (in the above example one has to extend the taxonomy to enable a *witch* to be a *person*). More generally, the complete lattice constraint is troublesome with regard to independent (non-disjoint) subset definition. In order to define types for N independent sets, 2^N-1 types must appear in the taxonomy.

- Finally, some negative properties about a concept (e.g. that a concept does not belong to some types) could be very useful.

---

[*]: The notion of *minimal form,* also appearing in Cosylog, is introduced only for pretty-printing convenience but does not affect in any case soundness and completeness of the results.

Generally speaking, we will call *minimal form* of a conceptual system S the lowest subset of S -named S'- such that S' implies S/S' having regard to conceptual theory axiomatic part and user-defined knowledge. S/S' is also called the *implicit conceptuel system* of S.

Up from now and for concise out-displays, all results are going to appear in their minimal form. For instance, the minimal form of

$$\left\{ \begin{array}{llll} isa(C1,child), & isa(C1,person), & isa(X,witch), & isa(X,witckedqueen), \\ isa(X,queen), & rel(C1,knows,X), & rel(C1,likes,X) \end{array} \right\}$$

is

$$\{isa(C1,child), \quad isa(X,wickedqueen), \quad rel(C1,knows,X), \quad rel(C1,likes,X)\}$$

4   COSYLOG

Cosylog adds to Prolog a convenient knowledge representation structure which is a slightly adapted form of *conceptual graphs* defined in [SOWA 84]. This simple knowledge representation structure can support many others used in knowledge processing such as the formalism of KL-ONE [BRACHMAN 84]. In Cosylog, a concept -the *object* of the representation- consists of :

a) a **type** which is in fact a set of positive and negative features and denotes a part of the univers to which the concept belongs. A feature can be a subfeature of another and two features can be **excluded**, as *male* and *female*. We define a type either as a set of non excluded features or as the special type $\perp$. One can define the partial order $\leq$ over the set of types by :

$$t_1 \leq t_2 \Leftrightarrow \left\{ \begin{array}{l} \quad \quad t_1 = \perp \\ or \\ \{F_i\}_{(i=1..n)}, \ \ t_2 = (G_k)_{(k=1..m)} \\ \textit{for any } k \textit{ there exists } i \textit{ such as} \\ F_i \textit{ is a subfeature } G_k \textit{ or } F_i = G_k \end{array} \right.$$

It is easy to prove that the order $\leq$ defines a complete lattice over the set of types. Indeed the user does not having to care about such a requirement. The greatest element is the empty set, noted $\top$, and the least type is $\perp$.

b) a **referent** which plays role of concept identifier. It will be either a Prolog variable(the concept is *generic*) or a Prolog constant(the concept is *individual*).

Concepts are linked by binary relations which may be **functional, inverse-functional, bi-functional**(a functional relation which its inverse relation is also functional), **symmetrical** and **transitive**.

Cosylog is also able to deal with a large kind of *Constraints Satisfaction Problems* thanks to an augmented type semantic that one may give to intended features. This yields a Cosylog constraints satisfaction module able to make consistency checking, forward checking and inferencies under *Complete World Assumption* induced by *Cosylog symbolic hierarchical domains*. The conceptual theory of Cosylog is the following :

- **Conceptual description** : Two concepts are equal if and only if they have the same referent (variable or constant). In a conceptual description, one can specify the predicates :
  - *isa(C,F)*,
  - not *isa(C,F)*
  - *rel(C1,R,C2)*.

- **Knowledge structure** : The nature of each relation is defined with the predicates :
  - *functional(R)*,
  - *inv-functional(R)* (a relation can be both functional and inv-functional).
  - *transitive(R)*,
  - *symmetrical(R)*.

Features may be structured using the three relations :
  - $F1 \leq F2 \ \ (F1 \Rightarrow F2)$,
  - *disjoint(F1,F2)* $(F1 \Rightarrow not \ F2)$.
  - $D \equiv \{E_1, ..., E_n\}$ (domain declaration)

- **Axiomatic** :

Knowledge semantics : $\forall R, C1, C2, C3$ *functional(R)* $\wedge$ *rel(C1,R,C2)* $\wedge$ *rel(C1,R,C3)* $\supset$ *C2=C3*

$\forall R, C1, C2, C3$ *inv-functional(R)* $\wedge$ *rel(C2,R,C1)* $\wedge$ *rel(C3,R,C1)* $\supset$ *C2=C3*

$\forall R, C1, C2, C3$ *transitive(R)* $\wedge$ *rel(C1,R,C2)* $\wedge$ *rel(C2,R,C3)* $\supset$ *rel(C1,R,C3)*

$\forall R, C1, C2$ *symmetrical(R)* $\wedge$ *rel(C1,R,C2)* $\supset$ *rel(C2,R,C1)*

Type semantic : $\forall F1, F2, F3$ $F1 \leq F2 \wedge F2 \leq F3 \supset F1 \leq F3$

$\forall F1, F2, C$ $F1 \leq F2 \wedge isa(C,F1) \supset isa(C,F2)$

$\forall F1, F2, C$ *disjoint(F1,F2)* $\wedge$ *isa(C,F1)* $\supset$ *not isa(C,F2)*

Augmented semantic : $\forall D \equiv \{E_1, ..., E_n\}_{(n \in \mathbf{N},\, n \geq 1)}$

$E_i \leq D \wedge disjoint(E_i, E_k)$ for $(i,k)_{i \neq k} \in [1,n]^2$

- bottom-up checking $\forall C, D \equiv \{E_1, ..., E_n\}_{(n \in \mathbf{N},\, n \geq 1)}$

$(not\ isa(C,E_i)$ where i ranges $[1,n]\ ) \supset not\ isa(C,D)$

- top-down checking $\forall C, D \equiv \{E_1, ..., E_n\}_{(n \in \mathbf{N},\, n \geq 1)}$

$isa(C,D) \wedge .(not\ isa(C,E_i)$ where i ranges I such that $I \in \Gamma_{\{1,...,n\}}^{n-1})^{*}$

$\supset isa(C,E_k)$ with $\{k\} = \{1, ..., n\} / I$

Overall coherence : $\forall F,$ *not disjoint(F,F)*

$\forall F1, F2, F3$ $F1 \leq F2 \wedge disjoint(F2,F3) \supset disjoint(F1,F3)$

It should be noticed that constraints on features definition are totally natural (resulting from the fact that one does not define a feature which would correspond to an always empty set of objects). The user may define his features as freely as possible, and errors will be filtered by the two last axioms. So the *conceptual model* (user-defined knowledge) will be both easy to establish and rich enough to encode a large part of knowledge.

Syntactically, a Cosylog program is made of feature and relation declarations and a set of clauses containing conceptual descriptions. An example of *conceptual description* could be:

- **A**: man : fair__haired : not handsome >wife> (mary : woman <mother< X)

This describes a generic concept whose referent is **A** having the features man, fair-haired and not handsome which is the first argument of a relation wife whose second argument is the individual concept mary. The concept mary which can be referred to by this name in other clauses, is said here to have the feature woman and to be the second argument of a relation mother coming from X. Formally this description is equivalent to:

$$\left\{ \begin{array}{lll} isa(A,man), & isa(A,fair\_\_haired), & not\ isa(A,handsome) \\ rel(A,wife,mary), & isa(mary,woman), & rel(X,mother,mary) \end{array} \right\}$$

Let us look at a small example: the simulation of a marriage bureau. This bureau has to match its clients according to their aspirations. Each couple will be represented by a relation wife between the husband and the wife (wife is bi-functional). Let us define the predicates match(CLIENT__LIST) which is true if each client (in CLIENT__LIST) has been placed in a couple. The program makes use of the predicate take(ELT,LIST1,LIST2) which is true if LIST1 minus ELT is equal to LIST2 :

---

*: Γ_E^m is the subset of 2^E restricted to elements with cardinal m

```
match(nil)
match(A:man >wife >B:woman . STOCK) ← take(B,STOCK,REMAIN)
                                  & match (REMAIN).
match(A:woman <wife <B:man . STOCK ← take(B,STOCK,REMAIN)
                                  & match (REMAIN).


take(ELT,ELT.END,END).
take(ELT,KEPT.END,KEPT.REMAIN) ←take(ELT,END,REMAIN).
```

Cosylog simulation marriage bureau program

Let us suppose the marriage bureau has to marry Peter, a simple man looking for a sweet blonde, John, a clutured man expecting a beautiful woman, Mary, a brunette liking cultivated man, and Betty, a sweet and fair-haired woman looking for a not selfish man. This is translated into the following goal:

```
← match(   peter :man :simple  >wife>  * :fair-haired :sweet
         . john :man :cultured  >wife>  * :beautiful
         . mary :woman :dark__haired  <wife<  * :cultured
         . betty :woman :fair__haired :sweet  <wife<  * :not selfish
         . nil).
```

If part of the associated *conceptual model* is:

```
functional(wife).        disjoint(fair__haired, dark__haired).
inv__functional(wife).   disjoint(simple cultured).   disjoint(man,woman).
```

Cosylog simulation marriage bureau conceptual model

the goal has a unique solution, the following formulas being successively proved (~A is the concept of referent A):

```
match(~ peter.~john.~mary.~betty.nil).
~take(~betty,    ~john.~mary.~betty.nil, ~john.~mary.nil).
  ~take(~betty, ~mary.~betty.nil,  ~mary.nil).
     ~take(~betty, ~betty.nil,    nil).
~match(~john.~mary.nil).
   ~take(~mary, ~mary.nil,    nil).
   ~match(nil).
```

But major results are the following informations about concepts:

```
peter:man:simple:not selfish      >wife> betty:woman:sweet:fair__haired
john:man:cultured                 >wife> mary:woman:dark__haired:beautiful
```

Cosylog simulation marriage bureau solution

(let us hope for general happiness that Peter is not too selfish and Mary beautiful, the program has made some hzardous assuptions).

We will illustrate Cosylog's ability in combinatorial problems upon a classical example (the zebra problem):

-   In a street are five houses. In the first, lives a Norwegian. Milk is drunk in the middle house. An Englishman lives in the red house. The Spanish has a dog. One drinks coffee in the green house. The Ukrainian drinks tea. The Old-Gold smoker has snails. The Kool smoker lives in the yellow house. The wine drinker smokes Gitanes. The Japanese smokes Craven. The blue house is near the Norwegian's one. The green house is on the right of the white one. The horse owner lives near the Kool smoker. The Chesterfield smoker lives near the owner of the fox. Who drinks water and where is the zebra ?

To solve this problem, the combinatorial explosion has to be mastered (in order to check only a very small part of the 25 billion possible arrangements). Colmerauer wrote a solution in Prolog II using the freeze mechanism. However, Cosylog allows more straightforward and more efficient solutions. This fact is due to its constraints satisfaction module which stays the current conceptual system constantly consistent according to the conceptual theory axiomatic part it uses and user-defined knowledge it knows. In operationally words, this means that all fireable rules(extracted from axiomatic) are applied as soon as possible. This entails a constraints handling in order to prune the *search space* in a a-priori manner.

```
COSYLOG DECLARATIONS
        bi-function(color)              bi-function(tobacco)
        bi-function(nationality)        bi-function(animal)
        bi-function(beverage)


COSYLOG CLAUSES
solution(~m1>nationality>~norwegian.~m2.
                ~m3>beverage>~milk.~m4.~m5.nil) ←
                & house(*>nationality>~english>color>~red)
                & house(*>animal>~dog        >nationality>~spanish)
                & house(*>beverage>~tea      >nationality>~ukrainian)
                & house(*>animal>~snail       >tobacco>~oldgold)
                & house(*>tobacco>~gitanes    >beverage>~wine)
                & house(*>tobacco>~craven     >nationality>~japenese)
                & beside(*>color>~blue,       *>nationality>~norwegian)
                & right-of(*>color>~green
                        >beverage>~coffee  *>color>~white)
                & beside(*>tobacco>~kool
                        >color>~yellow,      *>animal>~horse)
                & beside(*>tobacco>~chesterfield,   *>animal>~fox)
                & house(*>beverage>~water)
                & house(*>animal>~zebra).


        right-of(~m2,~m1).                right-of(~m3,~m2).
        right-of(~m4,~m3).                right-of(~m5,~m4).


        house(~m1).  house(~m2).  house(~m3).  house(~m4).  house(~m5).
```

Relational Cosylog program of the zebra problem

We must add to the problem that each characteristic applies to one and only one house and that each house has a unique color, pet, nationality, tobacco and drink of its occupant On the first program we propose, this can be enforced in using five bi-functional relations, one for each type feature. Giving a relation f, this means that the equality $f(H) = T$ has one and only one solution for all known houses H. For instance, the first program can be read as :

it exists a house H_i such that *nationality(H_i) =english* and *color(H_i) =red,*

...

it is right that it exists a house H_k such that *color(H_k) =blue* and H_k is inside a house H_j where lives a norwegian man...

When running the goal solution(*), we obtain the only solution after 156 ms[*]. The fails occurs after 288ms. For implementation reasons, our Cosylog interpreter/compiler do not handle in an efficient way concepts which have individual referent(due to the lack of global variable in VM/Prolog).

```
solution(     ~m1>color>        ~yellow
              >nationality>  ~norwegian
              >beverage>     ~water
              >tobacco>      ~kool
              >animal>       ~fox
         .~m2>color>         ~blue
              >nationality>  ~ukrainian
              >beverage>     ~tea
              >tobacco>      ~chesterfield
              >animal>       ~horse
         .~m3>color>         ~red
              >nationality>  ~english
              >beverage>     ~milk
              >tobacco>      ~oldgold
              >animal>       ~snail
         .~m4>color>         ~white
              >nationality>  ~spanish
              >beverage>     ~wine
              >tobacco>      ~gitanes
              >animal>       ~dog
         .m~5>color>         ~green
              >nationality>  ~japenese
              >beverage>     ~coffee
              >tobacco>      ~craven
              >animal>       ~zebra
     .nil).
```

Relational Cosylog solution of the zebra problem

---

[*] Cosylog interpreter/compiler is implemented with the IBM language VM/Prolog. All Cosylog programs are executed with an IBM 3090 computer.

We propose an other program for this problem, more efficient, which illustrate others Cosylog features. All zebra features are going to collect into five Cosylog domains. This yields a very natural and declarative way for ensure *disjunction* between all features of a same nature.(see above the *axiomatic part*). Each of the five Cosylog generic *house_concepts* has a type which is an element of the five domains cartesian product. When enforcing the fact that all house_concepts must be different regarding to their respectively type, we set up a lot of symbolic constraints use delay mechanism which are handled in an active way in order to reduce the search space as soon as possible when eliminating(by *type concept restriction*) all combinations which violate the constraints. The first naive, but more declaratively, solution consists to set-up constraints (extracted from the given problem statement) and generate type concept thanks to a user-generator.

The following program do not use any additional generator when taking advantage of Cosylog ability to reason efficiently with Complete world assumption(*domain consistency checking*). One have just to make sure that the program is given a minimal initial set of features allowing it to index directly all the twenty-five zebra characteristics.

The predicate present(F,LH,CDR__LH) give the characteristic F to one of the five houses.of the list LH. CDR__LH represent all houses in the right of the house is given F.

```
COSYLOG DECLARATIONS :
        color      ≡    {red,green,white,blue,yellow}
        nationality ≡   {english,spanish,japanese,norwegian,ukrainian}
        beverage   ≡    {coffee,water,milk,tea,wine}
        tobacco    ≡    {chesterfield,craven,gitanes,kool,oldgold}
        animal     ≡    {horse,dog,snail,fox,zebra}

        english ≤ red      snail ≤ oldgold     coffee ≤ green     craven ≤ japenese
        red ≤ english      oldgold ≤ snail     green ≤ coffee     japenese ≤ craven
        dog ≤ spanish      kool ≤ yellow       gitanes ≤ wine     ukrainian ≤ tea
        spanish ≤ dog      yellow ≤ kool       wine ≤ gitanes     tea ≤ ukrainian

COSYLOG CLAUSES :
        solution(L)  L = H1;norwegian.H2.H3;milk.H4.H5.nil
                & all__different(L,color.nationality.beverage.tobacco.animal)
                & beside(norwegian,blue,L)
                & beside(kool,horse,L)
                & beside(fox,chesterfiels,L)
                & right__of(white,green,L)
                & present(wine,L,*)
                & present(snail,L,*)
                & present(spanish,L,*).

        beside(A,B,L) ← right__of(A,B,L).
        beside(A,B,L) ← right__of(B,A,L).

        right__of(A,B,L) ← present(A,L,HOUSE;B,*).

        present(X, H1 ; X    .Q                                           , Q).
        present(X, *         .H2 ; X   .   Q                              , Q).
        present(X, *         .*        .   H3;X   .Q                      , Q).
        present(X, *         .*        .   *       .H4 ; X    .   Q        , Q).
        present(X, *         .*        .   *       .   *       .   H5 ; X    .Q   , Q).
```

Domain Cosylog program of the zebra problem

The fact that english is both more and less specific than red means that these two features are synonyms (they correspond in this problem to the same set of houses). The unique solution of the goal solution(*) is obtained in only 39 milliseconds. One of its minimal forms is :

```
solution(   H₁:water :fox :norwegian :yellow  . H₂:blue :chesterfield :horse :ukrainian .
            H₃:snail :red :milk                . H₄:wine :spanish :white .
            H₅:zebra :green :craven            . nil).
```

A domain minimal form Cosylog solution of the zebra problem

Cosylog has proved to be useful as the base component of a natural language understanding system [BERINGER 88b]. In this system, thanks to the rich *knowledge structure* of Cosylog, a large part of syntactic knowledge is embedded in the conceptual model. This is an easy way to express knowledge which is used efficiently. The current implementation in pure VMPROLOG (an IBM product) is quite efficient: a compiler-interpreter written partially in a more basic language could have very good performance.

CONCLUSION AND PERSPECTIVES

The CLP(C.T.) scheme identifies a class of logic programming languages which offer a powerful representation language and a natural and declarative way to explicit conceptual knowledge (the *conceptual model*). Such languages enable both easier programming (part of the program being expressed once and for all in the conceptual model) and more efficient programs (constraints are applied as soon as possible).

Moreover, the CLP(C.T.) scheme enables direct and concise specification of a large class of Prolog extensions. Thanks to that scheme, we have been able to compare some known extensions (which have been proven to be CLP(C.T.) languages) and to show their limitations. Being efficient and offering an advanced respresentation language, Cosylog is probably the most accomplished of the existing CLP(C.T.) languages.

The CLP(C.T.) scheme appears to be a promising research framework and deserves some further studies. First of all, we intend to develop this formal modal and, in particular, its operational semantics. Then, in studying the known constraint satisfaction algorithms, we will try to determine the optimal compromise between, on one hand, the expressiveness of the conceptual language, and, on another hand, the efficiency of the constraint satisfaction module. Finally, we will try to compare our approach with the interesting works about combination of Prolog and an object representation language.

ACKNOWLEDGMENTS

This research has been carried out at the firm *Electronique Serge Dassault* and partially supported by a grant of the *Association Nationale pour la Recherche Technique (ANRT)* -National Association for Technical Research in France-. One of the authors is now at the *Centre de Recherche en Informatique de Montreal (CRIM)* -Montreal Computer Science Research Center- with a postdoctoral grant of the Department of Foreign Affairs of France.

BIBLIOGRAPHY

Ait-Kaci H., Nsar R (1986): **LOGIN: a logic programming language with built-in inheritance**, Journal of Logic Programming, num. 3 pp.. 185-215.

Beringer H. (1988a): **Graphs in Logic Programming for Natural Language Analysis**, in Dahl V. & Saint-Dizier P. eds., "Natural Language Understanding and Logic Programming II", North Holland, Amsterdam pp. 203-224.

Beringer H; (1988b): **Traitement automatique des ambiguités structurales du Français utilisant la théorie Sens-Texte**, PhD Thesis, Université de Paris 6, 20 October 1988.

Boyer M; (1988): **Towards Functional Logic Grammars**, in Dahl V. & Saint-Dizier P. eds., "Natural Language Understanding and Logic Programming II", North Holland, Amsterdam pp. 45-62.

Brachman R., Schmolze J; (1984): **An overview of the KL-ONE Knowledge Representation system**, Cognitive Science.

Colmerauer A. (1987): **Opening the PROLOG III Universe**, Byte Magazine 12(9), August 1987.

Dincbas M., Lepape J.P. (1984): **Metacontrol of Logics Programs in Metalog**, in Procs. FGCS 84 pp. 361-370 Nov.1984.

Dincbas M., Van Hentenryck P. (1986): **Algorithmes d'unification étendue pour l'intégration des langages fonctionnelles et logiques**, Procs of "Seminaire de Programmation en Logique", Trégastel, France, 21-23 May.

Fages F. (1983): **Formes Canoniques dans les algèbres booléennes, Application à la démonstration automatique en logique du premier ordre**, Ph.D. Thesis, Université Pierre et Marie Curie - Paris 6 - 28 June 1983.

Goebel R. (1985): **The Design and Implementation of DLOG, a Prolog-based Knowledge Representation System**, New Generation Computing num.3 pp 385-403, OHMSHA. and Springer-Verlag.

Heintze N.C., Jaffa r J., Michaylov S., Stuckey P.J., Yap R., Yee C.N. (1987): **The CLP(R) Programmer's manual**, Monash University TEchnical Report No. 73, June 87.

Hullot J.M. (1980): **Compilation de formes canoniques dans des théories équationnelles**, Ph.D. Thesis of Paris Sud University, France, 14 November 1980.

Jaffar J., Lassez J.L., Maher M.J. (1984): **A theory of complete logic programs with equality**, Journal of Logic Programming 3:221-223.

Jaffar J., Lassez J.L. (1987): **Constraint Logic Programming**, Procs. Conference on Principle of Programming Languages, Munich, 87.

Kornfeld W. (1983): **Equality for Prolog**, procs. IJCAI, Karlsruhe, Germany, August 1983.

McCord M. (1985): **Semantics of Natural Language : LFL**, IBM Europe Institute, Oberlecht, Austria.

Montini G. (1987): **Efficiency considerations on built-in taxonomic reasoning in Prolog**, Procs. IJCAI, Milan, August 1987.

Mukai K., Yasukawa H. (1985): **Complex Indeterminates in Prolog and its application to Discourse Models**, New Generation Computing num.3 pp441-463, OHMSHA. and Springer-Verlag.

Sowa J.F.   (1984): **Conceptual structures, Information processing in mind and machine,** The systems programming series, Addison Wesley.

Van Hentenryck P. and Dincbas M. (1987): **Forward Checking in Logic Programming,** in "Fourth International Conference on Logic Programming", p 229-256, Melbourne, Australia, May 1987, MIT Press.

Constraint Hierarchies
and Logic Programming

Alan Borning†, Michael Maher‡, Amy Martindale†, and Molly Wilson†

†Computer Science Dept, FR-35   ‡IBM T.J. Watson Research Ctr.
University of Washington   P.O. Box 704
Seattle, WA 98195   Yorktown Heights, NY 10598
         internet: borning@cs.washington.edu, mjm@ibm.com,
               amy@cs.washington.edu, molly@cs.washington.edu

Abstract

Constraint Logic Programming (CLP) is a general scheme for extending logic programming to include constraints. It is parameterized by $\mathcal{D}$, the domain of the constraints. However, CLP($\mathcal{D}$) languages, as well as most other constraint systems, only allow the programmer to specify constraints that must hold. In many applications, such as interactive graphics, page layout, and decision support, one needs to express *preferences* as well as strict requirements. If we wish to make full use of the constraint paradigm, we need ways to represent these defaults and preferences declaratively, as constraints, rather than encoding them in the procedural parts of the language. We describe a scheme for extending CLP($\mathcal{D}$) to include both required and preferential constraints, with an arbitrary number of strengths of preference. We present some of the theory of such languages, and an algorithm for executing them. To test our ideas, we have implemented an interpreter for an instance of this language scheme with $\mathcal{D}$ equal to the reals. We describe our interpreter, and outline some examples of using this language.

1   Introduction

Recently there has been considerable research on extending logic programming to include constraints. This extension significantly increases the expressiveness of such languages. Constraint Logic Programming [8] is a general scheme for such extensions, and is parameterized by $\mathcal{D}$, the domain of the constraints. The language that arises from a fixed set of constraints over $\mathcal{D}$ can be denoted by CLP($\mathcal{D}$). In place of unification (which can be viewed as testing the satisfiability of equations over the Herbrand universe), constraints are accumulated and tested for satisfiability over $\mathcal{D}$, using techniques appropriate to the domain. Several such languages have now been implemented, including Prolog III [4], CLP($\mathcal{R}$) [7, 9] and CHIP [5]. The formal semantics of such languages differ mainly in the choice of underlying domain and constraints, as was shown formally in [8]. It was also shown that for every language that can be obtained from the CLP scheme for solution-compact domains $\mathcal{D}$, numerous desirable properties of the declarative and operational semantics hold—properties that had been considered characteristic of logic programming. In particular, CLP languages have coincident logical, fixedpoint, and operational semantics.

Independent of logic programming, constraints have proven useful for a variety of applications, including geometric layout, physical simulations, user interface design, document formatting, algorithm animation, and design and analysis of mechanical devices and electrical circuits. (See [10] for a survey.) Many such applications require some notion of defaults and preferences. If we wish to make full use of the constraint paradigm, we need ways to represent these defaults and preferences declaratively, as constraints, rather than encoding them in the procedural parts of the language.

Consider an interactive graphics example from our own work on ThingLab [3]. Suppose we have a line with a point constrained to lie at its midpoint. If we pick up one end of the line with the mouse and move it about, the constraint will ensure that the midpoint relation remains satisfied. However, without some notion of defaults and the ability to specify preferences, the other end of the line could flail wildly about the screen, without violating the midpoint constraint. To prevent this, we want to specify that parts of the figure should remain stationary unless otherwise required to move. There is a further problem, however. Given the discussion so far, we might also have the midpoint remain stationary, with the line pivoting about it. This isn't what most users expect; they want the endpoint of the line to be less movable than the midpoint. Early versions of ThingLab implemented these defaults in an *ad hoc* fashion as part of the constraint satisfaction algorithm. Later, to allow such defaults and preferences to be specified explicitly and declaratively, we devised a theory of *constraint hierarchies* [1], which allows a user to specify not only constraints that must hold, but also weaker constraints at an arbitrary number of strengths. The constraint hierarchy scheme is parameterized by a comparator $\mathcal{C}$ that allows us to compare different possible solutions to the hierarchy and select the best ones. We have also implemented several algorithms for satisfying such hierarchies within ThingLab [1, 6].

Defaults and preferences arise naturally when trying to use constraint logic programming for interactive graphics, as well as for other applications, for example, decision support systems. On the other hand, some of our interactive graphics applications require such general programming language capabilities as conditionals and recursion, which are already elegantly provided by logic programming. We are thus led to an integration of CLP and constraint hierarchies. The result, described in this paper, is a Hierarchical Constraint Logic Programming scheme $HCLP(\mathcal{D}, \mathcal{C})$, parameterized both by the domain $\mathcal{D}$ of the constraints and by the comparator $\mathcal{C}$. In addition to the benefits listed above, the integration allows us to build on CLP's firm theoretical foundation.

In the remainder of the paper, we first present a theory of constraint hierarchies, which extends and modifies our previous theory for use in a logic programming framework. We then describe $HCLP(\mathcal{D}, \mathcal{C})$, give examples of its use, and describe a formal semantics for this family of languages. We also present an algorithm for solving HCLP programs. This algorithm is general for the domain $\mathcal{D}$ of constraints, but specific to a particular comparator $\mathcal{LPB}$. ($\mathcal{LPB}$ is the locally-predicate-better comparator, which will be defined in Section 2.) We also describe a prototype implementation of $HCLP(\mathcal{R}, \mathcal{LPB})$, where $\mathcal{R}$ is the domain of real numbers.

2   Constraint Hierarchies

The domain $\mathcal{D}$ determines the constraint predicate symbols $\Pi_{\mathcal{D}}$ of the language. A constraint is of the form $p(t_1, \ldots, t_n)$ where p is an n-ary symbol in $\Pi_{\mathcal{D}}$ and each t_i is a term. A *labelled constraint* is a constraint labelled with a strength, written sc, where s is a strength and c is a constraint. In HCLP programs we give user-definable symbolic names to the different strengths of constraints. In both the HCLP theory and in the implementation, we then map each of these names onto the integers $0 \ldots n$, where n is the number of non-required levels. Strength 0 is always reserved for required constraints.

A *constraint hierarchy* is a multiset of labelled constraints. Given a constraint hierarchy H, let C_0 denote the required constraints in H, with their labels removed. In the same way, we define the sets $C_1, C_2, \ldots$ (C_k will be empty for k greater than the number of non-required levels). Note that if $i < j$ then the constraints in C_i are stronger (more preferred) than those in C_j.

A *solution* to a constraint hierarchy H will consist of a valuation for the free variables in H, i.e., a function that maps the free variables in H to elements in the domain $\mathcal{D}$. We wish to define the set S of all solutions to H. Clearly, each valuation in S must be such that after it is applied all the required constraints hold. In addition, we want each valuation in S to be such that it satisfies the non-required constraints as well as possible, respecting their relative strengths. To formalize this desire, we first define the set S_0 of valuations such that all the C_0 constraints hold. Then, using S_0, we define the desired set S by eliminating all potential valuations that are worse than some other potential valuation using the comparator *better*. (In the definition $c\theta$ denotes the result of applying the valuation θ to c.)

$$
\begin{aligned}
S_0 &= \{\theta \mid \forall c \in C_0 \ c\theta \text{ holds}\} \\
S &= \{\theta \mid \theta \in S_0 \land \forall \sigma \in S_0 \ \neg better(\sigma, \theta, H)\}
\end{aligned}
$$

There are many plausible candidates for comparators. We insist that *better* be irreflexive and transitive:

$$\forall \theta \forall H \ \neg better(\theta, \theta, H)$$

$$\forall \theta \forall \sigma \forall \tau \forall H \ better(\theta, \sigma, H) \land better(\sigma, \tau, H) \rightarrow better(\theta, \tau, H)$$

However, in general, *better* will not provide a total ordering—there may exist θ and σ such that θ is not better than σ and σ is not better than θ. We also insist that *better* respect the hierarchy—if there is some valuation in S_0 that completely satisfies all the constraints through level k, then all valuations in S must satisfy all the constraints through level k:

$$
\begin{aligned}
&\text{if } \exists \theta \in S_0 \land \exists k > 0 \text{ such that} \\
&\quad \forall i \in 1 \ldots k \ \forall p \in C_i \ p\theta \text{ holds} \\
&\quad \text{then } \forall \sigma \in S \ \forall i \in 1 \ldots k \ \forall p \in C_i \ p\sigma \text{ holds}
\end{aligned}
$$

We now define several different comparators. In the definitions we will need an error function $e(c\theta)$ that returns a non-negative real number indicating how nearly constraint c is satisfied for a valuation θ. This function must have the property that $e(c\theta) = 0$ if and only if $c\theta$ holds. For any domain $\mathcal{D}$, we can use the trivial error function that returns 0 if the constraint is satisfied and 1 if it is not. For a domain that is a metric space, we can instead use its metric in computing the error: for example, the error for $X = Y$ would be the distance between X and Y.

The first of the comparators, *locally-better*, considers each constraint in H individually.

Definition. A valuation θ is *locally-better* than another valuation σ if, for each of the constraints through some level $k-1$, the error after applying θ is equal to that after applying σ, and at level k the error is strictly less for at least one constraint and less than or equal for all the rest.

$$locally\text{-}better(\theta, \sigma, H) \equiv$$
$$\exists k > 0 \ \text{ such that}$$
$$\forall i \in 1 \ldots k - 1 \ \forall p \in C_i \ \ e(p\theta) = e(p\sigma)$$
$$\wedge \ \exists q \in C_k \ \ e(q\theta) < e(q\sigma)$$
$$\wedge \ \forall r \in C_k \ \ e(r\theta) \leq e(r\sigma)$$

Next, we define a schema *globally-better* for global comparators. The schema is parameterized by a function g that combines the errors of all the constraints C_i at a given level.

Definition. A valuation θ is *globally-better* than another valuation σ if, for each level through some level $k - 1$, the combined errors of the constraints after applying θ is equal to that after applying σ, and at level k it is strictly less.

$$globally\text{-}better(\theta, \sigma, H, g) \equiv$$
$$\exists k > 0 \ \text{ such that}$$
$$\forall i \in 1 \ldots k - 1 \ \ g(\theta, C_i) = g(\sigma, C_i)$$
$$\wedge \ g(\theta, C_k) < g(\sigma, C_k)$$

Using *globally-better*, we now define three global comparators, using different combining functions g. The weight for constraint p is denoted by w_p. Each weight is a positive real number.

$$
\begin{aligned}
weighted\text{-}sum\text{-}better(\theta, \sigma, H) \ &\equiv \ globally\text{-}better(\theta, \sigma, H, g) \\
\text{where} \ \ g(\tau, C) \ &\equiv \ \sum_{p \in C} w_p e(p\tau)
\end{aligned}
$$

$$
\begin{aligned}
worst\text{-}case\text{-}better(\theta, \sigma, H) \ &\equiv \ globally\text{-}better(\theta, \sigma, H, g) \\
\text{where} \ \ g(\tau, C) \ &\equiv \ \max\{w_p e(p\tau) \mid p \in C\}
\end{aligned}
$$

$$
\begin{aligned}
least\text{-}squares\text{-}better(\theta, \sigma, H) \ &\equiv \ globally\text{-}better(\theta, \sigma, H, g) \\
\text{where} \ \ g(\tau, C) \ &\equiv \ \sum_{p \in C} w_p e(p\tau)^2
\end{aligned}
$$

We define *locally-predicate-better* to be *locally-better* using the trivial error function that returns 0 if the constraint is satisfied and 1 if it is not. Finally, we define *unsatisfied-count-better* to be *weighted-sum-better* using the trivial error function and weights of 1 on each constraint.

We end this section with a few comments on the comparators. The definitions of the global comparators include weights on the constraints. For the local comparators, adding weights would be futile, since the result would be the same with or without the weights. The global comparators *weighted-sum-better*, *worst-case-better*, and *least-squares-better* are derived from the standard statistical measures of deviation L_1-*norm*, L_∞-*norm*, and L_2-*norm* respectively. The *locally-better* comparator is derived from the concept of a *vector minimum* (or *pareto-optimal point*, or *nondominated feasible solution*) in multiobjective linear programming problems [11]. Finally, the standard linear programming problem of minimizing an objective function subject to a set of linear inequality conditions can be easily expressed as a constraint hierarchy. The linear inequality conditions are represented as required constraints, and the objective function translates to a default constraint that the value of the objective function be zero.

3   Constraints in Logic Programming

In standard logic programming (as exemplified by Prolog), rules are of the form

$$p(\mathbf{t}) \; :- \; q_1(\mathbf{t}), \ldots, q_m(\mathbf{t}).$$

where $p, q_1, \ldots, q_m$ are predicate symbols, and $\mathbf{t}$ denotes a list of terms. In CLP, rules are of the form

$$p(\mathbf{t}) \; :- \; q_1(\mathbf{t}), \ldots, q_m(\mathbf{t}), c_1(\mathbf{t}), \ldots, c_n(\mathbf{t}).$$

where $p, q_1, \ldots, q_m$ are as before, and $c_1, \ldots, c_n$ are constraints. Operationally, we can think of executing the Prolog part of the program in the usual way, accumulating constraints on logic variables as we go, and either verifying that the constraints are solvable or else backtracking if they are not. The program can terminate with substitutions being found for all variables in the input, or with some constrained variables still unbound, in which case the output would include the remaining constraints on these variables.

In HCLP, rules are of the form

$$p(\mathbf{t}) \; :- \; q_1(\mathbf{t}), \ldots, q_m(\mathbf{t}), s_1 c_1(\mathbf{t}), \ldots, s_n c_n(\mathbf{t}).$$

where s_i indicates the strength of the corresponding constraint c_i. Symbolic names are given to the different strengths of constraints. The user defines an arbitrary number of names and their corresponding strengths. One strength, the "required" strength, is special, in that the constraints it labels *must* be satisfied. The other strengths all denote non-required constraints. If the s_i are all required, then clearly the program is equivalent to the same program in standard CLP with the strengths omitted.

Operationally, goals are executed as in CLP, temporarily ignoring the non-required constraints, except to accumulate them. After a goal has been successfully reduced, there may still be non-ground variables in the solution. The accumulated hierarchy of non-required constraints is solved, using a method determined by the comparator $\mathcal{C}$, thus further refining the values of these variables. Additional answers may be produced by backtracking. As with CLP, constraints can be used multi-directionally, and the scheme can accomodate collections of constraints that cannot be solved by simple forward propagation methods. (For example, our current implementation can handle simultaneous linear equations.)

4 HCLP Examples

The following example is illustrative of a wide class of interactive graphics programs. We have a horizontal line displayed on the screen, and we are moving one endpoint with the mouse (Figure 1). There is a required constraint that the line be horizontal, a preference that one endpoint of the line follow the mouse, and a weaker preference that the endpoints of the line remain fixed. This weak preference gives stability to the line as it is moved, so that, for example, it doesn't suddenly triple in length as we move the endpoint by some small distance.

The HCLP$(\mathcal{R}, \mathcal{C})$ rule below expresses the desired update behavior. It takes as arguments terms representing the old and new states of the horizontal line, and a third term that is the x-y distance by which one endpoint should be moved. Any or all of the terms may contain variables. However, in typical use in an interactive graphics application, the old state of the line and the displacement would be ground, while the new state of the line would be a variable, whose value would be computed as a result of satisfying the constraints.

Figure 1: Moving an endpoint of a horizontal line

```
/* set up symbolic names for constraint strengths */
levels([require, strong, prefer, default, weak]).

move_horiz_end2(line_segment(OldX1,OldY1,OldX2,OldY2),
            line_segment(NewX1,NewY1,NewX2,NewY2),
            delta(DX,DY)) :-
  require OldY1 = OldY2, require NewY1 = NewY2,
  prefer OldX2 + DX = NewX2, prefer OldY2 + DY = NewY2,
  default OldX1 = NewX1, default OldY1 = NewY1,
  default OldX2 = NewX2, default OldY2 = NewY2.
```

Suppose now we anchor the other end of the horizontal line, so
that this other end becomes difficult to move (Figure 2). We'll use a
strong preference rather than a required constraint, so that the anchor
can be moved if needed by using an even stronger mouse constraint.
Since in this version the anchor constraints are stronger than the mouse
constraints, now the line will stretch in the x direction, following the
mouse, but its y position will remain constant. In other words, the
mouse constraint on the new x value of *end2* will be satisfied, but the
mouse constraint on the new y value will be overridden by the stronger
constraint that it be the same as the old y value.

```
move_horiz_end2_anchor_end1(
        line_segment(OldX1,OldY1,OldX2,OldY2),
        line_segment(NewX1,NewY1,NewX2,NewY2),
        Displacement) :-
  move_horiz_end2(line_segment(OldX1,OldY1,OldX2,OldY2),
              line_segment(NewX1,NewY1,NewX2,NewY2),
              Displacement),
  strong OldX1 = NewX1, strong OldY1 = NewY1.
```

In a similar manner, we can (without any hard thinking required)
translate all of the ThingLab examples given in [3] into HCLP. For
the more complex examples, the HCLP code becomes tediously long.
However (as with ThingLab), we envision such code being written automatically by the interactive graphics application, rather than by a

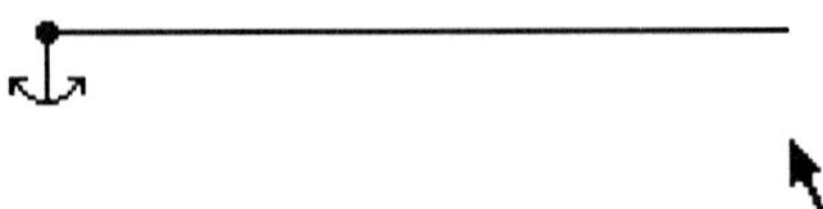

Figure 2: Moving an endpoint of an anchored horizontal line

person. For cases when a programmer is writing code, we have also designed a pre-processor to support a notion of objects in HCLP.

If we could do nothing beyond expressing previously implemented interactive graphics examples in HCLP, of course, the current research would not be of great interest. However, since we have the full power of logic programming available to configure a network of constraints dynamically, we can do considerably more. For example, in [2] we describe a user interface example in which we use a recursive rule to set up constraints between each node of a tree and a view of that node on the display.

5   HCLP Theory

5.1   Definitions

In this section we develop some of the theory of $\text{HCLP}(\mathcal{D}, \mathcal{C})$. Although many of these results are analogs of results for CLP, some analogs do not hold for HCLP, for reasons discussed below. Due to space limitations some definitions have been omitted. For undefined notation or terminology see [8].

We write $P \models_{\mathcal{D}} Q$ if Q holds in every model of P that has the same universe as $\mathcal{D}$ and assigns the same meaning to function symbols and constraint predicate symbols as $\mathcal{D}$. We use $(\exists)$ to denote existential closure. A conjunction of constraints C is said to be *consistent* (or *satisfiable*) if there are values (from $\mathcal{D}$) for the free variables $\mathbf{y}$ such that every constraint is true in $\mathcal{D}$, that is, $\emptyset \models_{\mathcal{D}} \exists \mathbf{y} C$.

A *variable renaming* is an invertible substitution, that is, a substitution α such that for some substitution α^{-1}, $\alpha \circ \alpha^{-1} = \alpha^{-1} \circ \alpha = \varepsilon$ (ε is the identity substitution). A *variant* of a syntactic object is the result of applying a variable renaming to that object. By a *new variant* we will refer to a variant that has no variables in common with the current context. The equivalence relation $\sim$ is defined by $A \sim A'$ iff A and A' are variants of each other.

As previously discussed, an HCLP *rule* takes the form

$$p(\mathbf{t}) :- q_1(\mathbf{t}), \ldots, q_m(\mathbf{t}), s_1 c_1(\mathbf{t}), \ldots, s_n c_n(\mathbf{t})$$

We can view a rule logically as

$$\forall \mathbf{x}\, p(\mathbf{t}) \leftarrow q_1(\mathbf{t}) \wedge \ldots \wedge q_m(\mathbf{t}) \wedge c_1(\mathbf{t}) \wedge \ldots \wedge c_n(\mathbf{t})$$

where $\mathbf{x}$ is a list of the free variables in $\mathbf{t}$. (Note that the labels have been removed from the constraints.) In fact, the logical semantics we will give uses only required constraints, but we take this view of a rule to compare with other possible logical semantics.

An HCLP($\mathcal{D}, \mathcal{C}$) *program* is a collection of rules. A *goal* takes the form $\langle G, H \rangle$ where G is a multiset of atoms and H is a constraint hierarchy such that the multiset of required constraints is consistent. We let B be the set of goals modulo variable renaming. Instead of working directly with elements of B, it suffices to work with new variants of a member of the equivalence class. This observation allows us to express some definitions in a simpler way.

5.2 Formal Semantics of HCLP

The formal operational semantics of HCLP is very close to the operational semantics for logic programming languages. In this section we define the operational semantics and examine its relationship to declarative semantics of HCLP.

A *derivation* for a program P and initial goal G_0 is a (finite or infinite) sequence of goals $\{G_i\}$. Consecutive goals are related in the following manner: for some $A' \in G$ where $G_i = \langle G, H' \rangle$, and some variant $A \leftarrow B_1, \ldots, B_n, H$ of a rule of P where A and A' have the same predicate symbol,

$$G_{i+1} = \langle (G - \{A'\}) \cup \{B_1, \ldots, B_n\}, H' \cup \{A = A'\} \cup H \rangle$$

where $\{A = A'\}$ denotes the set of required constraints obtained by equating each argument of A with the corresponding argument of A'.

A derivation is *successful* if some G_i takes the form $\langle \emptyset, H \rangle$. In this case H is called the *final constraint hierarchy*. A goal is *finitely failed* if it has no successful derivation and every derivation according to a fair computation rule is finite.

Recall that B denotes the set of goals modulo variable renaming. For a program P we define the success set SS (a subset of B), and the function T_P, which maps a set of goals I to the set of all goals that can be obtained by one-step deductions from I.

$$SS = \{\langle G, H \rangle \mid \langle G, \emptyset \rangle \text{ succeeds with final hierarchy } H\}$$

$$T_P : \wp(B) \to \wp(B) \qquad (\wp(B) \text{ denotes the power set of } B.)$$

T_P is defined as follows: for $I \subseteq B$,

$$T_P(I) = \{\langle G, H \rangle \mid$$
$$G = \{p_1(s_1), \ldots, p_n(s_n)\}$$

for $j = 1, \ldots, n$ there is a new variant of a rule of P,
$$p_j(t_j) :- p_{j,1}(t_{j,1}), \ldots, p_{j,n(j)}(t_{j,n(j)}), H_j$$
$$\langle \{p_{j,1}(r_{j,1}), \ldots, p_{j,n(j)}(r_{j,n(j)})\}, H'_j \rangle \in I$$
$$F_j = H_j \cup \{p_j(s_j) = p_j(t_j)\} \cup H'_j \cup \bigcup_{k=1}^{n(j)} \{p_{j,k}(t_{j,k}) = p_{j,k}(r_{j,k})\},$$
$$H = F_1 \cup \ldots \cup F_n,$$

and the collection of required constraints in H is consistent$\}$

Let $T_P \uparrow \omega = \bigcup_{n=0}^{\infty} T_P^n(\emptyset)$ and $T_P \downarrow \omega = \bigcap_{n=0}^{\infty} T_P^n(B)$. It is straightforward to show that T_P is continuous on the complete lattice of subsets of B under the inclusion ordering. Consequently T_P has a least fixedpoint, which is equal to $T_P \uparrow \omega$. This allows us to give a fixedpoint characterization of the successful goals for a program and the final constraint hierarchies they compute.

Proposition: SS is the least fixedpoint of T_P.

As described above, a solution to a constraint hierarchy is a valuation. v is a *computed solution* for $\langle G, H' \rangle$ iff $\langle G, H' \rangle$ has a successful derivation with final constraint hierarchy H, and v is a solution of H. Our next result is a soundness result for the computation of solutions. We extend it to give a logical criterion for the existence of a computed solution. This can be viewed as a soundness and completeness result for successful derivations. However, there is no direct converse of part (a) of the theorem, that is, there is no corresponding completeness result. We use P_0 to denote the program P with non-required constraints omitted.

Theorem:
(a) If v is a computed solution for $\langle G, H \rangle$ then $P_0 \models_{\mathcal{D}} v(G \wedge C_0)$.
(b) $\langle G, H \rangle$ has a computed solution iff $P_0 \models_{\mathcal{D}} (\exists)(G \wedge C_0)$.

To see why there is no corresponding completeness result, consider the goal $\langle p(X), \emptyset \rangle$ for the program P

```
p(X) :- strong_prefer X=0.
```

Then P_0 is simply p(X). If we take v to be the valuation that assigns 2 to X then $P_0 \models_{\mathcal{D}} v(p(X))$ but the computed solution will assign 0 to

X. The incompleteness here is due to using P_0 rather than P. However using P has even worse problems—a computed solution may not be sound. For example the program Q

```
p(X) :- strong_prefer X=0, weak_prefer X≠0.
```

is logically a tautology (with respect to $\mathcal{D}$). Hence although the computed solution would assign 0 to X we do not have $Q \models_{\mathcal{D}} p(0)$. The simplicity of this example can suggest some obvious possible remedies. However these do not work on other examples. Ultimately, the problem lies in attempting to characterize the solutions of a constraint hierarchy logically when they are defined in a manner that is essentially meta-logical.

In the theorem below we show that there is soundness and completeness for finitely failed computations. We also have a characterization of the finite failure set in terms of the function T_{P_0}.

Theorem: Let D be a satisfaction-complete theory for $\mathcal{D}$. The following are equivalent:
(a) $\langle G, H \rangle$ is finitely failed by the program P
(b) $P_0{}^*, D \models \neg(G \wedge C_0)$
(c) $\langle G, C_0 \rangle \notin T_{P_0} \downarrow \omega$

6 An Algorithm for Interpreting HCLP Programs

In this section we sketch an algorithm for interpreting $\text{HCLP}(\mathcal{D}, \mathcal{LPB})$ programs. A complete description is given in [2]. In addition, we have written a proof of correctness for the algorithm, which we plan to publish separately [12]. The algorithm works for any constraint domain $\mathcal{D}$, but is specific to the locally-predicate-better comparator.

The algorithm has two phases. In the first phase, the algorithm attempts to reduce a goal using only predicates and required constraints, while building up a hierarchy of non-required constraints. We assume the existence of a $\text{CLP}(\mathcal{D})$ interpreter for interpreting the predicates and required constraints during this phase. In the second phase, the hierarchy of constraints is solved to further refine the values of the remaining unbound variables, resulting in an *answer*. An answer consists of bindings for some (possibly all) of the variables in the initial goal, and constraints on the remaining variables. Additional answers are produced by backtracking.

Each answer represents one or more locally-predicate-better solutions to the constraint hierarchy. For example, the answer **x=2** represents the single valuation that maps **x** to 2, while the answer **y>5** represents an infinite set of valuations, with each member of the set mapping **y** onto a different number greater than 5. We make this distinction between answers and solutions since, on the one hand, we obviously want our algorithm to return **y>5** rather than an infinite number of solutions. On the other hand, it is easier to define the comparators in terms of solutions rather than answers.

During its second phase, the algorithm uses a recursive procedure *Solve*. Each invocation of *Solve* represents a node in an implicit search tree of possible non-required constraints to satisfy next. A number of data structures are maintained by each invocation of *Solve*, including *Answer* (a set of unlabelled constraints that represents the answer computed so far), and *Untried* (a multiset of labelled constraints that have not yet been dealt with). Let s be the strongest strength of the constraints in *Untried*. For each constraint c in *Untried* with strength s, *Solve* adds c to the current answer, refines *Untried* by removing constraints that either have become unsatisfiable by the assumption that c holds or that are implied by the current answer, and then recursively calls itself with the remaining untried constraints. The base case is reached when the hierarchy is empty.

Each leaf in the implicit tree represents an answer to the goal. Upon request, the algorithm will backtrack to find alternate answers. These can arise in two ways. First, it is possible that the constraint hierarchy produced by the current choices of rules has more than one answer. Second, it is also possible that a goal can be satisfied in more than one way at the rule level: by using different rules to solve a goal, a new constraint hierarchy may be obtained. All answers to the current hierarchy are given before an attempt is made to resatisfy the goal. There is a unique computation tree associated with every answer, but the answers themselves are not always unique.

Here is a trivial example in HCLP($\mathcal{R}, \mathcal{LPB}$) to illustrate the algorithm's behavior upon backtracking.

```
banana(X) :- bean(X), weak_prefer X>6.
bean(X) :- strong_prefer X=1.
bean(X) :- required X>0, required X<10, weak_prefer X<4.
```

The first answer to ?-**banana(A)** would be produced by selecting the first of the **bean** clauses, yielding the hierarchy **strong_prefer A=1**, **weak_prefer A>6**. There is a single answer to this hierarchy, namely **A=1**. Upon backtracking, the second **bean** clause is selected, resulting in the hierarchy **required A>0, required A<10, weak_prefer A<4, weak_prefer A>6**. This hierarchy has two answers. The first is **A>0, A<4**. Upon backtracking the second and final answer **A>6, A<10** would then be found.

To test our ideas, we have written an interpreter for HCLP($\mathcal{R}, \mathcal{LPB}$) in CLP($\mathcal{R}$). The first phase is accomplished via a meta-interpreter. As with most Prolog meta-interpreters, it accepts a goal and either satisfies it immediately, or looks up the goal in the rule base, reduces it to subgoals, and recursively solves the subgoals. Required constraints are passed on to the CLP($\mathcal{R}$) solver immediately, while non-required constraints are simply pushed onto a stack. Non-required constraints that are part of the body of some rule are only added to the stack if that rule (minus the non-required constraints) succeeds. Upon completion of this phase, variable bindings and required constraints are maintained within the environment, and the stack of non-required constraints is passed as a constraint hierarchy to the second phase.

The implementation of the second phase is a straightforward incorporation of the above algorithm into CLP($\mathcal{R}$). The search tree described above is built implicitly by the interpreter, and alternate answers are returned upon backtracking. The stack of constraints is represented as a flat Prolog list. The non-required constraints that have already become true or unsatisfiable due to bindings established by required constraints are removed from this list. The list is then sorted by the levels of the constraints. (The order in which answers to the hierarchy are found is dependent on the order of the constraints at a given level. However, all such answers are equally valid.) This second phase takes advantage of Prolog's backtracking capabilities to try various combinations of constraints.

The interpreter is small (2 pages of CLP($\mathcal{R}$) code) and clean. We haven't concerned ourselves yet with efficiency, and the second phase of the interpreter is slow.

7 Conclusions

In this paper we have described an extension to the CLP($\mathcal{D}$) scheme that allows preferential as well as required constraints to be expressed. The work is recent, and we are currently exploring a number of extensions to it.

- We plan to design and implement algorithms for comparators that use an error metric based on the underlying domain, in addition to $\mathcal{LPB}$.

- The theory as described above selects among all the solutions arising from a single choice of HCLP rules, but doesn't try to select among solutions arising from alternate choices of rules. This sometimes results in unintuitive answers. We have been extending the HCLP theory to allow comparing solutions arising from alternate rule choices, and plan to implement such an extended language.

- We are exploring alternatives to the technique described in Section 4 for representing objects and state in HCLP. We also plan to add some rudimetary interactive graphics capabilities to our prototype.

- Finally, we are investigating the relation between HCLP and non-monotonic logic.

Acknowledgements

Thanks for many useful discussions, and comments on drafts of this paper, to Greg Barnes, Alan Bundy, Rob Duisberg, Bjorn Freeman-Benson, Joxan Jaffar, Ken Kahn, Catherine Lassez, Jean-Louis Lassez, David Maier, Geoff Phipps, Vijay Saraswat, Peter Stuckey, and Dan Weld. This research was sponsored in part by the National Science Foundation under Grant Nos. IRI–8604923 and IRI–8803294, by the Washington Technology Center, by fellowships from Apple Computer for Molly Wilson and Amy Martindale, by IBM (for Michael Maher), and by Rank Xerox (for Alan Borning while a visiting scientist at Rank Xerox EuroPARC during summer 1988).

References

[1] Alan Borning, Robert Duisberg, Bjorn Freeman-Benson, Axel Kramer, and Michael Woolf. Constraint Hierarchies. In *Proceedings of the 1987 ACM Conference on Object-Oriented Programming Systems, Languages, and Applications*, pages 48–60. ACM, October 1987.

[2] Alan Borning, Michael Maher, Amy Martindale, and Molly Wilson. Constraint Hierarchies and Logic Programming. Technical Report 88-11-10, Computer Science Department, University of Washington, November 1988.

[3] Alan H. Borning. The Programming Language Aspects of Thing-Lab, A Constraint-Oriented Simulation Laboratory. *ACM Transactions on Programming Languages and Systems*, 3(4):353–387, October 1981.

[4] Alain Colmerauer. An Introduction to Prolog III. Draft, Groupe Intelligence Artificielle, Universite Aix-Marseille II, November 1987.

[5] M. Dincbas, P. Van Hentenryck, H. Simonis, A. Aggoun, T. Graf, and F. Bertheir. The Constraint Logic Programming Language CHIP. In *Proceedings FGCS-88*, 1988.

[6] Bjorn Freeman-Benson and John Maloney. The DeltaBlue Algorithm: An Incremental Constraint Hierarchy Solver. In *Proceedings of the Eighth Annual IEEE Phoenix Conference on Computers and Communications*, Scottsdale, Arizona, March 1989. IEEE. Also published as Technical Report 88-11-09, Computer Science Department, University of Washington, November 1988.

[7] N. Heintze, J. Jaffar, S. Michaylov, P. Stuckey, and R. Yap. The $CLP(\mathcal{R})$ Programmer's Manual. Technical report, Computer Science Dept, Monash University, 1987.

[8] J. Jaffar and J-L. Lassez. Constraint Logic Programming. In *Proceedings of the 14th ACM Principles of Programming Languages Conference*, Munich, January 1987. ACM.

[9] J. Jaffar and S. Michaylov. Methodology and Implementation of a CLP System. In *Proceedings of the 4th International Conference on Logic Programming*, 1987.

[10] William Leler. *Constraint Programming Languages*. Addison-Wesley, 1987.

[11] Katta G. Murty. *Linear Programming*. Wiley, 1983.

[12] Molly Wilson. A Proof of Correctness of an Algorithm for Executing Constraint Hierarchy Logic Programs. To be submitted for publication, 1989.

Parallel Constraint Satisfaction
in Logic Programming:
Preliminary Results of CHIP within PEPSys

Pascal Van Hentenryck*

European Computer-Industry Research Centre (ECRC)

Arabellastr. 17, 8000 Munich (F.R.Germany)

Abstract

Consistency techniques on finite domains are one of the constraint-solving techniques included in the constraint logic programming language CHIP. They allow the solving of many discrete combinatorial problems with a short development time and an efficiency comparable to procedural programs. Nevertheless most of these problems remain computationally expensive and the emergence of parallel computers opens a new area for research: the combination of parallel and constraint programming in the logic programming framework. This paper reports a first step in that direction. It shows that *or*-parallelism and consistency techniques on finite domains can be combined to yield an efficient parallel language for discrete combinatorial problems. In particular, this combination, together with the higher-order optimization predicates available in CHIP, gives rise to a parallel depth-first branch and bound approach. An implementation in PEPSys, a complete parallel logic programming system developed at ECRC, has been designed and preliminary results on real-life problems show effective, sometimes superlinear, speedups.

---

*This research emerged as a result of two large projects currently being pursued at ECRC: the CHIP and PEPSys projects.

1 Introduction

Many real-life problems in different areas such as operations research, hardware design, and artificial intelligence can be seen as constrained search problems. Most of them are $\mathcal{NP}$-complete, which means there is no hope to design an efficient (polynomial) algorithm for solving them.

Logic programming is a convenient language for stating these problems thanks to its relational form and nondeterminism. Its relational form makes it adequate to state constraints while its nondeterminism abstracts the tree search away from programmers. Unfortunately, standard logic programming languages such as Prolog are also very inefficient for solving them because they are based on a generate and test paradigm.

Therefore much research has been devoted during the last years to improving the efficiency of logic programming for combinatorial problems. This has led to the definition of several constraint programming languages (e.g., [5; 10; 14; 29]). These languages combine the declarative aspects of logic programming with the efficiency of constraint-solving techniques and open new application areas for logic programming. Among these languages is CHIP, a constraint logic programming language developed at ECRC [10]. CHIP extends usual logic programming languages by providing three new computation domains: (1) finite domains, (2) boolean terms, and (3) rational terms. CHIP also provides efficient constraint-solving techniques on each new computation domain, i.e., consistency techniques on finite domains, boolean unification for boolean terms, and a symbolic simplex-like algorithm for rational terms. It has been applied to numerous real-life problems, mainly from operations research and hardware design. CHIP drastically reduces the programming effort for these applications, yet it preserves most of the efficiency of specialized programs written in a procedural language.

Concurrently to the above research, much attention has been devoted to parallelizing Prolog. The motivation behind this research stems from the emergence of commercial multiprocessor computers and the declarative aspects of logic programming which, in principle, liberates programmers from managing parallelism. Different computation models have been proposed to exploit either *or*-parallelism (e.g., [3; 4; 18; 22; 31]) either *and*-parallelism (e.g., [7; 13]) or a combination of both (e.g., [33]). Several of these models have been successfully implemented and show promising results [2; 6; 18]. Among them is PEPSys, a parallel logic programming system developed at ECRC [1]. PEPSys combines *or*- and independent *and*-parallelism and is one of the most efficient implementations available.

The results in these two different directions, together with the fact that most constrained search problems are computationally expensive, were a major impetus to develop a parallel implementation of CHIP. Of particular interest is the "finite domains and consistency techniques" part of CHIP which has a large variety of applications in discrete combinatorial problems and offers large potentiality for parallelism. Currently solving a discrete combinatorial problem in parallel requires either the writing of a specialized program in a procedural language (e.g., [16; 21; 30]) or the use of a special-purpose package [11]. The first approach is programming-intensive; solving a discrete combinatorial problem in sequential requires much programming effort and parallelism further increases the programming complexity. Special-purpose packages relieve programmers from managing parallelism but they are, at the moment, rather inefficient. Compared to the above approaches, a parallel version of CHIP[1] is very appealing. Not only it reduces the programming effort to the sequential part itself simplified by the use of CHIP but it should also result in a good efficiency provided that the overhead of parallelism is kept small. It is therefore of much interest to study if the sequential efficiency of CHIP can be preserved in a parallel implementation.

This paper reports a first step in that direction: the design and implementation of an *or*-parallel version of CHIP. It shows that the principles behind the sequential implementation can be generalized to support *or*-parallelism while keeping the overhead small. In particular, basic operations on domains remain fast, constant time operations. A prototype implementation has been realized on a Siemens MX500 (equivalent to a sequent balance 8000) by extending PEPSys [6]. *Or*-parallelism together with consistency techniques and higher-order optimization predicates of CHIP naturally give rise to a parallel branch and bound approach. This approach has been applied to several real-life problems from operations research and show effective, sometimes superlinear, speedups. To our knowledge, this research is the first attempt to combine *or*-parallelism and constraint-solving in the logic programming framework.

The rest of this paper is organized as follows. Section 2 gives a brief overview of finite domains and consistency techniques. Section 3 identifies different opportunities for parallelism in CHIP. Section 4 shows how to exploit *or*-parallelism together with finite domains and consistency techniques. Finally, section 5 contains results on the N-queens problem and on two real-life discrete combinatorial problems:

---

[1]In the following, by CHIP, we mean the "finite domains and consistency techniques" part of CHIP.

the graph-coloring and cutting-stock problems.

2 Finite Domains and Consistency Techniques

2.1 Domains-variables

The basic feature of CHIP for solving discrete combinatorial problems is the ability to work on domain-variables, i.e., variables ranging over a finite domain [27]. Domains can be either a set of natural numbers or a set of constants. CHIP can also cope with arithmetic terms over domain-variables which are constructed from natural numbers, domain-variables over natural numbers and the operators $+$, $-$, $\times$ and $/$.

2.2 Constraints over Finite Domains

CHIP provides a large variety of constraints on domain-variables. It contains not only **arithmetic** but also **symbolic** and even **user-defined** constraints. Arithmetic constraints define the usual relations on arithmetic terms over domain-variables (e.g., $\geq$, $\leq$, $=$, $\neq$). Symbolic constraints are part of the originality of CHIP and define symbolic relations between several variables. An example of symbolic constraint is

- `element(Nb,List,Var)` which holds if `Var` is the Nb^{th} element of `List`; this constraint can be used when `Nb` and `Var` are domain-variables or constants and `List` is a list of constants.

This symbolic constraint often allows more natural problem statements and more efficient problem-solving.

Beside these primitive constraints, programmers can also define their own constraints as logic programs and tell the system how to handle them using forward and lookahead declarations.

2.3 Higher-order extensions

CHIP includes some higher-order extensions for finding solutions optimizing (i.e., minimizing or maximizing) some evaluation function. These predicates are used for solving combinatorial optimization problems. For instance, the predicate `minimize(Goal,Function)`, where `Goal` is a predicate and `Function` is an arithmetic term over domain-variables, can be used to find the solution of `Goal` which minimizes `Function`.

2.4 Consistency Techniques

All constraints involving domain-variables are solved through consistency techniques, a paradigm emerging from AI to solve discrete combinatorial problems (e.g., [12; 19; 20]). The principle behind these techniques is to use constraints to reduce the domains of variables and hence the search space. Different kinds of pruning (i.e., reduction of the domains) have been identified and efficient ways to achieve them have been devised. A theoretical framework has been proposed to embed these techniques inside logic programming and serve as basis for the implementation of the built-in constraints and the general control mechanism [24; 25; 26]. Consistency techniques are usually not able to solve the constraints by their own. It follows that solving a discrete combinatorial problem using them consists in iterating the following two steps

1. propagating the constraints as far as possible

2. making a choice

until a solution is reached.

3 What Parallelism to Exploit?

In this section, we review the main opportunities for parallelism arising in CHIP. As is well-known, there are mainly two kinds of parallelism inside logic programming: *and-* and *or*-parallelism. However, since the computational model of CHIP differs substantially from the one of Prolog, it is appropriate to reconsider that issue. As mentioned previously, the computational model of CHIP for solving discrete combinatorial problems is best viewed as the iteration of two steps: propagation and choices. Both steps provide opportunities for parallelism, three of them being considered now.

First, a constraint can be solved in parallel. This opportunity for parallelism arises inside the forward and lookahead declarations. Indeed, these control mechanisms solve a constraint by trying out different combinations of values for the variables appearing inside the constraint and these combinations could possibly be tried in parallel. This kind of parallelism is implicit in the bitwise forward-checking version of [12] and is expected to be of small granularity in most cases.

Second, the constraints can be propagated in parallel. During the propagation step, several constraints have to be considered and we might think of propagating them in parallel. This leads to a kind of *and*-parallelism. Once again this parallelism is expected to be of small granularity in most cases[2] and to introduce some synchronization problems since several constraints might share the same variable. It has attracted several researchers in the AI community (e.g., [23]). There are also theoretical limitations for its exploitation [15].

Third, choices can be made in parallel. This is the usual *or*-parallelism of Prolog except that CHIP has much more to offer in that context than usual logic languages. Indeed, choices can take various forms from instantiation (i.e., giving a value to a variable), to domain-splitting (i.e., dividing the domain of a variable in several parts), and to case analysis (i.e., using constraints for making choices). In all cases, a choice means choosing among different alternatives and the basic idea here is to explore several of them simultaneously. This parallelism has attracted many researchers outside the logic programming community (e.g., [11; 16; 30]) and can be of large granularity. It is particularly appealing when combined with the higher-order optimization predicates available in CHIP as it gives rise naturally to parallel depth-first branch and bound algorithms. These algorithms require searching (implicitly) throughout the entire search space; hence exploring different branches in parallel can lead to a significant improvement in efficiency. Parallelism has also an interesting side-effect on branch and bound algorithms. It introduces either a depth-first component in a best-first branch and bound or a breadth-first component in a depth-first algorithm. Therefore anomalies (e.g., superlinear speedups) can be observed [17]. For depth-first branch and bound algorithms, parallelism might allow to find early a good (or even optimal) solution that would otherwise require a long time. This solution can then be used to prune the search space, avoiding spending time in parts of the tree which are not worth exploring.

Among the above sources of parallelism, *or*-parallelism seems the most promising. It applies to the whole computation and not to a specific part of it (e.g., the constraint propagation). It can also be of large granularity and thus more amenable to implementation on a multiprocessor computer. Finally, it amounts to adding a breath-first component which can be valuable for the class of problems considered. Therefore we decided to restrict ourselves in a first prototype to the combination of *or*-parallelism and constraint-solving. The purpose of the prototype was to identify the potential incompatibilities between constraint and parallel programming if any and to study how much can be gained through parallelism for this class of problems in the framework of logic programming. The constraint imposed on the prototype is rather standard now in the area of parallel logic programming: the efficiency of the

---

[2]This is not the case for *and*-parallelism in general.

implementation when run on a single processor has to be comparable to a good sequential implementation.

4 Supporting *Or*-Parallelism in CHIP

In order to support *or*-parallelism, it is necessary to adapt the current implementation schemes of CHIP. This section reviews the problems raised by *or*-parallel CHIP and proposes several solutions to it.

4.1 The Problem

The computation of a logic language can be seen as tree whose root node is the initial goal and other nodes are obtained by reducing a goal using SLD-resolution or an extension of it. Different branches of the tree come from the different clauses used to reduce a goal. Prolog explores the computation tree using a depth-first search with chronological backtracking. In other words, when Prolog can apply several clauses to reduce a goal, one of them is selected. The remaining clauses will be tried on backtracking. In *or*-parallel Prolog, different processors are used to explore several branches of the tree in parallel, i.e., they try simultaneously several clauses for reducing the same goal. The main problem raised by *or*-parallel Prolog is how to represent different bindings of the same variable on different branches of the computation tree. Different schemes have been proposed to deal with that problem (e.g., [3; 31; 32; 33]). In addition to the binding problem, CHIP introduces a further difficulty due to domain-variables. Let us illustrate the problem through an example. Suppose X is ranging over $\{1,...,10\}$ and the constraint $X \neq 3$ has to be solved. In theory, this constraint is solved by binding X to a new variable Y ranging over $\{1,2,4,...,10\}$. However, for efficiency and memory reasons, the implementation scheme of CHIP removes the value 3 from the domain of X and trails the modification to undo it on backtracking. Therefore the new problem to be solved by *or*-parallel CHIP is how to represent different states of the same domain on different branches of the tree[3]. Although this problem looks similar to the binding problem of Prolog, it has a main difference. In Prolog, a variable is free or bound. When the variable is bound, it never changes value. This is not the case for domain-variables. The domain fields (i.e., the fields representing the domain of a variable) can be updated several

---

[3]A similar problem arises with the constraints. Since the solution is the same in both cases, we only discuss domains in the paper.

times. It follows that existing binding schemes do not apply directly although they provide useful insights on the present issue.

4.2 A Copy Solution

A straightforward solution to the above problem consists of requiring that *or*-parallel CHIP follows precisely the theory, i.e., each time the domain of a variable is updated, a new variable ranging over the reduced domain is created and the variable is bound to this newly created variable. This solution enables existing binding schemes of *or*-parallel Prolog to be used for solving our problem. Its basic advantage is its simplicity. Its drawback is the unacceptable overhead it induces. In sequential CHIP, basic operations on domain-variables requires constant time and do not depend on the length of the domains. This property is obviously violated by the copy solution. Since we aim at an efficiency on a single processor comparable to a good sequential implementation, a better scheme has to be devised.

4.3 Avoiding Copying

In order to avoid copying the domains, a new data structure local to a process, the domain area, is introduced. It contains the state of domains for the branch the process is working on. When a domain-variable is created, its domain is stored in the domain area instead of in the global stack for the sequential implementation. It follows that each process has its own view of the domains and modifications of the domain fields only occur in the domain area without affecting the view of other processes. The use of a domain area makes sure that all basic operations on domains (e.g., testing if a value is in a domain) remains constant-time operations.

The main overhead of this approach arises when switching tasks. In that case, the process has to update the contents of the domain area to reflect the state of the domains at the branch point it is grabbing work from. The update of the domain areas is achieved by using the usual value-trail which has been generalized for that purpose to include three fields:

- the entry in the domain area;

- the old value of the entry;

- the new value of the entry.

The *old value* field is necessary to restore the previous value of the entry on backtracking while the *new value* field is needed to update domain areas at switching tasks.

4.4   Avoiding Trailing

Since the value-trail is used not only on backtracking but also to update the domain areas, it is necessary to make sure that it contains all necessary information to achieve these two activities. An obvious way to enforce this requirement consists of trailing all modifications to the domain fields. However this simple solution would induce a severe overhead and requires much more memory for the parallel version than for the sequential one. Moreover the size of the value-trail directly defines the cost of switching tasks and thus reducing the amount of trailing decreases the cost of switching tasks. For these reasons, special care has been devoted to avoid trailing. The sequential optimizations have been generalized to make sure that the amount of trailing of *or*-parallel CHIP is proportional to the one of sequential CHIP.

4.5   Relation with the SRI Model

The above scheme has some similarities with the SRI model [31]. Each process (resp. worker in the SRI model) has a local data-structure for storing the domains (resp. bindings) which make sure that the basic operations on domains (resp. variables) remains constant time operations. The basic overhead arises at task switching due to the need to update the domain area (resp. the binding array). However there are also some important differences between them.

The SRI model distinguishes between conditional and unconditional bindings. Only conditional bindings are recorded into the binding array and trailed. Conditional bindings are directly stored into the variable cell. This distinction comes from the single assignment property of the logical variable. Once bound, a variable never change value. This is not true for domain fields which can be updated several times and differently on different branches. It follows that all the domain fields have to store in the domain area.

The scheme does not assume a global address space as does the SRI-model. During dereferencing, a worker in the SRI model can access other workers' stacks. Since access to a non-local stack is transparent in that model, it is necessary to have a global address space. Conversely the domain area does not contain references but only pure data (i.e., the value of the domain fields) so that no global address space is necessary.

Finally, it is worth noting that our scheme is independent of the binding scheme used for the variables.

4.6   Implementation Details

The above proposal has been implemented on a Siemens MX500 (equivalent to a Sequent balance 8000) by extending the PEPSys system [1; 6]. The PEPSys system contains four different parts: a parallel abstract machine which is an extension of the WAM to support *or-* and *and-*independent parallelism, a compiler which generates abstract instructions from the PEPSys code, an emulator of the abstract machine written in C as well as a scheduler responsible for distributing work among the processors. All four parts of the system have been modified to support *or-*parallel CHIP. A set of new abstract instructions has been defined to support the execution of CHIP. The code generation and the emulator have been extended to handle them. Most of the existing instructions have been modified to accommodate domain-variables and the new data-structures required for constraint-solving. Finally, the scheduler has been generalized to update the domain areas. Typical degradations for *or-*parallel CHIP are of the same order than those observed for *or-*parallel Prolog [1; 18] and are thus easily overcome through parallelism.

5   Preliminary Results

Several programs from simple puzzles to real-life discrete combinatorial problems have been solved using the system. We report here on three problems: the N-queens problem, real-size graph-coloring problems and a real-life cutting stock problem. The last two problems illustrate the use of parallel depth-first branch and bound in logic programming. The results are given for a Siemens MX500 whose Elementary Processor is an NS30302 giving an equivalent of 0.7 VAX780 MIPS.

5.1   N-queens Problem

The problem amounts to placing N queens on a N * N chessboard so that they do not attack each other. The generalized forward-checking version of [28] is used to compute all solutions, the only change being that the predicate `indomain/1` is replaced by its parallel version `par_indomain/1`. These predicates are used to give to a variable a value from its domain. In the sequential version, alternative values are tried out on backtracking while, in the parallel version, several values can be

N	T_1	T_2	T_3	T_4	T_5	T_6	T_7	T_8
8	11.74	6.35	4.53	3.52	3.12	2.85	2.37	1.91
10	204.67	104.24	71.46	54.59	43.02	36.86	31.98	28.25

Table 1: Execution Times for all Solutions to the N-queens Problem

N	S_2	S_3	S_4	S_5	S_6	S_7	S_8
8	1.85	2.59	3.33	3.76	4.11	4.95	6.14
10	1.96	2.86	3.74	4.65	5.55	6.40	7.24

Table 2: Speed-up on the N-queens Problem

explored simultaneously. This program first states all the constraints and then generate values for the variables. The generation of constraints is of course purely sequential. The execution results in seconds and the speed-ups are given for N = 8 and 10 and for 1 to 8 processors in Tables 1 and 2. For comparison purposes, we also give in Table 3 the times and speedups of the 8-queens problem in PEPSys using the program which applies tests as soon as possible.

First note that the time for the 8-queens problem on one processor is close to the time of PEPSys on 6 processors. This implies that the search space is much smaller for *or*-parallel CHIP than for *or*-parallel Prolog. Despite that fact, a speedup of 6.14 is achieved on 8 processors. The speedups are of course better for the 10-queens problems whose search space is much larger (e.g., 7.24 on 8 processors).

5.2 Graph-Coloring Problems

We now turn to a real-life problem from operations research: the graph-coloring problem. The purpose is to find the chromatic number of a graph, i.e., the smallest number of colors necessary to color a graph so that two adjacent vertices are colored with a different color. The program used comes from [8; 26] where the generator has been modified to explore choices in parallel. The sequential version of this program is comparable to, or better than, specific algorithms written in a procedural language when the graph density is not too high ($\leq 70\%$). It is therefore of much interest to observe the behaviour of the parallel

	1	2	3	4	5	6	7	8
Time	61.65	31.56	21.82	16.77	13.65	11.42	9.76	8.60
Speedup	1	1.96	2.83	3.68	4.52	5.41	6.33	7.18

Table 3: Times and Speedups for 8-queens Problem in PEPSys

N	T_1	T_6	S_6
1	3263	297	10.98
2	419	84	4.98
3	1225	60	20.41
4	545	108	5.04
5	350	72	4.86
6	1269	239	5.30
7	292	61	4.78
8	424	99	4.28
9	786	148	5.31
10	490	47	10.42
11	1091	206	5.29
12	4054	714	5.67
13	386	80	4.82
14	966	183	5.27
15	318	83	3.83
16	657	122	5.38
17	568	131	4.33
18	1306	237	5.51
19	1546	283	5.46
20	1789	239	7.39

Table 4: Results for the Graph-coloring Problem

version. For that purpose, 20 graphs with 60 vertices and a density of 50% have been randomly generated. A specific instance then includes 60 domain-variables ranging from 1 to 60, 885 disequations and the evaluation function. The results are reported in Table 4. T_1 and T_6 are the times in seconds on 1 and 6 processors while S_6 represents the speed-up for 6 processors.

It can be seen that *or*-parallel CHIP produces effective speedups over the sequential version. Four super-linear speed-ups have been obtained, all of them coming from the early finding of the optimal solution. For instance, a speed-up of more than 20 on 6 processors has been achieved. 9 instances exhibit speedups better than 5, 6 instances between 4 and 5 and 1 instance a speedup of 3.83. Note also that the poor speedups are obtained for easy problems (i.e., those which are solved quickly in sequential).

	1	2	3	4	5	6	7	8
Time	277	141	99	74	62	52	46	42
Speedup	1	1.96	2.79	3.74	4.46	5.32	6.02	6.44

Table 5: Results on the Cutting-Stock Problem

5.3   A Cutting-Stock Problem

The last example reported in this paper is the cutting-stock problem presented in [9]. We only consider the symbolic version described in that paper with a normal labeling procedure. The problem includes 4 domain-variables ranging from 1 to 72, 28 domain-variables ranging over set of natural numbers, 9 arithmetic constraints (i.e., linear inequalities), 28 symbolic constraints (i.e., `element` constraints), and an evaluation function. Only the first four domain-variables need to be instantiated to get a solution. Hence we expected poor results for this problem because of the small granularity of the parallelism. Table 5 shows the results.

Surprisingly, the resulting speedups are quite satisfactory. We obtain a speedup of 6 with 7 processors and of 6.44 for 8.

6   Conclusion

In this paper, we have considered the issue of exploiting parallelism and constraint-solving together in the logic programming framework. Starting with the computational model of CHIP for discrete combinatorial problems, different opportunities for parallelism have been identified. The most promising alternative, the combination of *or*-parallelism and consistency techniques on finite domains, has been considered in detail. Not only does this combination provide large potentialities for parallelism but it also gives rise to a parallel depth-first branch and bound approach when used together with the higher-order optimization predicates of CHIP. The problems raised by an *or*-parallel CHIP have been defined and several possible solutions have been proposed. Among them was an efficient scheme which makes sure that all operations on domains remain constant time operations and preserves most of the efficiency of the sequential implementation. This scheme has been embedded inside the PEPSys system. *Or*-parallel CHIP is the first language combining constraint-solving and *or*-parallelism in the logic programming framework. Various examples have been tried ranging from puzzles to real-life examples. The speedups obtained are very promising and clearly indicate that a parallel constraint logic programming language based on consistency techniques would be a valuable tool for solving discrete combinatorial problems.

Acknowledgments

This research would not have been possible without the valuable work done both in the CHIP and PEPSys team. I would like to thank all members of these teams. In particular, I am indebted to Jacques Chassin de Kergommaux for many valuable discussions about parallelism and for constant feedback and support about this research. I greatly benefited from the work of Abder Aggoun on the compilation of CHIP in the SEPIA system. Mehmet Dincbas provided not only support and encouragement but also contributed in many ways to an efficient implementation of CHIP. Finally, the support of Alexander Herold, Herve Gallaire and Jean-Claude Syre is greatly appreciated.

References

[1] U. Baron and al. The Parallel ECRC Prolog System PEPSys: An Overview and Evaluation Results. In *FGCS'88*, Tokyo, November 1988.

[2] J. Chassin, J.C. Syre, and H. Westphal. Implementation of a Parallel Prolog System on a Commercial Multiprocessor. In *ECAI*, pages 278–283, Munich, August 1988.

[3] A. Ciepielewski, B. Hausman, and S. Haridi. Or-parallel Prolog Made Efficient on Shared Memory Multiprocessors. In *Symposium on Logic Programming*, August 1987.

[4] W.F. Clocksin and H. Alshawi. A Method for Efficiently Executing Horn Clause Programs Using Multiple Processors. *New Generation Computing*, 5:361–376, 1988.

[5] A. Colmerauer. Opening the Prolog-III Universe. *BYTE Magazine*, 12(9), August 1987.

[6] J. Chassin de Kergommeaux and P. Robert. An Abstract Machine to implement efficiently OR-AND parallel Prolog. To appear in Journal of Logic Programming.

[7] D. DeGroot. Restricted And-Parallelism. In *FGCS-84*, pages 471–478, Tokyo, Japan, 1984.

[8] M. Dincbas, H. Simonis, and P. Van Hentenryck. Solving Large Combinatorial Problems in Logic Programming. *Journal of Logic Programming.* (To appear).

[9] M. Dincbas, H. Simonis, and P. Van Hentenryck. Solving a Cutting-Stock Problem in Constraint Logic Programming. In *Fifth International Conference on Logic Programming*, Seattle, WA, 1988.

[10] M. Dincbas, P. Van Hentenryck, H. Simonis, A. Aggoun, T. Graf, and F. Berthier. The Constraint Logic Programming Language CHIP. In *FGCS'88*, Tokyo, Japan, December 1988.

[11] Raphael Finkel and Udi Manber. DIB - A Distributed Implementation of Backtracking. *ACM Transactions on Programming Language and Systems*, 9(2):235–256, April 1987.

[12] R.M. Haralick and G.L. Elliot. Increasing Tree Search Efficiency for Constraint Satisfaction Problems. *Artificial Intelligence*, 14:263–313, 1980.

[13] M. Hermenegildo. An Abstract Machine for Restricted AND-parallel execution of logic programs. In *Third International Conference on Logic Programming*, pages 25–39, London, July 1986.

[14] J. Jaffar and J-L. Lassez. Constraint Logic Programming. In *POPL-87*, Munich (FRG), January 1987.

[15] S. Kasif. On the Parallel Complexity of Some Constraint Satisfaction Problems. In *AAAI-86*, pages 349–353, Philadelphia, PA, August 1986.

[16] V. Kumar, K. Ramesh, and V. Nageshwara Rao. Parallel Best-First Search of State-Space Graphs: A Summary of Results. In *AAAI-88*, pages 122–127, Saint Paul, Minnesota, 1988.

[17] T.H. Lai and S. Sahni. Anomalies in Parallel Branch and Bound Algorithms. *CACM*, 27(6):594–602, March 1987.

[18] E. Lusk and al. The Aurora Or-Parallel Prolog System. FGCS'88.

[19] A.K. Mackworth. Consistency in Networks of Relations. *AI Journal*, 8(1):99–118, 1977.

[20] U. Montanari. Networks of Constraints : Fundamental Properties and Applications to Picture Processing. *Information Science*, 7(2):95–132, 1974.

[21] C. Roucairol. *Du sequentiel au parallele: la recherche arborescente et son application a la programmation quadratique en variables 0.1.* PhD thesis, Universite Pierre et Marie Curie, Paris, Juin 1987.

[22] E. Shapiro. An OR-Parallel Execution Algorithm for Prolog and its FCP Implementation. In *Fourth International Conference on Logic Programming*, pages 311–337, Melbourne, Australia, May 1987.

[23] M. Swain and P. Cooper. Parallel Hardware for Constraint Satisfaction. In *AAAI-88*, pages 682–686, Saint Paul, Minnesota, 1988.

[24] P. Van Hentenryck. A Framework for Consistency Techniques in Logic Programming. In *IJCAI-87*, Milan, Italy, August 1987.

[25] P. Van Hentenryck. *Consistency Techniques in Logic Programming.* PhD thesis, University of Namur (Belgium), July 1987.

[26] P. Van Hentenryck. *Constraint Satisfaction in Logic Programming.* MIT Press, Cambridge, Ma, 1989.

[27] P. Van Hentenryck and M. Dincbas. Domains in Logic Programming. In *AAAI-86*, Philadelphia, PA, August 1986.

[28] P. Van Hentenryck and M. Dincbas. Forward Checking in Logic Programming. In *Fourth International Conference on Logic Programming*, pages 229–256, Melbourne, Australia, May 1987.

[29] P. Voda. The Constraint Language Trilogy: Semantics and Computations. Technical report, Complete Logic Systems, North Vancouver, BC, Canada, 1988.

[30] B. Wah and Y. Ma. Manip: A Muticomputer Architecture for Solving Combinatorial Extremum-Search Problems. *IEEE Transactions on Computers*, 33, May 1984.

[31] D.H.D. Warren. The SRI Model for Or-Parallel Execution of Prolog. Abstract Design and Implementation Issues. In *International Symposium on Logic Programming*, pages 46–53, September 1987.

[32] D.S. Warren. Efficient Prolog Memory Management for Flexible Control Strategies. In *IEEE International Symposium on Logic Programming*, pages 198–202, Atlantic City, NJ, February 1984.

[33] H. Westphal, P. Robert, J. Chassin, and J.C. Syre. The PEPSys Model: Combining Backtracking, AND- and OR-parallelism. In *International Symposium on Logic Programming*, pages 436–448, September 1987.

CLP(Σ^*): Constraint Logic Programming with Regular Sets

Clifford Walinsky[1]

Abstract

Many implementations of PROLOG currently incorporate string-handling procedures, but these procedures often violate the relational foundations of logic programming. CLP(Σ^*) provides a logic-based formalism for incorporating strings into logic programming in a more expressive manner than the standard collection of string-handling procedures. When files in secondary storage are viewed as containers of (possibly very long) strings, CLP(Σ^*) also provides a logic-based method for file-handling—a deficiency of PROLOG implementations.

CLP(Σ^*), a new constraint logic programming language presented in this article, describes membership constraints on regular sets. In addition to a examination of the CLP(Σ^*) language, we provide formal links with the CLP "scheme" by describing a decidable theory. A prototype implementation has been constructed in PROLOG. This prototype has demonstrated that flexible constraint scheduling is required to ensure terminating evaluation of all constraints. We describe the scheduling criteria for termination and efficient evaluation.

---

[1]Author's address: Dept. Math & Computer Science, Bradley Hall, Dartmouth College, Hanover, NH 03755.

1. Introduction.

CLP(Σ^*) is an instance of the Constraint Logic Programming (*CLP*) scheme [10, 11] specialized to the domain of regular sets [9]. The CLP scheme has previously been extended to the domain of infinite rational trees [13] in the PROLOG-II language [7], and real numbers in the CLP($\mathbb{R}$) language [12]. CLP(Σ^*) extends the scheme to regular sets, whose elements are strings generated from a finite alphabet Σ. As in the CLP($\mathbb{R}$) language, CLP(Σ^*) permits uninterpreted function symbols to appear in terms. For simplicity, however, this article does not deal with uninterpreted function symbols, though their inclusion is essential and must be handled carefully.

We first describe the CLP(Σ^*) language. An example of a constraint is

$$A \; in \; (X \cdot \text{"ab"} \cdot Y),$$

which states that any string bound to variable A must contain the substring "ab". The right-hand sides of constraints are regular expressions incorporating variables. If the constraint above is satisfied by a string x, variable X will be bound to the prefix of x preceding "ab", while variable Y will be bound to the suffix of x following "ab". If there are multiple occurrences of "ab" within string x, multiple bindings to X and Y are possible and are retrieved through backtracking. In addition, the constraint can be used to construct strings. If variable X is bound to "12" and variable Y is bound to "34", while A is unbound, the constraint above is satisfied by binding A to "12ab34".

We also describe the model and corresponding theory of CLP(Σ^*). As the example above demonstrates, non-determinism is required to solve atomic constraints. For sets of constraints, PROLOG's literal selection rule must be made more flexible. With a flexible scheduling rule, evaluation of every constraint set terminates. We will also propose syntactic requirements on the language so that evaluation of atomic constraints always terminates.

One motivation for the development of CLP(Σ^*) is that many implementations of PROLOG currently possess string-handling facilities without strong connections to logic. Typically in these implementations strings are represented as packed arrays of characters, and certain procedures are made available to unpack (e.g., "suffix", "prefix", and "substring") and pack (e.g., "concat") strings. String handling capabilities are undoubtedly useful, but these procedures lack a logic-based semantics. For example, in most implementations, the query

```
prefix(P,"abc")
```

will not successively instantiate variable P to all prefixes of the string "abc". CLP(Σ^*) provides this missing basis of relational behavior and logical semantics. In fact the prefix relation can be described in CLP(Σ^*) with the clause

```
prefix(P,X) :- X in P·Σ*.
```

Regular expressions also permit expressiveness and conciseness far exceeding that possible using the procedures supplied in most string-handling implementations.

Input-output to text files can be implemented uniformly within the framework of CLP(Σ^*). Implementations of file-handling in PROLOG rely on procedures that have semantics seemingly unrelated to PROLOG's declarative semantics. For example, the "get" procedure reads the next (non-blank) character from the current input stream. If the current input stream contains "ABCD…," and the query is

```
get(C),lowercase(C),
```

the query will immediately fail. Is this behavior correct? Perhaps the input stream should be read until a lowercase letter is found. Without a firm logical basis for file-handling in PROLOG, we have no way of knowing what the appropriate result of the above query should be. In certain applications, the contents of a file residing in secondary storage can be regarded as a string of characters. Though not implemented in the current CLP(Σ^*) prototype, strings in main memory and secondary storage can be manipulated with constraints independent of their place of residence. The logic-based semantics of CLP(Σ^*) therefore ensures that file-handling possesses a logic-based semantics also.

We anticipate that CLP(Σ^*) will be useful primarily in text processing applications. However, there are other diverse areas where constraints are specified naturally with regular expressions. For example, Bishop and Snyder have devised a representation of access rights and their transfer within an information system [4]. Information systems are characterized with active "subjects", i.e., computer system users; passive "objects", i.e., computer system resources; and access rights between subjects and objects. A model of an information system can be depicted as a bipartite graph with edges labeled with access rights. Security of a hierarchical information system can be compromised when a subject of a given protection level can gain access to information located at a more sensitive level. In the following information system, for example, we can infer in the presence of collusion that user U2 (at a low security level) has read access to object O (at a high security level) via user U1's read access right.

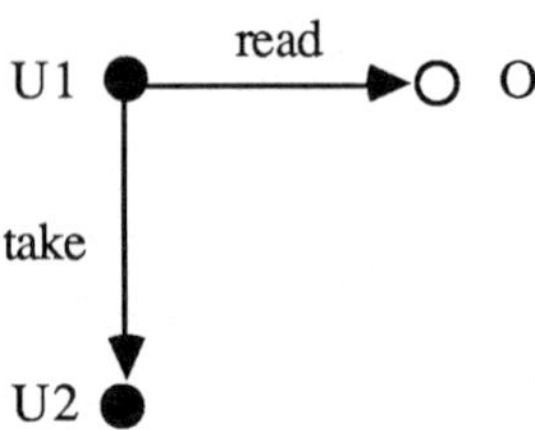

In general, an access right r can be obtained by subject x from y if there is a path between x and y labeled ("take" + "grant")$^*r$. More sophisticated inference rules are stated using regular expressions to encompass other possible security breaches [3].

Finally, development of CLP(Σ^*) demonstrates the generality of the CLP "scheme". But CLP(Σ^*) also points out weaknesses of this scheme. The constraint solver component of CLP(Σ^*) is independent of CLP($\mathbb{R}$). If every new instance of CLP is independent of all other instances, an implementation of all constraint solvers may be impractically large. To reduce size, some kind of sharing must occur between constraint solvers. Further development of instances of CLP will permit us to gain more insight into the problem of amalgamating constraint solvers. Solutions may be similar to constraint solvers devised for object-oriented systems [2].

2. The CLP(Σ^*) Language.

The following clauses are an example of a CLP(Σ^*) program, called Squeeze.

```
sqz(X,Z) :-
    X in (A·"□□"·("□")*·B), Z in (SA·"□"·SB),
    sqz(A,SA), sqz(B,SB).
sqz(X,X).
```

This program is intended to describe a relation sqz defined on pairs of strings so that sqz(x,y) is true if y has all extraneous spaces (denoted by □) occurring in x removed.

An *atomic constraint* is of the form x *in* e, where x is either a variable or string, and e is a regular expression possibly containing variables. For example, the atomic constraint

$$X \text{ in } (A \cdot "\square\square" \cdot ("\square")^* \cdot B)$$

occurs in program Squeeze.

By convention, all variables begin with uppercase letters. Variables range over strings formed from Σ. Variables within regular expressions are used to denote substrings, acting like the variables \$1, \$2, etc. that refer to fields of lines in AWK's [1] patterns and actions. The $CLP(\Sigma^*)$ constraint solver determines (most general) bindings for variables in order to satisfy constraints. For example, one binding produced by evaluation of the constraint below assigns the string "ab" to variable A, and "cd" to B.

$$"ab\square\square\square cd" \text{ in } (A \cdot "\square\square" \cdot ("\square")^* \cdot B).$$

A *clause* of a $CLP(\Sigma^*)$ program is of the form $A :- C$, where A is an atomic formula, and C is a (possibly empty) conjunction of atomic formulas and atomic constraints. The Squeeze program, for example, contains 2 clauses. In general, terms consisting of uninterpreted function symbols and regular expressions may occur in the heads of clauses. But for ease of presentation, we will not consider uninterpreted function symbols. Therefore, in this article, heads of clauses will contain only variables.

3. Meaning of $CLP(\Sigma^*)$ Programs.

In contrast to logic programming, the CLP scheme selects a specific domain for computation. For example, the field over $\mathbb{R}$ constitutes the model for $CLP(\mathbb{R})$. Selection of a specific domain enables development of efficient special-purpose constraint solvers. Similarly, $CLP(\Sigma^*)$ is a specialization of CLP's scheme to the domain of regular sets. In this section we will look at the algebraic structure of this domain.

Let $\mathbf{Reg}(\Sigma) = (\mathbf{R}(\Sigma); \cdot, +, ^*, 1, \emptyset)$ be an algebraic structure whose carrier is the collection of all regular sets formed of finite strings from alphabet Σ, denoted $\mathbf{R}(\Sigma)$. Given regular sets R_1 and R_2, the operations are defined below.

- $R_1 \cdot R_2 = \{xy \mid x \in R_1 \text{ and } y \in R_2\}$ is the pointwise concatenation of regular sets.
- $R_1 + R_2 = R_1 \cup R_2$.
- R_1^* is the least set R' such that $R' = 1 + (R' \cdot R_1)$.
- 1 is the set consisting of just the empty string, denoted ε.
- $\emptyset$ is the empty set.

$\varnothing$ is the additive identity element, while 1 is the multiplicative identity element. The collection of regular sets is closed under the operations listed above [9].

The definition of R^* can be made effective. The collection $\mathbf{R}(\Sigma)$ of regular sets, ordered by set inclusion, is a complete lattice with least element $\varnothing$, and greatest element Σ^*. Since + is a monotone operator, the Knaster-Tarski Theorem [16] provides that R^* also has the following formulation

$$R^* = \bigcup_{i=0}^{\infty} R^i,$$

where $R^0 = 1$, and $R^{i+1} = R^i \cdot R$.

A *regular expression* is just a finite expression composed from finite strings, and the operators listed in the signature of $\mathbf{Reg}(\Sigma)$. The set of strings (language) described by a regular expression e is usually denoted by $L(e)$.

It is well known that every regular set corresponds to a regular expression. Given a regular set R, suppose regular expression e describes R. The constraint X *in* e has a space of solutions equivalent to R. Therefore, every regular set can be described by a constraint. This characteristic of algebra $\mathbf{Reg}(\Sigma)$ is called "solution compactness," in the terminology of CLP.

Due to the closure properties of regular sets, the complement of a regular set (relative to Σ^*) is itself a regular set. So the complement of the solution space of any constraint X *in* e is itself describable by a constraint. Together with solution compactness, these two characteristics guarantee that constraints are expressive enough to describe every element of $\mathbf{Reg}(\Sigma)$.

4. Overview of the Constraint Solver.

Evaluation of CLP queries is very similar to evaluation of logic programming queries. However, unification used by a logic programming interpreter is replaced by constraint satisfaction in a domain other than the Herbrand Universe.

To illustrate the overall evaluation procedure, assume the current query is G under constraints C. Select a formula F from G. If F is an atomic constraint, and $F \cup C$ is satisfiable, recursively invoke the evaluation procedure on the new query $G - \{F\}$ under constraints $F \cup C$.

Otherwise, F is an atomic formula. Find variant $R :- G'$ of a clause for which R unifies with F under most general unifier μ, and recursively invoke the evaluation procedure on the new query

$$[G' \cup (G - \{F\})]\mu,$$

under constraints C.

Since the algebra $\mathbf{Reg}(\Sigma)$ has no limit elements, every ground atomic formula has a finitary cover [10]. The CLP scheme therefore guarantees correctness and completeness of this evaluation procedure. Furthermore, negation inferred from failure is correct for ground atomic formulas, and complete for canonical programs [14].

The next two sections describe in more detail how satisfiability of constraints is determined. The next section details the properties of the constraint solver that ensure termination for all conjunctions of constraints. The following section describes deduction rules for satisfaction of atomic constraints.

5. Evaluation of Conjunctions of Constraints.

Satisfaction of an atomic constraint x *in* e involves determination of a binding σ for the variables occurring in the constraint such that $x\sigma \in L(e\sigma)$. In fact, a given constraint may be satisfied by an infinite set of bindings, some more general than others. We formally define these notions next.

Definitions.

- Let $\leq$ be an ordering relation on idempotent substitutions. As described by Lassez, Maher and Marriott [15] and Eder [8], for substitutions σ and τ, $\sigma \leq \tau$ (σ more general than τ) if there is a substitution η such that $\sigma \circ \eta = \tau$.[2] Provably, $\leq$ is a partial order.

- Substitution τ is a *grounding* substitution for constraint x *in* e if τ maps every variable occurring in x *in* e to a string.

- Constraint x *in* e is *satisfied* if, for every grounding substitution τ for x *in* e, $x\tau \in L(e\tau)$.

- Substitution σ *satisfies* constraint x *in* e if $x\sigma$ *in* $e\sigma$ is satisfied.

- $\text{SAT}(x \ in \ e)$ is the most general set of substitutions that satisfy x *in* e. That is, if $\sigma \in \text{SAT}(x \ in \ e)$, there is no other substitution $\sigma' \in \text{SAT}(x \ in \ e)$ such that $\sigma' \leq \sigma$. Every substitution in $\text{SAT}(x \ in \ e)$ is a binding in the terminology used above.

---

[2] In accordance with convention, composed substitutions associate to the left; therefore, $x\tau \circ \sigma = (x\tau)\sigma$.

Examples.

SAT(X *in* "a"·("b")*) = {[X="a"], [X="ab"], [X="abb"],...}[3]

SAT("ab" *in* ("a")*·X) = {[X="b"], [X="ab"]}

SAT("a" *in* "a"+X) = {[X=X]} (the identity substitution).

We will defer our examination of the actual deduction rules used to obtain these bindings until the next section. For now, assume there a procedure that determines a satisfying binding σ for any constraint x *in* e whenever $\sigma \in$ SAT(x *in* e).

Most constraints of the form X *in* e^* are satisfied by an infinite number of substitutions for X (except when $L(e) = \{\varepsilon\}$). If the generation of strings is not controlled, a constraint solver may not terminate on unsatisfiable conjunctions of constraints. For example, the conjunction

$$X \ in \ ("a")^*, "a" \ in \ "b"$$

is unsatisfiable. When an unfair selection rule is employed, for example: "always solve atomic constraints within a conjunction from left-to-right, and backtrack from right-to-left," evaluation of the constraint above will not terminate. If the second conjunct had been selected first, the constraint solver would immediately fail. In fact, as demonstrated by the conjunction

$$X \ in \ "a"\cdot("a")^*, X \ in \ ("b")^*,$$

termination is only assured if a length limit on generated strings is enforced.

The constraint selection problem is resolved through a flexible, efficient scheduling strategy: *Those constraints that are capable of generating only a finite number of bindings are selected for evaluation.* Under this strategy, if every legal schedule contains a constraint that is capable of producing an infinite number of bindings, evaluation *flounders*: computation delays indefinitely. Floundered computations arise in other areas of logic programming, including evaluation of non-ground negated goals [5], non-linear algebraic constraints in CLP($\mathbb{R}$) [12], and evaluation of inequalities in PROLOG-II [6].

Syntactic examination of atomic constraints can determine when a finite set of bindings will be generated. The following proposition describes syntactic criteria sufficient to determine that a satisfiable constraint is incapable of generating an infinite number of bindings.

---

[3]$[X=e]$ describes a substitution mapping variable X to a string or variable e, and all other variables to themselves.

Proposition 1. SAT(x *in* e) is finite if either x is a string, or x is a variable but e contains neither variables nor closure operators.

PROOF: There are clearly two cases to consider.

(x is a variable) Then e contains neither variables nor closure operators. By simple induction on the number of operators in regular expression e, $L(e)$ is always finite. Therefore, SAT(x *in* e) must be finite also, because $\sigma \in$ SAT(x *in* e) if and only if $x\sigma \in L(e)$.

(x is a string "w") Consider any substitution $\sigma \in$ SAT("w" *in* e). Suppose σ maps a variable V to a string "v", where $|v| > |w|$. We claim that σ is not a most general substitution. According to Lemma 1 below, SAT("w" *in* e) must also contain all possible substitutions $\sigma_{v'}$ identical to σ, but with V mapped to an arbitrary string v'. Consider substitution σ' identical to σ, but with V mapped to itself. Then, for all strings v', $\sigma' \leq \sigma_{v'}$ and σ' satisfies "w" *in* e. Consequently, SAT("w" *in* e) contains only substitutions of the form

$$[V_1 = v_1, \ldots, V_k = v_k], \qquad (k \geq 0)$$

where $V_1, \ldots, V_k$ is a subset of the variables occurring in e, and each string v_i is no longer than w. SAT("w" *in* e) is therefore finite. ■

To obtain the converse, SAT(x *in* e) must always be infinite if x is a variable, and e contains either variables or closure operators. There are three ways in which the converse of Proposition 1 is violated. We describe these three possibilities through examples.

1) X *in* e^*, where $L(e) = \{\varepsilon\}$. This constraint is satisfied by the substitution $[X = \varepsilon]$.

2) X *in* Y. This constraint is satisfied by the substitutions $[X = Y]$ and $[Y = X]$.

3) X *in* e, where $L(e) = \Sigma^*$. This constraint is satisfied by the identity substitution.

Further examination of constraints at runtime could recognize these three situations. However, the additional scheduling flexibility does not seem to justify the increased runtime overhead.

Proof of Proposition 1 requires the following lemma.

Lemma 1. Let $e($"v"$)$ denote the expression resulting from substitution of string "v" for all occurrences of variable X in regular expression e. If, for strings w and v, substitution σ satisfies "w" *in* $e("v")$ and $|v| > |w|$ then, for all strings v', σ satisfies "w" *in* $e("v'")$.

PROOF: We perform induction on the number of operators in regular expression e.

BASIS:

(e is a string "u") Since "w" *in* "u"("v") is satisfiable and "u"("v") = "u", $w = u$. So, for all strings v', "u"("v'") = "u", and "w" *in* "u"("v'") is satisfiable.

(e is the variable X) Then $X("v") = "v"$, and "w" *in* $X("v")$ is unsatisfiable, because $|v| > |w|$.

(e is a variable Y, distinct from X) Then $Y("v'") = Y$, for all strings v', and σ satisfies "w" *in* $Y("v'")$ if σ satisfies "w" *in* $Y("v")$.

INDUCTION HYPOTHESIS: Assume the lemma is true for all regular expressions containing at most m operators.

INDUCTION: We now consider just the case of an expression e^*, where e contains m operators. Proofs for the other possible regular expression forms are simpler versions. Suppose σ satisfies "w" *in* $e("v")^*$, with $|v| > |w|$. Then, σ satisfies "w" *in* $e("v")^k$, for some $k \geq 0$. So $w = w_1 \cdots \cdot w_k$ and σ satisfies "w_i" *in* $e("v")$, for all $1 \leq i \leq k$. The induction hypothesis holds, and σ satisfies "w_i" *in* $e("v'")$, for all strings v'. Consequently, σ satisfies "w" *in* $e("v'")^*$. ∎

The scheduling strategy mandates that only constraints capable of generating a finite set of bindings will be selected from a conjunction for evaluation. This strategy is sufficient to obtain termination. Having selected an atomic constraint, the number of alternative bindings produced through evaluation will always be finite. And following evaluation, the number of atomic constraints decreases by one. Therefore, the entire search space that could be explored given any acceptable sequence of selected constraints is always finite.

6. Satisfaction of Atomic Constraints.

The previous section has described scheduling criteria on conjunctions of constraints. In this section, the criteria are used to devise a decidable procedure that determines bindings for atomic constraints. We first set a requirement on regular expressions, which results in a decidable deduction system: *Variables are not permitted within the scope of any closure expression.* This requirement will be utilized within the completeness and termination proofs of this section.

An expression e is ε-*free* if $\varepsilon \notin L(e)$. Because variables cannot appear within any closure expression e^*, it is possible to determine prior to runtime if e is ε-free: simply construct a finite automaton for e and determine if the automaton accepts ε. We will assume henceforth that subexpressions of all closure expressions are ε-free. This property will be crucial for the termination proof. If some expression e is not ε-free, it can be rewritten to an expression e' so that $L(e^*) = L((e')^*)$ and e' is ε-free. Details of the rewriting process will not be presented here.

Let $\sigma \vdash x$ *in* e denote the deduction that binding σ satisfies constraint x *in* e. We will use $\vdash x$ *in* e to indicate the deduction that the identity substitution satisfies x *in* e. Then $\sigma \vdash x$ *in* e according to the following rules.

$$\textit{Deduction Rules for Atomic Constraints}$$

(variable expressions) $\qquad [X="w"] \vdash "w" \textit{ in } X.$

(string expressions) $\quad \vdash "w" \textit{ in } "w" \quad$ and $\quad \dfrac{X\sigma = "w"}{\sigma \vdash X \textit{ in } "w"}.$

(alternation expressions) $\quad \dfrac{\sigma \vdash x \textit{ in } e_1}{\sigma \vdash x \textit{ in } e_1 + e_2} \quad$ and $\quad \dfrac{\sigma \vdash x \textit{ in } e_2}{\sigma \vdash x \textit{ in } e_1 + e_2}.$

(closure expressions) $\quad \vdash "\varepsilon" \textit{ in } (e)^* \quad$ and $\quad \dfrac{\vdash "w" \textit{ in } (e)^* \cdot e}{\vdash "w" \textit{ in } (e)^*}.$

(concatenation expressions)

$$\dfrac{\begin{pmatrix} w = w_1 \cdot w_2 \\ \sigma_1 \vdash "w_1" \textit{ in } e_1 \\ \sigma_2 \vdash "w_2" \textit{ in } e_2 \end{pmatrix}}{\sigma_1 \cup \sigma_2 \vdash "w" \textit{ in } e_1 \cdot e_2} \quad \text{and} \quad \dfrac{\begin{pmatrix} \sigma_1 \vdash X_1 \textit{ in } e_1 \\ \sigma_2 \vdash X_2 \textit{ in } e_2 \end{pmatrix}}{[X = (X_1 \sigma_1) \cdot (X_2 \sigma_2)] \vdash X \textit{ in } e_1 \cdot e_2}.$$

Conditional deduction rules are those listed above with a condition to be satisfied above the line and the conclusion below the line. The deduction rule for concatenation makes use of a partial operation, $\cup$, defined over idempotent substitutions. Given substitutions σ_1 and σ_2, $\sigma_1 \cup \sigma_2$ produces the most general idempotent substitution (if one exists) that is more specific than both σ_1 and σ_2. More formally, $\sigma_1 \cup \sigma_2 = \tau$ such that

- $\tau \geq \sigma_1$ and $\tau \geq \sigma_2$, and
- Whenever there is a substitution τ' with $\tau' \geq \sigma_1$ and $\tau' \geq \sigma_2$, $\tau' \geq \tau$.

Provably, $\sigma_1 \cup \sigma_2$ is unique up to renaming.

Deduction of a binding for a constraint of the form X *in* $e_1 \cdot e_2$ may be ill-defined in the event that either $X_1 \sigma_1$ or $X_2 \sigma_2$ is a variable. For then $X_1 \sigma_1 \cdot X_2 \sigma_2$ is not defined, and the substitution $[X = X_1 \sigma_1 \cdot X_2 \sigma_2]$ is undefined. However, when the constraint scheduling criteria are adhered to, this problem cannot arise. If $\sigma_1 \vdash X_1$ *in* e_1 and $X_1 \sigma_1$ is a variable, it must be either that e_1 contains a variable or a closure expression. But then the criteria for scheduling constraints should have prevented evaluation of X *in* $e_1 \cdot e_2$.

We next demonstrate soundness and completeness of the deduction rules.

Proposition 2. Suppose that constraint x *in* e is acceptable for evaluation according to the scheduling criteria. Then $\sigma \vdash x$ *in* e if and only if there is a substitution $\tau \in \text{SAT}(x$ *in* $e)$ and τ is more general than σ ($\tau \leq \sigma$).

PROOF: We will show that $\sigma \in \text{SAT}(x$ *in* $e)$ implies $\sigma \vdash x$ *in* e. The converse proof follows along the same lines, and we leave it to the reader. We perform induction on the number of operators in e.

BASIS:

e is a string "w".

> If x is a variable, then $\sigma = [x="w"]$. And, according to the deduction rules, $\sigma \vdash x$ *in* "w".
>
> If x is a string, then $x = "w"$ and σ is the identity substitution, which is also mandated by the deduction rules.

e is a variable Y.

> To be selected for evaluation, x must be a string. Say that $x = "w"$.

Then $\sigma = [Y="w"]$, which is again mandated by the deduction rules.

INDUCTION HYPOTHESIS: Assume that for every expression e containing at most n operators, $\sigma \in SAT(x \ in \ e)$ implies $\sigma \vdash x \ in \ e$.

INDUCTION: Consider an expression e consisting of $n+1$ operators.

$e = e_1 \cdot e_2$.

Suppose that $\sigma \in SAT(x \ in \ e_1 \cdot e_2)$.

If x is a string "w", then there are strings w_1 and w_2 such that $w = w_1 \cdot w_2$ where σ satisfies "w_1" $in \ e_1$ and "w_2" $in \ e_2$. Using the induction hypothesis, $\sigma \vdash$ "w_1" $in \ e_1$ and $\sigma \vdash$ "w_2" $in \ e_2$. Since $\sigma \cup \sigma = \sigma$, the deduction rules provide that $\sigma \vdash$ "w" $in \ e_1 \cdot e_2$.

If x is a variable X, then constraint scheduling prohibits variables or closure expressions within e. Consequently, $L(e)$ is finite. So $\sigma = [X="w"]$ for some string $w \in L(e_1 \cdot e_2)$. Therefore, there are strings w_1 and w_2 such that $w = w_1 \cdot w_2$ and both "w_1" $in \ e_1$ and "w_2" $in \ e_2$ are satisfied. But then $X_1 \ in \ e_1$ and $X_2 \ in \ e_2$ are satisfied by substitutions $\sigma_1 = [X_1="w_1"]$ and $\sigma_2 = [X_2="w_2"]$, respectively. Using the induction hypothesis, $\sigma_1 \vdash X_1 \ in \ e_1$ and $\sigma_2 \vdash X_2 \ in \ e_2$. Letting $\sigma = [X=(X_1\sigma_1) \cdot (X_2\sigma_2)]$, we have $\sigma \vdash X \ in \ e_1 \cdot e_2$.

$e = e_1 + e_2$.

$\sigma \in SAT(x \ in \ e_1 + e_2)$ if either $\sigma \in SAT(x \ in \ e_1)$ or $\sigma \in SAT(x \ in \ e_2)$. Without loss of generality, assume $\sigma \in SAT(x \ in \ e_1)$. Using the induction hypothesis, $\sigma \vdash x \ in \ e_1$, and therefore $\sigma \vdash x \ in \ e_1 + e_2$.

$e = (e_1)^*$.

According to the criteria for scheduling constraints, x must be a string. So let $x = "w"$. Furthermore, syntactic requirements prohibit variables from appearing within the scope of closure expressions. Since there are no variables in the constraint, whenever $SAT(x \ in \ (e_1)^*)$ is nonempty ($SAT(x \ in \ (e_1)^*)$ is satisfied), it can only contain the identity substitution.

Suppose now that $SAT("w" \ in \ (e_1)^*)$ is satisfied. Let $k \geq 0$ be the smallest number such that $SAT("w" \ in \ (e_1)^k)$ is satisfied. Then there are k substrings of w such that $w = w_1 \cdot w_2 \cdots \cdot w_k$ and for each w_i, $SAT("w_i" \ in \ e_1)$ is satisfied. Using the induction hypothesis, for each w_i, $\vdash "w_i" \ in \ e_1$. We now perform induction on k to show that $\vdash "w" \ in \ (e_1)^*$. If $k = 0$, $w = \varepsilon$ which implies $\vdash \varepsilon \ in \ \varepsilon$, and

and hence $\vdash"\varepsilon"$ *in* $(e_1)^*$. For the induction hypothesis, assume that for $k' = k-1$ and $k > 0$, $\vdash"w_1\cdot\ldots\cdot w_{k'}"$ *in* $(e_1)^*$. Since $\vdash"w_k"$ *in* e_1, we infer $\vdash"w_1\cdot\ldots\cdot w_{k'}\cdot w_k"$ *in* $(e_1)^*\cdot e_1$, using the deduction rule for concatenation. With $w = w_1\cdot\ldots\cdot w_{k'}\cdot w_k$, $\vdash"w"$ *in* $(e_1)^*\cdot e_1$. Therefore, $\vdash x$ *in* $(e_1)^*$. ∎

In the terminology of CLP, Proposition 2 states that the constraint satisfaction procedure—its constraint scheduling criteria and deduction rules—"correspond" to the algebra of regular sets. We still need to determine that the deduction rules constitute a decision procedure.

Proposition 3. The deduction rules for atomic constraints can be used to determine when a constraint x *in* e is unsatisfiable.

PROOF: If x *in* e is unsatisfiable, no possible application of the deduction rules can result in a determination that $\sigma \vdash x$ *in* e, according to Proposition 2. On the other hand, it may be that an infinite series of applications of the deduction rules are necessary to determine that x *in* e is unsatisfiable.

To eliminate this possibility, we first show that every application of a deduction rule reduces the size of a constraint. We consider just application of the rule for closure expressions, since this is the only rule that seems to produce a larger constraint. Indeed, to demonstrate $\vdash"w"$ *in* e^*, we may need to demonstrate $\vdash"w"$ *in* $e^*\cdot e$. According to the rule for concatenation, we next need to split w into substrings w_1 and w_2, and then demonstrate both $\vdash"w_1"$ *in* e^* and $\vdash"w_2"$ *in* e. Certainly, if $w_2 = \varepsilon$, a cycle results because w would be equal to w_1. But e is ε-free, so $"\varepsilon"$ *in* e is unsatisfiable. Therefore, $"w_2"$ *in* e is inferred only when $w_2 \neq \varepsilon$, and the size of w_1 will be less than the size of w.

Nontermination of a derivation could also result if an infinite number of alternative deduction rule applications are available. For every expression form, at most one deduction rule is applicable. Only the deduction rule for concatenation entails a variable number of alternative derivations. To demonstrate $\sigma \vdash"w"$ *in* $e_1\cdot e_2$, w is split into substrings w_1 and w_2, and derivations for $\vdash"w_1"$ *in* e_1 and $\vdash"w_2"$ *in* e_2 are attempted. But the number of alternatives is just the size of w, which is finite. ∎

Proposition 2 demonstrates that whenever a constraint is satisfiable the deduction rules terminate successfully. Proposition 3 demonstrates that termination is achieved even when a constraint is unsatisfiable. Therefore, the deduction rules constitute a decision procedure. Furthermore, simple induction on the structure of an expression e establishes that the number of alternative bindings for a constraint x in e is finite if and only if SAT(x in e) is finite. Both decidability and finiteness properties guarantee terminating evaluation of conjunctions under the constraint selection criteria of Section 5.

7. Summary.

CLP(Σ^*) represents an instance of the CLP scheme specialized to solving constraints on regular sets. We have described an algebra of regular sets, a procedure for deciding membership, and have shown that the theory corresponds to the algebra. A prototype constraint solver has already been written in PROLOG. A flexible, efficient constraint scheduling strategy ensures termination for unsatisfiable conjunctions. When we mandate that variables will not occur within closure expressions, the deduction procedure for atomic constraints has been shown decidable.

Having evaluated the prototype, a more efficient implementation will be pursued retaining the scheduling strategy suggested by the prototype. Strings can be represented compactly as packed arrays of characters. Packed array representation makes constraint solving independent of the actual location of strings. Consequently, strings can be located in secondary storage, and manipulated through constraints. Thus, solving constraints on strings provides a method for implementing file-handling constructs in a logic-based language.

Acknowledgements.

This work was funded by a grant from Dartmouth College. Much is also owed to IBM's CLP group for recognizing the existence of a general scheme, and proving its utility by implementing CLP($\mathbb{R}$). Our thanks to Joxan Jaffar, Jean-Louis Lassez, Michael Maher and Peter Stuckey for much useful advice. Also, thanks to Richard Hamlet for pointing out the unique expressive powers of regular expressions.

References.

[1] Aho, A.V., Kernighan, B.W. and Weinberger, P.J., *The AWK Programming Language,* Addison-Wesley (1988).

[2] Borning, A., et. al., "Constraint Hierarchies," *SIGPlan Notices,* 22(12): 48-60 (Dec. 1987).

[3] Bishop, M. "Hierarchical Take-Grant Protection Systems," (1981):109-122.

[4] Bishop, M. and Snyder, L., "The Transfer of Information and Authority in a Protection System," *Proceedings 7th Symposium on Operating Systems,* (Dec. 1979):45-54.

[5] Clark, K.L., "Negation as Failure," in: *Logic and Data Bases,* H. Gallaire & J. Minker (eds.), Plenum Press, New York (1978):293-322.

[6] Cohen, J., "Describing PROLOG by its Interpretation and Compilation," *Communications ACM,* 28(12):1311-1324 (Dec. 1985).

[7] Colmerauer, A., "Prolog and Infinite Trees," in: *Logic Programming,* K.L. Clark & S-A. Tarnlund (eds.), Academic Press (1982):231-251.

[8] Eder, E., "Properties of Substitutions and Unifications," *J. Symbolic Computation,* 1:31-46 (1985).

[9] Hopcroft, J.E. and Ullman, J.D., *Introduction to Automata Theory, Languages, and Computation,* Addison-Wesley, Ch. 2 and 3 (1979).

[10] Jaffar, J. and Lassez, J.L., "Constraint Logic Programming," *Proceedings 14th POPL,* (1987).

[11] Jaffar, J., Lassez, J.L. and Maher, M.J., "A Logic Programming Language Scheme," in: *Logic Programming: Relations, Functions and Equations,* D. DeGroot & G. Lindstrom (eds.), Prentice-Hall (1986).

[12] Jaffar, J. and Michaylov, S., "Methodology and Implementation of a CLP System," *Proceedings 4th Int'l Conf. on Logic Programming,* (1987):196-218.

[13] Jaffar, J. and Stuckey, P.J., "Semantics of Infinite Tree Logic Programming," *Theoretical Computer Science,* 46:141-158 (1986).

[14] Jaffar, J. and Stuckey, P.J., "Canonical Logic Programs," *J. Logic Programming,* 2:143-155 (1986).

[15] Lassez, J.L., Maher, M.J. and Marriott, K., "Unification Revisited," Foundations of Logic and Functional Programming, Trento, 1986, in: *LNCS,* no. 306, Springer-Verlag (1988):67-113.

[16] Tarski, A., "A Lattice-Theoretical Fixpoint Theorem and Its Applications," *Pacific J. Math.,* 5:285-309 (1955).

Extensions and Variations of Logic Programming

Narrowing Grammar

H. Lewis Chau

D. Stott Parker

Computer Science Department
University of California
Los Angeles, CA 90024-1596

ABSTRACT

We present a new kind of grammar. It combines concepts from logic programming, rewriting, lazy evaluation, and logic grammar formalisms such as Definite Clause Grammar (DCG). We call it *Narrowing Grammar*.

A narrowing grammar is a finite set of rewrite rules. It is directly executable, like most logic grammars. In fact, narrowing grammar rules can be compiled to Prolog and executed by existing Prolog interpreters as generators or acceptors. Unlike many logic grammars, narrowing grammar also permits higher-order specification and modular composition, and provides lazy evaluation. Lazy evaluation is important in certain language acceptance situations, such as in coroutined matching of multiple patterns against a stream.

This paper defines narrowing grammar and compares it with the successful and widely-used DCG formalism in logic programming. We show that pure DCG can be easily translated into narrowing grammar. Narrowing grammar enjoys the advantages of DCG, as well as its first-order logic foundation. At the same time, narrowing grammar can rank higher in aspects such as expressiveness and modularity.

Keywords: Logic Programming, Definite Clause Grammar, Logic Grammars, Parsing.

This work was done within the Tangram project, supported by DARPA contract F29601-87-C-0072.
Prolog code for the examples in this paper can be obtained by sending a message to the authors at chau@cs.ucla.edu or stott@cs.ucla.edu

1. Introduction

Since the development of metamorphosis grammar [5], the first logic grammar formalism, several variants of logic grammars have been proposed [1, 6, 10, 11, 16, 17, 19]. Among these we must mention Definite Clause Grammar (DCG), a successful and widely-used formalism for language analysis in logic programming. We assume that the reader is familiar with DCG and Prolog. Good introductions to DCG and Prolog can be found, for example, in [18, 20].

Most logic grammar formalisms mentioned above are *first-order*. Specifically, a nonterminal symbol in these formalisms cannot be passed as an argument to some other nonterminal symbol. For example, usually DCG does not permit direct specification of grammar rules of the form

```
goal(X)  --> X.†
```

This problem was pointed out as early as [12]. We will discuss later in the paper why this is more than just a minor problem, as it affects the convenience of use, extensibility, and modularity of grammars. Very recently Abramson [2] has commented on the problem, and has addressed it by using a new construct, *meta(X),* to define metarules that go beyond the limit of first-order logic grammar formalisms. We propose a higher-order solution.

Narrowing grammar is a formalism for writing rules. It combines concepts from logic programming, rewriting, lazy evaluation, and logic grammar formalisms such as DCG. The semantics of narrowing grammar are defined by a term-rewriting system that is an extension of Narain's Log(F) system [14]. This approach gives both a compact formal definition of narrowing grammar, and an efficient logic programming implementation. In this paper, we point out a number of advantages of narrowing grammar for language analysis.

As a brief introductory example, let us show how easily regular expressions can be defined with narrowing grammar. The regular expression pattern $a^+ b$ that matches sequences of one or more copies of a followed by a b can be specified with the grammar rule

---

† Some Prolog systems, including Quintus Prolog and Sicstus Prolog, have been extended to permit such rules. In these systems the rule shown above is translated to

```
goal(X,S0,S)  :- phrase(X,S0,S).
```

where `phrase/3` is a metapredicate that performs DCG compilation of its first argument (at run time) and then executes the result. See section 5.2 for further discussion.

```
pattern => ([a]+, [b]).
```

where we also define the following grammar rules:

```
(X+) => X.
(X+) => X, (X+).
([],L) => L.
([X|L1],L2) => [X|(L1,L2)].
```

Here '+' is the postfix operator defining the Kleene plus regular expression pattern, and the rules for ',' define pattern concatenation, very much like the usual Prolog rules for `append`. Lists are used to represent sequences, as in most logic grammars.

Narrowing grammar rules are used much like rewrite rules in [14], but with a special leftmost outermost term rewriting strategy described in the next section. With this strategy, the narrowing of `([a]+,[b])` to `[a,a,b]` along with the rules used in each step of the narrowing is as follows:

Rewritten term		*Rule used in rewriting*
`([a]+,[b])`		
$\rightarrow$	`(([a],[a]+),[b])`	`(X+) => X, (X+).`
$\rightarrow$	`([a|([],[a]+)],[b])`	`([X|L1],L2) => [X|(L1,L2)].`
$\rightarrow$	`[a|(([],[a]+),[b])]`	`([X|L1],L2) => [X|(L1,L2)].`
$\rightarrow$	`[a|([a]+,[b])]`	`([],L) => L.`
$\rightarrow$	`[a|([a],[b])]`	`(X+) => X.`
$\rightarrow$	`[a,a|([],[b])]`	`([X|L1],L2) => [X|(L1,L2)].`
$\rightarrow$	`[a,a,b]`	`([],L) => L.`

In a similar way, all other lists matching the pattern $a^+ b$ could be produced.

Narrowing grammar has a theoretical foundation in first-order logic. All pure narrowing grammar rules can be translated straightforwardly to pure Prolog clauses. This is advantageous since the full power of unification is exploited, and eventually it may be feasible for properties of a narrowing grammar to be verified using first-order logic theorem proving technology. At the same time, the higher-order specification and modularity of narrowing grammar enable some complex languages to be specified easily.

Section 2 defines narrowing grammar and section 3 shows how to implement it in Prolog. Section 4 then describes some of its interesting features, and section 5 goes on to compare narrowing grammar with the widely-used DCG formalism in logic programming, showing how it offers several important advantages.

2. Narrowing Grammar

Narrowing grammar is a clear and powerful formalism for describing languages. In this section we define narrowing grammar, and give examples showing how patterns can be specified with it.

2.1. Formalism of Narrowing Grammar

Definition 2.1

A *term* is either a variable, or an expression of the form $f(t_1,..,t_n)$ where f is a n-ary function symbol, $n \geq 0$, and each t_i is a term. A *ground term* is a term with no variables.

Definition 2.2

A *narrowing grammar* is a finite set of rules of the form:

$$LHS \Rightarrow RHS$$

where:

(1) LHS is any term except a variable, and RHS is a term.

(2)   If $LHS = f(t_1,...,t_n)$, then each t_i is a term in normal form (see definition 2.4 below).

Definition 2.3

Constructor symbols are functors (function symbols) that do not appear as any rule's outermost LHS functor.

A *simplified term* is a term whose outermost function symbol is a constructor symbol. By convention also, every variable is taken to be a simplified term. Note that no LHS of any rule can be a simplified term. In this paper we will assume the function symbols for lists (namely, the empty list [] and cons [_|_], following Prolog syntax) are constructor symbols. Much in the way that constructors provide a notion of 'values' in a rewrite system, constructors here provide a notion of 'terminal symbols' of a grammar.

Definition 2.4

A term is said to be in *normal form* if all of its subterms are simplified. Since every variable is taken to be a simplified term, a term in normal form can be non-ground.

Definition 2.5

Let p, q be terms where p is not a variable, and let s be a nonvariable subterm of p (which we write $p = r[s]$). If there exists a rule $(LHS => RHS)$ (which we assume has no variables in common with p), for which there is a most general unifier θ of LHS and s and $q = (r[RHS])\theta$ (the result of replacing s by RHS and applying the substitution θ), then we say p *narrows to* q.

A *narrowing* is a sequence of terms p_1, p_2, ..., p_n such that for each i, $1 \le i \le n-1$, p_i narrows to p_{i+1}. A narrowing is *successful* if p_n is simplified.

Generally speaking, a rewrite system will specify a mechanism for *selecting* a subterm s from a given term p, to determine what to narrow. This mechanism is then used successively with the actual rewriting mechanism to implement narrowing. Below we define *NU-narrowing,* a special leftmost outermost narrowing strategy for narrowing grammar.

Definition 2.6: NU-step

$p \rightarrow q$, or p narrows to q in a *NU-step* †, is defined concisely by the following clauses:

```
nu_step(P,Q)  ←  nonvar(P), (P => Q).
nu_step(P,Q)  ←  nonvar(P), ¬(P => Q), functor(P,F,N),
               functor(Q,F,N), subterm_nu_step(P,Q,1,N).

subterm_nu_step(P,Q,I,N)  ←  arg(I,P,A), arg(I,Q,A),
               plus(I,1,I1), subterm_nu_step(P,Q,I1,N).
subterm_nu_step(P,Q,I,N)  ←  arg(I,P,A), arg(I,Q,B),
               nu_step(A,B), unify_remaining(P,Q,I,N).

unify_remaining(_,_,N,N).
unify_remaining(P,Q,I,N)  ←  plus(I,1,I1), arg(I1,P,A),
               arg(I1,Q,A), unify_remaining(P,Q,I1,N).
```

We can view NU-step as a special leftmost outermost narrowing. The term p narrows to q in a NU-step if either $(p => q)$ is an instance of some rule (first clause), or if left-to-right unification of subterms of p followed by the replacement of a subterm by the result of a NU-step yields q (second clause). Note that the NU-step definition does not permit a narrowing to begin with a variable.

---

†The significance of the prefix '*NU-*' in '*NU-step*' comes from the fact that we use a special strategy to select a subterm for narrowing, and this strategy selects terms in a leftmost outermost, or *Normal* order, fashion. *Unification* is implicitly used left-to-right by this strategy.

We have used a logic program to define NU-step mainly out of interest in conciseness. Note that the definition is nondeterministic, since the `subterm_nu_step` predicate is nondeterministic. Nondeterminism permits NU-step to act both as an acceptor and as a generator.

Definition 2.7: NU-narrowing

A *NU-narrowing* is a narrowing $p_1, p_2, \ldots$ such that for each i, when p_i and p_{i+1} both exist, p_i narrows to p_{i+1} in a *NU-step*.

```
nu_narrowing(X,X).
nu_narrowing(X,Y) ← nu_step(X,Z), nu_narrowing(Z,Y).
```

Definition 2.8: simplification

A *simplification* is a *NU-narrowing* $p_1, p_2, \ldots, p_n$ if p_n is simplified and no other p_i is simplified.

```
simplification(X,X) ← simplified(X).
simplification(X,Y) ← ¬simplified(X),
                      nu_narrowing(X,Y), simplified(Y).
```

NU-narrowing is not just a leftmost outermost narrowing strategy. For instance, given the narrowing grammar rules:

```
a => c.
b => [].
c => c.
g(X,[]) => [].
```

then there is a NU-narrowing sequence

```
g(a,b), g(a,[]), []
```

but the only leftmost outermost narrowing is

```
g(a,b), g(c,b), g(c,b), ...
```

Definition 2.9:

A *stream* is a list of ground terms. A *stream pattern* is a term that has a NU-narrowing to a stream.

2.2. Specifying Patterns with Narrowing Grammar

We illustrate how useful patterns can be developed in narrowing grammar with a sequence of examples.

Example 2.0 : Regular Expressions

As we suggested earlier, regular expressions can be defined easily with grammar rules:

```
(X+) => X.
(X+) => X,(X+).

(X*) => [].
(X*) => X,(X*).

(X;Y) => X.
(X;Y) => Y.

([],L) => L.
([X|L1],L2) => [X|(L1,L2)].
```

The operators `+` and `*` define the familiar Kleene plus and Kleene star regular expressions, respectively. `;` is a disjunctive pattern operator, while `,` defines pattern concatenation.

Example 2.1 : Counting the Occurrences of a Pattern

Suppose we wish to count the number of times an uninterrupted sequence of one or more *a's* is followed by a *b* in a stream. This pattern can be represented by the regular expression `([a]+,[b])`, and we can count the number of its occurrences with the pattern

```
number( ([a]+,[b]), Total )
```

if we include the following grammar for `number`:

```
number(Pattern,Total) => number(Pattern,Total,0).
number(Pattern,Total,Total) => [end_of_file].
number(Pattern,Total,Count) =>
        Pattern, number(Pattern,Total,plus(Count,1)).
number(Pattern,Total,Count) =>
        [_], number(Pattern,Total,Count).
```

Here `Total` is unified with the number of occurrences of `Pattern` in a stream that is matched with the pattern `number(Pattern,Total)`, and `[end_of_file]` is a special terminal symbol that delimits the end of stream. We assume `plus(X,1)` that yields the value of `X+1` when simplified.

From the example above it is clear that the grammar rules have a functional flavor. Stream operators are easily expressed using recursive functional programs. In addition, `number` is *higher-order* because it takes an arbitrary pattern as an argument. The definitions for `+`, `*`, `;`, `,`, etc., above are also higher-order in that they have rules like

```
(X+) => X.
```

which rewrite terms to their arguments.

Example 2.2 : Coroutined Pattern Matching

Suppose we wish to count the occurrences of `[c]` as well as of `([a]+,[b])`. That is, we want to count the occurrences of multiple patterns in a stream. We use the pattern

```
number(([a]+,[b]),N1) // number([c],N2)
```

where we include the following grammar for `//`:

```
([X|Xs] // [X|Ys]) => [X|Xs//Ys].
([] // []) => [].
```

The operator `//` takes two patterns as arguments, narrows them to `[X|Xs]` and `[X|Ys]` respectively, and then yields `[X|Xs//Ys]`. Thus `//` is a pattern matching primitive that requires both argument patterns to generate or accept streams of the same length. This example shows that multiple patterns in a stream can be simultaneously generated or accepted (i.e., coroutined) easily with `//`.

Example 2.3 : Non-Context Free Languages

Consider the following grammar†:

```
s_abc => ab_c // a_bc.
ab_c => xy(a,b), [c]*.
a_bc => [a]*, xy(b,c).
xy(X,Y) => [].
xy(X,Y) => [X], xy(X,Y), [Y].
```

This grammar defines the non-context-free language $\{a^n b^n c^n \mid n \geq 0\}$ using only context-free-like constructions. The first rule for `s_abc` imposes simultaneous (parallel) constraints on streams generated by the grammar.

3. Compilation of Narrowing Grammar to Prolog

We describe an algorithm to compile narrowing grammars to Prolog programs. It turns out that SLD-resolution with left-to-right goal selection, the proof procedure commonly used in Prolog, will implement *NU-narrowing* on these programs. The compilation of a narrowing grammar rule into a Prolog clause combines information about the rule and the control of NU-narrowing when interpreting that rule. One interesting aspect of the compilation algorithm is its use of a suitable 'equality' predicate `equal(X,Y)`, which succeeds when `X` can be narrowed to `Y`.

---

† Fernando Pereira suggested this example.

Algorithm 3.1 : Compilation of Narrowing Grammar to Prolog

(1) For each n-ary constructor symbol c, $n \geq 0$, and for distinct Prolog variables $X_1, \ldots X_n$, generate the clause:

```
simplify( c (X₁,...,Xₙ), c (X₁,...,Xₙ) ).
```

(2) For each rule $f(L_1, \ldots, L_m) \Rightarrow RHS$, let $A_1, \ldots, A_m$, `Out` be distinct Prolog variables not occurring in the rule, and generate the clause:

```
simplify(f (A₁,...,Aₘ),Out)  :-
                        equal(A₁,L₁),
                        ...,
                        equal(Aₘ,Lₘ),
                        simplify(RHS,Out).
```

Algorithm 3.1 does not deal with 'impure' features in narrowing grammar rules, such as cuts. However, it is not difficult to extend the compilation to include such features.

Definition 3.1 : `equal(X,Y)`

```
equal(X,Y)  :- nu_narrow(X,Y).

nu_narrow(X,X)  :- !.
nu_narrow(X,Y)  :- simplify(X,Z),
                   nu_narrow_subterms(Z,Y).

nu_narrow_subterms(X,Y)  :-
                    functor(X,F,N),  functor(Y,F,N),
                    nu_narrow_subterms(X,Y,0,N).

nu_narrow_subterms(_,_,N,N).
nu_narrow_subterms(X,Y,I,N)  :-
                plus(I,1,I1),  arg(I1,X,A),  arg(I1,Y,B),
                nu_narrow(A,B),
                nu_narrow_subterms(X,Y,I1,N).
```

The table below lists some narrowing grammar rules together with the Prolog clauses resulting from their compilation†.

---

† Although the code produced by the compiler is not efficient, it can be optimized considerably. For example, partial evaluation alone will cause many `equal/2` subgoals to be replaced by unifications or `simplify/2` subgoals.

Narrowing Grammar Rules	Prolog Clauses

`match([],S) => S.`	`simplify(match(A,B),C) :-`
	`    equal(A,[]),`
	`    equal(B,S),`
	`    simplify(S,C).`

`match([X|L],[X|S]) =>`
`    match(L,S).`
	`simplify(match(A,B),C) :-`
	`    equal(A,[X|L]),`
	`    equal(B,[X|S]),`
	`    simplify(match(L,S),C).`

`(X+) => X.`	`simplify((A+),B) :-`
	`    equal(A,X),`
	`    simplify(X,B).`

`(X+) => X, (X+).`	`simplify((A+),B) :-`
	`    equal(A,X),`
	`    simplify((X,(X+)),B).`

`([],L) => L.`	`simplify((A,B),C) :-`
	`    equal(A,[]),`
	`    equal(B,L),`
	`    simplify(L,C).`

`([X|L1],L2) =>`
`    [X|(L1,L2)].`
	`simplify((A,B),C) :-`
	`    equal(A,[X|L1]),`
	`    equal(B,L2),`
	`    simplify([X|(L1,L2)],C).`

It should be clear that `simplify/2` guarantees its result (the second argument) will be simplified. That is, the function symbol of the result will be a constructor. Also, we can show that `simplify/2` behaves *like* NU-narrowing. Consider a derivation from the goal `simplify(`$f(t_1,...,t_m)$`,Z)` which uses the Prolog clause

```
simplify(f (X_1,...,X_m),Out) :-
    equal(X_1,Y_1) ,..., equal(X_m,Y_m), simplify(RHS,Out).
```

resulting from $f(Y_1,...,Y_m) => RHS$. In left-to-right Prolog derivation with this clause, the `equal/2` subgoals are satisfied first, each effecting either a unification (first clause of `nu_narrow/2`) or a recursive simplification (second clause of `nu_narrow/2`). These are followed by a derivation from the subgoal `simplify(`RHS`,Out)`, which also recursively effects a simplification of RHS. Concatenating these simplifications, we find that `simplify/2` effects a *simplification*. More formally:

Theorem 3.1: If X and Y are terms such that `simplify`(X,Y) succeeds, then `simplification`(X,Y) has a successful left-to-right SLD-derivation.

Proof :

We sketch a proof by induction on the length of a successful Prolog-derivation of `simplify`(X,Y). Because of the structure of the clauses for `simplify/2`, there must be a goal in this derivation that is an instance of `simplify`(Z,Y) for some term Z not equal to X. Since we know `simplify`(Z,Y) succeeds, then by the induction hypothesis, `simplification`(Z,Y) has a successful derivation. Now, we can show that each of the `equal/2` subgoals introduced in the derivation leads either to a unification or a derivation from a `simplify/2` subgoal, and these inductively give NU-narrowings. Since the composition of these NU-narrowings of arguments is a NU-narrowing, we can prove inductively that `nu_narrowing`(X,Z) has a successful derivation. Combining this with the result above about `simplification`(Z,Y), we find that `simplification`(X,Y) has a successful left-to-right SLD-derivation.

The converse of the theorem is true *if* we replace Prolog-derivation by left-to-right SLD-derivation, and we restrict the use of duplicate variables among arguments on the left hand sides of narrowing grammar rules in certain ways beyond the restrictions in Definition 2.2. One restriction is to require that only terms in normal form be passed to these arguments. This subject is studied in more detail in [4].

4. What is New about Narrowing Grammar

In this section we summarize several important features of narrowing grammar. Some of these features are novel in the context of grammar formalisms, while others are not. The combination of these features is certainly new and interesting, in any event.

4.1. New Model of Acceptance in Logic Grammar

Previously, we have described how grammar rules operate as pattern generators or specifiers. In this section, we show that they can also operate as acceptors. Our approach for pattern acceptance is to introduce a new pair of narrowing grammar rules specifying pattern matching. The entire definition is the following pair of rules for `match`:

```
match([],S) => S.
match([X|L],[X|S]) => match(L,S).
```

`match` can take a pattern as its first argument, and an input stream as its second argument. If the pattern narrows to the empty list `[]`, `match` simply succeeds. On the other hand, if the pattern narrows to `[X|L]`, then the second argument to `match` must also narrow to `[X|S]`. Intuitively, `match` can be thought of as *applying* a pattern (the first argument) to an input stream (the second argument), in an attempt to find a prefix of the stream that the grammar defining the pattern can generate.

Pattern acceptance is requested explicitly with `match`. As a simple example, consider the following derivation illustrating how `match` works:

```
match(([a]+,[b]), [a,a,b])
      →  match((([a],[a]+),[b]), [a,a,b])
      →  match(([a|([],[a]+)],[b]), [a,a,b])
      →  match([a|((([],[a]+),[b])], [a,a,b])
      →  match(((([],[a]+),[b]), [a,b])
      →  match(([a]+,[b]), [a,b])
      →  match(([a],[b]), [a,b])
      →  match([a|(([],[b])], [a,b])
      →  match((([],[b]), [b])
      →  match([b], [b])
      →  match([], [])
      →  []
```

There is a certain elegance to this; the rules of the grammar by themselves act as pattern generators, but when applied with `match` they act like an acceptor, or parser. This acceptance/generation duality is familiar to users of Definite Clause Grammar [16], and the ability to employ grammars both as acceptors and as generators has a number of uses [8].

4.2. Higher-order Specification, Extensibility, and Modularity

Narrowing grammar is higher-order. Specifically, narrowing grammar is higher order in the sense that patterns can be passed as input arguments to patterns, and patterns can yield patterns as outputs.

For example, the enumeration pattern `number(_,_)` defined in example 2.1 is higher-order, as its first argument is a pattern. The whole pattern `([a]+,[b])` can be used as an argument, as in:

```
number( ([a]+,[b]), Total ).
```

It is well known that a higher-order capability increases expressiveness of a language, since it makes it possible to develop generic functions that can be combined in a multitude of ways [7]. As a consequence, narrowing grammar rules are highly reusable and can be usefully collected in a library. In short, narrowing grammar is modular. Narrowing grammar is also extensible, since it permits definition of new grammatical constructs, as the `number` and `//` examples showed earlier.

4.3. Lazy Evaluation, Stream Processing, and Coroutining

Leftmost outermost reduction is also called normal-order reduction, and sometimes *lazy evaluation*. This name comes from the basic observation that outside-in evaluation of an expression tends to evaluate arguments of function symbols only on demand – i.e., only when the argument values are needed. That is, outside-in evaluation is 'lazy'.

Narain showed that compilation like that in section 3 is a technique for implementing lazy evaluation [13, 14]. Thus narrowing grammar rules are compiled to Prolog clauses in such a way that, when SLD-resolution with left-to-right goal selection interprets them, it directly simulates leftmost outermost narrowing, or lazy evaluation.

Lazy evaluation is intimately related with a programming paradigm referred to as *stream processing* [15]. Note that in this paper, a stream pattern is a term that will yield a list of ground terms under lazy evaluation. We are not aware of previous work connecting stream processing and grammars, although the connection is a natural one. Lazy evaluation and stream processing also have intimate connections with *coroutining* [9]. Coroutining is the interleaving of evaluation (here, narrowing) of two expressions. It is applicable frequently in stream processing. For example, narrowing of the stream pattern

```
([a]+, [b])
```

interleaves the narrowing of `[a]+` with the narrowing of `(_, [b])`. The sample narrowing of this pattern in section 1 shows the actual interleaving – first `[a]+` is narrowed for two steps, then `(_, [b])` for one step, then `[a]+` for two steps, and finally `(_, [b])` for two steps. The effect of leftmost outermost narrowing of the combined stream pattern is precisely to interleave these two narrowings.

A specific advantage of lazy evaluation in parsing, then, is that coroutined recognition of multiple patterns in a stream becomes accessible to the grammar writer. The coroutining rules

```
([X|Xs] // [X|Ys]) => [X|Xs//Ys].
([] // []) => [].
```

make explicitly coroutined pattern matching possible. Essentially `//` narrows each of its arguments, obtaining respectively `[X|Xs]` and `[X|Ys]`.

Having obtained simplified terms, it suspends narrowing of **Xs** and **Ys** until further evaluation is necessary. An immediate advantage of lazy evaluation here is reduced computation. Without lazy evaluation, both arguments would be completely simplified before pattern matching took place; failure to unify the heads of these completely evaluated arguments would then mean that many unnecessary narrowing steps on the tails of the arguments had been performed.

5. Comparison with Definite Clause Grammar

In this section we compare narrowing grammar with Definite Clause Grammar (DCG), a widely-used formalism of logic grammar. We show how pure DCG can be translated into narrowing grammar and how narrowing grammar and DCG differ. We also point out some limitations of first-order logic grammars.

5.1. Narrowing Grammar and Definite Clause Grammar

All pure narrowing grammar rules can be ultimately translated to pure Prolog clauses. As a consequence, the benefits DCG offers over things like Augmented Transition Networks listed in [16] are also enjoyed by narrowing grammar.

We show how a DCG rule can be translated into a narrowing grammar rule describing the same language.

How to Translate Definite Clause Grammar to Narrowing Grammar

(1) Essentially, DCG rules can be translated to narrowing grammar rules by changing all occurrences of `-->` to `=>` and by including the narrowing grammar definition for `','` as in section 2.2.

```
([],L) => L.
([X|L1],L2) => [X|(L1,L2)].
```

(2) Disjunction (`';'`) in DCG has the same semantics as in narrowing grammar but the latter can be defined at the grammatical level:

```
(X;Y) => X.
(X;Y) => Y.
```

(3) *Metamorphosis grammar* [5] permits rules of the form

```
LHS, T --> RHS
```

where *LHS* is a nonterminal and *T* is one or more terminals. We can capture the semantics of this rule in narrowing grammar by defining a constructor `replace(X,Y)` and one more rule for `match` as follows:

```
match([replace(X,Y)|L],S) => match(L,(Y,match(X,S))).
```

and transform the metamorphosis grammar rule to

```
LHS => [replace(RHS,T)].
```

Note, however, that with narrowing grammar T can be *any* pattern, not just a stream of terminals.

Example 5.1

Consider the following MG and NG rules which accept all strings of `[a]`'s and `[b]`'s which have an equal number of `[a]`'s and `[b]`'s.

```
ns --> [].                       ns => [].
ns --> na, ns, nb.               ns => na, ns, nb.
na --> [a].                      na => [a].
na,[term(nb)] --> nb, na.        na => [replace((nb,na),nb)].
nb --> [b].                      nb => [b].
nb --> [term(nb)].
```

The `[term(nb)]` 'terminal' permits the MG to treat the nonterminal `nb` temporarily as a terminal. Note that this artifice is not needed with NG.

A derivation showing how `match` works with the constructor symbol `[replace(_,_)]` is shown:

```
match(ns, [b,a])
        → match((na,ns,nb), [b,a])
        → match(([replace((nb,na),nb)],ns,nb), [b,a])
        → match((ns,nb), (nb,match((nb,na), [b,a])))
        → match(([],nb), (nb,match((nb,na), [b,a])))
        → match(nb, (nb,match((nb,na), [b,a])))
        → match([b], (nb,match((nb,na), [b,a])))
        → match([b], ([b],match((nb,na), [b,a])))
        → match([b], [b|match((nb,na), [b,a])])
        → match([], match((nb,na), [b,a]))
        → match((nb,na), [b,a])
        → match(([b],na), [b,a])
        → match([b|([],na)], [b,a])
        → match(([],na), [a])
        → match(na, [a])
        → match([a], [a])
        → match([], [])
        → []
```

5.2. Limitations of First-order Logic Grammars

The usual method for compiling DCG to Prolog does not permit direct specification of grammar rules of the form:

```
goal(X) --> ...,X,...
```

where x is a variable. Therefore, it is hard to write DCG rules that behave like `number` given earlier. This is a basic limitation of first-order logic grammars.

Abramson [2] has addressed this limitation by introducing a meta-nonterminal symbol, written *meta(X),* where X may be instantiated to any terminal or nonterminal symbol. During parsing, an X is to be recognized at the point where *meta(X)* is used in a grammar rule. Abramson suggested two ways to implement *meta(X).* The first method makes an interpretive metacall wherever *meta(X)* is used. (This is a special case of the approach used by the `phrase/3` metapredicate in Quintus and Sicstus Prolog.) The other approach is to preprocess the rules containing *meta(X)* so as to generate a new set of rules with no calls to *meta(X).* However, this preprocessing can generate extra nonterminals and rules.

The same problem was pointed out in [12], where Moss proposed a special translation technique by using a single predicate name for nonterminals. For instance, Moss translates the DCG rule

```
goal(X) --> X
```

to the Prolog clause

```
nonterminal(goal(X),S0,S) :- nonterminal(X,S0,S).
```

There is one final limitation. Even with the techniques suggested by Abramson and Moss, the lazy evaluation or coroutining aspects of narrowing grammar are not easily attained with first-order logic grammars. To attain them, a new evaluation strategy is needed for these grammars, implemented via either a meta-interpreter or a compiler like that in section 3.

6. Discussion and Conclusion

In this paper, we have shown how narrowing grammar, together with `match,` comprises a new formalism for language analysis. Narrowing grammar combines concepts from logic programming, rewriting, lazy evaluation, and logic grammar formalisms such as DCG. All narrowing grammar rules can be compiled to Prolog clauses in such a way that, when SLD-resolution with left-to-right goal selection interprets them, it directly simulates a kind of leftmost outermost narrowing called NU-narrowing.

Both narrowing grammar and DCG have a theoretical foundation in first-order logic. Since DCG can be translated directly to narrowing grammar, the benefits DCG offers over things like Augmented Transition Networks listed in [16] are enjoyed by narrowing grammar. Although we have shown how a pure DCG rule can be translated to a narrowing grammar rule, translation the other way is not trivial. We have also illustrated by examples that some problems are difficult to express with DCG but are very easy to express with narrowing grammar. 'Coroutined' matching of patterns is among these.

Narrowing grammar is modular, extensible and highly reusable, so saving rules in a library makes sense. These grammars extend the expressive power of first-order logic grammars, by permitting patterns to be passed as arguments to the grammar rules. As a consequence, some complex patterns can be specified more easily.

The main issue of implementation here that we have not addressed is *efficiency*. An interesting open problem is to devise improvements for the (relatively inefficient) implementation given in this paper. Efficient implementations are possible in many cases. For example, when we know we will use `match`, the definition

```
pattern => ([a]+, [b]).
```

can be replaced by

```
match(pattern,S) => t1(S).
t1([a|S]) => t2(S).
t2([a|S]) => t2(S).
t2(S) => t3(S).
t3([b|S]) => S.
```

More work on the issue of efficiency appears in [4].

Beyond standard applications of grammar, narrowing grammar has potential in new areas including specification, analysis, and verification of concurrent systems. It can be used in 'history-oriented' or 'object-oriented' specification of concurrent systems. In [3] we demonstrate this in more detail. Given a set of actors (automata, concurrent objects, etc.) $A_1,...,A_n$ we can produce narrowing grammars with starting patterns $S_1,...,S_n$ for these, and then use $S_1//...//S_n$ as a specification of valid histories for the entire system. To our knowledge, this aspect of narrowing grammar is unique.

Acknowledgement

Many people have contributed to the ideas in this paper, but we particularly would like to acknowledge the remarks of Paul Eggert, Sanjai Narain, Fernando Pereira, and the referees.

References

1. Abramson, H., "Definite Clause Translation Grammars," *Proc. First Logic Programming Symposium*, pp. 233-240, IEEE Computer Society, Atlantic City, 1984.

2. Abramson, H., "Metarules and an Approach to Conjunction in Definite Clause Translation Grammars: Some Aspects of Grammatical Metaprogramming," *Proc. Fifth International Conference and Symposium on Logic Programming*, pp. 233-248, MIT Press, 1988.

3. Chau, H.L. and D.S. Parker, "Executable Temporal Specifications with Functional Grammars," Technical Report CSD-880046, UCLA Computer Science Dept., Los Angeles, CA 90024-1596, June 1988.

4. Chau, H.L., "Narrowing Grammar: A New Scheme for Language Analysis," Ph.D. Dissertation, UCLA Computer Science Dept., Los Angeles, CA 90024-1596, 1989, forthcoming.

5. Colmerauer, A., "Metamorphosis Grammars," in *Natural Language Communication with Computers, LNCS 63*, Springer, 1978.

6. Dahl, V. and H. Abramson, "On Gapping Grammars," *Proc. Second Intl. Conf. on Logic Programming*, pp. 77-88, Uppsala, Sweden, 1984.

7. Darlington, J., A.J. Field, and H. Pull, "The Unification of Functional and Logic Languages," *Logic Programming: Functions, Relations, and Equations*, Prentice-Hall, 1986.

8. Gorlick, M.D., C. Kesselman, D. Marotta, and D.S. Parker, "Mockingbird: A Logical Methodology for Testing," Technical Report, The Aerospace Corporation, P.O. Box 92957, Los Angeles, CA 90009-2957, May 1987. To appear, *Journal of Logic Programming*, 1989.

9. Henderson, P., *Functional Programming: Application and Implementation,* Prentice/Hall International, 1980.

10. Hirschman, L. and K. Puder, "Restriction Grammar: A Prolog Implementation ," *Logic Programming and its Applications*, 1985.

11. McCord, M.C., "Modular Logic Grammars," *Proc. 23rd Annual Meeting of the Association for Computational Linguistics*, pp. 104-117, Chicago, 1985.

12. Moss, C.D.S., "The Formal Description of Programming Languages using Predicate Logic," Ph.D. Dissertation, Imperial College, London, 1981.

13. Narain, S., "A Technique for Doing Lazy Evaluation in Logic," *J. Logic Programming*, vol. 3, no. 3, pp. 259-276, October 1986.

14. Narain, S., "LOG(F): An Optimal Combination of Logic Programming, Rewrite Rules and Lazy Evaluation," Ph.D. Dissertation, UCLA Computer Science Dept., Los Angeles, CA 90024-1596, 1988.

15. Parker, D.S., "Stream Data Analysis in Prolog," Technical Report CSD-890004, UCLA Computer Science Dept., Los Angeles, CA 90024-1596, January 1989.

16. Pereira, F.C.N. and D.H.D. Warren, "Definite Clause Grammars for Language Analysis," *Artificial Intelligence*, vol. 13, pp. 231-278, 1980.

17. Pereira, F.C.N., "Extraposition Grammars," *American Journal for Computational Linguistics*, vol. 7, 1981.

18. Pereira, F.C.N. and S.M. Shieber, *Prolog and Natural-Language Analysis,* CSLI Stanford, 1987.

19. Stabler, E.P., "Restricting Logic Grammars with Government-Binding Theory," *Computational Linguistics*, vol. 13, no. 1-2, 1987.

20. Sterling, L. and E. Shapiro, *The Art of Prolog,* MIT Press, Cambridge, MA, 1986.

A Metalogic Programming Language

Stefania Costantini
Gaetano Aurelio Lanzarone

Universita' degli Studi di Milano,
Dipartimento di Scienze dell' Informazione
Via Moretto da Brescia 9, I-20133, Milano, Italy
Tel. +39-2-2772.222, Telex 335199 MI DSI I,
e-mail: logic@imisiam.bitnet

Abstract

A language called Reflective Prolog is presented, aimed at moving a step forward in the declarative representation of metaknowledge within the logic programming approach. Reflective Prolog is a metalogic programming and knowledge representation language which allows the definition of object-level and metalevel sentences, both expressed in Horn clauses extended with self-reference and metaevaluation capabilities. Namely, language entities can be described in the language itself, in order to represent metaknowledge, and a meta-evaluation level can be defined in a program, in order to express auxiliary deduction rules. Metasentences are processed by the language interpreter via an extended resolution procedure, with an efficiency comparable in principle to that of a Prolog interpreter. After stating the main objectives of the work and the relationship with the literature, the syntax and the procedural semantics of the language are described; how the model-theoretic semantics has been defined is also mentioned. An example is then discussed in order to illustrate the capabilities of Reflective Prolog. Since the interpreter of the language has been implemented, the architecture of the implementation, based on reflection mechanisms, is outlined. Directions of further reasearch are sketched in the conclusions.

Introduction

The importance of metaprogramming and metaknowledge representation is well known in the Logic Programming and in the Artificial Intelligence areas (see for instance [1]). The Logic Programming community has recognized and practically exploited (especially with the technique of metainterpreters) Prolog's features in this direction since its very beginning, and is in search of a systematization for a logic metaprogramming language since the seminal work of [3].

The present situation seems to be the following [17]. On the one hand, the implemented languages, like Metalog, lack a semantic definition, though a first attempt has been made very recently [23]. On the other hand, work is in progress to rationalize the metalogic features of Prolog and to give a precise meaning to metaprograms [11], in view of the definition of a suitable language.

In this paper we present a metalogic programming language which we have both syntactically and semantically defined [7], and fully implemented in a working prototype [2]. The objectives of our work, and the assumptions on which we have based our approach, are the following.

[1] The main objective is to improve the declarative expressive power of a logic programming language. We also agree with Gallaire's claim [9] that in order to gain ground in the real world, the logic programming approach has to provide more effective languages and tools. We believe that this is necessary especially for sophisticated applications like those in the Artificial Intelligence area, which is still dominated by Lisp and other formalisms. Some applications of the problem−solving capabilities of the language we are proposing have been shown in [5].

[2] It is advisable to maintain the language characteristics within computationally tractable bounds, amenable in principle to efficient implementations. We stayed within a first−order, Horn−clause, resolution−based language.

[3] It is important to achieve the added power of the language not at the expense of its logic basis. We gave up altogether the 'impure' metalogic predicates of Prolog and defined differently the metastructural features of the language [4]. Specifically, the language has been equipped with self−reference capabilities based on a full naming mechanism, similar to those of [19], and with a multilevel structure. The latter consists of a base (object and meta) execution level and a metaevaluation level; switching between levels is taken care of by an extended resolution algorithm, and has Feferman's logic reflection principles [8] as the semantic counterpart.

[4] The realization of the language should not simply be an implementation exercise, instrumental in obtaining the interpreter, but has to be based on a suitable computational architecture. We identified procedural reflection [21], [10] as the simple and powerful technique best fitting the deductive apparatus of the language.

1. The Language

Syntax and semantics of Reflective Prolog are fully defined in [7]; they are described here only by mentioning the main differences with respect to the usual definitions of definite programs [15].

The language defined by a Reflective Prolog program P consists of all the well-formed formulae in Horn-clausal form obtained from the alphabet of P. The main difference in the alphabet with respect to traditional Horn-clause languages is the presence of *metavariables* and *name constants*. Each metavariable is either a *function* metavariable (written with first character '$') or a *predicate* metavariable (written with first character '#'). Each name constant is either a *quoted* name constant (written enclosed in quotation marks) or a *bracketed* name constant (written enclosed in angle brackets). The alphabet contains the distinguished function symbols predication, predicate, function, functor, arity, args, and the distinguished unary predicates solve, theory_solve and theory_fact.

The definition of terms is extended to deal with self-reference: variables can be either object variables or metavariables, and there is a new class of terms, *name terms*, that are defined inductively as follows.

○ *Name constants* (either quoted or bracketed), described above.

○ *Function name terms*, which are of the form function(functor(ϕ), arity(I), args(α_1, ..., α_n)), where ϕ is a quoted name constant, I is a non-negative integer number and (α_1, ..., α_n) are name terms. The following abbreviations are available:

  – "$\phi(\alpha_1$, ..., $\alpha_n)$", where quotation is shifted from inside to outside the term and arity is omitted; e.g., "f(a)" is shortened for function(functor("f"), arity(1), args("a")).

  – "ϕ"(α_1, ..., α_n), "f"("a") for the above example, where arguments are extracted and arity omitted.

○ *Relation name terms,* which are of the form predication(predicate(ρ), arity(l), args(τ_1, ..., τ_n)), where ρ is a bracketed name constant, I is a non−negative integer number and (τ_1, ..., τ_n) are name terms. Abbreviations similar to those for function name terms are allowed, that is "ρ(τ_1, ..., τ_n)" (e.g., predication(predicate(<p>), arity(1), args("a")) can be shortened as "p(a)") as well as <ρ>(τ_1, ..., τ_n) (<p>("a")).

Name terms realize the ground representation of Reflective Prolog terms and atoms in the language itself: the definitions above introduce quoted name constants to denote constants, variables and function symbols (e.g. "c", "V", "fun"); brackteted name constants to denote predicate symbols (e.g. <pred>); function and relation name terms to denote terms and atoms respectively (e.g. "fun"("c","V") and <pred>("c","V"), which are sintactically equivalent to "fun(c,V)", "pred(c,V)").

Name terms are internally represented in the language interpreter in the form <ρ>(τ_1, ..., τ_n), because subterms are directly accessible, allowing easy inspection and composition/decomposition of metalevel terms (with no need of either run−time parsing or complex term manipulation, that a less expressive representation would require). Conversion among the different available forms is taken care by the language parser at program−consultation time.

Terms and atoms can be seen as divided into *metalevel terms (atoms)*, containing name terms and/or metavariables as subterms, and *object−level terms (atoms)*.

The notion of Reflective Prolog *definite clause* includes some syntactic restrictions. First, levels are distinct: if the conclusion of a clause is an object−level atom, the conditions must be object−level atoms as well and, conversely, if the conclusion is a metalevel atom, the conditions must be metalevel atoms. Moreover, being the language based on clear distinction between use and mention, a syntactic prevention against auto−mention is provided: atoms such as p(<p>), containing a reference to their own head predicate among the arguments, are not allowed.

A Reflective Prolog definite program is divided into a *metaevaluation level*, consisting of the clauses defining the distinguished predicate solve and its auxiliary predicates, and a *base level*, consisting of the remaining metalevel clauses and all the object−level clauses. Precisely, a predicate p belongs to the metaevaluation level if:

(i) its definition makes use of at least one of the distinguished predicates solve, theory_solve, theory_fact;

(ii) it is directly or indirectly used in the definition of solve; that is, it
either appears in the body of a solve clause, or it is directly or
indirectly used in the definition of some predicate q that appears in
the body of a solve clause.

The distinguished predicates can only be used in clauses at the
metaevaluation level, and cannot be nested, not even one within the
other. Metaevaluation predicates cannot be used at the base level.
Conversely, base-level predicates can be used at the metaevaluation
level, provided that the above-mentioned syntactic restrictions are
respected. All syntactic restrictions are verified at program-consulta-
tion time.

The unification algorithm is extended to deal with metavariables and
metalevel terms. Namely, rules for substitution are:

[1] any object-level variable V can be substituted by an object-level
term t distinct from V;

[2] any predicate metavariable #V can be substituted by a bracketed
name constant <t>;

[3] any function metavariable $V can be substituted by a metalevel
term t distinct from $V.

The extended unification algorithm has been proved to terminate
finitely, giving either an mgu for the expressions to be unified, or
reporting that they are not unifiable [7]. Relying on a flexible
representation of metalevel terms, extended unification can be easily
implemented as a straight extension of object-level unification, with
still linear complexity and only a slight overhead for the above-
specified "type-checking" in variable substitution.

Derivation by resolution is extended to state the role of base (object-
or meta-) level clauses as well as metaevaluation clauses in a proof.
Forms of reflection are introduced to shift from the base level to the
metaevaluation level and vice versa. The definition is the following,
where the notation ↑A is adopted, to indicate the relation name term
denoting the atom A (for instance, ↑p(a) stands for <p>("a")).

Definition. (Reflective SLD–Resolution, or RSLD–Resolution)

Let G be a definite goal $\leftarrow A_1,\ldots,A_m,\ldots,A_k$ and C a clause. If A_m is the selected atom in G, then G' is derived from G and C using mgu θ iff one of the following conditions holds:

(i)   C is $A \leftarrow B_1,\ldots,B_q$

      θ is an mgu of A_m and A

      G' is the goal $\leftarrow (A_1,\ldots,A_{m-1},B_1,\ldots,B_q,A_{m+1},\ldots,A_k)\theta$

(ii)   C is $solve(\alpha) \leftarrow S_1,\ldots,S_w$,

      $A_m \neq solve(\delta) \wedge A_m \neq theory\_solve(\delta) \wedge A_m \neq theory\_fact(\delta)$

      θ is an mgu of $\uparrow A_m$ and α

      G' is the goal $\leftarrow (A_1,\ldots,A_{m-1},S_1,\ldots,S_w,A_{m+1},\ldots,A_k)\theta$

(iii) A_m is $solve(M)$

      C is $A \leftarrow B_1,\ldots,B_q$

      θ is an mgu of M and $\uparrow A$

      G' is the goal $\leftarrow (A_1,\ldots,A_{m-1},B_1,\ldots,B_q,A_{m+1},\ldots,A_k)\theta$

(iv) A_m is $theory\_solve(M)$

      C is $A \leftarrow B_1,\ldots,B_q$

      θ is an mgu of M and $\uparrow A$

      G' is the goal $\leftarrow (A_1,\ldots,A_{m-1},B_1,\ldots,B_q,A_{m+1},\ldots,A_k)\theta$

(v) A_m is $theory\_fact(M)$

      C is $A \leftarrow$

      θ is an mgu of M and $\uparrow A$

      G' is the goal $\leftarrow (A_1,\ldots,A_{m-1},A_{m+1},\ldots,A_k)\theta$

To explain, the definition considers the following different possibilities about the selected goal A_m.

[1] $A_m \neq solve(\delta)$, $theory\_solve(\delta)$, $theory\_fact(\delta)$. The goal A_m can be proved in two ways. First, (similar to classical SLD–Resolution) using the clauses defining the corresponding predicate (case (i)): for instance, if $A_m = p(a,b)$, the clauses defining the predicate p, whose head unifies with p(a,b). Second, the clauses defining the solve predicate, whose head argument unifies with $\uparrow A_m$, can be used (case (ii), *upward reflection*): in the above example, clauses with head solve(<p>("a","b")), or solve(<p>($X,$Y)) or solve(#P("a",$K)), and so on.

[2] $A_m = solve(\delta)$. Again, there are two choices. First, using the clauses defining the predicate solve itself, similarly to any other goal (case(i)). Second, using the clauses defining the predicate corresponding to the atom denoted by the argument δ of solve (case (iii), *downward reflection*): for instance, if $A_m = solve(<q>("X","b"))$, the clauses defining the predicate q, whose

224

head unifies with q(X, b). That is, each goal generated at the metaevaluation level can be tried at the metaevaluation level, as well as at the base level.

[3] A_m = theory_solve(δ). The clauses defining the predicate corresponding to the atom denoted by δ can be used (case(iv), *downward reflection*): if for instance A_m = theory_solve(<h>("k")), the clauses defining the predicate h, whose head unifies with h(k). That corresponds to proving at the base level the (dereferenced) argument of theory_solve.

[4] A_m = theory_fact(δ). A fact is searched at the base level that matches the (dereferenced) argument of theory_fact. For instance, theory_fact(#P("a")) matches the representation <h>("a") of a fact h(a), instantiating #P to <h>.

The resolution procedure implemented in the Reflective Prolog interpreter follows a generalized depth–first strategy, where cases (i) and (iii) have higher priority than (ii): each goal is first attempted at the base level and then at the metaevaluation level. It is worth noting that, given a selected atom A_m in a definite goal G, the new selected atom A_m' in the new goal G' obtained as described above is treated in the same way: that is, an *RSLD–Refutation* is in general obtained by an interleaving between base level and metaevaluation level.

The following is a simple example of a Reflective Prolog program.

```
/* metaevaluation level */
    solve(#P($X,$Y)):-symmetric(#P),theory_solve(#P($Y,$X)).
/* base level */
    /* metalevel */
    symmetric(<friend>).
    /* object-level */
    friend(giorgio,mary).
    friend(lucia,albert).
```

The solve rule defines symmetry: (the objects denoted by) $X and $Y are in the relation (denoted by) #P in the theory, provided that the theory contains the assertions of #P being symmetric and it can be proved that $Y and $X are in #P.

Queries can concern both object–level and metalevel predicates. For instance, the query ?–symmetric(#P) instantiates #P to <friend>; the query ?–friend(albert,lucia) fails at the base level, causing the application of the solve rule, which first proves symmetric(<friend>) and then attempts theory_solve(<friend>("lucia","albert")), determining a shift–down to friend(lucia,albert) that succeeds.

This formulation avoids the problem of circular application of symmetry when expressed at the object–level, since the call to theory_solve results in directly proving its argument at the base level; in addition, exclusion of the metaevaluation rule when it is no longer needed significantly improves efficiency.

At this point, a comparison with other approaches is in order.

The distinguished predicate solve is not an axiomatization of provability, but expresses only what is beyond the normal behaviour. The distinguished predicate theory_solve stands for provability in the theory, but it is engendered by the interpreter rather than explicitly defined: it is a way for a theory to refer implicitly to its own inference mechanism.

Reflective Prolog is not an amalgamated language in the sense of [3]: the provability relation is not explicitly expressed in the language, and it is not the case that no theorem is provable that cannot be proved either in the language or in the metalanguage. The different levels are distinct, but procedurally and semantically integrated. The flexibility and power of their interaction through the extended resolution makes new theorems provable, which cannot be proved in the base–level or in the metaevaluation level only.

The metaevaluation level of Reflective Prolog is basically different from a Prolog metainterpreter, for the following reasons. First, base–level resolution need not be reproduced at the metaevaluation level, with the consequent gain in efficiency and conciseness. Second, different metaevaluation rules can be easily integrated, relying on the fact that each goal is metaevaluated when needed. On the contrary, with a Prolog metainterpreter it is necessary to explicitly state which goals are to be metaevaluated and which ones can be directly evaluated: possible uses of metaknowledge in a proof must therefore be identified in advance. Third, since base clauses and metaevaluation clauses are treated in the same way by the interpreter, there is no run–time overhead related to upward and downward reflection (other than referencing–dereferencing a goal). Fourth, the interpreter performs run–time checks to prevent auto–reference, forcing immediate failure of calls, such as p(<p>), that could be attempted via backtracking on the solve rules, leading to infinite loops; solving the same problem in Prolog metainterpreters is not at all straightforward.

To summarize, Reflective Prolog provides an automathic ("when needed") form of reflection (considered an open problem in [16]). This overcomes the "non insignificant control problem" [3] of when to use reflection, that contrasts with the principle of expressing knowledge in declarative form and leaving the procedural aspects to the deductive apparatus of the language [13]. Augmenting resolution with implicit reflection leads to reintroduce a declarative attitude in the definition of metaknowledge, without sacrificing efficiency.

The declarative semantics of the language has been defined in a model–theoretic fashion: a least model semantics has been provided, based on the definition of a concept of *Least Reflective Herbrand Model* of a theory. Starting from a notion of Extended Herbrand Interpretation of a Reflective Prolog definite program P (introduced to deal with name terms and distinguished predicate symbols), a Reflective Herbrand Model for P is defined to be an Extended Herbrand Interpretation which is a model for the theory P' obtained by applying to P the first of the *Reflection Principles* introduced in [8]. The Least Reflective Herbrand Model has then been characterized (similarly to the classical Horn–clause language semantics [15]) as the fixpoint of a suitable mapping, in order to provide a link between the declarative and procedural semantics of a Reflective Prolog definite program.

2. An example

The declarative representation of the transitivity property of a binary relation in Prolog:

```
r(X,Y):-r(X,Z),r(Z,Y).
```

cannot be procedurally used without problems, since with the depth–first strategy the interpreter may undergo an infinite branch before examining success branches. The problem is the application of the recursive clause twice consecutively: it has to be interleaved with the application of different clauses (facts); using a flag for this purpose [18] is awkward. Although in some cases a transitive relation can be defined in terms of transitive closure of a subrelation, this is not feasible for every relation. Even for those relations that can be defined as closures, it is not always possible to represent all the intended connections. Given for example the clauses:

```
parent(a,b).
parent(c,d).
```

```
ancestor(b,c).
ancestor(X,Y):-parent(X,Y).
ancestor(X,Y):-parent(X,Z),ancestor(Z,Y).
```

the solutions (a,d) and (b,d) to the query ?- ancestor(X,Y) cannot be obtained unless the following clause is added to the database (determining repetitions in answers):

```
ancestor(X,Y):-parent(Z,Y),ancestor(X,Z).
```

But also in this case, adding the fact ancestor(c,e) the same query cannot obtain the answers (a,e) and (b,e).

The problem occurs not only with Prolog, but also with other representation and inference systems [20]. One solution to determine the couples belonging to a transitive (as well as symmetric and/or reflexive) relation, is that of representing the relation couples by means of composable sets (as in [20]), and defining a suitable metainterpreter which uses them to infer those couples not explicitly asserted [6].

A simpler solution, which is possible in Reflective Prolog, is the following.

```
/* metaevaluation level */
solve(<ancestor>($AL)):-fact(<ancestor>($AL)).                    [1]
solve(<ancestor>($X,$Y)):-fact(<ancestor>($X,$Z)),               [2]
                          solve(<ancestor>($Z,$Y)).

fact(<ancestor>($AL)):-theory_fact(<ancestor>($AL)).
fact(<ancestor>($AL)):-theory_fact(<parent>($AL)).

/* base level */
parent(a,b).
parent(c,d).
ancestor(b,c).
ancestor(c,e).
```

Rules [1] and [2] define transitivity of the relation ancestor in a way that prevents loops by forcing each transitive step to be performed on facts; the predicate fact gives the possibility of considering both ancestor and parent facts.

For instance, the query ?- ancestor(a,e) is proved by means of subsequent applications of rule [2] and a final application of rule [1], precisely in the following way.

○ On failure of the goal at the object level, the consequent shift–up leads to selection of rule ⒈ that fails because neither the fact ancestor(a,e) nor the fact parent(a,e) exist in the database. The extended unification algorithm provides a special feature for name terms, i.e. it is able to unify <ancestor>("a","e") and <ancestor>($AL) by binding $AL to ["a","e"].

○ Selection of rule ⒉ results in attempting
fact(<ancestor>("a",$Z)), solve(<ancestor>($Z,"e")).
The first subgoal succeeds via the second alternative of fact, that is
fact(<ancestor>("a",$Z)):–theory_fact(<parent>("a",$Z))
that instantiates $Z to "b".

○ Then solve(<ancestor>("b", "e")) is attempted, leading in a similar way to solve(<ancestor>("c","e")) that succeeds via rule ⒈ and the first alternative of fact, concluding the proof.

To further develop the example, it can be noted that a family has actually a tree structure, where ancestors are connected to descendants by paths (a *metaphor* can be stated between the two concepts, to follow the terminology of [12]). In fact, the definition of path–finding in a generic directed acyclic graph, shown below, is appearently analogous to ancestor determination.

```
solve(<path>($AL)):–fact(<path>($X,$Y)).                    ⒈
solve(<path>($X,$Y)):–fact(<path>($X,$Z)),
                      solve(<path>($Z, $Y)).                ⒉
fact(<path>($AL)):–theory_fact(<path>($AL)).
fact(<path>($AL)):–theory_fact(<arc>($AL)).
```

Hence, ancestor finding could also be obtained by adapting path finding, adding the following part:

```
solve(#P($AL)):–map(#P,#Q),solve(#Q($AL)).                  ⒊
solve(#P($X,$Y)):–symmetric(#P),
                  theory_solve(#P($Y,$X)).                  ⒋
map(<parent>,<arc>).
map(<ancestor>,<path>).
symmetric(<map>).
parent(a,b).
parent(c,d).
ancestor(b,c).
ancestor(c,e).
```

Suitable facts map family concepts into tree concepts (and vice versa, in that map is declared as symmetric), and metaevaluation rule [3] engenders the mapping. Rule [4] concerning symmetry is the same as in the previous section.

Notice that composition of different solve clauses is obtained simply by justaposition, while composition of metainterpreters needs elaborate techniques [22].

Rather than mapping one solution onto the other, a common general structure can be identified, expressed by the rules below.

```
solve(#P($AL)):-fact(#P($AL)).                          [1]
solve(#P($X,$Y)):-transitive(#P),fact(#P($X,$Z)),
                  solve(#P($Z,$Y)).                      [2]
fact(#P($AL)):-theory_fact(#P($AL)).
fact(#P($AL)):-subsumes(#P,#Q), theory_fact(#Q($AL)).
```

Rules [1] and [2] define in general the transitivity of a relation, relying on the explicit declaration of a predicate being transitive. fact takes subsumption (intended as set inclusion of relation extensions) into account in facts lookup, stating that if a predicate #P subsumes another predicate #Q, then #P($AL) (where $AL denotes the argument list) holds in the theory if #Q($AL) holds. It also relies on explicit declaration of subsumption.

Supposing that the above theory is available, for instance in a system library, ancestor determination as well as path-finding can be obtained by adding to that theory a suitable definition of the base level, containing the object facts plus metalevel declarations of transitivity (for ancestor and path respectively) and subsumption (of parent by ancestor and of arc by path). In the family case for instance, the base level to be added is the following.

```
subsumes(<ancestor>,<parent>).
transitive(<ancestor>).
parent(a,b).
parent(c,d).
ancestor(b,c).
ancestor(c,e).
```

In substance, the general theory of transitivity constitutes a metaphor for both families and directed acyclic graphs powerful enough not to require to be adapted, but only to be used. Put aside the problem of how to recognize such abstractions, in Reflective Prolog it is possible to express and make use of them.

The Reflective Prolog interpreter also has the ability to expand and include in the data base some consequences of the program during program consultation, guided by directives expressed as metasentences. In the example, a directive transitive_closure(#P) can be defined (and then called over <ancestor>), that expands the definition of its argument, adding to the database all the facts obtained as transitive closure from those already present. In this case, any subgoal concerning ancestor is solved in just one step. Trading off time against space is left to the user; in both cases, expressiveness and conciseness in theory definition are not affected.

3. The implementation

Reflective Prolog has been implemented on the basis of a Horn clause language with procedural reflection, formerly developed (in Quintus Prolog on the IBM 6150 workstation) in our Department.

The procedural reflection architecture allows program execution to develop (on demand) along an arbitrary number of levels; at each level, the deductive apparatus of the basic formalism (in this case Horn clauses) is fully available. Shifting by procedural reflection to the next upper level, a program can look at and/or modify its own computational state. The state is explicitly modeled as the representation of the database and the proof tree (the latter including the binding environment) "frozen" at the moment of the shift-up.

Procedural reflection is a too low-level concept for direct use in applications, but is useful as an implementation tool for more advanced formalisms. It has been used for several features, like inspection and modification of variable bindings, necessary for the implementation of basic primitives of Reflective Prolog, namely extended unification and referentiation/dereferentiation. Furthermore, control predicates (like 'cut', 'fail') have been realized by procedural reflection, via access to the control part of the model (proof tree). These predicates do not have a high-level counterpart in Reflective Prolog, being related to aspects that are not explicit in the language.

Prolog's metalogic predicates for term inspection/manipulation are of course unnecessary in Reflective Prolog since explicit representation of terms and atoms is available, only the syntactic identity '==' is retained, realized via unification as in Prolog.

A prototype of the Reflective Prolog interpreter is actually working

[2], and includes a parser of the language (realized with the DCG approach), for translating programs and goals into a suitable internal form.

4. Conclusive remarks

In this paper we have presented Reflective Prolog, a metalogic programming language. The main objective was to show how better expressiveness, flexibility and computational power can be achieved in the context of a Horn−clause, resolution−based language with a firm semantic ground: syntactically, by introducing self−reference capabilities; computationally, by integrating forms of reflection in derivation.

The possibility is being investigated of making some aspects of the inference process explicit, so as to allow high−level forms of control (thus eliminating the need of predefined predicates like 'cut', 'fail'). The difficult is not in technical feasibility, but in the identification of: (i) what aspects to make explicit, and how to cope with them semantically; (ii) in which form they should be represented in a program, so as to preserve conceptual clarity, and to allow easy manipulation.

One theoretical open problem concerns the introduction of negation, in a semantically sound way. Recent investigations suggest [14] that the availability of a distinguished predicate, like solve, standing for provability, could help safely introducing 'negation as failure' in the language.

Presently, Reflective Prolog has no construct for the representation and manipulation at the metalevel of object−level clauses. Work is under way to define constructs able to include in the language the representation and use of several theories. However, in our opinion a proper use of theories is mainly related to hypothetical reasoning or reasoning involving multiple agents; in fact we think that the Reflective Prolog multilevel structure overcomes in other cases the need of using theories that arises in formalisms lacking this structure.

We are also carrying on studies and experiments on applying Reflective Prolog to sophisticated problem solving and intelligent reasoning. For example, some forms of non−monotonic reasoning seem amenable to elegant representation, but more work is needed to present results.

Acknowledgements

This work has been partly supported by IBM Italia S.p.A in the context of a joint study with the Computer Science Department of the University of Milan, and partly by the Italian Ministry of Public Education.

References

[1] L. Aiello, G. Levi, *The Uses of Metaknowledge in AI systems*, in: P. Maes and D. Nardi (eds.), Meta–level Architectures and Reflection, North–Holland 1988, 243–254.

[2] R. Barki, G. Casaschi, S. Costantini, P. Dell'Acqua and G.A. Lanzarone, *The Implementation of Reflective Prolog*, Internal Report, University of Milano, Computer Science Department, 1989.

[3] K. A. Bowen, R. A. Kowalski, *Amalgamating Language and Metalanguage in Logic Programming*, in: K.L. Clark and S.–A. Tarnlund (eds.), *Logic Programming*, Academic Press, 1982, 153–172.

[4] S. Costantini, G. A. Lanzarone, *Towards Metalogic Programming*, in: Proceedings of *Computational Intelligence 88,* Milano, September 26–30, 1988, 41–52 (in course of publishing by North–Holland).

[5] S. Costantini, G. A. Lanzarone, *Problem Solving in Metalogic Programming*, in: Proceedings of IPCCC 89 – IEEE *Eighth Annual International Phoenix Conference on Computers and Communications,* Phoenix, Arizona, March 22–24, 1989.

[6] S. Costantini, G. A. Lanzarone, *On the Properties of Relations in Prolog and Beyond*, Internal Report n. 32/88, University of Milano, Computer Science Department, 1988 (appeared in italian in: Proceedings of AICA Conference, 1988).

[7] S. Costantini, *Formal Definition of Reflective Prolog*, Internal Report n. 49/89, University of Milano, Computer Science Department, 1989.

[8] S. Feferman, *Transfinite Recursive Progressions of Axiomatic Theories*, Journal of Symbolic Logic, n. 27, 1962, 259–316.

[9] H. Gallaire, *Boosting Logic Programming,* (invited talk) in: J.–L. Lassez (ed.), Proceedings of the Fourth International Conference on Logic Programming, MIT Press 1987, 962–988.

[10] R. Ghislanzoni, L. Spampinato and G. Tornielli, *Reflection as a Tool for Integration: an Exercise in Procedural Introspection,* Proceedings of the Tenth International Joint Conference on Artificial Intelligence, Milano, August 23–28, 1987, 44–47.

[11] P.M. Hill, J.W.Lloyd, *Analysis of Meta–programs*, in: [17], 27–42.

[12] B. Indurkhya, *Constrained Semantic Transference: A Formal Theory of Metaphors,* in: A. Prieditis (ed.), *Analogica,* Pitman 1988, 129–157.

[13] R. A. Kowalski, *Logic for Problem Solving,* North–Holland Elsevier, New York, 1979.

[14] V. Lifschitz, *Negation as Failure and Introspective Reasoning,* Invited Talk, Third International Symposium on Methodologies for Intelligent Systems, Torino, Italy, October 12–15, 1988.

[15] J.W. Lloyd, *Foundations of Logic Programming,* (2nd Ed.), Springer–Verlag, 1987.

[16] P. Maes, *Introspection in Knowledge Representation,* Proceedings of the 7th European Conference on Artificial Intelligence, Brighton, UK, 1986.

[17] Meta88, *Proceedings of the Workshop on Meta–programming in Logic Programming,* Bristol, June 22–24, 1988.

[18] D. Nute, *A Programming Solution to Certain Problems with Loops in Prolog,* ACM SIGPLAN Notices, vol. 20, n. 8, August 1985, 32–37.

[19] D. Perlis, *Languages with Self–Reference I: Foundations,* Artificial Intelligence, vol.25, 1985, 301–322.

[20] S.C. Shapiro, *Symmetric Relations, Intensional Individuals, and Variable Binding,* Proceedings of the IEEE, vol. 74, n.10, October 1986, 1354–1363.

[21] B. C. Smith, *Reflection and Semantics in LISP,* Xerox PARC ISL–5, Palo Alto, 1984.

[22] L. Sterling, A. Lakhotia, *Composing Prolog Meta–Interpreters,* Proceedings of the 5th International Logic Programming Conference, Seattle, 1988.

[23] V.S. Subrahmanian, *Foundations of Metalogic Programming,* in: [17], 53–66.

Abduction Compared with Negation by Failure

K. Eshghi *
Hewlett Packard Laboratories,
Filton Road, Stoke Gifford, Bristol BS12 6QZ

R. A. Kowalski
Department of Computing,
Imperial College of Science and Technology
180 Queens Gate, London SW7 2BZ

Abstract

Horn clause logic programming can be extended to include abduction with integrity constraints. In the resulting extension of logic programming, negation by failure can be simulated by making negative conditions abducible and by imposing appropriate denials and disjunctions as integrity constraints. This gives an alternative semantics for negation by failure, which generalises the stable model semantics of negation by failure.

The abductive extension of logic programming extends negation by failure in three ways: (1) computation can be performed in alternative minimal models, (2) positive as well as negative conditions can be made abducible, and (3) other integrity constraints can also be accommodated.

---

*   This paper was written while the first author was at Imperial College.

Introduction

The term "abduction" was introduced by the philosopher Charles Peirce [1931] to refer to a particular kind of hypothetical reasoning. In the simplest case, it has the form:

> From A and A ← B
> infer B as a possible "explanation" of A.

Abduction has been given prominence in Charniak and McDermot's [1985] "Introduction to Artificial Intelligence", where it has been applied to expert systems and story comprehension.

Independently, several authors have developed deductive techniques to drive the generation of abductive hypotheses. Cox and Pietrzykowski [1986] construct hypotheses from the "dead ends" of linear resolution proofs. Finger and Genesereth [1985] generate "deductive solutions to design problems" using the "residue" left behind in resolution proofs. Poole, Goebel and Aleliunas [1987] also use linear resolution to generate hypotheses. All impose the restriction that hypotheses should be consistent with the "knowledge base".

Abduction is a form of non-monotonic reasoning, because hypotheses which are consistent with one state of a knowledge base may become inconsistent when new knowledge is added. Poole [1988] argues that abduction is preferable to non-monotonic logics for default reasoning. In this view, defaults are *hypotheses* formulated within classical logic rather than *conclusions* derived within some form of non-monotonic logic. The similarity between abduction and default reasoning was also pointed out in [Kowalski, 1979].

In this paper we show how abduction can be integrated with logic programming, and we concentrate on the use of abduction to generalise negation by failure.

Conditional Answers Compared with Abduction

In the simplest case, a logic program consists of a set of Horn Clauses, which are used *backward* to reduce goals to subgoals. The initial goal is solved when there are no subgoals left.

In Query-the-User [Sergot, 83], a subgoal can be solved by asking the user whether the subgoal holds and receiving an answer "yes". In more sophisticated versions of query-the-user, if the user doesn't know the answer, then the solution can be regarded as being conditional on the answer being "yes".

Consider the following simple example:

Locomotion(x fly) ← Bird(x) & Normal-bird(x)
Locomotion(x walk) ← Ostrich(x)
Bird(x) ← Ostrich(x)
Ostrich(John)

Given the goal ←Locomotion(John y) query-the-user would generate an unconditional answer Locomotion(John walk) and a conditional answer Locomotion(John fly) if Normal-bird(John). Abduction would, in place of the conditional answer, generate the hypothesis Normal-bird(John) justifying the conclusion Locomotion(John fly).

In the propositional case, given a query ←Q and theory T, a *conditional answer* is a clause of the form $Q \leftarrow \Delta$ such that $T \vDash Q \leftarrow \Delta$.

Under the same conditions, abduction generates Δ such that $T \cup \Delta \vDash Q$

Conditional answers and abductive hypotheses can be implemented by means of the same backward reasoning mechanism. We believe that abduction is more appropriate in a knowledge assimilation framework [Kowalski, 1979] when the theory undergoes change for other reasons.

We restrict the hypotheses that can be generated by abduction by insisting that their predicate symbols should belong to a set A of predicate symbols, called *abducible* predicates. An atom is *abducible* if its predicate symbol belongs to A. Some authors consider more liberal syntactic forms for hypotheses. However, these can be reduced to the simpler case of abducible atoms, by using Poole's naming device [Poole 88].

In this paper we restrict our attention further to the generation of *variable-free hypotheses*. As we shall see later, this is the analogue of restricting the selection of negative subgoals to variable-free literals in negation by failure. It is possible to liberalise this restriction. But in this case it is necessary to introduce skolem constants into hypotheses [Cox and Pietrzykowski, 1986].

Integrity Checking

The generation of abductive hypotheses can be restricted by means of integrity constraints. Thus when we have the theory T, the integrity constraints I and the abductive hypotheses Δ, we insist that T$\cup\Delta$ must satisfy I. The simplest form of integrity constraint is a denial; and the simplest notion of constraint satisfaction is logical consistency.

Suppose we add to our original example the denial

    $\leftarrow$ Ostrich(x) & Normal-bird(x).

The denial functions as an integrity constraint which causes the rejection of the abductive hypothesis Normal-bird(John) and of the conclusion Locomotion(John fly) that it justifies.

Integrity constraints which are denials can be checked (inefficiently) by reasoning backward from the denials. The constraints are satisfied if there is no refutation. Thus, in theory at least, the addition of denials as integrity constraints does not necessitate any extension of the theorem-proving techniques used to execute Horn clause programs.

In practice, however, it is generally more efficient to check consistency incrementally by reasoning forward from abductive hypotheses regarded as updates to the theory. Such forward reasoning from updates is the basis for the Consistency Method [Sadri & Kowalski 1988] for checking integrity in deductive databases.

In this paper we shall use a restricted version of the consistency method, to test the consistency of abductive hypotheses. We shall see that this version of the method is similar in behaviour to the behaviour of ordinary negation by failure.

The Abduction Framework

We can now state the general specification (and declarative *semantics*) for abduction:

<T,I,A> is an abduction framework iff

T is a Horn clause theory (without denials),

I is a set of integrity constraints,

A is a set of predicate symbols, called *abducible* predicates.

Given the abduction framework <T,I,A>, the hypothesis set Δ is *an abductive solution* for the existentially quantified conjunction of atoms Q iff

Δ is a set of variable free *abducible* atoms,

$T \cup \Delta \vDash Q$

$T \cup \Delta$ satisfies I.

For integrity constraints which are denials, $T \cup \Delta$ satisfies I if and only if $T \cup \Delta \cup I$ is consistent. Later we will define satisfaction for more general kinds of integrity constraints.

Alternative Hypotheses

In general there may be several alternative collections of hypotheses that satisfy the integrity constraints but are mutually inconsistent. This can happen, for example, in situations where Reiter's (1980) Default Logic would derive multiple conclusions holding in alternative extensions. Consider the following formulation of one of his examples:

Support(x Pacifism) ← Quaker(x) & Normal-quaker(x)
Support(x Defence) ← Republican(x) & Normal-republican(x)
← Support(x Pacifism) & Support(x Defence)
Quaker(Nixon)
Republican(Nixon)

Using the following default rules:
Conclude Normal-quaker(x) if Normal-quaker(x) is consistent
Conclude Normal-republican(x) if Normal-republican(x) is consistent,

in Default Logic, it is possible both to derive the conclusion Support(Nixon Pacifism) and to derive the conclusion Support(Nixon Defence). But it is not possible to derive the conjunction of the two conclusions. This anomally arises because the extensions used to derive the two conclusions separately are mutually inconsistent. With an appropriate reformulation of the example, circumscription (McCarthy 1986) avoids the anomaly at the expense of deriving the weaker conclusion

Support(Nixon Pacifism) xor Support(Nixon Defence)

where "xor" is exclusive "or".

Using abduction, making Normal-republican and Normal-quaker abducible, in response to the query ←Support(Nixon x) we obtain two alternative conclusions:

Support(Nixon Pacifism), justified by the hypothesis
Normal-quaker(Nixon) and
Support(Nixon Defence), justified by the hypothesis
Normal-republican(Nixon).

The two conclusions are incompatible with one another, but each is consistent on its own. Moreover, the alternative hypotheses under which the conclusions hold have been made explicit.

By making hypotheses explicit, abduction provides more information than either Default Logic or Circumscription. Thus, in this example, we might try to resolve the conflict between the alternative theories by gathering more information, perhaps by performing a "discriminating experiment" in an attempt to refute one of the hypotheses. This contrasts with approaches such as prioritized circumscription, [Lifschitz, 1986] which require that a priority between competing hypotheses be assigned in advance.

Both Poole and Finger-Genesereth show that there is a close connection between alternative hypotheses generated by abduction and alternative extensions in Reiter's Default Logic. The main difference is that abductive hypotheses are explicit and only determine partial extensions of the knowledge base, whereas default logic generates maximal extensions which are implicit. Reiter in the conclusion of his recent survey of non-monotonic reasoning [Reiter 1987] suggests that it might be profitable to view default reasoning as a kind of hypothesis formulation.

The purpose of this paper is to show that abduction is a generalisation of negation by failure. In particular, we will show that the situation where abduction generates alternative, mutually inconsistent sets of hypotheses corresponds to the case where a logic program which is not locally stratified (Przymuszynski 1988) has several stable models (Gelfond and Lifschitz 1988).

The simulation of negation by failure

The remainder of this paper concerns the use of abduction to generalise negation by failure. As touched upon in the previous sections of this paper, abduction has many other applications. A further discussion of these is beyond the scope of this work.

Consider the following variant of our earlier example. Notice that Ab1 is the complement of the predicate Normal-bird used earlier and that (v) below was expressed earlier as a denial.

    (i)   Locomotion(x fly) ← Bird(x) & not Ab1(x)

    (ii)   Locomotion(x walk) ← Ostrich(x) & not Ab2(x)

    (iii) Bird(x) ← Ostrich(x)

    (iv) Ostrich(John)

    (v)   Ab1(x) ← Ostrich(x)

The following search space is obtained using SLDNF [Clark 1978, Lloyd 1987] to find John's mode of locomotion:

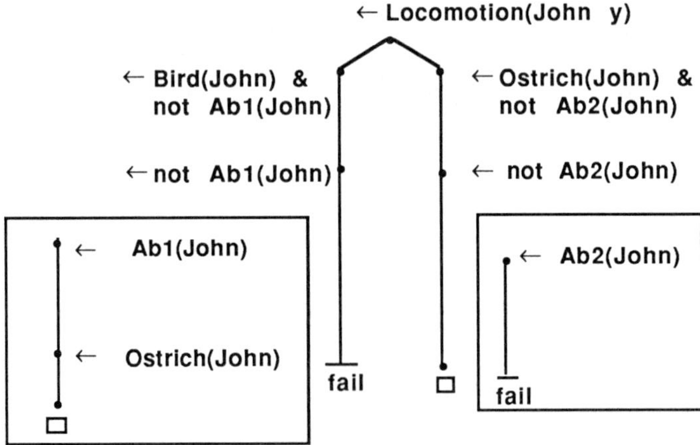

In the above figure (following a notation suggested by Chris Hogger), the box shaped enclosures depict the subsidiary search spaces for negation by failure.

Using a simple transformation (to be elaborated later), we can convert a logic program L which uses negation by failure to a corresponding abduction framework <L*,I,A>. First, for every predicate symbol P in L, we introduce an additional, new predicate symbol P*.

a) L* is the set of all clauses obtained from L by replacing every occurrence of a negative condition not P(x), where x can be a vector of variables, by a positive condition P*(x). (Clauses in L which contain no negative conditions appear in L* unchanged).

b) I is the set of all denials of the form

$$\leftarrow P^*(x) \ \& \ P(x)$$

for all P* introduced by (a).

c) A is the set of all P* introduced by (a).

Notice that the integrity constraints in I express only half of a definition of P* as the complement of P. We will introduce integrity constraints corresponding to the other half later.

Applied to the program (i)-(v) above, the transformation yields the new program:

$$\text{Locomotion}(x \ \text{fly}) \leftarrow \text{Bird}(x) \ \& \ \text{Ab1}^*(x)$$
$$\text{Locomotion}(x \ \text{walk}) \leftarrow \text{Ostrich}(x) \ \& \ \text{Ab2}^*(x)$$
$$\text{Bird}(x) \leftarrow \text{Ostrich}(x)$$
$$\text{Ostrich}(\text{John})$$
$$\text{Ab1}(x) \leftarrow \text{Ostrich}(x)$$

the integrity constraints

$$\leftarrow \text{Ab1}^*(x) \ \& \ \text{Ab1}(x)$$
$$\leftarrow \text{Ab2}^*(x) \ \& \ \text{Ab2}(x)$$

and the abducible predicates Ab1* and Ab2*. Notice that Ab1* is just the predicate Normal-bird used earlier.

With the same goals as before, we now obtain the following search space:

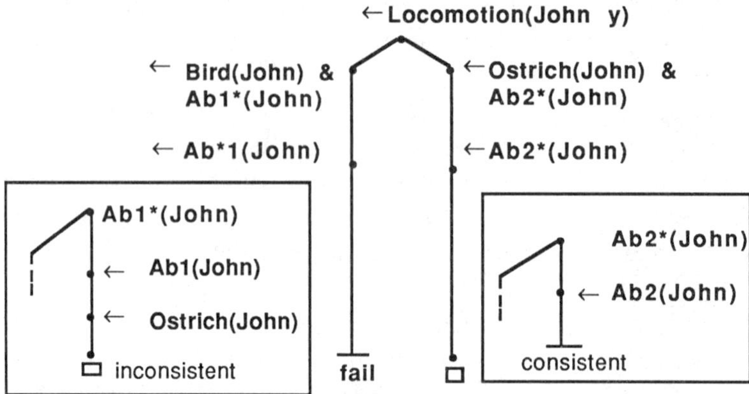

Thus we obtain the same answer as negation by failure, but with an explicit record of the hypothesis **Ab2***. Notice too that the search space is almost identical to the one generated by negation by failure. There are two differences: First, there is an extra step involved in reasoning forward from the abductive hypothesis, resolving with an integrity constraint, before deriving the denial which is the top clause in the corresponding subsidiary search space for negation by failure. Second, there is an additional branch also generated by reasoning forward from the abductive hypothesis. This branch retraces in a forward direction the path originally generated backward from the initial goal to the abductive subgoal.

In the restricted version of the consistency method which we use in this paper, these branches will not be explored. However, at the end of the paper we will present examples where exploring such branches is necessary to ensure consistency.

Nested Negation

The following example illustrates the need for further integrity constraints relating abducible predicates to their complements. It also illustrates, more simply than the Hanks-McDermott (1987) example, further semantic anomalies of Default Logic and Circumscription. Notice that our example has the form of a stratified logic program:

$$p \leftarrow \text{not } q$$

$$q \leftarrow \text{not } r$$

The program has two minimal models {q} and {p, r}.

As in Reiter's Quaker-Republican example, Default Logic derives alternative, mutually inconsistent conclusions, and circumscription derives a weak, disjunctive conclusion. In considering their more complex example, Hanks and McDermott argue, in effect, that only the first of the two models is intuitively correct. They do not consider negation by failure which computes the one, "intended" model, but not the other. (In order to apply negation as failure to the Yale Shooting Problem, it is necessary to transform a sentence of the form $a \vee b \leftarrow c$ to a clause of the form $a \leftarrow c$ & not b . It is this transformation from a clause with disjunction to one with negation by failure which eliminates the unintended model).

Transforming the example into an abduction framework, we obtain the clauses and integrity constraints:

$$p \leftarrow q^*$$
$$q \leftarrow r^*$$
$$\leftarrow q^* \& q$$
$$\leftarrow r^* \& r$$

where q^* are r^* are abducible.

Like Default Logic and unlike negation by failure, abduction derives two mutually incompatible conclusions:

q supported by the hypothesis r^* and
p supported by the hypothesis q^*.

We can eliminate the second, "unintended" conclusion by including extra integrity constraints , as discussed in the following section.

More general forms of integrity constraints

The preceding example illustrates the need for integrity constraints other than denials. Such constraints are common in the field of deductive databases. Eshghi [1987] also discusses the use of such constraints in a abductive formulation of the plan-formation problem. He uses metalevel constraints of the form "p must be provable if q is provable". Reiter [1987] proposes a similar metalevel interpretation of constraints within a modal logic. Sadri and Kowalski [1988] rewrite integrity constraints as denials using negation by failure. Interpreting negation by failure as non-provability gives their integrity constraints a similar metalevel character. Noel [1988] and Small [1988] have also proposed metalevel interpretations of integrity constraints.

In this paper, we shall consider, in addition to integrity constraints which are denials, only metalevel constraints which are disjunctions of the form

$$\text{Demo}(T \cup \Delta \ \ P^*(t)) \lor \text{Demo}(T \cup \Delta \ \ P(t))$$

where $\text{Demo}(A \ B)$ means the conclusion named B is provable from the theory named A and t is a variable-free term. A theory $T \cup \Delta$ *satisfies* such a disjunctive integrity constraint if and only if at least one of $P^*(t)$ or $P(t)$ is provable from $T \cup \Delta$.

In practice, because P^* is abducible and does not occur in the conclusion of any clause, the disjunctive integrity constraint in effect forces $P^*(t)$ to be added to Δ if $P(t)$ cannot be proved from $T \cup \Delta$. As we shall see below, the constraint is triggered during the consistency checking stage when a clause G of the form

$$\leftarrow P^*(t) \ \& \ C$$

is derived and the variable-free abducible atom $P^*(t)$ is selected. Activation of the constraint causes a subsidiary search space with top clause $\leftarrow P(t)$ to be constructed. If the search space contains a refutation then $P^*(t)$ is not provable from $T \cup \Delta$ and the clause G has no successor. If the search space contains no refutation then $P^*(t)$ is added to Δ and G has a successor which is C.

Notice that, in practice, some form of finite failure will be needed to detect the failure of the subsidiary search space to contain a refutation. Notice too that further abductions may be made during the course of generating a successful refutation.

The Nested Negation Example Reconsidered

Returning now to our propositional example

$$p \leftarrow q^*$$
$$q \leftarrow r^*$$
$$\leftarrow q \ \& \ q^*$$
$$\leftarrow r \ \& \ r^*$$

augmented with additional integrity constraints

$$\text{Demo}(T \cup \Delta \ q) \lor \text{Demo}(T \cup \Delta \ q^*)$$
$$\text{Demo}(T \cup \Delta \ r) \lor \text{Demo}(T \cup \Delta \ r^*)$$

we obtain the following search space:

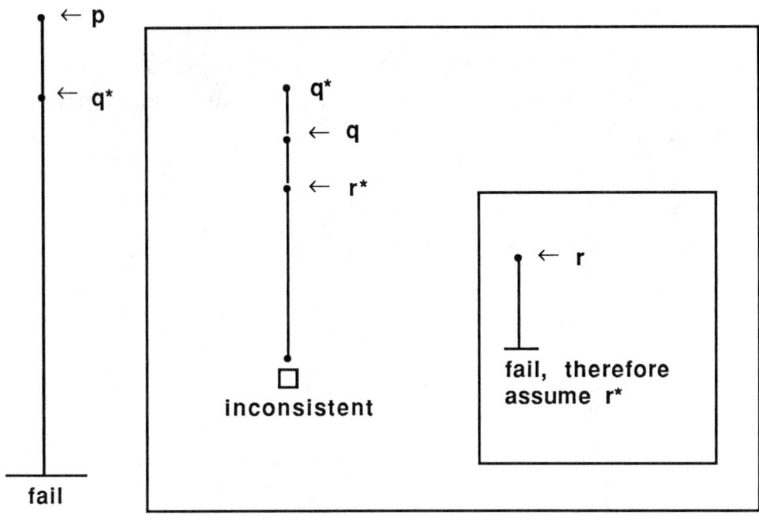

Here the innermost subsidiary search space corresponds to the application of the disjunctive integrity constraint for r and r*. To satisfy this constraint, we must show that either r or r* is provable from $T \cup \Delta$. Since the attempt to prove r fails, we must ensure that r* is provable. But r* is an abducible atom. The only way to make it provable is to add it to Δ. But this means that our original assumption q* is inconsistent. Notice that except for the first step of the attempt to show q* is consistent, the search space is identical to the search space for negation by failure. This shows, therefore, that like negation by failure, abduction with appropriate integrity constraints avoids the Hanks-McDermott problem.

In the sequel we shall assume that the abduction framework which results from transforming a logic program includes a potentially infinite set of disjunctive integrity constraints having the form

$$\mathrm{Demo}(T \cup \Delta \quad P^*(t)) \vee \mathrm{Demo}(T \cup \Delta \quad P(t))$$

for every abducible predicate P* and for every variable-free term t. Where the context makes the intended meaning clear, we will avoid writing the integrity constraints explicitly.

Non-stratified Negation

Abduction can deal with cases where ordinary negation by failure is semantically and operationally inadequate. Consider, for example, the non-stratified program

$$p \leftarrow not\ q$$

$$q \leftarrow not\ p.$$

Using the corresponding abduction framework, we obtain the following search space:

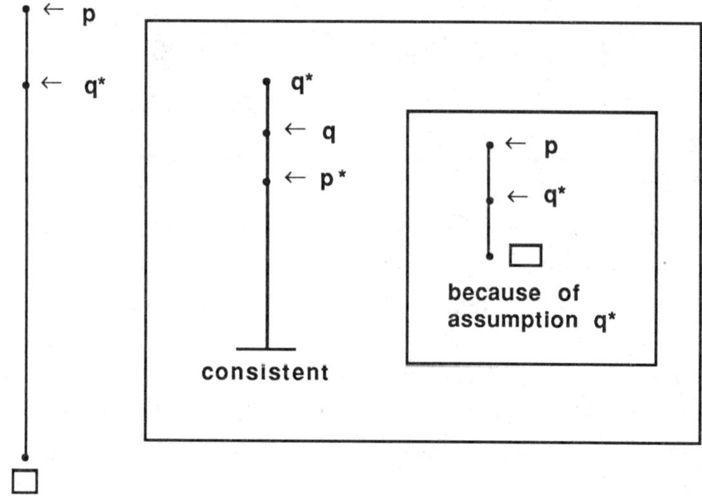

Here the refutation in the innermost subsidiary search space makes use of the hypothesis q^* which is assumed to hold *unless* it is inconsistent. The search space computes $\Delta = \{q^*\}$ which corresponds to the stable model $\{p\}$. Because p and q are symmetric in this example, it is similarly possible to compute an alternative $\Delta = \{p^*\}$ corresponding to the alternative stable model $\{q\}$. Thus abduction is semantically well-defined and operationally well behaved in this case, where negation by failure is not.

Before defining the abduction procedure more precisely for the negation by failure case, consider this elaboration of the preceding example:

$$r \leftarrow p \text{ and } q$$
$$p \leftarrow \text{not } q$$
$$q \leftarrow \text{not } p$$

Here p and q are abductive consequences supported by incompatible hypotheses. As a consequence r is not an abductive consequence. This example shows that it is necessary to keep an explicit record of the hypotheses generated when solving subgoals, so that they can be checked for mutual consistency when solving conjoint subgoals.

A Restricted Version of the Abduction Procedure

We now define a restricted version of the abduction procedure, which is general enough to deal correctly with all of the preceding examples. The proof procedure is a generalisation of SLDNF.

Let T be a Horn clause theory, A a set of abducible predicates of the form P^* (i.e. distinguished by the superscript "*"), and I a set of integrity constraints of the form

$$\leftarrow P^*(x) \,\&\, P(x)$$
$$\text{Demo}(T \cup \Delta \quad P^*(t)) \vee \text{Demo}(T \cup \Delta \quad P(t)),$$

for all abducible predicates P^* and for all terms t from the Herbrand universe of T. (We call these the integrity constraints for the atom $P^*(t)$). Let the abducible predicates P^* not occur in the conclusions of clauses of T. Analogously with SLDNF, let R be a safe computation rule (one that selects an abducible atom only if it contains no variables). Finally let Δ_1 be a set of abducible atoms satisfying the integrity constraints for these atoms. (Initially Δ_1 is empty).

An abductive derivation from $(G_1 \, \Delta_1)$ to $(G_n \, \Delta_n)$ is a sequence

$$(G_1 \, \Delta_1), (G_2 \, \Delta_2), \dots , (G_n \, \Delta_n)$$

such that, for each i, $1 \leq i < n$, G_i has the form $\leftarrow l \,\&\, l'$, where (without loss of generality) R selects l, and l' is a (possibly empty) collection of atoms, and

    abd1)   if l is not abducible, then

            $G_{i+1} = C$ and $\Delta_{i+1} = \Delta_i$

            where C is the resolvent of some

            clause in T with the clause G_i on the selected literal l;

abd2)   if l is abducible and $l \in \Delta_i$, then

$G_{i+1} = \leftarrow l'$ and $\Delta_{i+1} = \Delta_i$; and

abd3)   if l is abducible, $l \notin \Delta_i$,
l has the form k^*, and
there is a consistency derivation
from $(\{\leftarrow k\}\ \Delta_i \cup \{k^*\})$ to $(\{\ \}\ \Delta')$,
then $G_{i+1} = \leftarrow l'$ and $\Delta_{i+1} = \Delta'$,
(where $\{\ \}$ is the empty set).

A *refutation* is an abductive derivation to a pair $(\square\ \Delta')$.

Note:

(1)   Case (abd3) makes implicit the use of the step from k^* to $\leftarrow k$ obtained by resolving with the denial $\leftarrow k\ \&\ k^*$, which was made explicit before in our earlier examples.

(2)   We shall define a consistency derivation to be a finite sequence of pairs $(F_i\ \Delta_i)$ where F_i is a set of clauses representing the tips of a search tree. Every step in the derivation involves selecting a branch of the search tree from which to continue the search, selecting a literal from the tip of the branch and attempting to extend the branch by resolution or abduction. If the branch cannot be extended (i.e. the branch "fails"), it is removed from the search tree. The derivation successfully terminates when there are no branches left in the search space.

Thus a consistency derivation is effectively a search space of abductive derivations all of whose branches finitely fail. None-the-less, we need separate definitions for consistency derivations and abductive derivations because of the different ways abductive hypotheses are treated in the two cases. In particular, in the case of abductive derivations we want abductive subgoals to succeed, in the case of consistency derivations we want them to fail.

Let T, A, l, R and Δ_1 be given as in the definition of abductive derivation. A *consistency derivation* from $(F_1\ \Delta_1)$ to $(F_n\ \Delta_n)$ is a sequence

$$(F_1 \; \Delta_1), (F_2 \; \Delta_2), ..., (F_n \; \Delta_n)$$

such that, for each i, $1 \le i < n$, F_i has the form $\{\leftarrow k \; \& \; k'\} \cup F'_i$, where (without loss of generality) the clause $\leftarrow k \& k'$ has been selected (to continue the search), R selects k, and

> con1) if k is not abducible, then
>
> $$F_{i+1} = C' \cup F_i' \text{ and } \Delta_{i+1} = \Delta_i$$
> where C' is the set of all resolvents
> of clauses in T with the selected clause on the
> selected literal, and $\square \notin C'$;

> con2) if k is abducible, $k \in \Delta_i$,
> and k' is not empty, then
>
> $$F_{i+1} = \{\leftarrow k'\} \cup F_i' \text{ and } \Delta_{i+1} = \Delta_i; \text{ and}$$

> con3) if k is abducible, $k \notin \Delta_i$, and
> k has the form l^*, then
> if there is an abductive derivation
> from $(\leftarrow l \; \Delta_i)$ to $(\square \; \Delta')$
> then $F_{i+1} = F'_i$ and $\Delta_{i+1} = \Delta'$;
> otherwise, if k' is not empty, and there is no
> such derivation then
>
> $$F_{i+1} = \{\leftarrow k'\} \cup F_i', \text{ and } \Delta_{i+1} = \Delta_i \cup \{l^*\}.$$

It is clear from the definition that the notion of abductive derivation is a generalisation of SLDNF.

Correctness

In general, because of the presence of disjunctive, metalevel integrity constraints, a theory T will not ordinarily, by itself, satisfy all of its integrity constraints. These constraints can only be satisfied by generating additional abductive hypotheses. However, the abduction procedure can only generate finitely many abductive hypotheses, and this, in general, is not adequate to satisfy the potentially infinite number of integrity constraints.

The abductive framework corresponding to the unstratified program

$$r \leftarrow \text{not } r$$
$$p \leftarrow \text{not } q$$

shows another limitation of the abduction procedure. Although there is an abductive derivation from $(\leftarrow p \ \{ \ \})$ to $(\Box \ \Delta')$, $\Delta' = \{q^*\}$, q^* is inconsistent with the framework, because the clause

$$r \leftarrow \text{not } r$$

alone is inconsistent with the integrity constraints. Because the consistency derivation is a restricted form of forward reasoning from an abductive hypothesis, it can only hope to detect inconsistencies which involve the hypothesis.

As a consequence we define the *correctness* of an abduction procedure to mean that for every abductive framework $<T, I, A>$, such that $T \cup I$ is consistent, whenever there exists an abductive derivation from $(\leftarrow Q \ \{ \ \})$ to $(\Box \ \Delta')$, then there exists a (possibly infinite) Δ such that $\Delta' \subseteq \Delta$ and $T \cup \Delta$ satisfies all the integrity constraints. In the locally stratified case, we can prove the following

Theorem: If the abduction framework corresponds to the transformation of a locally stratified logic program, then the restricted abduction procedure is correct.

The restricted abduction procedure is also correct for a wider class of programs, which includes for example the framework corresponding to the program

$$p \text{ if not } q$$
$$q \text{ if not } p,$$

as shown earlier. However, the proof procedure needs to be extended to deal correctly with other cases, as the following example shows.

The abduction framework corresponding to the program

$$r \leftarrow \text{not } r$$
$$r \leftarrow q$$
$$p \leftarrow \text{not } q$$
$$q \leftarrow \text{not } p$$

has a derivation from $(\leftarrow p \ \{\ \})$ to $(\square \ \Delta')$, $\Delta' = \{q^*\}$, but the only Δ such that $T \cup \Delta$ satisfies the integrity constraints $\Delta = \{p^*\}$, which is not a superset of Δ'.

At the moment we do not have a general criteria to decide for what types of program the restricted abduction procedure is correct. We conjecture that an appropriate adaptation of the Consistency Method for proving integrity would be sufficient to guarantee correctness in general.

The Relationship with Stable Model Semantics

At the time of writing this paper, the stable model semantics (Gelfond and Lifschitz, 1988) seems to be the most general semantics for logic programs. It can be shown that there is a one-to-one correspondence between stable models and abductive hypotheses Δ satisfying the integrity constraints for negation by failure:

Theorem: Let L be a logic program, and let $< L^*, \ I, \ A >$ be the corresponding abductive framework.

a) For any stable model M of L, there is a Δ such that $L^* \cup \Delta$ satisfies I, where Δ is defined by:
$$d^* \in \Delta \text{ iff } d \notin M.$$

b) For any Δ such that $L^* \cup \Delta$ satisfies I, there is a stable model M of L, where M is defined by:
$$m \in M \text{ iff } m \text{ belongs to the Herbrand base of L and}$$
$$L^* \cup \Delta \models m.$$

Gelfond and Lifschitz regard a logic program as having a well-defined semantics if and only if it has a unique stable model. The abductive approach, on the other hand, assigns a semantics to programs having multiple stable models. This is possible because, whereas stable models M are only implicit, the corresponding hypotheses Δ are explicit.

Conclusion

In this paper we have concentrated on a special case of abduction corresponding to negation by failure. We have shown that, in this special case, the semantics of abduction corresponds to, and generalises, the stable model semantics. We have also defined a restricted version of the abduction procedure, which closely resembles, and generalises, SLDNF. We have shown that the restricted procedure is correct for a class that includes locally stratified programs, and we have conjectured that the procedure can be made correct in general by adapting the Consistency Method for proving database integrity to the problem of proving the consistency of abductive hypotheses. In a related paper [Kowalski and Sadri, 1989] we have investigated similar problems from the opposite point of view, showing that in certain cases abduction with integrity checking can be replaced by negation by failure.

Acknowledgements

We are grateful to Fariba Sadri and Marek Sergot for many useful discussions. This research was supported by the Science and Engineering Research Council.

References

Bowen, K.A., and Kowalski, R.A., [1982]: "Amalgamating Language and Metalanguage in Logic Programming" Logic Programming (Clark, K.L., and Tarnlund, S.-A., eds). Academic Press, pp 153-172.

Charniak, E., and McDermott, D., [1985]: "Introduction to Artificial Intelligence" Addison-Wesley Publishing Company.

Clark, K.L., [1978]: "Negation as failure". Logic and Data Bases (Gallaire, H., and Minker, J., eds.) Plenium Press, pp. 293-322.

Cox, P.T., and Pietrzykowski, T., [1986]: "Causes for events: their computation and applications". Proc. CADE-86, (J.H. Siekmann, ed.) Spinger-Verlag, lecture notes in computer science, pp 608-621.

Eshghi, K., [1988]: "Abductive Planning with event calculus", Proc. Fifth International Logic Programming Conference, MIT Press.

Finger, J.J., and Genesereth, M.R., [1985]: "RESIDUE: A deductive approach to design synthesis. STAN-CS-85-1035, Stanford University.

Gelfond, M., and Lifschitz, V. [1988]:- The Stable Model Semantics for Logic Programming. In Proceedings of the Fifth International Logic Programming Conference and Symposium. (R. Kowalski and K. Bowen, eds.) MIT Press, Cambridge, Mass. pp. 1070-1080.

Hanks, S. and McDermott, D., [1987]: "Default reasoning, nonmonotonic logics, and the frame problem", AI Journal.

Kowalski, R.A., [1979]: "Logic for Problem Solving", Elsevier North Holland, New York.

Kowalski, R.A. and Sadri, F. [1989]: "Logic programming without integrity constraints", Department of Computing, Imperial College.

Lifschitz, V., [1986]: "Pointwise Circumscription", AAAI 1986.

Lloyd, J.W., [1987] "Foundations of Logic Programming", Second Edition, Springer-Verlag.

McCarthy, J., [1986]: "Applications of circumscription to formalising common sense knowledge". Artificial Intelligence, Vol. 28, No. 1, pp. 89-116.

Noel, P.,[1988] :"Semantic constraints in first order theories: a definition and its application", Phd. Thesis, Unveristy of Manchester

Peirce, C.S., [1931]: "Collected papers of Charles Sanders Peirce". Vol. 2, 1931-1958 (C. Hartshorn et al, eds.) Harvard University Press

Poole, D. L., Goebel, R.G., and Aleliunas [1987]: "Theorist: A logical reasoning system for defaults and diagnosis. In N. Cercone and G. McCalla, eds. The Knowledge Fronteer: Essays in the Representation of Knowledge, Spinger-Verlag, pp. 331-352.

Poole, D.L. [1988]: "A logical framework for default reasoning". AI Journal, August 88.

Przymusinski, T.C., [1988]:- "On the Declarative Semantics of Deductive Databases and Logic Programs", In Foundations of Deductive Databases and Logic Programming (J. Minker, ed.) Morgan Kaufman, Los Altos, Ca. pp. 193-216.

Reiter, R., [1980]: "A logic for default reasoning" Artificial Intelligence, Vol. 13, pp. 81-132.

Reiter, R.,[1987]: "Nonmonotonic reasoning", Annual Review of Computer Science , 1987

Reiter, R., [1988]: "On integrity constraints" To appear in Theoretical aspects of reasoning about knowledge II, Asilomar, Ca. March 6-9, 1988.

Sadri, F., and Kowalski, R.A., [1988]: "A theorem-proving approach to database integrity". In Foundations of Deductive Databases and Logic Programming (J. Minker, ed.) Morgan Kaufmann, Los Altos, Ca., pp. 313-362.

Sergot, M.J. [1983]: "A query-the-user facility for logic programming" Integrated Interactive Computer Systems (P. Degano and Sandewell, E., eds.) North Holland Press, pp. 27-41.

Small, C., [1988] "Guarded default databases: An approach to the control of incomplete information". Birkbeck College, University of London.

Extending the Semantics of Logic Programs to Disjunctive Logic Programs

Jorge Lobo[1]   Jack Minker[1,2]   Arcot Rajasekar[1]

Department of Computer Science[1]
and
Institute for Advanced Computer Studies[2]
University of Maryland
College Park, Maryland 20742

Abstract

Van Emden and Kowalski proposed a fixpoint semantics based on model-theory and an operational semantics based on proof-theory for Horn logic programs. They prove the equivalence of these semantics using fixpoint techniques. The main goal of this paper is to present a unified theory for the semantics of Horn and disjunctive logic programs. For this, we extend the fixpoint semantics and the operational or procedural semantics to the class of disjunctive logic programs and prove their equivalence using techniques similar to the ones used for Horn programs.

1   Introduction

The main goal of this paper is to present a unified theory for the semantics of Horn and disjunctive logic programs. We present a declarative and a procedural semantics that embed the semantics of Horn programs as presented in [vEK76] and [AvE82]. In [vEK76, AvE82], two approaches to the semantics of Horn programs were studied. A fixpoint semantics based on the model theory of first-order logic and an operational semantics based on proof-theory form the core of these papers. Proof of equivalence between model-theory and proof-theory using fixpoint techniques instead of Gödel's Completeness Theorem is among the important contributions presented in [vEK76] and [AvE82]. In this paper we extend the fixpoint semantics and the operational or procedural semantics to a broader class of logic programs which include disjunctive logic programs. We prove the equivalence of the two semantics using techniques similar to the ones used in [vEK76, AvE82].

Fixpoint semantics is based on operators that transform elements of a given lattice to elements in the same lattice. Van Emden and

Kowalski in [vEK76] define an operator that applies to a lattice formed by sets of atoms using set inclusion as partial order. In our paper we use sets of positive clauses instead of atoms to apply the concepts in [vEK76] to the extended theory. Procedural semantics in logic programming uses implementation-independent proof procedures and describe the semantics of the programs as the theorems provable through the given procedures. SLD-resolution (SL-resolution for Definite clauses) is used as a basis for the procedural semantics of Horn theories. One of the underlying characteristics of SLD-resolution is that it has a very simple operational interpretation. Horn programs are formed of clauses that consist of two parts, an antecedent that consists of a conjunction of atoms and a consequent that consists of an atomic formula. SLD-resolution considers the consequent of a clause to be a problem that can be solved by reducing it to the subproblems given in the antecedent. Here, we present a procedural semantics for the extended class of programs that keeps the problem-subproblem operational flavor of SLD-resolution. The paper is organized as follows. In the rest of this section we present some preliminary definitions about logic programming and fixpoint theory. Section 2 contains the fixpoint semantics for disjunctive programs. In Section 3 we present the procedural semantics and its equivalence with the fixpoint semantics.

1.1 Preliminaries: Logic Programs

A *disjunctive logic program* P is a finite set of clauses of the form $A_1 \vee \ldots \vee A_n \leftarrow B_1 \wedge \ldots \wedge B_m$ where $n \geq 1$, $m \geq 0$, and the As and Bs are atomic formulas. The disjunction of atoms $A_1 \vee \ldots \vee A_n$ is called the *head* of the clause. The conjunction of atoms $B_1 \wedge \ldots \wedge B_m$ is called the *body* of the clause. We assume that all variables that occur in a clause are universally quantified in front of the clause. A *definite Horn* clause is a clause where $n = 1$. A *Horn* program, or logic program, consists of only definite Horn clauses. An *indefinite* or *disjunctive* clause is one where $n \geq 2$. A logic program is also called disjunctive if it contains a disjunctive clause. A *positive* clause or *assertion* is a clause with an empty body. The *Herbrand Universe* U_P of a logic program P, is the set of all ground terms that can be formed from the constants and function symbols in P (if there are no constants in P an arbitrary constant is placed in U_P). The *Herbrand Base* of a logic program P, $HB(P)$, is defined as the set of all ground atoms that can be formed by using predicates from P with terms from the Herbrand Universe U_P as arguments [Llo84]. An *Herbrand interpretation* I for

P is a subset of the Herbrand Base of P, in which all atoms in I are assumed to be *true* while those not in I are assumed to be *false*. A *Herbrand model* of P is a Herbrand interpretation of P that makes all clauses in P true. We use either the notation $C = A_1 \vee \ldots \vee A_p$ or $C = \{A_1, \ldots, A_p\}$ to represent a positive clause. This allows us to consistently use the relations $\in$ and $\subseteq$ between atoms and clauses. Also, when we use the relation $=$ between clauses we assume the set equality relation.

1.2 Preliminaries: Fixpoint Theory

Let S be a set and the relation $\leq$ be a binary relation on S and assume $\leq$ forms a partial order on the elements of S (i.e. $\leq$ is reflexive, transitive and antisymmetric.) If X is a subset of S, then $a \in S$ is an *upper bound* of X if $\forall x \in X$, $x \leq a$. $a \in S$ is the *least upper bound (lub)* of X of S if a is an upper bound of X and for all upper bounds a' of X, we have $a \leq a'$. We can define a *greatest lower bound (glb)* of X in a similar manner. S is a *complete lattice* if $lub(X)$ and $glb(X)$ exists for every subset X of S. An operator $T : S \rightarrow S$ is said to be *continuous* if for every chain $x_1 \leq x_2 \leq \ldots$ of elements of S, $T(lub\{x_1, x_2, \ldots\}) = lub\{T(x_1), T(x_2), \ldots\}$. Given $x \in S$, x is a *fixpoint (fp)* of T if $T(x) = x$. x is the *least fixpoint (lfp)* of T if $x \leq x'$ for all fixpoints x' of T. For an operator T, we define the ordinal powers of T as follows:

$$T \uparrow 0 = glb(S)$$
$$T \uparrow \alpha = T(T \uparrow (\alpha - 1)), \text{ if } \alpha \text{ is successor ordinal}$$
$$T \uparrow \alpha = lub\{T \uparrow \beta : \beta < \alpha\}, \text{ if } \alpha \text{ is a limit ordinal.}$$

The next theorem contains a well known property of continuous functions.

Theorem 1.1 *(see [Llo84])*
For a continuous operator $T : S \rightarrow S$, $lfp(T) = T \uparrow \omega$, where ω is the first limit ordinal. []

2 Declarative Semantics

2.1 Model-State Semantics

Among all the models of a program P we are interested in the minimal models since they have a close relation with fixpoint semantics. A model M of P is *minimal* if there is no proper subset M' of M such that M' is a model of P. Every Horn program P has a unique minimal model M_P. The intended meaning of P could be characterized by any of its models but there is a strong reason that makes M_P its intended interpretation. That is, the atoms in M_P are precisely those that are logical consequences of P [vEK76]. We can generalize this statement and say that every positive ground clause that is a logical consequence of P is subsumed by an atom in M_P. Hence, all logical consequences of a Horn program P are fully characterized by its minimal model M_P. A different situation occurs when we extend Horn programs to disjunctive programs. In this case we can have a clause that is a logical consequence of P but none of its subclauses are. For example, take the simple disjunctive program $P = \{A \vee B\}$ where $A \vee B$ is a logical consequence of the program P. But neither A nor B are consequences of P. We refer to such clauses as *minimal* clauses of the program P. We are interested in capturing such logical consequences in our semantics. In the case of Horn programs this is made through models which are subsets of the Herbrand Base. For disjunctive programs we need a set of minimal clauses. Our first step is to extend the definition of the Herbrand Base to cover the disjunctive cases.

Definition 2.1 *[MR] Given a disjunctive logic program P, the Extended Herbrand Base of P, $EHB(P)$, is the set of all positive clauses that can be formed with distinct atoms from $HB(P)$.* []

The need of the Extended Herbrand Base is also reflected in the minimal models of a program. In contrast to Horn programs, disjunctive programs may have more than one minimal model. For the program P in the previous example, the minimal models are $\{A\}$ and $\{B\}$. We want to condense this information in a unique simple structure. For this, we extend the definitions of interpretations and models to *states* and *model-states*.

Definition 2.2 *For a disjunctive logic program P*

1. *A state of P is a subset of the Extended Herbrand Base of P, $EHB(P)$.*

2. *A model-state of P is a state S of P, such that*

   (a) *Every minimal model of P is a model of S.*

   (b) *Every model of S is a model of P.* []

Now, we can collapse the information contained in the minimal models of a disjunctive program to its minimal model-states.

Definition 2.3 *A model-state S of a program P is minimal iff there is no model-state of P which is a subset of S.* []

The following two theorems justify the choice of minimal model-states as the intended meaning of logic programs.

Theorem 2.1 *Every disjunctive logic program P has a unique minimal model-state MS_P (the least model-state.)*

Proof: By Definition 2.2 a model M is a minimal model of a model-state of program P iff M is a minimal model of P. Assume M_1 and M_2 are minimal model-states of a program P to prove $M_1 = M_2$. Let C be a clause in M_1. Hence, $M_2 \vdash C$ since every minimal model of M_1 is a minimal model of M_2. Since M_2 is a set of positive clauses then there is a clause $C' \in M_2$ such that $C' \subseteq C$. If $C' = C$ then $C \in M_2$. If $C' \subset C$ and $C' \in M_2$, using a similar argument we know that there is $C'' \in M_1$ such that $C'' \subseteq C' \subset C$. Therefore, $M_1 - \{C\}$ is a model-state contradicting that M_1 is minimal. We can use a similar argument to prove that every clause in M_2 is also in M_1. []

Theorem 2.2 *For every positive ground clause C which is a logical consequence of a logic program P, there is a clause in MS_P that subsumes C.*

Proof: Direct from Part 2 of the model-state definition. []

The set MS_P has been identified by [YH85] following a different approach. They define for each predicate Q in a program P, the set $PIGC[Q]$ which contains the minimal clauses where the predicate Q occurs in clauses which are derivable from P. Taking the union of the $PIGC$ sets over all the predicate symbols in P we obtain MS_P.

2.2   Fixpoint Semantics

The power set of the Herbrand Base of a program P, $2^{HB(P)}$, is a complete lattice under the set inclusion relation. Van Emden and Kowalski [vEK76] define a closure operator that maps a Herbrand interpretation to a Herbrand interpretation of a program P. They have shown that the operator is continuous for Horn programs and hence has a least fixpoint. The least fixpoint is also shown to define the intended meaning of a Horn program P in the sense that the least fixpoint of the program is the least model M_P of P. Here, we use the power set of $EHB(P)$, $2^{EHB(P)}$, (i.e. the set of all states of a program P) with the partial order set inclusion, $\subseteq$, as the complete lattice underlying the fixpoint semantics of disjunctive programs. The closure operator that maps states to states of a program P is defined as follows:

Definition 2.4 *[MR] For a program P, a mapping $T_P : 2^{EHB(P)} \to 2^{EHB(P)}$ is defined as follows. Let S be a state of a program P, (i.e., S is a subset of EHB(P)), then*

$T_P(S) = \{\, C \in EHB(P) \mid C' \leftarrow B_1, B_2, \ldots, B_n$ is a ground instance of a program clause in P, $\{B_1 \vee C_1, \ldots, B_n \vee C_n\} \subseteq S$ where $\forall i, 1 \leq i \leq n$, C_i can be null, $C'' = C' \vee C_1 \vee \ldots \vee C_n$ and C is the smallest factor of $C''\,\}$. []

The smallest factor of a ground clause C' is defined as the clause C such that C contains only distinct atoms and $C \Leftrightarrow C'$. Since C in the above definition contains only distinct atoms it will be in EHB(P).

Example 2.1 *Consider the program*
$P = \{p(X) \vee q(f(X)) \leftarrow r(X)\,,\ t(X) \leftarrow q(X),$
$\qquad p(b) \vee q(b)\,,\ r(a) \vee s(a)\}$ *and the state*
$S_1 = \{p(b) \vee q(b)\,,\ r(a) \vee s(a)\}$ *then*
$T_P(S_1) = \{p(b) \vee q(b), r(a) \vee s(a), p(a) \vee q(f(a)) \vee s(a), p(b) \vee t(b)\}$.
$T_P(T_P(S_1)) = \{p(b) \vee q(b)\,,\ r(a) \vee s(a),\ p(a) \vee q(f(a)) \vee s(a),\ p(b) \vee t(b)\,,\ p(a) \vee t(f(a)) \vee s(a)\}$. []

Minker and Rajasekar [MR] prove that for a program P, the mapping T_P is continuous. Hence, $T_P \uparrow \omega$ is its least fixpoint. The next theorem shows that for a program P the least fixpoint of T_P contains all positive clauses that are derivable from the program P. First, we have to distinguish between the terms *derivability* and *provability*. We say a disjunctive program P derives a clause C if there is a finite sequence $C_1, C_2, \ldots, C_k$ of clauses such that C_i is either a clause in P or a resolvent of clauses preceding C_i, and $C_k = C$. A clause is provable from a program when it is a logical consequence of the program. In the case of Horn programs the notions of provability and derivability coincide. For disjunctive programs this is not valid. With respect to the semantics we are developing, we are only interested in the intended meaning of a program in the *derivable* sense. That is, our intended semantics will achieve a state that contains all (and only) the clauses which are derivable from a logic program. Since any provable clause also has a sub-clause that is derivable, we feel justified in restricting our intended meaning of a logic program to derivable clauses without loss of generality.

Theorem 2.3 *[MR] Given a program P,*
$$lfp(T_P^I) = \{C \mid C \ derivable \ from \ P\}. \qquad \qquad []$$

Next, we establish the equivalence between the fixpoint and model semantics for logic programs. For a program P, we denote $MM(P)$ the set of minimal models of P. The following theorem is due to Minker [Min82].

Theorem 2.4 *[Min82] A positive clause C is a logical consequence of a program P iff C is true in every minimal model of P. That is,*
$$P \vdash C \ \ iff \ \ \forall M \in MM(P), \ M \models C. \qquad \qquad []$$

Using the above theorem and Theorem 2.3 we have the following result:

Lemma 2.1 *[MR] Given a program P,*
$$\forall M \in MM(P), \ M \models C \ iff \ lfp(T_P^I) \vdash C. \qquad \qquad []$$

The next theorem follows directly from the lemma:

Theorem 2.5 *Let P be a logic program and S be a state of P.*
   i) S is a Model-State for P iff $S \Rightarrow T_P^I(S)$.
   *ii) MS_P is the minimal Model-State for P iff $MS_P = can(lfp(T_P^I))$
where for a given set of positive ground clauses S, the canonical set of
S, can(S), is defined as $can(S) = \{C|C \in S \ and \ \neg\exists C' \ s.t. \ C' \in S$
and C' is a sub-clause of C \}.*

Proof: Directly from Lemma 2.1 and definitions of model-state and minimal model-state. $\qquad \qquad []$

3   Procedural Semantics

In this section we are concerned with the procedural semantics of logic programs. Procedural interpretations provide implementation-independent proof procedures for deriving inferences from logic programs. We describe two procedures that extend SLD-resolution [Hil74], SLO-resolution and SLOP-resolution. Complete proof procedures for indefinite theories that use resolution based on model elimination [Lov78] are highly expensive due to ancestry resolution and factoring. SLO-resolution is a straightforward extension of SLD-resolution for disjunctive programs and reflects the underlying idea behind SLOP-resolution. SLOP-resolution is a non trivial extension of SLD and intends to minimize ancestry resolution based upon the syntactic structure of a program.

Definition 3.1 *A goal is of the form:* $\leftarrow C_1, \ldots, C_n \qquad n \geq 0$ *where the C's are positive clauses.* $[]$

Definition 3.2 *Given a positive clause $C = A_1 \vee \ldots \vee A_p$, we say that C θ-subsumes a clause D if θ is the most general unifier for $\{A_1 = D_1, \ldots, A_p = D_p\}$ where $D_1 \vee \ldots \vee D_p$ is a subclause of D.* $[]$

Definition 3.3 *Let P be a disjunctive logic program, G be a goal. An SLO-derivation from P with top-goal G consists of a (possibly infinite) sequence of goals $G_0 = G, G_1, \ldots$, such that for all $i \geq 0$, G_{i+1} is obtained from $G_i = \leftarrow C_1, \ldots, C_m, \ldots, C_n$ (where the Cs are positive clauses) as follows:*

(1) C_m is a clause in G_i. (C_m is called the selected clause)
(2) $C \leftarrow B_1, \ldots, B_q$ is a program clause in P
(3) C θ-subsumes C_m.
(4) G_{i+1} is the goal
$$\leftarrow (C_1, \ldots, C_{m-1}, B_1 \vee C_m, \ldots, B_q \vee C_m, C_{m+1}, \ldots, C_k)\theta. \qquad []$$

Notice that when the body of the program clause is empty G_{i+1} is equal to $\leftarrow (C_1, \ldots, C_{m-1}, C_{m+1}, \ldots, C_k)\theta$.

Definition 3.4 *An SLO-refutation from P with top-goal G is a finite SLO-derivation of the null clause $\square$ from P with top-goal G. If $G_n = \square$, we say the SLO-refutation has length n.* $[]$

Example 3.1 *Let P be the following program:*
$$P = \{t(X) \leftarrow p(f(X)),\ p(X) \leftarrow m(X),\ p(f(X)) \leftarrow q(X),$$
$$q(X) \leftarrow m(f(f(X))),\ q(X) \leftarrow p(X),\ m(0) \vee m(f(f(X))) \leftarrow\}$$
An SLO-refutation for the goal $\leftarrow t(0)$ is given below

$$\leftarrow \underline{t(0)}$$
$$\text{using } t(X) \leftarrow p(f(X))$$
$$\leftarrow \underline{p(f(0))} \vee t(0)$$
$$\text{using } p(f(X)) \leftarrow q(X)$$
$$\leftarrow \underline{q(0)} \vee p(f(0)) \vee t(0)$$
$$\text{using } q(X) \leftarrow m(f(f(X)))$$
$$\leftarrow m(f(f(0))) \vee \underline{q(0)} \vee p(f(0)) \vee t(0)$$
$$\text{using } q(X) \leftarrow p(X)$$
$$\leftarrow \underline{p(0)} \vee m(f(f(0))) \vee q(0) \vee p(f(0)) \vee t(0)$$
$$\text{using } p(X) \leftarrow m(X)$$
$$\leftarrow \underline{m(0)} \vee p(0) \vee \underline{m(f(f(0)))} \vee q(0) \vee p(f(0)) \vee t(0)$$
$$\text{using } \underline{m(0) \vee m(f(f(X)))} \leftarrow$$
$$\square \qquad\qquad []$$

The following two theorems establish the soundness and completeness of SLO-resolution. The proofs are similar to the soundness and completeness proofs of SLD-resolution [Llo84]. A formal description of these proofs can be found in [Raj].

Theorem 3.1 *(Soundness [Raj]) Let P be a logic program, $G = \leftarrow C_1, \ldots, C_k$ be a goal and $\theta_1, \ldots, \theta_n$ be substitutions obtained from an SLO-refutation from P with top-goal G then $\forall((C_1 \wedge \ldots \wedge C_k)\theta_1 \ldots \theta_n)$ is a logical consequence of P.* []

Theorem 3.2 *(Completeness [Raj]) Let P be a program and C be a ground clause which is derivable from P then there is an SLO-refutation from P with top-goal C.* []

The main drawback in SLO-resolution comes in Step 4 where the size of the selected clauses in the goal increases in each step. This problem is due to ancestry resolution. The selected clause in the derived goal is copied to keep track of ancestry information. However, there are cases where we are able to determine what part of the selected clause might be needed in subsequent derivations using the syntactic structure of the program. We define a partition of the predicates in the program and extend SLO-resolution to SLOP-resolution (SLO-resolution using program Partitions) that improves the use of ancestry information. Another disadvantage of SLO-resolution is the absence of failure derivations. All the derivations succeed or are infinite. The problem can be solved by not allowing repetition of subgoals in a refutation. We need the following definitions before we present SLOP-resolution.

Definition 3.5 *Given a program P,*

1. *A definition of a relation symbol R is the subset of P consisting of all clauses where R occurs in the head.*

2. *R is disjunctive in P if R occurs in the head of a disjunctive clause.*

3. *A relation Q **refers** to a relation R if there is a clause in P with Q in the head and R either in the head or the body.*

4. *The dependency graph of a program P is the directed graph representing the relation **refers**.* []

Example 3.2 *The strongly-connected components for the program P in Example 3.1 are:*
$$S_1 = \{m\}, \ S_2 = \{p, q\}, \ S_3 = \{t\}. \qquad \qquad []$$

Let $S_1, \ldots, S_n$ be an enumeration of the strongly connected components of the dependency graph of P. We say that a partion S_i is disjunctive if there is a disjunctive relation symbol that belongs to S_i otherwise we say it is definite. The partition function ρ_P : $\{A(t_1, \ldots, t_l)| \text{ atoms in } P\} \to \{S_1, \ldots, S_n\}$ is defined as follows:

$$\rho_P(A(t_1, \ldots, t_l)) = S_i \ iff \ A \in S_i.$$

We now extend the relation **refers** to the strongly connected components of P.

Definition 3.6 *Given two strongly connected components S, S', we say that S **strongly refers** to S' if there is a relation symbol $R \in S$ and a relation symbol $Q \in S'$ such that R **refers** to Q.* $\qquad []$

This new relation is acyclic and can be extended to a partial order among the strongly connected components. The main result is that we can isolate ancestry resolution inside each strongly connected component and between immediate successors with respect to the **refer** relation.

Definition 3.7 *Let P be a disjunctive logic program, G be a goal. Assume that $\leq$ is the reflexive and transitive closure of the relation* **strongly refer**. *An SLOP-derivation from P with top-goal G consists of a (possibly infinite) sequence of goals $G_0 = G$, $G_1, \ldots$, such that for all $i \geq 0$, G_{i+1} is obtained from* $G_i = \leftarrow C_1, \ldots, C_m, \ldots, C_k$ *as follows:*

(1) C_m is a clause in G_i. (C_m is called the selected clause)
(2) $C \leftarrow B_1, \ldots, B_q$ is a program clause in P
(3) C θ-subsumes C_m.
(4) $G_{i+1} = \leftarrow (C_1, \ldots, C_{m-1}, B_1 \vee D_1, \ldots, B_q \vee D_q, C_{m+1}, \ldots, C_k)\theta$
    where D_i is a subset of C_m that contains all the atoms
    *A in C_m such that either B_i **refers** to A*
    or $\rho_P(A) \leq \rho_P(B_i)$ and $G_i \neq G_{i+1}$. $\qquad []$

Definition 3.8 *An SLOP-refutation from P with top-goal G is a finite SLOP-derivation of the null clause $\square$ from P with top-goal G.*

$$[]$$

In Step 4 of a SLOP-derivation we solve both the problems associated with SLO-resolution. By choosing $D_i \subseteq C_m$ we are reducing the size of clauses in the goal and thus reducing ancestry resolution checking. The infinite derivation problem is taken care of by making sure that the new goal derived is different from the previous one. The reduction in ancestry resolution may be seen in the following example.

Example 3.3 *Let P be as in Example 3.1. An SLOP-refutation for the goal $\leftarrow t(0)$ is given below*

$$\leftarrow \underline{t(0)}$$
$$using\ t(X) \leftarrow p(f(X))$$
$$\leftarrow \underline{p(f(0))} \vee t(0)$$
$$using\ p(f(X)) \leftarrow q(X)$$
$$\leftarrow \underline{q(0)} \vee p(f(0))$$
$$using\ q(X) \leftarrow m(f(f(X)))$$
$$\leftarrow m(f(f(0))) \vee \underline{q(0)} \vee p(f(0))$$
$$using\ q(X) \leftarrow p(X)$$
$$\leftarrow \underline{p(0)} \vee m(f(f(0))) \vee q(0) \vee p(f(0))$$
$$using\ p(X) \leftarrow m(X)$$
$$\leftarrow \underline{m(0)} \vee p(0) \vee \underline{m(f(f(0)))} \vee q(0) \vee p(f(0))$$
$$using\ m(0) \vee m(f(f(X)))$$
$$\square \qquad\qquad\qquad\qquad\qquad\qquad\qquad\qquad\qquad []$$

Comparing Examples 3.1 and 3.3, we can notice the size difference between the subgoals. The immediate consequence of this reduction is the reduction in the number of choices in the two non-deterministic steps in a SLOP-resolution, (i.e., θ-subsumption and the program clause selection.)

Theorem 3.3 *Given a logic program P and a goal $G = \leftarrow C_1, \ldots, C_k$. Then, there is an SLOP-refutation from P with top-goal G and substitutions $\theta_1, \ldots, \theta_n$ iff $\forall (C_1 \wedge \ldots \wedge C_n)\theta_1 \ldots \theta_n$ is a logical consequence of P.*

Proof: (sketch) We use Theorems 3.1 and 3.2 for this proof. We prove that there is an SLO-refutation for G iff there is an SLOP-refutation for G. The *if* part follows immediately since we can directly transform an SLOP-derivation in an SLO-refutation. For the *only-if* part we have to observe that any shortest SLO-refutation of G can be transformed into an SLO-refutation that select larger literals (with respect to relation $\leq$) first. Then, we can transform this refutation to an SLOP-refutation. $\qquad\qquad []$

In general, θ-subsumption between clauses is not unique. This introduces a new nondeterministic step (Step 3) not present in SLD-resolution. There are some heuristics that can be used to guide the subsumption. We currently have an implementation of SLO-resolution in PROLOG which gives priority to the most-recently added atoms of a goal clause while doing θ-subsumption. We also include a mechanism which checks for repetition of goals as described in Step 4 of an SLOP-derivation.

Acknowledgements

We wish to express our appreciation to the National Science Foundation for their support of our work under grant number IRI-86-09170 and the Army Research Office under grant number DAAG-29-85-K-0-177.

References

[AvE82] K.R. Apt and M.H. van Emden. Contributions to the Theory of Logic Programming. *J.ACM*, 29(3):841–862, 1982.

[Hil74] R. Hill. *LUSH Resolution and its Completeness*. Technical Report DCL Memo 78, Department of Artificial Intelligence, University of Edinburgh, August 1974.

[Llo84] J.W. Lloyd. *Foundations of Logic Programming*. Springer–Verlag, 1984.

[Lov78] D.W. Loveland. *Automated Theorem Proving: A Logical Basis*. North–Holland Publishing Co., 1978.

[Min82] J. Minker. On Indefinite Databases and the Closed World Assumption. In *Lecture Notes in Computer Science 138*, pages 292–308, Springer-Verlag, 1982.

[MR] J. Minker and A. Rajasekar. A Fixpoint Semantics for Disjunctive Logic Programs. To appear in Journal of Logic Programming.

[Raj] A. Rajasekar. *Semantics for Disjunctive Logic programs*. PhD thesis, University of Maryland, Department of Computer Science. in preparation.

[vEK76] M.H. van Emden and R.A. Kowalski. The Semantics of Predicate Logic as a Programming Language. *J.ACM*, 23(4):733–742, 1976.

[YH85] A. Yahya and L.J. Henschen. Deduction in Non-Horn Databases. *J. Automated Reasoning*, 1(2):141–160, 1985.

LEXICAL SCOPING
AS UNIVERSAL QUANTIFICATION

Dale Miller
Department of Computer and Information Science
University of Pennsylvania
Philadelphia, PA 19104–6389 USA

Abstract: A universally quantified goal can be interpreted intensionally, that is, the goal $\forall x.G(x)$ succeeds if for some new constant c, the goal $G(c)$ succeeds. The constant c is, in a sense, given a scope: it is introduced to solve this goal and is "discharged" after the goal succeeds or fails. This interpretation is similar to the interpretation of implicational goals: the goal $D \supset G$ should succeed if when D is assumed, the goal G succeeds. The assumption D is discharged after G succeeds or fails. An interpreter for a logic programming language containing both universal quantifiers and implications in goals and the body of clauses is described. In its non-deterministic form, this interpreter is sound and complete for intuitionistic logic. Universal quantification can provide lexical scoping of individual, function, and predicate constants. Several examples are presented to show how such scoping can be used to provide a Prolog-like language with facilities for local definition of programs, local declarations in modules, abstract data types, and encapsulation of state.

1. Introduction

In [9], first-order Horn clause programs were extended by allowing implications in the body of clauses and in goals (queries). That extended logic was used to provide a simple and dynamic notion of modular logic programming. This paper extends the logic presented in that paper by permitting universal quantification as well as implications in goals and the body of clauses. The addition of such universal quantifiers strengthen the modular program constructions described in [9] since it makes it possible to provide scope to individual, function, and predicate constants.

The logic described in this paper is related to logics considered by many researchers in logic programming and, most recently, in theorem proving and type theory. See [3, 5, 7, 8, 14] for the description of closely logics applied to logic programming. Similar logics, especially higher-order versions, have been used as meta languages in specifying and implementing theorem provers [2, 18, 19]. The logic presented here is most closely related to the *first-order hereditary Harrop formulas* presented in [14]: it differs only in that we shall provide for more liberal forms of universal quantification in the body of program clauses. This logic, as well as several other extension to Horn clauses, are part of the experimental logic programming language λProlog [17]. The examples in this paper were developed and tested using the LP2.7 [13] and the eLP [1] implementations of λProlog.

Although the scoping concepts described in this paper follow naturally from simple proof-theoretical considerations, the resulting notions of "module" and "abstract datatype" differ significantly from those notions found in other programming languages. In our setting, logic programs defined in a given modules are not necessarily closed: the meaning of the programs defined in them may depend on the context in which they are used. Similarly, the mechanism for supplying security in abstract datatypes is described as a "runtime check"; it cannot, in general, be done at compile time. For proposals of more static notions of modules and abstract datatypes for logic programs, see [4, 15, 20, 21].

2.   The logic programming language $\mathcal{L}$

Consider a logic that contains constants and variables for individuals, functions, and predicates. Let A, D, G be syntactic variables that range over the following classes of formulas.

$$A := \text{atomic formula}$$
$$D := A \mid G \supset A \mid D_1 \wedge D_2 \mid \forall x\, D$$
$$G := A \mid D \supset G \mid G_1 \wedge G_2 \mid \forall y\, G$$

The universal quantifier $\forall x\, D$ is over individuals only, while the universal quantifier $\forall y\, G$ is over individuals, functions, and predicates. Let $\mathcal{D}$ be the set of D-formulas and let $\mathcal{G}$ be the set of G-formulas that, in both cases, do not contain free function or predicate variables. The role of free function and predicate variables is restricted only to the construction of D-formulas and G-formulas. During the interpretation of this logic (see Section 4) the only free variables that need to be considered are those that are individual variables. A formula in $\mathcal{G}$ is a *goal* or *query*. A formula in $\mathcal{P}$ is a *definite clause* or *program clauses*, and a finite subset of $\mathcal{P}$ is a *program*.

While this language is not, strictly speaking, first-order, it is far from having the complex meta theory or theorem proving problems associated with higher-order logics and logic programming languages (accounts of which are in [12, 14, 16]). As we shall show, a constrained form of first-order unification makes it possible to implement complete theorem provers and interpreters for $\mathcal{L}$.

Simple modifications of the proof theory discussions in [9] show that $\mathcal{P} \vdash_I G$ (where $\vdash_I$ denote intuitionistic provability) if and only if the sequent $\mathcal{P} \longrightarrow G$ has a cut-free proof in which every sequent in the proof has an antecedent that is a subset of $\mathcal{D}$ and a succedent that is a member of $\mathcal{G}$. Furthermore, cut-free proofs for $\mathcal{P} \longrightarrow G$ can be searched for in a goal-directed fashion (see [14] for a more formal treatment of the relation between logic programming and goal-directed search). Since intuitionistic provability admits goal-directed theorem provers in this setting, we shall refer to the triple $\mathcal{L} = \langle \mathcal{D}, \mathcal{G}, \vdash_I \rangle$ as a logic programming language.

In presenting example programs and goals of $\mathcal{L}$, we shall use a slightly extended version of usual Prolog syntax [22]. In particular, we use the symbol **=>** for implications at the top-level of goals. Thus, we have two notations for implication: **=>** is the converse of **:-**. When denoting Horn clauses, explicit quantifiers are generally not needed, while in $\mathcal{L}$, quantifiers in both D- and G-formulas must often be made explicit. In these cases, we use the syntax **all x,y,z** to denote universal quantification (of the three variables **x**, **y**, and **z**). We will use the following convention on naming bound variables: if the quantification occurs positively in a G-formula or negatively in a D-formula, we shall use a token with a lower case initial letter for the name of the quantified variable, otherwise we use a token with an upper case initial letter. This convention is only to aid readability: there is no logical status for the names of bound variables. When a token with an upper case initial letter is not explicitly quantified, it will be assumed to be universally quantified at the top of the formula it occurs in.

There are at least two different ways to interpret the goal $\forall x. G(x)$. The *extensional* interpretation is motivated by the semantics of universal quantification: $\forall x. G(x)$ is true of $\mathcal{P}$ if for all terms t, $G(t)$ is true of $\mathcal{P}$. (Often an additional predicate is supplied to restrict the domain of t). This interpretation of universal quantification is used often in database applications. See [6] for a formal treatment of this interpretation of universal quantification.

In this paper, we shall, however, use an *intensional* interpretation of universal quantification that is motivated by proof theory: $\forall x.G(x)$ follows from $\mathcal{P}$ if $G(c)$ follows from $\mathcal{P}$ for some constant c that does not occurs in G or $\mathcal{P}$. That is, $\forall x.G(x)$ follows if it follows generically. This interpretation of universal quantification in goals is similar to the interpretation of implications in goals used in this paper: the goal $D \supset G$ follows from program $\mathcal{P}$ if G follows for the augmented program $\mathcal{P} \cup \{D\}$.

3.   Two simple examples

For a simple example, consider the familiar sterile jar problem. Assume that a jar is sterile if every germ in it is dead, that a germ in a heated jar is dead, and that a given jar has been heated. What reasoning is necessary to establish that the given jar is sterile? The intensional interpretation of the quantification will work here. Let $\mathcal{P}$ be the following program:

```
sterile(Y) :- all x\ (germ(x) => in(x,Y) => dead(x)).
dead(X)    :- heated(Y), in(X,Y), germ(X).
heated(j).
```

Consider proving the goal ?- `sterile(j)`. Backchaining on the first clause above yields the goal

```
    ?- all x\ (germ(x) => in(x,j) => dead(x)).
```

Given the intensional interpretation of universal quantification, we proceed by selecting a constant, say g, that does not occur in $\mathcal{P}$ or in the goal. We now attempt to prove the goal

```
    ?- germ(g) => in(g,j) => dead(g).
```

This goal succeeds if the goal `dead(g)` follows from the augmented program $\mathcal{P} \cup \{\texttt{germ(g)}, \texttt{in(g,j)}\}$. It is easy to see that this in fact follows by simple backchaining steps. After this goal succeeds, the two clauses `germ(g)` and `in(g,j)` are removed from the current program: the constant `g` is similarly removed (discharged).

Interpreters for $\mathcal{L}$ must use unification and free variables carefully. For example, there is no substitution for X such that the goal

```
    ?-  all y\(p(f(y)) => p(X)).
```

would succeed from the empty program. If we naively simplify this goal using the motivation above, we would first generate a new constants, say `c`, and then try to prove `p(X)` from `p(f(c))`. But this reduced problem is satisfied with the substitution of `f(c)` for `X`. Notice, however, that the result of applying this substitution to the goal above, namely

```
?- all y\(p(f(y)) => p(f(c))).
```

does not yield a provable goal. The unsoundness arise from the fact that when `c` was selected, the future instantiations of `X` must be restricted to be terms that cannot contain the constant `c`. This restriction, which blocks the only route to a proof of the above goal, is central to most of the uses made of universals in goal in this paper.

In general, whenever a new constant is used to instantiate a universal goal, all free variables, in the goal and the program, must be restricted so that the substitution terms that will eventually instantiate them will not contain that new constant. Free variables generated by subsequent backchaining steps, however, may be instantiated with terms containing this new constant. An interpreter that restricts substitution variables for free variables as motivated above is described in the next section.

4.   An interpreter for $\mathcal{L}$

In order to interprete logic programs in $\mathcal{L}$, it is necessary, in some fashion, to keep track of notions such as the "current goal," the "current program," the "current set of constants," and restrictions on free variables. Interpreters for Horn clauses only need to keep track of the first of these: there the current program and set of constants remains unchanged during a computation, and the restriction on free variables do not need to be made. In the description of an interpreter for $\mathcal{L}$ given below, a *signature* is used to denote the current set of constants, an *assignment* is used to encode the restrictions on free variables, and a *sequent* is used to connect a program to a goal.

A *signature* is a (possibly infinite) non-empty set of individual, function, and predicate constants such that there are denumerably many individual, denumerably many function, and denumerably many predicate constants of our logic that are not in the signature. The interpreter described below will need to select constants that are not already mentioned in a given signature: this last restriction on signatures makes this possible. Let Σ be a signature. A Σ-*assignment* is a finite list $\mathcal{A} = \langle t_1 : \Sigma_1, \ldots, t_n : \Sigma_n \rangle$ where $\Sigma_1 \subseteq \ldots \subseteq \Sigma_n \subseteq \Sigma$ and for $i = 1, \ldots, n$, t_i is a first-order term or atom all of whose individual, function, and predicate constants are members of Σ_i. If for some $i = 1, \ldots, n$, x occurs free in t_i then x is *assigned by* $\mathcal{A}$. If σ is a substitution, then $\sigma \langle t_1 : \Sigma_1, \ldots, t_n : \Sigma_n \rangle$ is the structure $\langle \sigma t_1 : \Sigma_1, \ldots, \sigma t_n : \Sigma_n \rangle$. If this structure is also a Σ-assignment, σ is $\mathcal{A}$-*feasible* (the value of Σ is not needed to determine $\mathcal{A}$-feasible). The expression $\mathcal{A} + \mathcal{A}'$ denotes the concatenation of the two lists $\mathcal{A}$ and $\mathcal{A}'$, and the expression $\mathcal{A} + t : \Sigma'$ denotes $\mathcal{A} + \langle t : \Sigma' \rangle$. The concatenation of two assignments is not necessarily another assignment.

The restrictions on free variables described in the previous section was given in a negative sense: a free variable is restricted to *not* be instantiated with terms containing certain constants. Σ-assignments express this restriction in an equivalent but positive fashion: if x is free in t and the pair $t : \Sigma'$ is a member of a Σ-assignment $\mathcal{A}$, then x can be instantiated with an term whose constants are from the set Σ'. The restriction on variables comes from the fact that only $\mathcal{A}$-feasible subsitutions will be used in the interpreter (see the BACKCHAIN transition below) and the fact that Σ' may be a proper subset of Σ.

A $\Sigma, \mathcal{A}$-sequent is a pair $\mathcal{P} \longrightarrow G$ where $G \in \mathcal{G}$, $\mathcal{P}$ is a finite subset of $\mathcal{D}$, all constants in formulas of $\mathcal{P} \cup \{G\}$ are members of Σ, and all free variables of those formulas are assigned by $\mathcal{A}$. A *state* (of the interpreter) is a triple $\langle \Sigma, \mathcal{A}, \mathcal{S} \rangle$ where Σ is a signature, $\mathcal{A}$ is a Σ-assignment, and $\mathcal{S}$ is a finite set of $\Sigma, \mathcal{A}$-sequents. These sequents specify what remains to be proved. A *success state* is a state in which the set of sequents is empty.

We assume the usual notions of substitution into first-order (quantified) formulas, first-order unification, and most general unifiers (see, for example, [22]). Simultaneous substitutions are denoted as $[x_1 \mapsto t_1, \ldots, x_n \mapsto t_n]$.

A simple *elaboration* function elab that maps $\mathcal{D}$ to finite subsets of $\mathcal{D}$ is defined using the equations

- elab$(A) = \{A\}$,
- elab$(G \supset A) = \{G \supset A\}$,
- elab$(D_1 \wedge D_2) = $ elab$(D_1) \cup $ elab(D_2),
- elab$(\forall x (D_1 \wedge D_2)) = $ elab$(\forall x . D_1) \cup $ elab$(\forall x . D_2)$, and
- elab$(\forall x . D) = \{\forall x . D' \mid D' \in $ elab$(D)\}$ (provided D is not conjunctive).

Elaboration simply breaks a D-formula into its conjuncts, mini-scoping outermost universal quantifiers if possible. The logical consequences of D and elab(D) are the same, and a proof involving D differs in trivial ways from a proof involving elab(D).

The following transition rules, indicated by $\Longrightarrow$, describe the heart of a non-deterministic interpreter. $\uplus$ denotes disjoint union.

AND: $\langle \Sigma, \mathcal{A}, \{\mathcal{P} \longrightarrow G_1 \wedge G_2\} \uplus \mathcal{S}\rangle \Longrightarrow \langle \Sigma, \mathcal{A}, \{\mathcal{P} \longrightarrow G_1, \mathcal{P} \longrightarrow G_2\} \cup \mathcal{S}\rangle$.

This transition simply translates the logical connective $\wedge$ into an AND-node in the interpreter's search space.

AUGMENT: $\langle \Sigma, \mathcal{A}, \{\mathcal{P} \longrightarrow D \supset G\} \uplus \mathcal{S}\rangle \Longrightarrow \langle \Sigma, \mathcal{A}, \{\text{elab}(D) \cup \mathcal{P} \longrightarrow G\} \cup \mathcal{S}\rangle$.

A implication in a goal is thus an instruction to augment the program with the antecedent of the implication. To simplify the presentation of backchaining below, we augment the programs clauses in elab(D) instead of D.

GENERIC: $\langle \Sigma, \mathcal{A}, \{\mathcal{P} \longrightarrow \forall x.G\} \uplus \mathcal{S}\rangle \Longrightarrow \langle \Sigma \cup \{c\}, \mathcal{A}, \{\mathcal{P} \longrightarrow [x \mapsto c]G\} \cup \mathcal{S}\rangle$, provided that $c \notin \Sigma$.

A universal quantifier in a goal causes a new constant to be added to the current signature. Notice that the assignment $\mathcal{A}$ does not change; that is, the range for substitution terms for free variables does not change with this addition.

BACKCHAIN: Consider the state $\langle \Sigma, \mathcal{A}, \mathcal{S}\rangle$ where $\mathcal{S}$ is the set

$$\{\{\forall x_1 \ldots \forall x_n (G_1 \wedge \ldots \wedge G_m) \supset A\} \cup \mathcal{P} \longrightarrow A'\} \uplus \mathcal{S}'$$

for some set $\mathcal{S}'$ and for $n, m \geq 0$. Let $z_1, \ldots, z_n$ be new individual variables (that is, variables not assigned by $\mathcal{A}$) and let θ be the renaming substitution $[x_1 \mapsto z_1, \ldots, x_n \mapsto z_n]$. If θA and A' are unifiable, let σ be their most general unifier. Then the state

$$\langle \Sigma, \sigma(\mathcal{A} + z_1 : \Sigma + \ldots + z_n : \Sigma), \sigma(\{\mathcal{P} \longrightarrow \theta G_1, \ldots, \mathcal{P} \longrightarrow \theta G_m\} \cup \mathcal{S}')\rangle$$

arises from $\langle \Sigma, \mathcal{A}, \mathcal{S}\rangle$ provided that σ is $\mathcal{A}$-feasible. If $m = 0$ then the set of sequents has diminished by one. (The application of σ to a set of sequents, say $\mathcal{S}$, is the set of sequents resulting from applying σ to all formulas in all the sequents of $\mathcal{S}$.)

Backchaining in $\mathcal{L}$ is essentially the same as it is with Horn clauses. The main difference is that the new variables $z_1, \ldots, z_n$ must be assigned: they are allowed to be instantiated with any term involving constants in the current signature.

No transition can be applied to a success state. The following theorem is stated without proof.

Theorem.   *Let G be a member of $\mathcal{G}$, $\mathcal{P}$ be a finite subset of $\mathcal{D}$, Σ a signature that contains at least the individual, function, and predicate constants occurring in G and in formulas of $\mathcal{P}$, and let $x_1, \ldots, x_n$ be a list of individual variables occurring free in G and in formulas of $\mathcal{P}$. There is a substitution σ such σG is intuitionistically derivable from $\sigma \mathcal{P}$ if and only if there is a series of transitions that carries the state $\langle \Sigma, \langle x_1 : \Sigma, \ldots, x_n : \Sigma \rangle, \{\mathcal{P} \longrightarrow G\} \rangle$ to the success state*

$$\langle \Sigma', \langle t_1 : \Sigma, \ldots, t_n : \Sigma \rangle + \mathcal{A}, \emptyset \rangle$$

such that the substitution $[x_1 \mapsto t_1, \ldots, x_n \mapsto t_n]$ is more general than σ.

The intuitionistic logic used in this theorem is higher-order, although the higher-order aspects of that logic that are used are very weak.

We can now describe a simple, depth-first, deterministic interpreter for $\mathcal{L}$. First, we must consider the third component of a state and the antecedent of sequents as lists instead of sets. AUGMENT concatenates elaborated clauses to the front of an antecedent. When given a non-success state, the first sequent is used to determine which transition to consider. If the succedent of that sequent is an implication, apply AUGMENT; if it is a conjunction, apply AND; if it is universally quantified, apply GENERIC. The choice of constant used in GENERIC is immaterial (as long as it is not in the current signature). Finally, if the succedent is an atom, then we need to backchain. Here, we select a D-formula from the antecedent in a left-to-right order. The only backtrack points we must store are those involved with the selection of a clause: these backtrack points will be returned to following the depth-first discipline.

Notice that first-order unification does not need to be modified, although before a unifier is used in BACKCHAIN, it must be checked for $\mathcal{A}$-feasibility. This check, which provides the security used to implement data abstraction describe later, is done at runtime. Although there may be static, comile-time checks that might tell us that in certain programs feasibility of substitutions do not need to be checked, runtime checks would be necessary, in general. Also the cost of checking feasibility of substitutions is similar to the cost of doing the occur check in unification: the entire terms involved in a unifier must be transversed in order to determine that certain constants do not occur with them. It is, of course, possible to modify first-order unification so that only $\mathcal{A}$-feasible substitutions are produced. See [10, 11] for an account of how this can be accomplished. Skolem functions provide only one of several implementation techniques.

5. Local declaration of programs

A standard way to write the **reverse(L,K)** program in Prolog
is to first write a tail recursive auxiliary function **rev(L,K,Acc)**. Although this second program is intended to be used only locally in the
definition of **reverse**, there is no way in simple Horn clause logic or
in most Prolog implementations for the scope of **rev** to be localized to
just the definition of **reverse**. Making use of the universal quantification of predicates and of implications in goals, we can write a version
of **reverse** where **rev** is given local scope. Consider the following
D-formula.

```
reverse(L,K) :-
  all rev\(
          (all L\        (rev([],L,L)),
           all X,L,K,M\(rev([X|L],K,M)  :- rev(L,K,[X|M])))
          => rev(L,K,[]))
```

(Notice that the variables L and K are bound with different scopes in
this clause.) In attempting to prove the goal **reverse([1,2,3],K)**
from this clause, an interpreter would first generate a new predicate
symbol, say c, then add the Horn clauses

```
c([],L,L).
c([X|L],K,M) :- c(L,K,[X|M]).
```

to the current program, and then try to prove c([1,2,3],K,[]). After the answer substitution K = [3,2,1] is discovered, both c and the
new clauses pertaining to c would be discharged.

Given this style of programming, there is another way that **reverse** can be written. One way to reverse a list, say [a,b,c], is to
start with the atom rv([],[a,b,c]) and forwardchain over the clause

```
rv([X|N],M)  :- rv(N,[X|M]).
```

The goal rv([c,b,a],[]) is provable in this way. Obviously, for any
list L, if we start with the atomic fact rv([],L) and forwardchain
over the above clause, we can prove the atomic goal rv(K,[]) where
L and K are reverses of each other. While this is a natural approach to
specifying **reverse**, it is not possible to code it directly in Horn clauses
since it describes the **reverse** predicate as relating a list contained in
a program and one contained in a goal. Using $\mathcal{L}$, this algorithm can
be specified directly as follows.

```
reverse(L,K) :-
  all rv\ (
            (               rv([],K),
             all X,N,M\(rv([X|N],M) :- rv(N,[X|M])))
        => rv(L,[]))
```

In attempting to prove the goal `reverse([1,2,3],K)` from this clause,
an interpreter will again generate a new predicate symbol, say `c`, then
add the Horn clauses (where quantification is made explicit)

```
      c([],K).
all X,N,M\(c([X|N],M) :-c(N,[X|M])))
```

to the current program, and then try to prove goal `c([1,2,3],[])`.
Notice here that the goal is closed while the program is open: the free
variable in the program, the variable `K` in the first clause of `c`, will
be instantiated to the list `[3,2,1]` by the interpreter in the process
of establishing the goal `c([1,2,3],[])`. In the first clause above, `K`
should not be assumed to be universally quantified: that clause is,
instead, an open atomic formula.

For two more simple examples, consider how to specify goals that
fail in all program contexts or that succeed only once in all program
contexts. A predicate, say `fail`, will fail if there are no clauses defining
it. In a dynamic setting where implications allow new clauses to be
added, there is no guarantee that clauses defining `fail` are not added
during some computation. The goal `all p\ p`, however, will fail in
all programming contexts: when the interpreter encounters this goal,
it must select a new null-ary predicate, say `c`, and then attempt to
prove `c`, an attempt that must fail since `c` is new. Similarly, the goal
`all p\(p => p)` will succeed exactly once in all programming context:
again the interpreter will need to select a new null-ary predicate, say
`c`, then assume `c` and then attempt to prove `c`, which will, of course,
have exactly one proof in all programming contexts.

6.   A mechanism for abstract data types

Universals in goals can provide a scope for constants within goal
formulas. It would, of course, be useful to have a similar scoping
mechanism that works over program clauses. A notion of "local" declaration for constants in a collection of program clauses is presented
below.

Assume that the variable y is free in the formula D but not in the
formulas G. The interpreter attempting to prove $\forall y(D \supset G)$ will then

introduce a new constant for y, say k, and restrict all the current free variables so that they cannot be instantiated with terms containing k. The program code $[y \mapsto k]D$ can use the constant k to build data structures but any answer substitutions for this compound goal cannot make reference to k. It is in this sense that data abstraction can be accomodated in $\mathcal{L}$.

Before presenting some examples, it is helpful to simplify a problem of scoping. In the discussions above, the scope of y is, in a sense, only over D while we needed to use the universal quantifier $\forall y$ over the compound formula $D \supset G$ even though y is not free in G. To provide for a more natural scoping mechanism, we shall allow limited forms of existential quantification over D formulas. This example could thus be written more naturally as $(\exists y \; D) \supset G$. This use of existential quantification is also justified by the intuitionistic equivalence

$$(\exists x \; D) \supset G \quad \equiv \quad \forall x(D \supset G),$$

provided x is not free in G.

To be precise, let E be a syntactic formula variable whose range is determined by

$$E := D \mid \exists y \; E,$$

where the quantifier $\exists y$ is over individuals, functions, and predicates. The phrase "program clause" will now refer to any E formula all of whose free variables are individual variables. The interpreter would also need to make the following transition:

LOCAL: $\quad \langle \Sigma, \mathcal{A}, \{\mathcal{P} \longrightarrow (\exists x.E) \supset G\} \uplus \mathcal{S}\rangle \implies \langle \Sigma \cup \{c\}, \mathcal{A}, \{\mathcal{P} \longrightarrow ([x \mapsto c]E) \supset G\} \cup \mathcal{S}\rangle$, provided that $c \notin \Sigma$.

The following existentially quantified set of Horn clauses provide an implementation of the stack data type in which the constructors for stacks are not available to programs making use of this implementation.

```
exists emp, stk\(
          empty(emp),
  all S,X\( enter(X,S,stk(X,S)) ),
  all S,X\( remove(X,stk(X,S),S) )
  ).
```

Let this E-formula be denoted by the symbol `stack`. In a sense, `stack` represents a module with a local declaration. The only "exportables" constants of this module are the three predicates `empty`, `enter`, and `remove`.

A goal of the form `stack => G` is attempted by introducing two new constants that will play the role of the stack constructors, disallow the current free variables of `G` (and of the current program) to contain these constructors, and introduce three atomic clauses to implement `empty`, `enter`, and `remove`. After this point, any new free variables (introduced by subsequent backchaining steps) can be instantiated with stack objects: this is how stacks would be used in computations.

This approach to programming is, of course, very desirable since it can be used to guarantee that a client program of `stack` does not examine and manipulate stacks in any way other than those supplied by the predicates `empty`, `enter`, and `remove`. This allows different implementations of those predicates to be substituted for the module `stack`. For example, those operations could be implemented as a queue by the following code (the term `qu(L,K)` is a difference list construction):

```
exists qu\(
    all L\( empty(qu(L,L))),
 all X,L,K\( enter(X,qu(L,[X|K]),qu(L,K))  ),
 all X,L,K\( remove(X,qu([X|L],K),qu(L,K)) )
 ).
```

A search program written in $\mathcal{L}$ that uses `enter` and `remove` for storing and retrieving choice points could switch between a depth-first and breadth-first search by switching between these two implementations of those predicates.

7. Encapsulation of state

In this section, we shall make our logic language slightly higher-order in the sense that we shall allow quantification over propositional variables in D-formulas and permit predicate constants to appear within terms. Operationally speaking, we are making this extension to allow goal formulas to be passed around as arguments and to be dynamically called. Various higher-order extensions to logic programming have been analyzed in the papers [12, 14, 16]. The extension mentioned above is part of the much more general theory of *higher-order hereditary Harrop formulas* described in [14]. Although there is not sufficient space here to present details, it suffices to say that when propositional variables are not permitted as the head of definite clauses and when there are no logical constants embedded inside the terms of the logic (both cases are true of the examples below), then the straightforward operational meaning of these extended definite clauses can be given a proof theoretic semantics.

The following is an implementation of a switch data type where a switch's value has a scope. Consider the following program clauses:

```
exists sw\(
            sw(off),
    all G\( set_on(G)   :- sw(on)  => G ),
    all G\( set_off(G)  :- sw(off) => G ),
    all V\( status(V)   :- sw(V) )
  ).
```

The value for this switch is stored as the argument for the local, one-place predicate **sw**. The switch is initially set off by the first line. The predicates **set_on** and **set_off** take a goal formula as their argument (hence, the need for the higher-order extensions), set the switch either on or off by extending the program, and then call their arguments. Propositional variables allow a kind of "continuation passing" style of programming.

Notice that as a series of **set_on** and **set_off** predicates are called, there is an accumulation of all the previous settings of the switch. In a sense, when the switch gets set, it becomes more non-deterministic. In order to get the more deterministic and coventional notion of a switch we must consider various schemes for reducing non-determinism. There seems to be two natural choices for doing this. First, implication could be interpreted as redefining instead of augmenting. Many of the previous examples still have interesting meaning under such a reinterpretation of implication. The other choice, used here, is to provide the deterministic version of the intepreter with such control primitives as the "deterministic" declaration or cut (!).

As it is implemented above, the **status** predicate is the only way the value of the current switch can be determined. If the goal ?- **status(U)** is called, **U** will be bound to the most recent setting of the switch. Notice, however, that the call ?- **status(on)** succeeds if the switch had been set on at some point. If **status** were reimplemented using cut as

```
    all U,V\( status(V)   :- sw(U), !, U = V )
```

only the last value of the switch could ever be retrieved (by the deterministic interpreter).

Notice that, in general, the entire history of how this switch is set must be maintained since completing a goal such as **set_on(G)** requires a previous switch value to be reinstated. If the deterministic version of **status** is used and it is known that the goals called as continuations in **set_on** and **set_off** never fail, then previous settings of the switch are not needed. In this case, **set_on** and **set_off** could be implemented using a side-effect to change the argument of the local predicate **sw**.

For a final example, consider the following simple exercise in using a similar form of encapsulation.

```
make_account(Acc,Amt,G) :- all reg\ (
  (  reg(Amt),
     all Inc, H,  Val, Tmp\(
       add_money(Acc,Inc,H) :-
          reg(Val), Tmp is (Val + Inc), reg(Tmp) => H),
     all Dec, H, Val, Tmp\(
       wd_money(Acc,Dec,H) :-
          reg(Val), Tmp is (Val - Dec), reg(Tmp) => H ),
     all H, Val\(
       print_amt(Acc,H) :-
          reg(Val), write(Val), nl, H)
  => G).
```

The goal **make_account(john,100,G)** would call the goal G in an environment where there is an "account" named john that is initialized with the amount 100. This account is stored as a local predicate, which stores the balance (or state) of the account, and three "methods" for adding to, subtracting from, and printing that account's balance. The continuation G is given access to the three predicates **add_money**, **wd_money**, and **print_amt**. If G itself calls **make_account**, a new local predicate and three new "methods" are created to implement the new account.

The following is a very simple interpreter for treating the named accounts used as objects. In this example, the only continuation called is the predicate **transact**.

```
transact :-
  write(">>- "), read(Entry), do(Entry).
do(mk_acc(Name,Amt)) :- make_account(Name,Amt,transact).
do(add(Name,Amt)) :- ad_money(Name,Amt,transact).
do(wd(Name,Amt)) :- wd_money(Name,Amt,transact).
do(print(Name)) :- print_amt(Name,transact).
do(quit).
```

The following is a simple interaction with this transaction program.

```
?- transact.
>>- mk_acc(john,10).
>>- mk_acc(mary,20).
>>- add(john,5).
>>- print(john).
15
>>- wd(mary,10).
>>- print(mary).
10
>>- quit.
?-
```

Again, if the continuation **transact** never fails (that is, the user only types in correct information), then only the most recent state of an account is examined.

Acknowledgements. I would like to thank John Hannan, Frank Pfenning, and several of the attendees of the GULP Advanced School on Foundations of Logic Programming, September 1988 for their helpful comments and criticism of the work described in this paper. This work is supported in part by grants ONR N00014-88-K-0633, NSF CCR-87-05596, and DARPA N00014-85-K-0018.

8. References

[1] C. Elliott and F. Pfenning, eLP, a Common Lisp implementation of λProlog, January 1989.

[2] A. Felty and D. Miller, Specifying Theorem Provers in a Higher-Order Logic Programming Language, Proceedings of the Ninth International Conference on Automated Deduction, Argonne, IL, 23 – 26 May 1988.

[3] D. Gabbay and U. Reyle, N-Prolog: An Extension to Prolog with Hypothetical Implications. I, Journal of Logic Programming 1, 1984, 319 – 355.

[4] L. Giordano, A. Martelli, and G. Rossi, Local Definitions with Static Scope Rules in Logic Programming, Proceedings of the FGCS International Conference, Tokyo, 1988, pp. 389-396.

[5] L. Hallnäs and P. Schroeder-Heister, A Proof-Theoretic Approach to Logic Programming. I: Generalized Horn Clauses (unpublished).

[6] J. Lloyd and R. Topor, Making Prolog More Expressive, Journal of Logic Programming 1(3), October 1984, 225 – 240.

[7] L. McCarty, Clausal Intuitionistic Logic I. Fixed Point Semantics, Journal of Logic Programming 5(1), March 1988, 1 – 31.

[8] L. McCarty, Clausal Intuitionistic Logic II. Tableau Proof Procedure, Journal of Logic Programming 5, 93 – 132, 1988.

[9] D. Miller, A Logical Analysis of Modules in Logic Programming, Journal of Logic Programming 6 (1989), 79 – 108.

[10] D. Miller, Solutions to λ-term equations under a mixed prefix (submitted, January 1989).

[11] D. Miller, Unification under a mixed prefix (unpublished, December 1988).

[12] D. Miller and G. Nadathur, Higher-order Logic Programming, Proceedings of the Third International Logic Programming Conference, London, June 1986, 448 – 462.

[13] D. Miller and G. Nadathur, LP2.7, a C-Prolog and Quintus Prolog implementation of λProlog (July 1988).

[14] D. Miller, G. Nadathur, F. Pfenning, and A. Scedrov, Uniform Proofs as a Foundations for Logic Programming, Annals of Pure and Applied Logic (to appear).

[15] L. Monteiro and A. Porto, Contextual Logic Programming, Proceedings of the Sixth International Logic Programming Conference, Lisbon Portugal, June 1989.

[16] G. Nadathur, A Higher-Order Logic as the Basis for Logic Programming, Ph.D. dissertation, University of Pennsylvania, May 1987.

[17] G. Nadathur and D. Miller, An Overview of λProlog, Fifth International Conference on Logic Programming, MIT Press, 1988.

[18] L. Pauslon, The Foundation of a Generic Theorem Prover, Journal of Automated Reasoning (to appear).

[19] F. Pfenning, Partial Polymorphic Type Inference and Higher-Order Unification, Proceedings of the 1988 ACM Conference on Lisp and Functional Programming.

[20] D. Sannella and L. Wallen, A Calculus for the Construction of Modular Prolog Programs, Proceedings of the 1987 Symposium on Logic Programming, San Francisco, 1987.

[21] G. Smolka, TEL (Version 0.9), Report and Unser Manula. SEKI Report SR-87-11, FB Informatik, Universität Kaiserslautern, W. Germany, 1987.

[22] L. Sterling and E. Shapiro, *The art of Prolog: advanced programming techniques*, MIT Press, Cambridge MA, 1986.

Contextual Logic Programming

Luís Monteiro and **António Porto**

Departamento de Informática
Universidade Nova de Lisboa
2825 Monte da Caparica
Portugal

Abstract

The notion of contextual logic programming is proposed as an extension to the logic programming paradigm. It is tied to the development of a structuring theory for logic programming in which modules, called here units, are sets of context-dependent predicate definitions, and the proof of a certain kind of formulae, called extension formulae, requires extending the context of proof with definitions in a unit. Precise top-down and bottom-up derivation relations are presented, in terms of rules stating how formulae can be derived in varying contexts. A possible-worlds declarative semantics of the proposed notions is given, where the "information content" of contexts, called situations, are seen as possible worlds, and units as specifying transitions between worlds. Several extensions to the basic theory are discussed, like parameterized units and two-level contexts.

1   Introduction

In this paper we present and discuss a possible extension to the logic programming paradigm that deals with structuring of programs and derivations in a coordinated way. The purpose is twofold. On the one hand, to address software engineering concerns of modularity, flexibility, reusability, etc. On the other hand, to provide a computational model for contextual reasoning, so prevalently needed for most Artificial Intelligence tasks such as natural language interpretation, question answering, planning, etc. Because of the central and unifying role played in it by the notion of context, we call this new approach *contextual logic programming*.

Consider the following clause, written in a Prolog-like syntax, adapted from an example in [7]:

```
author(Person) <- wrote(Person, Something).
```

No conclusions can be derived from this clause unless further information concerning the predicate `wrote/2` is supplied. So the program `authors` consisting of this clause alone has an empty minimal model, and from that point of view is indistinguishable from the empty program. However, when placed in some contexts the two programs behave differently. In a context where there is the information `wrote(plato,republic)` the program `authors` allows us to conclude `author(plato)`, while clearly no such conclusion can be reached from the empty program.

We call the definition of the predicate `author/1` context-dependent, since it relies on the context to provide the definition of `wrote/2`. In the context we may have information about writers of theatrical plays, computer programs or musical pieces, and the same definition of authorship applies to them all. In this way we have achieved some form of modularity by splitting up the logical specifications into different "units", as we shall call them, like the unit `authors`. We have also gained in generality, by keeping the general definitions apart from the data to which they apply, and in reusability, since a unit like `authors` may be reused in several contexts.

A unit `books` containing information about writers of books is showed next:

```
books:
   wrote(plato,republic).
   wrote(homer,iliad).
   author(Person)  <-  authors >> author(Person).
```

The third clause, containing in its body the "context-extension formula"

```
authors >> author(Person)
```

states that an author is whatever is declared as such in the unit `authors`. When the unit `books` is asked about what authors there are, by means of the query `author(Who)`, the formula `authors >> author(Who)` must be proved. This consists in proving the "inner" formula `author(Who)` in the unit `authors`, in the context formed by the unit `books`. This means that the definition for `author/1` will be looked for in `authors`, but since `wrote/2` is not defined there, its definition must be found in the current context. As expected, the possible answers to the query are `plato` and `homer`.

Instead of saying that `author(Who)` is proved in `authors` in the context of `books`, we shall say that it is proved in the context `books` "extended" with `authors`, and denote this extended context by the sequence `authors.books`. In general, to prove an atomic formula in a context U.C we just prove the formula in U, using the context C when appropriate. This means that if the formula's predicate is defined in U then we use that definition (and only that definition), otherwise the formula will be proved in C. To prove an extension formula U>>G in a context C we prove G in U.C.

The null sequence λ represents the "empty" context. Asking `books` what authors there are consists in proving the formula `books>>author(Who)` in the empty context, which in turn consists in proving `author(Who)` in the empty context extended with `books`, that is in `books`.

The derivation relation for this system of contextual programming is thus a relation Context ⊢ Formula, stating that Formula is derivable in Context. In fact we shall define two derivation relations, a "top-down" derivation on which the operational semantics is based, and a bottom-up derivation useful for establishing the connection with the declarative semantics. As an example we show the top-down derivation of the formula `books >> author(plato)` from the empty context:

$$
\begin{array}{rcl}
\lambda & \vdash & \texttt{books >> author(plato)} \\
\texttt{books} & \vdash & \texttt{author(plato)} \\
\texttt{books} & \vdash & \texttt{authors >> author(plato)} \\
\texttt{authors.books} & \vdash & \texttt{author(plato)} \\
\texttt{authors.books} & \vdash & \texttt{wrote(plato,Something)} \\
\texttt{books} & \vdash & \texttt{wrote(plato,Something)} \\
\sqrt{} & & \texttt{\{ Something = rcpublic \}}
\end{array}
$$

Declaratively, we have seen that a unit cannot be characterized by its minimal model alone. One possibility is to associate with a unit the set of all of its models. For example, a model of `authors` must satisfy the constraint that if it contains information about who has written what, it also contains the information that he or she is an author. This is in contrast with the models of the empty unit, which are subject to no restriction whatsoever.

We prefer a characterization of the declarative semantics in terms of "situation-transformation operations", where by a "situation" we mean roughly the "information content" of a context, formalized as a subset of the Herbrand base. For example, the transformation associated with `authors` maps information about who has written what to information about authorship. We have thus a possible-worlds semantics, with situations acting as possible worlds and units as specifying transitions between worlds. Atomic formulae and clauses are interpreted in the usual way, except that the interpretation is relative to each situation. On the other hand, an extension formula U>>G is true in a situation S if G is true in the situation in which S is transformed by the denotation of U.

The field of contextual logic programming can be understood as the exploitation of contextual dependencies in logic programming, and is linked to the study of general situation-transformation operations. For the most part we shall limit ourselves in this paper to the kind of transformation exemplified above, called "context-extension" transformations. We shall propose a syntax for the resulting language and develop its basic theory. This consists of the notions of top-down and bottom-up derivations, together with a declarative and a fixed-point semantics, in the style of the corresponding theory for Horn clause logic. We state, but for lack of space do not prove, the equivalence between the proposed semantic definitions.

Besides the basic theory of context extension, other useful notions will be presented in a more informal way: predicate hiding, predicate extension, parameterized units, unit links, context freeing and two-level contexts. The paper ends with short sections on implementation and related work by other authors.

2   Basic Theory

In this section we describe our basic theory of contextual logic programming, an extension to Horn clause logic. In later sections additional constructs are introduced.

2.1   Syntax

Besides the sets Pred, Fun, Var of predicate, function and variable names, we need a set Un of *unit names*. We assume that these sets are finite or denumerably infinite. With every $u \in$ Un is associated a finite subset of Pred, called the *sort* of u and denoted by $[u]$.

Terms, atomic formulae and clauses are defined in the usual way, except that clauses may contain *extension formulae* in their bodies. The syntax for extension formulae is u>>G, where u is a unit name and G is a finite set of atomic or extension formulae, interpreted as the *conjunction* of its elements. If g and G are respectively an atomic or extension formula and a conjunction, we write (g,G) instead of $\{g\} \cup G$. The *null* formula is denoted by Δ, standing for true.

If g is an atomic formula $p(t_1,...,t_n)$, we sometimes write name(g) for the predicate name of g, namely p. By a p-clause we mean a clause $h \leftarrow G$ such that name(h)=p. We say a set of clauses defines p if the set contains some p-clause.

A *unit* is a formula of the form u:U, where $u \in$ Un and U is a finite set of clauses such that the set of predicates defined in U is $[u]$. We call u the *name* of the unit and U its *body*. A *system of units* is a set $\mathcal{U}$ of units such that no two distinct units in $\mathcal{U}$ have the same name. For a unit in $\mathcal{U}$ with name u, we denote its body by $|u|_{\mathcal{U}}$, or simply $|u|$ if $\mathcal{U}$ is understood. In the sequel we will often abuse language and refer to u as a unit in $\mathcal{U}$ when in fact we mean the unit u:|u|.

For examples of units see the introduction.

2.2 Top-down derivation

A program is viewed statically as a finite set of units, as captured by the concept of a system of units. The dynamic view of a program corresponds to the derivation of formulae in contexts, to whose definition we now turn.

Context names are defined as arbitrary sequences of unit names, intended to record the history of the formation of the contexts. Thus the set of context names is Cn=Un*. We represent context names by juxtaposition. For example, if u,v∈ Un, uv∈ Cn. The empty sequence λ is the name of the *empty* context. The context resulting from *extending* the context c with unit u is uc.

Instead of characterizing the notion of top-down derivation, we favour here a more structured approach in a style akin to the one advocated by Plotkin [8], and define a top-down derivation relation. For any context name c and formula G, we denote by $c \vdash_{\mathcal{U}} G\,[\theta]$ the fact that there is a *top-down derivation* of G in c from $\mathcal{U}$ with substitution θ. We reserve the symbol ε to denote the empty (identity) substitution. The result of applying θ to G is written $G\theta$. In the sequel we write $\vdash$ instead of $\vdash_{\mathcal{U}}$ if $\mathcal{U}$ is understood.

The *top-down derivation relation* $\vdash_{\mathcal{U}}$ is defined by rules of the form

$$\frac{\text{Assumptions}}{\text{Conclusion}}\quad \text{Conditions}\,,$$

asserting the Conclusion whenever the Assumptions and Conditions hold. Thus $\vdash_{\mathcal{U}}$ is the smallest relation satisfying the following rules.

Null formula

$$\frac{}{c \vdash \Delta\,[\varepsilon]}$$

The null formula is derivable in every context with empty substitution.

Conjunction

$$\frac{c \vdash g\,[\theta] \qquad c \vdash G\theta\,[\sigma]}{c \vdash (g,G)\,[\theta\sigma]}$$

To derive a non-empty conjunction, derive each conjunct in turn.

Atomic formula (I)

$$\frac{uc \vdash G\theta\,[\sigma]}{uc \vdash g\,[\theta\sigma]}\quad h\leftarrow G \text{ in } |u|,\ \theta = \mathrm{mgu}(g,h)$$

To derive an atomic formula in a context whose most recent unit defines the respective predicate, reduce the formula in the unit and derive the body of the clause used in the reduction. (Of course, the clause h←G is a variant of a clause in |u| with no variables in common with g.)

Atomic formula (II)

$$\frac{c \ \vdash \ g \, [\theta]}{uc \ \vdash \ g \, [\theta]} \qquad name(g) \notin [\![u]\!]$$

If the name of an atomic formula has no definitions in the most recent unit, derive the formula in the immediately preceding context.

Extension formula

$$\frac{uc \vdash G \, [\theta]}{c \vdash u{>}{>}G \, [\theta]}$$

To derive an extension formula, derive the "inner" formula in the context extended with the unit mentioned in the extension formula.

Given a system of units $\mathcal{U}$, the *operational semantics* of a formula g as determined by the top-down derivation relation is the set of all substitutions θ such that $\lambda \vdash_{\mathcal{U}} g\,[\theta]$, where λ is the name of the empty context. Note that this set is empty unless g has the form u>>G for some unit in $\mathcal{U}$ with name u.

The reader should check that the derivation presented in the introduction respects the above rules.

2.3 Bottom-up derivation

The operational semantics of logic programming in general, and of our context-extension proposal in particular, is based on the notion of top-down derivation. The notion of bottom-up derivation, to which we now turn, is more useful in connection with the declarative semantics.

The symbol $\vdash_{\mathcal{U}}$ denotes bottom-up derivation from $\mathcal{U}$, and as for the top-down derivation we write simply $\vdash$ if $\mathcal{U}$ is understood. We only need to define c $\vdash$ g for a context c and an atomic or extension formula g, since we have c $\vdash$ G if and only if c $\vdash$ g for every conjunct g∈ G. For a given set U of clauses, let inst(U) denote the set of all (possibly non-ground) instances of U. The relation $\vdash$ is the smallest relation satisfying the following conditions:

- If uc $\vdash$ g for every g∈ G and (h←G)∈ inst(|u|), then uc $\vdash$ h.
- If c $\vdash$ g and name(g)∉ [[u]] then uc $\vdash$ g.
- If uc $\vdash$ g for every g∈ G then c $\vdash$ u>>G.

The relationship between top-down and bottom-up derivations is described by the following result.

Theorem 1) If $c \vdash g_0$ and g_0 is an instance of g, there is a substitution θ such that $c \vdash g[\theta]$ and g_0 is an instance of $g\theta$.

2) If $c \vdash g[\theta]$ then $c \vdash g\theta$.

2.4 Declarative semantics

An interpretation of a first order language consists of a non-empty set D, called the domain of the interpretation, together with an assignment for each n-ary function symbol of a function from D^n to D, and an assignment for each predicate symbol of a subset of D^n. We extend this notion by providing a suitable interpretation for unit names. For simplicity, we shall confine our discussion in the sequel to Herbrand interpretations, where the domain and the interpretation of function symbols is fixed once and for all.

The domain of a Herbrand interpretation is the Herbrand universe H, the set of all terms t built with the function symbols in Fun. We assume that there is at least a nullary function symbol, to make H non-empty. Each function symbol f, of arity n, is interpreted as the function from H^n to H which maps any sequence of n terms $(t_1,...,t_n)$ to the term $f(t_1,...,t_n)$. A Herbrand interpretation is then an assignment of a subset of H^n to every predicate symbol of arity n. It is customary to identify such an interpretation with the set of all ground atomic formulae $p(t_1,...,t_n)$ such that $(t_1,...,t_n)$ is in the subset of H^n assigned to p by the interpretation. Thus a Herbrand interpretation is essentially a subset I of the Herbrand base B, which is the set of all ground atomic formulae. The set of all Herbrand interpretations is $\wp(B)$, the powerset of B.

In our system we need to consider several subsets of the Herbrand base simultaneously, called here *situations*. The reason is that we need to interpret in one situation statements that refer to other situations. For example, an extension formula u>>G is true in a situation S if every formula in G is true in the situation obtained from S according to the specifications contained in |u|.

Thus a predicate symbol is not in general assigned a single predicate, since this depends on the situation under consideration. The previous remarks also suggest that unit names should denote situation-transformation operations, that is functions from $\wp(B)$ to $\wp(B)$. As a first approach, then, an interpretation of a system of units is an assignment for each unit name of a transformation of $\wp(B)$. We can interpret this semantics in terms of a possible-worlds model, where situations are seen as possible worlds and units as specifying transitions between worlds.

The situation S' in which S is transformed by the denotation of u is determined by first finding the predicates defined by u in the situation S, and then updating S with those predicates. The denotation of u in an interpretation I is then a function u_I which when applied to a situation S gives the predicates defined by u in that situation. The resulting situation S' is the update of S by $u_I(S)$. We now make these ideas precise.

For $P \subseteq \mathrm{Pred}$ and $S \subseteq B$, the *restriction* of S to P is the set

$$S \lceil P = \{p(t_1,\ldots,t_n) \in S : p \in P\}.$$

We write $S\lceil{-}P$ instead of $S\lceil(\mathrm{Pred}{-}P)$, and to simplify the notation we abbreviate $S\lceil P$ to S_P and $S\lceil{-}P$ to S_{-P}. If U is a set of clauses, $\mathrm{ground}(U)$ is the set of all ground instances of clauses in U. A function $f : \wp(X) \to \wp(Y)$ is continuous if, for every $W \subseteq X$ and $y \in Y$, $y \in f(W)$ if and only if there is a finite subset W_0 of W such that $y \in f(W_0)$. The set of all continuous functions from $\wp(X)$ to $\wp(Y)$ is denoted by $[\wp(X) \to \wp(Y)]$.

An *interpretation* I is an assignment, for each $u \in Un$, of a continuous function

$$u_I : \wp(B_{-[u]}) \to \wp(B_{[u]}).$$

The *update* of $S \subseteq B$ by $u \in Un$ according to I is

$$S[u_I] = S_{-[u]} \cup u_I(S_{[u]}).$$

Thus the updated situation consists of the predicates not defined by u together with those redefined by u. Note that the "update by u" is a continuous function from $\wp(B)$ to $\wp(B)$.

Given a situation S, a formula f and an interpretation I, we denote by

$$S \models_I f$$

the fact that f *is true in* S *with respect to* I. The relation $\models_I$ is defined by the following clauses, depending on the form of f:

- $S \models_I F$, where F is a set of formulae, if and only if $S \models_I f$ for every $f \in F$.

- $S \models_I u{:}U$ if and only if $S[u_I] \models_I U$.
  A unit is true in a given situation if all the clauses in the unit body are true in the situation updated by the denotation of the unit name.

- $S \models_I g \leftarrow G$ if and only if $S \models_I g_0 \leftarrow G_0$ for all $g_0 \leftarrow G_0 \in \mathrm{ground}(g \leftarrow G)$.
  A clause is true if all its ground instances are true.

- $S \models_I g \leftarrow G$, where $g \leftarrow G$ is ground, if and only if $S \models_I g$ when $S \models_I G$.
  A ground clause is true if the head is true when the body is true.

- $S \models_I u \text{>>} G$ if and only if $S[u_I] \models_I G$.
  An extension formula is true if the "inner" conjunction is true in the situation updated by the denotation of the unit name.

- $S \models_I g$, where g is a ground atomic formula, if and only if $g \in S$.
  A ground atomic formula is true in a given situation just in case it belongs to the situation.

An interpretation I is a *model* of a system of units $\mathcal{U}$ if every unit in $\mathcal{U}$ is true in every situation with respect to I.

The set

$$\mathfrak{S} = \prod_{u \in Un} [\wp(B_{-[\![u]\!]}) \to \wp(B_{[\![u]\!]})]$$

of all interpretations is partially ordered by

$$I \sqsubseteq J \quad \Leftrightarrow \quad u_I(S) \subseteq u_J(S) \text{ for every } u \in Un \text{ and } S \in \wp(B_{-[\![u]\!]}).$$

$\mathfrak{S}$ is an algebraic lattice whose least and greatest elements $\perp$ and T are given respectively by $u_\perp(S) = \varnothing$ and $u_T(S) = B_{[\![u]\!]}$ for every $u \in Un$ and $S \in \wp(B_{-[\![u]\!]})$. The lub of a non-empty set $\{I_\alpha : \alpha \subset A\}$ of interpretations is the interpretation I such that

$$u_I(S) = \bigcup \{u_{I_\alpha}(S) : \alpha \in A\}$$

for every $u \in Un$ and $S \in \wp(B_{-[\![u]\!]})$.

Theorem Any system of units $\mathcal{U}$ has a minimal model $M = M_{\mathcal{U}}$.

2.5 Fixed-point semantics

The transformation $T = T_{\mathcal{U}} : \mathfrak{S} \to \mathfrak{S}$ associated with a system of units $\mathcal{U}$ maps an interpretation I to the interpretation $T(I)$ such that

$$u_{T(I)}(S) = \{ g : \exists\, g \leftarrow G \in \text{ground}(|u|).\ S[u_I] \models_I G \}.$$

Theorem I is a model of $\mathcal{U} \Leftrightarrow T(I) \subseteq I$.

The minimal model of a system of units is then its least fixed point.

The following result establishes the relationship between the declarative semantics based on the truth relation $\models_M$ with respect to the minimal model M and the relation $\vdash_{\mathcal{U}}$ for the bottom-up derivation. To state the theorem we need a new definition. The situation $S_{c,I}$ associated with a context name c in the interpretation I is defined inductively as follows:

- $S_{\lambda,I} = \varnothing$.
- $S_{uc,I} = S_{c,I}[u_I]$.

Theorem Given a system of units $\mathcal{U}$ with minimal model M,

$$c \vdash_{\mathcal{U}} g \quad \Leftrightarrow \quad S_{c,M} \vDash_M g$$

for every context name c and ground atomic or extension formula g.

The relation between the declarative semantics and the operational semantics as described by the derivation relation is as follows.

Theorem For any extension formula u>>G and substitution θ,

$$\lambda \vdash_{\mathcal{U}} u>>G\,[\theta] \quad \Leftrightarrow \quad u_M(\varnothing) \vDash_M G_0$$

for every ground instance G_0 of $G\theta$, where M is the minimal model of $\mathcal{U}$. (Note that $u_M(\varnothing) = \varnothing[u_M]$.)

3 Extensions to the basic theory

In order to have a practical and powerful contextual logic programming system, the above-exposed basic theory will certainly have to be enlarged. We present in this section, in a rather informal and introductory way, some useful notions that we think should be considered for this enlarged theory. Some are fairly trivial, while others may have far-reaching consequences.

Some other important notions need to be explored but are not addressed in here. A notable example is that of meta-level facilities.

3.1 Predicate hiding

When extending a context c with a unit u containing a definition for a predicate p, this will become the definition to be used in the new context uc to prove atomic formulae for p, eventually overriding an existing definition for p in c. Now imagine a further extension of uc with a unit v that contains p-calls, p not being defined in v. (We will refer by "p-call" an atomic formula whose predicate name is p, ocurring in the body of a clause.) These p-calls will be solved using the current definition for p that was introduced by u. This may in general be undesirable; one programmer may have written units in c and also written v but not u, and intend the connection through p-calls to be made between v and c regardless of u. One way around this problem is by "hiding" definitions such as that for p in u, so that they will be "seen" by p-calls originating in u but will be "invisible" to p-calls from units introduced by further context extensions of uc, such as v. Indeed, predicate definitions in a unit should be hidden by default, according to sound software engineering principles, and only those predicates intended to be called from other units (generally fewer) should be declared as "visible".

So, let us assume there is a function visible : Un $\to$ $\wp$(Pred) associating with each unit u a subset of $[\![u]\!]$. The derivation relation must now be considered to have an extra argument, say the *mode* with possible values int and ext, stating respectively whether or not the formula to be proved originated in the top unit of the current context (i.e. whether the formula is internal or external to the current unit).

The essential changes are in the rules for an atomic formula. Representing the mode argument inside parentheses after the derivation sign, they would now be:

$$\frac{\text{uc } \vdash_{(int)} G\theta\,[\sigma]}{\text{uc } \vdash_{(M)} g\,[\theta\sigma]} \qquad \begin{array}{l} (\ M{=}int \ \lor \ name(g){\in}visible(u)\ ) \\ \land\ h{\leftarrow}G \text{ in } |u| \ \land \ \theta = mgu(g,h) \end{array}$$

$$\frac{\text{c } \vdash_{(ext)} g\,[\theta]}{\text{uc } \vdash_{(M)} g\,[\theta]} \qquad \begin{array}{l} (\ M{=}ext \ \land \ name(g){\notin}visible(u)\ ) \\ \qquad \lor \qquad name(g){\notin}[\![u]\!] \end{array}$$

3.2 Predicate extension

There are good reasons, stemming from both software engineering considerations and the needs of experimental programming, for having separate (partial) definitions that can be dynamically combined in different ways into actual definitions for a *single* predicate. Within our framework of context extension, this corresponds to the notion of allowing a unit not just to introduce *new* predicate definitions while extending a context, but also to *extend* existing predicate definitions in the context. This is shown in the following example, where the definition of the predicate `eats/1` in the unit `my_dog` extends any definition for the same predicate that may exist in the context.

```
dog:
   ...
   eats(meat).
   ...

my_dog { extends eats/1 }:
   ...
   eats(canned_food).
   ...
```

The possible answers to the query `dog>>my_dog>>eats(What)` are `canned_food` and `meat`, while in the absence of the extension declaration the only answer would be `canned_food`.

In practice it is essential to introduce some form of commitment into logic programming languages, such as the cut in Prolog. A major implication is that predicates must then be considered to be defined by *sequences* of clauses rather than sets. This directly affects the notion of predicate extension, for it becomes crucial to decide whether the new clauses for a predicate are to be put before or after the existing clauses in its current definition. We may then decide to have two kinds of predicate extension, say "upwards" and "downwards".

3.3 Parameterized units

One very useful extension of the basic theory concerns the use of parameters in units, in order to pass unit names to definitions inside a unit. This can be accomplished by using a general term rather than just a constant to refer to a unit, encoding the unit name as the main functor and the parameters as arguments. For example, the units `authors` and `books` may be rewritten as follows, where the first has a parameter to be instantiated with the name of the unit containing the required information:

```
authors(Works):
  author(Person)  <-  Works >> wrote(Person,Something).

books:
  wrote(plato,republic).
  wrote(homer,iliad).
```

To know what authors of books there are we now ask the question to `authors`, instructing it to look for the relevant information in `books`, i.e. we try to prove the formula `authors(books) >> author(Who)`. In the first step the proof reduces to that of `author(Who)` in the unit `authors` with the parameter `Works` instantiated to `books`.

A point to discuss is whether we want completely general parameters, which can occur anywhere in the code of a unit, or just parameters to transmit unit descriptions to be used in extension formulas, as in the example above.

3.4 Unit links

We may want to assert the existence of pre-defined links between units, namely in the sense that one unit "requires" some other unit, that is, before being used in a context extension it will require an extension of the context with the required unit.

Take the previous example of `my_dog`. Instead of having to explicitly mention the unit `dog` in formulas such as `dog>>my_dog>>eats(What)`, one could just use the formula `my_dog>>eats(What)` if the unit `my_dog` was declared to require `dog`.

It is interesting to be able to combine this type of link between units with the use of parameters. An alternative way of programming the `authors` example is as follows:

```
authors(Works) { requires Works } :
   author(Person)  <-  wrote(Person,Something).
```

This notion of unit links is related to that of inheritance in object-oriented systems. The exact connection needs to be investigated.

3.5   Context freeing

Sometimes it may be necessary to prove some formula completeley out of the current context, to free the proof from current definitions and rely exclusively on those introduced by the formula alone. This can be easily achieved if a connective is introduced along with the corresponding inference rule to prove something from the empty context. For example:

Context-freeing formula

$$\frac{\lambda \vdash g\,[\theta]}{c \vdash\ ?g\,[\theta]}$$

Of course this is only useful when the inner formula g is itself an extension formula.

3.6   Two-level contexts

In general the context may change several times during a derivation, and we may wish at some point and for some reason to come back to a previous context, to prove a formula in there. This implies the need for some way of remembering past contexts and the ability to revert to them. Here is a possible solution.

We use the unary operator > prefixed to a formula to remember the context in which the proof of the formula started, and the prefix operator < applied to a formula to indicate that the formula should be proved in the more recently saved context. As an example let us redefine once again the `authors` and `books` units:

```
authors:
   author(Person)  <-  < wrote(Person,Something).

books:
   wrote(plato,republic).
   wrote(homer,iliad).
```

The formula `authors>>books(>author(Who))` may be interpreted as querying the database `books` about what authors there are, in the context of the general definition in `authors`. The proof leads to that of `>author(Who)` in the context `books.authors`, which consists in proving `author(Who)` in the same context but saving the context for future reference. Since `author/2` is not defined in `books`, the formula must be proved in `authors`, which calls for proving `<wrote(Person,Something)`. This in turn requires proving `wrote(Person,Something)` in the saved context `books.authors`, providing the answers `plato` and `homer` since `wrote/2` is defined in `books`.

Technically this solution relies on extending our notion of context to a two-level construction. At one level there are *definitional* contexts built as sequences of units (the previous notion of context), and at another level one has a *historical* context, built as a sequence of definitional contexts, which is the more general context that is the argument of the derivation relation. The historical context behaves as a stack of past definitional contexts that were explicitly recorded through the embedded proof of formulas prefixed by >.

The basic inference rules have to be trivially changed by turning what was the (definitional) context into the top of the historical context. For example (using c.C to denote the historical context whose top definitional context is c) the rule for the extension formula becomes

$$\frac{uc.C \vdash G\,[\theta]}{c.C \vdash u \!\!>\!\!> G\,[\theta]}$$

Two new rules have to be introduced for < and >, as follows.

$$\frac{c.c.C \vdash g\,[\theta]}{c.C \vdash \!\!>\!g\,[\theta]} \qquad\qquad \frac{C \vdash g\,[\theta]}{c.C \vdash \!\!<\!g\,[\theta]}$$

4   Implementation

We have been experimenting with the use of a contextual logic programming system incorporating the basic mechanisms and the extensions exposed in section 3. Two implementations have been realized, both targeted for rapid prototyping of different computational models rather than sheer speed.

One of the implementations is based on a pre-processor that transforms clauses in units written in the new language (an extension to Prolog) into standard Prolog clauses, which basically have an extra argument to carry through the derivation the representation of the context as a list of unit names.

The other implementation is done on top of Alpes Prolog [4], an extension to Prolog developed specifically for prototyping architectural solutions to logic programming environments.

Of course a lot of work needs to be done in terms of designing an efficient implementation at the abstract machine level. Still, the current experimental implementations are sufficient to run large programs. As an example, we are able to run an interactive knowledge system with a natural language interface that was rewritten using the new contextual logic programming methodology.

5   Related work

A theory of modules for logic programming based on the logic deduction theorem was developed by Miller [5]. Our own work was at first inspired by Miller's proposal, but we decided from the outset not to rely completely on the deduction theorem. Instead our main motivation was the idea of describing the semantics of units by continuous transformations of the powerset of the Herbrand base, of which the kind of transformation determined by the deduction theorem was but a particular case, and probably not the most interesting one. The declarative semantics of Miller's theory is also in terms of a possible-worlds model, where the set of all worlds is the set of all programs in Miller's sense. In our semantic definition, possible worlds are arbitrary subsets of the Herbrand base. This simplification is due to the fact that we use unit names in extension formulae rather than the units themselves.

O'Keefe [6] defines a module as essentially a set of Horn clauses, and presents several operations for composing modules. The semantics of a module is defined in terms of a continuous transformation of the powerset of the Herbrand base, and the semantics of the module operations as operations on the corresponding transformations.

McCabe [3] proposes a notion of object as a labeled theory, and proceeds to show how some common object-oriented programming notions can be defined in this framework. Class templates, rules and methods, messages, simple, multiple and differential inheritance, among others, are analysed, but objects with state are not considered. The semantics is defined by translating the language to Horn clause logic. Other approaches based on the object-oriented paradigm were followed by Gallaire [1], Stabler [9] and Zaniolo [10].

The work on Eqlog by Goguen and Meseguer [2] also concerns modularity. Like in O'Keefe's proposal, two different languages are needed for defining the basic modules and their composition. Unlike it, it requires a strict type discipline, but also allows functions along with predicates. As noted by Miller [5], Eqlog's notion of importing is one of accumulation, a module being imported by another one when it is enriched with new definitions. This contrasts with the private uses of modules typical of the context extension paradigm.

Acknowledgements

We want to thank Paola Mello, Antonio Natali, and Cristina Ruggieri for all the useful discussions we had about these topics, and all the other people at Enidata, Università di Bologna and Universidade Nova de Lisboa who performed the implementation work that led to a flexible working version of a contextual logic programming system. We also thank the referees for their suggestions.

This work was partially supported by Esprit Project P973, Junta Nacional de Investigação Científica e Tecnológica, Instituto Nacional de Investigação Científica and Gabinete de Filosofia do Conhecimento.

References

[1] Gallaire, H. 1986. Merging objects and logic programming: relational semantics. *Proc. AAAI-86*, Philadelphia, PA.

[2] Goguen, J.A., and J. Meseguer. 1984. Eqlog: Equality, Types and Generic Modules for Logic Programming. In D. DeGroot and G. Lindstrom (eds.), *Functional and Logic Programming*, Prentice-Hall, 295-363.

[3] McCabe, F. 1988. *Logic and objects — Part one: The language.* (2nd. edition) Research report DOC 86/9, Imperial College, London.

[4] Mello, P; A. Natali; C. Ruggieri. 1988. *Contexts as binding environments in Alpes Prolog.* Esprit Project P973 Alpes Technical Report, DEIS, University of Bologna and Enidata S.p.A.

[5] Miller, D. 1986. A Theory of Modules for Logic Programming. In *Proceedings of the 1986 Symposium on Logic Programming*, 106-114. IEEE Computer Society Press. Washington, D.C.

[6] O'Keefe, R. 1985. Towards an Algebra for Constructing Logic Programs. In *Proceedings of the 1985 Symposium on Logic Programming*, 152-160. IEEE Computer Society Press. Washington, D.C.

[7] Pereira, F.C.N., and S.M. Shieber. 1987. *Prolog and Natural-Language Analysis.* CSLI Lecture Notes No. 10. Center for the Study of Language and Information, Stanford University, Stanford, CA.

[8] Plotkin. G.D. 1981. *A structural approach to operational semantics.* Technical report DAIMI FN-19, Computer Science Department, Aarhus University.

[9] Stabler, E.P., Jr. 1986. Object-oriented programming in Prolog. *AI Expert*, October 1986, 46-57.

[10] Zaniolo, C. 1984. Object oriented programming in Prolog. *Proc. International Symposium on Logic Programming*, Atlantic City, NJ.

Extensions of Warren Abstract Machine

THE DESIGN OF AN ABSTRACT MACHINE FOR EFFICIENT IMPLEMENTATION OF CONTEXTS IN LOGIC PROGRAMMING

Evelina Lamma, Paola Mello, Antonio Natali

Dipartimento di Elettronica, Informatica e Sistemistica
Universita' di Bologna
Viale Risorgimento 2
40136 Bologna - ITALY
email: boari%bodeis.infnet@icineca2.bitnet

ABSTRACT

The main aim of this paper is to show how dynamic and flexible mechanisms of context handling in logic programming can be implemented by using a compiled approach and thus become useful constructs to build real applications. In particular, the paper focuses on the design of an abstract machine for context implementation. This abstract machine has been designed as an extended Warren Abstract Machine, where new data structures and new instructions have been added to deal with contexts.

INTRODUCTION

One of the main limitations of some logic programming languages is the lack of powerful concepts to structure the program into different modules, units or theories (i.e. sets of definite clauses) that can be statically or dynamically composed.
As already pointed out in [1], [3], [4], [5] units and their composition can be very useful to handle hypothetical reasoning, to simulate the assert and retract behaviour in a more declarative way and, in synthesis, to broaden the application area of logic programming towards Artificial Intelligence applications. Many different proposals exist on this subject (see for example [1], [4], [9], [11], [12]) with different ways of defining and composing units. Nevertheless, very few proposals ([1], [4]) try to implement unit combination efficiently by using compilation techniques.
The main goal of this paper is to show that a compilation approach can be successfully pursued by designing an extended Warren Abstract Machine [13] - called Contextual Warren Abstract Machine (C-WAM)- supporting very powerful and flexible forms of unit combination. The unit combination mechanisms introduced in this work and implemented in C-WAM by adding a new stack, new registers, and some new instructions to the WAM, are an extension of the basic mechanism proposed by Monteiro and Porto in *contextual logic programming* ([11]). In contextual logic programming, program execution corresponds to the proof of goals with respect to contexts, i.e. ordered sets of units, that can vary dynamically. In this work the concepts of binding-time (eager or lazy) for predicates, dynamic unit creation, and lexical or dynamic scope for units have been introduced to the basic mechanisms presented in [11] to make a good trade-off between

readabilty, flexibility and efficiency. A formal description of contextual logic programming is beyond the scope of this paper and is presented in [11].

Even if the C-WAM supports a particular policy of context handling, its design could constitute a sort of *guide-line* to implement different forms of unit combination proposed in other works. In particular, we feel that the concepts of binding-time, the interpretation of a context as a binding environment, the run-time representation of unit instances are not tailored simply to implement the particular policy of unit combination presented here.

1. CONTEXTS IN LOGIC PROGRAMMING

1.1 Basic Concepts

Contextual logic programming is deeply and formally described in [11], where a possible-world declarative semantics is given. Since the main aim of this work is to present the C-WAM design, the basic mechanisms of contextual logic programming are here only sketched. Let us consider an extended logic programming system - subsuming Prolog - where separate *units* can be defined as first-class objects and dynamically combined. Rather than evaluate a goal *g* by simply using a fixed and statically determined set of clauses, as happens in pure Prolog, *g* is evaluated in contextual logic programming [11] by using a variable set of clauses determined by the *current context of proof*. More precisely we define as:

unit: an ordered set of definite clauses univocally identified by a Prolog constant;

context: an ordered list of units that varies during execution and that determines the overall set of clauses to be considered in the proof of a goal. In particular, if the current context is $[U_N, U_{N-1}, ..., U_1]$ the ordered set of clauses considered is:

$<U_N$ clauses> $\qquad <U_{N-1}$ clauses> $\qquad .... \qquad <U_1$ clauses>

The built-in predicate $U_N >> G$ (*context-extension operator*), where U_N is the name of a unit and *G* a goal, forces the proof of the goal *G* in a new context, *C1*, obtained by conceptually "stacking" the U_N clauses on top of the previous context *C*. The underlying system guarantees automatic discarding of the U_N clauses at the end of the proof of *G*, both in the case of success or failure. In the following example:

unit list1:	**unit eq1:**
member(X,[Y|_]):- eq1 >> equal(X,Y).	equal(X,X).
member(X,[_|Z]):- member(X,Z).	

the top goal: *list1 >> member(a,[a,b,c])* has the top down derivation:

[] |- list1 >> member(a,[a,b,c])

[list1] |- member(a,[a,b,c])

[eq1,list1] |- equal(a,a)   success

A more generic definition of *member/2* can be obtained by omitting the context extension operator in its body.

unit list2:

member(X,[Y\|_]):- equal(X,Y).

member(X,[_\|Z]):- member(X,Z).

permutation([],[]).

permutation(L,[X\|P]):- del(X,L,L1),permutation(L1,P).

The top goal: *eq1>>list2>>member(a,[a,b,c])* has the following top down derivation:

[] |- eq1>>list1 >> member(a,[a,b,c])
[eq1] |- list1>>member(a,[a,b,c])
[list1,eq1] |- member(a,[a,b,c])
[list1,eq1] |- equal(a,a)
[eq1] |- equal(a,a)   *success*

If one desires to use *member/2* with a different definition for *equal/2* it is sufficient to call *member/2* with a different context, e.g. by using the top goal:

eq2 >> list2 >> member(a,[a,b,c]) where:

unit eq2:
equal(*,_).
equal(?,_).
equal(X,X).

1.2 Contexts as Binding Environments

The concept of context can be mapped in the concept of *binding environment*, a common notion in traditional programming languages to bind a name to a value for some period during execution of a program. The context, in fact, is the mean for associating predicate calls to predicate definitions. With reference to binding policies three problems have to be solved:

- How to determine the predicate definition for a predicate call, given a context;
- What part of the context to take into account in solving bindings;
- How to determine the current context when an extension takes place.

1.2.1 Predicate Definition

When the current context C is extended with a unit U each predicate p/n locally defined in U can either extend or override the previous definition of p/n present in C. The default policy adopted here is overriding. Extension of the definition of the predicate p/n can be obtained only by explicitly writing in U the declaration: *$extends(p/n)*. More formally, let us define as *Sp(U,p/n)* the ordered set of clauses in a unit U having head with the same functor p and arity n (i.e. the local definition of p/n in U). Given a context *Ctx* defined as $[U_N,...,U_i,...,U_1]$, where U_N is the most recent unit added to the context, and U_1 the least recent, and a predicate p/n, *Def(Ctx,p/n)* denotes the definition of the predicate p/n in *Ctx*:

Def(Ctx,p/n)=

{} if Ctx = []

Sp(head(Ctx),p/n) if Ctx <> [] and
    Sp(head(Ctx),p/n) <> {} and
    head(Ctx) does not extend p/n

Sp(head(Ctx),p/n) U Def(tail(Ctx),p/n)
    if Ctx <> [] and
    (Sp(head(Ctx),p/n) = {} or
    head(Ctx) extends p/n)

Use of the *$extends* declaration avoids replication of the code in some cases. For example, all the occurrences of the unit *eq2* could be replaced by the context extension *eq1>>eq2_II* where *eq2_II* is:

unit eq2_II:
$extends(equal/2).
equal(*,_).
equal(?,_).
In fact Def([eq2_II,eq1],equal/2) = Def([eq2],equal/2)).

To support information hiding, a predicate definition *p/n* is exportable from a unit *U* (i.e. visible outside it) only if the declaration *$visible(p/n)* is present in *U*. Of course, to deal with *$visible* declarations, *Def(Ctx,p/n)* has to be modified accordingly , together with the examples presented above.

1.2.2 Eager and Lazy bindings

Let us consider a predicate call *p/n* within a unit U_i and the context *Ctx* $[U_N,...U_i...,U_1]$. The binding of *p/n* is lazy if the definition of *p/n* is determined by the whole context *Ctx*, i.e. *Def(Ctx,p/n)*. We will refer to *Ctx* also as Lazy Context (LC). The binding of *p/n* is eager, if the definition of *p/n* is determined by the part $[U_i...,U_1]$ of the context starting from U_i, i.e. *Def([U_i,...,U_1],p/n)*. We will refer to this part of *Ctx* also as Eager Context (EC). Each predicate call is bound with reference to LC if prefixed by # (*lazy goal*), otherwise it is bound with reference to EC (*eager goal*). For example, in unit *list1*, *member/2* and *equal/2* subgoals are eager goals. Goals appearing in context extensions are always considered as lazy (e.g. *equal/2* subgoal in *list1*) even if not prefixed by #. To better understand the difference between eager and lazy goals let us consider the following unit:

unit eq3:
equal(X,X).
equal([X|A],[Y|B]) :- permutation([X|A],[Y|B]).
The top goal: *eq3 >> list2 >> member([a,b],[[b,a],c])* has the following derivation where the first list represents EC and the second one LC:

[] [] |- eq3 >> list2 >> member([a,b],[[b,a],c])
[eq3] [eq3] |- list2 >> member([a,b],[[b,a],c])
[list2,eq3] [list2,eq3] |- member([a,b],[[b,a],c])
[list2,eq3] [list2,eq3] |- equal([a,b],[b,a])
[eq3] [list2,eq3] |- equal([a,b],[b,a])
[eq3] [list2,eq3] |- permutation([a,b],[b,a])   failure

The eager goal *permutation/2* in *eq3* is bound with respect to the eager context [eq3] and then fails. Changing the order of *eq3* and *list2* in the context does not solve the problem (*equal/2* will fail). The best solution, to avoid explicit naming of the unit *list2* inside *eq3*, is to consider *permutation/2* subgoal as lazy:

unit eq4:
equal(X,X).
equal([X|A],[Y|B]) :- #permutation([X|A],[Y|B]).
The top goal: *eq4 >> list2 >> member([a,b],[[b,a],c])* has the following derivation:

[] [] |- eq4 >> list2 >> member([a,b],[[b,a],c])
[eq4] [eq4] |- list2 >> member([a,b],[[b,a],c])
[list2,eq4] [list2,eq4] |- member([a,b],[[b,a],c])

[list2,eq4] [list2,eq4] |- equal([a,b],[b,a])
[eq4] [list2,eq4] |- equal([a,b],[b,a])
[eq4] [list2,eq4] |- #permutation([a,b],[b,a])
[list2,eq4] [list2,eq4] |- del(b,[a,b],L1),permutation(L1,[a])   .... *success*
In this case, the lazy goal *permutation/2* is solved with reference to the lazy
context [list2,eq4] and the right definition is found in *list2*. From the practical point
of view, the predicate definition for an eager goal called in a unit U, can no longer
be modified or extended by new context extensions occurring after the extension
involving U. The predicate definition for a lazy goal called in a unit U can, instead,
be defined, overidden or extended, if needed, by new context extensions occurring
after the extension involving U. In [11] only eager binding is introduced. Here lazy
binding has been added to obtain a more dynamic way of structuring and combining
units, necessary, for example, to support inheritance mechanisms [8].

1.2.3 How to determine the Current Context in Context Extension

The context extension operator $U>>G$ extends the current context *Ctx* with U, as
said in section 1.1. Since in section 1.2.2 two different contexts have been introduced,
i.e. eager and lazy, we have to determine which is the current context. This choice
is fundamental when a context extension takes place. In this proposal the current
context is represented by the eager context.
This choice leads to adoption of a "cactus model" of the context extension, since it
seems safer [10], while the choice of selecting the lazy context as the current context
leads to a "linear model". However a "linear model" of the binding environment
can easily be obtained through a lazy evaluation of the extension operator. Moreover,
in order to support a more static, efficient and safe view of programs, with respect
to the basic mechanisms sketched in section 1.1, we add two kinds of unit here,
dynamic and *lexical* that produce different behaviours when extending the context.
Dynamic and lexical units are respectively defined by using the built-in predicates:

create(<unit_name>,<unit_code>)

define(<unit_name>,<unit_code>)

where <unit_name> is an atom and <unit_code> a list of definite clauses or a
reference to a file where the unit code is stored.
The main difference between dynamic and lexical units is that when the goal $U>>G$
is executed, if U is dynamic the new current context is obtained by extending the
current (eager) one with U, while if U is lexical the new current context is obtained
by extending with U the eager context present when U was created. Thus U is said to
be "lexically scoped" by analogy with "closure" definitions in the LISP language [15].
Let us consider the top goal: *eq2 >> list2 >> member(*,[a,b,c])* where *eq2* and *list2*
are supposed to be dynamically scoped. The following derivation will take place:

[] [] |- eq2 >> list2 >> member(,[a,b,c])*
[eq2] [eq2] |- list2 >> member(,[a,b,c])*
[list2,eq2] [list2,eq2] |- member(,[a,b,c])*
[list2,eq2] [list2,eq2] |- equal(,a)*
[eq2] [list2,eq2] |- equal(,a)*   *success*
Let us suppose, now, that unit *list2* must always use the definition of *equal/2*

present in *eq1*. Then unit *list2_II* can be defined as a lexically-scoped unit having the same source code as *list2*, and also having [eq1] as "fixed" context (e.g. by calling the top goal: *eq1 >> define(list2_II, <list2_code>)*).

For the top goal: *eq2 >> list2_II >> member(*,[a,b,c])* the following derivation will take place:

[] [] |- eq2 >> list2_II >> member(,[a,b,c])*
[eq2] [eq2] |- list2_II >> member(,[a,b,c])*
[list2_II,eq1] [list2_II,eq1] |- member(,[a,b,c])*
[list2_II,eq1] [list2_II,eq1] |- equal(,a)*
[eq1] [list2_II,eq1] |- equal(,a)   failure (backtracking)*

The same effect is obtained by directly calling *eq1>>equal(X,Y)* in *list1*, but the solution with lexical scope is more efficient, as will be clear in section 3.

In some cases it can be useful not only to extend the current context, but also to *switch* to a different, new context. This effect can be directly obtained, without the introduction of a new operator, by using context extension and lexical units. It is sufficient to assume the existence of a primitive unit, called *top*, with no predicate definition and lexically scoped in the empty context []. The switching of the context to $[U_N,..,U_1]$ is obtained by the goal: $top>>U_1>>...>>U_N>>G$. Each "top goal" *TG* has to be considered as *top>>TG*.

2. INFERENCE RULES

In this section we sketch the inference rules used by the extended Prolog machine supporting contexts in order to better explain the context handling mechanisms presented in section 1 and the implementation based on the C-WAM described in section 3, whose design was inspired by these rules. A meta-interpreter for contexts can be straightforwardly written in Prolog by translating these inference rules. For the sake of simplicity, \$extends-\$visible declarations and create/1-define/1 built-in predicates are not taken into account. We denote with:

g an atomic goal. From an operational point of view we denote a procedure call like p(t1,...,tn) with *g*;

G an atomic goal or a conjunction of atomic goals;

e, k, j answer subsitutions; *e* is the empty answer substitution;

(kj) the composition of the answer substitutions *k* and *j*;

{G}j the application of the substitution *j* to the formula *G*;

mgu(g,h) the most general unifier of the atomic formulas g and h;

The atomic clauses have the conventional body "true", which always holds;

Units = {u | u is a unit name};

|u| = {c | c is a clause in u};

||u|| = {p | p is the name of a predicate defined in u};

Contexts = {c | c is a list of unit names (e.g. $[u_1,u_2,..u_N]$)}.

To support both eager and lazy binding for a goal *G* occurring in a unit *U*, both the eager context EC and the lazy context LC have to be maintained at each resolution step. These two contexts constitute the Binding Environment (BE), represented as a two-element list of contexts (i.e. [EC,LC]). To deal with lexically-scoped units we have to associate a context with lexically-scoped units.

We denote with *closure: Units—> (Contexts U {nil})* the function that, given a unit *u*, returns the corresponding context if *u* is lexically scoped. If *u* is dynamic, the result nil is returned. In the following seven inference rules, *BE /-$_k$ G* means that *G* is derivable from the Binding Environment BE, with answer substitution *k*. The first three rules are very similar to those of standard pure Prolog.

(1)**TRUE**

$$\overline{\text{BE } \vdash_e \text{true}}$$

(2)**CONJUNCTION:**

$$\frac{\text{BE } \vdash_k G1 \ ; \ \text{BE } \vdash_j \{G2\}k}{\text{BE } \vdash_{kj} (G1,G2)}$$

(3)**ATOMIC GOAL I:**

$$\frac{h{:}{-}G \text{ in } |u|; \ k = mgu(g,h); \ [[u|C],LC]\vdash_j \{G\}k}{[[u|C],LC] \vdash_{kj} g}$$

This rule applies if a clause for the atomic goal *g* is defined in the unit *u* representing the top of the current eager context [u|C].

(4)**ATOMIC GOAL II:**

$$\frac{name(g) \text{ not in } ||u||; \ [C,LC]\vdash_k g}{[[u|C],LC] \vdash_k g}$$

This rule applies if no clause for the atomic goal *g* is defined in the unit *u* at the top of the current eager context [u|C]. In this case a definition for *g* is sought in C.

(5)**EXTENSION WITH DYNAMICALLY-SCOPED UNITS:**

$$\frac{u \text{ in Units}; \ closure(u) = nil; \ [[u|EC],[u|EC]]\vdash_k G}{[EC,LC] \vdash_k u{>}{>}G}$$

This rule extends the current eager context EC by stacking up *u*, which is dynamically scoped. The lazy context is made equal to the new eager context.

(6)**EXTENSION WITH LEXICALLY-SCOPED UNITS:**

$$\frac{closure(u) = EC1; \ [[u|EC1], [u|EC1]] \vdash_k G}{\text{BE } \vdash_k u{>}{>}G}$$

This rule extends the context *EC1* associated with a lexically-scoped unit *u* by stacking up *u* on it. Both the eager and lazy contexts are set to the resulting context.

(7)**LAZY GOALS:**

$$\frac{[LC,LC] \vdash_k G}{[EC,LC] \vdash_k \#G}$$

This rule forces the proof of the lazy goal #G in the current lazy context LC, which becomes the new eager context.

3. THE CONTEXT ABSTRACT MACHINE

In this section, the abstract machine designed for contextual logic programming (referred to as Context Warren Abstract Machine or C-WAM in the following) is presented. To maintain full compatibility with Prolog, C-WAM has been conceived as an extension of the Warren Abstract Machine [13]. The memory organization has been changed in order to support modularity and dynamic allocation of units. A new stack, representing the binding environment, has been added along with two new instructions to expand/contract it. Moreover, the structure of both the choice point and the environment of the WAM have been extended to consistently handle new registers. From the implementation point of view, each (sub)goal appearing in a unit U can be classified as:

1. *local* if a local predicate definition for it exists in U;
2. *eager* if no local predicate definition for it exists in U;
3. *lazy* if it is prefixed by the # operator.

The difference between these goals can be interpreted in terms of *binding time*. Bindings for local goals can be solved at unit creation-time since they are always solved in the unit in which they appear. Bindings for eager goals of a unit U can be solved:

- when the current context is extended with the unit U (i.e. at unit extension-time) if U is dynamically scoped;
- when unit U is defined (i.e. at unit creation-time) if U is lexically scoped.

Bindings for lazy goals, instead, can be solved only when they are called.

3.1 Generation of the unit code for C-WAM

The first issue faced in designing C-WAM is how to represent unit code and the units belonging to the current context. We will refer to them as *unit instances*. When the creation of an instance of a unit u is required (e.g. the goal $u >> g$ is invoked), two different choices might be adopted:

- <u>code copying</u>: a new private "copy" of u code is made, specialized with respect to the current context. For each instance of u, the code of u is copied once the references for eager goals have been solved with respect to the current binding environment;
- <u>code sharing</u>: different instances of u share the same, reentrant code. Each instance of u refers to a different binding environment.

These alternative choices are respectively similar to the mechanisms of structure copying and structure sharing in traditional Prolog implementations. In C-WAM, code sharing has been adopted since it allows a more compact use of the memory: the code need not be replicated for each unit instance. This is particularly evident when a recursion involving context extensions is executed. In particular, each instance of a unit u, shares the same code and has a private set of references for eager goals in u, all solved at unit extension-time. This choice has the drawback that an overhead is paid at extension-time also for eager goals that will never be called. Another possibility could be to leave unbound eager goals at extension time and solve them only when they are called, as happens for lazy goals. This choice, adopted for default theories of MetaProlog [2] implies an overhead that increases with the number of eager calls. This overhead becomes unacceptable if recursion is heavily used. The best solution should be to solve references for eager goals the first time they are called and then record the references for subsequent calls. This solution can be straightforwardly obtained from the implementation here presented.

Let us, from now on, consider only dynamically-scoped units; for lexically-scoped units see subsection 3.5.

C-WAM maintains a global table, T, where, for each unit U, the address of its compiled code is reported. The compiled code of a dynamically-scoped unit U is produced when a *create(U,<source>)* is called, and is constituted by:

1. the C-WAM code of the procedures defined in U;
2. a table for the visible procedures defined in U (*$visible* declaration) where for each procedure name the corresponding address is reported;
3. the type of unit (e.g dynamically-scoped in this case);
4. the number NE of predicates corresponding to eager goals called in U;
5. the number NP of procedures of U that extend others (*$extends* declaration).
6. a local table, *ET*, with dimension NE+NP where for each eager goal or extending predicate an offset number is associated;

In both dynamically- and lexically-scoped units, calls to local goals are compiled into **call P,n** or **execute P** instructions, as for standard WAM. In fact, for local goals, the right address for P is already known at compile-time.

In a dynamically scoped unit u, calls to an eager goal are compiled into one of the following instructions:

call_e Pi, m   execute_e Pi

where the *Pi* reference is found at extension-time, i.e. when an instance of u is created by using $u >> G$. Calls corresponding to a lazy goal q/n in both dynamically- and lexically-scoped units are compiled in:

call_l q/n, m   execute_l q/n

where the right addresses for q/n will be solved only at execution-time, i.e. when the instructions are executed.

If the type of goal cannot be determined at compile-time, a call to the *call/1* procedure, suitably extended, is produced. For each extending procedure p/n (*$extends* declaration) **try_me_else** instructions are used to allocate a choice point even if the p/n is deterministic. When backtracking occurs, other definitions for p/n will be sought in the current context C (inter-unit backtracking) by using the same mechanisms adopted for eager goals. The instruction **trust_ext Pi** is inserted to dynamically explore an alternative code for p/n in the current context. The reference Pi is left unsolved at compile-time and will be solved only at extension time.

3.2 Run-time structures and memory organization

To support contexts, C-WAM has to represent and consistently maintain the binding environment (i.e. the eager and lazy context). The eager context can always be obtained by popping some unit instances from the lazy context. This property guarantees efficient implementation by using only one stack (called context stack) and two different registers called EC and LC, pointing respectively to the top of the eager and lazy context (see section 3.3). Each object on the context stack is an *instance environment*. Every time the context is extended with a unit u, an instance environment for u is allocated at the top of the context stack. The instance environment consists of:

1. A vector of cells (P0..Pn), whose dimension is statically determined (see section 3.1) by the number of eager goals and extending procedures occurring

in the unit code. This vector is the run-time structure corresponding to the local table *ET* of *u*. Each offset *i* in *ET* corresponds to a cell, *Pi*, in the instance environment;

2. A reference (*unit_ref*) to the code of *u* in the code area;
3. A cell (*prev_ec*) where the value of EC is saved;
4. A cell (*prev_lc*) where the value of LC is saved.

Instance environments are for different instances of the same unit what environments are for different executions of the same clause body. Each *Pi* cell is bound at extension-time. Binding *Pi* requires each instance environment to be inspected, starting from EC, and searching for some visible code - in the corresponding unit - for the predicate associated with *Pi* until some code is found, or an instance of the primitive unit *top* is reached. If some code is found, its address is stored in *Pi* together with a reference to the instance environment where the search ends with success. Otherwise, the address of a failing procedure is inserted. The context stack grows whenever an extension $U >> G$ occurs and shrinks when G is deterministically solved or definitely fails. Since the context stack behaves like the local one we are investigating a more compact solution where instance environments are allocated on the local stack.

3.3 Registers

The C-WAM register set is composed of the WAM registers together with new registers, introduced to deal with contexts. The LC register determines the lazy context currently in use as the chain of instance environments starting from it. The EC register determines the eager context currently in use as the chain of instance environments starting from it. The value of EC and LC is modified whenever the context is extended. EC may also vary when an eager or lazy call is executed or an alternative procedure for an extending predicate is executed. Since the program counter can now be seen as the pair <P,EC> (<program pointer, eager context>), also for EC a continuation register (CEC), saved in the environment, is introduced. Register C refers to the top of the context stack in order to consistently handle backtracking. In fact, even if the instance of U can be logically discarded at the end of the goal, $U >> G$, by restoring the old values of EC and LC saved in the instance environment, it might be necessary to physically maintain the U instance on the context stack if G has not been deterministically solved. EC, LC, CEC and C are added to the choice point to support backtracking.

3.4 Instructions

The C-WAM instructions are the WAM instructions - suitably extended for handling contexts - plus some new instructions.

3.4.1 Instructions to allocate/deallocate instance environments

The new instruction: **allocate_contx** allocates a new instance environment on the top of the context stack (starting from the location pointed by the C register) for the

unit *u*, whose name has been inserted in a particular machine register (called CU).
get, put and **unify** instructions must admit this register as argument. The actions
performed by this instruction can be summarized as follows:

- It finds the address *ac* of *u* code in the global table *T* if *u* has already been
created, otherwise it fails;
- It allocates an instance environment for *u* with dimension *n*, determined from
the *u* code;
- It inserts *ac* in the *unit_ref* slot of the instance environment;
- It stores, in the P0,..,Pn-1 cells, the addresses and environments to be
used to solve eager goals and extending procedures of *u* according to the
mechanisms presented in subsection 3.1. These addresses could be determined, for the sake of efficiency, the first time eager goals are called;
- It inserts the value of EC and LC respectively in the *prev_ec* and *prev_lc* slot,
and updates both EC and LC with the new value of C.

The new instruction: **deallocate_contx** logically deallocates the instance
environment, *ie*, indicated by LC and restores the old values of EC and LC saved
in *ie*. *ie* will be physically discarded (i.e. the value of C will be set to the old value
of LC saved in *ie*) only if no choice point exists referring to it. More precisely,
if register B refers to the last choice point on the local stack, *ie* is physically discarded
only if $(C = LC)$ and $(LC > LC(B))$, where $LC(B)$ is the value of LC saved in the last
choice point. Let us consider, by way of example, the compilation of the clause:
p(U,G,X) :- U >> G, q(X).

```
p/3     allocate 1
        get_x_variable  A3,A0
        get_x_variable  A0,A1   % G in A0
        get_y_variable  Y0,A2   % X saved in the environment
        put_x_value  A3,CU      % name of the unit in CU
        allocate_contx
        call  call/1, 1
        deallocate_contx
        put_y_value  Y0,A0
        deallocate
        execute  q/1
```

In order to save the value of register A0 an environment is allocated on the context
stack. Compilation of the subgoal $U >> G$ consists of a few instructions that first load
a reference to *U* in the CU register, then call the *call/1* procedure suitably extended
in order to deal with contexts.

3.4.2 Call and execute instructions

Since in C-WAM the address code is represented by the pair <P,EC> and the
continuation by the pair <CP,CEC>, all C-WAM control instructions deal with
EC and CEC in a similar way as WAM control instructions deal with P and CP.
Standard **call** and **execute** WAM instructions are maintained to deal with local goals.
call_e Pi,n and **execute_e Pi** instructions (used for eager calls in dynamically-scoped
units) modify the value of the program counter register P and the register EC with
the values stored in the Pi offset of the current instance environment (i.e. that

indicated by the current EC).

call_l p/n,m and **execute_l p/n**, used for lazy calls in both dynamically- and statically-scoped units, search for the procedure *p/n* along the lazy context. To perform this search, the value of EC is made equal to the value of LC and some visible code for *p/n* is sought in the unit corresponding to the current instance environment. This search continues recursively by updating the value of EC with that of the *prev_ec* slot until some visible code for *p/n* is found or an instance environment for *top* is reached. If some code is found, it is executed, otherwise backtracking occurs.

3.4.3 Indexing instructions

For each extending procedure *p/n* - i.e. a procedure for which a declaration *$extends(p/n)* exists - the compiled code always allocates a choice point (by using the **try_me_else** instruction) even if *p/n* is deterministic. The code for the last clause of *p/n* is preceded by the **retry_me_else** instruction and followed by the new instruction **trust_ext Pi**. This instruction is like the WAM **trust** with the only difference that P and EC registers are set to the values stored in the Pi offset of the current instance environment (i.e. that pointed by the current EC), in order to perform inter-unit backtracking. If no alternative code has been found in the current context (i.e. the address code of a failing procedure has been inserted in the Pi offset) a failure is generated and standard backtracking occurs.

3.5 Compilation of lexically-scoped units

In a lexically-scoped unit U, not only local but also eager goals and extending procedures can be bound at compile-time by performing the same operations (e.g. the search in the eager context) done at extension-time for dynamically-scoped units. This justifies why lexically-scoped units are more efficient than dynamically-scoped ones. The price paid is a more complex compilation phase together with the production of new specialized codes that sometimes can be very large. When a *define(U_N,<U_N_code>)* goal is executed, for each unit instance U_i belonging to the current eager context [U_{N-1},...,U_1,top], a new code (*spec_U_i*) is produced by specializing the code of the corresponding unit (U_i) with respect to the values found in the P cells of the U_i instance. This specialization process starts from the less recent unit instance (i.e. U_1) and stops with the most recent (i.e. U_{N-1}). Since U_1 is specialized with respect to the context [top], eager and extending references are set to a failing built-in procedure. Eager references and extending procedures occurring in U_i - for each value *i* greater than *1* - are substituted in *spec_U_i* by the address of the corresponding procedure found in [spec_U_{i-1},..,spec_U_1]. Finally, the code for U_N is produced in a similar way. In U_N code, the list of addresses corresponding to the specialized codes [spec_U_{N-1},...,spec_U_1,top] is recorded (U_N closure). When extending the context with the lexical unit U_N the **allocate_contx** instruction allocates N+1 instances on the context stack for *top, spec_U_1,...,spec_U_N*. In this way the chain of instance environments present when U_N was defined is restored in a more compact form. In fact, instance environments for specialized units, U_N included, have no P cell, since all references are already solved in the specialized code. Another possibility is to deal with lexical units as was done for dynamic ones, by translating the extension $U_N >> G$, where U_N is lexical, into $top>>U_1>>...>>U_N>>G$. In this way, no specialized code is produced during U_N compilation.

4. RELATED WORKS

Many proposals exist that extend logic programming with the concepts of modules and contexts (see, for example [4], [9], [11]). Our previous work on contexts presented in [4] was less general than the one discussed here. In particular, only dynamically-scoped units and lazy goals were supported. A detailed discussion of these proposals and their comparison with the one presented here in terms of expressive power, flexibility and declarative semantics is beyond the scope of this paper. Its main aim of is, in fact, to define an abstract machine that efficiently supports a set of powerful context mechanisms. For this reason, our work is very similar, to Bacha's MetaProlog implementation (see [1], [2]) even though some remarkable differences exist. Some analogies/differences with Bacha's work are related to the basic mechanisms provided for unit definition and combination and can be summarized as follows:

1. Both in Meta-Prolog and in our proposal dynamic unit creation is provided;
2. In MetaProlog both "permanent" and "temporary" theories exist. Permanent theories are always present in the system and can be accessed via their names, while temporary theories are without names and are only accessible in the environments where the variables bound to their internal representation exist. In our proposal, units can be assimilated to permanent theories while temporary theories are not provided;
3. In MetaProlog, theories are organized in a hierarchical tree, when they are created. In our proposal you can obtain the same effect by using lexically-scoped units;
4. In MetaProlog the concept of dynamic context extension does not exist. A limited form of dynamic combination of theories in MetaProlog can be obtained by using virtual theories, but the set of theories composing the virtual theory has to be explicitly and completely specified. However, the same effect of MetaProlog: *demo(T1+T2+T3, Goal)* can be obtained by the goal: *top>>T3>>T2>>T1>>Goal*;
5. In MetaProlog no declaration like *$visible* exists to support information hiding, but this declaration is very useful to solve eager and lazy goals more efficiently;
6. In MetaProlog lazy binding is not provided. As written in [2], if a theory *Ti* redefines a predicate *p/n*, all its descendants can inherit the new *p/n* definition, but the ancestor theories of *Ti* retain the old definitions of *p/n*. This can be the right choice in some cases and corresponds to our policy of eager binding. However, in some cases a more dynamic view of programs is necessary as in object-oriented programming [14] where late binding is adopted. Let us consider the following example (inspired to the one in [1]):

unit ancestor:

unprejudiced :- #premarital_sex(right).

premarital_sex(wrong).

unit child:

premarital_sex(right).

Without lazy binding the goal *top >> ancestor >> child >> unprejudiced* fails even if in the *child* unit the belief about premarital sex has changed.

With respect to the implementation, the following differences between our proposal and MetaProlog can be pointed out:

1. In MetaProlog the code area is eliminated: the code of theories is in the heap area. We do not adopt this choice since we have no temporary theories;

2. We adopt an explict representation of the context as a set of unit instances. The code of each unit U is composed of the procedures explicitly defined in U. Access to the right code for the procedures called but not defined in U is performed by searching in the current context. MetaProlog, instead, represents all the procedures for the same predicate p/n in a single data structure $R(p/n)$ independently of the unit they belong to;

3. While in MetaProlog each goal p/n is solved at execution-time, i.e. when the goal is invoked, by searching for the right code in $R(p/n)$, in our proposal this happens only for lazy goals. The right code for local and eager goals is found, in fact, at compile- and extension-time respectively;

4. The difference in code representation determines two different searching algo rithms to find the right code for a predicate call p/n. In our proposal the search takes place along a single branch of the tree, i.e. along the current context, as happens for the algorithm described in [1]. While in our case the right branch is straighforwardly determined by the current context, in MetaProlog the branch has to be determined by the algorithm in a more complex way. However, this overhead is balanced in MetaProlog by the fact that only the theories where p/n is defined are taken into account.

CONCLUSIONS

This paper proves that expressive and flexible mechanisms for the definition of units and their static or dynamic combination can be implemented by using a compiled approach based on an extended Warren Abstract Machine. The context mechanisms here presented have to be applied to real, complex problems. For this reason we are experimenting with them, in an interpreted version, in the context of the ALPES Esprit Project n. 973 so as to build an advanced programming environment for Prolog. Contexts and lazy goals are proving to be very useful in defining the ALPES basic architecture and in structuring environment tools [7]. The ideas expressed in this paper have been partially implemented. In particular, the Context Abstract Machine has been designed and both the emulator and the compiler are in course of implementation. The first, partial results show that standard Prolog programs run on C-WAM with a small overhead mainly due to the new registers introduced and require a greater memory space to allocate environments. When contexts are used, the number of units constituting the program is immaterial, while the dimension of the current context greatly influences performance. In fact the execution times of both context extensions and lazy calls in the majority of cases are proportional to the current context dimension. Eager and local calls, instead, are independent of the context dimension. These first performace results together with the compiled code of the examples presented here can be found in [6].

Acknowledgements

The authors are deeply indebted to Luis Monteiro and Antonio Porto since this work has been possible because of their original ideas on contextual logic programming. We are also grateful to the referees for their remarks on the draft paper. The work here presented has been partially supported by ALPES Esprit P973, MPI 40%, and CNR. The work of the second author has been supported by ENIDATA S.p.a.

REFERENCES:

[1]   H. Bacha: "Meta-level Programming: a Compiled Approach", in *Proc. 4th ICLP*, Australia, MIT Press, 1987.

[2]   H. Bacha: "Meta-Prolog design and Implementation", in *Proc. 5th Int.l Conf. and Symp. on Logic Programming*, The MIT Press, 1988.

[3]   K.A. Bowen: "Meta-Level Programming and Knowledge Representation", *New Gen. Computing*, Vol.3, Springer-Verlag, 1985.

[4]   M.Cavalieri, E. Lamma, P.Mello: "An extended Prolog Machine for Dynamic Context Handling", in *Proc. ECAI88*, Pitman Publishing, August 1988.

[5]   H. Kauffman, A. Grumbach: "MULTILOG: MULTIple worlds in LOGic Programming", in *Proc. ECAI-86*, Brighton (UK), North-Holland, 1986.

[6]   E. Lamma, P. Mello, A.Natali: "Contexts in an Extended Warren Abstract Machine: Performance Results", *DEIS Technical Report*, (being drafted).

[7]   P.Mello, A.Natali, C.Ruggieri: "The architecture of the ALPES environment", *ESPRIT Technical Report*, November 1988.

[8]   P. Mello: "Inheritance as Combination of Horn Clause Theory", in *Proc. of the Workshop on Inheritance Hierarchies in Knowledge Representation and Programming Languages*, Viareggio (I), February 1989.

[9]   D.Miller: "A Theory of Modules for Logic Programming", in *Proc. 1986 Symp. on Logic Programming*, Salt Lake City (USA), September 1986.

[10]   L. Monteiro, *personal communication*, October 1988.

[11]   L. Monteiro, A. Porto, "Contextual Logic Programming", in *Proc. 6th ICLP*, Lisbon (P), The MIT Press, 1989.

[12]   K. Nakashima: "Knowledge Representation in Prolog/KR", in *Proc. of Int.l Symp. on Logic Programming*, Atlantic City, February 1984.

[13]   D.H.D. Warren: "An Abstract Prolog Instruction Set", *SRI Technical Note 309*, SRI International, October 1983.

[14]   P. Wegner, S.B. Zdonik: "Inheritance as an Incremental Modification Mechanism or What Like Is and Isnt Like", in *Proc. ECOOP88*, and in *LNCS*, Vol. 322, Springer-Verlag, 1988.

[15]   P.H.Winston, B.K.P.Horn: "LISP", Addison-Wesley, 1984.

An extension of WAM for K-LEAF:
a WAM-based compilation of conditional narrowing

P.G. Bosco, C. Cecchi, C. Moiso

CSELT
Via Reiss Romoli 274 - 10148 TORINO - ITALY

1. Introduction

K-LEAF [3] is a well-founded first-order logic+functional language whose execution mechanism, based on outermost SLD-resolution, provides a complete and efficient conditional equation solver, equivalent to conditional narrowing. In our approach to logic plus functional programming integration, K-LEAF, besides being itself a richer extension of Prolog, can be considered a high-level intermediate language for the implementation of IDEAL, an higher-order logic plus functional language [2], designed in order to offer in a unified and coherent environment the most appealing features of Prolog and of modern functional languages: full invertibility, non-determinism, higher-order functions and predicates, lazy-evaluation and typing.
The huge gap between the powerful computational model of IDEAL and the quite simple structure of the low level underlying abstract machine is filled through a two-step compilation process: 1) an IDEAL program is compiled into a flat set of K-LEAF clauses. 2) A K-LEAF program is compiled into K-WAM, an extension of the WAM [8] devised to efficiently implement the outermost resolution strategy (so as to achieve an abstract machine for both *fully invertible lazy evaluation* of functions and *conditional narrowing*). This paper analyses in some detail the extensions of the WAM to cope with K-LEAF outermost strategy and the related compilation schemes. Some performance results of this WAM-based implementation are provided, along with comparisons with implementations of purely functional languages.

2. Syntax and abstract execution mechanism of K-LEAF

The K-LEAF syntax is based on Horn Clause Logic with Equality, extending pure Prolog in order to express *non-terminating conditional* term rewriting systems with *constructors*.
Given a set V of variables, C of constructors, F of functions and P of predicates symbols, a K-LEAF program consists of a set of clauses whose syntax is defined by the following grammar:

Clause ::= Head :- Body. | Head.
Body ::= Atom | Atom, Body
Term ::= x | k(Term,...,Term) $\{x \in V \text{ and } k \in C \cup F\}$
Data-term ::= x | c(Data-term,...,Data-term) $\{x \in V \text{ and } c \in C\}$
Atom ::= p(Term,...,Term) | $\{p \in P\}$ <u>relational atom</u>

$$Term \equiv Term \qquad\qquad\qquad\qquad \underline{\text{strict-equality test}}$$
$$Head ::= f(Data\text{-}term,...,Data\text{-}term)=Term\,| \quad \{f \in F\} \quad \underline{\text{functional head}}$$
$$p(Data\text{-}term,...,Data\text{-}term) \qquad \{p \in P\} \quad \underline{\text{relational head}}$$

no multiple occurrences of the same variable in the arguments of f and p; in functional heads $var(rhs) \subseteq var(lhs)$

In order to guarantee confluency in function definition, the following additional constraints must be satisfied by a K-LEAF program: for each pair of functional heads of the form $f(d1,...,dn)=t$ and $f(d1',...,dn')=t'$, $(d1,...,dn)$ and $(d1',...,dn')$ are not unifiable. A K-LEAF *goal* is a conjunction of atoms to be proved w.r.t. the program clauses.

The operational semantics is *conditional narrowing*, that in [3] has been proved equivalent to the denotational semantics expressed in terms of algebraic CPOs. The execution mechanism that underlies the implementation, on the other hand, is *outermost SLD-resolution on homogeneous* (also called *flat*) *form* [3].

As described in [4] (basic-)conditional narrowing can be efficiently recasted into SLD-resolution on a transformed program where functional nestings are eliminated by recursively replacing each functional call $f(t1,...,tn)$ with a fresh variable v, named *produced variable*, and adding the functional atom $f(t1,..,tn)=v$ in the antecedent of the clause: the '=' symbol must be considered as an ordinary predicate and the axiom $x=x$ must be added to the transformed program. Therefore, in spite of some independent effort in "direct" implementation of narrowing, WAM can directly support conditional narrowing without extensions. An innermost strategy can be easily realized through the usual leftmost selection rule of Prolog, as long as the flat literals are put in the right order by the flattening procedure. But, in general, the unlimited possibility of resolving functional atoms with $x=x$ has, as a serious drawback, a large amount of useless computation.

From a theoretical point of view, the elimination of the reflexive clause causes the loss of completeness, unless functions are constrained to be *everywhere-defined*. The introduction of an *outermost* selection strategy according to which a functional atom is resolved only when its produced variable would be bound to a non-variable term, eliminates all redundant resolutions against $x=x$. As, now, the choice of functional atoms to resolve is *dynamically* performed (during unification), we must extend the WAM with a suspension/ reactivation mechanism for functional atoms.

The outermost strategy we considered for the implementation is specified by the following rules:

- all the *relational atoms* and *strict-equality tests* must be resolved: even if their selection order is immaterial, we adopted as default strategy for these atoms the left-to-right Prolog one;
- a functional atom is resolved only if the resolution of an atom A against a clause $H :- B$ *requires* its produced variable v (i.e. v is unified with non-variable term). To achieve better efficiency, through earlier detection of failures, the atoms required by a relational head or the lhs of a functional head are resolved before the atoms in B; those required by the rhs of a functional head are evaluated immediately after B;
- if a produced variable does not occur in the current goal to be resolved (and, thus, it can no longer be required by a resolution), its producer is eliminated (*elimination rule*);

Let us consider the following program (which is already in homogeneous form):

       1) p(1,2) :- q(0).   3) f(1)=1.
       2) q(0).   4) f(2)=1.

and the goal $?- p(f(x),x)$ transformed into $?- p(v,x),f(x)=v$.
$p(v,x)$, which is the only relational atom in the goal, is resolved with (1), so to obtain $?-f(2)=1,q(0)$. with the mgu $\sigma=\{v:=1;x:=2\}$: σ requires the value of v , because it binds v to 1. The resolution of $\sigma(f(x)=v)$, i.e. the producer of v, is performed before the resolution of the relational atom $q(0)$ occurring in the body of (1). Its resolution with (4) succeeds and, then, the overall computation succeeds after the resolution of $q(0)$ against (2).

In some cases, e.g. during the resolution of strict-equality tests, the resolution of a functional atom is required even if the produced variable is still unbound. In these situations we want that, after the resolution of such a functional atom, its produced variable is bound either to a non-produced variable or to a term whose outermost functor is a constructor (i.e. it is in *head-normal-form* , hnf in the following).

3. Basic compilation scheme for outermost strategy

The efficiency of the implementation is related to the efficiency in recognizing the produced variables and finding their producers: this is realized through a new WAM-type of term, called *prodvar*, which denotes the occurrence of a produced variable and links it to its producer. Moreover, by means of these links between variables and producers, the elimination rule is no longer considered, because a functional atom is implicitly eliminated as soon as in the current goal there are no longer occurrences of its produced variable. A *prodvar(C,T=V)* joins the (internal representation of the) functional atom T and the produced variable V, while C is a control flag needed to avoid the duplication of the resolution of $T=V$ (it is bound iff $T=V$ has been already resolved); *prodvars* can also be seen as a logical version of the functional closures in [7].

The syntactic unification algorithm is replaced by a version *extended* to handle *prodvars*: when a *prodvar pv* must be unified with a term t then: 1) the algorithm performs the unification between the produced variable associated to pv and t ; 2) if t is not a variable, pv is inserted into a global list, called *force-list*. The functional atoms (associated to the *prodvars*) collected in the *force-list* during a unification are those that are considered *required* in the above definition: in case of unification success, the one required by the lhs (resp. rhs) are resolved to their hnf (through a *meta-call* predicate) before (resp. after) the evaluation of the clause body.

The basic compilation scheme of K-LEAF (as well as the K-WAM described in next Section) has been formally derived from the partial evaluation of the K-LEAF interpreter written in Prolog w.r.t. actual K-LEAF clauses. The compilation scheme for K-LEAF is an extension of the Prolog one: most changes concern the compilation of the single clause, where the instructions dealing with the extended unification for outermost strategy and resolution to hnf must be introduced. The other aspects (i.e. the backtracking, indexing, environment management and procedure activation/ return) are fully inherited from Prolog. A n-ary function g is compiled into an n+1-ary procedure g_f (i.e. $g(d)=v$ is transformed into $g\_f(d,v)$).

Original WAM unification instructions have been enhanced to collect into the *force-list* the functional atoms required by the unifier. The force-list is pointed by two state registers (**hd** and **tl** head and tail, respectively), and is built on the heap. The *prodvars* collected into the force-lists are resolved through the non-deterministic system predicate *force* (defined in the Sect. 4).

As compared to the Prolog compilation scheme of the clause, the K-LEAF compiler adds some instructions which initialize (the *initreg* instructions) and return (the *close* instructions) the *force-lists*, and the calls to the predicate *force*. The activations of the required functional atoms are performed when the head's unification is completed, i.e., when all the actual arguments of the caller, stored in the temporary A-registers, are treated and possibly moved to permanent registers on the control stack. Therefore required atoms need to be temporarely collected during head's unification; the order of activation of the producers must reflect the (left-to-right) order in which they are met in head's unification, hence the insertion of an element into the *force-list* must be performed from the tail. In clauses defining functions, a second *force-list* can be necessary, since the *prodvars* met in the unification of the functional-head rhs must be forced after the execution of the body. A further register **hd1** is used for temporarely saving the pointer to the first *force-list* when the unification of the rhs starts, and the second *force-list* is initialized by resetting **hd** and **tl**. With this organization, in the execution of the unification instructions no distinction between the lhs and rhs case is necessary, since the insertion of *prodvars* always must be performed at the tail of the current force list, pointed to by **tl**. Clauses with relational heads need only one force-list "forced" before the body, while the general compilation scheme of those with functional heads is:

init_reg1	initialize **hd** and **tl**
<lhs unification>	get & unify instructions operate on **tl**
init_reg2	**hd** -> **hd1**, reset **hd** and **tl**
<rhs unification>	get & unify instructions operate on **tl**
close1 (a1)	**hd** -> **a1** : put rhs force-list in a1
get_var_y yj a1	save **a1** in permanent register
close2 (a1)	**hd1** -> **a1** : get lhs force-list
call force/1	force lhs prodvars
<compilation of the body>	
put_value_y yj a1	get rhs force-list from permanent register
call force/1	force rhs prodvars.

Several optimizations are performed:
- the instructions initializing/returning/forcing the *force-list* of atoms required by either the *lhs* of a functional head or a relational head are inserted if there is at least a constructor in them;
- the instructions initializing/returning/forcing the *force-list* of atoms required by the *rhs* of a functional head are only inserted if in the rhs there is either a variable, or a function call not at the outermost position;
- clauses without bodies need at most one list: the atoms required by the rhs are inserted after those required by the lhs;

The compilation of the rhs of functional heads must guarantee that the

resolution of a functional atom binds its produced variable at least to hnf. The treatement depends on the type of the outermost symbol in the rhs:
- <u>function call</u>: it is directly flattened as the last atom in the body;
- <u>constructor</u>: no further instructions are needed as the rhs is already in hnf ;
- <u>variable</u> (e.g. X): a) if it occurs as an argument in the lhs, the *get_value* instruction is replaced by the *get_result* one: along with performing unification, the instruction *get_result X expected-result* inserts X in the current force-list, if it is a *prodvar*, even if *expected-result* is unbound; b) if X occurs within a structure, the instruction *execute_hnf X* is added at the end of the compilation of the body: it dereferences X and evaluates X if it is a prodvar, otherwise a *proceed* is performed. In the latter case *get_result* is not sufficient to guarantee the hnf of the result, since after the rhs unification, X may be further instantiated to a *prodvar* by the execution of the first *force* call and the *prodvar* may fail to be detected when the *get_result* instruction is executed.

The second aspect peculiar to the compilation of K-LEAF programs is the generation of *prodvars*: if a function call is met in the body (resp. in the rhs of a functional head, but not at the outermost position), the compiler generates the instruction *put_prodvar* (resp. *get_prodvar*).
We show the compilation of the standard *naive-reverse* function. It will be used in the following to exemplify the refinement of the basic scheme. K-WAM code is preceded by an abstract Prolog-like description.

rev([])=[].
rev([E|L])=app(rev(L),[E]).

rev(A1,R) :- initlist,A1=[],R=[],closelist(FL),force(FL).
rev(A1,R) :- initlist,A1=[E|L],closelist(FL),force(FL),app(pv(rev(L)),[E],R).

1	rev	switch_on_term	$cl1 , $cl2 , $fail	13	unify_var_y	y3
2	$ch1	try_me_else	$ch2	14	get_var_y	y2 , a2
3	$cl1	init_reg1		15	close1	
4		get_nil	a1	16	call	force/1 , 3
5		get_nil	a2	17	put_prodvar	rev_f/2 , a1
6		close1		18	unify_value_y	y3
7		execute	force/1	19	put_list	a2
8	$ch2	trust_me_else_fail		20	unify_value_y	y1
9	$cl2	init_reg1		21	unify_nil	
10		allocate	3	22	put_value_y	y2 , a3
11		get_list	a1	23	deallocate	
12		unify_var_y	y1	24	execute	app_f/3

4. The implementation of the Extended WAM.

The data structures of the WAM are unchanged in the K-WAM. In addition, 4 new registers are necessary (**hd, tl, hd1, pv**; the first three introduced in the previous Section, **pv** being used in *switch* operations). The instruction set of the WAM is strictly included in that of the K-WAM.
It is assumed that Prolog terms are represented as tagged pointers: *tags*

range over *{REF_TAG,CNS_TAG,LST_TAG,STR_TAG}* corresponding to variable, constant, list , structure, respectively.

<u>The actual representation of suspended functional atoms.</u>
A *prodvar* term is represented as a structure on the heap, with a reserved functor. The introduction of a new tag for *prodvars* would be more efficient with respect to the adopted representation in that, both space on the heap and time in accessing the components would be saved. The chosen representation allows the least modifications of an existing WAM implementation.

A term *prodvar(C, Atom)* (where $Atom = f(V, t_1,...,t_n)$) and C is a control variable for the sharing mechanism) is represented by a (tagged pointer to a) sequence of $n+2+3$ locations on the heap of the abstract machine, *3* for the representation of the structure *prodvar(C, Atom)* and $n+2$ for the functional atom, as detailed in Figure 1.

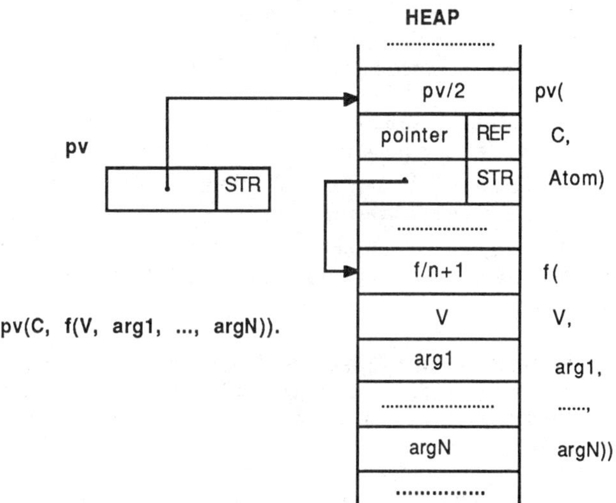

Figure 1: The representation of a *prodvar*

With the chosen representation of a *prodvar*, it is easy to access the value of the flag C,   the producer $f(V,t_1,...,t_n)$ and the produced variable V. The functional atom has in fact the result argument in the first position (so as to facilitate the access to the result in dereferencing). Therefore, in the dynamic activation of the producer, its arguments are *put* in the A-registers in the proper order, with the produced variable in the last position.

In the K-WAM, three versions of dereferencing are necessary: DEREF (same as WAM dereferencing, but for the case of evaluated *prodvar*, where the dereferencing of the produced variable is performed), REQUIRE (same as DEREF, but for the case of unevaluated *prodvar*, where the *prodvar* structure is inserted into the tail of the current *force-list* and the dereferenced result variable is returned) and SWITCH_DEREF (same as DEREF, but for the case of unevaluated *prodvar*, in which the dereferenced produced variable is assigned to the register **pv**, and the *prodvar* structure itself is returned).

The modifications of the standard WAM instructions simply amount to choosing the appropriate form of dereferencing for each class of instructions. Precisely, with respect to the classification of the WAM instructions, the modifications are the following:

- *procedural* instructions: are unchanged in the K-WAM;
- *get* instructions (format: get_What {arg} reg$_j$): *get_var* instructions are not changed, while in the others, the argument in reg$_j$ is dereferenced with REQUIRE before being unified with *arg*, or with a list constructor in *get_list*. In *get_value* instructions, the extended general unification is executed, where REQUIRE is used for dereferencing terms to be unified with instantiated values;
- *put* instructions: unchanged;
- *unify* instructions: same modifications as for *get* instructions;
- *indexing* instructions: the *switch_on_term* dereferences a$_1$ with SWITCH_DEREF: in the case of unevaluated *prodvar* it leaves the dereferenced value of the produced variable in the register **pv**: *switch_on_cons* and *switch_on_struct* use **pv** instead of a$_1$ for branching.

The modifications in the indexing instructions account for the case where the switch value (stored in a$_1$) dereferences to an unevaluated *prodvar* : the produced variable V may be already bound and that binding must be used in branching to the appropriate clause; however, register a$_1$ must still hold the *prodvar* structure for the correct execution of the clause code (which, for instance, may start with a *get_const c a$_1$*, requiring the insertion of the *prodvar* in the *force-list.*).

In the following, we describe in a Pascal-like language the procedures for extended dereferencing in K-LEAF. The standard versions for Prolog are first reported and the extensions refer to these. Terms are considered as elements of a type on which the selectors *tag* and *addr* are defined. If *a=addr(term)* then *mem[a]* is the contents of the cell pointed to by *a* in the memory of the abstract machine, with no distinction among the structures stack, heap, trail etc., whilst by *heap[a]* (for instance) it is denoted the contents of a heap location, provided that *a* is a reference to the heap.

The following auxiliary routines are referred to in the programs below:

IS_BOUND(ref):	checks if a value is stored in *mem[ref]*;
BIND(ref,val):	*mem[ref] := val*;
TRAIL(ref):	puts *ref* (which has been bound) in the current trail list;
ARITY(functor):	gets the arity of *functor*;
GET_PV(addr, res):	*addr* is the pointer to a *prodvar* structure. The contents of the heap cell for the produced variable V is accessed and stored in *res*;
PUT_FORCE_LIST(p):	adds an element to the tail of the current force list by operating on the register **tl**. The added element holds the *prodvar p*.
NEXT-HEAP-ARG:	refers to the heap-cell pointed to by register **s** which represents a structure argument. It increments **s**;
PV:	Is the identifier for the distinguished functor in a *prodvar*.

Prolog Dereferencing:

DEREF(term, res) ::=
        res := term;
        <u>while</u> tag(res) = REF_TAG and IS_BOUND(res) <u>do</u> res := mem[addr(res)] <u>od</u>

K-LEAF Dereferencing:

DEREF(term, res) ::=
        res := term;
        <u>*while*</u> *tag(res)* ∈ *{ REF_TAG,* STR_TAG *} <u>do</u>*
        <u>if</u> tag = REF_TAG
            <u>then</u> <u>if</u> IS_BOUND(res) <u>then</u> *res := mem[addr(res)]* <u>else</u> <u>break</u>
            <u>else</u> <u>begin</u>   (* res is a structure *)
                    addr := addr(res);
                    <u>if</u> heap[addr] = PV <u>then</u> (* *res* is a *prodvar* *)
                        <u>if</u> IS_BOUND(heap[addr + 1]) <u>then</u> GET_PV(addr, res)
        ==>   <u>else</u>   <u>break</u>
                    <u>else</u> <u>break</u>
                    <u>end</u>
    <u>*od*</u>

REQUIRE(term, res) ::=
        As DEREF, but for the row marked by ==>, which becomes:
                <u>else</u> <u>begin</u>   PUT_FORCE_LIST(tl, addr); GET_PV(addr, res) <u>end</u>

SWITCH_DEREF(term, res) ::=
        As DEREF, but for row ==>, which becomes:
                <u>else</u> <u>begin</u> GET_PV(addr, **pv**); DEREF(**pv**, **pv**); <u>break</u>; <u>end</u>

As an example of the modifications required to obtain the K-LEAF
get/unify instructions, we report a Pascal-like procedure for the instruction
get_cons; the other *get* instructions are similar.

GET_CONST(const,i) ::= (* Unify register a_i with *const* *)
    REQUIRE(a[i], a[i]); (* standard WAM instruction: DEREF instead of REQUIRE *)
    <u>case</u> tag <u>of</u>   CNS_TAG : <u>if</u> a[i] ≠ const <u>then</u> FAIL;
                    REF_TAG: mem[a[i]] := const; TRAIL(a[i]);
                    STR_TAG, LST_TAG : FAIL;   <u>fo</u>

The extensions discussed so far are 'conservative', in the sense that any
Prolog program compiled according to the WAM scheme can be equivalently
executed by K-WAM. A number of benchmarks were performed to measure
the overhead (in execution time) introduced by the extension: it is about 5%
for programs not using the data type *structure*, whilst it is about 15% for
programs which make heavy use of structures. The additional overhead is
due to the representation of *prodvars* in terms of structures. If the former
were represented with a reserved tag we would achieve a uniform overhead
of about 5% for all data.

<u>The forcing mechanism.</u>

The operation of *forcing* a list of *prodvar*s is implemented in WAM code (i.e. by means of a compiled Prolog procedure) with the support of a special instruction that corresponds to a meta-call, as outlined in Figure 2. It has a functional atom $f(V,t_1,...,t_m)$ as parameter in a_2, loads the registers a_1 to a_m with the arguments t_1 to t_m, loads a_{m+1} with V, the result variable (whose dereferenced value may be instantiated at the moment of call), accesses the entry point of the code for f in the symbol-table and jumps to that address, after having defined the state register **cp** (continuation program counter) as for an ordinary WAM *call* instruction. In order to achieve an acceptable efficiency in the meta-call, we found it convenient to organize the symbol table so as to include an entry for each atom/arity pair, and to include a 'code pointer' for each entry .

<u>The FORCE predicate:</u>	<u>The Extended META-CALL</u>
force([]).	*call_k*:
	cp := p;
force([PV|Rest]) :-	DEREF(a[2], term);
force_pv(PV),	<u>if</u> tag(term) $\neq$ STR_TAG <u>then</u> ERROR;
force(Rest).	call_k1: addr := addr(term);
	arity := arity(heap[addr]);
force_pv(pv(C, Atom)) :-	<u>for</u> i = 1 to arity - 1 <u>do</u>
var(C) ->	a[i] := heap[addr + i + 1];
C = done,	a[arity] := heap[addr + 1];
call_k(Atom) ;	index := index(heap[addr]);
true.	**p** := symb_tab[index].TOPCODE;

Figure 2: Implementation of *force*.

Sharing of functional subterms causes multiple references to the same *prodvar* structure in one or more *force-lists*. In the *force* predicate, a functional atom is called only if its control variable is unbound, and it is bound (and trailed) before the call. Thus, if the same *prodvar* is referenced by other force-list entries only one invocation of the associated functional atom takes place. Forcing is implemented as a sequence of WAM instructions, rather than as a single instruction, since backtracking can occur at forced atoms.

<u>The new K-WAM instructions.</u>

Along with the WAM instructions, extended as explained above, the K-WAM includes:

a) instructions for the management of the force list, as described in the previous Section, plus optimized versions which skip the *force* executions when the closed *force-list* is empty;

b) the *get/put_prodvar* pair for the data-type *prodvar*, similarly to the WAM pairs for constants, lists and structures; *get_prodvar* is a unification instruction for the functional head rhs;

c) instructions *get_result_x/y* for unification for the functional head rhs;

d) a set of *forcing* instructions for getting the hnf of terms and for the efficient execution of procedures with a strict first argument (see Sect. 5).

get-prodvar f/n+1, x_i :
It is similar to the WAM _get_structure_ executed in _write-mode_. It constructs
a _prodvar_ on the heap. If $\overline{x}_i$ dereferences to an unbound variable, x_i is
bound to the _prodvar_; otherwise the _prodvar_ result variable V is bound to x_i
and the whole structure is added to the **tl** of the current _force-list_.
put-prodvar f/n+1, a_j:
it loads the register a_j with a _prodvar_ term. It sets the _write-mode_ (similarly
to _put_structure_) for the subsequent construction of the arguments of the
function call onto the heap.
get-result-y y_i a_j:
it is used in rhs compilation to guarantee the hnf of the result (see its
specification in Section 3). There are _x_ and _y_ versions, according to the
classification of the first argument. We report the code for the _y_ version.

    GET_RESULT_Y(i,j) ::= (* y_i, a_j *)
        DEREF(a[j], u);   (* a[j] is the expected result; it never contains _prodvars_ *)
        REQUIRE(y[i], v);   (* y[i] is the actual result. It may be a _prodvar_ *)
        UNIFY(u, v);

5. The actual compilation scheme.

The outermost strategy implemented by the basic compilation scheme is
optimal w.r.t. failures. On the other hand, even with sharing of functional
calls, it is very inefficient for normal function evaluation: if a _prodvar_ is
required by _n_ alternative resolutions of a call, then its evaluation is
performed _n_ times in _n_ independent OR-branches. We developed a
compilation scheme to overcome this drawback, without loosing the
advantages of outermost strategy. It can be applied to a wide class of
functions defined by cases. We adopted a version of the pattern compilation
proposed by Augustsson for Lazy-ML [1]. It is obtained by generating new
clauses which evaluate (to their hnf) the arguments _always-required_ by a
procedure, once for all, before the attempt of unifying the computed values
against the corresponding patterns in the clause heads (this method is
recursively applied to the newly produced clauses). A simple
characterization of always-required arguments is:
  Given a procedure (with more than one clause) defining the n-ary
  predicate _p_ (resp. function _f_), its i-th argument is _always-required_ if all
  the i-th formal arguments in the head patterns are non-variables terms.

For instance, _rev_ always-requires its first argument:

rev(A1,R) :- eval_hnf(A1),aug_1(A1,R).   aug_1([],[]).
                                              aug_1([E|L],R) :- app(pv(rev(L)),[E],R).

1	rev	allocate	2		6	call	force/1 , 3
2		init_reg1			7	put_value_y	y1 , a1
3		get_hnf	y1 , a1		8	put_value_y	y2 , a2
4		get_var_y	y2 , a2		9	deallocate	
5		close1_skip_call			10	execute	aug_1/2

Get_hnf is a variant of *get_var_y*, but it also inserts the argument in the force-list if it is a *prodvar*.

Aug_1 is similar to the original definitions of *rev*. But when it is invoked, the first argument is always at least in hnf; therefore its unification against *[]* or *[./.]* never requires a functional atom.

This scheme causes an optimization in the code generated during the compilation of transformed clauses: the instructions to inizialize/return/ evaluate the force-list of atoms required by the lhs unification can be omitted even if in the pattern there are some constants or structures (with logical-variables as arguments), provided that the corresponding arguments are forced to hnf in the clauses introduced by the transformation.

The introduced scheme avoids that *always-required* arguments are evaluated as many times as the number of unifiable clauses but, on the other hand, it introduces another overhead, because it doubles the number of resolutions even if no functional atoms are required by unification. We further optimized this compilation scheme to avoid this drawback, at least when the patterns of all the clauses in a procedure require the first argument.

The *switch-on-term* instruction is extended (it becomes *switch-on-prodvar*): an additional case is added to deal with an unevaluated *prodvar*:

```
proc/n : switch_on_prodvar      $cons $list $stru $pv
    $var: try_me_else           $else

          ...

    $pv: save n                         (allocate + save a_1 to a_n on the stack)
         force_switch               (eval to hnf a_1)
         restore                    (restore a_1 to a_n + deallocate)
         execute proc/n
```

The new branch is entered only when we actually have to force a *prodvar*, otherwise the original clauses are directly activated.

A further improvement can be obtained by avoiding to build *prodvars* for *always-required* function calls. If a function call $f(t1,...,tn)$ occurs as an *always-required* argument in a context $C[f(t1,...,tn)]$, the corresponding *prodvar* is not generated, but the context is transformed into the conjunction $(f(t1,...,tn,V),C[V])$. If a variable X occurs as an *always-required* argument in a context $C[X]$, the context is transformed into the conjunction $(eval\_hnf(X),C[X])$, where *eval_hnf* is compiled into the K-WAM instruction *call_hnf* (see Sect. 6). This transformation is performed to guarantee that, when a call is evaluated, all its *always-required* arguments are already in hnf (it is avoided if X is the first argument since this case is dealt by the *switch-on-prodvar* scheme).

The *context-sensitive* flattening avoids building *prodvars* immediately required as soon as the outer call is evaluated. In certain situations, it must introduce auxiliary functions, as it is shown in the following example. Let *q2* do not *always-require* its first argument.

    q1(X) :- q2(rev(g)).

is abstractly compiled into:

    q1(X) :- q2(pv(rev1)).   rev1R) :- g(R1),rev(R1,R).

Note that the flattening $q(X) :-g(R),q2(pv(rev(R)))$ is not correct, w.r.t. the

K-LEAF non-strict semantics, because the resolution of *g(R)* would always be performed even if *rev* is not evaluated.
The actual compilation of *naive-reverse* function is:

```
rev(Pv,R) :- prodvar(Pv),!, eval_hnf(Pv),rev(Pv,R).
rev([],[]).
rev([E|L],R) :- rev(L,R1),app(R1,[E],R).
```

```
1   rev  switch_on_prodvar  $cl1,$cl2,$fail,$cl3    13       call               rev_f/2,3
2   $ch1 try_me_else         $ch2                    14       put_unsafe_value   y3 , a1
3   $cl1 get_nil             a1                      15       put_list           a2
4        get_nil             x2                      16       unify_value_y      y1
5        proceed                                     17       unify_nil
6   $ch2 trust_me_else_fail                          18       put_value_y        y2 , a3
7   $cl2 allocate            3                       19       deallocate
8        get_list            a1                      20       execute            app_f/3
9        unify_var_y         y1                      21  $cl3 save               2
10       unify_var_x         x1                      22       force_switch
11       get_var_y           y2 , a2                 23       restore
12       put_var_y           y3 , a2                 24       execute            rev_f/2
```

The compiler for K-LEAF is based on the three described schemes:
- context-sensitive flattening when an argument is *always-required*;
- compilation a` la Augustsson for sequential patterns (with the *switch-on-prodvar* optimization);
- the most general scheme, based on run-time accumulation and resolution of required functional atoms, to deal with non-sequential patterns, one-clause procedures and unification against the rhs of functional heads.

The following example requires the combination of the three schemes:

```
f(0,X) = X.
f(1,[]) = [].
f(1,[E|F]) = [E|f(g,F)].
```

```
f(Pv,L,R) :- prodvar(Pv),!,eval_hnf(Pv),f(Pv,L,R).
f(0,A2,R) :- initlist,get_result(A2,R),closelist(FL),force(FL).
f(1,A2,R) :- eval_hnf(A2),aug_0(A2,R).
```

```
1   f    switch_on_prodvar $bl,$fail,$fail,$cl3    14       get_var_y        y2 , a3
2   $ch1 try_me_else       $ch2                    15       close1_skip_call
3   $cl1 init_reg1                                 16       call             force/1,2
4        get_cons          &0 , a1                 17       put_value_y      y1 , a1
5        get_var_x         x1 , a3                 18       put_value_y      y2 , a2
6        get_result_x      x2 , a1                 19       deallocate
7        close1_skip_execute                       20       execute          aug_0/2
8        execute           force/1                 21  $cl3 save             3
9   $ch2 trust_me_else_fail                        22       force_switch
10  $cl2 init_reg1                                 23       restore
11       allocate          2                       24       execute          f_f/3
12       get_cons          &1 , a1                 25  $bl  switch_on_cons   4 ,$fail
13       get_hnf           y1 , a2                                           0,$cl1 | 1,$cl2
```

```
aug_0([])=[].                          str1_1(F)=f(g,F).
aug_0([E|F])=[E|str1_1(F)].

aug_0([],[]).                          str1_1(F,R) :- g(R1),f(R1,F,R).
aug_0([E|F],R) :-  initlist,R=[E|pv(str1_1(F))],
                   closelist(FL),force(FL).
```

1	aug_0	switch_on_term	$cl1 , $cl2 , $fail	1	str1_1	allocate	3
2	$ch1	try_me_else	$ch2	2		get_var_y	y1 , a1
3	$cl1	get_nil	a1	3		get_var_y	y2 , a2
4		get_nil	x2	4		put_var_y	y3 , a1
5		proceed		5		call	g_f/1, 3
6	$ch2	trust_me_else_fail		6		put_unsafe_value	y3 , a1
7	$cl2	init_reg1		7		put_value_y	y1 , a2
8		get_list a1		8		put_value_y	y2 , a3
9		unify_var_x	x3	9		deallocate	
10		unify_var_x	x4	10		execute	f_f/3
11		get_list a2					
12		unify_value_x	x3				
13		unify_var_x	x5				
14		get_prodvar	str1_1/2 , x5				
15		unify_value_x	x4				
16		close1_skip_execute					
17		execute	force/1				

The described compilation is independent of the possible way arguments are characterized as *always-required*: user annotations (already exploited by the compiler) as well as complex strictness-analysis tools developed for functional languages [6] can be adopted.

6. K-WAM instructions for the optimized compilation scheme.

The Augustsson compilation of patterns requires the hnf of terms, without any actual matching against instantiated values. A set of K-WAM instructions (*get_hnf, unify_hnf*) is devised for this purpose and implemented in terms of the primitive REQUIRE. Moreover, variants of *call_k*, called *call_hnf* (with *_x* and *_y* versions) are used in place of *init_list/ get_hnf/ close/ force* when it is known that the length of the *force-list* is is at most one.

```
get_hnf (i,j)  ::=              (* y_i, a_j *)
        REQUIRE(a[j], y[i]);


unify_hnf (i)  ::=              (* y_i *)
        if (READ_MODE) then
                begin term := NEXT_HEAP_ARG; REQUIRE(term, y[i]); end
        else (* WRITE_MODE *) y[i] := MAKE_HEAP_UNBOUND;
```

```
call_hnf_x (i) ::=                (* xᵢ *)
    DEREF(x[i], x[i]);
    addr = addr(x[i]); functor := heap[addr];
    if functor = PV then begin   c_flag := heap[addr+1];
                                 TRAIL(c_flag); BIND(c_flag, DONE);
                                 term := heap[addr+2]; (* get the functional atom *)
                                 cp = p;
                                 goto call_k1;
                  end;
```

The correct treatement of an head rhs may require a forcing instruction at the end of the execution of a clause (*execute_hnf_x/_y*). Its definition is analogous to that of *call_hnf*. In addition it executes a deallocate operation and, if the argument is already in hnf, a *proceed* action is taken. Finally it is provided the low-level description of the *switch_on_prodvar* instruction.

```
switch_on_prodvar ::= (* (a[1],) (@var,) @const, @struct, @list, @pv *)
    SWITCH_DEREF(a[1], term);
    if tag(term) = STR_TAG and  heap[addr(term)] = PV then  (* unevaluated prodvar *)
       begin   a[1] := pv; (*  save in a[1] the dereferenced result variable of the prodvar ,
                     set by  SWITCH_DEREF in the register pv  *)
               pv  = term; (* load the argument of the subsequent force_switch in pv *)
               c_flag := heap[addr(term) + 2];
               TRAIL(c_flag); BIND(c_flag, DONE);  (* Bind and trail the control-flag *)
               FETCH(@pv); goto @pv            (* Select the clause for case prodvar  *)
       end
    else      <Perform a switch_on_term action>.
```

The *force_switch* instruction is a variant of *call_k* that operates on the register **pv** instead of a_2 (in general a_2 holds the second argument of the procedure when a *switch* instruction is executed).

7. Benchmarks

Simple benchmarks have been run on the IDEAL/K-LEAF system 1) in order to get a flavour of the overhead imposed by lazy evaluation in the context of K-WAM code and 2) in order to compare the performance of outermost resolution with lazy evaluation of functions.
The C-emulated K-WAM was run on a VAX 8700. Runtimes are expressed in milli-seconds.

Examples:
  revN: Naive reverse of a list of N elements, in functional style
  revIN: Naive reverse (functional) of a list of N elements in inverted mode
  fibN: Nth. fibonacci number
  walkN: Non-naive functional rev. of a list of N elements repeated N times

The execution times in Table 1 refer to outermost compilation, with simple strictness analysis, as described in Sect. 5. In the compilation of *fib*, the first argument could not be inferred as *always-required*, due to the absence of a constructor in the head of the recursive case. By adding a strictness annotation to the *fib*'s argument, which is equivalent to inferring the *always-required* status, *fib* is compiled as in Prolog, hence the ratio is close to 1.

A more significant benchmark showing good performance w.r.t. conventional languages has been represented by an *invertible* event-driven logic simulator described in [5].

Query	Time K-LEAF	Time PROLOG	Ratio
rev40	82.5	28.5	2.9
rev20	2.25	0.75	3.0
revI40	1200	397	3.01
revI20	165	60	2.75
fib15	285	135	2.1
fib10	22.5	12.7	1.77
walk300	3037	2850	1.06
walk200	1282	1275	1.00

TABLE 1

We experimented the expansion in C-code of the extended WAM instructions as an approximation to native code generation, in order to extimate the achievable performance on several machines.

Table 2 reports the execution times (in seconds) of some C-expanded K-LEAF programs, and compares them with corresponding programs in Quintus Prolog 2.2, Lazy ML [1], and C-language, under Sun3/280. The programs are *queensN* (the C-implementation is imperative and makes use of arrays), *fibN*,*walkN* and *revN* (with the list constructor strict in both arguments).

Query	K-LEAF	Quintus	Lazy ML	C
queens9	5.5	13.18	7.5	1.0
fib29	22.4	46.7	11.8	4.8
walk300	0.6	1.0	0.55	0.4
5*rev300	1.75	1.65	//	//

TABLE 2

Even though we tested this approach on a small set of programs and we have not yet a well engineered system for C-code generation, the above figures suggest that the approach of C-compilation is viable, with the great advantage of portability and scalability to new RISC machines.

The drawback of C-expansion approach, besides a significant increase of the total compilation time, is the occupation of the generated code: in fact, the average size of the C-object file is the double of the code produced by the Quintus Prolog compiler.

K-WAM extensions are orthogonal to OR-parallel WAM extensions; an OR-parallel implementation of K-LEAF has been already developed for a distributed architecture.

Acknowledgment

This work has been partially supported by ESPRIT 415 (Parallel Architectures and Languages for Advanced Information Processing).

References

[1] **L. Augustsson**, Compiling lazy functional languages Part II, PhD thesis, Chalmers University of Technology, Goteborg (1987).

[2] **P.G. Bosco and E. Giovannetti**, IDEAL: An Ideal DEductive Applicative Language, <u>Proc. 1986 Symp. on Logic Programming</u> (IEEE Society Press, 1986), 89-94.

[3] **P.G. Bosco, E. Giovannetti, G. Levi, C. Moiso and C. Palamidessi**, A complete semantic characterization of K-LEAF, a logic language with partial functions, <u>Proc. 1987 Symp. on Logic Programming</u> (IEEE Society Press, 1987), 318-327.

[4] **P.G. Bosco, E. Giovannetti and C. Moiso**, Narrowing vs. SLD-resolution, <u>J. of Theoretical Computer Science</u>, Vol. 59, no 1-2 (North-Holland, 1988), 3-23.

[5] **P.G. Bosco, C. Cecchi and C. Moiso**, Exploiting the full power of logic plus functional programming, <u>Proc. 5th Conf. and Symp. on Logic Programming</u> (MIT Press, 1988), 3-17.

[6] **G.L. Burn**, Abstract interpretation and the parallel evaluation of functional languages, PhD Thesis, University of London (1987).

[7] **S. Narain**, A technique for doing lazy evaluation in logic, <u>Proc. 1985 Symp. on Logic Programming</u> (IEEE Society Press, 1985), 261-269.

[8] **D. H. D. Warren**, An Abstract Prolog Instruction Set, <u>Tech. Note 309</u>, SRI International (Oct.1983).

Miscellaneous Theory

Projections instead of variables
A category theoretic interpretation of logic programs

Andrea Asperti   Simone Martini

Università di Pisa
Dipartimento di Informatica
Corso Italia, 40, I-56125 Pisa
Italy

{asperti, martini}@di.unipi.it.uucp

Abstract

The paper proposes a categorial interpretation of logic programs, based on the topos theoretic semantics for first order logic. By interpreting the syntax of terms in a suitable category, we show how variables can be eliminated in favor of projections, a much more handy tool which avoids all problems related to name clashes. In that category, a substitution can be described as a composition of morphisms, and a most general unifier is a universal construction (a pullback). Computing pullbacks (unifiers) is thus reduced to symbolic manipulation of categorial terms without variables, in the spirit of the Categorical Abstract Machine for functional languages. We can then give an algorithm for Categorical SLD-Resolution (CSLD-Res.), which proves to be simpler then usual SLD-resolution. We propose a generalization of the semantic notions for logic programs, allowing the interpretation domain to come from any topos and not only from **Set**. For this interpretation we prove that CSLD-Res. is a sound and complete inference rule.

1. Introduction

Given a semantic universe D, the classical, set-theoretic interpretation of an n-adic predicate A^n is that of a relation, that is a subset of D^n. In general, a given formula $B(\Omega)$ with free variables in $\Omega=\{x_1, ...,x_m\}$ is interpreted with the subset of D^m such that B holds in the model for every tuple in that subset. For example the interpretation of B(f(x)) is the set of all d in D such that [f](d) is in (realizes) B (where [f] is of course the interpretation of f). This is clearly described in Category Theory: every predicate is interpreted as a subobject of a domain D, that is a (class of equivalence up to isomorphisms of a) monic arrow. As for the interpretation of the atom B(f(x)), it is obtained by "pulling back" (finding the inverse image of) the mono for B, with respect to the interpretation of f . As it is always the case, the categorial approach to semantics naturally leads to avoid any unnecessary concreteness, and in

---

Research partially supported by Joint Collaboration Contract ST2J-0374-C(EDB) of EEC

particular the concept of an environment for variables. A term t with free variables in a set $\Omega = \{x_1, \ldots, x_m\}$ is interpreted as an operation which accepts in input m data and constructs a new data , that is as an arrow form D^m to D . Fixed an interpretation for all the constants and functions of the language, the inductive interpretation of a term t with variables in $\Omega = \{x_1, \ldots, x_m\}$, is the following:

(i) $\qquad [x_i]\Omega = p^m_i \quad$ where $p^m_i : D^m \to D$ is the i-th projection.

(ii) $\qquad [f^n(t_1, t_2, \ldots, t_n)]\Omega = [f^n] \circ {<} [t_1]\Omega, \ldots, [t_n]\Omega {>}$

The basic idea of this work is to lift up to the syntactic level the representability of variables by means of projections expressed by (i). The relevance of such an operation is clear: we obtain a language where the very concept of variable is avoided, together with all the related problems, from the "trifle" of variable name clashes, to the need of defining a meta syntactic operation of substitution. The idea of eliminating variables by means of combinators (in our case projections) is not new in computer science. In 1972 De Bruijn developed a formalism for eliminating problems caused by α-conversion in λ-calculus, and its work has been recently revisited and developed by Cousineau, Curien and Mauny [5], [6]. Our work goes in the same direction of the Categorical Abstract Machine: without having in mind Curien's philosophy of making syntax akin to semantics, we would have never written this work. Anyway, at the best of our knowledge, these studies have been confined only to functional languages. This paper can be regarded as a first step towards an extension of their results to Logic Programming.

The use of projections instead of variables gives an equivalent syntactic formulation of HCL: we show how to go back and forth from the two formalisms. Of course all this work would have been just a twist, if it could have not been possible to give a direct description of unification in our new formalism (the only categorial unification algorithm proposed so far in literature [3], [12] is actually still based on a syntax with variables). We prove that in our Syntactic Category a unifier of two terms is just an equaliser, and that its computation can be performed by using simple, well know properties, of this categorial construction. At the moment we have only a toy (but working!) implementation (yes, a Prolog meta-interpreter), but we are confident in the implementative interest of our approach.

The structure of the work is as follows: in section 2 we define the syntactic category $\mathbf{CC_S}$ associated to a ranked alphabet S, which is, informally, the smallest cartesian category build up from the signature S. We prove that there is a bijection between every homset $\mathbf{CC_S}[X^n, X]$ and the set of terms of signature S with at most n free variables. Moreover also substitutions become arrows in $\mathbf{CC_S}$, and the application of a substitution to a term is just the composition of two arrows. We prove that a mgu of two terms is an equaliser of the associated arrows in $\mathbf{CC_S}$. In section 3 we generalize the notion of model for a logic program, allowing the choice of any *topos* as ambient in which one can define interpretations. In section 4 we define the procedural semantics of a logic program, by giving an algorithm for Categorical SLD-Resolution (CSLD-Res.), which proves to be simpler then usual SLD-resolution. We prove that CSLD-Res. is a sound and complete inference rule.

2. Projections instead of variables

Let S be a single sort signature, that is a set of operators and their arities. As usual we call *constant* an operator whose rank is 0, and write f^n for a n-ary operator. Given a set of variables V, let $T_S(V)$ be the set of terms over S in variables from V. In this section we show how every term in $T_S(V)$ can be interpreted as an arrow in a suitable Cartesian Category CC_S. If U is any *finite* set of variables, we prove that there is a bijection between $T_S(U)$ and a suitable hom-set of CC_S. Using projections instead of variables allows us to dispense with the tedious problem, both theoretical and practical, of renaming variables to avoid name clashes. Moreover we obtain a uniform handling of terms and substitutions in the category CC_S since both are just arrows of the category. The application of a substitution to a term is just their composition.

2.1 The category CC_S

We start by defining for any single sort signature S a typed language CL_S (the Cartesian Language associated to S). The types of CL_S are the product types generated from two constants T and X, and these are also the objects of the category CC_S. The arrows of CC_S are equivalence classes of terms of CL_S with respect to a suitable congruence relation. For avoiding confusion between the terms in CL_S and the terms in $T_S(V)$ we shall call the former *elements*, and we shall use Greek letters for ranging over them.

2.1.1 Definition *Let S be a single-sort first order signature. The Cartesian Language CL_S associated to S is the typed language defined as follows :*

Types: 1) T is a type 2) X is a type 3) if A, B are types then AxB is a type

Elements: *1) if c is a constant in S then $c: T \to X$*

      2) if f^n is an n-ary function in S, then $f^n: X^n \to X$
          where $X^n = ((TxX)...)xX$ with n copies of X
      3) $id_A: A \to A$
      4) $!A: A \to T$
      5) $fst_{A,B}: AxB \to A$, $snd_{A,B}: AxB \to B$
      6) if $\tau: A \to B$ and $\tau': B \to C$ then $\tau' o \tau: A \to C$
      7) if $\tau: C \to A$ and $\tau': C \to B$ then $<\tau,\tau'>: C \to AxB$

Let $=$ be the minimal congruence relation on the elements of CL_S which contains the following equations :

category: i) $id_B \, o \tau = \tau$ ii) $\tau \, o id_A = \tau$ iii) $(\tau'' o \tau') o \tau = \tau'' o (\tau' o \tau)$

terminal: i) $!B \, o \tau = !A$ (for $\tau: A \to B$)

product: i) $fst_{A,B} \, o <\tau,\tau'> = \tau$ ii) $snd_{A,B} \, o <\tau,\tau'> = \tau'$

         iii) $< fst_{A,B} \, o \tau, \, snd_{A,B} \, o \tau > = \tau$

We shall use the notation $[\tau]$ for the equivalence class of τ w.r.t. $=$.

2.1.2 Definition *The category* CC_S *has for objects the types of* CL_S *and for arrows from* X^m *to* X^n *the equivalence classes* $[\tau]$ *of elements* τ: $X^m \to X^n$. *The identity on an object* A *is just* $[id_A]$, *and composition is defined as follows:* $[\tau'] \circ [\tau] = [\tau' \circ \tau]$.
It is easy to check that CC_S is indeed a category.

2.1.3 Proposition *The category* CC_S *is cartesian.*
Proof: T is the terminal object; terminal) expresses the fact that there is exactly one arrow !B from any given object to T . The product of two types A and B is AxB, with $[fst_{A,B}]$ and $[snd_{A,B}]$ as projections; equations product-i)-iii) state that this is indeed a categorial product.

With a little abuse of notation we shall often write τ instead of $[\tau]$ for an arrow in CC_S, and we shall endure in calling it an element: usually it will be clear from the context if we are referring to τ as an arrow of CC_S or as an element of CL_S.

Remark The category CC_S is nothing else but the Cartesian Category *freely generated* by S, if S is regarded as a graph. Let **Cart** be the category of Cartesian Categories, with functors which preserve the cartesian structure "on the nose" as morphisms; let **Graph** be the usual category of graphs, and U: **Cart**→**Graph** be the obvious forgetful functor. Then there is an adjunction (CC_ , U, φ) : **Cart** →**Graph** .

It is also interesting to consider the rewriting system obtained by orientating the previous equations from left to right. A *reduction* is a sequence of elementary reduction steps; a term is *in normal form*, if it is no more reducible. The process of reduction is terminating and confluent; two equivalent elements have the same normal form, which thus provides a canonical representative in every equivalence class $[\tau]$.

Now we define a function which translates terms into elements of CC_S .
2.1.4 Definition *For any finite set* $\Omega = \{x_1, \ldots x_m\}$ *of variables,* $\mathcal{F}_\Omega$: $T_S(\Omega) \to CC_S[X^m, X]$ *is defined as follows:*
$\mathcal{F}_\Omega(x_i) = snd \circ fst^{m-i}$ *(for simplicity we omit the types of the projections)*
$\mathcal{F}_\Omega(c) = c \circ !X^n$ *for* c *constant symbol in* S
$\mathcal{F}_\Omega(f^n(t_1, t_2, \ldots, t_n)) = f^n \circ \langle \mathcal{F}_\Omega(t_1), \ldots, \mathcal{F}_\Omega(t_n) \rangle$

Example: Let $\Omega = \{x, y\}$.
$\mathcal{F}_\Omega(f(x, g(y, x))) = f \circ \langle \mathcal{F}_\Omega(x), \mathcal{F}_\Omega(g(y, x)) \rangle$
$= f \circ \langle snd \circ fst, g \circ \langle \mathcal{F}_\Omega(y), \mathcal{F}_\Omega(x) \rangle \rangle$
$= f \circ \langle snd \circ fst, g \circ \langle snd, snd \circ fst \rangle \rangle : (TxX)xX \to X$

$\mathcal{F}_\Omega$: $T_S(\Omega) \to CC_S[X^n, X]$ is actually a bijection. The idea for defining the inverse function $\mathcal{H}_\Omega$: $CC_S[X^n, X] \to T_S(\Omega)$ is the following: first extend the language of CC_S by introducing "variables" x_i: $T \to X$ for any $x_i \in \Omega$.

Then, for any element $\tau \in CC_S[X^n,X]$ consider the term $\tau' = \tau \circ \langle\langle id_T, x_1\rangle,...,x_n\rangle: T \to X$. As a matter of fact the normal form of τ' does not contain any projections. Thus, when reading composition as application, we have just a term of T_S. Let $\mathcal{H}_\Omega: CC_S[X^n,X] \to T_S(\Omega)$ the map we have just informally defined. It is not difficult to show that $\mathcal{F}_\Omega$ and $\mathcal{H}_\Omega$ define a bijection.

Example Consider the term $f \circ \langle$ snd $\circ$ fst, $g \circ \langle$ snd, snd $\circ$ fst $\rangle\rangle$: $(TxX)xX \to X$. Let $\Omega = \{x,y\}$, $x: T \to X$, and $y: T \to X$. Then :

$f \circ \langle$ snd $\circ$ fst, $g \circ \langle$ snd, snd $\circ$ fst $\rangle\rangle \circ \langle\langle id_T,x\rangle,y\rangle =$

$\quad = f \circ \langle$snd $\circ$ fst $\circ \langle\langle id_T,x\rangle,y\rangle$, $g \circ \langle$snd, snd $\circ$ fst $\rangle \circ \langle\langle id_T,x\rangle,y\rangle \rangle$

$\quad = f \circ \langle x$, $g \circ \langle$snd $\circ \langle\langle id_T,x\rangle,y\rangle$, snd $\circ$ fst $\circ \langle\langle id_T,x\rangle,y\rangle \rangle \rangle$

$\quad = f \circ \langle x$, $g \circ \langle y , x \rangle \rangle$

Thus $\mathcal{H}_\Omega(f \circ \langle$ snd $\circ$ fst, $g \circ \langle$ snd, snd $\circ$ fst $\rangle\rangle) = f(x,g(y,x))$.

2.2 Substitution as composition

In this section we study the correspondent of a substitution in the category CC_S. As a remarkable fact, a substitution simply becomes an arrow in CC_S and the application of a substitution to a term is just the composition of two arrows.

2.2.1 Definition *Let* $\Theta = (x_1/t_1, ...,x_n/t_n)$ *be a substitution. Let* $\Omega = \{y_1,...y_m\}$ *be a set of variables which contains all the variables in* $t_1, ...,t_n$. *We associate to* Θ *an arrow* $S_\Omega(\Theta): X^m \to X^n$ *defined as follows:*

$$S_\Omega(\Theta) = \langle !X^m, \mathcal{F}_\Omega(t_1),...,\mathcal{F}_\Omega(t_n)\rangle \quad (X^m = TxX...xX)$$

Suppose now that s is a term with variables in $\Omega' = \{x_1, ...,x_n\}$: the instantiation of s by Θ is simply described in the category CC_S as the composition $\mathcal{F}_{\Omega'}(s) \circ S_\Omega(\Theta)$, as it is stated in the following lemma:

2.2.2 Lemma *Let* $\Theta = (x_1/t_1, ...,x_n/t_n)$ *be a substitution. Let* $\Omega = \{y_1,...y_m\}$ *be a set of variables which contains all the variables in* $t_1,...,t_n$. *Let s be a term with variables in* $\Omega' = \{x_1, ...,x_n\}$; *then:* $\mathcal{F}_{\Omega'}(s) \circ S_\Omega(\Theta) = \mathcal{F}_\Omega(s\Theta)$.

Proof By induction on the structure of s .

If s is a constant, the result is immediate.

If $s = x_i$ then $\mathcal{F}_{\Omega'}(s)$ is the i-th projection $p^n_i : X^m \to X$, thus

$$\mathcal{F}_{\Omega'}(s) \circ S_\Omega(\Theta) = p^n_i \circ \langle !X^m, \mathcal{F}_\Omega(t_1),...,\mathcal{F}_\Omega(t_n)\rangle = \mathcal{F}_\Omega(t_i) = \mathcal{F}_\Omega(s\Theta)$$

If $s = f(s_1,...,s_k)$ then

$$\begin{aligned}
\mathcal{F}_{\Omega'}(s) \circ S_\Omega(\Theta) &= f \circ \langle \mathcal{F}_{\Omega'}(s_1),..., \mathcal{F}_{\Omega'}(s_k)\rangle \circ S_\Omega(\Theta)\\
&= f \circ \langle \mathcal{F}_{\Omega'}(s_1) \circ S_\Omega(\Theta) ,..., \mathcal{F}_{\Omega'}(s_k) \circ S_\Omega(\Theta) \rangle\\
&= f \circ \langle \mathcal{F}_\Omega(s_1\Theta),..., \mathcal{F}_\Omega(s_k\Theta) \rangle\\
&= \mathcal{F}_\Omega(f(s_1\Theta,..., s_k\Theta))\\
&= \mathcal{F}_\Omega(s\Theta) \quad\quad\quad \text{q.e.d.}
\end{aligned}$$

As a corollary to lemma 2.2.2 we have that composition of substitutions is composition of arrows in CC_S :

2.2.3 Corollary *Let* $\Theta = (x_1/t_1, ...,x_n/t_n)$ *and* $\Gamma = (y_1/s_1, ...,y_n/s_n)$ *be substitutions such that all the variables which appear in* $t_1, ...,t_n$ *are in*

$\Omega = \{y_1,...y_m\}$. *Let Ω' be a set of variables which contains all the variables in $s_1,...,s_n$. Then, for any substitution Θ' such that $\Theta' = \Theta\,\Gamma$, $\mathcal{S}_{\Omega'}(\Theta') = \mathcal{S}_{\Omega}(\Theta) \circ \mathcal{S}_{\Omega'}(\Gamma)$.*

Proof:
$$\begin{aligned}
\mathcal{S}_{\Omega}(\Theta) \circ \mathcal{S}_{\Omega'}(\Gamma) &= \,\langle!X^n,\mathcal{F}_{\Omega}(t_1),...,\mathcal{F}_{\Omega}(t_n)\rangle \circ \mathcal{S}_{\Omega'}(\Gamma) \quad \text{by def. of } \mathcal{S}_{\Omega}\\
&= \,\langle!X^q, \mathcal{F}_{\Omega}(t_1) \circ \mathcal{S}_{\Omega'}(\Gamma),...,\mathcal{F}_{\Omega}(t_n) \circ \mathcal{S}_{\Omega'}(\Gamma)\rangle\\
&= \,\langle!X^q, \mathcal{F}_{\Omega'}(t_1\Gamma),...,\mathcal{F}_{\Omega'}(t_n\Gamma) \quad\quad\quad \text{by lemma 2.2.2}\\
&= \mathcal{S}_{\Omega'}(\Theta\Gamma)\\
&= \mathcal{S}_{\Omega'}(\Theta')
\end{aligned}$$

The converse of lemma 2.2.2 is :

2.2.4 Lemma *Let $g = <g_1,...,g_n>: X^q \to X^n$, $f: X^n \to X^m$, be two elements in CC_S. Let $\Omega = \{x_1,...x_q\}$, $\Omega' = \{y_1,...,y_n\}$ be two set of variables, and $\Theta = (y_1/\mathcal{H}_{\Omega}(g_1),...,y_n/\mathcal{H}_{\Omega}(g_n))$. Then $\mathcal{H}_{\Omega}(f \circ g) = (\mathcal{H}_{\Omega'}(f))\Theta$.*

Proof : $\mathcal{S}_{\Omega}(\Theta) = g$, thus by lemma 2.2.2 we have
$$f \circ g = \mathcal{F}_{\Omega'}(\mathcal{H}_{\Omega'}(f)) \circ \mathcal{S}_{\Omega}(\Theta)) = \mathcal{F}_{\Omega}((\mathcal{H}_{\Omega'}(f))\,\Theta)$$
and thus
$$\mathcal{H}_{\Omega}(f \circ g) = \mathcal{H}_{\Omega}(\,\mathcal{F}_{\Omega}((\mathcal{H}_{\Omega'}(f))\,\Theta)\,) = (\mathcal{H}_{\Omega'}(f))\Theta$$

2.3 Unification as computing equalisers (pullbacks)

In this section we consider the problem of unificating terms when they are regarded as elements in CC_S , and outline an unification algorithm based upon well known constructions of Category Theory [2], [10], namely *pullbacks* and *equalisers*. A description of unification in the framework of Category Theory has been already considered by Rydeheard and Burstall ([3], [12]), following a suggestion of Goguen. The main (essential) difference from our approach is that they still work with variables.

2.3.1 Definition *Given a pair of morphisms f, $g \in C[a,b]$, an **equalizer** of f and g is a pair $(e, i \in C[e,a])$ such that :*
i) $f \circ i = g \circ i$
ii) *for all $h \in C[c,a]$, $f \circ h' = g \circ h'$ implies $\exists! k \in C[c,e]$ $i \circ k = h$.*

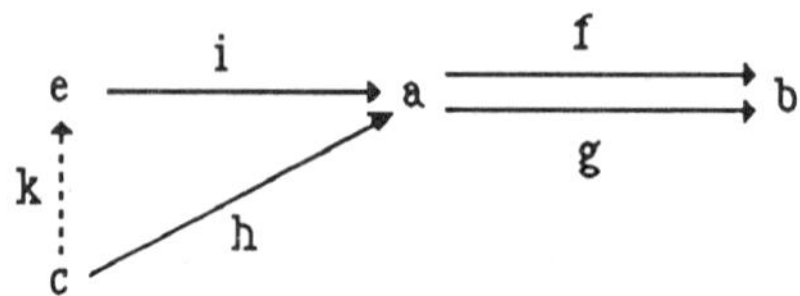

Pullbacks generalize equalisers to pairs of morphisms with different sources.

2.3.2 Definition *Given two arrows $f: b \to a$ and $g: c \to a$ with common target a, the **pullback** of (f,g) is a pair of arrows $(p: bx_ac \to b$, $q: bx_ac \to c)$, such that*
1) $f \circ p = g \circ q: bx_ac \to a$
2) for all $(d, h: d \to b, k: d \to c)$, such that $g \circ k = f \circ h$, there exists a unique arrow $<h,k>_a : d \to bx_ac$ such that $p \circ <h,k>_a = h$, and $q \circ <h,k>_a = k$.
A typical pullback diagram is the following:

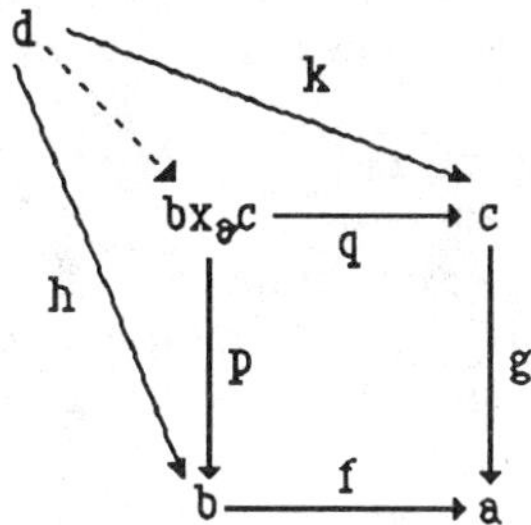

The lower "square" is also called *pullback square*.

A pullback of two arrows f: b→a and g: c→a can be simply expressed as an equaliser:

2.3.3 Lemma *(p: d→b, q: d→c) is a pullback of f: b→a and g: c→a if and only if <p,q> : d→bxc is an equaliser of f ∘fst: bxc→a , g ∘snd: bxc→a (where fst and snd are the projections of the product bxc).*
Proof: easy.

For lack of space we cannot enter in all the details of the categorial unification algorithm, but we only state a few properties of equalisers and pullbacks which should suggest the way for computing them. The first lemma reduces the computation of an equaliser of a pair of arrows <f,f'>: b→axa' and <g,g'>: b→axa' to the computations of an equaliser of f,g and an equaliser of "an instantiation" of f', g'; the second lemma reduces the computation of the equaliser of two arrows f∘g, f∘k, to the computation of the equaliser of g and k (in case f is a mono). Finally we have a lemma for the base case of unification of a term f with a projection. Note that while the first two lemmas holds in every category, the third lemma is specific of **CC$_S$** .

2.3.4 Lemma *If h: c→b is the equaliser of f: b→a and g: b→a ,*

$$c \xrightarrow{\ h\ } b \underset{g}{\overset{f}{\rightrightarrows}} a$$

and k: d→c is the equaliser of f'∘h : c→a' and g'∘h : c→a',

$$d \xrightarrow{\ k\ } c \underset{g'∘h}{\overset{f'∘h}{\rightrightarrows}} a'$$

then h ∘k: d→b is the equaliser of <f,f'>: b→axa' and <g,g'>: b→axa'

$$d \xrightarrow{\ h∘k\ } b \underset{<g,g'>}{\overset{<f,f'>}{\rightrightarrows}} axa'$$

Proof Obviously $<f,f'> \circ h \circ k = <g,g'> \circ h \circ k$, so we have only to prove that it is universal. Suppose now that $l: d' \to b$ is another arrow such that $<f,f'> \circ l = <g,g'> \circ l$; then

$$1) \quad f \circ l = g \circ l$$
$$2) \quad f' \circ l = g' \circ l$$

By universality of h, there exists a unique $r: d' \to c$ such that $l = h \circ r$. From 2) we obtain $f' \circ h \circ r = g' \circ h \circ r$, so by universality of k, there exists a unique s, such that $r = k \circ s$ and thus $l = h \circ k \circ s$ for this unique s .

2.3.5 Lemma *If $f: b \to a$ is monic, then $k: d \to c$ is the equaliser of $f \circ g$: $c \to a$ and $f \circ h: c \to a$, iff it is the equaliser of $g: c \to b$ and $h: c \to b$.*
Proof: immediate.

Note that in the category $\mathbf{CC_S}$ every term associated to a symbol of the signature S is monic.
Now we consider the problem of unificating a term with a projection in the category $\mathbf{CC_S}$. Without loss of generality, we can suppose that the involved projection is $snd: X^n xX \to X$.
2.3.6 Lemma *Let $fst \in CC_S[X^n xX, X^n]$, $snd \in CC_S[X^n xX, X]$ be the two projections associated to the product $X^n xX$. Let $f \in CC_S[X^n xX, X]$. f and snd have an equalizer h (in $\mathbf{CC_S}$) if and only if:*
i) either $f = snd$, and then $h = id$
ii) or there exists f' such that $f = f' \circ fst$, and then $h = <id, f'> \in CC_S[X^n, X^n xX]$.
Proof: The if part is an easy diagram chase. As for the converse, it follows by properties of composition in $\mathbf{CC_S}$, and the existence of normal forms.

We now relate most general unifiers with equalisers and pullbacks in $\mathbf{CC_S}$. The following results show how variables can be safely eliminated in the context of unification, and motivate the title of the paper.
2.3.7 Theorem *Let r, s be two terms with variables in $\Omega = \{x_1, ..., x_n\}$; let $\Theta = (x_1/t_1, ..., x_n/t_n)$ be a m.g.u. for r and s, and let $\Omega' = \{y_1, ... y_m\}$ be the set of variables in $t_1, ..., t_n$. Then $S_{\Omega'}(\Theta)$ is the equaliser in $\mathbf{CC_S}$ of $F_\Omega(r)$ and $F_\Omega(s)$.*
Proof Since $F_\Omega(r) \circ S_{\Omega'}(\Theta) = F_{\Omega'}(r\Theta) = F_{\Omega'}(s\Theta) = F_\Omega(s) \circ S_{\Omega'}(\Theta)$, then $S_{\Omega'}(\Theta)$ unifies $F_\Omega(r)$ and $F_\Omega(s)$; we must only prove that it is universal.
Suppose that $g: X^q \to X^n$ is another term in $\mathbf{CC_S}$ such that $F_\Omega(r) \circ g = F_\Omega(s) \circ g$. Let $g_i = p^n_i \circ g$ where $p^n_i : X^n \to X$ is the i-th projection. Then $g = <g_1, ..., g_n>$. Let $\Omega'' = \{z_1, ..., z_q\}$ be a set of fresh variables, and consider the substitution: $\Theta' = (x_1/H_{\Omega''}(g_1), ..., x_n/H_{\Omega''}(g_n))$. By lemma 2.2.2 $r\Theta' = H_{\Omega''}(F_\Omega(r) \circ g) = H_{\Omega''}(F_\Omega(s) \circ g) = s\Theta'$, thus Θ' is a unifier of r and s; since Θ is a m.g.u. there exists Γ such that $\Theta' = \Theta \Gamma$. We can suppose Γ be a substitution for all (and only) the variables $\{y_1, ... y_m\}$ which appear in $t_1, ..., t_n$, i.e. $\Gamma = (y_1/s_1, ..., y_m/s_m)$ (such a

Γ is unique). By lemma 2.2.3, we have $S_{\Omega'}(\Theta) \circ S_{\Omega''}(\Gamma) = S_{\Omega''}(\Theta') = g$. The unicity of $S_{\Omega''}(\Gamma)$ is a consequence of the unicity of Γ.   q.e.d.

2.3.8 Theorem *Let r, s be two terms with variables respectively in two disjoint sets $\Omega_r = \{x_1, ..., x_n\}$ and $\Omega_s = \{y_1, ..., y_m\}$; let $\Theta = (x_1/t_1, ..., x_n/t_n, y_1/s_1, ..., y_m/s_m)$ be a m.g.u. for r and s, and let $\Omega' = \{z_1, ..., z_p\}$ be the set of variables in $t_1, ..., t_n, s_1, ..., s_m$. Let $\Theta_r = (x_1/t_1, ..., x_n/t_n)$, $\Theta_s = (y_1/s_1, ..., y_m/s_m)$. Then $(S_{\Omega'}(\Theta_r), S_{\Omega'}(\Theta_r))$ is the pullback in CC_S of $F_{\Omega_r}(r)$ and $F_{\Omega_s}(s)$.*
Proof: easy by theorem 2.3.7 and the relation between pullbacks and equalisers expressed by lemma 2.3.3.

The usefulness of theorem 2.3.8 should be clear: in SLD resolution, when we unify an atom of the goal with the head of a clause, we are dealing with terms with disjoint sets of variables. Thus, the categorial counterpart of SLD resolution is more naturally based on pullbacks, instead of equalisers.

3. Categorial semantics

The definitions of atom (atomic formula) and program can be rephrased in our formalism as follows. Given a set AT of *atom symbols*, an *atom* is a pair (A^n, τ^m), where A^n is an atom symbol of arity n, and $\tau^m \in CC_S[X^m, X^n]$; the integer m will be called the *degree* of the atom. A *conjunction with degree* m is a tuple $(B_1^{n_1}, \tau_1^m)(B_2^{n_2}, \tau_2^m)...(B_k^{n_k}, \tau_k^m)$, $k \geq 0$, of atoms with common degree m; when k=0 the conjunction is *empty*. A *program clause* (simply a *clause* from now on) is a pair $((A^n, \sigma^m), G)$ where (A^n, σ^m) is an atom, and G is a conjunction with degree m. A clause $((A^n, \sigma^m), (B_1^{n_1}, \tau_1^m)...(B_k^{n_k}, \tau_k^m))$ will be usually written as $(A^n, \sigma^m) \leftarrow (B_1^{n_1}, \tau_1^m)...(B_k^{n_k}, \tau_k^m)$. A clause with an empty conjunction is a *fact*; a *formula* is either a conjunction or a clause; a *program* is a set of clauses. Given a conjunction $G \equiv (B_1^{n_1}, \tau_1^m)...(B_k^{n_k}, \tau_k^m)$ with degree m and an element $\sigma \in CC_S[X^p, X^m]$, we can *instantiate* G with σ: $G\sigma = (B_1^{n_1}, \tau_1^m \circ \sigma)...(B_k^{n_k}, \tau_k^m \circ \sigma)$. Note that $G\sigma$ is a conjunction with degree p.

It is well known how the "usual" semantics of a first order language can be generalized to categories different from **Set**, and still having enough structure to interpret relations and logical connectives. In the general case of a full first order language, this can be achieved in a *topos* (see [7] for an introduction, or [8] for a deeper treatment). Topoi have been introduced in the late sixties, as a class of categorial structures satisfying many of the "standard" properties of sets and functions, like the notion of subset and the existence of the power set; they provide a sound categorial environment for any attempt to generalize the semantic notions of a logic. Many of the following definitions and results can be obtained in any category with finite limits only, as long as Horn clause logic is concerned. In view of the discussion above, however, sticking to topoi seems more acceptable from a methodological point of view. On the other hand, in trying to write a paper readable also for non categorists, we introduce explicitly all the concepts and definitions we need, by using only the existence of finite limits in a topos. We recast in the following the usual semantic notions for logic programs [1]. Σ will always denote a topos.

3.1 Definition A *universe in Σ* for the signature S is a cartesian functor $H: \mathbf{CC_S} \rightarrow \Sigma$.

Since a universe H is a functor, giving H amounts both to fix an object H(X) of Σ interpreting the distinguished object X of $\mathbf{CC_S}$, and to fix the interpretation of constants (as arrows from the terminal object of Σ to H(X)) and function symbols. Moreover, since H preserves the cartesian structure, H defines also the interpretation for terms as arrows with the due source and target. We can then define the *category of universes in a topos* Σ, $\mathbf{Univ_\Sigma}$, as the category of the cartesian functors from $\mathbf{CC_S}$ to Σ and natural transformations as morphisms.

Example An important example of universe in the topos **Set** is given by the hom-functor on the terminal object: $\mathbf{CC_S}[T,\_]: \Sigma \rightarrow \mathbf{Set}$. We shall call this functor HU_S. It is not difficult to prove that HU_S is cartesian and hence is a universe in **Set**. The motivation for its name is given by the following
3.2 Proposition *HU_S is initial in $\mathbf{Univ_{Set}}$ (it is the Herbrand Universe over S).*
Proof Let H be any cartesian functor from $\mathbf{CC_S}$ to **Set**. By the Yoneda lemma, $\text{Nat}[\mathbf{CC_S}[T,\_], H] \cong H(T)$. Hence there is a unique natural transformation from HU_S to H, since H(T) is the singleton, for H cartesian.

As for the interpretation of atom symbols, which is a relation in **Set**, we can use a subobject, the categorial concept for a subset:
3.3 Definition *Let Z be an object of a category C.*
(i) A subobject of Z is an object X of C and a monic $m \in C[X,Z]$. Subobjects with isomorphic domain are identified.
(ii) Given two subobjects of Z, $m \in C[X,Z]$ and $n \in C[Y,Z]$, $m \subseteq n$ iff there exists an arrow $i \in C[X,Y]$ such that $m = n \circ i$ (in this case i is itself a mono).

Let Sub(Z) be the collection of all subobjects of Z; it is readily seen that "$\subseteq$" is a partial order on Sub(Z).

3.4 Definition *An interpretation in Σ for CC_S is a pair (H, I), where H is a universe in Σ and I is a map associating to each atom symbol A^n a subobject of $H(X^n)$.*

In the sequel we will often say "an interpretation" for "an interpretation in some topos Σ". In order to give a meaning to an atomic formula (A^n, σ^m), we need a way of "composing" the mono $I(A^n) \in \Sigma[Y, H(X^n)]$ with the interpretation of the element σ, that is the arrow $H(\sigma) \in \Sigma[X^m, H(X^n)]$. This can be easily achieved by using the existence of pullbacks in Σ.

3.5 Definition *Let (H,I) be an interpretation for CC_S.*
(i) An atom (A^n,σ^m) is interpreted by the mono $[(A^n,\sigma^m)]$ defined by the following pullback (in Σ):

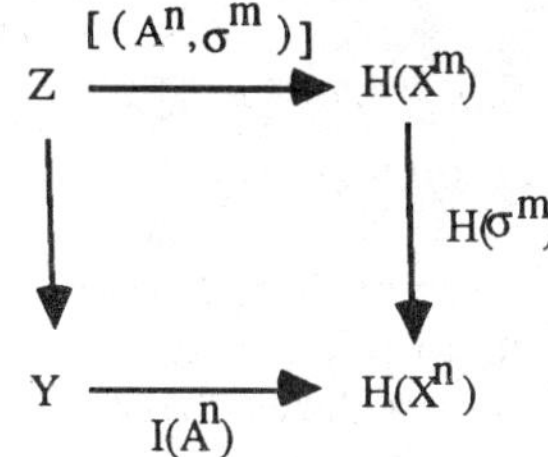

(ii) A conjunction $(B_1{}^{n}1,\tau_1{}^m)(B_2{}^{n}2,\tau_2{}^m)\dots(B_k{}^{n}k,\tau_k{}^m)$ with degree m, $k\geq0$, is interpreted by the limit of the following diagram (in Σ):

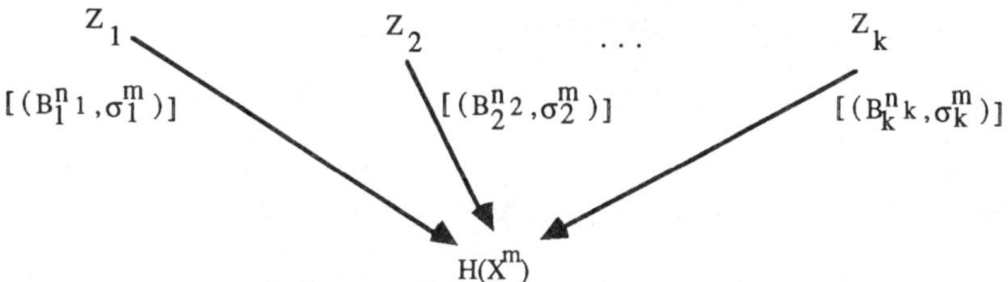

This is given by an object Z and a mono in $\Sigma[Z,H(X^m)]$, denoted by $[(B_1{}^n1,\tau_1{}^m)\dots(B_k{}^nk,\tau_k{}^m)]$.

The intuition behind (i) of definition 3.5 should be clear: By pulling back $I(A^n)$ along $H(\sigma)$ we are selecting among all m-tuples of points of $H(X^m)$ those which, when substituted for the free positions of the element σ, yield an n-tuple in the interpretation of $I(A^n)$. As for (ii) this is the standard interpretation of the conjunction of a finite family of monos in a topos.

3.6 Remarks (i) The interpretation of the empty conjunction with degree m is id_{X^m}, since the limit of a diagram consisting in a single object is (isomorphic to) that object.
(ii) The interpretation (following 3.5(ii)) of a conjunction with a single atom $(B_1{}^n1,\tau_1{}^m)$ coincides with the interpretation of the same atom following 3.5(i). This again follows easily by the definition of limit.

Also the following definition of validity is equivalent to the usual topos theoretic validity.

3.7 Definition *Let (H,I) be an interpretation. The notion of **validity in (H,I)** for a formula α (notation: (H,I) $\models \alpha$) is defined as follows.*
(i) A conjunction G is valid in (H,I) iff $[G] = id_{X^m}$.
(ii) A clause $(A^n,s^m)\leftarrow(B_1{}^n1,s_1{}^m)(B_2{}^n2,s_2{}^m)\dots(B_k{}^nk,s_k{}^m)$ is valid in (H,I) iff there exists a monic $m\in\Sigma[Z,Y]$ such that the following diagram commutes.

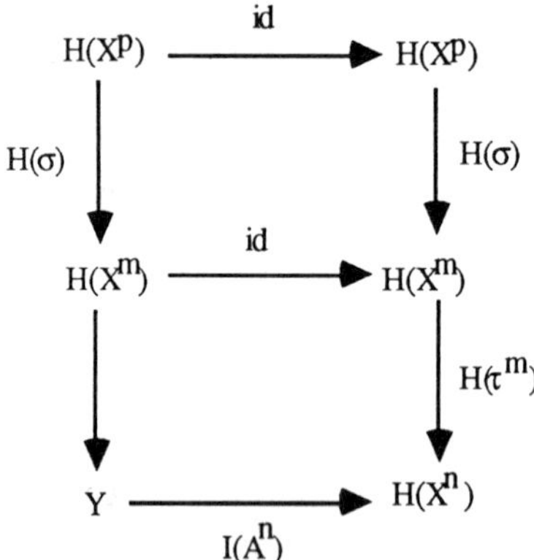

$$[(B_1^{n}1,\sigma_1^{m}),(B_2^{n}2,\sigma_2^{m}),...,(B_k^{n}k,\sigma_k^{m})] \qquad Z \xrightarrow{\ m\ } Y \qquad [(A^n,\sigma^m)]$$
$$H(X^m)$$

*(iii) A set of clauses P is valid in (H,I) iff every clause of P is valid in (H,I); we say in this case that (H,I) is a **model** of P: (H,I) |= P.*

In view of the ordered structure of $Sub(H(X^n))$ mentioned after definition 3.3, (ii) above is equivalent to require $[(B_1^{n}1,\sigma_1^{m})...(B_k^{n}k,\sigma_k^{m})] \subseteq [(A^n,\sigma^m)]$. The following lemma shows that definition 3.7 formalizes well the intended notion of validity.

3.8 Lemma *Let (H,I) be an interpretation.*
(i) The empty conjunction is valid in (H,I)
(ii) (H,I) |= $(A^n,\sigma^m)\leftarrow$ iff (H,I) |= (A^n,σ^m)
(iii) (H,I) |= $(B_1^{n}1,\sigma_1^{m})(B_2^{n}2,\sigma_2^{m})...(B_k^{n}k,\sigma_k^{m})$ iff for every $1 \leq i \leq k$, (H,I) |= $(B_i^{n}i,\sigma_i^{m})$

Proof (i) By remark 3.6(i). (ii) easily follows from (i).As for (iii), the "if part" is trivial: the limit of a diagram containing only identities is the identity. As for the "only if" part, suppose we have a diagram like the one of definition 3.5 with, as limit, the object $H(X^n)$ with arrows $id_{X^m} \in \Sigma[H(X^n),H(X^n)]$, by hypothesis, and $f_i \in \Sigma[H(X^n),Z_i]$, $1 \leq i \leq k$, making the diagram commute. All the f_i's are monic, as can be readily seen by using the fact that all arrows in the starting diagram are monics. By this, as subobjects, $H(X^n) \subseteq Z_i \subseteq H(X^n)$; hence every Z_i is isomorphic to $H(X^n)$.

The following lemma proves that any instantiation of a valid atom is valid.
3.9 Lemma *If (H, I) |= (A^n,τ^m), then for any X^p and any $\sigma \in CC_S[X^p,X^m]$, (H,I)|= $(A^n,\tau^m \circ \sigma)$.*
Proof We show that the outer square in the following diagram is a pullback:

$$
\begin{array}{ccc}
H(X^p) & \xrightarrow{\ id\ } & H(X^p) \\
\downarrow{\scriptstyle H(\sigma)} & & \downarrow{\scriptstyle H(\sigma)} \\
H(X^m) & \xrightarrow{\ id\ } & H(X^m) \\
\downarrow & & \downarrow{\scriptstyle H(\tau^m)} \\
Y & \xrightarrow{\ I(A^n)\ } & H(X^n)
\end{array}
$$

The bottom square is a pullback, by hypothesis; the top square is trivially shown to be a pullback. Hence the outer rectangle is a pullback, by standard properties.

In order to be satisfied by the previous definition we have to show, at least, that if the ambient topos is **Set**, then the models defined in 3.7 are exactly the "standard", set-theoretical models.

3.10 Proposition *Let P be a program.*
(i) For any set theoretical model of P M = <D, Const_asgm, Funct_asgm, Atom_asgm>, there exists a model $(H_M, I_M)\models P$.
(ii) For any $(H,I)\models P$, where $H\in Univ_{Set}$, there exists a set theoretical model of P $<D_H, Ca_H, Fa_H, Aa_H>$.

Proof (i) One have $(H_M, Atom\_asgm)\models P$, where $H_M : CC_S \to$ **Set** is defined as: $H_M(X)=D$; $H_M([c]:T\to X) = const_c:\{*\}\to D$ (where $const_c(*) =$ Const_asgm (c)), for any c constant symbol in S; $H_M([f]:X^m\to X^n) =$ Funct_asgm(f), for any f function symbol in S.
(ii) Let (H,I) be a model in **Set** for P. Then $<H(X), Ca_H, Fa_H, I>$ is a set-theoretical model of P, where $Ca_H(c)=H([c])$ and $Ca_H(f)=H([f])$.

3.11 Definition *Let P be a program.*
*(i) A conjunction G is a **logical consequence** of P in Σ (write: $P\models_\Sigma G$), iff G is valid in every model of P defined over universes in Σ.*
*(ii) A conjunction G is a **logical consequence** of P (write: $P\models G$), iff for any topos Σ, $P\models_\Sigma G$.*

3.12 Definition *Let (H, I) be an interpretation, P be a program and G a conjunction with degree m. An element $\sigma\in CC_S[X^p, X^m]$, for some p, is a **correct witness** for $P\cup\{G\}$ iff $P\models G\sigma$.*

4. Procedural Semantics

This section is concerned with the procedural categorial semantics of logic programs. The procedural counterpart of a correct witness is a *computed witness*, which is defined using categorical SLD-resolution (CSLD for short). We prove that every computed witness is correct (soundness), and moreover we show how completeness w.r.t. interpretations in **Set** can be obtained. Beyond the similarities with standard SLD-resolution, we stress the *novelty* of our approach. By avoiding the rather annoying concept of substitution, and all the problems related to clash of variable names, we get rid of the need of a methodical use of variants in the definition of SLD-resolution; unification becomes the computation of a pullback, and the instantiation of a term by a substitution is simply the composition of two elements. While devising *efficient* algorithms for computing pullbacks (unifiers) in CC_S is still an open problem, the coding of the usual one (corresponding to the "implementation" of lemmas 2.3.4-6) does not create problems. The approach suggests a simple implementation strategy based on term rewriting, which seems to be promising of good performances.

We suppose the reader has a good knowledge of the usual definition of SLD resolution [9], so we start straight away by defining its *categorial* counterpart, in which, by building on the results of section 2, composition of elements and pullbacks are used instead of substitutions and mgu's, respectively. We shall use the standard definition of **computation rule.**

4.1 Definition *Let G be the goal $\leftarrow(A_1,\mu_1)...(A_m,\mu_m)...(A_k,\mu_k)$, C be the clause $(A,\mu)\leftarrow(B_1,\rho_1)...(B_q,\rho_q)$ and R be a computation rule. The goal G' is **derived** from (is the **resolvent of**) G and C using (σ,τ) via R iff the following conditions hold:*

(a) A_m is the atom of the goal selected by R

(b) $A =A_m$ and (σ,τ) is the pullback of (μ_m,μ) (in CC_S)

(c) G' is the goal $\leftarrow(A_1,\mu_1\circ\sigma)...(A_{m-1},\mu_{m-1}\circ\sigma)(B_1,\rho_1\circ\tau)...(B_q,\rho_q\circ\tau)$ $(A_{m+1},\mu_{m+1}\circ\sigma)...(A_k,\mu_k\circ\sigma)$

Note the different use of σ and τ for instantiating atoms of the old goal G, and atoms in the body of C, respectively. Note also that all the compositions in the elements of the atoms of G are well defined, and that the goal G' has degree p, if $\sigma,\tau\in CC_S[X^p,X^r]$, for r degree of G.

4.2 Definition *Let P be a program, G be a goal and R a computation rule. A **Categorical SLD-derivation** (CSLD-derivation) of $P\cup\{G\}$ via R consists of a sequence $G_0=G,G_1,...$ of goals, a sequence $C_1,C_2,...$ of program clauses and a sequence $(\sigma_1,\tau_1),(\sigma_2,\tau_2),...$ of pairs of elements, such that each G_{i+1} is derived from G_i and C_{i+1} using $(\sigma_{i+1},\tau_{i+1})$ via R. C_i is called **input** clause at stage i.*

Note here one of the main features of our approach: In the usual definition, each C_i must be a *suitable variant* of the corresponding program clause, so that C_i does not have any variables which already appears in the derivation up to level i-1. The elimination of variables performed in section 2 in favor of projections, allow the use of the clause *as it is.*

4.3 Definition *A **Categorical SLD-refutation** of $P\cup\{G\}$ via R is a finite CSLD-derivation which has the empty clause $\square$ as the last goal in the derivation. If $G_n = \square$, we say that the refutation has length n.*

4.4 Definition *Given a CSLD refutation of $P\cup\{G\}$ via R , if $(\sigma_1,\tau_1),(\sigma_2,\tau_2), ...,(\sigma_n,\tau_n)$ is the sequence of pullbacks used in the refutation, the element $\sigma_1\circ\sigma_2\circ...\circ\sigma_n$ is a **computed witness** for $P\cup\{G\}$.*

4.5 Theorem *(Soundness) If the element σ is a computed witness for $P\cup\{G\}$, then $P/=G\sigma$ (that is σ is a correct witness).*

Proof Let G be the goal $\leftarrow (A_1,\mu_1),...,(A_k,\mu_k)$, and (σ_1,τ_1), $(\sigma_2,\tau_2)...,(\sigma_n,\tau_n)$ the sequence of pullbacks used in the refutation of $P\cup\{G\}$ via R . Let $\sigma=\sigma_1\circ\sigma_2\circ\sigma_n$; we have to show that $(A_1,\mu_1\circ\sigma),...,$

$(A_k,\mu_k{\circ}\sigma)$ is a logical consequence of P. The result is proved by induction on the length n of the refutation.

case n=1 : then G is a goal of the form $\leftarrow(A,\mu)$, P has a fact $(A,\rho)\leftarrow$, and (σ,τ) is the pullback of (μ,ρ). Then $(A,\mu{\circ}\sigma) = (A,\rho{\circ}\tau)$; $P{\models}(A,\rho)$, by hypothesis; hence $P{\models}(A,\rho{\circ}\tau)$, by lemma 3.9.

case n+1 : suppose the result holds for all R-computed witnesses which come from refutation of length n. Suppose $(\sigma_1,\tau_1),(\sigma_2,\tau_2)...,(\sigma_{n+1},\tau_{n+1})$ is the sequence of pullbacks used in a refutation of $P{\cup}\{G\}$ of length $n+1$, and let $\sigma' = \sigma_2 \circ ... \circ \sigma_{n+1}$, $\sigma = \sigma_1 \circ \sigma'$. Let $(A,\mu)\leftarrow(B_1,\rho_1),...,(B_q,\rho_q)$ be the first input clause, and A_m be the selected atom of G. The first resolvent $\leftarrow(A_1,\mu_1\circ \sigma_1),..., (B_1,\rho_1\circ \tau_1),...,(B_q,\rho_q\circ \tau_1),...,(A_k,\mu_k\circ \sigma_1)$ has a refutation of length n, and thus by induction hypothesis the computed witness $\sigma' = \sigma_2 \circ ... \circ \sigma_{n+1}$ must be a correct witness, that is $P{\models}(A_1,\mu_1\circ \sigma),..., (B_1,\rho_1\circ \tau_1\circ \sigma'),...,(B_q,\rho_q\circ\tau_1\circ\sigma'),...,(A_k,\mu_k\circ \sigma)$. In particular, for every $i{\neq}m$, $P{\models}(A_i,\mu_i\circ \sigma)$ by lemma 3.8(iii), and also $P{\models}(B_1,\rho_1\circ \tau_1\circ \sigma'),...,$ $(B_q,\rho_q\circ\tau_1\circ\sigma')$. But then $(A,\mu \circ \tau_1\circ \sigma') = (A,\mu_m\circ\sigma_1\circ \sigma') = (A,\mu_m\circ\sigma)$ is also a logical consequence of P. q.e.d.

The reader has certainly recognized in the argument of the previous theorem the same reasoning for the soundness of usual SLD-resolution. This is possible since our generalized models behave in the right expected way with respect to validity of formulas. The same happens for completeness:

4.6 Theorem *(completeness) Let P be a program and G be a goal. For every correct witness σ for $P{\cup}\{G\}$, there exists a computation rule R, an R-computed witness τ for $P{\cup}\{G\}$ and an element ρ such that $\sigma=\tau \circ \rho$.*

Proof *(sketch)* Suppose $P{\models}G\sigma$; in particular $P{\models}_{Set}G\sigma$, hence $(HU,M){\models}G\sigma$, where M is the interpretation of the least Herbrand model. We can then mimic all the standard results leading to completeness: success set equal to least Herbrand model, lifting lemma, refutations with identity substitutions. All what is needed is a "rephrasing" of the results in the categorial framework, which is straightforward by the results of section 2.

The validity of the previous theorem is, in a sense, expected: By *enlarging* the class of models of a formalism (see proposition 3.10) one never looses completeness. The stronger result that *fixed any topos* Σ, if $P{\models}_\Sigma G\sigma$ then σ is an instance of a computed witness, does not hold. A counter-example is the topos **FinSet**, whose objects are the finite sets and morphisms are the functions. If the above implication did hold, finite validity $(P \models_{FinSet}G)$ would imply validity $(P \models G)$, by 4.5 above. The following counterexample (due to C. Palamidessi) shows this cannot be the case. Let $P=\{A(x,x),$ $A(x,y){:}{-}A(sx,sy), B{:}{-}A(sx,0)\}$; then $P \models_{FinSet}B$, but not $P{\models}B$. It remains open to characterize the class of topoi for which strong completeness does hold, like **Set**. This problem appears connected to that of finding the class of topoi which admit initial structures.

5. Conclusions

We have developed in this paper a categorial interpretation of logic programs inspired by the idea that terms are arrows in suitable categories. At the syntactic level we have free categories, where the existence of a pullback describes the existence of a mgu between two terms; at the semantic level we have topoi, where atoms are interpreted as subobjects and logical connectives are described via the algebraic structure of these. Besides the single technical achievements, we suggest that categories could provide a better environment where clarify many of the theoretical problems logic programming is facing, for instance integrating Logic and Functional Programming, and imposing a Type Structure on Logic Programs.

The main focus of the paper has been the procedural interpretation; we believe in the possibility of avoiding variables in CSLD-resolution and of symbolically reducing substitutions. One of the future research directions will be to study what can be retained of this approach when the syntactic category CC_S is replaced by categories with "more structure", like categories with functional objects and evaluation morphisms (Cartesian Closed Categories). We stress how our syntactic approach has been suggested by the semantic intuition, outlined in section 3. Here much remains to be done, from a deeper understanding of the *categories of models* one can define over a topos, to the investigation of possible links with intuitionistic logic. In this semantic investigation it will be fruitful to clarify the relations of our approach with more general categorial interpretation of logic, like Burstall and Goguen's institutions [6] and Meseguer's logic programming languages [11].

6. References

[1]   Apt, K.R. "Introduction to Logic Programming", to appear in *Handbook of Theoretical Computer Science*, J. van Leeuwen (ed.), North-Holland.

[2]   Asperti A., Longo G. *Categories and Type Structures*. Book, in preparation.

[3]   Burstall R.M., Rydeheard D.E. *Computational Category Theory*, Prentice-Hall, 1988.

[4]   Curien P.L. *Categorical Combinators, Sequential Algorithms and Functional Programming*, Res. Notes in Theoretical Computers Science. Pitman, London, 1986.

[5]   Cousineau G., Curien P.L., Mauny M. "The Categorical Abstract Machine", Proc. ACM Conf. on *Functional Programming Languages and Computer Architecture*, Nancy 1985. Springer LNCS 201, *Sci. Comp. Programming*.

[6]   Goguen J, Burstall R.M. "Institutions: Abstract model theory for computer science", TR-CSLI-85-30, prel. vers. in *Logics of Programmings* LNCS 164.

[7]   Goldblatt R. *Topoi. The Categorial Analysis of Logic*, Studies in Logic and the Foundations of Mathematics. Vol. 98, North Holland, Amsterdam, 1984.

[8]   Johnstone P.T. *Topos Theory*, L.M.S. Mon. n. 10 , Academic Press, London 1977.

[9]   Lloyd J.W. *Foundations of Logic Programming*, Springer-Verlag, New York, 1984.

[10] Mac Lane S. *Categories for the Working Mathematician*, Springer-Verlag, NY, 1971.

[11] Meseguer J. "What is logic programming? What is a logic?", Proc. *Logic Colloqium 87*, Granada, to appear.

[12] Rydeheard D.E., Burstall R.M. "A Categorical Unification Algorithm", Proc. Summer Conf. on *Category Theory and Computer Programming* 1985. LNCS 240.

On the safe termination of
PROLOG programs

Krzysztof R. Apt[1,2]

Roland N. Bol[1]

Jan Willem Klop[1,3]

Abstract

We systematically study loop checking mechanisms for logic programs by considering their soundness, completeness, relative strength and related concepts. We introduce a natural concept of a *simple loop check* and prove that no sound and complete simple loop check exists, even for programs without function symbols. Then we introduce a number of sound simple loop checks and identify a natural class of PROLOG programs for which they are complete. In this class a limited form of recursion is allowed. As a by-product we obtain an implementation of the closed world assumption of Reiter [R] and a query evaluation algorithm for a class of logic programs without function symbols.

1. Introduction

PROLOG has been advocated as a programming language which allows us to write executable specifications. Unfortunately, when interpreting correct specifications written in the form of a logic program as a PROLOG program, a divergence usually arises... This is due to the fact that the PROLOG interpreter uses a depth-first search and consequently can enter an infinite branch and miss a solution.

The problem of detecting such a possibility of divergence is obviously undecidable as PROLOG has the full power of recursion theory. Consequently this problem has been taken care of by developing a number of useful heuristics on how to avoid a possibility of non-termination.

Another possible approach to this problem has been based on modifying the underlying computation mechanism that searches through the corresponding SLD-trees by adding a capability of pruning. Pruning an SLD-tree means that at some point the interpreter is forced to stop its search through a certain part of the tree, typically an infinite branch. Every method of pruning SLD-trees considered so far has been based on excluding some kind of repetition in the SLD-derivations, because such a repetition makes the interpreter enter an infinite loop.

---

[1] Centre for Mathematics and Computer Science
P.O.Box 4079, 1009 AB Amsterdam, The Netherlands

[2] Department of Computer Sciences, University of Texas at Austin,
Austin, Texas 78712-1188, USA

[3] Department of Computer Sciences, Free University of Amsterdam
De Boelelaan 1081, 1081 HV Amsterdam, The Netherlands

That is why pruning SLD-trees has been called *loop checking*. Such modifications of PROLOG interpreters were considered in the literature (see e.g. [B], [BW], [Co], [PG], [SGG]), but no results were proved about them, with a notable exception of [SGG].

In this paper we systematically study loop checking mechanisms by analyzing their soundness (no computed answer substitution to a goal is missed), completeness (all resulting derivations are finite), relative strength and related properties. We introduce a natural subclass of loop checking mechanisms, called *simple* loop checks, obtained when their definition does not depend on the analyzed logic programs. We prove among others that no sound and complete simple loop check exists even in the absence of function symbols.

Then we introduce a number of intuitive simple loop checks which are all sound and identify a natural class of *restricted* programs without function symbols for which these loop checks are complete. Restricted programs allow a restricted form of recursion (hence the name).

To better understand the relevance of the problems studied here, consider the following example. Let P be the following simple-minded PROLOG program computing in the relation *tc* the transitive closure of the relation *r*:

P = { tc(x,y) ← r(x,y).

   tc(x,y) ← r(x,z),tc(z,y). }

Suppose we add to P the following facts about r: r(a,a)←, r(a,b)←, r(b,c)←, r(d,a)←. Then if we ask:

- tc(a,b) we get the answer 'yes';
- tc(a,c) the program gets into an infinite loop (whereas we should get the answer 'yes');
- tc(a,d) the program gets into an infinite loop (whereas we should get the answer 'no');
- tc(b,d) we get the answer 'no'.

Thus P is not the right program for computing the transitive closure. One solution is to write a different program, which is not straightforward - see for example the program in [CM], section 7.2. In fact, Kunen [K] recently proved that any such program must use either function symbols or negated literals.

In our solution, we change the underlying interpreter by adding to it a simple loop check, and retain the above program, which turns out to be restricted. (In contrast, this solution cannot be applied to an alternative version of P obtained by replacing the second clause by tc(x,y) ← tc(x,z),tc(z,y), as the resulting program is not any more restricted.)

As a by-product of these considerations we obtain an implementation of the *closed world assumption* of Reiter [R] and of a query evaluation mechanism for definite deductive databases which are restricted programs. The closed world assumption (CWA in short) is a way of inferring negative information in deductive databases. Reiter [R] showed that in the case of definite deductive databases (DB in short) it does not introduce inconsistency. However, even though CWA is correctly defined for DB, there is still the problem of how it can be implemented, since it calls for the use of the following rule (or rather metarule):

$$\text{if } DB \nvdash \varphi \text{ then } DB \vdash \neg\varphi,$$

that is: deduce $\neg\varphi$ if φ cannot be proved from DB using first order logic.

The problem is how to determine for a particular ground atom (or *fact* in short) that there is no proof of it. When DB is a restricted program, to infer $\neg A$ for a fact A it suffices to use Clark's [Cl] *negation as (finite) failure* rule augmented with an appropriate loop check.

A more general problem is that of query processing in DB: given an atom A, compute the set $[A]_{DB}$ of all its ground instances $A\theta$ such that $DB \vdash A\theta$. Indeed, when A is ground and $DB \nvdash A$, the query processing problem reduces to the problem of deducing $\neg A$ by means of CWA. When DB is a restricted program, to compute $[A]_{DB}$ for an atom A, it suffices to collect all computed answer substitutions in the SLD-tree with leftmost selection rule and $\leftarrow A$ as root, pruned by a sound and complete loop check.

In the full version of this paper we shall analyze several other loop checks, including those based on a subsumption check (see [CL], [SGG]). These loop checks are complete for different classes of programs.

2. Loop checking

Throughout this paper we assume familiarity with the basic concepts and notations of logic programming as described in [L]. For two substitutions σ and τ, we write $\sigma \leq \tau$ when σ is more general than τ and for two expressions E and F, we write $E \leq F$ if F is an instance of E. We then say that F is *less general* than E. An SLD-derivation step from a goal G, using a clause C and an mgu θ, to a goal H is denoted as $G \Rightarrow_{C, \theta} H$.

The purpose of a loop check is to prune every infinite SLD-tree to a finite subtree of it containing the root. One might define a loop check as a function from SLD-trees to SLD-trees, directly giving the pruned tree. However, this would be a very general definition, allowing practically everything. We shall use therefore a more restricted definition according to which for a program P:
- a node in an SLD-tree of $P \cup \{G\}$ (for some goal G) is *pruned* if all its descendants have been removed. (Note the terminology: the pruned node itself remains in the tree.)
- by pruning some of the nodes we obtain a pruned version of the SLD-tree.
- whether a node is pruned or not only depends upon its ancestors in the SLD-tree, that is on the SLD-derivation from the root up to this node. (Note: throughout the paper, by an SLD-derivation we mean an SLD-derivation in the sense of [L] or an initial fragment of it.)

Therefore, we can define a loop check as a function on the SLD-derivations instead of on the SLD-trees. However, for convenience we do not define it as a function from derivations to derivations, but as a set of derivations (depending on the program): the derivations that are pruned exactly at their last node. Such a set of SLD-derivations L(P) can be extended in a canonical way to a function $f_{L(P)}$ from SLD-trees to SLD-trees by removing from an SLD-tree all the descendants of the nodes in {G | the SLD-derivation from the root to G is in L(P)}. In the remainder of this article, we shall usually make this conversion implicitly.

We shall also study an even more restricted form of loop check, called simple loop check, in which the set of pruned derivations is independent of the program P. In other words, a loop check is a function, having a program as input and a simple loop check as output. This leads us to the following definitions.

DEFINITION 2.1.
Let L be a set of SLD-derivations.
$RemSub(L) = \{D \in L \mid L$ does not contain a proper subderivation of D\}
L is *subderivation free* if $L = RemSub(L)$. $\qquad\qquad\qquad\square$

In order to render the intuitive meaning of a loop check L: 'every derivation $D \in L$ is pruned *exactly* at its last node', we need that L is subderivation free. Note that RemSub(RemSub(L)) = RemSub(L).

In the following definition, by a *variant* of a derivation D we mean a derivation D' in which in every derivation step, atoms in the same positions are selected and the same program clause is used. D' may differ from D in the renaming that is applied to these program clauses for reasons of standardizing apart and in the mgu used. It has been shown that in this case every goal in D' is a variant of the corresponding goal in D (see [LS]).

DEFINITION 2.2.
A *simple loop check* is a computable set L of SLD-derivations such that
- for every derivation D: if $D \in L$ then for every variant D' of D: $D' \in L$;
- L is subderivation free. □

The first condition here ensures that the choice of variables in the input clauses in an SLD-derivation does not influence its pruning. This is a reasonable demand since we are not interested in the choice of the names of the variables in the derivations.

DEFINITION 2.3.
A *loop check* is a computable function L from programs to sets of SLD-derivations such that for every program P, L(P) is a simple loop check. □

DEFINITION 2.4.
Let L be a loop check. An SLD-derivation D of $P \cup \{G\}$ is *pruned by L* if L(P) contains a subderivation D' of D. □

EXAMPLE 2.5 (based on Example 8 in [B], see also [vG1]).
A first attempt to formulate the *Contains a Variant of Atom* (*CVA*) check might be: 'A derivation is pruned at the first goal that contains a variant A of an atom A' that occurred in an earlier goal.' Note that we have to allow here that A and A' are variants: if we required A=A' then we would violate the first condition in definition 2.2.

The intuition behind this loop check is the following. We wish to prove A' by resolution. If we find out after some resolution steps that in order to prove A' we need to prove a variant A of A', then there are two possibilities. One is that there is a proof for A. Then this proof could also be used as a proof for A', by applying an appropriate renaming on it. So we do not need the proof of A' that goes via A. The other possibility is that there is no proof for A. In that case, the attempt to prove A' via A cannot be successful. So in both cases there is no reason to continue the attempt to prove A' via A.

The derivation step $\leftarrow B,A \Rightarrow_{B \leftarrow} \leftarrow A$ shows that the first formulation of the CVA check is not precise enough: it does not capture the intuition that the proof of A' *goes via* A. A should be the result (after one or more derivation steps) of resolving A', or a further instantiated version of A' (if A' is not immediately selected).

Therefore we define CVA = RemSub($\{ D \mid D = (G_0 \Rightarrow_{C_1,\theta_1} G_1 \Rightarrow \ldots \Rightarrow G_{k-1} \Rightarrow_{C_k,\theta_k} G_k)$ such that for some i and j, $0 \leq i \leq j < k$, G_k contains an atom A that is
- a variant of an atom A' in G_i and
- the result of an attempt to resolve $A'\theta_{i+1}\ldots\theta_j$, the further instantiated version of A' that is selected in $G_j \}$).
We shall now give an illustration of the use of this loop check.

Let P = { A(0) ←   (C1)
          B(1) ←   (C2)
          A(x) ← A(y)   (C3)
          C ← A(x),B(x)   (C4) },
let G = ← C.

That the informal justification of the loop check CVA is incorrect, is shown by applying it to two SLD-trees of P∪{G}, via leftmost and rightmost selection rule respectively, which gives us:

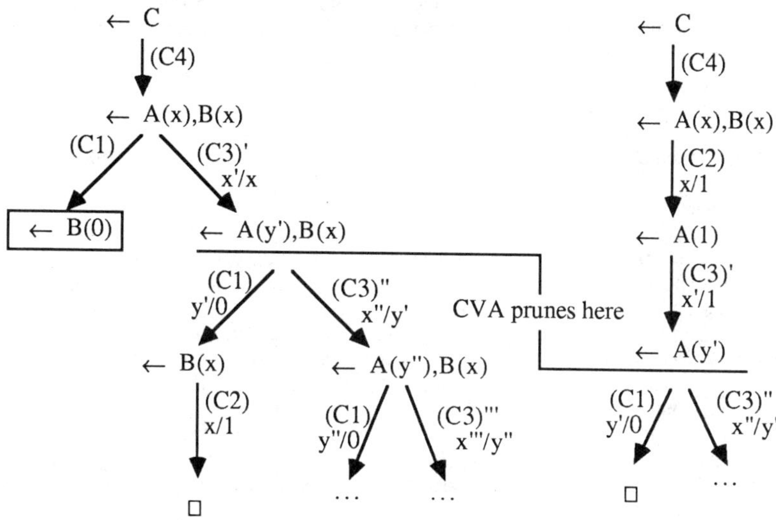

figure 1

Here and elsewhere a substitution θ acting on one variable only, say x, is denoted by $x/x\theta$. A failed node, i.e. a node without a successor in the SLD-tree, is marked by a box around it.

A detailed analysis shows why the goal $G_3 = \leftarrow A(y')$ in the rightmost tree is pruned by the CVA check. Clearly, a variant of $A(y')$ occurs in an earlier goal: $A(x)$ in G_1. So we take i=1. In G_1, $A(x)$ is not yet selected, so j>i. In fact j=2, for in G_2 the atom $A(1)$, which is a further instantiated version of $A(x)$, is selected. Indeed, $A(y')$ is the result of resolving $A(1)$. Therefore the derivation is pruned at G_3 by the CVA check. (In this case, $A(y')$ is the direct result of resolving $A(1)$, but in general there may be any number of derivation steps between G_j and G_k.)   □

Indeed, this loop check has not worked properly here: all successful derivations have been pruned. Clearly, this is an undesirable property for loop checks. On the other hand, all infinite derivations are pruned, as intended. In the next section, we shall give formal definitions of these and related properties of loop checks.

3. Some general considerations

In this section some basic properties of loop checks are introduced and some natural results concerning them are established.

3.1. Soundness and completeness
The most important property is definitely that using a loop check does not result in a loss of success. Since we intend to use pruned trees instead of the original ones, we need at least that pruning a successful tree yields again a successful tree.

Even stronger, because we use here a PROLOG-like interpreter augmented with a loop check as the *only* inference mechanism, we do not want to lose any individual solution. That is, if the original tree contains a successful branch (with some computed answer substitution), then we require that the pruned tree contains a successful branch with a more general answer substitution.

Finally, we would like to retain only shorter derivations and prune the longer ones that give the same result. This leads to the following definitions, where for a derivation D, |D| stands for its length, i.e. the number of goals in it.

DEFINITION 3.1.1.
i) A loop check L is *weakly sound* if for every program P and every goal G, and for every SLD-tree T of $P \cup \{G\}$: if T contains a successful branch, then $f_{L(P)}(T)$ contains a successful branch.
ii) A loop check L is *sound* if for every program P and every goal G, and for every SLD-tree T of $P \cup \{G\}$: if T contains a successful branch with a computed answer substitution σ, then $f_{L(P)}(T)$ contains a successful branch with a computed answer substitution σ' such that $G\sigma' \leq G\sigma$.
iii) A loop check L is *shortening* if for every program P and every goal G, and for every SLD-tree T of $P \cup \{G\}$: if T contains a successful branch D with a computed answer substitution σ, then either $f_{L(P)}(T)$ contains D or $f_{L(P)}(T)$ contains a successful branch D' with a computed answer substitution σ' such that $G\sigma' \leq G\sigma$ and $|D'|<|D|$. $\qquad\square$

The following lemma is an immediate consequence of these definitions.

LEMMA 3.1.2. *Let L be a loop check.*
    i) If L is shortening, then L is sound.
    ii) If L is sound, then L is weakly sound. $\qquad\square$

The purpose of a loop check is to reduce the search space for top-down interpreters. We would like to end up with a finite search space. This is the case when every infinite derivation is pruned.

DEFINITION 3.1.3.
A loop check L is *complete* if every infinite SLD-derivation is pruned by L. $\qquad\square$

We must point out here that in these definitions we have overloaded the terms 'soundness' and 'completeness'. These terms do not refer here only to loop checks, but also to interpreters for logic programs (with or without a loop check). Such an interpreter is sound if the answer it gives (if it gives one) is correct w.r.t. the intended model or the intended theory of the program. An interpreter is complete if it finds every correct answer within a finite time.

3.2. Interpreters and loop checks

When a top-down interpreter is augmented with a loop check, we obtain a new interpreter. The soundness and completeness of this new interpreter depends on the soundness and completeness of the old one, as well as on the soundness and completeness of the loop check. However, these relations are not trivial. In particular, it is not true that adding a complete loop check to a complete interpreter yields again a complete interpreter.

These relationships are expressed by the following lemma's. For each of them, an intuitive meaning is provided in terms of interpreters. We refer here to two interpreters: one searching the SLD-tree depth-first left-to-right (as the PROLOG interpreter does), and one searching breadth-first. Without a loop check, both interpreters are sound w.r.t. CWA. The breadth-first interpreter is also complete.

The (quite simple) proofs are omitted in this section. They will appear in [BAK], the full version of this paper.

LEMMA 3.2.1. *Let P be a program, A a ground atom and L a weakly sound loop check. Then for every SLD-tree T of $P \cup \{\leftarrow A\}$, $P \vdash_{CWA} \neg A$ iff $f_{L(P)}(T)$ contains no successful branches.* $\quad\square$

Thus an interpreter augmented with a weakly sound loop check remains sound w.r.t. CWA. Since $f_{L(P)}(T)$ may be infinite, nothing can be said about completeness.

LEMMA 3.2.2. *Let P be a program, A an atom and L a sound loop check. Then for every SLD-tree T of $P \cup \{\leftarrow A\}$ and for every ground substitution θ, $P \vdash A\theta$ iff $f_{L(P)}(T)$ contains a successful branch with a computed answer substitution τ such that $\tau \leq \theta$.* $\quad\square$

Thus an interpreter augmented with a sound loop check remains sound. Moreover, a breadth-first interpreter remains complete .

COROLLARY 3.2.3. *Let P be a program, A a ground atom and L a weakly sound and complete loop check. Then for every SLD-tree T of $P \cup \{\leftarrow A\}$, $P \vdash_{CWA} \neg A$ iff $f_{L(P)}(T)$ is finite and contains no successful branches.* $\quad\square$

Thus an interpreter augmented with a weakly sound and complete loop check becomes complete w.r.t. CWA.

COROLLARY 3.2.4. *Let P be a program, A an atom and L a sound and complete loop check. Then for every SLD-tree T of $P \cup \{\leftarrow A\}$ and for every ground substitution θ, $P \vdash A\theta$ iff $f_{L(P)}(T)$ is finite and contains a successful branch with a computed answer substitution τ such that $\tau \leq \theta$.* $\quad\square$

Thus a depth-first interpreter augmented with a sound and complete loop check becomes complete . This also means that a sound and complete loop check can be used to implement query processing as defined in the introduction. Indeed, given a program P and an atom A with an SLD-tree T of $P \cup \{\leftarrow A\}$, it suffices to traverse the finite tree $f_{L(P)}(T)$ and collect all computed answer substitutions.

3.3. Comparing loop checks
After studying the relationships between loop checks and interpreters, we shall now analyze a relationship between loop checks. In general, it can be quite difficult to compare loop checks. However, some of them can be compared in a natural way: if every loop that is detected by one loop check, is detected at the same derivation step or earlier by another loop check, then the latter one is *stronger* than the former.

DEFINITION 3.3.1.
Let L_1 and L_2 be loop checks.
L_1 is *stronger than* L_2 if for every program P every SLD-derivation $D_2 \in L_2(P)$ contains a subderivation D_1 such that $D_1 \in L_1(P)$. □

In other words, L_1 is stronger than L_2 if every SLD-derivation that is pruned by L_2 is also pruned by L_1. Note that the definition implies that L_1 is stronger than itself.
The following theorem will prove to be very useful. It will enable us to obtain soundness and completeness results for loop checks which are related by the 'stronger than' relation, by proving soundness and completeness for only one of them.

THEOREM 3.3.2. *Let L_1 and L_2 be loop checks, and let L_1 be stronger than L_2.*
   i) If L_1 is weakly sound, then L_2 is weakly sound.
   ii) If L_1 is sound, then L_2 is sound.
   iii) If L_1 is shortening, then L_2 is shortening.
   iv) If L_2 is complete then L_1 is complete.
PROOF. Straightforward. □

Now we have a more clear view of the situation. Very strong loop checks prune derivations in an 'early stage'. If they prune too early, then they are unsound. Since this is undesirable, we must look for weaker loop checks. But a loop check should preferably be not too weak, for then it might fail to prune some infinite derivations (in other words, it might be incomplete). Of course, the 'stronger than' relation is not linear. Moreover, loop checks exist that are neither sound nor complete.

3.4. Sound and complete loop checks
The question is now: do there exist sound and complete loop checks? Obviously, there cannot be such a loop check for logic programs in general, as logic programming has the full power of recursion theory. (Remember that according to the definition, a loop check is computable.) So our first step is to rule out programs that compute over an infinite domain. We shall do so by restricting our attention to programs without function symbols. This restriction leads to a finite Herbrand Universe, but other solutions (typed functions, bounded term-size property [vG2]) are also possible here.
Note that our definitions so far referred to arbitrary programs and SLD-derivations. In the sequel, we shall consider only certain classes of programs (like the ones with a finite Herbrand Universe) and SLD-derivations (like the derivations via leftmost selection rule). The definitions we introduced can be extended in an obvious way so that we can use terminology like 'complete w.r.t. leftmost selection rule'.
In the sequel, we shall write 'complete' instead of 'complete in the absence of function symbols'. So our question can be reformulated as: is there a sound

and complete loop check? Before answering this question for loop checks in general, we shall answer it for simple loop checks.

THEOREM 3.4.1. *There is no weakly sound and complete simple loop check.*
PROOF. For every $n>0$, let $P_n = \{\ S(i,i+1)\leftarrow\ |\ 0\leq i<n\ \}\ \cup\ \{\ A(0)\leftarrow,$ $A(x)\leftarrow A(y),S(y,x),\ B(n)\leftarrow\ \}$ and let $G=\leftarrow A(x_0),B(x_0)$. Let L be a complete loop check and T_n an SLD-tree of $P_n\cup\{G\}$ via leftmost selection rule. (T_n is fixed modulo the names of the variables.)
T_n has an infinite branch with goals of the form $\leftarrow A(x_i),S(x_i,x_{i-1}),$ $...,S(x_1,x_0),B(x_0)$ $(i\geq 0)$. The side-branches that are the result of applying the clause $A(0)\leftarrow$ instead of $A(x)\leftarrow A(y),S(y,x)$ are all finitely failed, except for the one successful branch that begins at $\leftarrow A(x_n),S(x_n,x_{n-1}),...,S(x_1,x_0),B(x_0)$.

L is complete, so the infinite derivation that is the result of always selecting the recursive clause $A(x)\leftarrow A(y),S(y,x)$ is pruned by L. Since L is simple, the goal at which pruning takes place is independent of P_n. In particular it is independent of n, since n does not occur in this derivation. Suppose that the pruned goal is $\leftarrow A(x_i),\ S(x_i,x_{i-1}),...,S(x_1,x),B(x)$. (Note that according to the definition of a loop check, taking other variable names does not influence the level at which pruning takes place.) Then for $n\geq i$: T_n contains a successful branch and $f_L(T_n)$ does not. Hence L is not weakly sound. $\quad\square$

Taking the whole program into account gives us an opportunity to define a shortening (so a fortiori sound) loop check which is complete. Moreover, this loop check is stronger than *every* other shortening loop check. Strange as it may seem, this one is also impractical. It is like solving a puzzle by trial and error. You can save effort if you can avoid the trials that lead to an error. In order to know exactly which trials to avoid you decide to solve the puzzle first. Then you know.

DEFINITION 3.4.2.
$STRONG(P) = RemSub(\{D = G\Rightarrow...\ |$ for no σ, D is an initial fragment of a shortest refutation of $P\cup\{G\}$ with a computed answer substitution $\sigma\})$. $\quad\square$

THEOREM 3.4.3. *i) STRONG is a shortening loop check.*
ii) STRONG is stronger than any shortening loop check.
iii) STRONG is complete.
PROOF. The proof will appear in [BAK]. $\quad\square$

So far, we have not been very successful in defining useful sound and complete loop checks. In the next section, we shall restrict our attention to simple loop checks. They will be shortening, but as shown above, they cannot be complete (in the absence of function symbols). Nevertheless, we shall introduce a natural class of programs for which they are complete.

4. Some simple loop checks

In this section, we introduce some simple loop checks. For each of them, there exist two versions: the first one is weakly sound, the second one shortening. The second, shortening version is obtained by adding an extra condition to the first one. By this construction, the first one is always stronger than the second one.

Starting with the Contains a Variant of Atom check (defined for arbitrary selection rules), we can make three independent modifications of it.

1. Adding this extra condition, dealing with the computed answer substitution 'generated so far'. A neat formulation of this condition can be obtained by the use of *resultants* instead of goals in SLD-derivations. When considering a derivation $G_0 \Rightarrow_{C1,\theta 1} G_1 \Rightarrow \ldots$, to every goal $G_i = \leftarrow S_i$ there corresponds the resultant $R_i = S_0\theta_1\ldots\theta_i \leftarrow S_i$. Resultants were introduced in [LS].

2. Replace *variant* by *instance*. This yields the *Contains an Instance of Atom (CIA)* check. This check is still unsound: it is even stronger than the CVA check. Besnard [B] has introduced a weakly sound version of this loop check. This check and related ones (derived from CVA; shortening versions) are discussed in [BAK].

3. Replace *atom* by *goal*. This yields the *Equals Variant of Goal (EVG)* check. Informally, this loop check prunes a derivation as soon as a *goal* occurs that is a variant of an earlier goal. Replacing 'variant' by 'instance' again yields the *Equals Instance of Goal (EIG)* check. The shortening versions are called *Equals Variant of Resultant (EVR)* and *Equals Instance of Resultant (EIR)*. These checks are discussed below.

   Taking goals instead of atoms as a basis for a loop check yields two independent choices again.

   3a. Whereas equality between atoms is unambiguous, equality between goals is much less clear. In SLD-derivations, we regard goals as lists, so both the number and the order of occurrences of atoms is important. However, we may also regard them as multisets, where the order of the occurrences is unimportant. We might even consider regarding them as sets, but that proves to be impractical: the difference between the derivation steps $\leftarrow A,A \Rightarrow \leftarrow A$ and $\leftarrow A \Rightarrow \leftarrow A$ is then no longer visible. Regarding goals as sets in our loop checks would require regarding goals as sets in SLD-derivations, which would result in too many undesirable effects.

   So we shall consider *two* EVG checks: EVG_L (for list) and EVG_M (for multiset). The same holds for EIG, EVR and EIR. We shall refer to these eight loop checks as the *equality* checks.

   3b. Finally, we may replace "G_2 *is* a variant/instance of G_1" by "G_2 *is subsumed by* a variant/instance of G_1". We define 'G_1 subsumes G_2' as '$G_1 \subseteq G_2$'. Thus we can make a distinction between 'subsumed by a variant' and 'subsumed by an instance'. Usually in literature, 'subsumed by a variant' is not considered, 'subsumed by an instance' is simply called 'subsumed'. See e.g. [CL]. Subsumption can also be defined for resolvents.

   This yields the *subsumption* check. Since this modification is again independent of the others, there are in total 2x2x2=8 subsumption checks. These checks are discussed in [BAK].

We now study the equality checks in more detail. At first we give a formal definition of the weakly sound versions. Then we introduce an extra condition that makes these checks shortening. Finally we identify a natural class of programs for which the equality checks are complete.

In fact, we should give a definition for each equality check. This would yield eight almost identical definitions. Therefore we compress them into two definitions, trusting that the reader is willing to understand our notation. The equality relation between goals regarded as lists is denoted by $=_L$; similarly $=_M$ for multisets. We begin with the weakly sound versions.

DEFINITION 4.1.

For Type $\in \{L,M\}$, the *Equals Variant/Instance of Goal$_{Type}$* check is the set of SLD-derivations EVG/EIG$_{Type}$ = RemSub($\{D \mid D = (G_0 \Rightarrow_{C1,\theta1} G_1 \Rightarrow \ldots \Rightarrow G_{k-1} \Rightarrow_{Ck,\theta k} G_k)$ such that for some i, $0 \leq i < k$, there is a renaming/substitution τ such that $G_k =_{Type} G_i\tau\})$. $\square$

We shall prove later that these loop checks are weakly sound. However, they are not sound (see Example 4.3). We can make them sound, and even shortening, by adding the condition that τ and $\theta_{i+1}\ldots\theta_k$ also agree on the variables of the intermediate goal $G_0\theta_1\ldots\theta_i$. So the extra condition is: $G_0\theta_1\ldots\theta_k = G_0\theta_1\ldots\theta_i\tau$. (Note: in this equality it is irrelevant whether goals are lists or multisets.) It will appear that this condition works not only for EVG and EIG, but for all other loop checks studied in this section, as well.

Note that adding this condition is equivalent to the replacement of the condition $G_k =_{Type} G_i\tau$ by the condition $R_k =_{Type} R_i\tau$, where R_k and R_i are the resultants corresponding to the goals G_k and G_i.

DEFINITION 4.2.

For Type $\in \{L,M\}$, the *Equals Variant/Instance of Resultant$_{Type}$* check is the set of SLD-derivations EVR/EIR$_{Type}$ = RemSub($\{D \mid D = (G_0 \Rightarrow_{C1,\theta1} G_1 \Rightarrow \ldots \Rightarrow G_{k-1} \Rightarrow_{Ck,\theta k} G_k)$ such that for some i, $0 \leq i < k$, there is a renaming/substitution τ such that $G_k =_{Type} G_i\tau$ and $G_0\theta_1\ldots\theta_k = G_0\theta_1\ldots\theta_i\tau\})$. $\square$

The following example shows the difference between the goal-based and resultant-based equality checks. The example is such that the other variations (variants or instances, goals regarded as lists or as multisets) do not play a role here.

EXAMPLE 4.3.

Let P = { p(a) $\leftarrow$,   (C1)
        p(y) $\leftarrow$ p(z)   (C2) },
let G = $\leftarrow$ p(x).

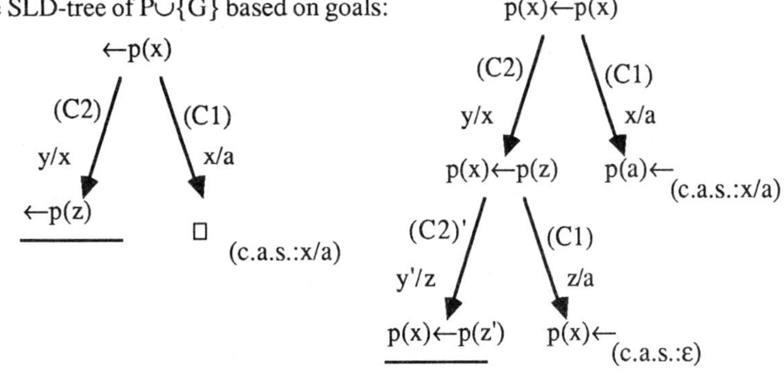

figure 2

Without the condition $G_0\theta_1...\theta_k = G_0\theta_1...\theta_i\tau$ we would only obtain x/a as the computed answer substitution, whereas we also should obtain the empty substitution. This shows that the EVG and EIG loop checks are not sound.

In the leftmost tree $\leftarrow p(z)$ is a variant of $\leftarrow p(x)$, so the derivation is pruned by EVG at that goal. However, the corresponding resultant $p(x)\leftarrow p(z)$ is clearly not a variant of $p(x)\leftarrow p(x)$, therefore the derivation is not yet pruned by EVR. However, after another application of (C2), the resultant $p(x)\leftarrow p(z')$ occurs, which is a variant of $p(x)\leftarrow p(z)$. At that point the derivation is pruned by EVR.

The rightmost tree in figure 2 shows an 'SLD-tree' in which the goals are replaced by the corresponding resultants. Note that a successful branch in a resultant-based SLD-tree does not end by the empty goal $\square$, but by the instance of the initial goal that was 'proved' by this branch. $\qquad\square$

LEMMA 4.4. *All equality checks are simple loop checks.*
PROOF. Straightforward. $\qquad\square$

We now prove that the equality checks based on resultants are shortening and that the equality checks based on goals are weakly sound. According to Theorem 3.3.2 it is sufficient to focus on the strongest checks in both classes: the EIR_M and the EIG_M checks. We need the following lemma.

LEMMA 4.5. *Let P be a program. Let G_1 and G_2 be goals such that $G_1 =_M G_2$. Suppose D_1 is an SLD-derivation of $P \cup \{G_1\}$ with computed answer substitution σ. Then there exists an SLD-derivation D_2 of $P \cup \{G_2\}$ with computed answer substitution σ and $|D_1|=|D_2|$ via every selection rule.*
PROOF. By the soundness and strong completeness of SLD-resolution, see [L]. $\qquad\square$

THEOREM 4.6. *i) The loop check EIR_M is shortening.*
    ii) The loop check EIG_M is weakly sound.
PROOF. i) Let D be an SLD-refutation of G_0 with computed answer substitution σ. If D is pruned by EIR_M then we have to find in every SLD-tree containing D an SLD-refutation D' of G_0 with computed answer substitution σ' such that $G_0\sigma' \leq G_0\sigma$, $|D'|<|D|$ and D' is not pruned by EIR_M. We prove this by induction on the length l of the refutation D. We have $l \geq 1$. For $l=1$, D cannot be pruned. Now suppose the theorem is true for every refutation of G_0 of length $\leq l$. Let D be a refutation of length $l+1$. Suppose that D is pruned by EIR_M. Then we have $D = (G_0 \Rightarrow_{C_1,\theta_1} G_1 \Rightarrow ... \Rightarrow G_{i-1} \Rightarrow_{C_i,\theta_i} G_i \Rightarrow_{C_{i+1},\theta_{i+1}} G_{i+1} \Rightarrow ... \Rightarrow G_{k-1} \Rightarrow_{C_k,\theta_k} G_k \Rightarrow_{C_{k+1},\theta_{k+1}} G_{k+1} \Rightarrow ... \Rightarrow \square)$, and for some substitution τ: $G_k =_M G_i\tau$ and $G_0\theta_1...\theta_k = G_0\theta_1...\theta_i\tau$.

By Lemma 4.5 we have a refutation of $G_i\tau$ with a computed answer substitution $\theta_{k+1}...\theta_l$. Now we can obtain an unrestricted (in the sense of [L]) SLD-refutation D_1 of G_0 (that is in the step $G_{i-1} \Rightarrow_{C_i,\theta_i\tau} G_i\tau$ we do not use an mgu), which is shorter than D. Using the Mgu Lemma of [L], we have an SLD-refutation D_2 of G_0 with the same length as D_1 and a computed answer substitution $\sigma_2 \leq \theta_1...\theta_i\tau\theta_{k+1}...\theta_l$. (Lemma 4.5 and the proof of the Mgu Lemma show that for every SLD-tree containing D, such a derivation D_2 can be constructed.) D_2 is an SLD-refutation of G_0 which is shorter than D, so by the induction hypothesis there exists an SLD-derivation D_3 of G_0 with computed answer substitution σ_3 such that $G_0\sigma_3 \leq G_0\sigma_2$ and D_3 is not pruned by EIR_M. Now we can take $D'=D_3$ and we have $G_0\sigma' = G_0\sigma_3 \leq G_0\sigma_2 \leq G_0\theta_1...\theta_i\tau\theta_{k+1}...\theta_l = G_0\theta_1...\theta_i\theta_{i+1}...\theta_k\theta_{k+1}...\theta_l = G_0\sigma$.

ii) Note that the extra condition $G_0\theta_1...\theta_k=G_0\theta_1...\theta_i\tau$ was only used to prove that $G_0\sigma' \leq G_0\sigma$. □

COROLLARY 4.7. *i) EVR and EIR are shortening.*
ii) EVG and EIG are weakly sound.
PROOF. By Theorem 4.6 and Theorem 3.3.2. □

For completeness issues, it is sufficient to consider the weakest of the equality checks: the EVR_L check. We know that EVR_L is not complete - Theorem 3.4.1 presents a counterexample that holds for every simple loop check. However, for the EVR_L check this counterexample can be simplified. The program in Theorem 3.4.1 consists of a collection of ground facts and one recursive clause. Clearly, this clause is the 'core' of the counterexample. It appears that for EVR_L, we need only this clause for a demonstration of its incompleteness. Moreover, we need only the propositional structure of the clause: i.e. we may remove the arguments.

EXAMPLE 4.8.
Let $P = \{ A \leftarrow A,S \}$.
Then for 'the' SLD-tree T of $P\cup\{\leftarrow A\}$ via leftmost selection rule, $f_{EVRL}(T)$ is infinite. Indeed, every descendant of the initial goal has one occurrence of S more than its parent goal, so it cannot be a variant of any of its ancestors. □

Obviously, the problem is that the atom A in the goal is allowed to generate infinitely many S-atoms, which are never selected, thereby making the goal wider and wider. We now introduce a class of programs for which this phenomenon cannot occur and we prove that EVR_L is complete for these programs. The necessary restriction is obtained by allowing at most one recursive call per clause and allowing such a call only after all other atoms in the body of the clause have been completely resolved. In order to avoid unnecessary complications, we shall put the atom that causes the recursive call (if present) at the end of the body of the clause, and consider only derivations via the leftmost selection rule. For a formal definition, we use the notion of the *dependency graph* D_P of a program P.

DEFINITION 4.9.
The *dependency graph D_P* of a program P is a directed graph whose nodes are the predicate symbols appearing in P and
$(p,q) \in D_P$ iff there is a clause in P using p in its head and q in its body.
D_P^* is the reflexive, transitive closure of D_P. When $(p,q) \in D_P^*$, we say that p *depends on* q. For a predicate symbol p, the *class of p* is the set of predicate symbols p 'mutually depends' on: $cl_P(p) = \{q \mid (p,q)\in D_P^* \text{ and } (q,p)\in D_P^* \}$. □

DEFINITION 4.10.
Given an atom A, let *rel(A)* denote its predicate symbol.
A program P is called *restricted* if in every clause $A_0\leftarrow A_1,...,A_n$ $(n\geq 0)$ of P, $rel(A_i)$ does not depend on $rel(A_0)$ for $i = 1,...,n-1$. □

Note that this definition allows at most one recursive call per clause. Thus (disregarding the order of atoms in the bodies) restricted programs include so called linear programs, which contain only one recursive clause and in this clause only a single recursive call occurs. The 'transitive closure' program from the introduction is restricted. Note also that programs of which all clauses have a body with at most one atom are restricted.

We now prove that EVR_L is complete w.r.t. leftmost selection rule for restricted programs. An interesting feature of restricted programs is that in each SLD-derivation, goals have a number of atoms which is bounded in advance. We shall show that this implies that modulo the 'being a variant of' relation, the number of possible goals in a given SLD-derivation is finite.

In the rest of this section, P is a restricted program without function symbols and G is a goal in L_P. By the *length* of a goal G, $|G|$, we mean the number of atoms of G. The maximum length of the goals in a derivation is easily predictable from the program and the initial goal. This can be done by defining (simultaneously) the *weight*-function on goals and predicate symbols (or rather the classes of predicate symbols).

DEFINITION 4.11.
Let P be a restricted program.
Then the function *weight* is defined as:
i) for a goal $G=\leftarrow A_1,\ldots,A_n$ $(n\geq 1)$ in L_P,

$weight(G) = \max\{weight(rel(A_i))+n-i \mid i=1,\ldots,n\}$;
ii) for a predicate symbol p of P, $weight(p) =$

$\max(\ \{weight(\leftarrow A_1,\ldots,A_n) \mid$

$A\leftarrow A_1,\ldots,A_n \in P,\ n>0,\ rel(A)\in cl_P(p),\ (rel(A_n),p)\notin D_P^*\}\ \cup$
$\{1+weight(\leftarrow A_1,\ldots,A_{n-1}) \mid$

$A\leftarrow A_1,\ldots,A_n \in P,\ n>1,\ rel(A)\in cl_P(p),\ (rel(A_n),p)\in D_P^*\}\ \cup$
$\{1\}\ )$. $\qquad\qquad\square$

Note that in the definition of weight(p), clauses of the form $A\leftarrow B$, with $cl(rel(A))=cl(rel(B))$ are not considered - they do not affect the length of goals appearing in a derivation. Moreover, if the predicate symbols p and q are mutually dependent, then weight(p)=weight(q).

The fact that P is restricted ensures that the weight-function is well-defined: if weight(p) is defined in terms of weight(q), then $(q,p)\notin D_P^*$, hence weight(q) is not defined in terms of weight(p). Intuitively, the weight of a goal G majorizes the length of all goals which appear in an SLD-derivation of $P\cup\{G\}$ using leftmost selection rule. More precisely, we have the following lemma's.

LEMMA 4.12. $|G|\leq weight(G)$.
PROOF. Let $G=\leftarrow A_1,\ldots,A_n$ $(n\geq 1)$. Then $weight(G) \geq weight(rel(A_1))+n-1 \geq n = |G|$. $\qquad\qquad\square$

LEMMA 4.13. *Let* $G \Rightarrow_C H$ *be a derivation step w.r.t. P. Then* $weight(G) \geq weight(H)$.
PROOF. Since the weight of a goal does only depend on the predicates appearing in it, and not on the arguments of these predicates, we prove this fact for the case of programs written in the propositional logic. Let $G = \leftarrow A_1,\ldots,A_n$; then $weight(G) = \max\{weight(A_i)+n-i \mid i=1,\ldots,n\}$, and let $C = A_1\leftarrow B_1,\ldots,B_m$. Then the goal $H = \leftarrow B_1,\ldots,B_m,A_2,\ldots,A_n$ and therefore $weight(H) = \max(\{weight(B_i)+m+n-1-i \mid i=1,\ldots,m\} \cup \{weight(A_{i-m+1})+m+n-1-i \mid i=m+1,\ldots,m+n-1\}) = \max(\{weight(B_i)+m+n-1-i \mid i=1,\ldots,m\} \cup \{weight(A_i)+n-i \mid i=2,\ldots,n\})$. Two cases arise.
i) $weight(H) = \max\{weight(A_i)+n-i \mid i=2,\ldots,n\}$.

Then clearly $weight(H) \leq weight(G)$.

ii) weight(H) = max{weight(B_i)+m+n-1-i | i=1,...,m} (hence m>0). We will show that in this case weight(H) $\leq$ weight(A_1)+n-1 (which is $\leq$ weight(G)). Subtracting n-1, it suffices to show that max{weight(B_i)+m-i | i=1,...,m} $\leq$ weight(A_1). Again two cases arise.

iia) (rel(B_m),rel(A_1))$\notin D_P^*$. Then because of the existence of C, weight(A_1) $\geq$ weight($\leftarrow B_1,...,B_m$) = max{weight(B_i)+m-i | i=1,...,m}.

iib) (rel(B_m),rel(A_1))$\in D_P^*$. Then weight(A_1) $\geq$ 1+weight($\leftarrow B_1,...,B_{m-1}$) = 1+max{weight($B_i$)+m-1-i | i=1,...,m-1} = max{weight(B_i)+m-i | i=1,...,m-1}. Also weight(A_1) = weight(B_m)+m-m, since rel(B_m) $\in$ clp(rel(A_1)). Now we have proven the claim that max{weight(B_i)+m-i | i=1,...,m} $\leq$ weight(A_1). $\quad\square$

COROLLARY 4.14. *Let $D = G_0 \Rightarrow G_1 \Rightarrow G_2 \Rightarrow ... \Rightarrow G_i \Rightarrow ...$ be an SLD-derivation. Then for every goal G_i in D: $|G_i| \leq weight(G_0)$.*
PROOF. By induction on i. The induction basis is provided by Lemma 4.12, the induction step by Lemma 4.13. $\quad\square$

So weight(G_0) is the desired maximum length of goals occurring in any SLD-derivation of $P \cup \{G_0\}$. Now we shall formalize the 'being a variant of' relation on resultants.

DEFINITION 4.15.
We define the relation ~ as the 'being a variant of' relation on resultants. Let G be a goal and let k$\geq$1. Then $\sim_{G,k}$ stands for the restriction of the relation ~ to resultants $G_1 \leftarrow G_2$ such that G_1 is an instance of G and $|G_2| \leq k$. $\quad\square$

LEMMA 4.16. *For every goal G and $k \geq 1$, $\sim_{G,k}$ is an equivalence relation.*
PROOF. Straightforward. $\quad\square$

The following lemma is crucial for our considerations.

LEMMA 4.17. *Suppose that the language L has no function symbols and finitely many predicate symbols. Then for every goal G and $k \geq 1$, the relation $\sim_{G,k}$ has only finitely many equivalence classes.*
PROOF. The proof is straightforward. It will appear in [BAK]. $\quad\square$

We can now prove the desired theorem.

THEOREM 4.18. *The loop check EVR_L is complete w.r.t. leftmost selection rule for restricted programs.*
PROOF. Let P be a restricted program and let G_0 be a goal in L_P. Let k=weight(G_0). Consider an infinite SLD-derivation $D = G_0 \Rightarrow_{C_1,\theta_1} G_1 \Rightarrow ... \Rightarrow G_{k-1} \Rightarrow_{C_k,\theta_k} G_k \Rightarrow ...$ of $P \cup \{G_0\}$. By Corollary 4.14 for every i$\geq$0: $|G_i| \leq k$. Every goal G_i is a goal in L_P and hence every resultant $G_0\theta_1...\theta_i \leftarrow G_i$ belongs to an equivalence class of $\sim_{G_0,k}$. Since L_P satisfies the conditions of Lemma 4.17, $\sim_{G_0,k}$ has only finitely many equivalence classes, so for some i$\geq$0 and j>i ($G_0\theta_1...\theta_i \leftarrow G_i$) and $G_0\theta_1...\theta_j \leftarrow G_j$ are variants. This implies that D is pruned by EVR_L. $\quad\square$

COROLLARY 4.19. *All equality checks are complete w.r.t. leftmost selection rule for restricted programs.*
PROOF. By Theorem 4.18 and Theorem 3.3.2. $\quad\square$

Now combining Corollary 3.2.3 and Corollary 3.2.4 with Corollary 4.7 and Corollary 4.19, we conclude that all equality checks lead to an implementation of CWA for restricted programs without function symbols. Moreover, the equality checks based on resultants also lead to an implementation of query processing for these programs.

References

[AvE] K.R. APT and M.H. VAN EMDEN, *Contributions to the Theory of Logic Programming*, J. ACM, vol. 29, No. 3, 1982, 841-862.

[B] Ph. BESNARD, *Sur la Detection des Boucles Infinies en Programmation en Logique*, in: Actes "Séminaire de Programmation en Logique", Trégastel, 1985 (in French).

[BAK] R.N. BOL, K.R. APT and J.W. KLOP, *An Analysis of Loop Checking Mechanisms for Logic Programs*, Technical Report, Centre of Mathematics and Computer Science, Amsterdam, 1989. (In preparation)

[BW] D.R. BROUGH and A. WALKER, *Some Practical Properties of Logic Programming Interpreters*, in: Proceedings of the International Conference on Fifth Generation Computer Systems, (ICOT eds), 1984, 149-156.

[Cl] K.L. CLARK, *Negation as Failure*, in: Logic and Data Bases, (H. Gallaire and J. Minker, eds), Plenum Press, New York, 1978, 293-322.

[CL] C.L. CHANG and R.C. LEE, *Symbolic Logic and Mechanical Theorem Proving*, Academic Press, New York, 1973.

[CM] W. CLOCKSIN and C. MELLISH, *Programming in PROLOG*, Springer-Verlag, New York, 1981.

[Co] M.A. COVINGTON, *Eliminating Unwanted Loops in PROLOG*, SIGPLAN Notices, Vol. 20, No. 1, 1985, 20-26.

[vG1] A. VAN GELDER, *Efficient Loop Detection in PROLOG using the Tortoise-and-Hare Technique*, J. Logic Programming 4:23-31 (1987).

[vG2] A. VAN GELDER, *Negation as Failure Using Tight Derivations for General Logic Programs*, in: Foundations of Deductive Databases and Logic Programming (J. Minker ed), Morgan Kaufmann, Los Altos, 1988, 149-176.

[K] K. KUNEN, *Some remarks on the Completed Database*, Technical report, Computer Sciences Department, University of Wisconsin, Madison, U.S.A., 1988.

[L] J.W. LLOYD, *Foundations of Logic Programming*, Second Edition, Springer-Verlag, Berlin, 1987.

[LS] J.W. LLOYD and J.C. SHEPHERDSON, *Partial Evaluation in Logic Programming*, Technical Report CS-87-09, Dept. of Computer Science, University of Bristol, 1987.

[PG] D POOLE and R. GOEBEL, *On Eliminating Loops in PROLOG*, SIGPLAN Notices, Vol. 20, No. 8, 1985, 38-40.

[R] R. REITER, *On Closed World Data Bases*, in: Logic and Data Bases, (H. Gallaire and J. Minker, eds), Plenum Press, New York, 1978, 55-76.

[SGG] D.E. SMITH, M.R. GENESERETH and M.L. GINSBERG, *Controlling Recursive Inference*, Artificial Intelligence 30:343-389 (1986).

Average Time Analyses Related to Logic Programming

Nachum Dershowitz
Department of Computer Science
University of Illinois
Urbana, IL, USA

Naomi Lindenstrauss
Department of Computer Science
The Hebrew University
Jerusalem, Israel

Abstract

Logic programs are known to be amenable to parallelization. Our work is an attempt to quantify the magnitude of speed-up one can expect from parallel execution of a logic program.

To make average case analysis tractable we look separately at two aspects of logic program execution: the "subgoaling" aspect, which involves trying to prove a goal by using matching to reduce it to other goals and finally to *true*, and the "goal reduction" aspect, involving full unification.

In the first case we assume that the and-or tree determined by a goal can be constructed by matching only, and show—using the generating function approach of Flajolet— that the average cost of evaluating such trees in parallel tends to a constant as the size tends to infinity, but that the same is true, though with a larger constant, for "clever" sequential evaluation.

For the second aspect we use the generating function methods to obtain partial results about unification, which suggest that, although unification may be "difficult", it very often is not.

1   Introduction

Logic programs, that is Horn-clause programs, are known to be amenable to parallelization. Our interest is in quantifying the magnitude of speed-up one can expect from parallel execution of a logic program.

To make average case analysis tractable, we look separately at the "subgoaling", or "rewriting", aspect of logic program execution, and at the "goal-reduction", or "narrowing" (cf. [7]), aspect. The former involves trying to prove a goal by using matching to reduce it to other goals and finally to *true*; the latter requires full unification.

In the first case, we assume that the and-or search tree for a given goal can be constructed by using matching only (that is, when the head of a clause in the program is unified with a subgoal, the variables in the subgoal behave like constants—no term is substituted for them). It seems that programs are "often" of this form (cf. [3]), or one may say at least that unification is frequently used only to accumulate an answer in a variable and does not affect the structure of the tree. The tree obtained has inner nodes that are labeled either *and* or *or*, and leaves that are either instances of unit clauses in the program, and hence can be replaced by *true*, or subgoals that cannot be reduced, and hence can be replaced by *false*. The arity of *and* and *or* nodes can vary, in general, but we can replace such a tree with varyadic nodes by an equivalent tree in which all inner nodes have arity 2.

This leads us to consider binary trees representing Boolean expressions consisting of *and, or, true,* and *false.* The *length* of an expression is defined as the total number of occurrences of the above symbols in it. Note that the length always is odd in our case. The evaluation of such an expression can be performed by different methods. We consider three:

- The "naive" ("call by value") method, which evaluates both E_1 and E_2 before evaluating $and(E_1, E_2)$ or $or(E_1, E_2)$.

- The "clever" sequential method (as in Prolog), which starts by evaluating the first argument of an *and* or *or*, evaluating the second argument only if necessary (for instance if we know that E_1 evaluates to *false*, we know the value of $and(E_1, E_2)$ without evaluating E_2).

- The parallel method, which begins evaluating both arguments of an *and* or *or* in parallel, and stops when it is possible to evaluate the whole expression.

We define the appropriate cost functions, and consider the cumulative costs of evaluating the expressions of length $2n + 1$ by the above methods. These values will be denoted respectively by C_{2n+1} , S_{2n+1} , and P_{2n+1} . For example, P_{2n+1}, will be the cost for evaluating all Boolean expressions of length $2n + 1$ by the parallel method. The number of all Boolean expressions of length $2n + 1$ will be denoted by N_{2n+1}. Now we consider the average values

$$\frac{C_{2n+1}}{N_{2n+1}} , \quad \frac{S_{2n+1}}{N_{2n+1}} , \quad \frac{P_{2n+1}}{N_{2n+1}}$$

For the "naive" method the cost is equal to the length of the expression, so

$$\frac{C_{2n+1}}{N_{2n+1}} = 2n + 1$$

For the parallel and "clever" sequential cost we get, by using the generating function methods of Flajolet, the results

$$\frac{P_{2n+1}}{N_{2n+1}} \longrightarrow 4 \quad as\ n \to \infty$$

$$\frac{S_{2n+1}}{N_{2n+1}} \longrightarrow 16 \quad as\ n \to \infty$$

This means that, when evaluating a long Boolean expression , "on the average" we'll only have to go to approximately depth 4 in the tree representing it when we use the parallel method, and—more surprisingly— will only have to consider approximately 16 nodes when we use the "clever" sequential method. That is, we get the suggestive result that the speed-up we can expect by passing from a "clever" sequential method of evaluation to a parallel one in this case is only by a constant factor.

The same kind of analysis can be applied to Boolean expressions which contain *not* in addition to *and, or, true,* and *false.* We obtain analoguous results with 5 and 20 replacing 4 and 16.

Regarding the relative costs of sequential and parallel unification aspect, the well-known result of [2] shows that it is improbable that unification will lend itself to efficient parallelization. There it is proved that unification is complete for polynomial time even if input terms are represented as trees (as opposed to dags). This shows that there are cases in which unification is "difficult".

Practical experience, on the other hand, seems to suggest, that "on the average" unification is inexpensive. We have partial, theoretical results in support of this contention. Instead of considering terms composed of variables and functors taken from an arbitrary set of function symbols $f_0, f_1, f_2, \dots$ we assume that there are only three symbols—a constant 0, a functor s of arity 1, and a functor t of arity 2. We can establish a correspondence between f_i and

$$\underbrace{s(s(\dots s(0)\dots))}_{i \ times}$$

and represent $f_i(X_1, \dots, X_n)$, where $n > 0$ is the arity of f_i, as

$$t(s(s\dots s(0)\dots)), t(X_1, t(X_2, \dots, t(X_{n-1}, X_n)\dots)$$

This correspondence does not, however, preserve the size of a term. Also, only some of the terms in 0, s, t, and variables can be obtained in such a manner. (On the other hand, the more symbols there are, the more likely that unification will fail quickly.)

Define the size $|T|$ of a term T as the number of symbols appearing in it. We considered all different terms having the same size as having the same probability and obtained the following results:

Consider terms T_1 and T_2 in 0 and t such that $|T_1|+|T_2| = n$. Then the average cost (i.e. the number of nodes considered) for unifying T_1 and T_2 in the "naive" sequential method tends to 4 as $n \longrightarrow \infty$. If we consider terms in 0, t, and _ (a symbol denoting *different* variables) we get that the cost tends to 4 as $n \longrightarrow \infty$. If we look at terms T_1, T_2 composed of 0, t, and _ (where again _ denotes different variables) such that $|T_1| + |T_2| = n$ and compute the probability that unification between them will succeed, we find that the ratio of success tends to $\frac{1}{2\sqrt{2}} \approx 0.35$ as $n \to \infty$.

For terms that contain the functor s with arity 1 in addition to the above symbols we have analoguous results with

$$2 \quad \sim 2.15 \quad \sim 0.23$$

replacing the numbers

$$4 \quad 4 \quad \sim 0.35$$

which appear in the preceding paragraph.

In [3] it is proved that unification is complete for PTIME even if both terms are represented by trees and are linear (i.e. have at most one occurrence of each variable). In this case the difficulty arises from the fact that the two linear terms may have shared variables, and one has to perform the occur check before unifying a variable with a term containing variables.

We have the following partial result for terms in a constant 0, a binary functor t, and one variable X: Suppose all terms of the same size are equiprobable. The cost (average number of nodes considered) for an "occur check" (i.e. the cost of finding whether X is contained in a term T) for the "clever" sequential method tends to $2\sqrt{2} + 4 \approx 6.8$ as the size goes to ∞. In this "clever" method, if we want to find whether X occurs in $T = t(T_1, T_2)$, we first check T_1, and check T_2 only if we have not found an X in T_1.

Since the above results demonstrate that sequential execution is already very fast, there is no need for parallelization in these cases.

We also have a result that seems to indicate that doing away with the occur check may have a significant impact on the average running time. We saw that for terms in $0, t$ (or $0, t, s$) and different variables the average cost of "naive" sequential unification tends to a constant. We can use the following cost function to give an indication of the cost of the occur check in the "naive" sequential method:

$$cost(variable, term) \;=\; cost(term, variable) \;=\; length\ of\ term$$

$$cost(t(A, B), t(C, D)) \;=\; cost(A, C) \;+\; cost(B, D)$$

If the terms include s we also define

$$cost(s(A), s(B)) \;=\; cost(A, B)$$

In all other cases the cost is defined as 0. It turns out that in these cases the quotient C_n/N_n (where C_n is the sum of the costs for all pairs of terms T_1, T_2 for which $|T_1| + |T_2| = n$) behaves asymptotically like $k\,n$ for a suitable positive constant k, that is—adding the occur check in this setting makes unification much more expensive.

2   Evaluating Boolean expressions

We consider all Boolean expressions consisting of *and, or, true,* and *false.* The length of an expression is the number of the above symbols appearing in it (or, equivalently, the number of nodes in its binary-tree representation). This number is always odd.

Denote by N_n the number of expressions of length n. We begin by illustrating how its value may be derived by using generating functions. Consider the generating function

$$N(z) = \sum_{n=1}^{\infty} N_n\, z^n$$

We have

$$N(z) = \sum_{E} z^{|E|} =$$

$$= \sum_{E=true\ or\ E=false} z^{|E|} + \sum_{E=and(E_1,E_2)} z^{|E|} + \sum_{E=or(E_1,E_2)} z^{|E|} =$$

$$= 2z + 2z \sum_{E_1,E_2} z^{|E_1|}\, z^{|E_2|} = 2z + 2z N(z)^2$$

where summation over E means summation over all Boolean expressions.

So we get for N the equation

$$2zN^2 - N + 2z = 0$$

whose solution is

$$N = \frac{1 - \sqrt{1 - 16z^2}}{4z} \tag{1}$$

Since we are looking for a solution analytical at 0 we take the branch of the square root which is 1 at $z = 0$ ($N(0) = 0$). Hence

$$N_{2n} = 0 \qquad N_{2n+1} = \frac{1}{n+1} \binom{2n}{n} 2^{2n+1}$$

We define, recursively, the cost for "naive" evaluation of an expression by

$cost(true) = cost(false) = 1$
$cost(and(E_1, E_2)) = 1 + cost(E_1) + cost(E_2)$
$cost(or(E_1, E_2)) = 1 + cost(E_1) + cost(E_2)$

The cost for "clever" sequential evaluation of an expression is recursively defined by

$scost(true) = scost(false) = 1$

$$scost(and(E_1, E_2)) = \begin{cases} if\ val(E_1) = false : & 1 + scost(E_1) \\ if\ val(E_1) = true : & 1 + scost(E_1) + scost(E_2) \end{cases}$$

$$scost(or(E_1, E_2)) = \begin{cases} if\ val(E_1) = true : & 1 + scost(E_1) \\ if\ val(E_1) = false : & 1 + scost(E_1) + scost(E_2) \end{cases}$$

And, finally, the cost for parallel evaluation is recursively defined by

$pcost(true) = pcost(false) = 1$

$$pcost(and(E_1, E_2)) = \begin{cases} if\ val(E_1) = false\ and \\ pcost(E_1) < pcost(E_2) : & 1 + pcost(E_1) \\ if\ val(E_2) = false\ and \\ pcost(E_2) < pcost(E_1) : & 1 + pcost(E_2) \\ otherwise : & 1 + max(pcost(E_1), pcost(E_2)) \end{cases}$$

$$pcost(or(E_1, E_2)) = \begin{cases} if\ val(E_1) = true\ and \\ pcost(E_1) < pcost(E_2) : & 1 + pcost(E_1) \\ if\ val(E_2) = true\ and \\ pcost(E_2) < pcost(E_1) : & 1 + pcost(E_2) \\ otherwise : & 1 + max(pcost(E_1), pcost(E_2)) \end{cases}$$

Let C_n be the sum of the "naive" costs for evaluating all expressions of length n (it is easy to see that $C_n = n\, N_n$). Let S_n be the sum of the "clever" sequential costs for evaluating all expressions of length n. Let P_n be the sum of the parallel costs for evaluating all expressions of length n. We now consider the generating functions

$$C = \sum C_n\, z^n \qquad S = \sum S_n\, z^n \qquad P = \sum P_n\, z^n$$

The following computation enables us to express the relation between P and N in a simple form. The idea behind it is a kind of symmetry between *and* and *or*—the *and* requires a lot of work exactly in those cases in which the *or* requires a little and vice versa. We'll denote the truth value of an expression E by $val(E)$.

It is easy to check that in all cases

$$pcost(and(E_1, E_2)) + pcost(or(E_1, E_2)) = 2 + pcost(E_1) + pcost(E_2)$$

Hence

$$P = \sum P_n\, z^n = \sum_E pcost(E)\, z^{|E|} =$$

$$= 2z + z \sum_{E_1, E_2} pcost(and(E_1, E_2))\, z^{|E_1|+|E_2|} + z \sum_{E_1, E_2} pcost(or(E_1, E_2))\, z^{|E_1|+|E_2|} =$$

$$= 2z + z \sum_{E_1, E_2} (2 + pcost(E_1) + pcost(E_2))Z^{|E_1|+|E_2|} =$$

$$= 2z + 2zN^2 + 2zPN$$

Using the relationships $N = 2z + 2zN^2$ and $N(1 - 2zN) = 2z$, we get

$$P = \frac{N}{1 - 2zN} = \frac{N^2}{2z} =$$

$$\frac{1}{2z}\left(\frac{1 + 1 - 16z^2 - 2\sqrt{1 - 16z^2}}{16z^2}\right) = -\frac{1}{2z} + \frac{1}{4z^2} \cdot \frac{1 - \sqrt{1 - 16z^2}}{4z} \qquad (2)$$

and therefore

$$P_{2n} = 0$$

$$P_{2n-1} = \frac{1}{4}N_{2n+1} = \frac{1}{4} \cdot \frac{1}{n+1}\binom{2n}{n} 2^{2n+1}$$

Hence, the average parallel cost is

$$\frac{P_{2n+1}}{N_{2n+1}} = \frac{\frac{1}{4(n+2)}\binom{2(n+1)}{n+1} 2^{2n+3}}{\frac{1}{n+1}\binom{2n}{n} 2^{2n+1}} =$$

$$= \frac{(n+1)(2n+1)(2n+2)}{(n+2)(n+1)(n+1)} \longrightarrow 4 \quad \text{as } n \to \infty$$

This is a rather surprising result, because it says that when we rewrite a Boolean expression by the above method the average time asymptotically does not depend on the length of the expression.

For the generating function of the "clever" sequential cost S we get

$$S = \sum S_n z^n = \sum scost(E)\, z^{|E|} =$$

$$= 2z + \sum scost(and(E_1, E_2))\, z^{|E_1|+|E_2|+1} + \sum scost(or(E_1, E_2))\, z^{|E_1|+|E_2|+1} =$$

$$= 2z + \sum_{val(E_1)=false} (1 + scost(E_1))z^{|E_1|+|E_2|+1} +$$

$$+ \sum_{val(E_1)=true} (1 + scost(E_1) + scost(E_2))z^{|E_1|+|E_2|+1} +$$

$$+ \sum_{val(E_1)=true} (1 + scost(E_1))z^{|E_1|+|E_2|+1} +$$

$$+ \sum_{val(E_1)=false} (1 + scost(E_1) + scost(E_2))z^{|E_1|+|E_2|+1} =$$

$$2z + \sum (1 + scost(E_1))z^{|E_1|+|E_2|+1} + \sum (1 + scost(E_1) + scost(E_2))z^{|E_1|+|E_2|+1} =$$

$$= 2z + 2zN^2 + 3zNS = N + 3zNS$$

and therefore

$$S = \frac{N}{1 - 3zN} \tag{3}$$

We are interested in the behaviour of the average sequential cost

$$Q_n = \frac{S_{2n+1}}{N_{2n+1}}$$

The computation is more complicated in this case than in the parallel case, but it can be shown (by direct computation) that

$$Q_n = \frac{6 \cdot 18^n - 2 \sum_{k=0}^{n} N_{2k+1} \cdot 18^{n-k}}{N_{2n+1}}$$

and that it satisfies the recurrence relation

$$Q_{n+1} = \frac{18}{16} \cdot \frac{n+2}{n+\frac{1}{2}} Q_n - 2$$

(This, by the way, is a highly unstable relation for computation.) From this relation it can be proved that $Q_n \longrightarrow 16$ as $n \to \infty$. This shows that the "clever" sequential method is only worse by a factor of 4 than the parallel method for evaluating Boolean expressions.

In the case of parallel cost, it is not hard to compute the ratio $\frac{P_n}{N_n}$ from the relation between the generating functions P and N. For the sequential cost it is quite involved to get explicitly from the relation of the generating functions S and N a relation between the coefficients S_n and N_n. In other cases, direct computation is impossible. Fortunately, it turns out that the functional relation suffices for deriving information about the asymptotic behavior of the coefficients (cf. [1,5,4]).

We have here and in the next section the following setup. An enumerative generating function $N(z) = \sum N_n\, z^n$ is given which satisfies $N(z) = z \cdot \Phi(N(z))$, where $\Phi(X)$ is a polynomial. (Note that for an enumerative generating function all coefficients are non-negative reals.) Then the radius of convergence of N is $\rho = \frac{\tau}{\Phi(\tau)}$, where τ is the smallest positive real root of the equation $\Phi(X) = X\Phi'(X)$ and $\tau = N(\rho)$ (cf. [1]). In all the cases we consider $\Phi(X)$ will be a quadratic polynomial, so it will be easy to express N in terms of z directly and find ρ and τ directly.

We return now to the special case (1) of the Boolean expressions in *and, or, true*, and *false* considered above. In this case $\tau = 1$, $\rho = 1/4$. Introduce the following notation: for $\eta, r > 0$, $0 < \phi < \pi/2$, $\{z_1, ..., z_m\}$ points with $|z_k| = r$ for all k, define $\Delta(r, \eta, \phi, \{z_1, ..., z_m\})$ as

$$\{z \;:\; |z| \le r(1+\eta),\; |\arg(z - z_k) - \arg(z_k)| \ge \phi \text{ for } k = 1, ..., m\}$$

This domain is the indented disk in the following figure:

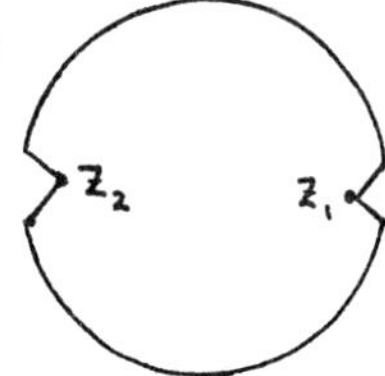

The function N is defined as a single valued function in $\Delta = \Delta(\rho, \eta, \phi, \{-\rho, \rho\})$ (for any η and ϕ) and is analytic in Δ except at $\pm\rho$. It has an expansion of the form

$$N(z) = \tau + c_1 \left(1 - \frac{z}{z_j}\right)^{1/2} + c_2 \left(1 - \frac{z}{z_j}\right) + O\left(\left|1 - \frac{z}{z_j}\right|^{3/2}\right) \tag{4}$$

for $j = 1, 2$, where we put $z_1 = \rho$ and $z_2 = -\rho$, valid for z in Δ near z_j. (For the validity of such a formula in more general settings, cf. [6].)

Suppose another generating function $F(z) = \sum F_n z^n$ is given and that by formal manipulation of the power series we get $F(z) = G(N(z))$ for a function $G(z)$ that is analytic in a neighborhood of

$$\Omega = N(\{z \ : \ |z| \le \rho\}) \quad \subseteq \{w \ : \ |w| \le \tau\} \tag{5}$$

Using Taylor's formula to expand $G(w)$ around $w = \tau$ we get

$$G(w) = G(\tau) + \frac{dG}{dw}\bigg|_{w=\tau}(w - \tau) + \frac{1}{2}\frac{d^2G}{dw^2}\bigg|_{w=\tau}(w - \tau)^2 + O(|w - \tau|^3)$$

Substituting $N(z)$ for w we get for z in the indented disk near ρ

$$G(N(z)) = G(\tau) + \frac{dG}{dw}\bigg|_{w=\tau}(N(z) - \tau) + \frac{1}{2}\frac{d^2G}{dw^2}\bigg|_{w=\tau}(N(z) - \tau)^2 + O(|N(z) - \tau|^3)$$

Using (4) for $\rho_1 = \rho$ we get (cf. [1])

$$F(z) = G(N(z)) =$$

$$= G(\tau) + \frac{dG}{dw}\bigg|_{w=\tau} \left(c_1 \left(1 - \frac{z}{\rho}\right)^{1/2} + c_2 \left(1 - \frac{z}{\rho}\right) + O\left(\left|1 - \frac{z}{\rho}\right|^{3/2}\right)\right) +$$

$$+ \frac{1}{2}\frac{d^2G}{dw^2}\bigg|_{w=\tau} \left(c_1^2 \left(1 - \frac{z}{\rho}\right) + O\left(\left|1 - \frac{z}{\rho}\right|^{3/2}\right)\right) + O\left(\left|1 - \frac{z}{\rho}\right|^{3/2}\right) =$$

$$= G(\tau) + \frac{dG}{dw}\bigg|_{w=\tau} c_1 \left(1 - \frac{z}{\rho}\right)^{1/2} + d \left(1 - \frac{z}{\rho}\right) + O\left(\left|1 - \frac{z}{\rho}\right|^{3/2}\right)$$

for suitable d.

Now we use an extension of Theorem 1 in [4]: Assume that, with the exception of a finite number of singularities $z_1, ..., z_m$ with $|z_j| = 1$ for $j = 1, ..., m$, $f(z)$ is analytic in $\Delta = \Delta(1, \eta, \phi, \{z_k\}_{k=1}^m)$, where $\eta > 0$ and $0 < \phi < \pi/2$, and that as z tends to z_j in Δ

$$f(z) = O(|z - z_j|^\alpha)$$

for some real α. Then the n-th Taylor coefficient of $f(z)$ satisfies

$$f_n = O(n^{-\alpha-1})$$

(The proof of the theorem and its extension uses Cauchy's formula for a suitable contour.)

Denote by γ_n the n-th coefficient of the development of $c_1(1 - z/\rho)^{1/2}$ into a power series around 0. Its absolute value behaves like $\rho^{-n}n^{-3/2}$ as $n \to \infty$. By the cited theorem

$$N_n = \gamma_n + O(n^{-5/2}\rho^{-n})$$

$$F_n = \frac{d\,G}{d\,w}\Big|_{w=\tau}\gamma_n + O(n^{-5/2}\rho^{-n})$$

so

$$\frac{F_n}{N_n} \longrightarrow \frac{d\,G}{d\,w}\Big|_{w=\tau} \qquad \text{as } n \to \infty$$

If we want to express the parallel cost function P appearing in (2) as a function of N we have to substitute $z = N/(2+2N^2)$ and get

$$P = N/(1-2zN) = N(1+N^2)$$

and thus we get

$$\frac{P_{2n+1}}{N_{2n+1}} \longrightarrow \frac{d}{d\,N}(N(1+N^2))\big|_{N=1} = (1+3N^2)\big|_{N=1} = 4$$

Similarly, for the "clever" sequential cost

$$S = \frac{N}{1-3zN} = \frac{N}{1 - \frac{3N^2}{2+2N^2}} = \frac{2N(1+N^2)}{2-N^2}$$

For $N < \sqrt{2}$, $S(N)$ is regular, so it is regular on a neighborhood of Ω (cf. (5)), so

$$\frac{S_{2n+1}}{N_{2n+1}} \longrightarrow \frac{d}{d\,N}\left(\frac{2N(1+N^2)}{2-N^2}\right)\Big|_{N=1} =$$

$$= \frac{(2-N^2)(2+6N^2) + 2N(1+N^2)2N}{(2-N^2)^2}\Big|_{N=1} = 16$$

In the case of Boolean expressions consisting of *not, and, or, true,* and *false* we get

$$N = z(2+N+2N^2) \ , \ \ \tau = 1 \ , \ \ \rho = \frac{1}{5}$$

$$P = \frac{N}{2}(2+N+2N^2)$$

$$S = N(2+N+2N^2)/(2-N^2)$$

In this case we cannot compute the coefficients explicitly, but the above method gives

$$\frac{P_n}{N_n} \longrightarrow \frac{d}{d\,N}\left(\frac{N}{2}(2+N+2N^2)\right)\Big|_{N=1} = (1+N+3N^2)\big|_{N=1} = 5$$

$$\frac{S_n}{N_n} \longrightarrow \frac{d}{d\,N}\left(\frac{N(2+N+2N^2)}{2-N^2}\right)\Big|_{N=1} = 20$$

Again the speed-up between the "clever" sequential case and the parallel case is 4.

3 Partial results about unification

In this section we present the proof of two of the results quoted in the introduction. Because of space limitations we cannot give the details of the other results we mentioned. The proofs are in principle similar to the arguments presented in the second half of the previous section. We note that in all of our examples in which F_n/N_n tends to a constant, the functions $G(w)$ which we use are rational functions or the quotient of two functions which are the sum of a polynomial and a square root of a polynomial. In order to check that $G(N(z))$ is analytic in a neighborhood of Ω (defined in (5)), we have to check that the polynomial in $N(z)$ which is under the square root does not vanish there and also that the denominator does not vanish there. In the case of rational functions it turns out that it is enough to check that the denominator of $G(w)$ does not vanish for $0 \leq w \leq \tau$, because N and F have non-negative coefficients, . The two cases in which the quotient F_n/N_n behaves asymptotically like $k\,n$ are proved similarly to the proof of case 2 of Theorem 3.3 in [1].

Case 1

Consider terms consisting of a constant 0, a unary functor s, a binary functor t, and a symbol $\_$ denoting *different* variables. Let N_n be the number of terms of length n. Then

$$N = \sum N_n\, z^n = \sum_T z^{|T|} = \sum_{T=0} z^{|T|} +$$

$$+ \sum_{T=\_} z^{|T|} + \sum_{T=s(T_1)} z^{|T|} + \sum_{T=t(T_1,T_2)} z^{|T|} =$$

$$= 2z + zN + zN^2 = z(2 + N + N^2)$$

$$\Phi(\tau) = 2 + \tau + \tau^2 = t\Phi'(\tau) = \tau(1 + 2\tau)$$

$$\tau = \sqrt{2} \quad , \quad \rho = \frac{\tau}{\Phi(\tau)} = \frac{1}{2\sqrt{2}+1}$$

Denote by $ucost(T_1, T_2)$ the cost for unifying two terms T_1 and T_2 by the "naive" sequential method, that is

- if at least one of the terms is a variable the unification succeeds with cost 1;
- if none of the terms is a variable and the main functors are different the unification fails with cost 1;
- if both terms are not variables and have the same functor the cost of the unification is 1 plus the costs for unifying the arguments.

Let U_n be the sum of the costs for unifying all the terms T_1 and T_2 such that $|T_1| + |T_2| = n$. Then

$$U = \sum U_n\, z^n = \sum_{T_1,T_2} ucost(T_1, T_2)\, z^{|T_1|+|T_2|} =$$

$$= \sum_{T_1=0} z^{|T_1|+|T_2|} + \sum_{T_2=0} z^{|T_1|+|T_2|} - \sum_{\substack{T_1=0 \\ T_2=0}} z^{|T_1|+|T_2|} +$$

$$+ \sum_{T_1=\_} z^{|T_1|+|T_2|} + \sum_{T_2=\_} z^{|T_1|+|T_2|} - \sum_{\substack{T_1=\_ \\ T_2=\_}} z^{|T_1|+|T_2|}$$

$$-2 \sum_{\substack{T_1=0 \\ T_2=\_}} z^{|T_1|+|T_2|} + 2 \sum_{\substack{T_1=t(S_1,S_2) \\ T_2=s(S_3)}} z^{|T_1|+|T_2|} +$$

$$+ \sum_{\substack{T_1=s(S_1) \\ T_2=s(S_2)}} (1 + ucost(S_1, S_2)) z^{|T_1|+|T_2|} +$$

$$+ \sum_{\substack{T_1=t(S_1,S_2) \\ T_2=t(S_3,S_4)}} (1 + ucost(S_1, S_3) + ucost(S_2, S_4)) z^{|T_1|+|T_2|} =$$

$$= 4zN - 4z^2 + 2z^2 N^3 + z^2 N^2 + z^2 U + z^2 N^4 + 2z^2 N^2 U$$

Therefore

$$U = \frac{4zN - 4z^2 + 2z^2 N^3 + z^2 N^2 + z^2 N^4}{1 - z^2 - 2z^2 N^2}$$

and substituting $z = \frac{N}{2+N+N^2}$ we obtain

$$U = \frac{4N^2 + 4N^3 + 5N^4 + 2N^5 + N^6}{4 + 4N + 4N^2 + 2N^3 - N^4}$$

Now we have to show that the denominator does not vanish for $0 \leq N \leq \tau = \sqrt{2}$, but this follows from the fact that its value for $N = 0$ is positive, and its derivative $4 + 8N + 6N^2 - 4N^3$ is positive for positive N if $6N^2 - 4N^3 > 0$, that is $N < 6/4 = 1.5$. We have

$$\left. \frac{dU}{dN} \right|_{N=\sqrt{2}} = \frac{13\sqrt{2} + 17}{(1 + \sqrt{2})^2} \approx 6.07$$

In order to get the average value of the cost we have to divide U_n by the number of pairs T_1, T_2 such that $|T_1| + |T_2| = n$ which is the coefficient of z^n in the series for $N(z)^2$, that is

$$\left. \frac{d}{dN} N^2 \right|_{N=\sqrt{2}} = 2\sqrt{2} \approx 2.83$$

So we get for the average cost ~ 2.15.

This means that the cost for unifying by the naive sequential method two terms T_1 and T_2 such that $|T_1| + |T_2| = n$ tends to ~ 2.15 as n tends to infinity.

Case 2

Now consider terms consisting of a constant 0, a binary operator t, and a variable X. The length of a term is the number of these symbols appearing in it. By N_n we denote the number of terms of length n. The enumerative generating function of these terms satisfies

$$N = \sum_{n=1}^{\infty} N_n z^n = \sum_T z^{|T|} =$$

$$= \sum_{T=X} z^{|T|} + \sum_{T=0} z^{|T|} + \sum_{T=t(T_1,T_2)} z^{|T|} = z(2 + N^2)$$

In this case $\Phi(X) = 2 + X^2$ and τ is the smallest positive solution of $\Phi(X) = X\Phi'(X)$, so $\tau = \sqrt{2}$ and $\rho = \frac{1}{2\sqrt{2}}$. The "clever" sequential cost of the occur check, that is the check if X appears in a term, is defined recursively by

$$cost(X) = cost(0) = 1$$

$$cost(t(T_1, T_2)) = \begin{cases} X \epsilon T_1 : & 1 + cost(T_1) \\ X \not\in T_1 : & 1 + cost(T_1) + cost(T_2) \end{cases}$$

Denote by C_n the sum of the costs for all terms of length n.

$$C = \sum C_n z^n = \sum_T cost(T) z^{|T|} =$$

$$= \sum_{T=0} cost(T) z^{|T|} + \sum_{T=X} cost(T) z^{|T|} + \sum_{T=t(T_1,T_2)} cost(T) z^{|T|} =$$

$$= 2z + \sum_{X \epsilon T_1} (1 + cost(T_1)) z^{1+|T_1|+|T_2|} + \sum_{X \not\in T_1} (1 + cost(T_1) + cost(T_2)) z^{1+|T_1|+|T_2|} =$$

$$= 2z + \sum z^{1+|T_1|+|T_2|} + \sum cost(T_1) z^{1+|T_1|+|T_2|} + \sum_{X \not\in T_1} cost(T_2) z^{1+|T_1|+|T_2|} =$$

$$= 2z + zN^2 + zCN + zC \sum_{X \not\in T_1} z^{|T_1|}$$

Denote $M = \sum_{X \not\in T} z^{|T|}$. This is the enumerative generating function for all terms in 0 and t and satisfies the relation

$$M = \sum_{X \not\in T} z^{|T|} = \sum_{T=0} z^{|T|} + \sum_{\substack{T=t(T_1,T_2) \\ X \not\in T_1, X \not\in T_2}} z^{|T|} = z + zM^2$$

We have

$$z = \frac{N}{2 + N^2} = \frac{M}{1 + M^2}$$

so

$$NM^2 - (2 + N^2)M + N = 0$$

$$M = \frac{2 + N^2 - \sqrt{4 + N^4}}{2N}$$

We take the branch of the square root which is 2 for $N = 0$ ($M(0) = 0$).

We have

$$C = N + zCN + zCM$$

$$C = \frac{N}{1 - zN - zM} = \frac{N}{1 - \frac{N}{2+N^2}(N + M)} = \frac{N(2 + N^2)}{2 - NM}$$

where M is considered a function of N. We have to show that as a function of N, C is analytic in Ω. In order to show this we'll show that for $|z| \leq \rho$ we have $4 + N^4 \neq 0$ and that the denominator does not vanish. But $N^4 + 4 = 0$ has the four solutions

$$N_1 = i + 1, \quad N_2 = i - 1, \quad N_3 = -i + 1, \quad N_4 = -i - 1$$

and the corresponding z values if in $|z| \leq \rho$ would be given by $z_j = N_j/\Phi(N_j)$ and be $z_1 = z_3 = 1/2$, $z_2 = z_4 = -1/2$, which are outside $|z| \leq \rho$.

Now suppose $2 = MN$. Then we get the contradiction

$$2 = (2 + N^2 - \sqrt{4 + N^4})/2 \quad \implies \quad N = 0$$

So

$$\frac{C_{2n+1}}{N_{2n+1}} \longrightarrow \frac{dC}{dN}\Big|_{N=\sqrt{2}} = 4 + 2\sqrt{2} \approx 6.8$$

(we differentiate M as function of N and get that its derivative at $N = \sqrt{2}$ is 0).

Acknowledgements

We are grateful to Stéphane Kaplan for pointing out how to pass from a relation between generating functions to a relation between the coefficients and to Yehoshua Sagiv and Catriel Beeri for helpful discussions.

References

[1] C. Choppy, S. Kaplan, M. Soria, *Algorithmic complexity of term rewriting systems*, Rewriting Techniques and Applications Proceedings 1987, Lecture Notes in Computer Science 256, 1987.

[2] C. Dwork, P. Kanellakis, J. Mitchell, *On the sequential nature of unification*, J. Logic Programming 1(1984), pp.35-50.

[3] C. Dwork, P. Kanellakis, L. Stockmeyer, *Parallel algorithms for term matching*, 8th International Conference on Automated Deduction Proceedings 1986, Lecture Notes in Computer Science 230, 1986.

[4] P. Flajolet, A. Odlysko, *Singularity analysis of generating functions*, INRIA Technical Report 826, 1988.

[5] P. Flajolet, J.S. Vitter, *Average-case analysis of algorithms and data structures*, INRIA Technical Report 718, 1987.

[6] A. Meir, J.W. Moon, *On the altitude of nodes in random trees*, Canadian Journal of Mathematics 30(1978), pp. 997-1015.

[7] U.S. Reddy, *On the relationship between logic and functional languages*, in *Logic Programming: Relations, Functions, and Equations*, D. DeGroot and G. Lindstrom, eds., 1985.

Polymorphic Higher-Order Programming in Prolog

Michael Hanus

Fachbereich Informatik, Universität Dortmund
D-4600 Dortmund 50, W. Germany
(uucp: michael@unidoi5)

Abstract

Pure logic programming lacks some features known from other modern programming languages, e.g., type systems for detection of particular programming errors at compile time and higher-order facilities for treating programs as data objects and writing more compact programs. On the one hand there are several proposals for polymorphic type systems for logic programming, and on the other hand Warren [35] has shown that higher-order programming can be simulated in first-order logic. But the integration of these proposals fails because Warren's first-order programs are ill-typed in the sense of the polymorphic type systems.

This paper presents a polymorphic type system for logic programming which allows the application of higher-order programming techniques. For Prolog-like applications of higher-order programming techniques it is possible to compute optimizations by abstract interpretation so that the polymorphic logic programs have the same operational efficiency as untyped Prolog programs.

1 Introduction

Pure logic programming is based on untyped first-order logic and does not permit detection of many programming errors at compile time. Therefore various attempts have been made to integrate types into logic programming. One research direction follows an *operational approach*: The main goal of the operational approaches is to ensure that predicates are only called with appropriate arguments at run time. This should be attained by a static analysis of the program. These approaches have only a syntactic notion of "type", i.e., types are sets of terms rather than subsets of carrier sets of interpretations (on which the declarative semantics of logic programs is based [22]). Type information is frequently inferred by a type inference algorithm (see, for instance, [25] [20] [38] [21] [15] [5] [37]). Mycroft and O'Keefe [27] have adapted the polymorphic type discipline of modern functional languages [8] to pure Prolog. In their proposal the programmer has to declare the types of functions and predicates and the types of variables in clauses are inferred by a type checker. Since they have put restrictions on the use of polymorphic types in function declarations and clauses, their programs "do not go wrong" in the sense of well-typedness. But these restrictions prevent the application of higher-order programming techniques in the sense of Warren [35] (see below). The type system was extended to subtypes on the basis of mode declarations by Dietrich and Hagl [10], but they have no semantic notion of a type, similarly to Mycroft and O'Keefe's work.

Another research direction, to which this papers belongs, follows a *declarative approach*: The programmer has to declare all types of functions and predicates that he wants to use in the program. These approaches have a formal semantics of a type, i.e., types represent subsets of carrier sets of interpretations. This influences the operational mechanism because correctness can only be ensured by a typed unification procedure. In many-sorted Horn logic [29] typed unification is the same as untyped unification, but in order-sorted logic [11] [33], polymorphically order-sorted logic [32], or in a logic with subtypes and inheritance [3] the unification procedure has to consider the types of terms.

Higher-order objects well-known from functional languages are another useful extension to pure logic programming. Aït-Kaci, Lincoln and Nasr [2] have proposed an untyped language with functions and relations which permits higher-order functions. Although they have presented an operational semantics for this language based on delayed evaluation of expressions, a declarative semantics is not defined. Generally, a semantically clean amalgamation of higher-order objects with logic programming techniques like unification is not trivial since the unification of higher-order terms is undecidable in general [12]. Miller and Nadathur [24] have defined an extension of first-order Horn clause logic to include predicate and function variables based on the typed lambda calculus. For the operational semantics it is necessary to unify typed lambda expressions which leads to a complex and semi-decidable unification [18]. The latter efficiency argument is our motivation to keep *first-order* Horn clause logic as our formal framework. But there is still another reason: Higher-order unification means solving equations between functions and guessing or computing new functions that satisfy the equations. This is a new feature not available in functional languages and, in our opinion, not necessary for programming. From a practical point of view it is sufficient to apply only user-defined functions to appropriate arguments at run time.

In order to integrate the higher-order facilities of functional languages into logic programming, Warren [35] has shown that first-order logic need not be extended because the usual higher-order programming techniques can be simulated in first-order logic by an axiomatization of an `apply` predicate. Since he is concerned with Prolog and its untyped logic, he does not have a clear distinction between first-order and higher-order objects. A type system may help to obtain this distinction. But the clauses for the `apply` predicate are not well-typed in the sense of the usual polymorphic type systems for logic programming [27] [10] [32] (see below).

Mycroft and O'Keefe [27] have also proposed an `apply` predicate for higher-order programming, but the precise meaning of the predicate is not defined. Prolog has also a predefined predicate `call` for the application of higher-order programming techniques [7], but the meaning of `call` cannot be described in first-order logic because the called predicate name must be instantiated to an atom at run time (a non-declarative restriction).

Hanus [14] has proposed a generalized polymorphic type system for logic programming based on a semantic notion of polymorphic types. Since the type system is rather general, it is necessary to consider the types of terms in the unification procedure. In this paper we show that Warren's first-order specification of the `apply` predicate is well-typed in the sense of [14]. Therefore this type system is a basis for the application of higher-order programming techniques in a typed framework. Moreover, we show that in most applications it is possible to compute optimizations by abstract interpretation so that the polymorphic logic programs can be executed with the same efficiency as untyped Prolog programs, i.e. the typed unification can be replaced by untyped unification without loss of soundness.

The next section gives an outline of the polymorphic type system of [14] and presents an example with higher-order predicates. In a further section we develop an optimization technique based on abstract interpretation to detect the cases where all type information can be omitted at run time.

2 Polymorphically typed logic programs

We are interested in an ML-like polymorphic type system for logic programming, i.e., types may contain type variables that are universally quantified over all types [8]. The programmer has to declare the types of all functions and predicates occurring in the program. The types of variables in clauses can be inferred by an ML-like type checker. Therefore the clauses of a program need not be annotated with type information by the programmer, but the type annotations are computed by the type checker. Moreover, the type checker can detect a lot of programming errors at compile time.

The typing rules are quite simple. First the programmer has to declare the *basic types* like *int* or *bool* and *type constructors* like *list* which he wants to use in the program. Each type constructor has a fixed *arity* (e.g., *list* has arity 1, denoted by *list*/1). We assume a given infinite set of *type variables* and we denote members of this set by α and β. A (*polymorphic*) *type* is a term built from basic types, type constructors and type variables (see [17] for the notion of term). A *monomorphic type* is a type without type variables. For instance, *list*(int) and *list*(α) are monomorphic and polymorphic types which denote lists of integers and lists of elements of an arbitrary type, respectively. A type τ_1 is an *instance* of another type τ_2 if τ_1 can be obtained from τ_2 by replacing type variables in τ_2 by other types. Two types τ_1 and τ_2 are *equivalent* if

τ_1 is an instance of τ_2 and τ_2 is an instance of τ_1, i.e., they are equal up to renaming of type variables.

Next the user has to declare the argument and result types of functions and predicates occurring in the program. A function declaration has the form

$$\textbf{func f}: \quad \tau_1, \ldots, \tau_n \to \tau$$

(where $\tau_1, \ldots, \tau_n, \tau$ are arbitrary types) and means that function $\textbf{f}$ takes n arguments of types $\tau_1, \ldots, \tau_n$ and produces a value of type τ. $\textbf{f}$ is called *constant* of type τ if $n = 0$. A predicate declaration has the form

$$\textbf{pred p}: \quad \tau_1, \ldots, \tau_n$$

(where $\tau_1, \ldots, \tau_n$ are arbitrary types) and means that predicate $\textbf{p}$ has n arguments of types $\tau_1, \ldots, \tau_n$. In order to compute the most general type of a term and to apply some optimization techniques (see below), we forbid overloading: For each function and predicate symbol there is only one type declaration. Note that there are no restrictions on the use of type variables in function declarations in contrast to [27].[1]

The type variables in a declaration are universally quantified over all types, i.e., functions and predicates can be used with an arbitrary substitution of types for type variables in the declaration. Hence we call a function or predicate declaration a *generic instance* of another declaration if it can be obtained from the other declaration by replacing each occurrence of one or more type variables by other types (cf. [8]). For instance, if there is the declaration

$$\textbf{pred append}: \quad list(\alpha), \; list(\alpha), \; list(\alpha)$$

for the predicate $\textbf{append}$, then

$$\textbf{pred append}: \quad list(int), \; list(int), \; list(int)$$

is a generic instance of the declaration.

According to [6], types are embedded in terms, i.e., each symbol in a term is annotated with an appropriate type expression. These annotations are useful for the unification of polymorphic terms (see below). The type annotations need not be provided by the user because most general type annotations can be computed. We assume a given infinite set Var of variable names distinguishable from type variables. A *typed variable* has the form $x{:}\tau$ where $x \in Var$ and τ is an arbitrary type. We call V an *allowed set of typed variables* if V contains only typed variables and $x{:}\tau, x{:}\tau' \in V$ implies $\tau = \tau'$. We call $L \leftarrow G$ a *polymorphic program clause* if there is an allowed set of typed variables V and $V \vdash L \leftarrow G$ is derivable by the inference rules in table 1. Note that there are no restrictions on the use of types and type variables in clauses in contrast to [27], [32] and similar type systems.[2] A

---

[1] In their type system each type variable occurring in the argument type of a function must also occur in the result type [26].

[2] In these type systems the left-hand side of a clause must have a type that is equivalent to the declared type of the predicate.

$$\text{Variable:} \qquad \overline{V \vdash x{:}\tau} \qquad\qquad (x{:}\tau \in V)$$

$$\text{Term:} \qquad \frac{V \vdash t_1{:}\tau_1,\ldots,V \vdash t_n{:}\tau_n}{V \vdash f(t_1{:}\tau_1,\ldots,t_n{:}\tau_n){:}\tau} \qquad \begin{array}{l} (f{:}\tau_1,\ldots,\tau_n \to \tau \text{ is a generic inst.}\\ \text{of a function declaration, } n \geq 0) \end{array}$$

$$\text{Literal:} \qquad \frac{V \vdash t_1{:}\tau_1,\ldots,V \vdash t_n{:}\tau_n}{V \vdash p(t_1{:}\tau_1,\ldots,t_n{:}\tau_n)} \qquad \begin{array}{l} (p{:}\tau_1,\ldots,\tau_n \text{ is a generic instance}\\ \text{of a predicate declaration, } n \geq 0) \end{array}$$

$$\text{Clause:} \qquad \frac{V \vdash L_0,\ldots,V \vdash L_n}{V \vdash L_0 \leftarrow L_1,\ldots,L_n} \qquad \begin{array}{l} (\text{each } L_i \text{ has the form } p(\cdots),\\ i = 0,\ldots,n) \end{array}$$

Table 1: Typing rules for polymorphic program clauses

polymorphic logic program is a finite set of polymorphic program clauses.

We give an example of a polymorphic logic program that defines the higher-order predicate map. The constant [] represents the empty list, and the function • concatenates an element with a list of the same type. We write [E|L] instead of •(E,L) (throughout this paper we use the Prolog notation for lists, cf. [7]). The literal map(P,L1,L2) should be satisfied if predicate P is satisfied for each pair of corresponding elements from lists L1 and L2. In order to define the type of map we introduce a type constructor *pred2* of arity 2 that denotes the type of binary predicates. The type of map is

    pred map: $pred2(\alpha,\beta),\ list(\alpha),\ list(\beta)$

For each binary predicate p of type "τ_1,τ_2" we introduce a corresponding constant λp of type "$pred2(\tau_1,\tau_2)$". The relation between each predicate p and the constant λp is defined by clauses for the predicate apply2. Hence we get the following example program for the predicate map (we omit type annotations in program clauses because they can be automatically inferred by an ML-like type checker [8]):

    type $bool,\ nat,\ list/1,\ pred2/2$
    func true : $\to bool$
    func false: $\to bool$
    func 0   : $\to nat$
    func s   : $nat \to nat$
    func []   : $\to list(\alpha)$
    func •   : $\alpha, list(\alpha) \to list(\alpha)$
    func λnot: $\to pred2(bool,bool)$
    func λinc: $\to pred2(nat,nat)$
    pred not: $bool,\ bool$
    pred inc: $nat,\ nat$
    pred map: $pred2(\alpha,\beta),\ list(\alpha),\ list(\beta)$

```
pred apply2:   pred2(α,β),  α,  β

clauses:
map(P,[],[]) ←
map(P,[E1|L1],[E2|L2]) ← apply2(P,E1,E2), map(P,L1,L2)
not(true,false) ←
not(false,true) ←
inc(N,s(N)) ←
apply2(λnot,B1,B2) ← not(B1,B2)
apply2(λinc,I1,I2) ← inc(I1,I2)
```

We can use this definition of map to compute a new list from a given one or to
search for predicates which relate two lists (see next section for operational
semantics):

```
?- map(λnot,[true,false,false],L)
L = [false,true,true]
?- map(P,[0],[s(0)])
P = λinc
```

Note that the last two clauses for the predicate apply2 are not well-typed
in the sense of [27] and similar type systems since apply2 has the declared
type "$pred2(α,β),α,β$" but is used in the clause heads with the specialized
types "$pred2(bool,bool),bool,bool$" and "$pred2(nat,nat),nat,nat$", respectively. Therefore such first-order axiomatizations of higher-order predicates
cannot be well-typed with the usual polymorphic type systems in a reasonable way.

We remark that it is also possible to permit lambda expressions which
can be translated into new identifiers and apply clauses for these identifiers
(see [35] for more discussion). If the lambda expressions have polymorphic
arguments that do not occur in the result (e.g., the length function on lists
length: $list(α) \rightarrow nat$), then typing of such expressions is no problem
because type variables in argument types that do not occur in the result
type are permitted in our type system in contrast to [27]. If the underlying
system implements indexing on the first arguments of predicates (as done in
most compilers for Prolog, cf. [36] and [13]), then there is no essential loss of
efficiency in our translation scheme for higher-order objects in comparison to
a specific implementation of higher-order objects [35].

Since our foundation is first-order logic, the predicate symbol map is semantically not interpreted as a higher-order predicate. The constants λnot
and λinc are also interpreted as values and not as predicates. But the first
apply2 clause ensures that in each model of the above program the constant
λnot and the predicate not are related together. From an operational point
of view the behaviour of our map program is similar to the behaviour of a
corresponding program in a higher-order language. To be more precise we
give a short outline of the semantics in the next section.

3 Declarative and operational semantics

First we give a short outline of the declarative semantics. The type variables in a clause vary over all possible types, i.e., a clause containing a type variable α is true for each type which is substituted for α. The carrier of an *interpretation* is a family of sets with one set for each (monomorphic) type. Function symbols are interpreted as functions on appropriate carrier sets, and predicates are interpreted as relations between appropriate carrier sets. This leads to a similar notion of *validity* and equivalent results as in many-sorted Horn clause logic [29]. Especially, an initial model can be constructed as the intersection of all Herbrand models where the carrier sets contain all ground terms with monomorphic types. We call a *goal* (goals have the same form as the right-hand side of a polymorphic program clause) *valid with respect to a program P* if it is valid in each interpretation which satisfies all clauses from P.

In [14] it is shown that resolution is a sound and complete proof procedure for polymorphic logic programs with goals that may contain type variables if the unification is extended to polymorphic terms. The unification of polymorphic terms can be reduced to common first-order unification [30] if the annotated types are treated as first-order terms. Type terms are distinguished from other terms by their position (type terms occur only after a colon ':'). For instance, a unifier of the polymorphic terms $[\,]{:}list(\alpha)$ and $\mathtt{v}{:}list(int)$ is the substitution that replaces α by int and $\mathtt{v}$ by $[\,]$. This could also be computed by a first-order unification algorithm if the symbol ':' is treated as a term constructor of arity 2. Therefore it is possible to translate polymorphic logic programs into Prolog programs (more details can be found in [14]).

Since we have an unrestricted type system, the unification procedure has to consider the types of polymorphic terms. Otherwise the resolution is not sound and produces ill-typed goals. For instance, assume that the above `map` program is given. We may ask for a predicate that relates two lists of naturals and apply this predicate to the constant 0:

```
?- map(P,[N1],[N2]), apply2(P,0,N3)
```

(P has type $pred2(nat, nat)$ and N1, N2 and N3 have type nat). If we omit all types at run time and solve the goal by the computation rule of Prolog, P, N1 and N2 are bound to λnot, `true` and `false`, respectively, and we obtain the ill-typed goal

```
?- apply2(λnot,0,N3)
```

Resolution with typed terms and typed unifiers is correct, since

```
apply2(P:pred2(nat, nat),N1:nat,N2:nat)
```

and

```
apply2(λnot:pred2(bool, bool),B1:bool,B2:bool)
```

are not unifiable. But

$$\texttt{apply2(P:}\mathit{pred2(nat,nat)}\texttt{,N1:}\mathit{nat}\texttt{,N2:}\mathit{nat}\texttt{)}$$

and

$$\texttt{apply2(}\lambda\texttt{inc:}\mathit{pred2(nat,nat)}\texttt{,I1:}\mathit{nat}\texttt{,I2:}\mathit{nat}\texttt{)}$$

are unifiable and therefore we obtain the well-typed goal

$$\texttt{?- apply2(}\lambda\texttt{inc:}\mathit{pred2(nat,nat)}\texttt{,O:}\mathit{nat}\texttt{,N3:}\mathit{nat}\texttt{)}$$

in the resolution process. This example demonstrates that types are necessary for soundness of resolution in general. But there are some cases where types are unnecessary in the resolution process. This should be shown in the next section.

4 Optimization

The unification procedure has to consider the types of polymorphic terms because of our unrestricted type system. Hence the polymorphic unification is more complex and less efficient than the unification in untyped logic languages. But Mycroft and O'Keefe [27] have shown that types can be completely omitted at run time if the program has particular restrictions. In section 2 we have seen that these restrictions prevent the application of higher-order programming techniques. Nevertheless, there are cases where all type information can be omitted at run time in the presence of clauses for an **apply** predicate. This section presents some sufficient criteria to omit type information in the resolution process. It is shown that in Prolog-like applications of higher-order predicates no type information is needed at run time.

4.1 General optimization techniques

First we review two optimizations mentioned in [14]. One optimization can be applied to most functions: A function symbol f is called *type preserving* if all type variables occurring in the argument type also occur in the result type. For instance, all function symbols in the above **map** program are type preserving, whereas the function

$$\textbf{func first:} \quad \mathit{pair}(\alpha,\beta) \to \alpha$$

is not type preserving. Since all type information of a type preserving function can be computed from the type declaration and the actual instantiation of the result type, the type annotations of arguments can be omitted at unification time. Hence only the direct result types of the arguments of predicates are needed in the above **map** program. For instance, we need instead of the completely typed goal

$$\texttt{map(P:}\mathit{pred2}(\alpha,\beta)\texttt{,[E1:}\alpha\texttt{|L1:}\mathit{list}(\alpha)\texttt{]:}\mathit{list}(\alpha)\texttt{,[E2:}\beta\texttt{|L2:}\mathit{list}(\beta)\texttt{]:}\mathit{list}(\beta)\texttt{)}$$

only the goal

$$\texttt{map(P:}\mathit{pred2}(\alpha,\beta)\texttt{,[E1|L1]:}\mathit{list}(\alpha)\texttt{,[E2|L2]:}\mathit{list}(\beta)\texttt{)}$$

for correctly typed unification.

All types can be omitted in the resolution proof of a predicate if the predicate is type-generally defined: Intuitively, a predicate is called *type-generally defined* if in each clause for the predicate all predicates in the body are also type-generally defined and the clause head has a most general type according to the type declaration of the predicate. Usually, a literal with predicate symbol p has a *most general type* if the types of the arguments are equivalent to the declared type of p. For instance, the clause head

$$\texttt{map}(\texttt{P}{:}pred2(\alpha,\beta),\texttt{[E1|L1]}{:}list(\alpha),\texttt{[E2|L2]}{:}list(\beta))$$

has a most general type, but not

$$\texttt{apply2}(\lambda\texttt{not}{:}pred2(bool,bool),\texttt{A1}{:}bool,\texttt{A2}{:}bool)$$

because the declared type of $\texttt{apply2}$ is "$pred2(\alpha,\beta),\alpha,\beta$".

In a well-typed program in the sense of Mycroft and O'Keefe each function must be type preserving and each predicate must be type-generally defined. This is the reason why these programs can be executed without dynamic type checking. As shown above, the first-order specification of an $\texttt{apply}$ predicate is not a type-general definition and therefore only the first optimization technique for type preserving functions is applicable to programs with higher-order predicates. In order to omit all types in this case, better optimization techniques are required.
In which cases does the untyped unification lead to ill-typed goals? Two conditions must be satisfied:

1. There is a predicate p and a clause for p where the head of the clause does not have a most general type w.r.t. the type declaration of p (otherwise all predicates are type-generally defined and all types can be omitted, see above).

2. At run time there is a call to this predicate and after the call some variables are bound to terms with specialized types (for instance, if the $\texttt{map}$ program of section 2 is given, a call of $\texttt{apply2(P,A1,A2)}$ bind variable P to $\lambda\texttt{not}$ which has type $pred2(bool,bool)$).

If type annotations should be omitted at run time, it must be ensured that these conditions cannot be satisfied. Therefore we need some knowledge about the run-time behaviour of the program. Since detailed run-time properties of Prolog programs are generally undecidable, we give sufficient criteria for the absence of the second condition.

We call a predicate p *type-specialized* if there is a program clause of the form

$$p(t_1{:}\tau_1,\ldots,t_n{:}\tau_n) \leftarrow L_1,\ldots,L_m$$

where $\tau_1,\ldots,\tau_n$ is not equivalent to the declared type of p. The *critical points of a program* are the calls of type-specialized predicates. We need a sufficient criterion to ensure that

- the unifiability of literals with clause heads does not depend on argument types, and

- no variable arguments in literals are bound to terms with specialized types while unifying the literal with a clause head.

In this case the argument types can be omitted at run time. A sufficient criterion for this property is *groundness of arguments*: If there is an argument of the predicate call which is a ground term and the corresponding argument in the clause head has a most general type, then the unification does not depend on the argument types and no variable argument is instantiated to a term with a specialized type. In the following we give a precise definition of this criterion.

Let p be a type-specialized predicate with declared type $\nu_1,\ldots,\nu_n$, $p(r_1{:}\rho_1,\ldots,r_n{:}\rho_n)$ be a literal that calls p and

$$p(t_1{:}\tau_1,\ldots,t_n{:}\tau_n) \leftarrow L_1,\ldots,L_m$$

be a clause for p. The type annotations $\rho_1,\ldots,\rho_n$ and $\tau_1,\ldots,\tau_n$ are not required for correct unification if the following conditions are satisfied:

1. There is an argument position i $(1 \leq i \leq n)$ such that ν_i contains all type variables occurring in the declared type $\nu_1,\ldots,\nu_n$.

2. $r_i{:}\rho_i$ is a ground term.

3. The term $t_i{:}\tau_i$ has a most general type w.r.t. ν_i, i.e., there is no term $t_i'{:}\tau_i'$ which is equal to $t_i{:}\tau_i$ up to type annotations so that τ_i' is an instance of ν_i, τ_i is an instance of τ_i', and τ_i is not equivalent to τ_i'.

By the first condition, the actual instantiation of type $\nu_1,\ldots,\nu_n$ is determined by the type of the i-th argument. This condition could be extended to more than one argument position that contain all type variables and are ground, but this would complicate the definition. The condition with one argument position is sufficient for our purpose of higher-order programming. The third condition ensures that each other well-typing of the i-th argument term of the clause head gives a type which is an instance of τ_i (the notion "*equal up to type annotations*" means that the terms become equal if all type annotations are deleted).

We show that the types of predicate arguments can be omitted if the above conditions are satisfied. If $p(r_1,\ldots,r_n)$ and $p(t_1,\ldots,t_n)$ are not unifiable, then $p(r_1{:}\rho_1,\ldots,r_n{:}\rho_n)$ and $p(t_1{:}\tau_1,\ldots,t_n{:}\tau_n)$ are not unifiable, too. Let $p(r_1,\ldots,r_n)$ and $p(t_1,\ldots,t_n)$ be unifiable. Then r_i is also unifiable with t_i. Since $t_i{:}\tau_i$ has a most general type (condition 3), ρ_i is an instance of type τ_i. Thus a most general unifier σ of $r_i{:}\rho_i$ and $t_i{:}\tau_i$ exists and does not instantiate any type variable in ρ_i (w.l.o.g. all type variables in $t_i{:}\tau_i$ are disjoint from type variables in $r_i{:}\rho_i$). $\sigma(\tau_1,\ldots,\tau_n) = \rho_1,\ldots,\rho_n$ because $\sigma(\tau_i) = \sigma(\rho_i) = \rho_i$ and the declared argument type ν_i contains all type variables of the declared type (condition 1). Therefore $p(r_1{:}\rho_1,\ldots,r_n{:}\rho_n)$ and $p(t_1{:}\tau_1,\ldots,t_n{:}\tau_n)$ are unifiable, too, and a most general unifier does not instantiate any variable argument in $p(r_1{:}\rho_1,\ldots,r_n{:}\rho_n)$ to a term with a specialized type. Hence the absence of argument types does not influence unifiability and the types of arguments can be omitted at run time.

Condition 3 is necessary for this optimization. For instance, a predicate p is declared by

> **pred** p: $list(\alpha)$, α

and the only call of predicate p is of the form $\texttt{p(}\square{:}list(bool)\texttt{,B:}bool\texttt{)}$. If the only clause for p is

> $\texttt{p(}\square{:}list(nat)\texttt{,O:}nat\texttt{)}\ \leftarrow$

then the clause is not applicable to literal $\texttt{p(}\square{:}list(bool)\texttt{,B:}bool\texttt{)}$. If we omit the argument types, then the clause would be applicable and the Boolean variable B would be instantiated to term 0 of type "nat". If the only clause for P has the form

> $\texttt{p(}\square{:}list(\alpha)\texttt{,X:}\alpha\texttt{)}\ \leftarrow$

then the argument types can be omitted because type variable α is instantiated to "$bool$". The argument types can also be omitted if there is a clause of the form

> $\texttt{p([O]:}list(nat)\texttt{,X:}nat\texttt{)}\ \leftarrow$

(we omit the type annotation of 0 because function '$\bullet$' is type preserving) since the term $\texttt{[O]:}list(nat)$ has a most general type.

The above three conditions can be checked at compile time if information about the groundness of variables at run time is available. Condition 3 can be checked by the use of a type checker that computes the most general type of a term. Groundness condition 2 can be verified if we know the modes of type-specialized predicates [23] [9] [34]: If the i-th argument of predicate p is in input mode, then $r_i{:}\rho_i$ is always ground at run time. Since we only need groundness information about some arguments and not the modes of all predicates, we prefer to use abstract interpretation techniques [1] to compute groundness information at compile time. Abstract interpretation have been applied to derive groundness information by Jones, Søndergaard [19] and Nilsson [28]. The results of abstract interpretation are sufficient for our purposes.

4.2 Application to logic programs with higher-order predicates

We have implemented the optimization techniques developed above and we have applied it to a number of logic programs with first-order axiomatizations of higher-order predicates. In the following we outline the implementation and the results.

To compute groundness information of variables we have implemented

Nilsson's abstract interpretation technique [28]. The computation of information is based on distinguished *program points*. The point before a literal L in the body of a clause or in a goal is called *calling point of L* and the point after L is called *success point of L*. Abstract interpretation of a logic program is started by supplying a goal pattern that describes possible initial goals and groundness information of these goals. Then the program is translated into a graph structure and groundness information is computed for each program point. For each critical program point (calling point of a type-specialized predicate) the above three criteria are checked. If these criteria are satisfied for each critical program point, then all type annotations of predicate arguments can be omitted.

For instance, assume that the above polymorphic logic program for the predicate `map` is given. The initial goal information is

```
map(P,L1,L2)   with ground P
```

which means that the `map` program is only started with a goal of the form `map(P,L1,L2)` where the first argument is a ground term. Now groundness information is computed for all program points. Since `apply2` is the only type-specialized predicate, the only critical program point is the calling point of literal `apply2(P,E1,E2)` in the second clause for the `map` predicate. The following groundness information is computed for this polymorphic clause (the list of ground variables is shown for each calling and success point of each literal in the clause body):

```
map(P:pred2(α,β),[E1|L1]:list(α),[E2|L2]:list(β))  ←
*** Ground variables:  [P]
     apply2(P:pred2(α,β),E1:α,E2:β),
*** Ground variables:  [P,α,β]
     map(P:pred2(α,β),L1:list(α),L2:list(β))
*** Ground variables:  [P,α,β]
```

(the type annotations of arguments of type preserving functions are omitted). We see that after a successful call of the `apply2`-literal the type variables α and β are also bound to monomorphic types since there are only `apply2`-clauses for monomorphically typed predicates. Next the three conditions are checked for the `apply2`-literal:

1. The declared type of `apply2` is "$pred2(\alpha,\beta),\alpha,\beta$" and therefore the type of the first argument contains all type variables occurring in the declared type.

2. The first argument of the `apply2`-literal is a ground term.

3. The first arguments of the heads of the `apply2`-clauses are $\lambda\text{not}{:}pred2(bool,bool)$ and $\lambda\text{inc}{:}pred2(nat,nat)$, respectively. Since these constants are declared with monomorphic types, these terms have most general types.

Hence all type annotations can be omitted at run time of this program since all functions are type preserving.

The actual implementation automatically checks all conditions. For condition 3 all types in term t_i:τ_i are deleted, the type checker is called for the term without type annotations to obtain a term t_i':τ_i' with most general type annotations, and it is checked whether τ_i and τ_i' are equivalent. Since the implementation language is Prolog, equivalence of type expressions can be decided by the use of the common meta-logical predicate *numbervars*.

It is easy to see that conditions 1 and 3 are satisfied by all clauses for an `apply` predicate in our implementation scheme for higher-order predicates: If an higher-order predicate which takes an n-ary predicate as argument should be defined, we have to declare a type constructor *predn* with arity n, a corresponding predicate

$$\textbf{pred apply}n: \quad predn(\alpha_1,\ldots,\alpha_n), \ \alpha_1, \ \ldots, \ \alpha_n$$

and for each n-ary predicate

$$\textbf{pred p}: \quad \tau_1, \ \ldots, \ \tau_n$$

a constant

$$\textbf{func } \lambda\text{p}: \quad \rightarrow predn(\tau_1,\ldots,\tau_n)$$

For each of these constants there is a clause

$$\texttt{apply}n(\lambda\text{p}{:}predn(\tau_1,\ldots,\tau_n),\text{A}_1{:}\tau_1,\ldots,\text{A}_n{:}\tau_n) \ \leftarrow \ \text{p}(\text{A}_1{:}\tau_1,\ldots,\text{A}_n{:}\tau_n)$$

The type of the first argument of `apply`n contains all type variables occurring in the declared type of p (condition 1). Since $predn(\tau_1,\ldots,\tau_n)$ is the declared type of constant λp, the term $\lambda\text{p}{:}predn(\tau_1,\ldots,\tau_n)$ has a most general type (condition 3). Condition 2 is dependent on the actual program, but the abstract interpreter gives precise information in most cases.

We have applied these optimization techniques to several polymorphic logic programs with higher-order predicates and obtained the following results:

- If higher-order predicates are used in a Prolog-like way, i.e., the `apply` predicate is only used with a non-variable first argument at run time (this is the only possibility in Prolog, otherwise a run-time error occurs), then this is recognized by the optimizer and no types are needed at run time. This means that in Prolog-like applications of higher-order predicates we have no overhead because of types.

- The cases where types are needed at run time are rare in practical programs. It occurs when somebody wants to *compute predicates* that could be applied to certain terms. This feature is not available in Prolog and it shows that our notion of higher-order programming has a declarative meaning and is type secure in contrast to Prolog. In these cases types are not superfluous but may reduce the search space (this is also an argument to include types in the computation process of order-sorted logic [16]).

5 Conclusions

We have presented a polymorphic type system for logic programming that allows the application of higher-order programming techniques. In most cases, polymorphic logic programs with higher-order predicates can be executed with the same efficiency as untyped logic programs if an optimization technique based on the computation of groundness information by abstract interpretation is used. The polymorphic logic language has a well-defined semantics based on first-order logic. Higher-order objects are specified by a name and distinguished clauses that defines the application of these objects to other ones. The necessary definitions can be automatically generated. This technique was proposed by Warren for untyped Horn clause logic.

Logic programming with higher-order functions was also proposed by Smolka [31]. In his language Fresh higher-order functional programming is combined with unification. To avoid the difficulties with higher-order unification, a name is associated with each function and equality between functions is defined as identity of associated names. This is similar to our approach except that Fresh is an untyped language.

The compilation of higher-order functions into first-order logic was also proposed by Bosco and Giovannetti [4], but in their language IDEAL type-checking is only performed for the source program and not for the target program. Clearly, the target program is not well-typed in the sense of [27] because of the clauses for the `apply` predicate.

Since higher-order logic programs can be translated into polymorphic logic programs, the use of higher-order objects is type secure in our framework. The typing rules are similar to functional languages and the type system ensures that a predicate is only called with appropriate arguments at run time. Hence our polymorphic logic language is a sound and clearly defined framework for higher-order programming in comparison with other ad-hoc approaches (`call` predicate in Prolog, `apply` predicate in [27]). Since we have restricted the domain of predicate variables to user-defined predicates, our theoretical foundation is first-order logic and not higher-order logic. The advantage of this restriction is an efficient operational semantics, and the occurrence of type variables in goals raises no problems (in contrast to [24]).

Further work remains to be done. From a practical point of view a type inference algorithm should automatically derive type declarations for predicates from the given program [37]. But the distinction between type errors and well-typings is not trivial because of our general type system.

References

[1] S. Abramsky and C. Hankin, editors. *Abstract Interpretation of Declarative Languages*. Ellis Horwood, 1987.

[2] H. Aït-Kaci, P. Lincoln, and R. Nasr. Le Fun: Logic, equations, and Functions. In *Proc. 4th IEEE Internat. Symposium on Logic Programming*, pp. 17–23, San Francisco, 1987.

[3] H. Aït-Kaci and R. Nasr. LOGIN: A Logic Programming Language with Built-In Inheritance. *Journal of Logic Programming (3)*, pp. 185–215, 1986.

[4] W. Bosco and E. Giovannetti. IDEAL: An Ideal Deductive Applicative Language. In *Proc. IEEE Internat. Symposium on Logic Programming*, pp. 89–94, Salt Lake City, 1986.

[5] M. Bruynooghe and G. Janssens. An Instance of Abstract Interpretation Integrating Type and Mode Inferencing. In *Proc. 5th Conference on Logic Programming & 5th Symposium on Logic Programming (Seattle)*, pp. 669–683, 1988.

[6] A. Church. A formulation of the simple theory of types. *Journal of Symbolic Logic*, Vol. 5, pp. 56–68, 1940.

[7] W.F. Clocksin and C.S. Mellish. *Programming in Prolog*. Springer, third rev. and ext. edition, 1987.

[8] L. Damas and R. Milner. Principal type-schemes for functional programs. In *Proc. 9th Annual Symposium on Principles of Programming Languages*, pp. 207–212, 1982.

[9] S.K. Debray and D.S. Warren. Automatic Mode Inference for Logic Programs. *Journal of Logic Programming (5)*, pp. 207–229, 1988.

[10] R. Dietrich and F. Hagl. A polymorphic type system with subtypes for Prolog. In *Proc. ESOP 88, Nancy*, pp. 79–93. Springer LNCS 300, 1988.

[11] J.A. Goguen and J. Meseguer. Eqlog: Equality, Types, and Generic Modules for Logic Programming. In D. DeGroot and G. Lindstrom, editors, *Logic Programming, Functions, Relations, and Equations*, pp. 295–363. Prentice Hall, 1986.

[12] W. Goldfarb. The Undecidability of the Second-Order Unification Problem. *Theoretical Computer Science 13*, pp. 225–230, 1981.

[13] M. Hanus. Formal Specification of a Prolog Compiler. In *Proc. of the Workshop on Programming Language Implementation and Logic Programming*, Orléans, 1988. Springer LNCS 348.

[14] M. Hanus. Horn Clause Programs with Polymorphic Types: Semantics and Resolution. In *Proc. of the TAPSOFT '89*, pp. 225–240. Springer LNCS 352, 1989.

[15] K. Horiuchi and T. Kanamori. Polymorphic Type Inference in Prolog by Abstract Interpretation. In *Logic Programming '87 (Tokyo)*, pp. 195–214. Springer LNCS 315, 1987.

[16] M. Huber and I. Varsek. Extended Prolog with Order-Sorted Resolution. In *Proc. 4th IEEE Internat. Symposium on Logic Programming*, pp. 34–43, San Francisco, 1987.

[17] G. Huet and D.C. Oppen. Equations and Rewrite Rules: A Survey. In R.V. Book, editor, *Formal Language Theory: Perspectives and Open Problems*. Academic Press, 1980.

[18] G.P. Huet. A Unification Algorithm for Typed λ-Calculus. *Theoretical Computer Science*, Vol. 1, pp. 27–57, 1975.

[19] N. Jones and H. Søndergaard. A semantics-based framework for the abstract interpretation of PROLOG. In S. Abramsky and C. Hankin,

editors, *Abstract Interpretation of Declarative Languages*, pp. 123–142. Ellis Horwood, 1987.

[20] T. Kanamori and K. Horiuchi. Type Inference in Prolog and Its Application. In *Proc. 9th IJCAI*, pp. 704–707. W. Kaufmann, 1985.

[21] F. Kluźniak. Type Synthesis for Ground Prolog. In *Proc. Fourth International Conference on Logic Programming (Melbourne)*, pp. 788–816. MIT Press, 1987.

[22] J.W. Lloyd. *Foundations of Logic Programming*. Springer, second, extended edition, 1987.

[23] C.S. Mellish. Some Global Optimizations for a Prolog Compiler. *Journal of Logic Programming (1)*, pp. 43–66, 1985.

[24] D.A. Miller and G. Nadathur. Higher-Order Logic Programming. In *Proc. Third International Conference on Logic Programming (London)*, pp. 448–462. Springer LNCS 225, 1986.

[25] P. Mishra. Towards a theory of types in Prolog. In *Proc. IEEE Internat. Symposium on Logic Programming*, pp. 289–298, Atlantic City, 1984.

[26] A. Mycroft. Private Communication, 1987.

[27] A. Mycroft and R.A. O'Keefe. A Polymorphic Type System for Prolog. *Artificial Intelligence*, Vol. 23, pp. 295–307, 1984.

[28] U. Nilsson. Towards an Abstract Interpretation Scheme for Logic Programs. In *Proc. of the Workshop on Programming Language Implementation and Logic Programming*, Orléans, 1988. Springer LNCS 348.

[29] P. Padawitz. *Computing in Horn Clause Theories*, volume 16 of *EATCS Monographs on Theoretical Computer Science*. Springer, 1988.

[30] J.A. Robinson. A Machine-Oriented Logic Based on the Resolution Principle. *Journal of the ACM*, Vol. 12, No. 1, pp. 23–41, 1965.

[31] G. Smolka. Fresh: A Higher-Order Language Based on Unification and Multiple Results. In D. DeGroot and G. Lindstrom, editors, *Logic Programming, Functions, Relations, and Equations*, pp. 469–524. Prentice Hall, 1986.

[32] G. Smolka. Logic Programming with Polymorphically Order-Sorted Types. In *Proc. First International Workshop on Algebraic and Logic Programming (Gaussig, G.D.R.)*, pp. 53–70. Akademie-Verlag (Berlin), 1988.

[33] G. Smolka, W. Nutt, J.A. Goguen, and J. Meseguer. Order-Sorted Equational Computation. SEKI Report SR-87-14, FB Informatik, Univ. Kaiserslautern, 1987.

[34] Z. Somogyi. A system of precise modes for logic programs. In *Proc. Fourth International Conference on Logic Programming (Melbourne)*, pp. 769–787. MIT Press, 1987.

[35] D.H.D. Warren. Higher-order extensions to PROLOG: are they needed? In *Machine Intelligence 10*, pp. 441–454, 1982.

[36] D.H.D. Warren. An Abstract Prolog Instruction Set. Technical Note 309, SRI International, Stanford, 1983.

[37] J. Xu and D.S. Warren. A Type Inference System For Prolog. In *Proc. 5th Conference on Logic Programming & 5th Symposium on Logic Programming (Seattle)*, pp. 604–619, 1988.

[38] J. Zobel. Derivation of Polymorphic Types for Prolog Programs. In *Proc. Fourth International Conference on Logic Programming (Melbourne)*, pp. 817–838. MIT Press, 1987.

Contributions to the View Update Problem

Francesca Rossi
Shamim A. Naqvi

MCC
3500 West Balcones Center Drive
Austin, Texas 78759

Arpanet address: rossi@mcc.com, shamim@mcc.com

Abstract

Fagin *et al.* [5] have proposed a semantically consistent approach to the problem of view updates in relational databases, namely the problem concerning the ambiguity arising from translating a view update to an update over the underlying base relations. Their approach, given a theory and an update, returns a set of new theories, as many as the number of alternatives, all accomplishing the given update. The disjunction of all these theories is then considered as the updated theory. In this paper we take this approach as a starting point, but we improve upon it by proposing a new, equivalent but less redundant definition of the updated theory, and by developing an algorithm for obtaining it. Moreover, in our approach, and in contrast to [5], the resulting database does not depend on the structure of the initial database. In particular, we adopt the idea of translating updates by appealing to the Clark completion [3] of the database. We are able to update any kind of derived predicate (even if recursively defined) and to embed in the old theory any sequence of general updates (even if conflicting, such as insertions and deletions about the same relation). Finally, we give an efficient proof procedure, called SLIL-resolution, that does not construct the new updated database; rather, it operates on the initial Horn database and on a priority data structure containing the clauses representing the update sequence.

1 Introduction

The problem of updating view predicates is quite different from that of updating base predicates. For example, adding a new fact $b(a)$ where b is a base predicate in a database T can be described as the unique new database $T' = T \cup \{b(a)\}$ (if we want minimality). The same holds for a deletion ($T' = T - \{b(a)\}$).

On the contrary, if we want to update a derived predicate, this same mapping is ambiguous, i.e., given T, there may exist different new minimal databases producing the desired result of the update. Consider, for example, the intensional database

$$p(x) \leftarrow b_1(x).$$
$$p(x) \leftarrow b_2(x).$$
$$q(x) \leftarrow b_1(x).$$

Assuming that neither $b_1(a)$ nor $b_2(a)$ is in T, the update $+p(a)$ may be satisfied in several ways. For example, we can add a new fact $p(a)$ to the definition of p as in Prolog and [11]. This approach implies that queries to the relation q will not see the effects of the updates to the relation p. However, the usual intuitive understanding of a logical database is such that the facts are seen as the description of the world and the rules as reasoning mechanisms using this description to derive new facts. This means that we would like to change only the world (i.e. the facts) and not the procedures (i.e. the rules) using it. This understanding forms the basis upon which different users share the same database through different sets of rules (views), and also share the updates defined through these views.

In the relational database literature concerned with this problem, called the *updatability problem of relational views* [4, 1], it is generally recognized that the base relations are to be updated but the problem is that semantic inconsistencies arise from this ambiguous mapping. For example, in the above case, an update $+p(a)$ can be achieved by updating either the base relation b_1 or the relation b_2.

Many different solutions to the view update problem can be found in the relational approach. Most of these solutions rely on choosing one alternative over all others but it is safe to say that no semantically consistent approach along these lines has been found to date.

Fagin *et al.* [5] have proposed an interesting method that considers all the alternatives, and defines an update not as a mapping from a theory to a new one, but from a theory to a disjunction of new theories (as many as the number of different alternatives), each one of which is obtained by applying one of the alternative ways to do the update to the given old theory. This method presents a semantically consistent picture of view updates, but there are at least four possible extensions of their work that can be considered.

First, the sentences of the database grow doubly exponentially with each update. A less costly update translation is needed. Second, only one update at a time is considered rather than a general sequence of updates. Third, in their approach it is recognized that rules should not be deleted because of an update. An adhoc method based on DBA assigned priorities is proposed to prevent such an event. However, the scheme remains adhoc and a systematic solution is needed. Finally, Fagin *et al.* state that "... the result of the update is dependent upon the way the logical database is constructed. More research should be done on that aspect to make our methodology more practical." In fact, the result of any update should be independent of the structure of the database, i.e. an algorithm for deriving the new database is needed.

A subsequent report by Fagin *et al.* ([6]) improves upon certain other aspects of the earlier proposal by introducing the concept of *flocks*. However, as far as the four above described problems are concerned, they only directly address the second one by considering *batch updates*, i.e., sets of insertions or of deletions but not both. Thus, a clarification of what happens in the case of sequences of updates in which an update contradicts some previous update is necessary.

In this paper we extend the proposal of Fagin *et al.* ([5, 6]) along the above four directions. First, we allow a sequence of insert/delete operations to be specified on the database. Also, no rule is changed by any update. We then present an algorithm that takes a given Horn theory, HDB, and a sequence of updates, and derives a unique new theory (not necessarily Horn), NDB, that accomplishes the updates. We show that NDB has the desired logical properties in that it logically entails all the additions and deletions to the database. The query answering process over NDB is considered; this must be a full first-order derivability relation since the formulae of NDB are, in general, non-Horn. However, they do not grow doubly exponentially with each update.

Appealing to a first-order derivability relation over NDB will be computationally prohibitive. In section 4 we present a more practical approach to the view update problem. In this approach the updates are kept in a stratified data structure, i.e., in a data structure with distinct levels. Each level represents a set of clauses denoting a positive or a negative update. Next, a new refutation procedure, called SLIL, is defined to operate over the clauses of the initial Horn theory, HDB, and the clauses in the priority data structure. SLIL uses the levels of the data structure judiciously only for certain specific actions during the proof process. We give complexity arguments to show the viability of SLIL-refutation over full first-order resolution. We also show that SLIL is sound with respect to derivability over NDB, and complete in the sense that every positive literal provable in NDB has an SLIL-proof.

2   Semantics of Updates

In this section we shall briefly explain the approach described in [5] and [6] and clarify the relationship between our approach and theirs. Fagin *et al.* consider a database as a consistent set of sentences, i.e., a theory. When this theory is updated, more than one theory could accomplish the desired update. These different theories can be partially ordered so as to consider only the minimal ones (with the least number of changes with respect to the original one), but even in this case we may have more than one resulting theory.

Consider a theory T. Let T^* be the set of logical consequences of T and $Mod(T)$ the set of all the models of T. Given a theory T, a theory S accomplishes the insertion of a sentence c in T if $c \in S$. S accomplishes the deletion of c from T if $c \notin S^*$. Also, S accomplishes an update to T minimally if S accomplishes the update and there is no other theory accomplishing the update with a smaller number of changes. A minimal theory accomplishing an update is defined as

- S accomplishes the deletion of c from T minimally iff S is a maximal subset of T consistent with $\neg c$;

- $S \cup c$ accomplishes the insertion of c into T minimally iff S is a maximal subset of T consistent with c.

Given a theory T and the set $\{T_1, \ldots, T_n\}$ of all the minimal alternative theories accomplishing an update to T, they suggest that there should be a unique resulting theory T' representing the update to T, that T' should be constructed from $T_1, \ldots, T_n$ and that it should be such that $Mod(T') = \bigcup_{i=1,\ldots,n} Mod(T_i)$. Then they consider the theory

$$T' = \bigvee_{i=1,\ldots,n} T_i = \{c_1 \vee \ldots \vee c_n : c_i \in T_i, i = 1, \ldots, n\}$$

and they show that this theory satisfies the required condition about its set of models. Also, they show that, given $T'' = \bigcap_{i=1,\ldots,n} T_i^*$, $Mod(T'') = Mod(T')$.

Since the deletion of rules is considered unacceptable, Fagin *et al.* propose a priority scheme, determined by the DBA, to prevent such an occurrence. However, no systematic, i.e., algorithmic, method is proposed to derive the new constructed logical database. As a first step towards a solution to this problem we think that it is necessary to avoid the consideration of all those theories that accomplish the desired update but that do not contain all the rules of the original theory.

In this sense, we say that a theory S accomplishes an update u to a theory T minimally if S accomplishes u minimally in the sense of [5] and [6] and it contains all the rules of T.

Consider for example the database containing the two clauses $p \vee \neg b$ and b; their approach would consider $T_1 = \{p \vee \neg b\}$ and $T_2 = \{b\}$ as the two minimal theories accomplishing the deletion of p, thus obtaining T' which is the empty set of sentences (because the sentence $p \vee \neg b \vee b$ is valid and hence not considered). In our approach, on the contrary, we would consider only one theory accomplishing the update, i.e. T_1.

Let $T_1, \ldots, T_n$ be alternative minimal theories to a theory T accomplishing an update (we shall show later how these alternative theories can be derived from the update and the theory T). Then, for an insertion, we define the resulting theory T' as

$$T' = \bigcap_i T_i \cup \bigvee_i (T_i - \cap_j T_j)$$

and for a deletion as

$$T' = \bigcap_i T_i \cup \bigvee_i \neg (T_i - \cap_j T_j)$$

for i and j to range over $1, \ldots, n$.

Note that the improvement over the previous definition of T' (as $\bigvee T_i$) comes from the fact that we push the disjunction of the theories to affect only the clauses added to T, instead of all the clauses of T. In fact, in this way we can avoid redundant disjunctive clauses in T'.

As an example, consider the database with the sentences $p \vee \neg b_1$, $p \vee \neg b_2$ and b_3, and the update asking for the insertion of p; in both approaches we have $T_1 = T \cup \{b_1\}$ and $T_2 = T \cup \{b_2\}$. But, while in their approach we have $T' = T_1 \vee T_2 = \{p \vee \neg b_1, p \vee \neg b_2, p \vee \neg b_1 \vee \neg b_2, p \vee \neg b_1 \vee b_3, p \neg b_2 \vee b_3, p \vee \neg b_2 \vee b_1, p \vee \neg b_1 \vee b_2, b_3 \vee b_2, b_1 \vee b_3, b_1 \vee b_2, b_3\}$, using our definition of T' we have $T_1 \cap T_2 = T$, so $T' = T \bigcup \{b_1 \vee b_2\}$.

Note that we do not change the semantics of updates by using this different approach. In fact, given the minimal theories $T_1, \ldots, T_n$ that accomplish an update, the following theorem shows that the model of T' is the intersection of the sets of logical consequences of $T_1, \ldots, T_n$.

The alternative theories $T_1, \ldots, T_n$, for a given T and an update, are equivalent insofar that they all accomplish the update. Thus, to answer a query in the new database we believe that one should appeal to logical entailment from the collection $T_1, \ldots, T_n$, i.e., a query is true in the resulting database iff it is entailed by each T_i. Thus, it is reasonable to consider always one model for a given theory (we will write $M(T)$ for the model of the theory T), which is the intersection of all its models. This means that, whenever a theory has more than one minimal model, we assign the empty model to it. In fact, as far as the user of that theory is concerned, no query will have a positive answer in such a theory.

Theorem 1 *Let $T_1, \ldots, T_n$ be alternative theories accomplishing an update to a theory T, and let T' be as defined above. Then*

$$M(T') = \bigcap_{i=1,\ldots,n} M(T_i). \blacksquare$$

In the next section we propose an algorithm to derive the new theory T' from a given theory T and an update sequence.

3 Derivation of the New Theory

To obtain the new theory T', we first represent any update as a set of possibly non-Horn clauses, and then we combine these clauses with the old theory. The next section describes the translation phase, while Section 3.2 describes an algorithm for the combination phase.

3.1 Translating Updates

A *(logical) database* is a collection of function-free *closed* clauses in which the base and derived predicate symbols are distinct. If all the clauses are Horn, then it is called a *Horn database* (denoted by HDB); otherwise it is called a *non-Horn database* (and will be denoted by NDB). All updates are assumed to be variable-free. The terms *database* and *theory* shall be used interchangeably. Derived predicates are denoted by using the letters $p, q, r, \ldots$, base predicates by using $b, b_1, b_2, \ldots$ and literals or atoms by using $A, B, \ldots$.

An *update* to a predicate p (where p here can be either derived or base) has the form $+p(a)$ if we want to add the tuple a to the relation defining p (and in this case it is called a *positive update*), or the form $-p(a)$ if we want to delete the tuple a (and in this case it is called a *negative update*).

We now show how to translate an update to an HDB predicate, say p, into a set of (possibly non-Horn) clauses. The basic idea is to interpret the rules defining the relation p as an *if-and-only-if* definition. Thus, if we have a rule of the form

$$p \leftarrow q_1, \ldots, q_n$$

then an update to p is interpreted as an update to the relations $q_1, \ldots, q_n$. The updates to $q_1, \ldots, q_n$ are similarly interpreted recursively and the translation terminates when either a base relation is reached or if the predicate symbol p is reached again, e.g., in case of recursively defined predicates. While a deeper unfolding of p is also possible, we think that our choice is a reasonable trade-off between the work required at update time and query time. In fact, we give the query answering process the minimum (i.e. the shortest clause) that it needs to accomplish the update to p, leaving it the choice to go deeper in the definition of p if it needs to do so.

We now give the procedure which returns the translation of an update α to HDB. Given HDB, first we obtain its Clark completion [3]. This can be done in a sequence of steps at the end of which the definition of each derived predicate p is the formula $p(x) \leftrightarrow F_1 \vee \ldots F_n$, where each F_i is of the form $B_{i1} \wedge \ldots \wedge B_{ik}$. Let us set $F_1 \vee \ldots \vee F_n = F(p)$ for the predicate p.

We start with a given update and we first replace it by the corresponding literal ($p(a)$ if the update is $+p(a)$, $\neg p(a)$ if the update is $-p(a)$). Let us denote this literal by Lit. Then we apply to Lit the following steps:

1. if p is a base predicate then return Lit;

2. if p is not recursive and there are no existentially quantified variables in $F(p)$ then

    (a) if $Lit = p(a)$ then replace Lit by $F(p)\theta$, where $\theta = \{x/a\}$; for each literal in $F(p)\theta$ start again from step 1;

    (b) if $Lit = \neg p(a)$ then replace Lit by $\neg F(p)\theta$, where $\theta = \{x/a\}$; for each literal in $\neg F(p)\theta$ start again from step 1;

3. if p is not recursive but there are existentially quantified variables in $F(p)$ then

    (a) if $Lit = p(a)$ then replace Lit by $F(p)\theta$, $\theta = \{x/a\} \cup \{y/f(a)$ for each existential variable y in $F(p)$ (f is a new Skolem function)$\}$; for each literal in $F(p)\theta$ start again from step 1;

    (b) if $Lit = \neg p(a)$ then replace Lit by $\neg F(p)\theta$, where $\theta = \{x/a\}$; for each literal in $\neg F(p)\theta$ start again from step 1;

4. if p is recursive (and possibly with existentially quantified variables):

   (a) if $Lit = p(a)$ then replace Lit by $F(p)\theta$, $\theta = \{x/a\} \cup \{y/f(a)$ for each existential variable y in $F(p)\}$; for each literal in $F(p)\theta$ except any literal containing p start again from step 1;

   (b) if $Lit = \neg p(a)$ then replace Lit by $\neg F(p)\theta$, where $\theta = \{x/a\}$; for each literal in $\neg F(p)\theta$ except any literal containing p start again from step 1;

As an example of the non-recursive case, the update $+p(a)$ for the database

$$p(x) \leftarrow b_1(x, y), b_2(y, z).$$
$$p(x) \leftarrow b_3(x).$$

gives the formula $(b_1(a, f(a)) \wedge b_2(f(a), g(a))) \vee b_3(a)$. On the contrary, for $-p(a)$ we get $\neg b_1(a, x) \vee \neg b_2(x, y)$ and $\neg b_3(a)$.

As an example of the recursive case, consider the following definition of p

$$p(x) \leftarrow b_1(x), p(x).$$
$$p(x) \leftarrow b_2(x).$$

In this case, $+p(a)$ is translated into $(b_1(a) \wedge p(a)) \vee b_2(a)$ while $-p(a)$ is translated into $\neg b_2(a)$ and $\neg b_1(a) \vee \neg p(a)$.

3.2   Composing Updates

In the previous section we have seen that each update u_i to a Horn logical database HDB can be transformed into a set of (in general, non-Horn) clauses C_i. Note that a clause representing a positive update is always of the form $B_1 \vee \ldots \vee B_n$, where every B_i is a positive literal, while a clause representing a negative update is always of the form $\neg B_1 \vee \ldots \vee \neg B_n$, where again every B_i is a positive literal.

Given HDB, an *update query* U for HDB is a formula of the form $\leftarrow u_1, \ldots, u_n$ where $u_1, \ldots, u_n$ are updates to predicates of HDB.

Let us now consider a Horn logical database HDB and an update query $U = \leftarrow u_1, \ldots, u_n$ to HDB, and let us call ADD the set of all the clauses representing positive updates of U, and DEL the set of all those clauses representing negative updates of U.

Now it is clear that the updates are mappings of HDB into a new database, say NDB. The question is how to define NDB. It may be tempting to think of NDB as the union of the sets HDB, ADD and DEL. However, whereas $HDB \cup ADD$ is consistent, in general DEL will contain clauses that contradict some clause in ADD or HDB. Our task is thus to give a new definition of NDB that maintains consistency while accomplishing all the desired updates.

The idea is to start with a given Horn database HDB and the update query $U = \leftarrow u_1, \ldots, u_n$ and to embed the clauses representing all these updates into HDB one at a time in the right sequence, i.e. from i=1 to i=n. Such an embedding is non-trivial because subsequent updates may *subsume*, *contradict*, *partially undo*, or be *unrelated to* the effects of prior updates.
In the sequel we consider Horn databases without any facts, i.e. intensional databases. This is not a restriction because it is easy to see that, given a Horn database with a set of facts $F = \{f_1, \ldots, f_k\}$, i.e. $HDB = IDB \cup F$, and an update query $U = \leftarrow u_1, \ldots, u_n$, it is equivalent to the intensional database IDB with the update query $\leftarrow +f_1, \ldots, +f_k, u_1, \ldots, u_n$.
The following is the *composition algorithm* that takes as input an intensional database HDB and a sequence of updates $u_1, \ldots, u_n$, and returns a new logical database, NDB. Recall that C_i is the set of clauses resulting from the translation of the update u_i as described in Section 3.1. NDB is defined as $HDB \cup S_n$, where S_n is incrementally constructed as follows:

- set S_0 to the empty set;

- for $i = 0, \ldots, n-1$, compute S_{i+1} from S_i in the following way:

  - set S_{i+1} to S_i;
  - for all c in C_{i+1}:
    * add c to S_{i+1};
    * consider the proof tree with root c and which uses clauses from $S_i \cup C_{i+1}$; for each branch with the empty clause as leaf, delete from S_{i+1} the clauses used in that branch;
    * delete from S_{i+1} all the clauses that are subsumed by some other clause.

We will write $HDB \longrightarrow_{u_1, \ldots, u_n} NDB$, or $HDB \longrightarrow_U NDB$ if $U = \leftarrow u_1, \ldots, u_n$.

Example: Let us suppose that HDB has these clauses:

$$p(x) \leftarrow b_1(x).$$
$$p(x) \leftarrow b_2(x).$$

Let the update sequence be $+p(a), -b_1(a)$. We have $C_1 = \{b_1(a) \vee b_2(a)\}$ and $C_2 = \{\neg b_1(a)\}$, so $S_1 = C_1$ and $S_2 = S_1 \cup C_2 = \{b_1(a) \vee b_2(a), \neg b_1(a)\}$.

Let the update sequence be $+p(a), +b_1(a)$. We have $C_1 = \{b_1(a) \vee b_2(a)\}$ and $C_2 = \{b_1(a)\}$, so $S_1 = C_1$ and $S_2 = S_1 \cup C_2 \setminus \{\text{subsumed clauses}\} = \{b_1(a)\}$.

Let the update sequence be $+p(a), -p(a)$. Now $C_1 = \{b_1(a) \vee b_2(a)\}$ and $C_2 = \{\neg b_1(a), \neg b_2(a)\}$, so $S_1 = C_1$ and $S_2 = S_1 \cup C_2 \setminus \{b_1(a) \vee b_2(a)\}$ (because this clause is used in the proof tree for both $\neg b_1(a)$ and $\neg b_2(a)) = \{\neg b_1(a), \neg b_2(a)\}$.

Let the update sequence be $-p(a), +p(a)$. In this case $C_1 = \{\neg b_1(a), \neg b_2(a)\}$ and $C_2 = \{b_1(a) \vee b_2(a)\}$, so $S_1 = C_1$ and $S_2 = C_1 \cup C_2 \setminus \{\text{subsumed clauses}\}$(which is exactly C_1) $= C_2 = \{b_1(a) \vee b_2(a)\}$.∎

The following theorems show that NDB is always consistent and, moreover, it has the right semantics, i.e. it accomplishes all the updates.

Theorem 2 *Given an update sequence $U =\leftarrow u_1,\ldots,u_n$ to HDB, the logical database NDB such that $HDB \longrightarrow_U NDB$ is consistent.*∎

The next theorem shows that given a database and an update to it, the new updated database accomplishes the update. Given an update u_i, let us write u_i' for u_i without the add/del sign. Thus u_i' is a ground atom.

Theorem 3 *Given HDB and $U =\leftarrow u_1,\ldots,u_n$, for every $i = 1,\ldots,n$ we have $NDB_i \vdash u_i'$ if u_i is a positive update, otherwise $\neg(NDB \vdash u_i')$.*∎

To show that if $HDB \longrightarrow_{u_1,\ldots,u_n} NDB$ then NDB logically entails all the desired updates in the right sequence, we first need to define the notion of *disjoint updates*.

Given a ground atom, say $p(\bar{c})$, we define the set $Unfold(p(\bar{c}))$ as:

- if p is a base predicate then $Unfold(p(\bar{c})) = \{p(\bar{c})\}$, or

- if p is a derived predicate and it is defined by the clauses (for simplicity, we write only the predicate symbols)

$$p \leftarrow p_{i1}, \ldots, p_{in_i}$$

for $i = 1, \ldots, k$, then

$$Unfold(p(\bar{c})) = \cup_{i=1\ldots k, j=1\ldots n_i, p_{ij} \neq p} Unfold(p_{ij}(\bar{c}_{ij}))$$

where $\bar{c}_{ij}$ is the instantiation of the arguments of p_{ij} corresponding to $\bar{c}$ (new variables are left as variables).

Two ground atoms A and B are *disjoint* if there do not exist C, D such that $C \in Unfold(A)$ and $D \in Unfold(B)$ and C and D unify. Two updates u_1 and u_2 are *disjoint updates* if, whenever they have different signs, then u'_1 and u'_2 are disjoint atoms.
The next theorem states that NDB can derive the consequences of an update, provided that no subsequent update in the given sequence affects it.

Theorem 4 *Given a Horn logical database HDB and an update query $U = (\leftarrow u_1, \ldots, u_n)$ for HDB, if*

- $HDB \longrightarrow_{u_1, \ldots, u_n} NDB$, *and*

- $\exists i \in \{1, \ldots, n\}$ *such that u'_i and u'_j are disjoint atoms $\forall j = i + 1, \ldots, n$,*

then $NDB \vdash u'_i$ if u_i is a positive update, otherwise $\neg(NDB \vdash u_i)$. ∎

From theorems 2 and 3 it follows that, first, a positive literal unaffected by updates and provable in HDB remains provable in NDB. Second, that a positive literal is provable from NDB but not from HDB alone if it is "implied" by updates. In particular, if a literal, say $p(a)$, was unprovable in HDB and there is no update which implies $p(a)$ (in the sense of theorem 3) then it remains the case that $\neg(NDB \vdash p(a))$. However, in general negative queries will require an extension of the CWA as in [9].
Note that there is more than one way to define the composition algorithm while maintaining consistency of the updated database and accomplishment of the updates. For example, a possible alternative to our algorithm can be described in an informal way as follows:

- set S_0 to the empty set;

- for $i = 0, \ldots, n - 1$, compute S_{i+1} from S_i in the following way:

    - set S_{i+1} to S_i;
    - for all c in C_{i+1}:
        * for all branches with root c and empty leaf, if c is positive, then delete the clauses that have been used in this branch and add c;
        * for all the branches with root c and non empty leaf, add the leaf;

      * delete from S_{i+1} all the clauses that are subsumed by some other clause.

It is possible to prove, for this new composition algorithm, that the obtained updated database NDB is consistent and accomplishes all the updates in the right sequence. A comparison of the two methods can be done by considering a minimality issue (w.r.t. number of clauses in the updated database), or the efficiency of answering queries in NDB. We feel that the first composition algorithm is better in terms of minimality (it adds a smaller number of clauses), but it is worse w.r.t. the query answering process in the updated database (because the alternative algorithm adds clauses that already embed some computation steps). However, our choice of describing in detail the less efficient alternative is based on two beliefs: that our algorithm is more intuitive, and that we will deal with the efficiency issues in the next section, by providing an alternative, to the composition approach, of answering queries in the old database while keeping track of the desired updates. In fact, the purpose of the composition algorithm is not to be efficient, but to show a systematic way of obtaining the updated database from the old one under a sequence of updates.

4   SLIL Resolution Procedure

Now that we know that NDB has the desired meaning (of HDB plus the updates in U), we can answer any query to the updated database by using a general resolution strategy over NDB. But we can also try to develop a new more efficient resolution procedure that is able to exploit the restricted class of non-Horn clauses resulting from our transformation. We now define this procedure.

We take inspiration from the SLI-resolution procedure defined in [8], but we use another notation while changing some rules and adding a new data structure in order to take care of the order-dependent nature of the updates and to treat them as constraining information. The result is called SLIL-resolution (Linear resolution with Selection function for Indefinite clauses and Levels of updates).

Given an update sequence $(u_1, \ldots, u_n)$ to HDB, we now want to answer a query $Q = \leftarrow q_1, \ldots, q_n$.

The order-dependence of the updates $u_1, \ldots, u_n$ can be explained by noticing that an update u_i may undo the effects of an update u_j, with $i < j$. The data structure that takes care of this problem is a sequence $SEQ = (L_1, \ldots, L_n)$ of levels, where each level L_i contains the set of clauses corresponding to the update u_i. This structure may be changed (not in the number of the levels, but in the content of each one of them) during the development of a proof. Note that each L_i can contain either clauses with only positive literals (if u_i is a positive update), or clauses with only negative literals (if u_i is a negative update).

Let DEL be the set of all the negative non-Horn clauses, i.e. the set of all the clauses c such that there exists a negative level L_i with $c \in L_i$, while ADD is the set of all the positive non-Horn clauses, i.e. of all those clauses occurring in some positive level.

Each clause c which is a Horn clause or a positive non-Horn clause will be given a number, called the *level number*, ln, such that $ln(c) = 0$ if $c \in HDB$, otherwise $ln(c) = i$ if $c \in L_i$.

The main idea is to resolve a literal A in the current resolvent with some clause in some level, say L_i, and then to check, before replacing A, if there is some clause in some negative level among $L_{i+1}, \ldots, L_n$ that contradicts this action. Checking of only the levels after L_i is based on the fact that an update may contradict only some past updates, but none of the future ones. So there is nothing in $L_1, \ldots, L_{i-1}$ that can contradict the chosen literal in L_i.

At each step i, $1 \leq i \leq m$, of the resolution procedure we have a goal G_i and a sequence $SEQ_i = (L_1, \ldots, L_n)$ of levels of non-Horn clauses. We also have a set of negative clauses CON_i that constrain the execution of the step.

The initial goal G_0 is set to Q, where Q is the given query, and SEQ_0 is set to the given SEQ. The general current goal G_i will be $g_1 \vee \ldots \vee g_n$.

We have two rules of inference:

(*Factoring*): $\exists$ indices j, k, with $1 \leq j < k \leq n$ and a substitution θ_i such that $g_j\theta_i = g_k\theta_i$. Then

$$G_{i+1} = \left(g_1 \vee \ldots \vee g_{k-1} \vee g_{k+1} \vee \ldots \vee g_n\right)\theta_i$$

and $SEQ_{i+1} = SEQ_i.\blacksquare$

(*Substitution*): there may be two cases:

- if $g_1 = b$ where b is a positive atom, and $\exists B_1 \vee \ldots \vee B_m \in (HDB \cup DEL)$ and θ_i such that $\neg g_1\theta_i = B_1\theta_i$, then

$$G_{i+1} = \left(B_2 \vee \ldots \vee B_m \vee g_2 \vee \ldots \vee g_n\right)\theta_i.$$

  If $B_1 \vee \ldots \vee B_m \in L_i$, then $L_i := L_i \setminus \{B_1 \vee \ldots \vee B_m\}$. SEQ_{i+1} is set to the current sequence $(L_1, \ldots, L_n)$;

- if $g_1 = \neg b$ where b is a positive atom, and $\exists B_1 \vee \ldots \vee B_m \in (HDB \cup ADD)$ and θ_i such that $\neg g_1 \theta_i = B_1 \theta_i$, then let us set $level = ln(B_1 \vee \ldots \vee B_m), AFTER(level) = \{L_j, \forall j > level\}$ and $CON_i = \{c \mid c \in L_k, L_k \in AFTER(level), c = \neg d_1 \vee \ldots \vee \neg d_h, \neg g_1 \theta_i = d_1 \theta_i\}$.

If $CON_i \neq \Phi$, i.e. there are clauses in subsequent levels that constraint the current "proof", then the levels are changed as follows. All levels $L_1, \ldots, L_{level}$ remain unchanged. All negative levels among $L_{level}, \ldots, L_n$ are changed using the following iterative algorithm.

For all $c = \neg d_1 \vee \ldots \vee \neg d_h \in CON_i$, if $c \in L_j$, then

$$L_j := L_j \setminus \{c\} \cup \{(\neg d_2 \vee \ldots \vee \neg d_n)\theta_i\}$$

Now, if $\square \notin L_i \forall i$, then

$$G_{i+1} = (B_2 \vee \ldots \vee B_m \vee g_2 \vee \ldots \vee g_n)\theta$$

and SEQ_{i+1} is set to the current sequence $(L_1, \ldots, L_n)$.■

When the factoring rule cannot be applied, and the substitution rule, if it can be applied, introduces the empty clause into some level, then we backtrack.

Example: Let us consider the Horn logical database consisting of the following two clauses

$$p(x) \leftarrow b_1(x).$$
$$p(x) \leftarrow b_2(x).$$

The first update query that we ask to this database is $\leftarrow +p(a), -p(a)$ followed by the query $\leftarrow p(a)$.

In this case we have $SEQ = (L_1, L_2)$, where $L_1 = \{b_1(a) \vee b_2(a)\}$ and $L_2 = \{\neg b_1(a), \neg b_2(a)\}$. $G_0 = \neg p(a)$ and $SEQ_0 = SEQ$. Now, $p(a)$ unifies with the head of the first rule with mgu $\theta = \{x/a\}$, so $level = 0, AFTER(0) = \{L_1, L_2\}, CON_0 = \Phi$. This means that no level is changed. Moreover, no level contains the empty clause, so $G_1 = \neg b_1(a)$ and $SEQ_1 = SEQ_0$.

Now, $b_1(a)$ unifies with a literal in L_1, so $level = 1, AFTER(1) = \{L_2\}, CON_1 = \{\neg b_1(a)\}$. Thus $L_2 := L_2 \setminus \{\neg b_1(a)\} \cup \{\square\} = \{\neg b_2(a), \square\}$. So, L_2 contains the empty clause, that means this branch of the proof tree has failed. But we may note that any other branch will lead us to a similar situation, so the entire proof of $p(a)$ fails.

Let us now consider another update query to the same database as before:

$$\leftarrow -p(a), +p(a).$$

followed by the same query as before.

It is clear that we want to show how our resolution procedure handles the cases where we have the same set of updates but in a different order. In this particular case, for example, the intuitive meaning is that, unlike the previous query, we want this one to succeed, i.e., we want to be able to deduce $p(a)$.

Following SLIL-resolution, we have $SEQ = (L_1, L_2)$, where now $L_1 = \{\neg b_1(a), \neg b_2(a)\}$, and $L_2 = \{b_1(a) \vee b_2(a)\}$. The first step is as in the previous case, so we end up with $G_1 = \neg b_1(a)$ and $SEQ_1 = SEQ$. Then, $b_1(a)$ unifies with a literal in L_2, so $level = 2, AFTER(2) = \Phi$ and $CON_1 = \Phi$. This means that no level is changed, so $G_2 = b_2(a)$ and $SEQ_2 = SEQ$.

Now, $\neg b_2(a)$ unifies with a literal in L_1, so $L_1 := L_1 \setminus \{\neg b_2(a)\} = \{\neg b_1(a)\}$. $G_{i+1} = \square$ and this means that the query succeeded, i.e. that p(a) can be deduced from the database. $\blacksquare$

The following theorem shows that SLIL-resolution is sound.

Theorem 5 *Given a non-Horn logical database NDB such that HDB $\longrightarrow_U NDB$ for some HDB and sequence of updates U, we have that $NDB \vdash A$ if A can be deduced from HDB and $(L_1, \ldots, L_n)$ using SLIL-resolution.* $\blacksquare$

It must be noted that the above theorem states that every positive literal provable under SLIL is also logically entailed by NDB. Thus, the soundness of SLIL is shown with respect to NDB. In particular, we can not consider the soundness issue based on the clauses in HDB together with the clauses in the levels since this collective set of clauses may be inconsistent.

SLIL-resolution is complete in the sense that every positive literal that is logically entailed by NDB has an SLIL-proof. Let us set M_{atoms} $(NDB) = \{A \mid NDB \vdash A \text{ and } A \text{ is a ground atom}\}$.

Theorem 6 *Given HDB, U and NDB such that $HDB \longrightarrow_U NDB$, a ground atom A can be deduced from HDB and $(L_1, \ldots, L_n)$ using SLIL-resolution if $A \in M_{atoms}(NDB)$.* $\blacksquare$

A special case of the SLIL proof procedure arises when the updates in the sequence $U = (u_1, \ldots, u_n)$ are disjoint. In fact, it can be proved that in this case we do not need the entire sequence of n levels, but only one level L_1 for all the clauses representing the positive updates and another level L_2 containing all the clauses representing the negative updates in U.

When the original database has been changed by a large number of updates, an equally large number of levels have to be considered by SLIL-resolution. In this case, some heuristic techniques can be of help in collapsing some of the levels while still preserving correctness. We plan to investigate this issue in our future research.

The worst drawback in using our approach of unfolding each update request into a set of positive or negative non-Horn clauses is the fact that the number and the length of the non-Horn clauses to be added may be large. Note, however, that in our case we deal only with a very restricted form of non-Horn clauses. In fact, every time we use a non-Horn clause, it comes out that we don't need to perform general unification, but only *matching*, due to the fact that positive non-Horn clauses are always ground and negative non-Horn clauses may not be ground but are checked only against ground subgoals.

Let us now examine in more detail what happens from the time and space complexity point of view.

Suppose that the definition of the predicate p to be updated consists of these clauses (we consider a simple definition; the others can be reduced to this form):

$$p \leftarrow b_{11}, \ldots, b_{1n_1}.$$
$$\vdots$$
$$p \leftarrow b_{k1}, \ldots, b_{kn_k}.$$

Then, a positive update $+p$ will be translated into

$$\left(b_{11} \wedge \ldots \wedge b_{1n_1}\right) \vee \ldots \vee \left(b_{k1} \wedge \ldots \wedge b_{kn_k}\right)$$

which in turn translates into $n_1 \times n_2 \times \ldots \times n_k$ clauses, each clause in the form of a disjunction of exactly k literals. If on the contrary we have a negative update $-p$, it is translated into

$$\left(\neg b_{11} \vee \ldots \vee \neg b_{1n_1}\right) \wedge \ldots \wedge \left(\neg b_{k1} \vee \ldots \vee \neg b_{kn_k}\right)$$

that is a collection of k negative clauses where each clause i has exactly n_i literals.

Thus, in the negative case we are linear in the definition of p (number and length of the clauses defining p), while in the positive case we add to the database non-Horn clauses whose length is linear in the number of clauses defining p and whose number can be exponential in the number of clauses defining p.

This means that the main problem is the positive case, but it can be partially solved by not unpacking the definition of p for obtaining the conjunctive form and so the non-Horn clauses, and then do the unpacking only when, and if, it is necessary for the resolution procedure.

Actually, the negative case does not lead to any space problems but can be heavy in time while answering the query because whenever we use the substitution rule we have to check all the negative clauses and their number may be very large. We can solve this problem by using an efficient pattern matching search technique that avoids looking at all the negative clauses (in fact we have to only look for all the clauses matching some already found base literal).

5   Conclusions

We believe that the work reported in [5] presents a semantically consistent picture of the view update problem. We have proposed various extensions of this work that improve certain aspects of that proposal along semantical and pragmatic directions. Our approach consists of:

- representing each update as a set of (in general, non-Horn) clauses;
- transforming the given database by *composing* its original clauses with these new non-Horn clauses;
- proving that the new database has the correct and complete semantic properties;
- providing an extension of SLD-resolution for answering queries in the new database.

However, we feel that more research is needed towards the goal of finding an efficient method. In case of a large number of updates, our SLIL procedure may get swamped by the number of levels. Perhaps heuristic techniques to collapse the number of levels, based upon Church-Rosser or other equivalence preserving properties of updates, can be considered.

Acknowledgements: We thank C. Zaniolo, R. Krishnamurthy and Oded Shmueli for reading the manuscript and suggesting several improvements to our presentation. Also, Francesca Rossi would like to thank the Italian National Research Council for supporting her visit at MCC.

References

[1] Bancilhon, F., Spyratos, N.,"Update Semantics of Relational Views", *ACM TODS 6, 4,* 1981.

[2] Chang, C., Lee, R., *Symbolic Logic and Mechanical Theorem Proving*, Academic Press, 1973.

[3] Clark, K., "Negation as Failure", in *Logic and Databases*, (eds. Gallaire, Minker and Nicolas), Plenum Press, NY, 1978.

[4] Dayal, U., Bernstein, P.A., "On the Updatability of Relational Views", *Proc. 4th VLDB*, 1978.

[5] Fagin, R., Ullman, J., Vardi, M.,"On the Semantics of Updates in Databases", *Proc. 2nd ACM PODS*, April 1983.

[6] Fagin, R., Kuper, G., Ullman, J., Vardi, M.,"Updating Logical Databases", *Advances in Computing Research, Vol. 3*, pp. 1-18, 1986.

[7] Manchanda, S., "A Dynamic Logic Programming Language for Relational Updates", University of Arizona, TR 88-2, 1988.

[8] Rajasekar, A., Minker J.,"A Fixpoint Semantics for Non-Horn Logic Programs", unpublished manuscript.

[9] Naqvi, S. A., "Some Extensions to the Closed World Assumption in Databases", International Conference on Database Theory, Rome, 1987.

[10] Reiter, R., "On Closed World Databases", in *Logic and Databases*, (eds. Gallaire, Minker and Nicolas), Plenum Press, NY, 1978.

[11] Wilkins, M. W.,"A Model-Theoretic Approach to Updating Logical Databases", in *Proc. 5th ACM PODS*, 1986.

[12] Winslett M., "A Framework for Comparison of Update Semantics", *Proc. 7th ACM PODS*, Austin, March 1988.

Parallel Implementations

Scheduling Or-parallelism in Aurora – the Manchester scheduler

Alan Calderwood*
Péter Szeredi[†‡]

Department of Computer Science
University of Manchester, Manchester M13 9PL, U.K.

Abstract

Aurora is a prototype or-parallel implementation of the full Prolog language for shared-memory multiprocessors. The role of the scheduler within this system is to synchronise the workers that explore the branches of the Prolog search tree in parallel and to distribute work between them. The basic philosophy behind the Manchester scheduler is to attempt to match workers with work in the best possible way, so that migration overheads can be minimalised.

The reader is first introduced to the basic notions of the SRI model used in the implementation of Aurora and to the basic principles of the Manchester scheduler. This is followed by a detailed description of the implementation issues. The data structures needed to realise the scheduling strategy are presented. The basic functions of the scheduler, i.e. those needed for pure Prolog programs, are discussed in detail. The issues of implementing cut, commit and side-effect built-in predicates are also described. Results (showing nearly linear speedups for some benchmarks) are presented and discussed. Finally, possible limitations of the current approach and directions for future work are outlined.

*Present address: Ceres Trading Systems, 90 London Road, London SE1, U.K.
[†]Present address: Department of Computer Science, University of Bristol, Bristol BS8 1TR, U.K.
[‡]On leave from SZKI, Donáti u. 35-45, Budapest, Hungary

1   Introduction

Aurora is a prototype or-parallel implementation of the full Prolog language for shared memory multiprocessors, currently running on Sequent and Encore machines. It has been developed in the framework of the Gigalips project [7], a collaborative effort between Argonne National Laboratory in Illinois, Manchester University and the Swedish Institute of Computer Science (SICS) in Stockholm. The Manchester group has recently moved to Bristol.

Aurora is based on the SRI model [9]. According to the SRI model the exploration of the Prolog search tree is done in parallel by several *workers*. Workers are abstract processing agents, currently implemented as operating system processes each running on a separate processor. Each worker uses the normal depth-first left-to-right search strategy to explore a *subtree* of the search tree by actually building it (creating choice-points during resolution) and destroying it (during backtracking). The component of a worker concerned with these actions is called the Prolog *engine*. A continuous piece of work executed by an engine is called a *task*. The other principal component of a worker is the *scheduler* which is concerned with providing the worker with a suitable task to work on, moving the worker over the tree to work, and synchronising with other workers.

One of the major issues arising in an or-parallel Prolog system is that of implementing alternative bindings to a variable. Workers exploring two branches with a common part share all the variables created on that common part and normally wish to assign different bindings to the same variable. The SRI model introduces a new data structure to support alternative bindings, the *binding array*. Each worker has its own binding array and uses it to store its bindings to shareable variables. Whenever an assignment is made to a shareable variable both its address and the value assigned are stored on the trail (similar to that in the WAM). This way the trail can be used to update a worker's binding array when it migrates over the tree, by deleting (deinstalling) bindings as it moves up the tree and adding (installing) bindings as it moves downwards. The major advantage of the SRI binding scheme is that there is only a small (constant time) overhead on accessing the value of a variable. However, when a worker moves to another part of the search tree, there may be significant overhead, which is proportional to the number of bindings recorded on the given path of movement.

The Prolog engine used in Aurora is based on SICStus Prolog version 0.3 [5]. There are three schedulers currently being designed or implemented: the Argonne scheduler [2], the Manchester scheduler and the wavefront scheduler [1]. The independent development of these schedulers was made possible by establishing a strict interface between the engine and the scheduler (cf. Sec. 4).

2 Philosophy of Manchester scheduler

Basically, the Manchester scheduler attempts to match workers with work as well as possible. At any stage of a computation one of two states may exist - either there may be insufficient work for all of the workers, resulting in some becoming idle, or there may be more work than available workers. The SRI model imposes an overhead on task switching proportional to the number of bindings to be installed/deinstalled. Thus, if a piece of work is to be made available for sharing then the idle worker which is the 'nearest' (in terms of bindings) should be given that work. Similarly, if a worker exhausts its current task then it should choose the nearest piece of shareable work.

The Argonne scheduler tries to implement this goal by a purely local strategy. Information about the availability of work is stored in the search tree itself and is used to "attract" workers without work to nodes where work is available. All workers that notice some work will migrate towards it, but only the first one to reach it will succeed in taking it. In contrast with this the Manchester scheduler makes the decision of matching the worker with work in advance, before any migration takes place. A worker looking for work will select the nearest piece of work first, reserving it for itself, and only then will start migrating towards it. A worker trying to release some work will choose the nearest idle worker and tell it to migrate to the work. Although this strategy is more complex and more difficult to implement than that used in the Argonne scheduler, we believe that it should lead to a better way of distribution of work between workers.

Both the Manchester and the Argonne schedulers follow the same fundamental despatching strategy, termed 'despatching on the topmost'. This may be regarded as a breadth-first strategy in that work may be shared only at the highest (topmost) possible point in the tree until all branches at that level have been or are currently being examined. When no more work is available for sharing at one level, work at the next level down the branches of the tree constitutes the new topmost set. Possible limitations of this strategy will be discussed later.

3 Data Structures

In the SRI model most of the main data objects are very similar to those in a sequential Prolog system such as the WAM. WAM choicepoints (which, in fact, correspond to nodes of the search tree) are expanded to include extra fields needed for or-parallel execution and are termed *nodes*. Initially, when a node is created it is *private* (i.e. not shared) and so the parallel fields need not be filled in. When a node is made *public* (i.e. accessible to all other workers), the additional data fields have to be initialised. The oldest private node on a worker's branch is termed the *sentry* node as it delimits the public/private boundary. It serves as a placeholder to maintain the correct topology of the tree and therefore requires that all of its parallel data fields be kept up to date.

A further subdivision of nodes is into *parallel* and *sequential*. In the current Aurora implementation, predicates in the Prolog source can be labelled as *sequential*, i.e. not supporting or-parallel execution. Thus when a node corresponding to a sequential predicate is made public, only one alternative from it may be executed at any one time. By default, all other predicates, and hence nodes, are parallel. A node which has alternatives remaining is termed *live*, in contrast to one which is exhausted and is hence *dead*.

The most important parallel fields in the nodes are the following:

`first_child`, `parent`, `next_sibling` - pointers describing the topology of the search tree.

`bit_map` - each bit in this field corresponds to a worker and if set to 1 indicates that the given worker is at or below that node in the tree.

`node_type` - a field containing a number of flags implemented as single bits:

- `TOPMOST` - meaning this node has no live parallel nodes above it (cf. despatching on topmost, Sec. 2),

- `CUT` - the subtree rooted upon this branch has been cut (cf. Sec. 6),

- `SUSPENDED` - the leftmost branch below this node is suspended (cf. Sec. 7).

`public_lock` - a lock associated with every public and sentry node. Locks are used here and in other data structures for synchronisation purposes.

`root_of_subtree_level` - for suspension (cf. Sec. 7)

In addition to the above information distributed in the search tree itself, the Manchester scheduler maintains two global arrays: the *worker* array and an array of *queues*, both indexed on a unique worker identifier number. The elements of the worker array store information on the workers themselves, comprising a current `sentry_node` field, a `migration_cost` field (used for idle workers and shows the number of bindings between their current node and the root), and a lockable `interrupt_message` area to allow one worker to communicate with another. The interrupt mechanism is asynchronous, so that the deposition of a message is distinct from a receiver's reading of it.

Each worker has a corresponding element in the array of queues. This contains a pointer to a *single* live `node` the worker currently has to share, an associated `lock`, a `grabbed` flag (indicating that some work has recently been taken from the node in the queue—cf. delayed re-release of work, Sec. 5.1) and a `migration_cost` field (the number of bindings between the `node` and the root). Note that the queue currently may hold only one pointer to shareable work. This restriction may be removed in future if alternative scheduling strategies are examined.

4 Interface between the scheduler and the engine

The interface consists of a set of *macros* on both the engine and scheduler side. The figure below shows the most important macros and illustrates the flow of control between the scheduler and the engine. Note that in order to simplify the presentation, not all parameters are shown — see [3] for full details.

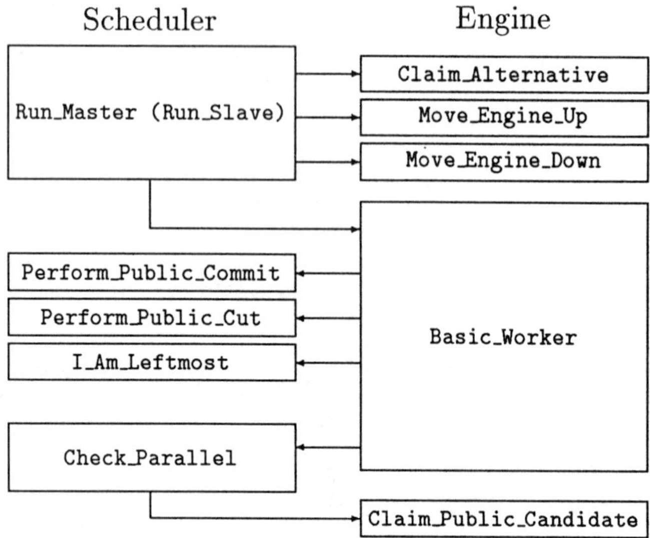

Figure: Engine/Scheduler Interface

The entry point to the scheduler is via the **Run_Master (Run_Slave)** macro. The only difference between these two macros is in the initialisation phase, thereafter both are identical. Whenever there is shareable work in the search tree (cf. sections 5.1, 5.2 and 5.3), the scheduler may call the **Claim_Alternative(WORKER,NODE,SENTRY)** macro to take an alternative from **NODE** on behalf of **WORKER** (who may be itself or an idle worker to whom the given piece of work is handed over) and to create a new sentry node **SENTRY**. The worker for whom the alternative was claimed will position itself at the appropriate node using the macros **Move_Engine_Up** and **Move_Engine_Down** (to have the engine update its binding array). Subsequently the scheduler will invoke the **Basic_Worker** macro to do actual work (i.e. Prolog execution).

Inside **Basic_Worker** the engine may invoke the scheduler to perform a cut or commit operation that affects the public part of the tree (**Perform_Public_Cut** and **Perform_Public_Commit**). In order to check if it is allowed to execute a built-in predicate with a side effect, the engine invokes **I_Am_Leftmost**. Furthermore, the engine has to check periodically if the worker has any duties concerning the parallel execution and for that reason it invokes the scheduler via the **Check_Parallel** macro. Inside this macro the scheduler checks whether the branch has been cut and also may try to extend the public part of the tree. The engine provides the `Claim_Public_Candidate` macro that can be used to determine if there are any parallel nodes in the currently private area of the worker that can be made public.

The following three sections give an outline of how the Manchester scheduler implements the scheduler side of this interface. Due to space limitations, some details (e.g. locking) are not covered (see [4] for the particulars of these).

5 Basic functions of the scheduler

There are two ways for a worker to get hold of a piece of work: another worker may *release* the work, (Sec. 5.1) or it may *grab* the work itself (Sec. 5.2). When a worker finishes working privately it has to perform *public backtracking* (Sec. 5.3). If it cannot find any work it becomes *idle* (Sec. 5.4).

5.1 Releasing work

Work at a node is released for sharing under two circumstances - either when a new node is made public, or when a currently shared, live, public node needs to be re-released (cf. delayed re-release, later in this section).

The scheduler uses the following algorithm to release work from a live *work node* to an idle worker. First it scans the array of workers determining if none, one, or more than one are idle. If no idle worker can be found, the work node address is written into the releasing worker's queue. If only one idle worker exists then the work is handed to it directly. If more than one idle worker exists then the best is chosen, as follows. The bit map of the parent of the work node is examined. If there are no idle workers in that bit map then the search continues at the next node above that whose bit map is different. This algorithm means that increasingly larger subtrees are considered for the presence of idle workers. If one is found, it is handed the work directly. If more than one is found in a subtree then the one whose migration cost is lowest is chosen.

In order to hand work to an idle worker an alternative is claimed for that worker from the work node, a sentry node is created and inserted at the right end of the sibling chain, maintaining the left-to-right ordering of the branches. Finally a HANDED_WORK interrupt is placed in the idle worker's message area, along with the address of the new sentry node.

If the alternative given to the worker were the last one then the releasing worker's queue has to be cleared and any workers in the subtree rooted upon this node should be informed that it would be appropriate to release some more nodes for sharing. This is accomplished, indirectly, by setting the TOPMOST flag in all nodes in the sibling chain (propagation of TOPMOST flags).

It is clear from the above description that if there are idle workers then choosing the best one and handing it the work is relatively expensive since the worker releasing the work is being delayed from performing its current task. For this reason the above algorithm has recently been modified so that as soon as one idle worker is found when initially scanning the worker array, it is told to perform the optimal release of work (possibly to itself).

A further idea being experimented with in the current version of the scheduler is that of delayed re-release. It is thought to be undesirable that a node being made public could result in several idle workers being handed all of the alternatives at that node in rapid succession. There is no guarantee that any of the selected clauses will be unifiable or even if they are, that they will lead to significant amounts of work. Workers will have been concentrated needlessly in one part of the tree and will tend to impede one another's actions. Delayed re-release is a simple attempt to ensure that work is shared in a controlled fashion, only being released to another idle worker when a first has established its computation at that node (reached its first invocation of the Check_Parallel macro).

5.2   Grabbing work

The scheduler attempts to grab work for its engine when it has failed to obtain any directly by public backtracking or following a suspension. The array of queues is scanned and if no work is available the worker becomes idle. If only one piece of work is found it is claimed. Where more than one queue is found to contain pointers to available work the nearest piece of work is chosen. The bit maps and queues are used in considering progressively larger subtrees and comparing migration costs, much as was described in the section on releasing work.

Grabbing an alternative involves the same sequence of events as handing an alternative to an idle worker: claiming an alternative, inserting the sentry node at the end of the sibling chain and possibly updating the queue and propagating the TOPMOST flags.

5.3 Public backtracking

Whenever the engine determines that it needs to backtrack to a node whose type is public then it regards itself as having finished its allotted task and exits to the invoking scheduler code. The scheduler sets its current node to point to the sentry node and performs public backtracking according to the following algorithm: It first removes the current node from the sibling chain, making it no longer part of the topology of the tree, but keeping its parent pointer valid. Before the scheduler can allow the node's stack space to be physically recovered it must wait until all idle workers positioned at the given node move away from it (cf. Sec. 5.4). When the bit map at the node shows no one else present, the node is marked as no longer being required, and its parent is made the new current node.

If this node is dead and has no children then the node was not being shared with another worker, so the public backtracking procedure can be repeated at the new current node. If the the current node is dead but has a child then the backtracking cannot proceed past this node and the worker will have to try to grab some work from somewhere else in the tree. Before doing so the scheduler checks if straightening can be performed: if the dead parent node has only one child now, the parent can be deleted from the topology of the tree by joining its parent and its only child with a direct parent-child link. The straightening operation has significant benefits since it simplifies and speeds up all further worker movements through the given path in the tree.

If the current node is not dead then the next alternative is claimed from it, the sentry node is inserted at the end of the sibling chain, a possible propagation of TOPMOST flags takes place and the engine is invoked with its new task.

5.4 Actions of idle workers

Despite their name, such workers are actually not inactive. An idle worker performs a number of actions inside a loop:

- If its current node is dead and has no children (which means that another worker is backtracking over the node), the idle worker moves up the tree until it finds either a live node or one with branching beneath it.

- It checks its interrupt area for a message indicating that it has been cut and must move up the tree (cf. Sec. 6), or that it has been handed some work by another worker (cf. Sec. 5.1).

- It tries to move to shadow an active (working) worker in the hope that it will release some work later on. For this purpose the bit maps in the children of the current node are used to determine whether there is an excess of active workers over idle ones in any of the subtrees rooted at these children. If this is so, the idle worker moves down one node to the child where this excess is the highest. If not, it looks up the tree and performs this check moving up one node if this will bring it closer to an unshadowed worker.

6   Cut and commit

Currently the system supports strict asymmetric cut (normal sequential Prolog semantics of cut) and cavalier symmetric cut (termed commit in the sequel) which cuts branches both to its left and right. The engine handles by itself cuts and commits which are entirely within its private region of the tree. If the node it wishes to cut to is public, however, then the appropriate scheduler macro must be used.

The scheduler is concerned with two aspects of 'cutting' to use a generic term: whether it is possible to perform the full cut, and how to perform the cut efficiently and synchronise with other concurrent cuts/commits. The first question is rather beyond the remit of this paper and is covered in detail in [6]. Basically, cavalier commits always proceed and attempt to do their full pruning of the search tree; cuts, in contrast, must be sensitive to the presence of other nested cuts of smaller scope, in which situation they may cut only the overlap of their own scope and that of the smallest nested cut.

The simplest, though by no means most efficient, way to ensure the maintenance of the cut's semantics is to require that a cut may proceed only when the branch issuing it is the leftmost at the node *beneath* the node to which it wishes to cut. Should it not be, then the execution of the cut could be suspended, which is what is currently implemented. A superior alternative would be to perform as much of the cut as possible, and then to continue with the task, having requested that the worker which prevented the completion of the full cut takes responsibility for it when appropriate.

Assuming that the cut can proceed it does so as follows. The scheduler starts processing the cut at the lowest public node and kills all of the sibling branches to its right. To kill a branch, it sets the CUT bit in the first node on that branch, reads the bit map, and interrupts the workers in the subtree one by one. It sets a MUST_DIE interrupt in each, together with the address of the parent node to which they should die back. Note that there is no need to kill all of the live nodes on a branch as the workers who have been cut handle this (see below). When all of the sibling branches have been killed, any remaining alternatives at the parent node are cleared, and the procedure continues with the next parent node, up to and including the cut node. Having processed the cut node the scheduler clears its queue and sets the TOPMOST bit in its sentry node.

A complication arises when the cutter finds that a branch it is trying to kill has an empty bit map. This can happen if each tip node in the given subtree is either suspended or some other worker is currently migrating to it (from outside the subtree). The cutter should try to clear up as much of the stack space as possible, bearing in mind that nodes to which some other worker may be migrating should not be marked as reclaimable. A simple recursive procedure, noting the presence of SUSPENDED bits handles this.

Performing a commit is almost identical to cut, the only difference being that sibling branches to the right and also those to the left of the cutter's are killed.

When a worker notices it has been killed by a cut or a commit it first clears its queue (to prevent any other workers wastefully claiming work from the queued node) and checks whether it is the only worker in the bit map of its current node. If so, it must try to reclaim all stack space at or below that node, as detailed above. If having done so it finds that its current node now has no children, (meaning that it has marked as reclaimable all of the subtree below) then it performs unconditional public backtracking. This is similar to normal public backtracking, except that no attempt is made to claim alternatives from live nodes encountered as these are now to be regarded as dead. If unconditional backtracking cannot proceed because a node is shared, then the worker switches over to simply moving upwards with no concern for reclaiming stack space. Thus the last worker out of a cut subtree has all the responsibility for space recovery. If during the backtracking a suspended branch is found to the right *or* to the left, then an attempt is made to clean up as much as possible, always bearing in mind that one or more workers may be migrating into this area.

It can be seen that cutting in the public part of the tree is a relatively expensive procedure, when it is considered that the worker doing the cutting is being held back from getting on with its task. For this reason, it is intended in future to use any available idle worker to perform the public cutting, allowing the busy worker to continue with more profitable computation.

7 Side effect predicates — suspension and resumption

One of the basic goals of the Aurora system is to implement all standard Prolog built-in predicates preserving their sequential semantics. This means that predicates with side effects should be executed in the same order as in sequential execution. Probably the only practical way to ensure this is to require the executing branch to be leftmost in the entire execution tree. This means that if a non-leftmost worker reaches a side effect predicate then the execution of the given branch should be suspended until it becomes the leftmost.

In the present system, suspension only occurs because of a cut or a side effect predicate being reached on a branch that is not the leftmost in some subtree (possibly the entire tree). This is established by scanning the tree upwards from the sentry node checking at each node on the branch whether there are any siblings to its left. If there are, then the SUSPENDED flag is set in the branch node and its `root_of_subtree_level` field is set to the level of the root of the subtree in which the worker wishes to be leftmost (to ensure the scanning can be continued properly when all the siblings to the left of the branch node cease to exist). Having completed the suspension process the worker moves out of the suspended branch and attempts to find a new task as outlined in Sec. 5.2.

Whenever a worker backtracks to a public node the scheduler checks whether its right sibling (if one exists) has a SUSPENDED bit set. If the suspended branch will now become leftmost (the backtracking worker has no siblings to its left) then the worker must check whether resumption is appropriate. It clears the `SUSPENDED` bit, reads the `root_of_subtree_level` field and continues the leftmost test, setting the `SUSPENDED` flag further up the tree if necessary. If, however, the suspended branch is found to be leftmost in its subtree then the backtracking worker resumes it. To do this, the worker moves down to the tip of the suspended branch, making all nodes public on the way (this is a requirement of the current Aurora engine). It sets the sentry node to be the tip node and invokes the engine. Resumption complicates slightly the release of work from the topmost node since the topmost node and the sentry node may not be adjacent now. The current implementation handles this.

8 Results

The following results were obtained on a Sequent Balance 8000 machine with 12 processors and 8 Mbytes of memory. The benchmarks used were `parse1` – `parse5`, natural language parsing parts of Chat-80 queries; `db4` and `db5`, the data base searching part of the fourth and fifth Chat-80 query; `house`, the "who owns the zebra" puzzle from ECRC; `8_queens2`, the naive (generate and test) version of the 8 queens problem from ECRC; `tina`, a holiday planning program from ECRC; `salt_mustard`, the "salt and mustard" puzzle from Argonne. These benchmarks are described in [8] along with more complete results. All of the programs were run using the `nopff` (no Page Fault Frequency adjustments) command to minimise page faulting. The run times given are the shortest obtained from several runs. Times (in seconds) are shown for 1, 4 and 8 workers with speedups given in italics after the times. For comparison, the results from both the Manchester scheduler (Table 1) and the Argonne scheduler (Table 2) are presented here.

Goal [*repetitions]	Workers		
	1	4	8
parse1 *20	11.33	4.33 *(2.61)*	3.95 *(2.86)*
parse2 *20	41.98	13.69 *(3.06)*	10.35 *(4.05)*
parse3 *20	9.68	4.00 *(2.42)*	3.69 *(2.62)*
parse4 *5	38.83	11.17 *(3.47)*	7.63 *(5.09)*
parse5	27.33	7.66 *(3.56)*	5.16 *(5.29)*
db4 *10	14.64	4.16 *(3.52)*	2.49 *(5.87)*
db5 *10	17.72	4.91 *(3.60)*	2.98 *(5.94)*
house *20	35.71	10.41 *(3.43)*	6.60 *(5.40)*
8-queens2	132.06	33.48 *(3.94)*	17.17 *(7.69)*
tina	101.23	26.03 *(3.88)*	14.05 *(7.20)*
salt-mustard	15.98	4.13 *(3.87)*	2.15 *(7.43)*

Table 1: Run times with the Manchester scheduler

Goal [*repetitions]	Workers		
	1	4	8
parse1 *20	11.10	4.39 *(2.53)*	4.78 *(2.32)*
parse2 *20	40.84	14.80 *(2.76)*	12.44 *(3.28)*
parse3 *20	9.49	4.51 *(2.10)*	4.32 *(2.19)*
parse4 *5	37.73	11.64 *(3.24)*	8.94 *(4.22)*
parse5	26.55	8.72 *(3.04)*	5.79 *(4.58)*
db4 *10	14.21	6.01 *(2.36)*	3.38 *(4.19)*
db5 *10	17.25	5.88 *(2.93)*	4.73 *(3.64)*
house *20	35.24	10.64 *(3.31)*	6.69 *(5.26)*
8-queens2	128.45	32.62 *(3.93)*	16.72 *(7.68)*
tina	98.13	25.50 *(3.84)*	13.50 *(7.26)*
salt-mustard	15.02	3.91 *(3.84)*	2.11 *(7.11)*

Table 2: Run times with the Argonne scheduler

It can be seen that both schedulers in their current, untuned states are capable of achieving reasonable speed-ups with 8 workers except for the first three parsing benchmarks (which are characterised by very fine grain parallelism, [8]). Note that the Manchester scheduler is slightly slower for one worker, perhaps because it employs more complex algorithms inside the **Check_Parallel** macro. In spite of this overhead, it runs significantly faster with 8 workers for problems with fine to medium grain parallelism (the first 8 rows of the table) while it is slightly slower for those problems distinguished by larger grain parallelism (the last three rows).

9 Discussion

The results presented show that the Manchester scheduler performs its tasks well, in particular extracting the parallelism from relatively fine grain problems significantly better than the Argonne scheduler.

It seems likely that the relatively simple-minded despatching on topmost strategy used in both schedulers may be sub-optimal for certain types of computation. Currently work can be shared only at the topmost node on a branch, and thus only when that node is fully exhausted may work be shared at the next appropriate node down each branch. This may be regarded as a breadth first scheduling strategy. However, if we have a program which requires the first solution from some search space, indicated by the presence of a large scope cut, then much of the work performed in breadth first or-parallel may not have been performed in the sequential execution of the same program. All parts of the search tree to the right of a branch which will issue a cut represent wasted work for an or-parallel system. In general, a procedure containing cuts will have a cut on all but the last clause, and therefore the further a branch is to the right in the search tree rooted upon that predicate's node the more likely it is to be cut at some point - the work becomes more speculative. It would therefore seem preferable in the scope of a cut to be able to abandon the dispatching on the topmost rule and be able concentrate workers to the left of the tree. Of course, if the cut does not encompass all of the search tree, then those parts which are outside of the scope of a cut are always preferable to those within.

The scheduling strategy may be made as complex as one wishes, for example using information from compilation and runtime profiling as input to some form of strategy module, but the main implication for the writer of the scheduler is the need to provide a completely general suspension and resumption mechanism. It would now seem necessary to be able to bring arbitrary amounts of work to the attention of all workers so that they may choose the best. The direct connection between shareable work and the worker who owns it is broken, rendering the continued use of bit maps and queues difficult at best. It seems likely that if such flexible scheduling strategies are worth employing (something yet to be proved) then a completely flexible method of publicising work available for sharing or resumption will be required. The approach expounded in this paper, whereby the closest piece of work or idle worker is chosen at a distance, would probably still be used. An obvious way of achieving these goals is to use a single linked list of work rather than queues. Idle workers would probably have to be linked into this as would all workers which did not have work currently to share - some form of placeholder would be required in order to maintain the ordering of individual workers in the tree. A scheduler using such a dynamic work data structure, the *wavefront*, has been proposed and is currently being implemented at SICS [1].

10   Conclusions

The philosophy and implementation of the Manchester scheduler have been described and the preliminary results seem very encouraging. It is intended that the suggestions for improvements made in this text will be implemented and some care taken to tune the system. The implementation of some simple form of suspension of speculative work will also be examined. It is too early to say whether much more general suspension and the inclusion in the scheduler of some form of dynamic strategy module will be worth the effort required. Such matters will be investigated, and to aid experimentation it may be useful to replace the queue mechanism with a more flexible work list scheme, whilst maintaining the greater part of the implementation.

11 Acknowledgements

The authors would like to thank their colleagues in the Gigalips project at Argonne National Laboratory, the Swedish Institute of Computer Science, and the University of Manchester. Thanks are due in particular to David Warren and Ross Overbeek.

The work was supported by the UK Science and Engineering Research Council.

References

[1] P. Brand. *The Wavefront scheduler.* Internal Report, Gigalips Project, 1988.

[2] R. Butler,T. Disz,E. L. Lusk,R. Overbeek and R. Stevens. *Scheduling OR-parallelism: an Argonne perspective.* In *Logic Programming, Proceedings of the Fifth International Conference and Symposium on Logic Programming, Seattle,* pages 1590–1605, MIT Press, 1988

[3] A. Calderwood. *Aurora – Description of Interfaces.* Internal Report, Gigalips Project, 1988.

[4] A. Calderwood. *Aurora – the Manchester scheduler.* Internal Report, Gigalips Project, 1988.

[5] M. Carlsson. Internals of SICStus Prolog version 0.6. Internal Report, Gigalips Project, 1987.

[6] B. Hausman, A. Ciepielewski and A. Calderwood. *Cut, commit and side effects in or-parallel Prolog. Proceedings of the FGCS '88 Conference,* ICOT, 1988.

[7] E. Lusk *et al.*, D. H. D. Warren *et al.*, S. Haridi *et al. The Aurora Or-Parallel Prolog System. Proceedings of the FGCS '88 Conference,* ICOT, 1988.

[8] P. Szeredi. *Performance Analysis of the Aurora Or-Parallel Prolog System.* Internal Report, Gigalips Project, 1989.

[9] D. H. D. Warren. The SRI Model for Or-Parallel Execution of Prolog. In *Proceedings of the 1987 Symposium on Logic Programming, San Francisco, California,* pages 92–102, IEEE, 1987.

Distributed Implementation of KL1 on the Multi-PSI/V2

Katsuto Nakajima

Yū Inamura   Nobuyuki Ichiyoshi

Kazuaki Rokusawa   Takashi Chikayama

Institute for New Generation Computer Technology

Abstract

KL1 is a stream AND-parallel logic programming language based on Flat GHC. This paper describes the implementation issues of a parallel KL1 system. The target machine of this system is a non-shared memory multi-processor, Multi-PSI/V2, in which up to 64 processing elements (PEs) are connected by a message passing network. The key issues are: (1) how to achieve efficient intra-PE and inter-PE garbage collection, (2) how to avoid making redundant copies of data objects over many processors, and (3) how to reduce the amount of inter-PE communication.

The well-defined semantics of KL1 allows incremental intra-PE garbage collection by the Multiple Reference Bit (MRB) technique and incremental inter-PE incremental garbage collection by the Weighted Export Counting (WEC) technique. We introduced a global structure management mechanism to avoid making duplicate copies of large data objects. Program codes are distributed and managed by this scheme. The communication required for inter-PE process control is minimized by the Weighted Throw Counting (WTC) scheme.

The implementation has been completed, the system is being used to research parallel software, and we are evaluating the performance for refining it and also for designing the future system, the parallel inference machine (PIM).

1   Introduction

The target of the Japanese fifth generation computer project is to build a parallel inference machine (PIM) [Goto 88], for running large-scale logic based programs. It aims to achieve hundreds of times the performance of the present computer systems by parallel processing. In the initial stage of the project, we realized that research in parallel software is important for designing a highly parallel inference architecture, because the architecture is influenced by the nature of application programs and little was known about it. The problem was that no machine existed that had the capability of running parallel application programs of a realistic size. The Multi-PSI machine was developed to fill this gap [Taki 88]. It also serves as a workbench for evaluating various new implementation techniques.

The Multi-PSI is a non-shared memory multi-processor, whose processing elements (PEs) are the CPUs of the personal sequential inference (PSI) machine, which are readily available. The Multi-PSI/V1 used the first version of the PSI as PEs, and the new Multi-PSI/V2 uses the more compact and faster version, PSI-II [Nakashima 87] as PEs. PEs (up to six in the Multi-PSI/V1 and up to 64 in the Multi-PSI/V2) are connected to each other to form a two-dimensional mesh network with message switching and automatic routing capabilities.

Our final target machine, the PIM, has a two-level architecture: the higher level is a network-connected multi-cluster architecture to make the system scalable, and the lower level is a shared memory multi-processor to build a high-performance cluster. As a PE in the Multi-PSI corresponds to a cluster in the PIM, the research of the language implementation on the Multi-PSI has been conducted to find the problems related especially to the inter-cluster processing and to employ various mechanisms to try to solve them.

After we developed a distributed implementation of the KL1 (Kernel Language Version 1), which is an AND-parallel logic programming language, on the Multi-PSI/V1 [Ichiyoshi 87], we continued with our research in efficient implementation, and came up with an improved implementation on the Multi-PSI/V2.

This paper describes the problems we faced in designing our KL1 implementation, presents the way we tried to solved these problems, and reports on the current status and the remaining problems.

2 KL1 Features and Implementation Issues

2.1 KL1 (Kernel Language Version 1)

KL1 (kernel language version 1) is a stream AND-parallel logic programming language based on Flat GHC. A KL1 program is made up of a collection of guarded horn clauses, whose form is:

$$\underbrace{H :- G_1, \ldots, G_m}_{\text{guard}} | \underbrace{B_1, \ldots, B_n}_{\text{body}}. \ (m > 0,\ n > 0)$$

where H is called the *head*, G_i the *guard goals*, and B_i the *body goals*. The vertical bar (|) is called the *commitment operator*. The logical reading of the clauses is the same as GHC [Ueda 86].

KL1 is provided with the following meta-programming functions so that it becomes a practical and efficient parallel language for describing not only application programs but also operating systems.

(1) Shōen mechanism: A shōen is a meta-logical unit to control and monitor the KL1 goals in it. It has a pair of streams, named the *control stream* and *report stream*. The control stream is used to start, stop or abort the goals from outside the shōen. Termination of all goals or events that occurred inside a shōen, such as a failure or an exception, are reported on the report stream from inside the shōen. Shōen can be nested to form a tree-like structure (shōen tree) whose leaves are KL1 goals.

(2) Resource management: The system should be safe from a user goal that wastefully runs such as an erroneous infinite loop. The shōen must be given resource for the execution through the control stream. The resource shortage is reported on the report stream.

(3) Priority pragma $(\ldots, B@priority(Prio), \ldots)$: Scheduling by using *priority* contributes to efficient problem solving. The shōen has a priority range and each goal inside it can have an individual priority within this range. The priority is specified by a priority pragma with a relative value in the allowed range.

(4) Throw goal pragma $(\ldots, B@processor(PE), \ldots)$: A throw goal pragma in the source program denotes load distribution. It also contributes to efficient execution on a multi-processor machine.

2.2 Implementation Issues for KL1

To execute KL1 on the network connected parallel machine, the following points should be kept in mind in designing the system.

2.2.1 Garbage Collection

As goals are not executed in a last-in-first-out manner, the stack mechanism used in most Prolog implementations is not suitable for a KL1 implementation. Therefore, heap-based memory management must be used for flexible memory use, although memory reclamation is generally inefficient with this scheme. The time spent in garbage collection (GC) may seriously affect the system performance. On a non-shared memory multi-processor, the degradation by GC should be considered more seriously, because naïve inter-PE GC might take time proportional to the length of the reference chains over many processors. Implementing low-cost incremental GC for inter-PE and intra-PE data is one of our major targets because incremental GC is better than non-incremental one in terms of the access locality, which leads to, for example, a good cache hit ratio.

2.2.2 Data Management

KL1 has a property where data objects that have been instantiated once can be copied, while keeping the program logic. To allow local access, data shared by PEs should be copied. However, uncontrolled copying leads to unnecessary data transfer.

2.2.3 Message Communication

Message passing communication is more expensive than communication on a shared memory. The communication delay is also large. We have to pay attention to reduce the amount of inter-PE communication and to maintain quick responses.

3 KL1-B and Its Implementation

3.1 Execution Model

KL1 programs are compiled into the sequence of a WAM-like abstract machine instruction set, KL1-B [Kimura 87]. It is a register-based in-

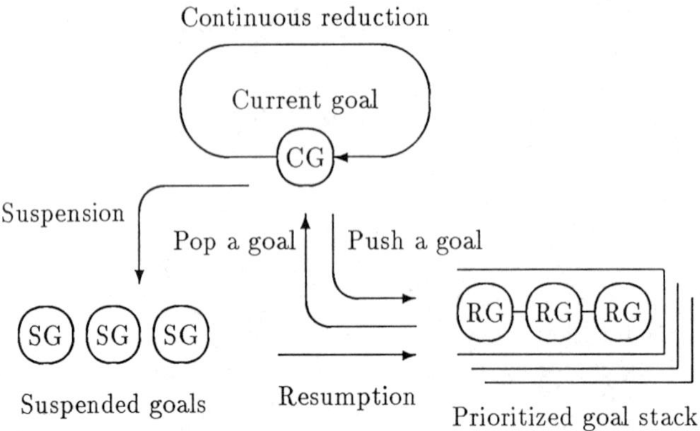

Figure 1: Goal State Transition

struction set and serves as an efficient interface between the language and machine architecture.

Goals in a PE are categorized as: (1) *ready goals* which are waiting for execution, (2) *current goal* which is being executed, or (3) *suspended goals* which are hooked on variables to be instantiated (Figure 1).

A reduction cycle is as follows. When a current goal calls a predicate, the guard parts of the clauses for the predicate are tried one by one. If no clause commits and at least one clause is suspended, the goal is hooked to the variable(s) that caused the suspension. If no clause commits and there is no suspended clause, a *failure* is reported on the report stream of the parent shōen with the goal information. In both cases, another goal is popped from the goal stack to be evaluated. If one of the clauses commits, all the body goals except for the leftmost one in the source code are pushed to the goal stacks according to the priority pragmas attached to the goals. The leftmost goal is chosen as the next one to be evaluated unless the goal stack of the higher priority has a goal. When a clause without body goals commits, another goal is popped from the current goal stack.

Every reduction cycle, request for (non-incremental) GC and message arrivals from the network are checked, and processed if necessary. This timing, called the *slit check*, is most suitable for switching the process because the PE is free from goal contexts.

3.2   Executing KL1-B

The KL1-B instructions, including some tens of instructions for built-in predicates, are directly interpreted by the microcode to attain a high execution speed as a practical tool for software research.

The microcode of the PE can perform various functions in parallel, such as tag insertion, two-way or multi-way branching on a tag, specially prepared counter and flag operation, ALU operation and memory access operation. The arguments for the unification are fetched on the registers every reduction cycle. Control information, such as the priority and the shōen resource, is cached on the registers as long as the execution context remains unchanged.

3.3   Goal Stack

Strict scheduling with priority can be managed by having only one prioritized goal stack in the system. However, the access contention on such a global resource leads to serious performance degradation. To avoid this, every processor has a prioritized goal stack, at the sacrifice of scheduling strictness. In our experience, local goal stack management is realistic and efficient enough to control the execution in the system in most cases. However, the maldistribution of high priority goals over PEs is possible and problematic, and needs to be solved by dynamic load balancing that we have not implemented yet.

3.4   Memory Management

As stated in 2.2.1, efficient GC is vital in a KL1 implementation. We have developed the MRB technique [Chikayama 87] for intra-PE incremental GC. In this scheme, the pointer has one-bit information to indicate whether it is the only pointer to the referenced data. Even with the one-bit counter, more than 60% of the garbage cells are collected in various benchmark programs in our evaluation. Collected cells are linked in the free lists to be reused. We have several individual free lists for records of various sizes[1].

When records in a free list are exhausted, a pre-determined number of new records are created on the heap top and linked to the free list. In our current implementation, fragmentation among the free lists is resolved only by local (non-incremental) GC because, though records in

---

[1]In the current implementation, the sizes are from 1 to 8, 16, 32, 64, 128 and 256. A record over 256 words is allocated on the heap top.

a long free list can be split and used as smaller pieces, they cannot be used for larger records. Free list handling operation is too frequent to employ fragment reconstruction techniques such as the buddy system [Knowlton 65].

4   Inter-PE Processing

Goals with throw goal pragmas are distributed by throw_goal messages over many processors. Distributed goals communicate with each other through the shared variables by read or unify messages. This section discusses how the shared data is accessed from outside the PE, and how the distributed goals are monitored or controlled in these situations.

4.1   Inter-PE Data Management

4.1.1   Copying Shared Data

When a goal is thrown to another PE, its arguments are also carried with it. If the argument is an atomic value, the value itself is sent with the goal. If it is an unbound variable, a pointer to the variable is created and carried. For a structure argument, there are three reasonable choices. One is to create and carry a pointer to the structure (0-level copying). The contents are read when they are actually used in a unification. The second is to copy all the elements of the structure including all nested substructures (infinite-level copying). The third is to copy all the elements at the surface level (1-level copying).

In a distributed system like the Multi-PSI where the cost of the inter-PE reference is relatively high, it is better to copy data for later accesses in many cases. However, an infinite-level copying may cause unnecessary duplication because the passive or active unification for the structure might fail at any level in the destination PE.

Following the policy of *on-demand* copying, we chose 0-level copying for the arguments of thrown goals and 1-level copying for those of unifications. It is one of the design decisions to be evaluated. At least, if it is known that the element of a structure will be read sooner or later (such as the tail of a stream), it is better to copy the elements at one time as long as they are bound to a value. This is left as a future optimization.

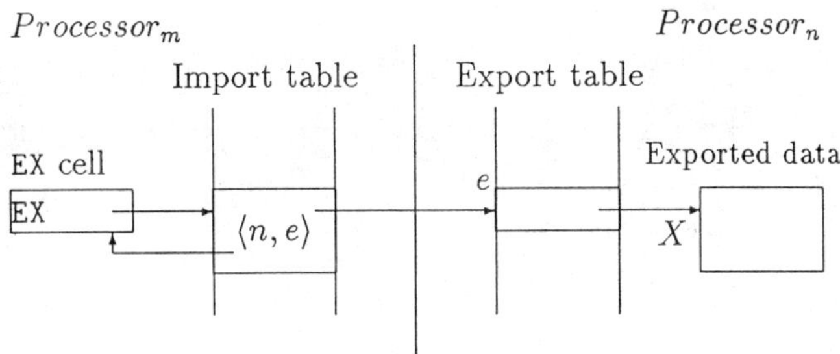

Figure 2: Export Table and Import Table

4.1.2 Export and Import Tables

When a PE exhausts its heap memory, garbage must be collected. If
the PE does not know whether a cell is referenced from other PEs or
whether it is garbage, the PE cannot perform GC for its memory without cooperation by all PEs. Global GC, where all PEs perform GC
at one time by exchanging marking messages and indicating the movements of object cells [Ali 86], can be a solution, but it is expected to be
very time consuming.

In a large scale non-shared memory multi-processor, local GC, where
the PE performs GC alone for its memory when exhausted, is desirable
in terms of the system performance. It is possible if the object cells
referenced from outside are represented by a kind of global ID for the
external PEs. The garbage collecting PE need only maintain the translation table according to the local object movements in local GC. The
table is called the *export table* (Figure 2). The object cells referenced
from the external PEs are said to be *exported*, and on the referencing
side, they are said to be *imported*. The global ID is represented in the
form $< pe, entry >$, where pe is a PE number and *entry* is the entry
position of the export table. The global ID is called the *external ID*.

4.1.3 Incremental Inter-PE GC by Weighted Export Count-
ing

To reclaim the garbage cells pointed to by the export table, the entries
of the table must be collected when they become garbage. We employed the weighted export counting (WEC) method [Ichiyoshi 88] to
perform inter-PE incremental GC. This scheme is based on the weighted
reference counting (WRC) principle [Watson 87] and has the following
features.

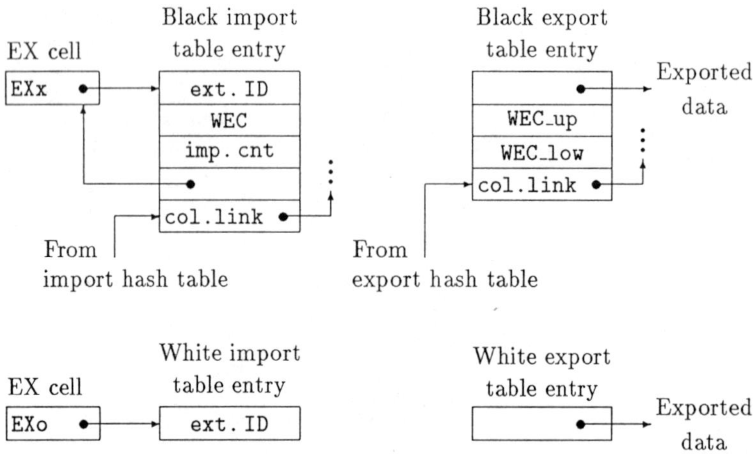

Figure 3: Export and Import Table Entries

- When an importing pointer is copied in the importing PE, its weight is split and no message is sent to the exporting PE to maintain the reference count.

- No racing occurs in terms of count (weight) zero checking at the exporting PE.

An integer representing a WEC value is attached to an exported pointer and is stored in the *import table entry* (Figure 3). Each entry for the imported pointers accumulates a WEC when the same pointer is imported again. The number of imports, the *import count*, is also counted. When the contents of the imported pointer are no longer needed, a `release` message is sent to the exporting PE to return the amount of the WEC. A `release` message is sent when: (1) an instantiated value is returned by an `answer_value` message in response to a `read` message, (2) the import count reaches zero by incremental GC by using the MRB mechanism, or (3) an imported pointer is known to be garbage after a local GC in the importing PE (see 4.1.6).

When an export entry receives a `release` message, the WEC in the entry is maintained. If it becomes zero, the entry is reclaimed. In this case, the exported object cell itself may also be reclaimed when the export table entry is known to be the single reference to the cell by the MRB mechanism.

4.1.4   Re-exporting

The same variable may be exported to the same PE. If the re-exported reference to a variable is given with a different external ID, it cannot be determined as a variable that was originally the same. Therefore, the importing PE may send `read` messages twice, and if the object is a structure data, it is brought twice by `answer_value`. This can be avoided by reusing the same export and import table entries. For this purpose, the *export hash table* and *import hash table* are provided on each side. The export hash table associates the exported object addresses with their external IDs, and the import hash table associates the imported external IDs and the import table entry.

4.1.5   White and Black Exports

Our external reference management with WEC has overhead in terms of maintaining both the WEC and import count, and of looking up the hash table to check the re-exporting. Fortunately, the MRB mechanism can be used to optimize them. To export a single reference pointer at a low cost, a simplified pair of export and import tables, called *white export* and *white import tables*, are used (Figure 3). The original tables are called the *black export* and *black import tables*. From our observation, pointers duplicated once will often be copied again later. In contrast, a single reference pointer is not likely to be duplicated after being exported. Thus, the white export and import tables do not have hash tables because the exported pointers are rarely exported again for the same reason.

The white import table can be considered as an import table for the pointers whose WEC and import count equals one, and its entries are released immediately when the imported pointers are collected by MRB GC[2]. Their white export entries are also released only when the `release` message is received. The effectiveness of this optimization depends heavily on the programs; however, the average characteristics are expected to be similar to that of MRB inside a PE.

4.1.6   Local Garbage Collection

The current implementation of local GC is based on the conventional copying GC scheme. The garbage collector moves all data cells reachable from the prioritized goal stacks and the export tables to a new heap area.

---

[2]If an imported pointer is copied, the MRB of both pointers is turned on so that the import table entry is not released when one of the pointers becomes garbage.

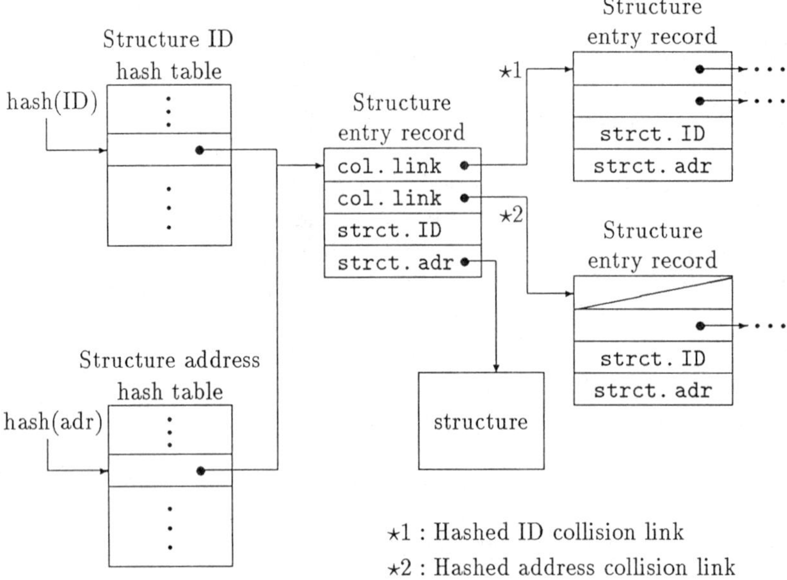

Figure 4: Structure Entry Records and Hash Tables

After copying, valid entries in the import tables are swept. If unmarked entries are found, **release** messages are sent to the exporting PEs to return their WECs.

The time spent in local GC can be a big factor in the total performance because PEs requesting a response from the garbage collecting PE have to wait for its termination[3]. One solution to improve the GC time is *generation GC* [Lieberman 83][Nakajima 88], which avoids moving long life objects at every GC. This is an on-going study.

4.1.7 Global Structure Management

In our export system, the external ID originates from the exporting PE. For example, if PE_B has a copy of the structure in PE_A, and PE_C has external references to both the original structure in PE_A and the copy in PE_B, their external IDs are not the same. PE_C will have two copies after reading them. If the structure is big and will live long, it

---

[3]Messages sent to the garbage collecting PE are buffered in the reserved memory area by the PE.

is inefficient in terms of both the memory space and the data transfer overhead. In the worst case, copies are created at each imports if a pair of mutually linked structures are read alternately along the loop.

To solve this problem, we introduced the *structure ID* for such structures, which is a global ID attached to an instantiated structure. By using this, what was originally the same structure is duplicated at most once in a PE even if it is imported from different PEs more than once.

When a `read` message is sent to a PE for a structure with a structure ID, only the ID is returned in the `answer_value` message. If the PE requesting `read` receives only the ID, it looks up the *structure ID hash table* (Figure 4) with the returned ID to search for the structure address if the PE already has the structure. If it is not found, a `read` message is sent again to copy it. Another hash table, the *structure address hash table*, is used to get the structure ID from the structure address when the PE returns the ID instead of the structure itself in the `answer_value` message.

The global structure management mechanism is used for the program code, because code pieces in a program are connected to each other and references to the same code piece can be imported from various PEs. The problem in this scheme is the collection of the garbage ID, which needs a kind of global GC scheme, and is left for future research.

4.1.8   Program Code Management

KL1 programs are described as a collection of *modules* which may contain several KL1 predicates. A module is the unit of compilation and is also used as the unit of code distribution to each PE. The predicate calls within a module are represented by relative pointers because they are constants in the module and are easy to move in local GC or to send to other PEs. Only the inter-module predicate calls use absolute address pointers which require address maintenance in data transfer. Absolute address pointers in a module are gathered at the top region in the module as an optimization in local GC. They must be swept in local GC. The rest (and the greater part) of the module, however, contains only atomic data, that is, KL1-B instructions (with the relative address operand, if necessary) and their full word constant operands following the instructions, and they need not be swept in GC.

On a loosely coupled multi-processor with many PEs, an on-demand loading mechanism for the program code is essential to save the memory area in the system. The following is how it is realized.

When a goal is thrown to another PE, the code address for the goal

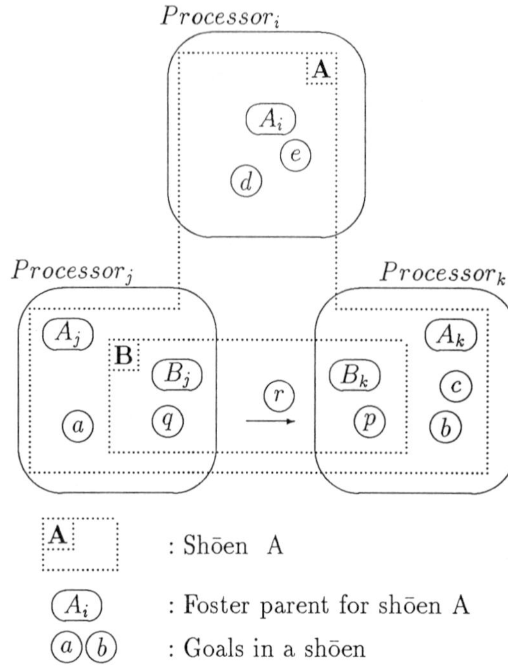

Figure 5: Shōen and Foster Parents

is encoded as a tuple of $<module,\ offset,\ structure\ ID>$, where *module* is an external reference to the code module in the exporting PE, and *offset* is the code location in the module. *Structure ID* is the global identification for the module. On the receiving side, *structure ID* is checked to see whether the received PE has the same ID or not by searching the structure ID hash table. If it has, *module* is translated to the module that it has, and the code address is calculated with *offset*. If it does not have the module, a variable is created and the received goal is hooked to wait for the module. A `read` message is sent to the exporting PE with the *structure ID*. When the exporting PE answers the `read`, the surface level (1-level) is encoded and the absolute addresses pointing to other modules in the PE are encoded as external references in the `answer_value`. When the `answer_value` message arrives, the variable on which the thrown goal is hooked is instantiated by the module and the goal is resumed.

4.2   Goal Control by Shōen and Foster Parent

A shōen and the goals belonging to it (*child goals*) must communicate to perform the execution control from the shōen, such as stopping and abortion, and to receive the report from the child goals, such as goal termination and resource shortage. To reduce the message traffic towards a shōen, we can employ a cache technique. When a goal is moved from the shōen PE (the PE that contains the shōen) to another, a *foster parent* is created on the PE to which the goal migrated [Ichiyoshi 87]. Only one foster parent is created for the shōen on each PE which has goals belonging to the shōen (Figure 5).

The foster parents have the *shōen status* (*running, stopped or aborted*), the *child count* (the number of child goals created on the PE), and the cached resource information of the shōen. Goal termination is checked at the shōen only when one of the foster parents sends a `terminated` message to report that its child count has reached zero.

The termination detection is one of the difficult problems in parallel computation systems, especially when messages may be in transit on the network as in the Multi-PSI. Even if all the foster parents report termination, the shōen is not necessarily terminated, because there are goals in transit.

Our solution for it is the weighted throw counting (WTC) scheme, which is, like the WEC scheme, an application of the WRC scheme. In this scheme, each shōen manages the amount of the count. The WTC is attached to a thrown goal or a `unify` message, and the foster parents accumulate WTC on receiving the messages. Foster parents can split it when they throw child goals. When all the goals in a foster parent terminate, the amount of WTC kept by the foster parent is returned to the shōen. The shōen can determine the true termination of the child goals when all WTC is returned.

For a full description of the WTC scheme, see [Rokusawa 88].

5   Conclusions and Future Works

This paper discussed the issues of implementing KL1 on a loosely coupled multi-processor, and described our decisions and the implementations on the Multi-PSI/V2. The major problems not discussed here are free list fragmentation, export/import table overflow, collection of the structure ID, and global GC or synchronized local GC.

The parallel operating system, *PIMOS* [Chikayama 88], and several application programs are now running on the Multi-PSI/V2. The peak performance on a single PE is 147 K reductions/sec for KL1 append (6.8μsec/reduction). The typical cost of throwing a goal is about 85μsec, and that of receiving is about 130μsec.

The system performance with large programs are being measured. We also have plans to evaluate the effectiveness of the various ideas in this implementation, such as white export and white import tables, global structure management, and incremental intra- and inter-PE garbage collection by MRB and WEC.

We want to extend this research to *load balancing*, one of the major topics in parallel processing. Currently, we are interested in: (1) defining the load, taking account of the priorities as well as the number of executable goals in a PE, and (2) coordinating the load locally by using only local information. The P^3 (processing power plane) scheme [Takeda 88] is a candidate for the load balancing mechanism on a scalable multi-processor system like the Multi-PSI.

Acknowledgments

We would like to thank the ICOT Director, Dr. K. Fuchi, and the chief of the fourth research laboratory, Dr. S. Uchida, for giving us the opportunity to conduct this research. We would also like to thank the researchers of ICOT and the cooperating companies, who have worked with us in designing and implementing the KL1 system on the Multi-PSI/V2.

References

[Ali 86] K. A. M. Ali and S. Haridi. Global Garbage Collection for Distributed Heap Storage Systems. International Journal of Parallel Programming, 15(5): 1986.

[Chikayama 87] T. Chikayama and Y. Kimura. Multiple Reference Management in Flat GHC. In *Proceedings of the Fourth International Conference on Logic Programming*, 1987.

[Chikayama 88] T. Chikayama, H. Sato and T. Miyazaki. Overview of the Parallel Inference Machine Operating System (PIMOS). In *Proceedings of the International Conference on Fifth Generation Computer Systems*, ICOT, Tokyo, 1988.

[Goto 88] A. Goto, M. Sato, K. Nakajima, K. Taki and A. Matsumoto. Overview of the Parallel Inference Machine Architecture (PIM). In *Proceedings of the International Conference on Fifth Generation Computer Systems*, ICOT, Tokyo, 1988.

[Ichiyoshi 87] N. Ichiyoshi, T. Miyazaki, and K. Taki. A Distributed Implementation of Flat GHC on the Multi-PSI. In *Proceedings of the Fourth International Conference on Logic Programming*, 1987.

[Ichiyoshi 88] N. Ichiyoshi, K. Rokusawa, K. Nakajima and Y. Inamura. A New External Reference Management and Distributed Unification for KL1. In *Proceedings of the International Conference on Fifth Generation Computer Systems*, ICOT, Tokyo, 1988.

[Kimura 87] Y. Kimura and T. Chikayama. An Abstract KL1 Machine and Its Instruction Set. In *Proceedings of 1987 Symposium on Logic Programming*, Sept. 1987.

[Knowlton 65] K. C. Knowlton. A Fast Storage Allocator. Commun. ACM, 8(10): 1965.

[Lieberman 83] H. Lieberman and C. Hewitt. A Real-Time Garbage Collector Based on the Lifetimes of Objects. Commun. ACM, 26(6): 1983.

[Nakajima 88] K. Nakajima. Piling GC — Efficient Garbage Collection for AI Languages. In *Proceeding of the IFIP WG 10.3 Working Conference on Parallel Processing*, 1988.

[Nakashima 87] H. Nakashima and K. Nakajima. Hardware Architecture of the Sequential Inference Machine : PSI-II. In *Proceedings of 1987 Symposium on Logic Programming*, Sept. 1987.

[Rokusawa 88] K. Rokusawa, N. Ichiyoshi, T. Chikayama, and H. Nakashima. An Efficient Termination Detection and Abortion Algorithm for Distributed Processing Systems. In *Proceedings of the 1988 International Conference on Parallel Processing*, Vol. I, 1988.

[Takeda 88] Y. Takeda, H. Nakashima, K. Masuda, T. Chikayama and K. Taki. A Load Balancing Mechanism for Large Scale Multiprocessor Systems and its Implementation. In *Proceedings of the International Conference on Fifth Generation Computer Systems*, ICOT, Tokyo, 1988.

[Taki 88] K. Taki. The Parallel Software Research and Development Tool: Multi-PSI system. Programming of Future Generation Computers, Elsevier Science Publishers B.V. (North-Holland), 1988.

[Ueda 86] K. Ueda. Guarded Horn Clauses: A Parallel Logic Programming Language with the Concept of a Guard. Technical Report TR-208, ICOT, 1986.

[Watson 87] P. Watson and I. Watson. An Efficient Garbage Collection Scheme for Parallel Computer Architectures. In *Proceedings of Parallel Architectures and Languages Europe*, June 1987.

A Performance Comparison of AND- and OR-Parallel Logic Programming Architectures

E. Tick

Institute for New Generation Computer Technology

Abstract

This paper details a performance comparison between KL1, a byte-code architecture for Flat Guarded Horn Clauses (FGHC) and Aurora, a byte-code architecture for Or-parallel Prolog. The architectures were measured executing a set of equivalent benchmarks. Timing emulators were used to measure raw execution speed to determine relative performances and speedups. Instrumented (high-level) emulators were used to measure gross characteristics of the benchmarks, such as number of procedures calls. Instrumented (low-level) emulators were used to measure detailed characteristics of memory referencing and coherent cache performance. The results of this study indicate that many problems are well-suited to Prolog's powerful unification and backtracking mechanism; however, Aurora is limited at the algorithm level by the primary weakness of OR-parallel search: that processes cannot communicate. On the other hand, most problems can exploit dependent AND-parallelism more easily than OR-parallelism, but the inefficiencies of the KL1 model (no backtracking, excessive use of memory) often overshadow the benefits of parallelism. There are a class of problems that perform equally well on both architectures and classes of problems that favor one or the other of the architectures. These results indicate that a high-performance system should have backtracking and full unification as well as dependent AND-parallelism.

1   Introduction

> " 'These suckers are all written in hexadecimal, see, 'cause the industry
> programmers are all washed-out computer hacks. That's how they think. But let
> me...run a few changes on it, translate it into a modern wetlanguage.' "
> Dogfight
> M. Swanwick and W. Gibson [5]

This paper compares the design and execution performance of Aurora [8] and KL1-B (called KL1 here) [7, 13], two parallel logic programming architectures which have been implemented on shared-memory multiprocessors. Aurora is an OR-parallel Prolog system retaining the full semantics of Horn Clause logic. KL1 is an AND-parallel FGHC system that is a committed-choice architecture. High-level analyses of these systems have been published [3, 1, 13, 12], but no low-level or comparative analysis, as presented here. This paper summarizes a portion of Tick[16], and all caveats, detailed descriptions, raw data, source listings, etc. can be found in that work.

A high-performance programming system enables the development of powerful (parallel, memory efficient, declarative, fast) algorithms, as well as the efficient execution of the architecture. The former without the latter results in a top-heavy system, e.g., GHC as compared to FGHC. In this case, the language is too complex to implement efficiently. The latter without the former results in the opposite: a language easily implemented, but inherently weak, e.g., FGHC as compared to parallel Prolog. Note that the examples of GHC, FGHC and Prolog given above are opinions not just of the author, but of the implementers of the languages themselves. It has been said that committed-choice languages are just "machine languages" with which to build more complex languages. A potential pitfall of this approach is the loss of efficiency due to levels of meta-interpretation and/or translation. On the other hand, it should be noted that Prolog may fall prey to the "top-heavy" problem stated above. The overheads of exploiting both AND- and OR-parallelism in Prolog may negate much of the gain. It is relatively clear, however, from the results of this study, that full unification, backtracking and dependent AND-parallel (stream communication) synchronization are all necessary in a high performance logic programming system.

The Aurora and KL1 system architectures were analyzed by studying the empirical results of executing a set of benchmark programs. The programs were compiled and run on parallel, abstract-machine emulators executing on a common host, the Sequent Symmetry multiprocessor [14]. Overall, the performances of the Aurora and KL1 systems for sequential, determinate code are closely calibrated and therefore allow a fair comparison of both raw timings and instrumented simulations. Calibration was performed with an **8-Queens** program that is identical in both FGHC and Prolog. Single PE execution on a Sequent Symmetry gave 13.16 seconds for Aurora and 13.00 seconds for KL1, less than a 2% difference. It can therefore safely be assumed that both systems are performing simple indexing and simple determinate computation equally well.

Each architecture is emulated at three levels of abstraction: raw timing, high-level instrumentation (e.g., number of procedure calls), and low-level instrumentation (e.g., bus traffic for shared-memory multiprocessor model). The former two sets of statistics help place the benchmarks in context whereas the latter statistics uncover the critical performance factors in the systems.

2 Benchmarks

Five pairs of benchmarks, summarized in Table 1, are analyzed in this paper. **Triangle** finds all (133) winning solutions to a triangular peg game (a shortened version from [4]). The FGHC program was automatically translated from the Prolog by the continuation-based method as described by Ueda [17]. **Puzzle** finds all (65) solutions to a puzzle packing problem (another shortened version from [4]). **Pascal** generates the 100th row of Pascal's Triangle, using integer bignums to represent the coefficients. The Prolog program uses a optimized form of M. Carlsson's hack for implementing AND-in-OR parallelism [2]. **Semigroup** generates all (313) members of a Bradt Semigroup, given a set of four generators, each a list of length 40 (see Overbeek [3]). **Queens** finds all (724) solutions to the 10-Queens problem. The Prolog uses constraints and the FGHC uses layered-streams [11].

2.1 High-Level Benchmark Characteristics

Table 1 first gives the number of static source lines for each program. Dynamic measures are given for the execution time on eight PEs (in seconds) on a Symmetry, the relative speed-up (su) on eight PEs, the number (in thousands) of procedure *entries* and millions of abstract-machine instructions executed, and the number (in millions) of abstract memory references made. The final two ratios are instructions per entry and reference per instruction. For Prolog, a procedure entry is either a reduction (procedure call) or backtrack. For FGHC, a procedure entry is either a reduction or suspension.

A major limitation of this study is that the programs are small. Although the amount of computation of the programs is sufficient to

bench	lines	sec	su	ent	instr(i)	ref	i/ent	ref/i
Prolog								
Tri.	86	12.0	7.7	58.7K	5.5M	20.9M	9.36	3.81
Semi.	126	18.6	3.2	15.4K	1.9M	11.4M	12.56	5.92
Puzzle	233	6.3	7.6	14.5K	1.9M	10.3M	13.27	5.34
Pascal	286	41.7	2.0	26.7K	2.4M	27.7M	8.93	11.61
Queen	37	14.3	5.6	33.5K	2.3M	14.8M	6.88	6.44
FGHC								
Tri.	182	49.3	5.8	32.0K	13.0M	28.2M	19.55	2.17
Semi.	104	87.5	4.8	29.2K	4.8M	25.1M	16.35	5.24
Puzzle	151	55.3	6.5	85.3K	15.6M	29.2M	18.30	1.87
Pascal	310	16.6	6.1	32.0K	5.0M	10.0M	15.68	1.99
Queen	43	27.3	6.8	36.2K	10.0M	17.3M	27.72	1.72

Table 1: Short Summary of Benchmarks on Eight PEs

exercise the cache simulators, the benchmarks do not have large working sets as do big applications. The programs all have significant parallelism and most can exploit that parallelism efficiently (with the exception of **Semigroup** and **Pascal** in Prolog). In general, the OR-parallel Prolog programs display less parallelism than the FGHC programs. Looking at procedure entries and raw execution time, in general, the Prolog programs do less work than the corresponding FGHC programs.

When FGHC performs more procedure entries it is characteristic of the lower semantic power of the language as compared to Prolog. Prolog can exploit full unification coupled with backtracking to solve many of these problems quite efficiently. FGHC is limited to one-way unification and must "emulate" backtracking at the source language level. Note that although **Triangle** performs more Prolog procedure entries, the Prolog executes about four times faster than FGHC. In **Puzzle**, the difference is more pronounced. In both programs, Prolog can use unification of logical variables to avoid the structure copying necessary in FGHC. Comparing **Queens**, we find that Prolog's ability to backtrack over unification gives it a 2:1 speed advantage, whereas the number of procedure entries are almost equal.

The remaining two benchmarks, **Semigroup** and **Pascal**, solve single solution problems. Prolog **Semigroup** uses a 2-3 tree to store the elements of the semigroup. This sequentializes the search for an element, but the search is quite efficient. KL1 uses a pipeline of filters to store the elements of the semigroup. This parallelizes the search for an element (different searches can be pipelined), at the cost of an inefficient (linear) search for each element. **Pascal** has no OR-parallelism, so that Aurora must simulate AND-parallelism via meta-interpretation [2], at great overhead. The overhead of exploiting AND-in-OR parallelism (FGHC is over twice as fast as Prolog on eight PEs) comes from the bookkeeping needed to execute many fine-grained processes. It should be noted that Carlsson et. al. [2] measured a *maximum* speedup of 2.2 for an AND-in-OR parallel compiler running on Aurora. Although the compiler had coarse-grain parallelism, 30% of the computation was sequential, thus limiting speedup. In general, FGHC can manage fine-grained processes much more efficiently than can Prolog, whereas Prolog can manage coarse-grained processes more efficiently than FGHC. The amount of such parallelism in real applications is a yet unanswered question.

2.2   Discussion

The algorithms chosen are sometimes different in each language, often in definition of data structures. In **Semigroup**, Prolog's use of 2-3 trees gives it a definite advantage over KL1. The KL1 pipeline process structure can conceivably be rewritten into a tree structure that will speedup up the search. In **Puzzle**, Prolog's use of logic variables obviates the need for copying large data structures, as is necessary in KL1. Because **Puzzle** and **Triangle** are all-solutions searches, *destructive arrays* cannot be used to represent the data structures in either language.

The nondeterminate benchmarks chosen in this study perform an all-solutions search. Given a problem space containing multiple solutions, all-solutions search is used to avoid unreliable measurements. If for instance only one solution is required from a multiple solution space, a *different* solution may be found when the *same* program is run on different numbers of PEs. This may result in either sublinear or superlinear speedups. This problem is one of determinacy—a good benchmark is a determinate benchmark. Nondeterminacy can cause high variance in performance measurements that is not attributable to the architecture or system, but rather to luck.

Unfortunately, choosing all-solutions search problems give OR- parallel Prolog an advantage over FGHC. Prolog can collect all solutions with builtin functions (such as `findall` and `bagof`) that backtrack over solutions more efficiently than can be simulated in FGHC. All-solutions search problems guarantee OR-parallel Prolog a source of easily exploitable parallelism. However, OR-parallelism in single-solution problems is not so easily uncovered by Prolog. As seen in Table 1, the Prolog solutions to the single-solution problems have the lowest speedup of all the benchmarks. These programs also have the least readability (declarativity) as a result of unrolling and other machinations needed to exploit the little parallelism which exists.

On average FGHC has greater parallelism than Prolog because the poor relative speedup of **Semigroup** and **Pascal** lowers the Prolog average. On a single PE, the ratio of Aurora to KL1 execution time is 1.2–7.5, but on eight PEs, this varies from 0.4–8.8. Most notable is **Pascal** in which KL1 gains an advantage via parallelism. **Semigroup** and **Queens** also illustrate the superior parallelism of KL1, but the underlying weaknesses cannot overtake Aurora. Note that the KL1 system measured here has subsequently been improved to execute about 10% faster (via compilation optimizations of fusing common instruction pairs). It is obvious from the measurements however that an improvement of *2–9 times* is necessary to become on par with Aurora. By "improvement" it is meant more efficient support, in compiler and architecture, of necessary programming paradigms. The two systems calibrate on a specific **Queens** algorithm that does not exercise all the programming styles needed in both languages.

3 Memory Referencing Characteristics

Understanding the general memory referencing characteristics of an architecture aids in improving the instruction set design and optimizing compiled code. For example, we shall see that KL1 has almost twice the percentage of instruction bytes referenced as Aurora, yet certainly Aurora is not twice as potent or densely encoded. This result points to, among other things, considering more efficient resumption policies and reevaluating the code generation policy meant to avoid lock conflicts for KL1 [7]. The memory referencing characteristics also aid the intuition in explaining the cache performance results of Section 4. Interpretations of all the statistics presented in this paper are the opinion of the author and hold specifically for tightly-coupled shared-memory multiprocessor hosts.

3.1 High-Level Characteristics

For the KL1 benchmarks, suspensions compose less than 10% of all procedure entries. Thus instructions per *reduction* and instructions per entry are the same. The average instructions per entry of 20 has little variance among the benchmarks. For Prolog, many programs have a significant amount of backtracking. Compared to KL1, the Prolog instructions per entry of 10 is lower because clause selection in KL1 counts as only one procedure entry, whereas in Prolog, shallow backtracking may count as many procedure entries. Prolog instructions per *reduction* is higher only for two programs: **Triangle** and **Puzzle**. For each of these programs, the KL1 code executes many more (smaller) procedures to simulate all-solutions search. The **Queen**s programs also perform all-solutions search, but the overhead is not so great because the search tree is very simple.

(WAM, Aurora, KL1) have (0.70, 1.37, 1.03) instruction references per instruction and (2.32, 5.26, 1.41) data references per instruction, respectively. The WAM has the lowest instruction reference frequency because real byte-code formats are used [15], whereas the Aurora and KL1 systems have all instructions on word boundaries. More interesting are data referencing characteristics, as discussed below.

Both KL1 and Aurora have high variances for data reference counts due to **Semigroup** and **Puzzle** respectively. Nonetheless, in general we can say that the KL1 instruction set has weaker *potency* than the WAM because it does not implement backtracking. Prolog is more semantically powerful (potent) than FGHC and its direct correspondence architecture is also more powerful (i.e., more work is performed by each individual instruction, on average). Suspension referencing of course increases the data references per instruction with respect to Prolog; however, the benchmarks studied do little synchronization. One exception is **Semigroup**, with 0.09 suspensions per reduction, and 4.24 data references per instruction. This is significantly higher than any of the other benchmarks measured. **Queens** also has a high suspension ratio, but still retains low data references per instruction.

On the other hand, Aurora displays significantly higher data references per instruction than the standard WAM. This however is not due to increased potency because both languages are Prolog. The benchmarks studied here do a significant amount of complex pattern matching and backtracking, thus increasing data referencing above that of the more "realistic" programs studied in [15]. **Puzzle** is the most intensive program of the group in this respect, with 10.15 data references per instruction. In addition, the overheads of the Aurora scheduler [1] also increase data referencing.

In summary, it is interesting to compare the performance of programming styles fostered by language definition. If FGHC encourages object-oriented programming style by the nature of stream communication, then the performance of object-oriented programs is important to study. Likewise the various uses of logical variables and backtracking that Prolog encourages are important to measure. This may seem obvious, but some of the benchmarks here have been criticized as un-

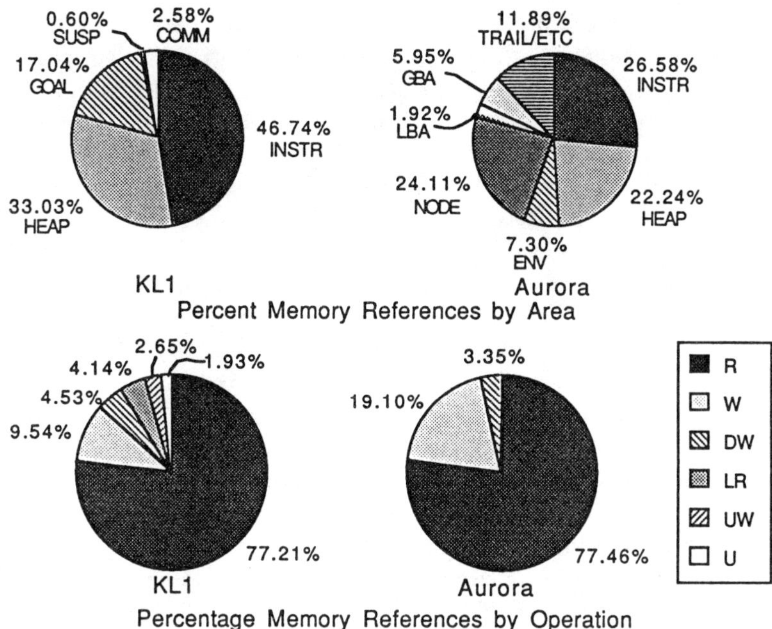

Figure 1: Memory Referencing Characteristics of KL1 and Aurora

fair because the paradigms used are inefficient in a particular language.
These criticisms are addressed in general as follows. The attributes of
Prolog that were abandoned in the committed-choice languages because
these attributes had sequential roots, are precisely the attributes that
permit Prolog to outperform the committed-choice languages on shared
memory multiprocessors. Of course, this study may again be criticized
on the grounds that the committed-choice languages are targeted for
massively parallel hosts.

3.2   Low-Level Characteristics

Figure 1 shows the memory references broken down by storage area and
memory operation, for each architecture. Aurora areas GBA and LBA
are the gobal and local binding arrays, respectively. Operation LR is
lock and read, U is unlock, UW is write and unlock, DW is direct write
(discussed in Section 4).

The KL1 and Aurora referencing characteristics are primarily skewed
by the large percentage of KL1 instruction references, 47% of all references compared to Aurora's 27%. (WAM, Aurora, KL1) have (3.46,
2.76, 1.14) data references per instruction reference, respectively. The

differences are due in part to the instruction formats, parallel overheads, and language potency. Aurora is the most efficiently encoded instruction set (more efficiently than the original WAM). However, Aurora has overheads of parallel execution: scheduler work is counted as data references with no instruction fetches made. Overall, Aurora therefore falls inbetween Prolog and KL1 in data references per instruction reference.

The over 2:1 ratio between Aurora and KL1 data references per instruction reference is also felt in the skewed read reference counts. Even given this bias however, KL1 and Aurora have almost the same percentage of reads. When instruction references are removed from the statistics, Aurora has 70% reads to KL1's 61%. In both cases, the read:write ratio is higher than Prolog (53% read data references [15]). The reason for this is not because the architectures are more efficient than Prolog, but because each has scheduling and synchronization overheads that require many reads. In Aurora, the scheduler generates control stack read traffic. In KL1, we measure 8.5% read data references to lock variables (during dereferencing and/or binding).

The data referencing characteristics of each architecture are now discussed in more detail. Note that these statistics are deceptive because bus traffic, the critical concern in a shared memory multiprocessor, is only indirectly related to the raw reference counts. Locality and sharing in the areas radically affects the bus traffic generated. For these benchmarks, the KL1 heap is referenced 62% on average, goals 32%, and communication 5%. Suspensions do not affect reference counts significantly. Aurora is more complex, with a balanced mix of references to heap (30%), environment (10%), control (node) (33%), trail (16%), and binding array areas (11%). This profile is radically different than that measured for Prolog (53% control, 23% environment, 20% heap, 3% trail). The differences are explained as follows. 11% of Aurora references are devoted to the binding arrays, so these references must be factored out when compared to Prolog. In addition, trailing in Aurora requires saving both an address and value, twice the storage requirements of the Prolog trail. In addition, the Aurora compiler generates efficient code that can reduce node referencing during shallow backtracking. The Prolog statistics were gathered on a system without such optimizations. These considerations help to calibrate the two variations of the WAM; however, the rather low environment data reference count in Aurora has not yet been explained. This is again possibly due to the sophistication of the Aurora compiler.

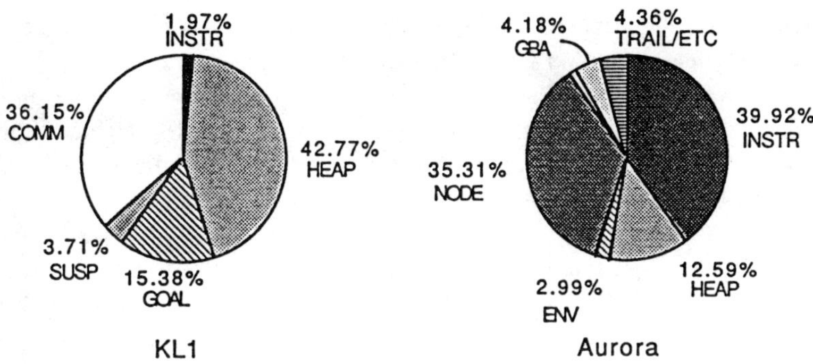

Figure 2: Bus Traffic Characteristics (by Area) of KL1 and Aurora

4   Bus and Cache Performance

To gain better understanding of the critical factors governing system performance, a multiprocessor coherent cache and bus model [6] was simulated *during* program emulation. Abstract-machine memory references were issued to a set of communicating cache simulators, one per PE. The copyback cache protocol includes: write allocation (if a write request misses in the cache, the target line is fetched from memory and allocated in the cache), invalidation (modifications to shared data cause invalidation of remote copies), and no-copy (when transferring a dirty line from one cache to another, shared memory is *not* updated). In addition to the standard memory operations, a *direct write* optimization is used. Direct write is effectively a memory write; however, if the write misses in the cache, the cache will *not* fetch the target line from memory. Instead, the line is allocated in the cache without initialization. Direct write is used when creating new data objects on the top of a memory stack of some sort. Since the architecture knows *a priori* that the memory will be overwritten, fetching of lines from memory can be avoided, and the cache allocated directly. This optimization is used in both the KL1 and Aurora systems for heap accesses.

The cache simulator utilizes an internal model of a shared memory multiprocessor to calculate the bus traffic generated by the benchmark program. In this paper, we present measurements of a model assuming eight instruction-data (I+D) caches coupled with a shared one-word wide bus, a simple non-overlapped bus manager, and an eight-cycle shared-memory access time, and a simple non-overlapped bus manager. The caches utilize four-word blocks and are four-way set-associative.

Figure 2 shows the average bus traffic profiles of the benchmarks measured in this study. These measurements are of simulations run with eight PEs, each with a 8192 word cache, except for **Semigroup** and and **Pascal**, run on two PEs. Note that a split I/D cache will likely give different results. Changing the memory access time assumption of eight cycles does not significantly affect the statistics [16], although bus width is critical. For example, on a two-word bus, KL1 bandwidth was reduced to 62–75% of the one-word bus traffic shown here.

Aurora's bus traffic characteristics vary greatly with each benchmark. Instruction bus traffic varies from 15–77%. Within data traffic, heap bus traffic varies from 1–39% and node bus traffic varies from 9–58%. The other areas are more stable across the benchmarks. KL1's bus traffic characteristics also vary with each benchmark. Instruction bus traffic varies from 0.1–4.9%. Within data traffic, suspension bus traffic varies from 0–10% and communication bus traffic varies from 10–56%.

The most significant difference between the architectures is the instruction bus traffic. Aurora generates a great deal of instruction bus traffic, whereas KL1 has almost none. It would therefore appear than KL1 has superior code locality. This may be due to the fact that KL1 does not backtrack, and in these benchmarks, does little synchronization. Thus execution is determinate and jumps are infrequent. With few jumps, the prefetch effect of four word cache blocks gives KL1 a very low instruction miss ratio. On the other hand, the Prolog programs are heavily backtracking. This however cannot explain why **Pascal** instruction traffic differs by a factor of 67, whereas Aurora makes only 68% of KL1's instruction requests!

Another interesting statistic is that Aurora heap bus traffic is on average 21% of all data bus traffic, compared to 44% for KL1. Similarly, Aurora environment bus traffic is on average 5% of all data bus traffic, compared to 16% for KL1. These results indicates in part that Prolog's stack-group storage management has superior spatial locality to KL1's heap-based storage management. The results also derive from Aurora's high scheduling overhead: the control stack alone generates 59% of all data bus traffic. The binding arrays and trail account for 15% more. One can roughly compare this to KL1's suspension and communication traffic of 41%. Thus the statistics reenforce the hypotheses that committed-choice languages require simpler management than do non-committed-choice languages (because there is no backtracking, nor multiple bindings of the same variable), but that committed-choice languages have less data locality because of the necessity for heap-based management. Specifically, OR-parallel Prolog requires high control-stack bus bandwidth because the individual PEs are walking around the OR-tree, executing the program. AND-parallel FGHC requires heap-based storage management because procedure environments

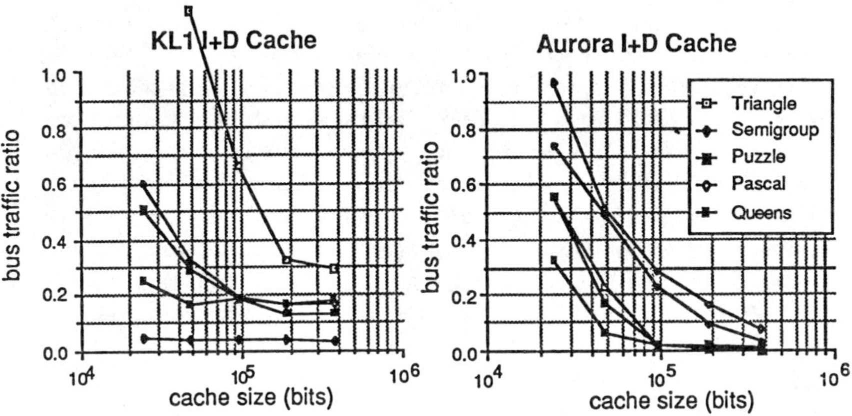

Figure 3: KL1 and Aurora Cache Performance: Bus Traffic Ratios

cannot be stored effectively on a true stack.

Scheduling weaknesses of both systems are illustrated by analyzing data bus traffic on two and eight PEs. Considering KL1 **Triangle**, communication bus traffic increases from 21% (two PEs) to 41% (eight PEs) of the total data bus traffic. Considering Aurora **Semigroup** and **Pascal**, node bus traffic increases from 28% and 9% (two PEs) to 75% and 79% (eight PEs), respectively. **Triangle** spawns many small tasks in KL1 that cause load-balancing problems resulting in high communication costs. Aurora **Semigroup** and **Pascal** simply don't generate enough tasks, resulting in (unintentionally) high scheduler costs. **Semigroup** is data intensive: data bus traffic is 85% (two PEs) and 95% (eight PEs) of total bus traffic. **Pascal** however is *not* data intensive: data bus traffic increases from 24% (two PEs) to 85% (eight PEs), a more severe problem. These characteristics are reflected in the code— computation of a group element in **Semigroup** is more expensive than adding two bignums in **Pascal**.

Figure 3 shows the relationship between increasing cache size and bus traffic ratio. Bus traffic ratio, as defined here, is the ratio of the total number of bus cycles to the total number of memory requests (see Matsumoto [9] for an alternative definition). Again, the simulations were run with eight PEs except for **Semigroup** and **Pascal** in Aurora which were run on two PEs. The **Semigroup** and **Pascal** bus traffic ratios on eight PEs are 0.2–0.3 higher (across all cache sizes) than on two PEs for Aurora because of scheduler difficulties. The cache sizes simulated are 32, 64, 128, 256, and 512 columns, corresponding to data areas of 512–8192 words. The plotted cache sizes assume a five byte data word and include the directory size as well.

Aurora achieves lower bus traffic ratios than KL1 as cache size increases. The KL1 curves (except for **Triangle**) flatten out almost precisely at 10^5 bits (2048 word cache), whereas Aurora continues to improve. Note that different benchmarks have drastically different behavior on the two systems, as we would expect from the high-level results in previous sections. For example, **Semigroup** and **Pascal** display higher bus traffic for a 2048 word cache in Aurora (even on two PEs) than in KL1. However, at 8192 words, Aurora can achieve lower bus traffic on two PEs, but still not on eight PEs (due to scheduling bandwidth). For **Triangle**, the roles are reversed, and Aurora has consistently lower bus traffic. **Puzzle** and **Queens** show almost equal performance for both systems on 512 word caches, but Aurora improves more rapidly with increasing cache size.

In general, KL1 performance is "flat," indicative of an architecture with a ever changing working set. KL1 monotonically walks through memory, referencing fresh areas on the way (until GC is incurred). Still, reasonable cache performance is achieved because the execution mechanism rereferences the same area frequently, as the walk through memory proceeds. Aurora performance is more "classical," i.e., bus traffic ratios continue to decrease gracefully with cache size. Most of the benchmarks have their entire working sets captured in caches of 2048 words and larger.

Comparing I+D-cache to D-cache statistics (not shown), Aurora and KL1 have opposite results. Aurora D-cache performance is *better* for all the benchmarks except **Semigroup**, than its I+D cache performance. KL1 performance is exactly opposite. This confirms the results shown previously that Aurora instruction referencing has lower locality than KL1 instruction referencing, and visa-versa for data referencing. Again, these characteristics can be explained by Aurora's more efficient stack-based storage model and its more "jumpy" code style.

These results do not compromise the viability of building a multiprocessors for either architecture, given an investment in a reasonable size cache. The results further indicate where the systems can be improved to get the most reduction in bus traffic.

5   Conclusions

This paper attempts to quantify some of the performance differences between committed-choice and non-committed-choice parallel logic programming language architectures. Specifically, the Aurora OR-parallel Prolog system is compared to the KL1 AND-parallel FGHC system for equivalent benchmark programs. Because the systems differ in both the type of parallelism exploited *and* the facility for non-determinate execution, separation of effects is difficult to analyze. Added are the differences of scheduling methods, garbage collection, and various other system support. In any case, this paper is one of the first detailed performance analyses and comparisons of parallel logic programming architectures.

The most important result of this study was a confirmation that indeed *(independent) OR-parallel architectures have better memory performance than (dependent) AND-parallel architectures.* The reasons are that OR-parallel architectures can exploit an efficient stack-based storage model whereas dependent AND-parallel architectures must resort to a less efficient heap-based model. For all-solutions search problems, a further result is that *non-committed-choice architectures have better memory performance than committed-choice architectures.* This is because backtracking architectures can efficiently reclaim storage during all-solutions search, thereby reducing working-set size. Committed-choice architectures, like functional language architectures, consume memory at a rapid rate. Incremental GC can alleviate some of penalty for this memory appetite, but incremental GC also incurs its own overheads [10]. Thirdly, for single-solution problems, *OR-parallel architectures cannot exploit parallelism as efficiently as dependent AND-parallel architectures can.* Although OR-parallel goals may exist, they are often too fine-grained for the excessive overheads necessary to execute them in parallel. In this respect, *dependent AND-parallel architectures can execute fine-grain parallelism more efficiently than can OR-parallel architectures.*

From the raw timings we saw that even with the anticipated improvement in KL1 speed due to compiler optimization, 2–9 times improvement (in support of necessary methods of programming) is needed to equal Aurora's speed. **Pascal** is the single exception where KL1 outperformed Aurora because the Argonne scheduler went crazy trying to find parallelism that did not exist. In any case, both systems calibrated on a simple determinate benchmark. There is no doubt however that the benchmarks favor Prolog. **Triangle** was translated from Prolog to FGHC, thereby incurring overheads. **Puzzle** in KL1 involves excessive structure copying. **Semigroup** in KL1 does not use a 2-3 tree as does Prolog. **Queens** uses layered-streams, thereby incurring suspensions. On the other hand, *is there a more natural or more efficient way to write these programs in FGHC?* Prolog-to-FGHC continuation-based translation, layered-streams, object-oriented programming, pipelined parallelism, etc. are all publicized methods of parallel FGHC programming. If there are better versions of these programs, it would be very enlightening to measure them.

A "bottom-heavy" system, such as KL1, makes a tradeoff between the ease of exploiting parallelism and the power of language constructs. Backtracking and full logical unification have been traded for stream-AND parallelism. On the other hand, Aurora makes a tradeoff between the power of language constructs and the availability of parallelism. This leads to dismal results for programs with little or no OR-parallelism like **Pascal**. There is a large class of problems, not represented here, requiring intelligent search strategies, e.g., **Maxflow** and **Bestpath**. These problems cannot be solved efficiently in OR-parallel.

Acknowledgements

This research was supported in full by NSF Grant No. IRI-8704576. I thank M. Sato, M. Matsumoto, A. Okumura and other ICOT members for helping with KL1. I also thank A. Ciepielewski of SICS whose help with Aurora was invaluable. The author is now at the University of Tokyo.

References

[1] R. Butler et. al. Scheduling OR-Parallelism: an Argonne Perspective. In *Int. Conf. and Symp. on Logic Prog.*, pages 1565–1577. MIT Press, August 1988.

[2] M. Carlsson et. al. A Simplified Approach to the Implementation of AND-Parallelism in an OR-Parallel Environment. In *5th Int. Conf. and Symp. on Logic Prog.*, pages 1565–1577. MIT Press, August 1988.

[3] T. Disz et. al. Experiments with OR-Parallel Logic Programs. In *4th Int. Conf. on Logic Prog.*, pages 576–600. MIT Press, May 1987.

[4] R. P. Gabriel. *Performance and Evaluation of Lisp Systems*. MIT Press, 1985.

[5] W. Gibson. *Burning Chrome*. Grafton Books, 1988.

[6] A. Goto, A. Matsumoto, and E. Tick. Design and Performance of a Coherent Cache for Parallel Logic Programming Architectures. In *16th Int. Symp. on Comp. Arch.*, June 1989.

[7] Y. Kimura and T. Chikayama. An Abstract KL1 Machine and its Instruction Set. In *Int. Symp. on Logic Prog.*, pages 468–477, August 1987.

[8] E. Lusk et. al. The Aurora Or-Parallel Prolog System. In *Int. Conf. on FGCS*, pages 819–830. Tokyo, November 1988.

[9] A. Matsumoto et. al. Locally Parallel Cache Design Based on KL1 Memory Access Characteristics. Technical Report 327, ICOT, 1987.

[10] K. Nishida et. al. Evaluation of the Effect of Incremental Garbage Collection by MRB on FGHC Parallel Execution Performance. Technical Report 394, ICOT, 1988.

[11] A. Okumura and Y. Matsumoto. Parallel Programming with Layered Streams. In *Symp. on Logic Prog.*, pages 224–233, August 1987.

[12] M. Sato and et al. KL1 Execution Model for PIM Cluster with Shared Memory. In *4th Int. Conf. on Logic Prog.*, pages 338–355. MIT Press, May 1987.

[13] M. Sato and A. Goto. Evaluation of the KL1 Parallel System on a Shared Memory Multiprocessor. In *IFIP Working Conf. on Parallel Processing*. North Holland, May 1988.

[14] Sequent Computer Systems, Inc. *Sequent Guide to Parallel Programming*, 1987.

[15] E. Tick. Data Buffer Performance for Sequential Prolog Architectures. In *15th Int. Symp. on Comp. Arch.*, May 1988.

[16] E. Tick. Performance of Parallel Logic Programming Architectures. Technical Report TR-421, ICOT, 1-4-28 Mita, Minato-ku Tokyo 108, Japan, September 1988.

[17] K. Ueda. Making Exhaustive Search Programs Deterministic: Part II. In *4th Int. Conf. on Logic Prog.*, pages 356–375. MIT Press, May 1987.

Parallel Languages

Pandora: Non-deterministic
Parallel Logic Programming

Reem Bahgat and Steve Gregory

Department of Computing, Imperial College
180 Queen's Gate, London SW7 2BZ, England

Abstract

Recent work suggests that it may be feasible to combine stream and-parallelism with don't-know non-determinism in a unified logic programming language or system. We present such a language Pandora, whose operational semantics is a generalization of Warren's Andorra model. Pandora extends Parlog with a deadlock handling mechanism and a simple non-deterministic fork primitive. Using these facilities, Pandora provides a programming paradigm of (don't-know) non-deterministic concurrent, communicating processes, which opens up interesting application areas that cannot conveniently be expressed in existing logic programming languages. We describe the use of Pandora in one such application: to solve finite domain constraint satisfaction problems, and suggest other application areas. We believe that Pandora can be implemented easily on parallel machines; some of the implementation issues are outlined here.

1. Introduction

Most of the logic programming languages that have been seriously implemented and used to date fall into one of two categories: (a) variants of Prolog, and (b) the parallel (or concurrent) logic programming (PLP) languages. The basic distinction is that Prolog features *don't-know non-determinism* (DKND); the PLP languages provide *dependent* or *stream and-parallelism* but are based on *committed choice non-determinism* (CCND). Recent work suggests that it may be feasible to combine DKND and stream and-parallelism in a single language or system. This is attractive for two reasons: (a) more parallelism can be exploited in the kinds of application currently written in Prolog; (b) combining DKND with a concurrent programming style may open up interesting new application areas to logic programming.

This paper describes a new proposal: Pandora, a language combining stream and-parallelism and DKND. It is closely related to Warren's Andorra model, which we outline below. The Pandora language is introduced in Section 2 and illustrated in Section 3 by an application in constraint logic programming. Some general application issues are noted in Section 4, and implementation in Section 5. Other closely related work is described in Section 6.

The Andorra model

Andorra [16, 18] is a computational model designed to transparently extract stream and-parallelism (as well as or-parallelism) from Prolog programs. It combines the idea of suspending goals until they are deterministic, as in the committed choice subset of P-Prolog [17], with a novel "deadlock breaking" policy to realize DKND.

In Andorra, execution alternates between two phases. In the *and-parallel* phase, all deterministic goals are evaluated concurrently. A deterministic goal is one for which it is known that there is no more than one matching clause. This is checked by simple run-time tests, intended to be deduced by a compile-time analysis. When no deterministic goals remain, a *non-deterministic* phase is started in which the leftmost goal is selected and a choice point created for it. For each or-branch, a new and-parallel phase is begun, running all deterministic goals until they are exhausted.

This summarizes Warren's original proposal, to which we shall refer as Pure Andorra. Pure Andorra can run a deterministic Prolog program with behaviour similar to that of a PLP language. However, Pure Andorra does not subsume the PLP languages, for the following reasons:

Problem 1. Forcing suspension.
In PLP languages, a goal is supposed to suspend until its arguments are sufficiently instantiated, e.g., reverse(X,Y) should suspend until X is bound. Pure Andorra may evaluate such a goal in the non-deterministic phase, and "guess" the value of X instead of waiting for it, as is desired.

Problem 2. Committed choice.
PLP languages make use of CCND relations, of which the archetype is merge. CCND goals reduce by making a committed choice, even when they are not deterministic. Pure Andorra will delay such goals until the non-deterministic phase and then evaluate them using DKND, which is not what is required.

Problem 3. Implicit determinism test.
Because it aims to implicitly extract parallelism from Prolog, Pure Andorra does not specify exactly what tests are performed to check that a goal is deterministic. But this choice profoundly affects the behaviour. For example, if the compiler cannot deduce that the goal reverse(X,Y) is deterministic when X is instantiated, it will not be run concurrently with

other goals but will be deferred to the non-deterministic phase.

Problem 4. Flat determinism test.
The simple nature of the determinism tests means that Pure Andorra can only simulate the behaviour of *flat* PLP languages. However, several implementations of Parlog, including Jim Crammond's [4], feature "deep guards" and sequential conjunction.

These considerations suggest that Prolog is insufficient as a programming language for Andorra if it is desired to run applications that are currently expressible in PLP languages. In the next section, we propose an alternative language that extends Parlog [6] to incorporate don't-know non-determinism, and has an operational semantics derived from Andorra. It is hence named Pandora (Parlog + Andorra).

Pandora is a language that provides explicit control of concurrency and non-determinism, answering the four problems with Pure Andorra identified above. There are two other important differences: (1) Pandora goes beyond the Andorra model by allowing a more general deadlock breaking mechanism, explained below; (2) Pandora is not necessarily intended to subsume Prolog, but rather to extend the role of Parlog with the minimum of complication.

2. Pandora: the language

Pandora extends Parlog in two ways. First, it provides a way to handle deadlock by invoking a specified Parlog computation. Second, it adds a non-deterministic fork primitive that causes an evaluation to split into multiple or-branches.

Deadlock relations

There are two basic kinds of relation in a Pandora program: and-parallel relations and deadlock relations. Both kinds of relation may call each other freely, except that a deadlock relation may not be called from a guard, either directly or indirectly. An *and-parallel relation* is defined by a normal Parlog procedure (which we shall call an *and-parallel procedure*), while a *deadlock relation* is defined by both an and-parallel procedure and a deadlock procedure. The two procedures defining a deadlock relation need not, in general, be logically equivalent.

A *deadlock procedure* has the same syntax as an and-parallel procedure except that it is headed by a declaration of the form deadlock r(?,...,^) instead of mode r(?,...,^). The annotations '?' and '^' respectively denote input and output arguments.

In normal computation, the operational semantics of Parlog is unaffected by the existence of deadlock procedures: only the and-parallel procedures of both kinds of relation are used. However, if a computation deadlocks, i.e., all goals are suspended, it need not be fatal. If the deadlocked resolvent contains any goals for deadlock relations, *one* such goal (the language does not specify which one) is reduced using its deadlock procedure instead of its and-parallel procedure.

Non-deterministic fork

The other extension in Pandora is a non-deterministic fork primitive:

$$\{conj_1; ...; conj_n\}$$

in which each $conj_i$ is a Pandora conjunction. {...} may only appear as the sole body goal in a clause of a deadlock procedure (output unification is treated as a body goal, so this is also prohibited in a clause containing a {...} fork). When executed, this causes the computation to split into n or-branches; in the ith or-branch the fork goal is replaced by the conjunction $conj_i$.

Don't-know relations

Deadlock relations provide a general mechanism for handling deadlock which, if combined with the non-deterministic fork primitive, yields Andorra-like behaviour. As a "syntactic sugar" to facilitate this combination, we introduce a further type of relation whose procedure can be compiled to a committed choice and-parallel procedure and a deadlock procedure; the compilation is explained in [1].

Don't-know relations have names that are distinct from all other, committed choice, relation names; they may be called anywhere except from a guard of a committed choice procedure. A don't-know relation is defined by an undeclared procedure which comprises a sequence of clauses. Each clause takes the form:

$$p(t_1,...,t_n) <\text{-} D : B.$$

D is a *det-guard*: a conjunction of goals for certain primitives, including at least unification (=); we also allow other primitives such as $<, >, =<, >=$. B is the clause body: any Pandora conjunction.

The purpose of det-guards is to delimit the conditions that are used to detect whether a goal is deterministic. Following the Andorra model, we wish to execute in and-parallel all don't-know relation goals that are deterministic. However, because of problem 3 above, we want the determinism test to be explicit, hence the following definition:

Definition. A goal for p is deterministic iff at least k-1 clauses have false (unsatisfiable) det-guards, where k is the number of clauses in p's procedure.

Given the restrictions on det-guards noted above, and the above definition of determinism, it is possible in most cases to test whether a don't-know relation goal is deterministic without binding any variables in the goal, i.e., just by inspecting its arguments.

Finally, we sketch the operational semantics of Pandora in the special case where deadlock relations are not used explicitly. A query may contain goals for both committed choice relations and don't-know relations. The computation starts with an and-parallel phase, during which committed choice and-parallel relation goals reduce in the normal Parlog manner. Also, don't-know relation goals are reduced provided they are deterministic by the above definition. If the computation deadlocks with some of the suspended goals being for don't-know relations, one such goal is selected and a choice point created for it; a new and-parallel phase is initiated for each or-branch.

3. Pandora for constraint logic programming

The Andorra model, and hence Pandora, runs non-deterministic programs in an interesting coroutining manner whereby non-deterministic goals are executed after deterministic ones. This "lazy non-determinism" can significantly reduce the search space in many cases [3], resulting in a more intelligent problem-solving behaviour than either a sequential execution, as in Prolog, or a fully eager parallel evaluation. This is because, in the latter cases, several choices may be made (by non-deterministic goals) before a failing goal is encountered; a chronological backtracking scheme will then backtrack to the most recent choice, which may well not be the one responsible for the failure. Lazy non-determinism makes it more likely that a failure is encountered immediately after the choice that caused it, i.e., before any further choices are made.

Constraint logic programming (CLP) systems have similar benefits: search can be reduced because certain test goals ("constraints") are executed before goals for user-defined relations. However, they do even better. Whereas constraints are traditionally used in a passive manner, as part of a "generate and test" strategy, CLP systems use them *actively*. That is, constraints can be solved (hence reducing the search space) by special techniques, earlier than would otherwise be possible.

One approach to CLP is described below. We then show how problems that are suited to this can also be solved in Pandora, by a special programming technique.

Domain variables

van Hentenryck and Dincbas [9] show that certain types of problem can usefully be specified by constraints on finite domains; in [5] they expand on this theme and introduce a language CHIP that features techniques to solve these as well as other kinds of constraints.

CHIP is a language that extends a sequential Prolog in several ways, including a special-purpose coroutining mechanism, *forward checking*. The most important feature is that a variable can be declared as a *domain variable*, ranging over a specified set of values. This set is the initial value of the variable's *possible set*. When certain "constraint" relations are executed, they can remove values from the possible set of their arguments. For example, the constraint $V \leq 1$ will remove all values greater than 1 from V's possible set. If a constraint results in the possible set becoming empty, it will fail. Moreover, if the possible set of a domain variable V is reduced to a singleton set $\{e\}$, V will be deterministically bound to e.

Domain variables in Pandora

First, consider a special case of domain variable: one that can only handle what Dincbas *et al.* [5] call *symbolic constraints* (i.e., equality ($=$) and inequality ($\neq$) constraints). We shall call this a *symbolic domain variable*.

A symbolic domain variable V ranging over $\{1,...,n\}$ can be represented in Pandora by a *symbolic domain vector*. This is an ordered collection of bits, for example $[B_1,...,B_n]$ where each B_i may take the value 0 or 1. If V is unbound, some (initially all) of $B_1,...,B_n$ are unbound variables; the B_i's ($1{\leq}i{\leq}n$) that are unbound represent the possible set of V. A unification $V = m$ succeeds if and only if m is in V's possible set. Corresponding to this is the unification $B_m = 1$, provided $1{\leq}m{\leq}n$. If this unification succeeds, the system should unify each of $B_1,...,B_{m-1},B_{m+1},...,B_n$ with 0.

Another interesting operation on a domain variable V is the inequality $V \neq m$, which removes m from V's possible set and deterministically binds V if it has one possible value left. The corresponding operation on a domain vector is the unification $B_m = 0$, provided $1{\leq}m{\leq}n$. In this case, the system should ensure that, if $B_1,...,B_{k-1},B_{k+1},...,B_n$ are all 0, B_k is unified with 1.

Dynamic domain variables

Unlike CHIP, it is not necessary in Pandora to insist that the size of a domain vector be known in advance, when writing a program. The relation symvec(B), defined below, implements a symbolic domain vector

B whose size need not be known until run time.

```
symvec(B) <- vec_le1(B), vec_ge1(B).
```

vec_le1(B) is the relation: B is a list of bits (0 or 1) such that *at most* one bit is 1. A goal for this relation should work actively in the following sense: if one of the bits is bound to 1, it should automatically unify the other members of the list with 0. vec_ge1(B) is the relation: B is a list of bits such that *at least* one bit is 1. A goal for this relation should also work actively: if all but one of the bits are bound to 0, it should unify the remaining member with 1.

We define vec_le1(B) by a recursive program that spawns a conjunction of goals for a bit_le1 relation. For example, vec_le1($[B_1,...,B_n]$) reduces to the conjunction:

$$\text{bit\_le1}(B_1,1,V), \ \text{bit\_le1}(B_2,2,V), \ ..., \ \text{bit\_le1}(B_n,n,V)$$

The arguments of a bit_le1 goal (the *i*th) are: the *i*th bit B_i; an identifier *i*, unique to that goal; and a variable common to all of the goals. bit_le1 is a don't-know relation defined by the procedure:

```
bit_le1(1,V,V).
bit_le1(0,_,_).
```

The *i*th bit_le1 goal becomes deterministic if B_i is instantiated. It also becomes deterministic if another bit B_j ($j{\neq}i$) is bound to 1 because then the *j*th goal will bind the common variable to its identifier *j*, eliminating the *i*th goal's first clause. This causes B_i to be unified with 0, as required.

The definition of vec_ge1 is rather similar: it comprises a conjunction of goals for a bit_ge1 relation, and again the first argument of bit_ge1 is the *i*th bit B_i. The second and third arguments link the goals together in a chain: the third argument of the *i*th goal is a variable shared with the second argument of the (*i*+1)th goal; the ends of the chain are two distinct constants, begin and end:

$$\text{bit\_ge1}(B_1,\text{begin},R_2), \text{bit\_ge1}(B_2,R_2,R_3), \ ..., \ \text{bit\_ge1}(B_n,R_n,\text{end})$$

bit_ge1 is a don't-know relation defined by another simple procedure:

```
bit_ge1(1,_,_).
bit_ge1(0,R,R).
```

The *i*th bit_ge1 goal becomes deterministic if B_i is instantiated. It also becomes deterministic if all other bits are bound to 0 because then the other bit_ge1 goals will succeed and unify their second and third argument variables. This makes the ith goal bit_ge1(B_i,begin,end), which eliminates its second clause and unifies B_i with 1, as required.

This completes our definition of symvec. The Pandora programs for vec_le1 and vec_ge1 are straightforward; they are defined in [1].

Pandora example: *n*-queens

van Hentenryck and Dincbas [9] present a solution to the *n*-queens problem using symbolic domain variables. In their program, the n columns of a chessboard are represented by n domain variables $X_1,...,X_n$, each of which ranges over $\{1,...,n\}$. X_i indicates the row of the queen in the ith column. When a queen is placed in the ith column, X_i is given a value and inequality constraints ($\neq$) are executed which reduce the possible set of other columns to exclude squares that are on the same row or diagonal as the queen just placed. Eventually, a column's possible set may be reduced to one row and its value decided deterministically, which reduces other columns' possible sets still further, and so on. This use of domain variables dramatically reduces the search space compared with a conventional "generate and test" method.

In Pandora we can use the symbolic domain vector already defined to construct a similar solution. Unlike domain variables, our domain vectors can *overlap*, which is very useful for many problems including this. We represent the chessboard by an $n*n$ array of bits, one for each square: 1 if the square has a queen, 0 otherwise. We use a domain vector for each column *and* each row: each square's bit thus belongs to two domain vectors. Additionally, all the squares in each diagonal are connected to a vector satisfying the vec_le1 property, to ensure that each diagonal has at most one queen on it. queens(S) is the relation: S is an $n*n$ array, represented as a list of lists, satisfying this property. It is defined by a recursive Pandora program. For the sake of simplicity, an instance of the queens procedure for $n = 3$ (which, of course, has no solution) appears below:

```
queens([[A1,A2,A3],[B1,B2,B3],[C1,C2,C3]]) <-
       symvec([A1,A2,A3]), symvec([B1,B2,B3]),
       symvec([C1,C2,C3]),                        % columns
       symvec([A1,B1,C1]), symvec([A2,B2,C2]),
       symvec([A3,B3,C3]),                        % rows
       vec_le1([B1,C2]), vec_le1([A1,B2,C3]),
       vec_le1([A2,B3]),                          % left diagonals
       vec_le1([A2,B1]), vec_le1([A3,B2,C1]),
       vec_le1([B3,C2]).                          % right diagonals
```

The paper by van Hentenryck and Dincbas gives statistics on the number of backtrackings exhibited by their program, compared with a conventional coroutining "generate and test" strategy. Our Pandora program reduces the search space still further, thanks to the use of overlapping domain vectors. This is because, during a search, either a column *or* a row may be left with all but one square ruled out; our program will deterministically assign a queen to this square. Their program does this only for columns. Table 1 presents the relevant statistics from [9] together with our results (ST is a coroutining generate and test strategy; GFF means Generalized Forward Checking, which is the most effective use of domain variables).

Number of queens	ST	GFF	Pandora
4	7	2	2
6	46	8	8
8	223	24	21
10	276	24	21
12	873	54	37
14	7262	349	258

Table 1 Number of backtrackings in *n*-queens problem

This example also illustrates a fundamental difference between Pandora and the forward checking scheme of Dincbas *et al.* In the latter, the non-deterministic generator and the constraints must be distinguished by the programmer and ordered so that constraints are executed before the generator is invoked to make a choice. On the other hand, Pandora is a concurrent language in which the order of goals is irrelevant. It is the Andorra computational model underlying the language which ensures that "constraints" (i.e., deterministic tests) are executed before any choice is made.

Numeric domain variables

For some applications the values of a domain variable are significant. CHIP [5] provides *numerical constraints* $<, >, \leq, \geq$ over natural numbers: for example, if V is a domain variable ranging over $\{2,3,5,7,11\}$ and the inequality $V \leq 6$ is executed, V's possible set is reduced to $\{2,3,5\}$. We can define in Pandora a *numeric domain vector* that has this ability.

A numeric domain vector is implemented by a goal multiset(Bits,Values,Constraints,Contents) which takes a list Bits = $[B_1,...,B_n]$ where each B_i is 0 or 1, and a list Values = $[V_1,...,V_n]$ of arbitrary values. Provided the Constraints argument is unbound, it outputs a list Contents containing those members of Values whose corresponding member of Bits is 1, i.e., Contents is $\{V_i : 1 \leq i \leq n \ \& \ B_i = 1\}$. More generally, the Constraints argument can be instantiated to a stream of messages of the form $\leq(N)$ or $\geq(N)$, etc. When a message such as $\leq(N)$ is sent to the multiset, each item with a value *V* that does not satisfy the constraint (*V>N* in this case) should be removed, by unifying the corresponding bit with 0.

multiset is defined by the following Pandora procedure:

```
mode multiset(?,?,?,^).
multiset([Bit|Bits],[Value|Values],Constraints,Contents)  <-
        item(Bit,Value,Constraints,Contents,Rest),
        multiset(Bits,Values,Constraints,Rest).
multiset([],[],_,[]).

mode item(?,?,?,^,?).
item(Bit,Value,Constraints,Contents,Rest)  <-
        bit(Bit),   item1(Bit,Value,Constraints,Contents,Rest).

bit(1).
bit(0).

mode item1(?,?,?,^,?).
item1(1,Value,_,[Value|Rest],Rest).
item1(0,_,_,Rest,Rest).
item1(Bit,Value,[Constraint|Constraints],Contents,Rest)  <-
        satisfied(Constraint,Value)  :
        item1(Bit,Value,Constraints,Contents,Rest).
item1(Bit,Value,[Constraint|_],Rest,Rest)  <-
        not satisfied(Constraint,Value) : Bit = 0.

mode satisfied(?,?).
satisfied(≤(N),Value) <- Value ≤ N.
satisfied(≥(N),Value) <- Value ≥ N.
```

An item goal is spawned for each member of the multiset. For example, multiset([B1,B2,B3],[10,20,30],C,Contents) reduces to the conjunction:

```
item(B1,10,C,Contents,R1),  item(B2,20,C,R1,R2),
item(B3,30,C,R2,[])
```

Each goal item(B,V,C,L,R) receives the entire stream C of constraint messages. If a constraint is received that is not satisfied by V, the item process unifies B with 0, outputs an empty difference list on (L,R), and terminates. A satisfied constraint message is ignored.

Note that item is defined by a conjunction of a don't-know relation bit and a committed choice relation item1. Both of these are essential here. If we omitted the bit goal, item could not be run non-deterministically. On the other hand, item1 could not be made a don't-know relation for several reasons. (1) It is never deterministic: it should reduce if either of the first or third arguments is instantiated. (2) In the non-deterministic phase, or-branches should not be made for the last two clauses, since this would mean "guessing" constraint messages. This could be avoided by creating an or-branch for all four clauses and leaving the last two suspended indefinitely, but this seems wasteful. (3) Deep guards are used for convenience; this could be avoided by reprogramming.

Our numeric domain vector can be defined as a conjunction of the above multiset and a symbolic domain vector, which constrains the multiset to contain just one value. numvec(Bits,Values,Constraints,Value) unifies Value with a member of the list Values that satisfies the Constraints messages:

```
numvec(Bits,Values,Constraints,Value)  <-
        symvec(Bits),
        multiset(Bits,Values,Constraints,[Value]).
```

A Pandora sort program that uses numeric domain vectors can be found in [1].

4. Applications: other issues

The deadlock relations of Pandora can be used explicitly by the programmer, and provide a powerful way to handle deadlock in a manner suited to the particular application. Such a deadlock breaking facility is necessary for several applications, e.g., discrete event simulation [2, 8].

One way in which deadlock relations can be used is in combination with the non-deterministic fork, to implement a heuristic search. This is a way to reduce the search space by intelligently selecting a non-deterministic goal to execute, when several are possible. What constitutes an intelligent choice will be specific to a particular application, so it clearly cannot be left to an implementation to decide.

In Pandora, a heuristic search can be obtained by making sure that the "best" goal is selected from all the don't-know goals available at the time of deadlock. To decide which goal is best, a heuristic function is computed, as follows. The deadlock procedure generated for a don't-know relation does not simply contain a non-deterministic fork; instead, it initiates two further phases of computation. First, it sends messages to all the deadlocked goals in order to gather information needed to compute a heuristic function. Second, the result of the function is communicated to all the goals, whereupon the "best" one enters a state in which, on deadlock, it can perform a non-deterministic fork.

We used this technique to program the first-fail heuristic, in which the goal chosen is the one with the fewest remaining consistent choices; in the *n*-queens problem, this results in a further dramatic reduction in the number of backtrackings.

5. Implementation

In designing Pandora, one of our objectives was to extend Parlog only as far as necessary to provide don't-know non-determinism. This policy allows us to exploit both the programming techniques and the implementation technology that has been developed for Parlog. From the description of the Pandora language in Section 2, it is clear that a Pandora implementation must extend Parlog in two ways: (1) to detect deadlock in a computation and handle this by invoking another computation; (2) to allow a computation to split into multiple alternative or-branches.

On top of Parlog

A prototype implementation of Pandora has been developed on top of Parlog and has been used to run the example programs in this paper, as well as others. It makes use of Parlog's control metacall to detect deadlock. Deadlock is handled by a metalevel Parlog program which retrieves the deadlocked goals and *copies* them to create multiple or-branches. This copying is a naive way to implement non-determinism, but it means that it is equally easy to explore alternative or-branches sequentially or in parallel. Moreover, we are mainly interested in applications in which the frequency of choice points is low (because of the Andorra computation rule), so the overhead of copying may be relatively insignificant.

An efficient implementation

Jim Crammond's abstract machine, known informally as JAM [4], is a parallel implementation of Parlog which exhibits good parallel speed-ups on shared memory multiprocessors. With some extensions to JAM we hope to achieve a practical parallel implementation of Pandora. The main extensions required are outlined below; details are deferred to a future paper.

During the and-parallel phase, goals reduce and suspend on variables in the normal way. Deadlock relations also suspend on a new system variable DEADLOCK. When deadlock occurs, i.e., when there are no more runnable processes, the suspension queue of DEADLOCK is inspected. If it is non-empty, one of the goals in the queue is chosen and its deadlock procedure code is activated. The other extensions required to JAM are a stack for choice points and a trail. A choice point comprises pointers to the main memory areas of JAM at the time of its creation. A process frame for a suspending process is copied only if it is woken up after a choice point while it was created before the choice point (conditional binding). The new process frame can be reused for child processes in the same way as in JAM (tail recursion optimization). In practice, not all information in the process frame needs to be copied.

6. Conclusions

Pandora provides a programming paradigm of (don't-know) non-deterministic concurrent, communicating processes. Following the Andorra model, the non-determinism is handled lazily; as well as being easy to implement, this yields an intelligent problem solving behaviour that appears to be well suited to many applications.

In Section 3 we demonstrated the use of Pandora for solving problems expressed as constraints on finite domains. This reduces the number of backtrackings (compared with a generate and test strategy) by performing extra consistency checks during forward computation. Because these checks are programmed in Pandora itself, the price paid is an increase in the number of reductions performed; in contrast, a special purpose CLP system such as CHIP includes a low-level mechanism to check consistency. For this reason, we have not attempted to compare the number of reductions or the absolute speed of our approach with that of CHIP.

We have also investigated the suitability of the language for other applications, including: (1) simulation and verification of communication protocols [11, 7]; (2) distributed discrete event simulation [8]. For all these applications, the Andorra computation rule is essential. However, Pure Andorra is insufficient: the concurrent facilities of parallel logic programming languages are needed as well.

Related work

The work of Haridi and Brand [8] is closely related to, although independent of, our own. Like us, their objective is to use the Andorra computational model as the basis of a language more expressive than Prolog, for similar reasons. Their language, Andorra Prolog, extends Prolog by adding features analogous to those of parallel logic programming languages, such as a commit primitive and a delay declaration. Whereas Pandora can be viewed as extending Parlog in the direction of Prolog, Andorra Prolog is best viewed as an extension of Prolog towards Parlog. We believe that the languages have broadly similar expressive power.

P-Prolog, cp(!,|,&) [12], and ANDOR-II [15] are all similar to Pandora in that they combine a committed choice parallel logic programming language with don't-know non-determinism. The crucial difference is that a process may perform a non-deterministic fork eagerly, even while other processes are running concurrently. While this method may yield more parallelism than Pandora, it is much more difficult to implement [18] and lacks the advantages of lazy non-determinism that we have described.

Saraswat [13] uses cp(!,|,&) as a concurrent constraint programming language to solve problems similar to those in Section 3. Indeed, his solution to the n-queens problem is a process network with a topology quite similar to ours. However, because his language forks eagerly, he had to explicitly program the lazy non-determinism. While this is possible, it makes the programs considerably more complex. Also, it is more difficult to construct programs from simple units, which is the approach we take in Section 3.

Other related work includes Parlog and Prolog United [3], Parallel NU-Prolog [10], and Somogyi's intelligent backtracking algorithm [14].

Future research

In the immediate future, we will complete the practical multiprocessor implementation of Pandora outlined in Section 5.

It is possible to extend Pandora with an even more powerful mechanism than the present one for handling deadlock; one option is to allow the deadlocked goals to be accessed and manipulated by a metalevel program. We intend to investigate whether this would be worthwhile and, if so, what changes are needed to the implementation.

At the language level, we will investigate other application areas suited to Pandora. We believe that Pandora may be suited to the solution of other varieties of constraint satisfaction problems than those considered to date. Another interesting subject is to design a higher-level language, as a front end to Pandora, to make it easy to solve constraint problems like those in Section 3.

Acknowledgements

Thanks are due to Per Brand, Seif Haridi, David Warren, Rong Yang, and several of our colleagues at Imperial College, for comments on earlier drafts of this paper. This research was supported in part by an SERC Advanced Research Fellowship.

References

[1] Bahgat, R.M.R. and Gregory, S. Pandora: non-deterministic parallel logic programming. Research report, Department of Computing, Imperial College, London, 1988.

[2] Broda, K. and Gregory, S. Parlog for discrete event simulation. In *Proceedings of the 2nd International Conference on Logic Programming* (Uppsala, July), S.A. Tarnlund (Ed.), Uppsala: Uppsala University Press, 1984, pp. 301-312.

[3] Clark, K.L. and Gregory, S. Parlog and Prolog united. In *Proceedings of the 4th International Conference on Logic Programming* (Melbourne, May), J.L. Lassez (Ed.), Cambridge, Mass.: MIT Press, 1987, pp. 927-961.

[4] Crammond, J.A. Implementation of committed choice logic languages on shared memory multiprocessors. PhD thesis, Heriot-Watt University, Edinburgh, 1988.

[5] Dincbas, M., Simonis, H. and van Hentenryck, P. Solving a cutting-stock problem in constraint logic programming. In *Proceedings of the 5th International Conference and Symposium on Logic Programming* (Seattle, August), R.A. Kowalski and K.A. Bowen (Eds.), Cambridge, Mass.: MIT Press, 1988, pp. 42-58.

[6] Gregory, S. *Parallel Logic Programming in Parlog*. Reading, Mass.: Addison-Wesley, 1987.

[7] Gregory, S., Neely, R. and Ringwood, G.A. Parlog for specification, verification and simulation. In *Proceedings of the 7th International Symposium on Computer Hardware Description Languages and their Applications* (Tokyo, August), C.J. Koomen and T. Moto-oka (Eds.), Amsterdam: Elsevier/North-Holland, 1985, pp. 139-148.

[8] Haridi, S. and Brand, P. Andorra Prolog: an integration of Prolog and committed choice languages. In *Proceedings of the International Conference on Fifth Generation Computer Systems* (Tokyo, November), 1988.

[9] van Hentenryck, P. and Dincbas, M. Forward checking in logic programming. In *Proceedings of the 4th International Conference on Logic Programming* (Melbourne, May), J.L. Lassez (Ed.), Cambridge, Mass.: MIT Press, 1987, pp. 229-256.

[10] Naish, L. Parallelizing NU-Prolog. In *Proceedings of the 5th International Conference and Symposium on Logic Programming* (Seattle, August), R.A. Kowalski and K.A. Bowen (Eds.), Cambridge, Mass.: MIT Press, 1988, pp. 1546-1564.

[11] Ringwood, G.A. The dining logicians. MSc thesis, Department of Computing, Imperial College, London, 1984.

[12] Saraswat, V.A. The concurrent logic programming language cp: definition and operational semantics. In *Proceedings of the Symposium on Principles of Programming Languages* (January), New York: ACM, 1987, pp. 49-62.

[13] Saraswat, V.A. cp as a general-purpose constraint language. In *Proceedings of the AAAI National Conference* (Seattle, July), 1987.

[14] Somogyi, Z., Ramamohanarao, K. and Vaghani, J. A stream and-parallel execution algorithm with backtracking. In *Proceedings of the 5th International Conference and Symposium on Logic Programming* (Seattle, August), R.A. Kowalski and K.A. Bowen (Eds.), Cambridge, Mass.: MIT Press, 1988, pp. 1142-1159.

[15] Takeuchi, A., Takahashi, K. and Shimizu, H. A parallel problem solving language for concurrent systems. In *Proceedings of IFIP Workshop on the Concepts and Characteristics of Knowledge-based Systems* (Mt. Fuji, Japan, November), M. Tokoro (Ed.), 1987.

[16] Warren, D.H.D. Personal communication, 1986.

[17] Yang, R. *P-Prolog: a Parallel Logic Programming Language.* Singapore: World Scientific, 1987.

[18] Yang, R. Programming in Andorra-I. Technical report, Department of Computer Science, University of Bristol, 1988.

Programming in Delta Prolog

José C. Cunha, Maria C. Ferreira, Luís Moniz Pereira

Departamento de Informática
Universidade Nova de Lisboa
2825 Monte da Caparica
Portugal

Abstract

We illustrate, through commented program examples, the constructs of Delta Prolog, a concurrent logic programming language founded on the Distributed Logic of L. Monteiro. The paper aims to show that a declarative programming style is available when using Delta Prolog. The style is similar to Prolog's, but in addition each problem can be expressed into parallelized components where a specification of their communication schemes may be present. We show this can be expressed initially without regard to the underlying computation strategy of Delta Prolog.

1 Introduction

Delta Prolog (Δ-Prolog for short) extends Prolog to include AND-concurrency and inter-process communication. The groundwork for Δ-Prolog originates with Distributed Logic (cf. Monteiro 84,86), which is neutral with regard to operational semantics. A first implementation extended C-Prolog (Pereira 83) with the main concepts previously devised, but with no coordinated interprocess backtracking strategy (Pereira et al. 84). Subsequently, a distributed backtracking algorithm and the choice operator were introduced in a new implementation (Pereira et al. 86,87). Improvements since then have concentrated on the distributed backtracking algorithm, its decentralization, treating the cut, overall clarity (Pereira et al. 88; Cunha 88) and efficiency, and portability of the implementation (Cunha et al. 87). Δ-Prolog's extension of Prolog is obtained, at the language level, by introducing three additional goal types: *splits, events,* and *choices*. At the implementation level, the extension is supported on Prolog and C; a small number of core primitives aids portability. Currently, Δ-Prolog supports distributed programs by means of the asynchronous execution of multiple instances of the extended C-Prolog interpreter.

A declarative programming style is available when using Δ-Prolog, similar to Prolog's, but in addition each problem can be expressed into parallelized components where a specification of their communication schemes may be present. At a later stage in the program design process, not shown here, some detailed knowledge of the computation strategy may be useful to obtain a more efficient execution; the programming style can influence the distributed backtracking of a concurrent program, inclusively by prefering alternative communication constructs. The extra knowledge required, if desired, to take better advantage of the more complex operational semantics is a direct consequence of the availability of new constructs which, additionally, allow more programming freedom vis-à-vis Prolog. A more detailed introduction to the language constructs as well as to its declarative and operational semantics is given in (Pereira et al. 88). Here we follow a more pragmatic approach, illustrated with commented examples showing how to :

- specify sequentiality constraints and the degree of parallelism allowable in each problem
- specify the suitable communication schemes to express inter-process cooperation that may be required for cooperative problem solving within a distributed programming setting
- exploit the several forms of non-determinism available in a Δ-Prolog program.

The rest of the paper is organized in sections for each of the above aspects. The emphasis is on the declarative programming style made possible by Δ-Prolog, sketched in the examples. The reader is directed to (Pereira et al. 84,86,87,88) for additional examples, variants of the main constructs, and the full operational semantics.

2 Sequentiality constraints and parallelism in Δ-Prolog programs

A Δ-Prolog program is a sequence of clauses of the form: H :- $G_1,...,G_n$. (n≥0). The *comma* is the *sequential* composition operator. Declaratively, the truth of goals in Δ-Prolog is order-dependant, so that H is true if $G_1,...,G_n$ are true in succession. Operationally, to solve goal H solve successively goals $G_1,...,G_n$. Also, whereas H is a Prolog goal, each G_i may be either a Prolog or a Δ-Prolog goal. The latter is either a *split* goal (for parallelism), an *event* goal (for inter-process communication) or a *choice* goal (for external non-determinism). A Δ-Prolog program without Δ-Prolog goals is and executes like a Prolog program, so Δ-Prolog is an extension to Prolog.

Parallel goal composition. Split goals are of the form $S_1 \; // \; S_2$, where $//$ is a right associative *parallel* composition operator and S_1 and S_2 are arbitrary Δ-Prolog goal expressions. In particular a,b//c//d,e stands for a,(b//(c//d)),e. Declaratively, $S_1 \; // \; S_2$ is true iff S_1 and S_2 are jointly true. The associativity of the $//$ operator reflects the declarative equivalence of A//(B//C) and (A//B)//C. Operationally, solving S1 // S2 corresponds to a concurrent resolution of goal expressions S1 and S2, i.e. to an arbitrary interleaving of their resolution steps, except that it must respect the semantics of sequential and-parallel composition and of event goals (cf. below). The execution model for the resolution of a split goal may be pictured as follows:

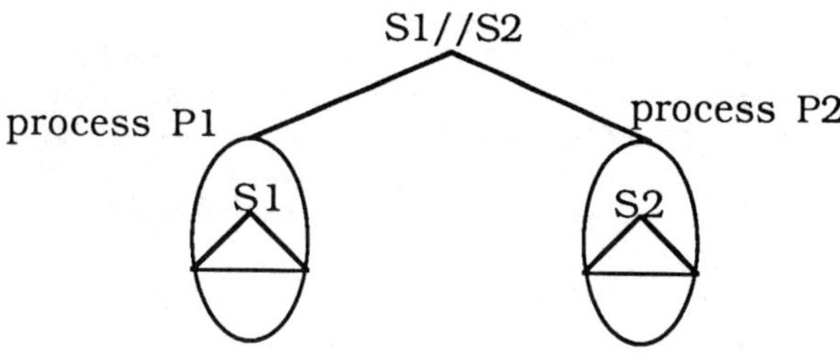

Remark: each goal expression (S1 and S2) is solved within a separate *process* and there is a basic assumption that these don't share memory. So if S1 and S2 have variable occurrences with common names, they must be unified when both processes terminate. Each process is implemented by an interpreter following a sequential depth-first search with backtracking as in Prolog. *Distributed backtracking* is an extension of the backtracking mechanism of Prolog, which is triggered by unification failure of the common variables in a split goal, the failure of a process, or the local backtracking into a previously solved split, event, or choice goal.

Quicksort example using difference lists.

A concurrent quicksort shows split goals may share variables. Slot-filling is unproblematic for free shared variables in split goals (SL in this case).

```
quicksort(U, S) :-qsort(U, S-[]).
qsort([A|U], S-L) :- part(U, A, Sm, La),
      qsort(Sm,S-[A|SL]) // qsort(La,SL-L).
qsort([], L-L).
part([X|Xs], A, Sm, [X|La]) :-  A<X,  part(Xs,A, Sm, La).
part([X|Xs], A, [X|Sm], La) :-  A>=X, part(Xs,A, Sm, La).
part([], _, [], []).
```

Declarative reading. The program has the same declarative reading as the corresponding Prolog program where "//" is replaced by the comma, and is interpreted as a conjunction of goals.

Operational semantics. We informally introduce the concept of derivation tree for a program and a goal (cf. [Pereira et al. 88] for a detailed rigorous definition). The nodes in the tree are labelled with resolvents, the root being the top goal. Given a node, a descendant node is obtained by selecting the leftmost goal G in its resolvent:

• if G is a Prolog goal, the node is the outcome of a resolution step involving a matching clause;

• if G is a Δ-Prolog goal of the form $G_1//G_2$, the node has 2 direct descendants, corresponding to the resolvents for the individual goals G_1 and G_2, each handled by a separate process.

Consider the top goal "quicksort([2,1,3],X)". Execution of part([1,3],2, Sm, La) is first completed, with substitutions Sm = [1] and

La = [3], and only then activation of the split goal qsort()//qsort() is allowed. The execution model of Δ-Prolog allows the parallel expansion of any of the current leaves in a derivation tree. A successful derivation is one such that every leaf is the empty resolvent.

3 Inter-process communication in Δ-Prolog

Besides communication through logical variables, Δ-Prolog offers a basic language mechanism for inter-process communication: *event* goals, which may be synchronous or asynchronous.

Synchronous event goals. There are two main types, X ? E : C   and X ! E : C where X is a term (the *message*), ? and ! are infix binary predicate symbols (the *communication modes*), E is bound to a Prolog atom (the *event name*), and C is a goal expression (the *event condition*), which may not evaluate Δ-Prolog goals. If C is the literal *true*, event goals may simplify to X ? E and X ! E. Two event goals are *complementary* iff they have the same event name, one of mode ? and the other of mode !. An event goal, say X?E:C, solves only with a complementary event goal, say Y!E:D, "simultaneously", whenever the latter is available in a parallel derivation (unavailability causes resolution of the goal to "suspend"). The two goals solve iff X and Y unify and then conditions C and D evaluate to true. A solved event goal is not by itself true or false. It can only be said that it was true *when* it solved with its complementary goal. Thus, the declarative semantics of Δ-Prolog does not assign an "absolute" truth value to a goal. In general, a goal is true for some combination sequences of events (or traces) that were true, and false for others.

Remarks:
   • Solving event goals is a form of "rendez-vous" of the two derivations solving the goals, with exchange of messages achieved by unification of X and Y and evaluation of conditions C and D. This basic synchronization mechanism of Δ-Prolog generalizes Hoare's and Milner's synchronous communication (Hoare 85; Milner 80) by using term unification for message exchange. No special significance is attached to the communication modes ! and ? (like "send" or "receive"), except that they are complementary in the sense above.
   • To preserve the declarative semantics, but only whenever there is no common memory implemented, it is required that after the two conditions' evaluation both X and Y be ground. Alternatively, as there is no shared memory, one could record any variables shared by X and Y and attempt to unify them upon termination of the processes solving the events (this is automatically done for the common variables in a split goal). A less strict condition would allow variables in the message as long as they result from unification of two anonymous variables (i.e. those with a single occurrence in a clause).
   • Failure of or local backtracking into an event goal causes distributed backtracking. An event name may not be shared by more than two active processes, otherwise completeness may be impaired (Pereira et al. 88).
   • For improved efficiency, synchronous communication with no backtracking involved is also supported in Δ-Prolog through the binary

predicates !!! and ???, where the above restriction does not apply. This means that there is no complete search strategy for the handling of the joint failure of two goals like T1!!!E and T2???E , i.e. when both of these event goals fail, then each corresponding process backtracks locally. Likewise, no distributed backtracking occurs when a process backtracks over a synchronous event goal of this type.

An example of a simple game of touch and go

Bidirectionality of communication in synchronous event goals is shown in the next program, a simple version of the game of "touch and go": a pursuer process tries to catch a fugitive process, and the processes invert their roles after each successful catch. The current positions for each process are exchanged in the synchronous event named "game". The approach and escape strategies for each process (in predicates new_position/2 and approach/6) are not detailed.

```
% top goal (where the pursuer starts at position (0,0))
      :- fugitive(go) // pursuer(0,0,go).

fugitive(stop) :- pursuer(0,0,go).
fugitive(go) :- new_position(X,Y), display_position(X,Y,'*'),
      fug(X,Y)&pur(A,B) ! game, am_I_caught(X,Y,A,B,T),  fugitive(T).
pursuer(_,_,stop) :- fugitive(go).
pursuer(X,Y,go) :- display_position(X,Y,'>'),
      fug(A,B)&pur(X,Y) ? game, catch_you(A,B,X,Y,NX,NY,T),
pursuer(NX,NY,T).
am_I_caught(X,Y,X,Y,stop).
am_I_caught(_, _, _, _, go).
catch_you(X, Y,  X,  Y,  _,   _, stop).
catch_you(X,Y,MX,MY,NX,NY,go) :- approach(X,Y,MX,MY,NX,NY).
```

An example of a simple filtering system

This is a system with three processes, where an intermediate process (with top goal filter/4) filters each result that is sent by a producer process (with top goal prod/2); next it sends it to a consumer process (cons/2). Note that event names can be variable parameters.

```
p(X) :- prod(X,e1) // filter(e1,e2,1,5) // cons(Y,e2).        % top goal
prod(X,To) :- a(X), X ! To.
a(1).        a(2).        a(3).        a(4).        a(5).

filter(From,To,Lower,Upper):- X ? From : (X>Lower, X<Upper), X ! To.

cons(X,From) :- X ? From.
```

Declarative reading. The relation defined by p(X) and the program is the set of all singletons (Xθ) for all substitutions θ such that Xθ is ground and is true in the minimal model of the program for the null trace (Monteiro 86; Pereira et al. 88). This corresponds to the substitutions {X=2}, {X=3} and {X=4}, obtained by successful resolution of event goals X!e1 and X?e1: (X>1, X<5) in the communication between the producer and the filter, and of event goals X!e2 and X?e2 in the communication between the filter and the consumer. The substitutions {X=1} and {X=5} are ruled out by the event condition. In (Monteiro 86) it is shown that a Δ-Prolog program possesses a rigorous definition of its refutation semantics, proven equivalent to its declarative and fixpoint semantics.

Operational semantics. Δ-Prolog is responsible for finding the successful derivations that are defined by a goal and program. A successful derivation tree has the empty resolvent in all of its leaves and a corresponding null trace (i.e. where all event goals have been successfully solved). The resolution rule of event goals is that, given a derivation tree with two leaves of the form:

$$X \; ? \; E : C \, , \, G_2, \, ..., \, G_n \qquad \text{and} \qquad Y \; ! \; E : D \, , \, G'_2, \, ..., \, G'_m$$

where event goals X?E:C and Y!E:D resolve with unifier θ obtained by first unifying X and Y and then solving C and D, then each leaf spawns a new node and resolvent with the respective forms:

$$(G_2, \, ..., \, G_n)\theta \qquad \text{and} \qquad (G'_2, \, ..., \, G'_m)\theta$$

Thus the rule defines a joint derivation step that "simultaneously" occurs in the processes that are responsible for the expansion of those branches in the derivation tree. If the conditions for event success are not fulfilled the corresponding derivation tree is not expandable anymore, i.e. the computation strategy must abandon it and try to explore alternative derivations.

Executing the filtering system, a derivation is produced whose leaves are headed by event goals:

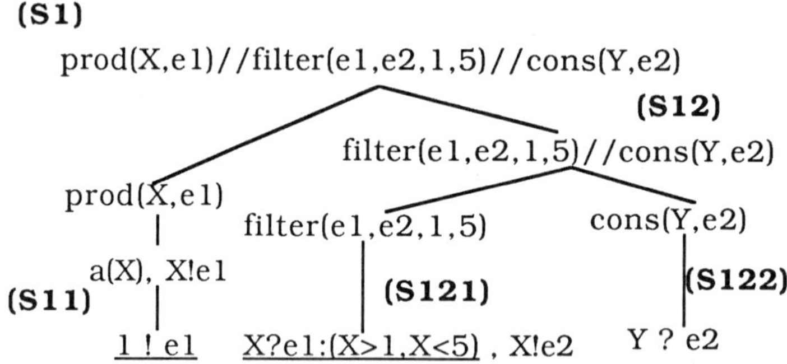

The rightmost leaf in the tree is *suspended* as no complementary event goal currently exists heading another leaf. Other leaves contain complementary leading event goals exist, but their joint resolution fails because the event condition (X>1, X<5) is not satisfied for X=1. A search strategy must now find the next derivation in the space of possible derivations. As we are modelling the expansion of each branch in the tree by processes following Prolog's sequential search strategy, the mechanism for searching alternative derivations involves two aspects:

• a local search is performed by each process relative to the doing and undoing of derivation steps of Prolog goals; this follows Prolog's depth-first search and uses local backtracking within each process; a gain is obtainable here, vis-à-vis a purely sequential system, as we have multiple Prolog processes that may be executing in parallel both in the forward and backward directions;

• a global coordination of the search is required whenever a joint derivation step (involving an event or a split goal) must be done or undone; this is done following a distributed backtracking strategy demanding the cooperation of all processes that may depend on the joint step.

The details of this distributed backtracking strategy are not explained here: cf. (Pereira et al. 88; Cunha 88). Its main purpose is to implement an exhaustive search for the set of successful derivations for a program and goal, where a distinction between local and global search is made and no centralized control component is required. The computation path of each process is sliced down into consecutive *segments*, identified as derivation paths between two consecutive Δ-Prolog goals (cf. the derivation tree for the example above, where each segment is identified by a diadic number which encodes a lexicographic ordering). The concept of segment allows concentrating on interaction points only, and ignore local backtracking within segments (which is dealt with by each process alone). An ordering amongst segments is defined that guides an exhaustive search through all alternative derivations. The global strategy is invoked only when a process, in local backtracking, reaches a previously solved Δ-Prolog goal, or when the conditions for success of a synchronous event fail.

The filtering example shows a simple case, where only 2 processes are involved in a failure: the consumer process, being suspended on its event goal, is not involved in the communication failure occurring at event named e1. So when the search strategy abandons the derivation tree shown, the branch for the consumer process is unnaffected by the search for alternatives involving the other processes. It is up to the producer to backtrack locally and try to offer alternative bindings to the event term X, while the filter process just waits for those alternatives by hanging at its event goal. In all cases the systematic approach is such that its decisions are based on the ordering among the segments involved (e.g. S11 and S121 in the example):

• the process of the lower segment in the ordering (S11) is forced to hang at its event goal;

• the other process is forced to backtrack and search for local alternatives.

In the filtering example, as no local alternatives are available within the filter process, search will ultimately force backtracking into the producer process. Thus a first solution is obtained where X=2, which is passed over to the consumer. If further solutions are requested, distributed backtracking forces the filter and consumer processes to relaunch their top goals (so that all their solutions become available again) while the producer backtracks locally (past event goal X ! e1) and obtains alternative bindings for X.

4-colour maps example

This program illustrates the creation and launching of a top goal for colouring the regions of planar maps, with at most four colours, such that no two adjacent regions have the same colour. The program consists in the construction and launching (in parallel for each region), of a region-specific parallel top goal that checks whether the colours of that region's bordering ones are different from the colour chosen for itself by the region. Failure to comply with the different-colour constraint ignites distributed backtracking, but affecting only the necessary regions. A top goal has the form

$$\text{:- region}(r_1, L_1, C_1) \ // \ ... \ // \ \text{region}(r_n, L_n, C_n).$$

where each r_i, L_i, C_i denotes a region name, a list of its adjacent region's names, and the region's solution colour. The four possible colours are expressed, say, by:

colour(green).   colour(yellow).   colour(red).   colour(blue).

Each region predicate call chooses a colour for the region and then sets up and executes in parallel all the tests required to check for colour compatibility with its neighbouring regions, in "Test".

```
region(R, B, C) :- setup_test(C, R, B, Test ), colour(C), Test.
setup_test(C, R, [], true).
setup_test(C, R, [B], Test_B ) :- create_test(C,R,B,Test_B).
setup_test(C, R, [B|L], (Test_B // Test_L) ) :-
      create_test(C, R, B, Test_B), setup_test(C, R, L, Test_L).
```

The creation of a test introduces, for efficiency, an assymmetry with respect to region names: regions with an alphabetically lower name "send" a request for the colour of their alphabetically higher bordering neighbour, receive from it its colour and test for colour similarity. Thus, the colour constraint is only tested by one of any two bordering regions, and not redundantly by both. For each frontier between two regions a unique event name is generated and used for communicating colour from one to the other.

```
create_test(C1, R, B, (colour(C2) ! Event : not C1=C2) ) :- R @≤ B, !,
      event_name(B,R, Event).
create_test(C1, R, B, (colour(C1) ? Event) ) :- event_name(R, B, Event).
event_name(R, B, Event) :- name(R, NR), name(B, NB),
      append(NR, NB, NE), name(Event, NE).
```

In the case of the map

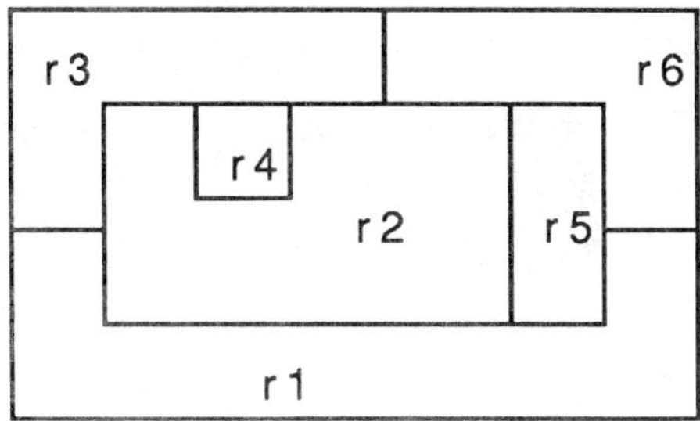

we have the top goal
:- region(r1,[r2,r3,r5,r6],C1)   // region(r2,[r1,r3,r4,r5,r6],C2) //
   region(r3,[r1,r2,r4,r6],C3)   // region(r4,[r2,r3],C4)   //
   region(r5,[r1,r2,r6],C5)   // region(r6,[r1,r2,r3,r5],C6).

The execution of, say, region(r5,[r1,r2,r6], C5), launches the Test:
colour(C5) ? r5r1 // colour(C5) ?r5r2 // colour(C6) ! r6r5 : not C5=C6.

Asynchronous event goals. These allow the sending and receiving of
Prolog terms as messages, using respectively the forms T ^^ E and T ?? E,
where E is bound to a Prolog atom (the *event name*) and T is a term. If T
is a non-ground term the receiver process obtains a local copy for each
variable in T, its instantiation reflecting the received message. The
semantics of these constructs is defined in a way comparable, respectively,
to the one for "write" and "read" in i/o streams. Currently no distributed
backtracking applies to event goals of this type although the distributed
backtracking strategy could be extended to deal with asynchronous
communication. An alternative is to simulate the asynchronous model in
terms of synchronous event goals and choice goals (cf. next section) using
an intermediate buffer . Thus asynchronous goals are mainly provided for
convenience and efficiency.

An example for an air-line reservation system
Multiple terminal processes interact with a database process responsible
for the management of a simple air-line reservation system , by processing
user requests of the forms:
    info(flight_number, Number_of_available_seats)
    reserve(flight_number, number_of_requested_seats, Answer)

"Number_of_available_seats" gives the available seats on the flight, and
Answer is 'YES' or 'NO'. Serialization is achieved by having the database
process (predicate dbase/1) first receive the terminal name for a user
process through an asynchronous event goal named "data". Then a single
synchronous event goal is used to support the reception of a request, its
processing (within the event condition) and the return of the results to the
user. The name of the synchronous event goal is the terminal name for
each user process, and is dynamically transmitted to the database process.

% top goal :- terminal(t1)//terminal(t2)//terminal(t3) // dbase([112,256,68]).

Each terminal solves the top goal "terminal(ttyn)" where ttyn is its terminal name.

terminal(Tty) :- read(X), Tty ^^ data, X ! Tty, write(X), nl, terminal(Tty).

The database process keeps a list (DB) with the current state of available seats for each flight, and solves, e.g., a top goal of the form "dbase([112,256,68])".

```
dbase(DB) :-  Next_tty ?? data, dbase(DB, Next_tty).
dbase(DB, Next_tty) :-
    Request ? Next_tty : dbprocess(Request,Next_tty,DB,New_DB),
    dbase(New_DB).
dbprocess(info(Flight, Seats), _, DB, DB) :-
    information(DB, Flight, Seats).
dbprocess(reserve(Flight, Seats, Response), _, DB, New_DB) :-
    reserve(Flight, Seats, DB, Response, New_DB).
dbprocess(_, Next, DB, DB) :-  write('unknown command from '),
    write(Next),  nl.
```

4 Non-determinism in Δ-Prolog   programs

Δ-Prolog programs exhibit the same types of non-determinism found in Prolog, namely a form of *internal* or *local non-determinism* corresponding to the possibility of unifying a Prolog goal with alternative clauses, the selection of any one such clause (within each process) being independent of the state of the environment (i.e. of any other processes). Concurrency and communication introduce additional forms of non-determinism in Δ-Prolog. In order to model *external* or *global non-determinism* (Francez et al. 79), where the environment can influence the choice of an event among a set of alternatives for commmunication, the language includes choice goals, based on its namesake introduced in (Hoare 85).

Choice goals. These have the form $A_1 :: A_2 :: ... :: A_n$ (n≥2), where :: is the *choice* operator, and the A_i are the *alternatives* of the goal. Each alternative has the form "G_e,B", where G_e is a synchronous event goal (the head of the alternative), sequentially conjuncted to a possibly empty goal expression B (body of the alternative). Declaratively, $A_1 :: A_2 :: ... :: A_n$ is true iff at least one alternative is true. Solving a choice goal consists in solving the G_e of any one alternative (whose choice is governed by the availability of a complementary goal for G_e) and then solving its body B. If no complementary events are available for any alternative the choice suspends. Operationally, the behaviour of *choice* is extended to deal with backtracking. Failure of the selected alternative or failure into the choice initiates a specific distributed backtracking discipline such that the remaining choice alternatives (if any) are considered for computation (the failed alternative being abandoned). If no alternatives remain to be explored then the whole choice goal fails.

An example of a counter object

This example is given in (Shapiro 83). It may be programmed as in (Pereira et al. 84) by using a backtracking strategy or, alternatively, it may use a choice goal as below. The top goal has the form ":-terminal // counter(0)" where terminal processes request operations on the object via a synchronous event. According to the request issued, a choice alternative is selected and executed.

```
terminal :- read(X),  do_it(X),  write(X),  nl,  next(X).
do_it( abolish ) :-        _ ! abolish.
do_it( up ) :-             _ ! up.
do_it( down ):-            _ ! down.
do_it( show(S) ) :-        S ! show.
do_it( clear ) :-          _ ! clear.
counter(S) :- (  _ ? clear,     counter(0)
          ::    _ ? up,         U is S+1,  counter(U)
          ::    _ ? down,       D is S-1,  counter(D)
          ::    S ? show,       counter(S)
          ::    _ ? abolish ).
next(abolish).
next(_) :-  terminal.
```

Touch and go with n pursuers

Here we allow n pursuers in the previous "touch and go" game and further specify that the game must be over on the first successful catch of the fugitive. The termination of the game could easily be modeled by having an arbiter process as a central coordinator (as an alternative a broadcast mechanism would be helpful, possibly using the logical variable as a communication channel). Instead an asynchronous event with name "stop" is used which indicates the end of the game: on being caught the fugitive process sends a term "end_of_game". This term is then successively received by each of the pursuers, as an alternative in a choice goal. Each pursuer starts with a brother process responsible for detecting the termination of the game (which it signals through a synchronous event named   after the pursuer identification (cf. variable Port)). This extra process is required because an asynchronous event goal may not be the head of an alternative in a choice goal.

```
% top goal for a game with 3 pursuers, each starting at (0,0)
     :- fugitive(go) //pursuers(0,0,1) //pursuers(0,0,2) //pursuers(0,0,3).
fugitive(stop) :- end_game ^^  stop.
fugitive(go) :- new_position(X, Y),
      display_position(X, Y, '*'),
      fug(X, Y) & pur(A, B)  !!! game,   % non-backtrackable event
      am_I_caught(X, Y, A, B, T), fugitive(T).

pursuers(X, Y, Identification) :- build_name(Identification, Port),
      pursuer(X, Y, Port) // termination(Port).
```

```
pursuer(X, Y, Port) :- display_position(X, Y, '>'),
    ( end_game ? Port
    ::
    fug(A, B) & pur(X, Y)  ???  game,        % non-backtrackable event
    catch_you(A, B, X, Y, NX, NY,_),  pursuer(NX, NY, Port)
    ).
termination(Port) :- end_game ?? stop, end_game ^^ stop,
    end_game ! Port.
```

Back to the air-line reservation system

The previous program for the air-line database forces each terminal process to hang waiting for the completion of its request on a synchronous event, while at the same time forcing all other terminals to hang, waiting to be served. This restriction can be lifted by decomposing the database process into three separate ones: the merge, responsible for receiving user requests, the database, responsible for their processing, and the split, responsible for the sending of results. Non-backtrackable synchronous events (denoted by !!! and ???) can be used here for efficiency reasons (just replace ! and ? in the text, respectively by !!! and ???).

```
% top goal :-  terminal(t1)   //   terminal(t2)   //   database([180,290])   //
               split([(Answer&Terminal)?s]).
```

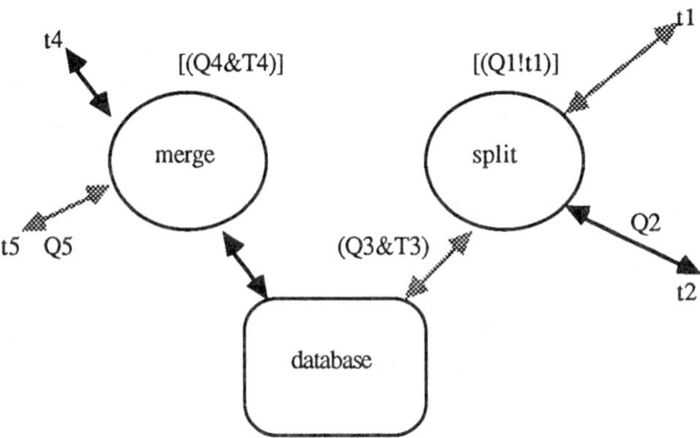

a) The terminal process sends a pair of the form "Question & T" to the merger process. "Question" is a user request and "T" is the terminal name where the answer is to be collected via an event.

```
terminal(T) :- read(Question), (Question&T) ! m, Answer ? T,
    write(Answer), terminal(T).
```

b) The merge process acts as a buffer process between the terminal processes and the database; it starts by receiving a first request and then cycles receiving additional requests or sending them for processing.

merge([]) :- (Question&Terminal) ? m, merge([(Question&Terminal)]).

merge([H|T]) :- (
    (Question&Terminal) ? m,
     append([H|T], [(Question&Terminal)], NL), merge(NL)
    ::
    H ! data, merge(T)
).

c) The database process
database(DB) :- (Question&Terminal) ? data,
    dbprocess(Question, Terminal, DB, NDB),
    (Question&Terminal) ! s , database(NDB).

d) The split process uses a choice goal in order to receive the replies to the user queries as they are produced by the database process or to send them to the terminal processes that are ready to get them. The choice alternatives must be dynamically built, as new replies to user queries are received by the split process (note that since process split has to keep an alternative for receiving further replies from the database process, every time a reply is received (on event named s), a new alternative has to be built for that event in order to allow a new communication, c.f. below, first clause of new_choice_list/3). A variant of the choice (*dynamic choice*), which allows a more flexible manipulation of the choice alternatives, is useful here. Its syntax is *choice_list(L, A)* , where A represents the heading event goal for the selected alternative (in the form (Term, Event_Type, Event_Name, Condition)) and L stands for a (non-empty) list of choice alternatives in the form (Term Event_Type Event_Name : Condition, Body).

split(L) :- choice_list(L,Alternative), new_choicelist(Alternative,L,NL),
    split(NL).

new_choicelist(((Answer&Terminal), ?, s , _), L,NL) :-
    remove(((Answer&Terminal)? s), L ,L1),
    append([(Answer ! Terminal), ((NAnsw&NTerm)?s)], L1, NL).
new_choicelist((Answer, !, Terminal, _), L,NL) :-
    remove((Answer ! Terminal), L , NL).

Non-attacking queens
   Two possible solutions to the problem of N non-attacking queens on a chessboard (Wirth 76) are discussed in the sequel.

(i) Central chessboard
   A single process (solving goal board/2) is responsible for keeping the current state of the chessboard and checking for the compatibility of queens' positions. Each queen has a fixed column number (J) and an associated process (solving goal queen/2 where NQueens is the number of queens) responsible for its placement along that column. This is achieved by choosing a line (predicate pick_line/2 not shown) and then offering the

queen's position to the chessboard process through event "qJ " (event name given by build_name/2).

```
queen(J, NQueens) :- build_name(J, Event), pick_line(NQueens, I),
     (I&J) ! Event.
```

The top goal is ":- queens(R,8)." and an initial setup takes place to launch the required processes.
```
queens(Result, NQueens) :-
     board(NQueens, Result) // set_up(NQueens, NQueens).
```

```
set_up(1, NQ) :- !, queen(1, NQ).
set_up(N, NQ) :- M is N-1, queen(N, NQ) // set_up(M, NQ).
board(NQ, R) :- build_choice(NQ, [],ChoiceList),
     accept_queens(ChoiceList,[], R, NQ).
```

The board process must build a list of alternatives for the communication of the queens' positions, where the order of communications is not a priori known. Initially the list (as given by build_choice/3) has the form [(_&_)?q1,(_&_)?q2,..., (_&_)?q8]. A dynamic choice goal is used for the non-deterministic selection of one of the available alternatives and then a test is performed (predicate accept/3) to check acceptance of the received queen position, depending on the current board configuration (being kept on the list PartialBoard). An accepted queen's position (I,J) is added to the PartialBoard and the board process recurses, considering only the remaining queens (ChoiceList being updated by predicate remove/3). A solution is found when all queens have been accepted. (Remark: operationally, failure to accept a queen triggers distributed backtracking and a queen process is ultimately forced to search for a new position by locally backtracking within pick_line, while the board process keeps the corresponding alternative open for communication).

```
accept_queens([], Result, Result, _).
accept_queens(ChoiceList, PartialBoard, Result, NQ) :-
     choice_list(ChoiceList, ((X&Y), ?, Event, _)),
     accept(PartialBoard, (X,Y), NQ),
     remove(ChoiceList, Event, NewChoiceList),
     accept_queens(NewChoiceList, [(X,Y)|PartialBoard], Result, NQ).
```

(ii) Chessboard as a ring token
An alternative solution could be devised where the processes representing the queens are connected in a ring structure. Each queen process has a local (possibly incomplete) view of the chessboard (using a suitable representation). This view reflects the current chosen position for the corresponding queen plus information exchanged with its neighbours. The exchange is achieved through events (suitably named by build_names/4) where the chessboards of the intervening queens are mutually unified, and so any incompatibility is ruled out by pattern matching (since disallowed positions are marked). A solution is found when a complete chessboard is detected. The exchanges take place according to a certain direction around the ring, although this need not be

fixed a priori (a choice goal could be used instead of the last two clauses for ring/5).

The top goal is ":- queens(Result,8).", which is analogous to the one given above, except for inexistence of the board process. Each queen process is specified by:

```
queen(J, Board,NQueens) :- build_ names(J, Right, Left, NQueens),
      direction(J, Direction), pick_line(NQueens, I), set_board(I,J,Board),
      ring(Direction, Board, Right, Left, NQueens).
```

```
ring(_,Board,_,_,NQ) :- all_queens_accepted(Board, NQ).
ring(right, Board, Right, Left, NQ) :- Board ! Left,
      ring(left, Board, Right, Left, NQ).
ring(left, Board, Right, Left, NQ) :- Board ? Right,
      ring(right, Board, Right, Left, NQ).
```

5 Conclusions

Δ-Prolog subsumes Prolog (a Δ-Prolog program without Δ-Prolog goals is and executes like a Prolog program) and extends it with non-deterministic AND-concurrency with distributed backtracking, plus interprocess communication without redefining unification. It does not enforce commitment, like the clause guards of Concurrent Prolog (Shapiro 83), Parlog (Clark Gregory 84) and Guarded Horn Clauses (Ueda 85), nor does it require synchronization mechanisms affecting unification semantics. A comparison of these languages and Δ-Prolog is found in (Butler et al. 86; Aparício 87). Currently, Δ-Prolog supports distributed programs through the asynchronous execution of multiple instances of an extended C-Prolog interpreter on a single processor. Research is being carried out on improvements of the computation strategy for Δ-Prolog.

Acknowledgements
To colleagues, ALPES, DEC, GFC, INIC, and JNICT.

References

Aparício, J.N. 1987. Concorrência na Programação em Lógica. M.Sc. thesis, Deptº de Informática, Universidade Nova de Lisboa.

Butler, R.; Lusk, E.; McCune, W.; Overbeek, R. 1986. Parallel logic programming for numeric applications. In *Proc. 3rd Int. Conf. on Logic Programming,*, pp 375-388, LNCS **225**, Springer-Verlag, New York.

Clark, K.; Gregory, S. 1984. Parlog: Parallel programming in logic. Research Report DOC 84/4, Imperial College, London.

Cunha, J.C.; Medeiros, P.; Carvalhosa, M. 1987. Interfacing Prolog to the operating system environment: mechanisms for parallelism and concurrency control. Technical report, Dept² de Informática, Universidade Nova de Lisboa.

Cunha, J.C. 1988. Execução Concorrente de uma Linguagem de Programação em Lógica. Ph.D. thesis, Dept². de Informática, Universidade Nova de Lisboa.

Francez, N.; Hoare, C.A.R.; Lehmann, D.J.; Roever. W.P. 1979. Semantics of nondeterminism, concurrency and communication. *J. Comp. Syst. Sci.* **19**, 290-308.

Hoare, C.A.R. 1985. *Communicating sequential processes.* Prentice-Hall, New Jersey.

Milner, R. 1980. *A calculus of communicating systems.* LNCS **92**, Springer-Verlag, New York.

Monteiro, L. 1984. A proposal for distributed programming in logic. In *Implementations of Prolog* (J.A. Campbell ed.), Ellis Horwood, Chichester.

Monteiro, L. 1986. Distributed logic: a theory of distributed programming in logic. Dept² de Informática, Univ. Nova de Lisboa.

Pereira, F. (ed.) 1983. C-Prolog User's Manual, DAI, Edinburgh.

Pereira, L.M.; Nasr, R. 1984. Delta-Prolog: a distributed logic programming language. In *Proc. of Fitfh Generation Computer Systems*, Tokyo.

Pereira, L.M.; Monteiro L.; Cunha J.C.; Aparício J.N. 1986. Delta-Prolog: a distributed backtracking extension with events. In *Proc. 3rd Int. Conf. on Logic Programming,*, pp 69-83, LNCS **225**, Springer-Verlag, New York.

Pereira, L.M.; Monteiro L.; Cunha, J.C.; Aparício, J.N.; Ferreira, M.C. 1987. Delta-Prolog User's Manual. Dep² de Informática, Univ. Nova de Lisboa.

Pereira, L.M.; Monteiro L.; Cunha, J.C.; Aparício, J.N. 1988. Concurrency and Communication in Delta-Prolog. Conf. Proc. IEE Int. Specialist Seminar on "The Design and Application of Parallel Digital Processors", pp. 94-104, Lisbon.

Shapiro, E.Y. 1983. A subset of Concurrent Prolog and its interpreter. Weizmann Science Institute, Rehovot.

Ueda, K. 1985. Guarded Horn clauses.. Report TR-103, ICOT, Tokyo.

Wirth, N. 1976. Algorithms + data structures = programs. Prentice-Hall.

Programming Environments

Towards Distributed Tools for Heterogeneous Logic Programming Environments

José A. S. Alegria, Artur M. Dias and Luís Caires

Departamento de Informática
Universidade Nova de Lisboa
2825 Monte da Caparica
PORTUGAL

Abstract

MACLOGIC is a logic programming environment based on Apple Macintosh personal computers which can also be used as an ergonomic *Interface-Station* to webs of sequential Prolog processes distributed across a shared local area network of heterogeneous processors. The name "MACLOGIC" suggests the interrupt-free event driven "logic" behind Macintosh applications, and the framework extends this "logic" with remote event posting. Participating distributed/local processes have a single private (priority) queue of events with communication achieved by remote/local event posting. Underlying protocols allow for the asynchronous mapping of interface related events in the *InterfaceStation* into terms to be interpreted by any "listening" Prolog process. Symmetrically, application related events may map into requests to one of the *InterfaceStation* managers or tools. A canonical term representation provides a standard mechanism for communication between heterogeneous Prolog implementations as well as communication with non-Prolog applications. This framework is the basis for the architecture of MACLOGIC's distributed editor and browser. MACLOGIC, nevertheless, can be used as a stand-alone logic programming environment.

1 Introduction

The MACLOGIC environment framework and prototype were designed with the purpose of supporting in the same physical setting both a top quality office automation environment and a research oriented distributed and heterogeneous Logic Programming environment. This common physical setup is currently constituted by an AppleTalk™ network of Apple Macintosh personal computers linked through a bridge to an Ethernet of various Unix™ workstations and servers, all under SUN's Network File System (NFS). In the future, we hope to support multiprocessors.

The "desktop" of the research environment relies on the Macintosh (Figure 1) working like a personal *InterfaceStation*, while computation greedy problem solvers may run distributed across the Unix servers, probably written in different and highly efficient commercial Prologs. The Unix machines play in the environment the role of *LogicServers*.

The environment interface resides on the Macintosh side and is implemented in C and in C-Prolog. The latter, after being ported from Unix to the Macintosh, was extended with a complete interface to the Macintosh toolbox [4, 5] and with a set of basic mechanisms supporting distributed communication between heterogeneous processes. Programming can be done directly on the Macintosh but executed either remotely or locally.

Personal desktop research environments

Postscript™
printer server

Shared local area network of powerful servers

Figure 1

Some of the tools are truly distributed, with part of their functionality implemented on the *InterfaceStation* side and the remaining on a *Logic-Server*. User programs, like the tools, can be distributed and have their user interface running on one *InterfaceStation*. These distributed tools and user programs can be written in any Prolog or language supporting our *Canonical Term Representation (CTR) and Remote Term Posting (RTP)* toolkits described later. These toolkits are crucial to our architecture and are at the heart of our distributed tools like our Browser and Editor, for instance.

Although the RTP protocol is currently implemented on top of the relatively slow **A**pplication **T**ransaction **P**rotocol of AppleTalk, it will be easy to port it to more efficient transport level protocols like "plain" TCP/IP or, better, *Versatile Message Transaction Protocol* (VMTP), a transport-level protocol designed by Cheriton to support remote procedure call, multicast and real-time communication [6].

Note that with this framework it will be possible to support within the same distributed environment both structure-sharing and non-structure-sharing components by supporting different communicating Prolog implementations. The ability to mix both strategies is likely to prove advantageous in large scale systems.

In this paper, we briefly introduce the main architectural principles implemented in the MACLOGIC distributed environment as well as their rationale. Its main services (managers and tools) are outlined, and the canonical term representation and remote term posting mechanism are discussed and application examples given. Finally, the outline of the distributed architecture of the MACLOGIC browser engine is provided. A more detailed account of the MACLOGIC project can be found in [1-3]. A preliminary implementation is available.

2   MACLOGIC'S Architecture

MACLOGIC's programming environment conceptual architecture centers around an environment knowledge base (EKB) supporting a general notion of browsing and editing. Programming is achieved by manipulating this EKB mainly through browsing and editing. Other static and dynamic tools further support the browsing process with diagnostic capabilities. Compilation, not yet available, is desirable for more efficient execution.

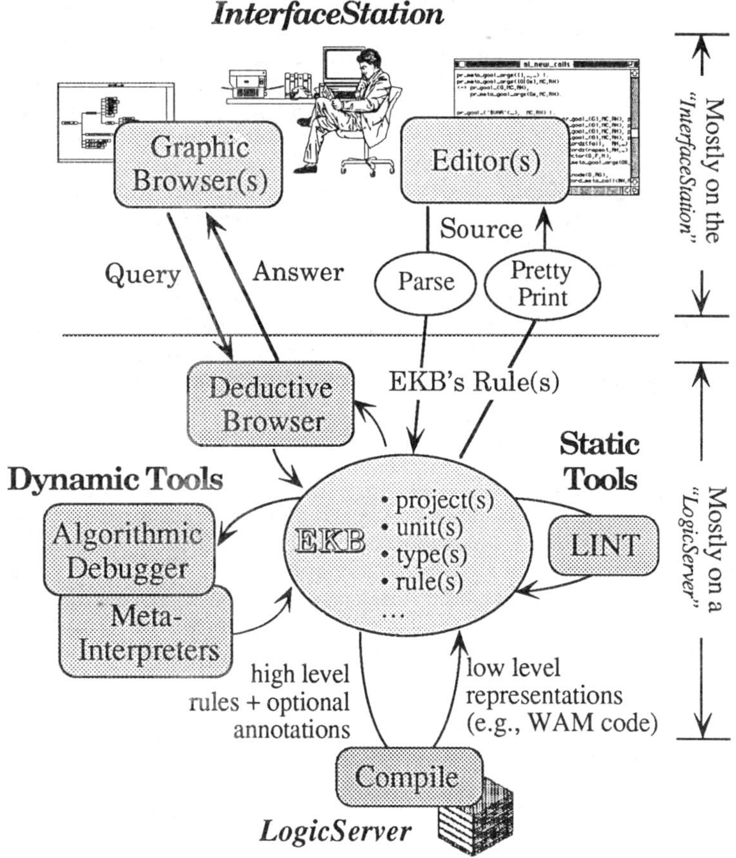

Figure 2

In Figure 2 we can see the main components in place. Here, a separation is made between components which are more of a "problem-solving" nature from those that are more of a "user-interaction" nature. Such separation is useful for distribution purposes: part reside on the *InterfaceStation*, the rest being distributed through a set of different and possibly heterogeneous *LogicServers*, relying perhaps on highly efficient albeit incompatible commercial Prologs. This division, however, is not mandatory. MACLOGIC can perfectly function as a stand-alone environment for development of less CPU-eager programs.

An advanced logic programming environment can and should support browsing as a deductive EKB process, furnishing the answer to questions about all meaningful environment relations, rather than just simple "pointer chasing" as in most classical programming environments (where browsing is limited to a set of pre-defined relations [8]). The EKB doesn't need to be fully explicit since useful information can be obtained using Prolog's meta-abilities. For convenience, however, it is desirable to have explicit high level representations for programming components such as predicates, clauses (rules), and predicate types, for the benefit of efficient static (LINT or static analyzer) and dynamic tools (debuggers and diverse meta-interpreters).

The interface requirements for such a general *deductive browsing* are obviously complex. The full power of natural language would be ultimately an asset. However, we have achieved a reasonable compromise by requiring from the EKB an intermediate binary view for every "browsable" relation. This has made possible the development of a generic *graphic browser* whose architecture is discussed later. A natural language based browser is also under development by members of our research group, following up on António Porto's work on semantic unification [14].

Furthermore, a general editing model for the EKB is required. Here, also, as long as editing actions on the binary view of a relation can be mapped back onto the original relation, generic editing is possible. Text editing is possible as long as "parsing" and "pretty-printing" properties are available for the relation in question.

MACLOGIC's execution environment makes available to user programs the full functionality of the *InterfaceStation* concept plus the capability of running distributed or on the Macintosh. Functionally, the environment interface provides a set of resident managers (catering for different types of interface services) and a set of tools for higher level user interaction. These have global names qualified by their respective *InterfaceStation* name. Among the managers we have the file system, window, menu, dialog, sound, speech, basic graphic and text editing ones. The programming environment's own editor and generic graphic browser can also be used by user processes for higher level user interaction.

MACLOGIC's event driven framework, supported by its remote term posting scheme, together with its managers and tools are basis for the distributed architecture.

3 MACLOGIC Environment Managers and Tools

MACLOGIC managers provide sophisticated user interaction mechanisms to Prolog processes. Without loosing flexibility and control, they provide

Macintosh interface mechanisms at a higher level freeing the Prolog programmer from the tricky and complex programming needed at low level interface programming [4,5]. They were themselves heavily used in building some of the MACLOGIC tools.

The managers supply primitives for the creation of entities which have a reasonable amount of autonomy and know how to behave in most circumstances. Their behavior is controlled by the underlying MACLOGIC support system. Only in some well defined conditions does an entity request from the Prolog process which created it, to perform an action using the remote term posting mechanism.

For example, MACLOGIC's Dialog Manager includes a predicate that creates and installs a list item on a dialog window (similarly to the Macintosh "Standard File Dialog"). Almost every user interaction with this list is handled by the system, including the operations of scrolling and selection of entries. The only special action we consider on this kind of item is double-clicking an entry. A high level event is generated and remotely/locally posted on the listening Prolog process to interpret.

MACLOGIC managers also provide Prolog processes with the ability to access or change the internal state of these entities and, of course, to destroy them.

3.1. MACLOGIC Main Managers

There follows a description of the principal features of the main managers.

Window Manager: There are several kinds of windows each one having its own manager. This manager controls window attributes that are not specific, like size, placement, set aside state (i.e., on the desktop), text font and text size. It can also control the relative front to back order of windows, obtain the list of all existent windows, and delete any window. Printing of any kind of window is also supported.

Text Window Manager: This manager supplies a predicate to create text editing windows that behave like a conventional Macintosh text editor. They support pretty display using text attributes like bold, italics, etc. Optionally, the window can be a display only window.

Predicates to manipulate the window's text are provided. They include selection, insertion, change, deletion, and bringing into view of text parts. One can also use input/output predicates to read and write from and to a text window in a similar way as for files. UNL's Rational Debugger [10, 13] uses most of these predicates.

Dialog Manager: Creates and maintains dialog windows. Several kinds of items are supported: push button, check boxes group, radio buttons group, static text, editing text, picture, icon, list, and pop up menu. Predicates are supplied to access and change some parts of the internal state of dialog items, namely any text associated with it, currently selected part, and enable/disable state. An enabled item can generate events that are remotely/locally posted to a Prolog process when clicked in a some special way that depends on the kind of item. There exists support for modal and modeless dialogs. Besides list creation, other predicates the Dialog manager supplies enable control of the list contents, selected entry, placement and size of lists. The richness of our dialogs allows us to build different environment control panels (e.g., for debugging control), simple list-based browsers, and even animation by means of fast replay of sequences of icons or pictures.

Menu Manager: This manager provides complete control over menus and menu items. It offers installation, extension and deletion of menus. The item attributes that are individually controllable are: check mark, item text, text style, enable/disable state, and item icon.

There are two categories of menu items: system items and Prolog items. System items correspond to commands the system should know how to perform. Prolog menu items correspond to events that are to be handled by a Prolog process by remote/local term posting. Since every system menu item has a unique and known reference number, the Menu manager predicates can make available the control of the command attribute that is associated with each.

Any newly created menu can be made a property of a particular window. It shows up only when its window owner is the front window.

File System Manager: Provides interface predicates to the file system. Allows changing to a different directory, exploring the contents of directories and volumes, obtaining the attributes of any file, and so on. Our browser uses this manager to implement the file system sub-browser.

Speech/Sound Manager: Supplies a very complete and interesting sound package. The Macintosh can be made to say loudly any sentence, the rate and the pitch of the voice being controllable. Furthermore, any sound resource can be played. Optionally, sound resources can even be played asynchronously.

3.2. MacLogic Tools

Currently, MacLogic's major tools are the editors and browsers. A Prolog LINT package (static analyzer) is underway, as well as a Prolog to PostScript prettyprinter. A more sophisticated graphic manager is also under design.

The MacLogic browser looks pretty much like many browsers available in Lisp environments. However, there are some major functional differences. Firstly, our browser supports different views of the current browser window. There are two such views: a local map and a local glossary to help interpret the meaning of the symbols displayed on the currently active browser window (Figure 3). Secondly, our browser supports nodes represented by atoms, icons and even pictures. Associated with each node there can be a type and a pop-up menu of possible operations. Finally, our browser is distributed and is capable of "graphically browsing" any relation.

A side-effect of the above is that we can browse the the browsing process's own "history". We can then answer questions every browser should answer: a) where am I, b) where did I came from, and c) where can I go.

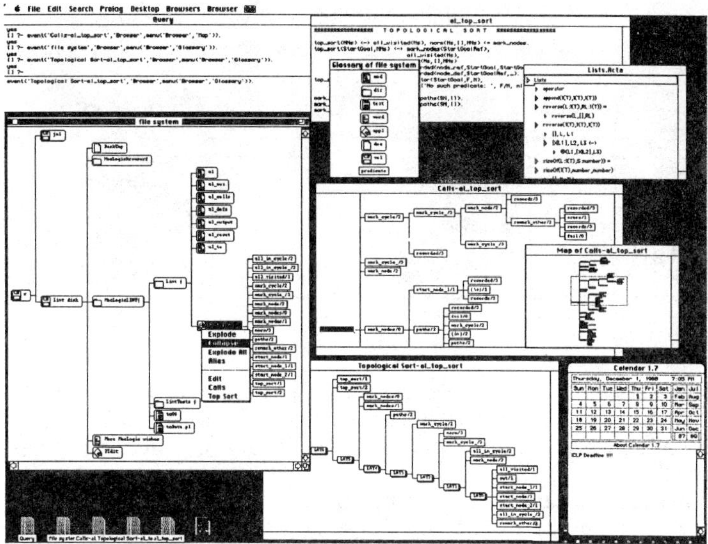

Figure 3

MACLOGIC has more than one editor. Firstly, it has a basic text editor with features expected from a Macintosh text editor. Secondly, it has a more sophisticated text editor which has an incorporated Prolog parser and is capable of using attributes like **bold** and *italics* for prettyprint Prolog code. With this editor one can detect errors quickly and have more visually appealing code windows. For instance, the editor can put all system predicates in **boldface**, other special predicate names in *italics*, etc. This editor has a distributed variant discussed later. Thirdly, it has an experimental outline based editor (Figure 4). Finally, the generic graphic browser can and should also be used as a generic structure editor.

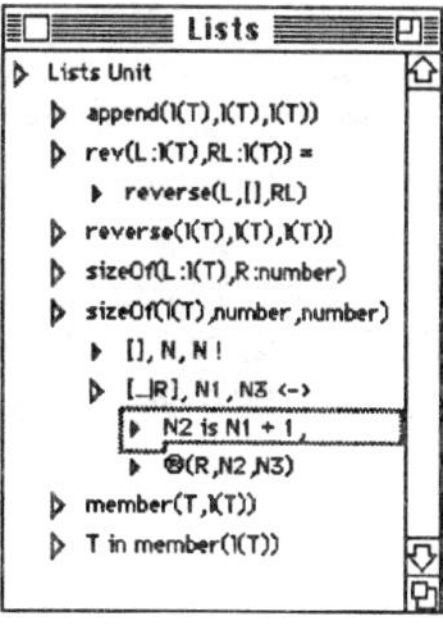

Figure 4

4   Canonical Term Representation (CTR)

In order to effectively establish any sort of communication between cooperating Prolog processes taking terms as **messages/events**, the standard representation (i.e. textual) for the later is obviously inadequate. A coding (**CTR**) of Prolog terms, taking into account both space and translation speed constraints, was devised and implemented to support communication between different C-Prolog instances running on different hardware.

Each C-Prolog term **T** is mapped into a sequence of 32 bit integers (i.e. C-Prolog `Sint`'s, the integers having the size of pointers) $\lceil$ **T** $\rceil$, as follows:

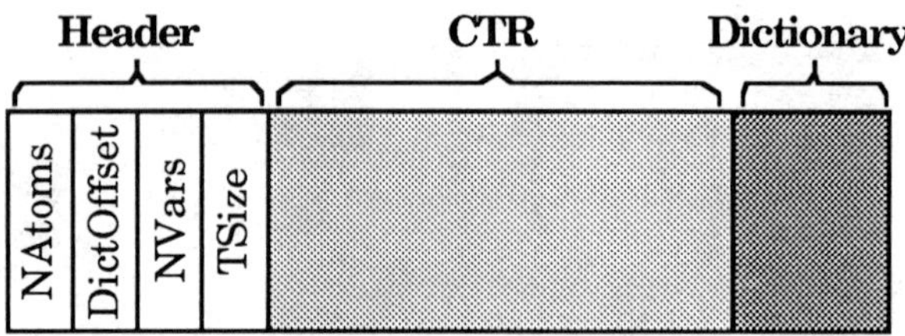

Figure 5

- **Dictionary** is a linear sequence of null terminated character strings.
- **NAtoms** indicates the number of atom names in the dictionary.
- **DictOffset** specifies the offset of the Dictionary (in 4 byte quantities) from the CTR.
- **NVars** specifies the number of mentioned unbound vars.
- **TSize** specifies the size needed above the global stack pointer to allocate the (structure shared) representation. This reduces checking time at read in.

The coding algorithm is straightforward. A single (structural inductive) pass is made over the term, keeping a (local) dictionary for atoms and variables while dumping the CTR into a buffer. After the pass terminates, the atom dictionary is appended, the `DictOffset` field computed, and the other header fields set.

The main concern in the development of this particular decoding algorithm was the minimization of calls to internal C-Prolog term construction built-ins. The code goes as follows:

- **TSize** is checked against **v1max - v1**.
- **v1** is increased by **NVars**.
- the atom dictionary is reconstructed from the atom's names (i.e. doing one lookup/1 for each name).
- decoding then proceeds doing a single pass over the CTR, as above.

This representation was chosen to eliminate data decompaction/compaction, and some test cases seem to imply that using the atoms' dictionary somehow compensates for the apparent waste of storage due to the exclusive use of **long** data; Furthermore, we think that the speed gain is significant (3 to 7 times speed increase (when reading files in CTR format) for just about 15 % storage increase). The typical example of booting C-Prolog using the above representation results in a 3.89 speed improvement, when compared with standard text file reading.

The following set of prolog primitives handling **CTR** streams is available in MACLOGIC. They are also the basis of MACLOGIC's fastload and fastsave mechanism. These primitives fail on errors producing an error message at the same time.

- **`csee(Atom,Var)`**.Open a new stream named atom **Atom** for reading, and set variable **Var** to its internal reference number (an integer, actually). **Var** must be unbound.
- **`ctell(Atom,Var)`**. Open a new stream named atom **Atom** for writing, and set variable **Var** to its internal reference number (again an integer). **Var** must be unbound.
- **`cwrite(Ref,Term)`**. Write term **Term** to the stream with reference number **Ref**.
- **`cread(Ref,Term)`**. Unify term **Term** with the next term read from stream with reference number **Ref**.
- **`ckill(Ref)`**. Close stream with reference number **Ref**.
- **`fastload(F)`**. Does a fast reconsult of a CTR file **F**.

Finally a few words on portability. **CTR** is also used in the MACLOGIC RTP implementation. Note, however, that machines can have different low level representations of data (as in the Macintosh/VAX case). Depending on the byte order used and on the internal representation of floating point numbers, some conversions must be made. An optimized version of RTP could perform some preliminary handshaking (on a definite format), and decide later who should do the conversions; however, our current prototype uses as standard the MC680XX format. Even if the communication is between two VAX based Prolog processes CTR conversions are made to and from the MC680XX standard. This will, however, be improved in the short term.

5   Communicating Sequential Prolog Processes by Remote Term Posting (RTP)

A very simple and efficient mechanism supports the communication between Prolog processes and the *InterfaceStation* or between themselves: the *remote term posting protocol*. We envisage Prolog programming on the *InterfaceStation* side to follow a similar pattern as that of standard application programming on a Macintosh. Each standard Macintosh application top level consists of an infinite loop fetching events from the Macintosh's event queue. For each event fetched a suitable routine is then invoked. To support pseudo-concurrent context switching, without bringing in the notion of interrupt, the application must periodically call a special routine **systemTask**, which gives the opportunity for the system to run some other code, like desk accessories, giving in this way a slight illusion of multitasking. Spectacular interactive applications are possible with just this clean event based approach and without involving any hard to explain interrupt concepts.

Similarly, MACLOGIC processes are perpetual processes running on a particular site with its own private event term queue. Here events are at a much higher level than normal Macintosh events. The former usually represent goals to be evaluated by the referred destination MACLOGIC process while the latter may be at the level of mouse tracking, something that in most cases a Prolog process shouldn't care about. MACLOGIC processes communicate by remotely and asynchronously "posting" event terms into each others' event term (priority) queue (Figure 6). A process can only manipulate its own queue and it can only ask the network meta-process to post event terms to other processes, including itself. Finally, the reply to a particular event term is attained by posting to the event term queue of the process supposed to receive the answer a special event term with standard name **reply** and corresponding pair *<question, reply>*. A few other event term names are pre-defined as well, like **unknown, unreachable** and **halt**. A reply term always informs if it is a success or a failure. Two-way pattern-matching, and synchronization, can easily be built on top of the basic RTP mechanism.

The Remote Term Posting protocol, currently implemented on top of the AppleTalk/EtherTalk Transaction Protocol (ATP) and on Unix™ systems using Columbia University Appletalk support over Ethernet based TCP/IP (known as CAP). The implementation of RTP on a given machine only assumes the existence of some network protocol performing node to node deliverance of a single packet with (preferably automatic) acknowledgment of reception. Fragmentation, reassembly of messages requiring multiple packets and also the maintenance of message ordering is of RTP's responsibility. Note, however, that message length is limited, in the present implementation, to five ATP packets (about 3Kbytes); more than enough for our purposes.

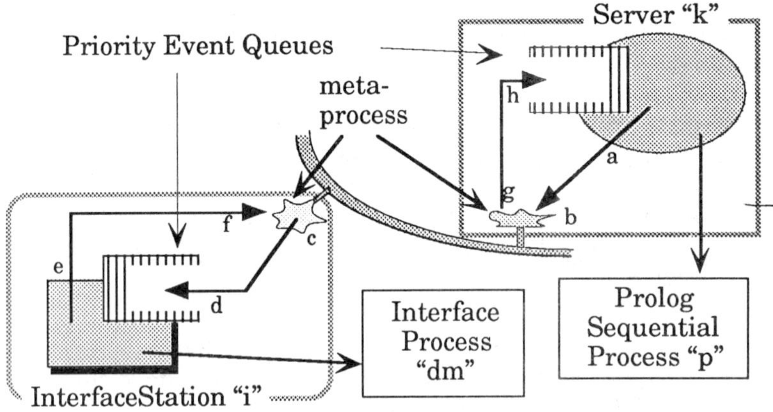

Figure 6

RTP enables MACLOGIC Prolog processes running in different processors or networked machines to cooperate by remotely and asynchronously posting terms to be dealt with by each other. When a given process, with identification "p", executes the MACLOGIC statement dm<:G (meaning *"remotely post term G on process dm's private event term (priority) queue"*) a pair <p,*G*>, will be delivered and posted on process dm's private event term queue. The process of remote term posting involves the following phases: the request (dm<:G) is made (step **a**) and the term G is converted to the CTR representation before it is transmitted (step **b**). Then on the site where the destination "dm" process is, the term G is converted back to its internal Prolog form proper to the type of Prolog implementation and underlying hardware (step **c**). Finally, the term is posted on the destination process event queue for processing (step **d**). In this case, if process "dm" has an answer to give, perhaps a standard term **reply** is later posted through the symmetric path **efgh** in p's own event term queue.

Since the Prolog code should not be interrupted, (remember the "free" event driven nature of MACLOGIC) the local (C-level) RTP event manager keeps a private bounded queue of incoming events. Usually, however, through the predicate `rtp_getnext/3` a process sees its "current" event (priority) queue as a normal clause data base. Therefore, the process can use all power of logic programming to select one or more "pending" event terms. Finally, the protocol supports group broadcasting, and full broadcasting. Note that the arrival of a higher priority remote term directly corresponds to entering a new break mode in Prolog to attend to it. The protocol can also have access to the identification (i.e. name) of all the listening processes in the network.

RTP events are represented in CTR format, and can carry two (user defined) attribute values (a 32 bit tag and a character string) which we call its *signature*.

The current set of low level RTP primitives are :

- **`mk_rtp_queue(Atom,Var1)`**. Opens an RTP queue for listening with name **Atom**. **Var1** returns the completion code. Although we could allow for multiple queues we prefer first to explore the simpler single queue approach!
- **`delete_rtp_queue(Var)`**. Closes an RTP queue. **Var** is the completion code.
- **`rtp_listeners(Var)`**. **Var** is unified with the list of all listening processes in all network sites in the form **[Atom1-Ref1,Atom2-Ref2...]** where **Atom$_i$** is the global process name, and **Ref$_i$** its (local) reference. **'$SELF$'-31** refers the caller (i.e. a process can post to itself).
- **`rtp_local_listeners(Var)`**. **Var** is unified with the list of local listening processes in the caller's site, in the form **[Atom1-Ref1, Atom2-Ref2,...]** where **Atom$_i$** is the global process name, and **Ref$_i$** its reference number.
- **PR <: Term**. Posts term **Term** into process **PR**'s queue. This is a commodity; instead of using a reference number as in `send/5`, the user should be allowed to use process names.
- **`rtp_getnext(Var1,Var2,Ref)`**. Extracts an event term from the local queue. **Var1** is the read in term, **Var2** is the sender's process name. If there are no pending events, **Var1=[]** and **Var2=0**. **Ref** is the event term unique reference (similar to the internal data base references).
- **`rtp_erase(Ref)`**. Erases pending event term with reference **Ref**.
- **Pr >: Term**. Waits for an event **Term** from process named **Pr**. If Pr is unbound, this primitive receives from any process unifying. Note that **>:/2** is blocking; never **[]** is returned.

Note that the above Prolog primitives never **fail** on errors, but rather return an incompletion code.

Consider this very simple example:

```
/*  process A : reader                      */
/*     reads terms from Source, assembles   */
/*     them in lists of 20 and sends the    */
/*     result to Dest                       */

reader(Source,Dest) :-
    mk_rtp_queue(Source,C),  start(Dest).
main :- repeat, work(L,20), Dest <: L,
fail.
work([],0).
work([H|T],N) :- FR :> H, N0 is N-1,
work(T,N).
```

As another example consider that user interaction on the MACLOGIC site `mac1` produces high level events: some of them can be handled locally like through the browser caching mechanism, discussed bellow. If required, however, they can migrate to a remote process. In this case, the event is sent as an event term, for instance

```
rp1 <: sons_of(tc,infer(_,_,_),L)
```

This could mean that MACLOGIC wants to know the immediate sons of predicate `infer/3` on module `tc` over the relation `calls`. After this call, MACLOGIC can go on asynchronously performing other tasks.

The remote Prolog process *rp1*, sends later back a **reply** message, like

```
mac1 <: reply(sons_of(tc,infer(_,_,_),L),
              [L=[f1(_),p_x(_,_)]]).
```

The term *reply(sons_of(tc,infer(_,_,_),L),[L=[f1(_),* *p_x(_,_)]]* is asynchronously posted into `mac1`'s own event term queue.

Instead of this fully asynchrounous scheme, more fine strategies can be implemented: MACLOGIC may sit waiting for its request **reply**, if that is needed (say, for two-way pattern-matching); or the **reply** command could be enhanced in order to cover some special features like

```
mac1 <: try_later(sons_of(tc,infer(_,_,_),L))).
```

Since we are not dealing with interrupts, the process top level must periodically call `rtp_getnext/3` (either directly or indirectly). However, a few scheduling shells are already available for user convenience.

Note that a communication scheme based on continuations can be trivially implemented: instead of a simple request/reply, the sender can tell the receiver to which process it should send the response.

This RTP approach is conceptually simple, is easy to implement and is highly efficient if we take advantage of new protocols such as VMTP [6]. The approach entirely avoids logically hard-to-explain concepts like interrupts. The approach, however, is not to be taken as an alternative to languages of the Concurrent Prolog heritage [16], Parlog [9] or Δ-Prolog [11,12,7]. It is, instead, a *minimal, clean* and *efficient* platform to build more problem oriented top level shells or protocols to support other communication disciplines. In particular, we are in the process of developing a *remote goal evaluation* facility on top of our RTP protocol and we may in the future develop a Δ-Prolog shell on top of it.

6 The Distributed Architecture of MACLOGIC Tools

We have produced a fully functional Prolog interpreter based on C-Prolog to run as an *inner* process. We have managed to "extract" the parser out of C-Prolog so as to use it close to the editor, to support local syntax checking. The inner part of the interpreter was adapted to communicate through our RTP protocol and it can now be used as the basis for "lighter" remote interpreter processes (Figure 7). However, some difficulties persist since much of the C-Prolog code is dependent on the existence of some kind of terminal (for displaying error messages, for example). The error handling scheme and the built-in tracer/debugger suffers from the same problem.

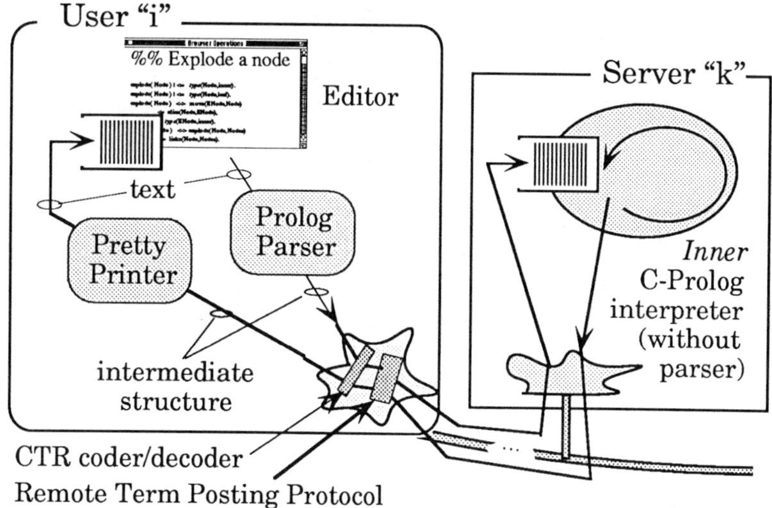

Figure 7

An inner Prolog process is one which communicates only through the canonical term representation. The underlying interpreter doesn't carry along the weight of the so called outer interpreter (parser/printer). These term streams are used to convey terms to be interpreted by the receiver. Responses are just special **reply** terms. These streams are therefore associated univocally with each component of the system. Event terms and argument terms are efficiently represented by the canonical term representation.

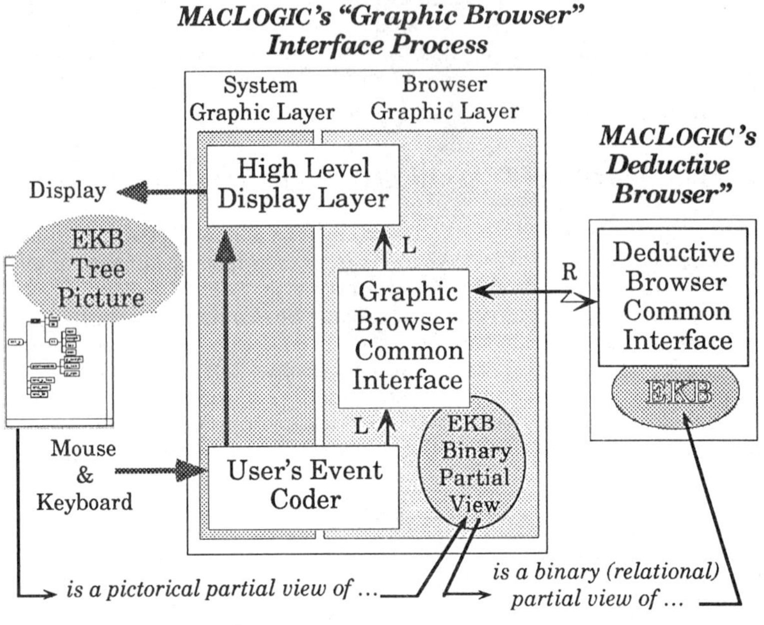

Figure 8

Editing is done on the *InterfaceStation* while interpretation may be done in another processor. Like in Smalltalk-80 [8] the user, with this editor, can directly perform questions to and modify the data base of the **remote** Prolog process. The menu operation **do** parses and sends for evaluation any text region selected. The answer is pasted in front of the selected region, becoming in turn selected.

Any instance of MACLOGIC's browser is composed of instances of two communicating processes (Figure 8). The first and most interesting one, known as the *Environment's Deductive Browser*, is a specialized Prolog process that provides a coherent interface to the *Environment Knowledge Base* (EKB). Through this component the system has a standard way of gathering and manipulating environment related information/knowledge. The second and perhaps more standard component, called the *Graphic Browser*, is just a convenient state-of-the-art graphical interface supporting a *direct interface* to the Deductive Browser. The Deductive Browser component is

implemented as an *Inner Prolog* process while the Graphic Browser
component is implemented in a mix of C (High Level Display Layer and
User's Event Coder) and Prolog (Graphic Browser Common Interface) and
the two communicate through a stream of event terms according to the
Remote (R)/Local (L) Term Posting protocol.

The Graphic Browser deals only with binary views of the EKB. In
order to browse a particular relation, one has to provide a binary
interpretation for it. All operations supported by the Graphic Browser are
directly passed on to the Deductive Browser for local interpretation. The
Graphic Browser is therefore kept universal and independent from the
semantic domain. Furthermore, since all relations are commonly represented
at the Graphic Browser level, one only needs to develop a display layer per
type of pictorical view (tree, graph, ...). Finally, caching mechanisms are
used to reduce communication between both graphic and deductive
components.

7 Future Work

On the scientific side, and within the ALPES project, we intend to investigate
the integration of the MACLOGIC framework and tools with the contextual
logic programming notions developed by Luís Monteiro and António Porto
at UNL [15]. This promises to be both complex and interesting. Also, we
hope to pursue our investigation on the RTP protocol, experiment with
systems involving both structure-sharing and non-structure-sharing implementations, and do performance oriented experiments. Finally, on the
practical side we intend to develop RTP/CTR packages for commercial
Prolog implementations running on Unix such as Quintus Prolog.

Acknowledgments

We would like to thank António Porto, Luís Trindade, Gabriel Dias and
Cristina Ribeiro for the development of the Deductive Browser. Finally, to
Luís Moniz Pereira we thank the research environment he has created against
all odds. Without him no Macs would be available much less MACLOGIC.

This work was supported by ESPRIT Project P973, Junta Nacional de
Investigação Científica, Instituto Nacional de Investigação Científica e
Gabinete de Filosofia do Conhecimento.

References

[1] Alegria, J. et al., *MACLOGIC: Rationale and Informal Specifications*,
     ESPRIT Project P973 ALPES report, Dept. Informática, UNL,
     July 1987.
[2] Alegria, J., *The MACLOGIC Programming Environment*,
     3rd Portuguese AI Conference, Braga, Portugal, October 1987.
[3] Alegria, J., *The Architecture of MACLOGIC*, Proceedings of the 5th
     ESPRIT Conference, North-Holland, pp. 737-748, Vol I, 1988.
[4] Apple Computer, Inc., *Inside Macintosh*, Volumes *1-5*,
     Addison-Wesley, 1985-1987.

[5] Apple Computer, Inc., *Human Interface Guidelines,*
Addison-Wesley, 1987.

[6] Cheriton, D.R., *VMTP: A Transport Protocol for the Next generation
of Communication Systems*, ACM SigComm 86, pp. 406-415.

[7] Cunha, J. et al., *Programming in Delta-Prolog*, in these Proceedings.

[8] Goldberg, A., *Smaltalk-80: The Interactive Programming
Environment*, Addison-Wesley, 1984.

[9] Gregory, S. *Parallel Logic Programming in PARLOG*,
Addison-Wesley, 1987.

[10] Pereira, L. M., *Rational Debugging of logic programs*,
Proceedings of the 3rd ICLP, London, July 1986.

[11] Pereira, L. M. et al., *Delta-Prolog: a Distributed Backtracking
Extension with Events*, Proceedings of the 3rd ILCP,
London, July 1986.

[12] Pereira, L. M. et al., *Concurrency and Communication in Delta-
Prolog*, Proceedings of the IEE Int. Specialist Seminar on the "Design
and Application of Parallel Digital Processors", Lisbon 1988.

[13] Pereira, L. M.; Calejo, M., *A Framework for Prolog Debugging*,
Proceedings of the 5th ICLP, Seattle Washington, August 1988.

[14] Porto, A., *Semantic unification for deduction in knowledge bases*,
Proceedings of the Workshop on Foundations of Deductive Data Bases
and Logic Programming, University of Maryland,
Washington D. C., 1986.

[15] Monteiro, L.; Porto, A. *Contextual Logic Programming*,
in these Proceedings.

[16] Shapiro, E., (ed.), *Concurrent Prolog: Collected Papers*,
MIT Press 1987.

THE NU-PROLOG DEBUGGING ENVIRONMENT

Lee Naish
Philip W. Dart
Justin Zobel

Department of Computer Science
University of Melbourne
Parkville 3052, Australia

lee@cs.mu.oz.au, philip@cs.mu.oz.au, jz@cs.mu.oz.au

ABSTRACT

One of the advantages of logic programming is that it is easy to reason about what is computed by a program (the declarative semantics) independently of how it is computed (the procedural semantics). As well as being useful for writing, transforming and understanding programs, these two alternative viewpoints are useful for testing and debugging programs. By taking full advantage of declarative and procedural semantics, we anticipate that very powerful programming environments can be constructed.

In this paper we describe the NU-Prolog Debugging Environment (NUDE). NUDE combines previous work with several new techniques for testing and debugging. It has three main components. First, several static program analysis tools are used for detecting program errors such as simple typing mistakes, type errors, infinite loops and floundering. Second, dynamic tools are provided for diagnosing incorrect behaviour of a query at run time. There are tools for diagnosing wrong answers, missing answers, infinite loops and floundering. Third, there is a mechanism which helps automate testing of programs to detect queries with wrong or missing answers. The three components are integrated into the NU-Prolog system, supporting a rapid test-debug-recompile cycle.

1. INTRODUCTION

One of the advantages of logic programming is that it is easy to reason about what is computed independently of how it is computed. That is, programs have a simple 'declarative' semantics as well as a 'procedural' semantics. Programs can be understood and, to a lesser extent, written using either or both viewpoints. These two ways of viewing a logic program are complementary. Reasoning about (partial) correctness and completeness is best done at the declarative level whereas reasoning about termination and efficiency requires a procedural view. The declarative semantics is more high level and has a very well developed theory, so the benefits of using it are considerable.

The two views are also complementary when testing and debugging logic programs. The topic of this paper is a system called NUDE (NU-Prolog Debugging Environment), which exploits the declarative and procedural semantics more fully than previous systems and is designed to make use of and support the unique features of NU-Prolog [Thom 88]. It consists of several testing and debugging tools which have been integrated into one system, running under NU-Prolog. Testing programs and finding bugs which cause incorrectness or incompleteness can be done with several tools based on the declarative semantics. Flexibility of input-output modes is used widely, and interaction with the user concerning the intended behaviour of the program is simplified. The tools used for finding bugs which cause loops or abnormal termination are based on the procedural semantics.

2. SEMANTICS OF NU-PROLOG

The NU-Prolog manual [Thom 88] gives a full description of the syntax, declarative semantics and procedural semantics of NU-Prolog. The syntax is Edinburgh Prolog syntax with some additions based on 'extended syntax' [Lloyd 84a]. These include constructs for implication (for example, `Goal1 => Goal2`), if-then-else, aggregate predicates which examine all solutions to a goal (for example `max(Term, Goal, MaxTerm)`), soundly implemented negation and logical quantification (`all Vars Goal` and `some Vars Goal`). Logical quantification, restricts the scope of variables which occur syntactically in the term `Vars`, to the formula `Goal`. If the same variable name occurs in distinct scopes it refers to distinct variables.

The declarative semantics of NU-Prolog is given by interpreting constructs of the language as formulas of first order logic. A detailed treatment of this subject is given in [Lloyd 84b]. Many built-in predicates of NU-Prolog (such as cut) are considered non-logical, and predicates which call them are not assigned any declarative semantics. There are advantages in avoiding non-logical code where possible, especially before a program has been fully debugged.

The default procedural semantics is the same as other Prolog systems: NU-Prolog normally selects the leftmost subgoal for evaluation first. However, NU-Prolog is able to 'delay' the execution subgoals until they are further instantiated, when they are 'woken'. Many system predicates delay until they have a finite number of solutions and the implementation of negation guarantees soundness by delaying until global variables are ground. 'when' declarations may also be used to make calls to user-defined predicates delay until some arguments or parts of arguments are non-variable or ground. A goal has 'floundered' if it has terminated with some subgoals delayed but insufficiently instantiated to be woken.

Procedural semantics are defined for all the non-standard constructs, such as implication and quantifiers, as well the standard constructs. However, this procedural semantics can be overridden if a predicate is declared 'pure'. In this case, the procedural semantics is not defined, allowing the NU-Prolog compiler to optimise the code in any way consistent with the declarative semantics.

Pure declarations should not be given for predicates containing non-logical code.

By default, NU-Prolog predicates are 'static'. That is, they can be only changed by redefining the whole predicate, (for example, with `consult`). Procedures can also be declared 'dynamic'. Dynamic predicates can be changed by adding or deleting individual clauses (for example, with `assert`).

3. EXISTING DEBUGGING TOOLS

The most common debugging tools for Prolog, tracing and 'spy points', are procedural debuggers based on the 'four port' model of Prolog execution. Users can step through, and also affect, the execution of the program. Probably the most advanced procedural debugger is the Transparent Prolog Machine [Eisenstadt 88]. This system represents the Prolog search and/or tree graphically, displaying information about procedure invocations, matches with clause heads, bindings to variables, et cetera.

There have also been several methods, proposed and implemented, for detecting possible errors by static analysis at compile time. The simplest of these are the 'style checkers', which detect such things as variable names which don't start with '_' (underscore) but occur uniquely in a clause. These programs can find many simple typing mistakes and some more serious errors. The more complex static analysis methods use declarations supplied by the programmer and analyse such things as input-output modes of procedures and what 'types' procedures have [Bruynooghe 82] [Mycroft 84] [Zobel 87].

Another kind of Prolog debugger which is gaining popularity is the 'declarative' (or 'algorithmic') debugger [Shapiro 83] [Lloyd 87] [Dershowitz 87] [Naish 88]. These debuggers are based on the declarative semantics of Prolog and diagnose wrong and missing answers. They ask the programmer what the correct behaviour is for certain calls, for example, whether they should succeed. The cause of incorrect behaviour is traced to a single incorrect clause or procedure. The BIM Prolog debugger enables the user to apply the same algorithms but does not explicitly ask the user questions, so it cannot capture any of the user's knowledge.

4. OVERVIEW OF NUDE

NUDE has three main components. The first consists of static program analysis tools, the second of dynamic tools to diagnose incorrect run-time behaviour, and the third is a mechanism for automatically testing a program. Prior to the implementation of NUDE, several of these tools existed independently, each with their own representation of programs. The first step in integrating the tools was to design a common way to access the program being debugged. An abstract data type was devised which gave the required functionality. Procedures were provided for: modifying the program, for example, consulting files, deleting a procedure and adding individual clauses; accessing parts of the program, such as details of clauses and declarations for given procedures; extracting program structure, such as what procedures are defined in what files and what procedures directly or indirectly call what other procedures; and miscellaneous tasks, for example printing clauses with the correct variable names, and listing procedures. Information which is relatively expensive to calculate, such as the call graph, is computed on demand then saved until the relevant parts of the program are changed. When available, the compiled code for procedures is loaded as well as the source. This is useful for manual testing and several debugging tools which run some code in the normal way.

The static program analysis tools in NUDE detect simple errors, such as misspelt variable and procedure names and missing arguments, as well as more subtle coding errors, for example, errors which result in programs always failing. These tools are also provided as a separate non-interactive style checker called *nit* [Thom 88]. *nit* can be used in the same way as other style checkers but, because of the extra analysis, more subtle errors can be discovered. Within NUDE, the static checks can be run interactively on the whole program, all procedures directly or indirectly called by a goal or a single procedure:

```
?- nit.                    ?- nit(Pred, Arity).
?- nit Goal.
```

The second component of NUDE consists of several dynamic tools for diagnosing incorrect behaviour of the program at run time. If a goal returns an incorrect answer, misses a correct answer, (apparently) doesn't terminate or flounders, one of four tools is used to diagnose the bug:

```
?- wrong Goal.             ?- loop Goal.
?- miss Goal.              ?- flounder Goal.
```

Before the dynamic analysis, relevant static checks are performed on the procedures called by the goal. In the case of incorrect and missing answers, a declarative debugger is invoked and the user is asked questions related to what answers should be returned by various parts of the computation. A database containing this information is built up which can be saved in and restored from files and modified to correct mistakes.

The third component of NUDE is a mechanism to help test the program for wrong and missing answers:

```
?- test Goal.                        ?- test(Pred, Arity).
```

Instances of the goal in the declarative debugger database are run. Other instances are generated by interpreting the goal.

The three components are integrated into the NU-Prolog system. The various tools interface with each other and parts of the NU-Prolog system such as spy points.

5. STATIC CHECKS

A variety of checks can be applied to programs in the absence of any goal. Some of these checks analyse the program by treating the body of each clause as a goal, while others look for inconsistencies within each clause. Briefly, the static checks applied in NU-Prolog are: type checking, loop detection, floundering analysis (all discussed in detail later), checking for inconsistencies other than type errors, and a stratifiability test.

Some of these static checks relate to programming style. For example, the existence of two procedures or functors with the same name and different arity (number of arguments) generates a warning; this is particularly useful if both arities are large. Similarly, the programmer is warned if two variables in the same clause have near-identical names. NUDE also checks the convention that a variable name begins with an underscore if and only if the variable only occurs once in a clause. Since NU-Prolog includes quantifiers to define scope, the same variable name in the same clause can refer to different variables; if this occurs, a warning is printed. All of these errors could occur in a 'correct' program, but could well arise from typographical mistakes, and should be pointed out to the user. Non-observance of these conventions can detract from the clarity of a program.

Other checks relate to program correctness. The programmer is warned if a procedure is declared but not used, or is used but not declared. Also, if a procedure is modified but not declared 'dynamic', or contains non-logical features but is declared 'pure', the error is reported; the semantics of procedures containing such errors is not defined. Similarly, if a clause contains a variable which is used within a negation but never used in subgoals which could instantiate that variable to a ground term, execution using that clause will always flounder, and so the user is warned. *nit* can also detect when a program is not stratifiable.

5.1. Infinite loops

In conventional Prolog systems, where sub-goals are always executed from left to right, the termination of a call to a procedure generally depends on which arguments are instantiated. Therefore, mode analysis is needed for useful termination analysis. Consider the following example:

```
append([], A, A).
append(H.A, B, H.C) :- append(A, B, C).

append3(A, B, C, ABC) :-
        append(B, C, BC), append(A, BC, ABC).
```

If `append3` is always called with its first two arguments instantiated to lists, `append` will always be called with its first instantiated to a list. In this mode, `append` has a finite number of solutions and will not cause an infinite loop. However, if `append3` is called with only its last two arguments instantiated, `append` will be called with its first and last arguments uninstantiated. In this mode, `append` has an infinite number of solutions and can cause an infinite loop (for example, if all solutions to `append3` are sought).

In NU-Prolog, this loop can be avoided by adding control information so that the two calls to `append` are not executed from left to right. Calls to `append` which have an infinite number of solutions can be delayed until they are further instantiated. [Naish 85] gives an algorithm which analyses potential infinite loops and generates control information to prevent them. For example, the control generated for `append` delays it until the first or last argument is instantiated. There is an implementation of a variation of this algorithm for NU-Prolog called *nac*.

The idea of the loop analysis code of NUDE is to compare the control information in the program with the control information required to prevent infinite loops. The current implementation is a simplification of this, more ideal approach. In the example above without control information, the user would be warned that the second clause of `append` may cause an infinite loop. With the control information added, the recursive call can delay instead of looping, and the system does not generate a warning. Most recursive procedures with no when declarations loop when run in some mode and cause warnings to be generated, even if the procedure is never used in that mode.

There is one other special case which the static loop checker detects, which is useful even when control information is not used. Clauses which contain a call to `repeat` but no call to cut cause a warning message.

5.2. Types

When programmers define a procedure, they intend that the procedure be applicable only to particular types. For example, although the definition of `append`, as given above, can succeed for non-lists, it is intended that `append` only succeed for lists. A procedure could include logic to restrict it to the intended types, but such a definition would be inefficient to execute, and type information would be distributed throughout a program. If type declarations rather than extra logic were used, the type information is made explicit, and the type declaration should be considered as part of the specification of the program. This is summed up in the equation Specification = Program + Types [Naish 87]. For example, if `append` has a type declaration stating that all of its arguments should be lists, then for the following definition of `append`

```
append([], A, a).            % 'a' should be 'A'
append(H.A, B, H.C) :- append(A, B, C).
```

it can be demonstrated that the first clause cannot succeed in the specification. Similarly, the use of `append` in the clause

```
last(E, L) :- append(_, E.nil, L). % 'nil' -> '[]'
```

is inconsistent with the type declaration (that is, it should never succeed). A programmer is unlikely to deliberately include useless clauses in a program, and it is therefore probable that something different was intended. Thus, although both of the faulty clauses above can succeed in the program, they are flagged as containing type errors because they cannot succeed in the "specification".

Two distinct type systems based on these principles have been implemented. Programs with optional type declarations on procedures are examined for clauses (or queries) which, according to the specification, should not take part in a successful execution. One, *regular* types, is based on a precise system of polymorphic types defined in a regular language. The other, *unrestricted* types, is based on types defined by arbitrary Prolog procedures, which have greater expressive power than regular languages, but in which type checking is incomplete.

5.2.1. Regular types

A system in which types are defined by a regular language has been implemented under NU-Prolog [Zobel 87] [Dart 88]. In this system, types can be defined as follows:

```
?- type $list(X) -> { [], X.$list(X) }.
?- type $list -> { $list($_) }.
?- type $odd -> { $_.[], $_.$_.$odd }.
?- type $even -> { [], $_.$_.$even }.
```

There are several predefined types, such as `$_` for 'don't care' and `$integer` for integers. In the definitions above, functors starting with '$' are type symbols. In type definitions, type symbols may have parameters, as in the definition of `$list(X)`; these parameters must be given a value when the type definition is used in a type declaration. Type declarations are of the form

```
?- type append($list, $list, $list).
?- type sumlist($list($integer), $integer).
?- type isOdd($odd).
?- type isEven($even).
```

In this example, arguments to `append` must be lists, the first argument of `sumlist` must be a list of integers and the second an integer, and the arguments of `isOdd` and `isEven` must be odd and even length lists respectively.

One of the advantages of using a regular language to define types is that algorithms exist for unification and comparison of such types. This type checker uses type unification to infer a type for each variable in a clause. These inferred types are compared to the declared type of the procedure containing the clause. If the inferred type is empty, or is disjoint from the declared type, the clause cannot be used in a successful execution without conflicting with a type declaration, and probably contains an error. For example, the clause

```
query :- odd(X), even(X).
```

has a type error, because the type unification of the types `$odd` and `$even` is empty.

This regular type system was developed as part of a separate system [Dart 88] in which declared types are automatically incorporated into the program, so that the new program embodies the original specification. Extra type checking code is added only where it is needed, so that the new program is not significantly less efficient than the original program. The extra tests in the code could be used to detect wrong answers at run time, or the need for extra tests could be reported to the user immediately, to indicate the possibility of type errors.

5.2.2. Unrestricted Types

The definition a type in [Naish 87] is more general than in other schemes. Types of procedures are specified by arbitrary Prolog goals rather giving the name of a type (which is defined in a restricted way) for each argument. This added flexibility compared to other type schemes means that more errors can potentially be detected. However, for any given implementation of this scheme, not all type errors will be detected; the problem of detecting clauses which cannot succeed is not decidable.

As a simple example of the extra power the scheme gives, the type information for `append` can specify that each argument is a list *and* the sum of the lengths of the first two arguments equals the length of the last argument:

```
?- append(A,B,C) type
       length(A,AL), length(B,BL), length(C,CL),
       plus(AL,BL,CL).
append([], A, A).
append(H.A, C, H.B) :-                 % C and B swapped
       append(A, B, C).

query(X) :- append([a,b], [b,c], X).  % X=[a, c]
```

Unlike other systems, our implementation is able to detect that `query` should never succeed. From the initial call to `append`, the system deduces that the length of `X` should be four. In the recursive call to `append`, although all the arguments are lists, their lengths are not compatible with the length of `X` being four. Any solution to `query` must therefore violate the type constraints somewhere in the execution, so an error is reported. The system does not report an error for the recursive clause of `append` because there are instances of it which succeeds correctly. Even when a clause can never succeed correctly, the system may not report an error because the implementation is necessarily incomplete.

The current implementation of the scheme is very simple, consisting of a meta-interpreter for programs and type declarations. The interpreter is run for each clause to be checked. If it fails, the user is warned that the clause should never succeed. Because the meta-interpreter only needs to be sound with respect to finite failure, calls to non-logical primitives and calls beyond a certain recursion depth are assumed to succeed. This ensures termination.

5.3. Groundness analysis

As stated earlier, a goal flounders if it terminates with delayed subgoals which are insufficiently instantiated to be woken. Analysis of the propagation of variable bindings in a program can detect likely causes of floundering during execution. For example, consider a definition of `member` which avoids repeated solutions.

```
member(H, H._).
member(E, H.L) :- not (E = H), member(E, L).

query :- member(heart-Val, [club-10, heart-4]).
```

Since sound negation is only be evaluated when its argument is ground, `query` will flounder. This problem can be identified by groundness analysis; this analysis can be extended to encompass extended syntax and evaluable predicates. For example, consider the program

```
increment(N, Nplus1) :- N is Nplus1 - 1.

query :- increment(5, X).
```

In this example, `query` will flounder, because `is` requires that the right-hand argument be ground. Analysis can demonstrate that `increment` can only propagate bindings from its second argument to its first. If the definition of `increment` is changed to

```
increment(N, Nplus1) :- plus(N, 1, Nplus1).
```

in which the call to `plus` will ground the first or third argument, but not both, then analysis can demonstrate that `increment` will propagate bindings in either direction.

6. DYNAMIC CHECKS

The dynamic tools, especially `wrong` and `miss`, use the declarative semantics of Prolog, so code which uses non-logical aspects of Prolog cannot easily be debugged using these tools. More conventional methods based on the procedural semantics are needed. We suggest that during the initial development and debugging of programs, the code should be kept as pure as possible. As well as simplifying debugging, this often results in better code. After the code has been debugged, low level efficiency details can be addressed and non-logical primitives can be added if it is felt necessary.

For each of the dynamic tools, the user is first asked if static checks should be performed. The choice of static checks depends on what dynamic check is being called. The simple checks, such as those concerning variable and functor names, are always applied, but the loop checker is only run with `loop` and the type checker is run with `miss` and `wrong`, et cetera. These checks are performed on the goal and all predicates indirectly called by it.

6.1. Wrong answers

Declarative or algorithmic debugging for Prolog was first presented in [Shapiro 83]. This was extended to allow coroutining and arbitrary first order logic formulas in the bodies of clauses in [Lloyd 87]. The theory behind declarative debugging is that the user has an *intended model* of the program but the completion of the program is not true in that model (that is, some procedure definitions are inconsistent with the intended model). If a wrong answer is returned, normally there is a clause which is false in the intended model; that is, for some instance of the clause, the body correctly succeeds but a call to the atom in the head should fail. The debugging algorithm finds such a clause instance.

NUDE interprets the goal and checks whether intermediate results are correct. To find out if a goal should succeed, the system queries the user. The response is stored in a database, so the user is not asked the same question repeatedly. The user can also indicate that the procedure in question has been completely debugged. The system will then just run the code and assume the answer is always correct. A similar but complementary idea is to have two definitions of a procedure; one assumed to be correct (the specification, which may be very inefficient) and another which may need to be debugged [Dershowitz 87]. Rather than asking the user questions, the specification code is run. A further extension is to allow users to make general assertions about the intended behaviour of the program [Drabent 88]. We plan to add these facilities to NUDE.

For a brief example of how the wrong answers diagnosis works, consider the buggy `append` procedure from section 5.2.2. Parts typed by the user are in **bold**.

```
?- wrong query(X).
Do static analysis? n
Do dynamic wrong answer analysis?      % defaults=yes
query([a, c])    Valid? n
append([a, b], [b, c], [a, c])       Valid? n
append([b], [c], [b, c])    Valid?

Incorrect Clause Instance:
append([a, b], [b, c], [a, c]) :-
       append([b], [c], [b, c]).

Matching Clauses:
append([H|A], C, [H|B]) :-
       append(A, B, C).

Do you want to edit append/3 ?
```

6.2. Missing answers

The method used to diagnose missing answers is similar in spirit to that for wrong answers. The bug normally returned is an 'uncovered atom'; that is, an atomic goal which should succeed, but the bodies of all clauses it matches with correctly fail. It indicates that an extra clause is needed in the procedure or one of the clauses needs to be made weaker. Diagnosing missing answers is actually a more difficult problem than diagnosing wrong answers and the algorithm is more complex. One of the consequences for users is that the questions asked by the system are not always yes/no questions. Sometimes the system asks if a goal is satisfiable (true for some values of the variables in it), then asks for particular instances which are valid. The user must provide answers to goals rather than just verify whether answers are correct.

Details of the algorithm used are given in [Naish 88]. It is based on the algorithms of Shapiro and Lloyd, but has several enhancements which reduce the number of questions asked. It is particularly important to reduce the number of questions where the user must provide valid instances of goals. One technique used to find valid instances of a goal is to call the goal (rather than ask the user). The user is then asked a yes/no question to make sure the answer is valid. If the answer is not valid, `wrong` is called. Missing answer bugs in top level goals are often caused by wrong answers somewhere deeper in the computation. Since wrong answers are easier to diagnose, this feature can avoid many difficult questions. `wrong` is also called when a negated goal misses an answer.

6.3. Infinite loops

Infinite loops are dealt with at run time by a meta-interpreter. The interpreter maintains a list of the ancestor calls, the clauses they were matched with and the current recursion depth. If the recursion depth reaches a multiple of some value (the default is 30) then the interpreter succeeds. A message is printed indicating the depth and the number of times each clause has been used in the branch of the proof tree. If the user is not convinced the loop has been found, the interpreter can continue the computation. If a call matches with any ancestor call then the interpreter succeeds and a message is printed in a similar manner.

Many infinite loops only occur after a substantial amount of backtracking, for example, after all solutions to a goal have been found. This is due the to practice of putting simple clauses such as facts (base cases) before recursive clauses. The interpreter dynamically changes the clause selection rule to avoid the extra backtracking and find the infinite loop as quickly as possible. Rather than always trying the first clause first, the interpreter tries the most recently used clause in the current branch of the tree first. Consider the following example:

```
reverse(L, R) :- reverse1(L, [], R).


        % first arg should be instantiated
reverse1([], R, R).
reverse1(H.L, R0, R) :- reverse1(L, H.R0, R).


        % logic correct but reverse causes loops
palindrome(LR) :- reverse(L, R), append(L, R, LR).
palindrome(LR) :- reverse(L, R), append(L, _.R, LR).


?- palindrome("able was I ere I saw elba").
```

With the standard order for executing calls and selecting clauses, the first call to `reverse` repeatedly generates longer and longer lists which cause append to (eventually) fail and backtrack. It takes $O(N^2)$ time to reach a recursion depth of N. With the modified clause selection rule, the first call to `reverse1` matches with the fact and succeeds, causing `append` to fail immediately. On backtracking, the second (recursive) clause of `reverse1` is selected. When the recursive call to `reverse1` is made, it is matched with the recursive clause first. This clause is chosen first for each subsequent call, so a recursion depth of N is reached after N+1 calls. Note that no call matches with any ancestor call due to the way the second argument of `reverse1` is constructed.

When the recursion gets deep enough, the interpreter will succeed and inform the user that the first clause of `palindrome` and `reverse` have been used once and all other calls used the second clause of `reverse1`. The bug can be fixed most simply by adding control information to `reverse1` so that calls to it delay until the first argument is instantiated. It is also desirable to change the order of subgoals in `palindrome`.

6.4. Floundering

In NU-Prolog, calls to both system and user-defined procedures can delay when they are not sufficiently instantiated; this can lead to floundering as discussed in Section 2. With sensible control information, NU-Prolog programs will often flounder when the goal has an infinite number of solutions. However, bugs in the program, both in the logic and in the control, can cause floundering in quite reasonable goals.

When a goal flounders in NU-Prolog, the system simply prints a message to that effect. The `flounder` procedure of NUDE interprets the goal then prints all goals which have been delayed but never woken. A future implementation will further simplify debugging by also printing the procedure from which the call was made.

6.5. Spy points

When a NU-Prolog procedure which has a spy point is executed, the call (and other information) is printed and the user has a large number of options (continue the computation, fail, turn off debugging partially or completely etc). One of the options, 'l', causes a user-defined procedure `spyHook` to be executed with the current call, port and other information. This facility is used as an interface between the four port debugger and the dynamic debugging tools of NUDE. At an exit (succeed) port, the 'l' option is equivalent to calling `wrong` with the current call. First the user is asked if static analysis is desired, then the declarative debugger is used. At a fail port, the 'l' option is equivalent to calling `miss`, and at a call port it is equivalent to calling `loop`.

This facility is very useful when the top levels of a program do various non-logical operations, such as initializing tables, reading data and writing results, but call logical code to do major parts of the computation. A spy point can be added to the logical code and the non-logical top level code can be called. When control enters the logical code, the 'l' option can be used to enter the declarative debugger. The technique is also useful for large programs if the user has a good idea as to which part of the program contains the bug. This can significantly reduce the number of questions put to the user.

7. AUTOMATIC TESTING

The testing mechanism has three phases. The first runs static checks on everything called by the goal. The second checks that the goal behaves consistently with all information in the declarative debugger database. The database contains atoms which are known to be satisfiable (they should succeed, possibly binding some variables), unsatisfiable (they should fail) and valid (they should succeed without binding any variables). Atomic goals are simply matched with the atoms in the database then run. If any goal instance fails incorrectly then `miss` is called and if any goal instance succeeds incorrectly then `wrong` is called.

Testing with each of the three kinds of atoms is optional. There are two reasons for this. Sometimes the user already knows that the program is consistent with the database for that goal (for example, that phase of testing may have already been completed successfully). Also, running some of the goal instances can cause infinite loops. Rather than preventing further testing of (partial) correctness, this can be ignored, at least temporarily. The infinite loop may disappear when the partial correctness bugs are fixed, or the loop may be because the program was run in a mode which will not be needed.

The third phase of testing interprets the goal. The user is asked whether each solution returned is valid. If the solution is valid the system continues searching for more solutions, otherwise `wrong` is called. If the goal eventually fails, `miss` is called to check if any solutions were missed. If the goal has an infinite number of solutions the system will keep generating solutions until the user is convinced that the procedure is correct or suspicious that some answers are being missed (these can then be checked separately). If Prolog's (unfair, depth first) search strategy was used, an infinite search space could result in some answers which are derivable from the program never being returned. This is clearly undesirable, so a fair search strategy is used, which guarantees that every answer will be returned eventually.

The most obvious fair search is breadth first. However, a much more efficient approach is to use a bounded depth first search with iterative deepening. For each successive depth, Prolog's backtracking mechanism can be used to search very quickly and with little space overhead. Whenever the search is stopped by the depth bound, a flag is set. If the flag is not set at all during the search at one depth, then the tree has been searched completely and the depth does not have to be increased further. Another desirable enhancement is to avoid repeatedly returning answers found near the root of the tree. This is achieved by checking the depth bound of the previous iteration when each solution is found. Answers found above the previous bound have been returned already, so they are ignored.

The `append` program of Section 5.2.2 is used again, to illustrate the third phase of testing.

```
?- test(append, 3).
Do static analysis? n
Test known valid instances? n
Test known satisfiable atoms? n
Test known unsatisfiable atoms? n
Generate solutions to goal?
Solution found: append([], A1, A1).
append([], A1, A1) Valid?
Solution found: append([A1], B1, [A1|B1]).
append([A1], B1, [A1|B1])  Valid?
Solution found: append([A1, B1], [B1|C1], [A1|C1]).
append([A1, B1], [B1|C1], [A1|C1]) Valid? n
```

When the wrong answer is found, debugging continues as in the previous example. After the procedure has been edited and the new version has been loaded the user is asked if they want `append` to be tested again. Because the system has captured some knowledge about the desired behaviour of the program, it can quickly check whether the bug has been corrected and whether the new code still behaves correctly for the other cases.

8. CONCLUSIONS

There is a great deal of work still to be done on NUDE. First, several of the tools discussed still need more work on implementation and/or integration with NUDE. The two type systems should be integrated, hopefully keeping the best features of each and several enhancements mentioned in this paper should be implemented. More consideration needs to be given to the debugging of very large programs and of parts of programs which contain non-logical code. Some features of the current system, such as the 'l' option on spy points and the ability to declare procedures correct, provide some support already. Another area for improvement is the treatment of code which is transformed in some way before execution, such as definite clause grammar rules. Currently NUDE only knows about the transformed code, whereas debugging may be better done at the original source code level.

NUDE could be improved by adding more tools along the same lines as the existing tools, and by using better algorithms for some of the tools. However, there may be more to be gained by putting more high-level knowledge about bugs into the system. NUDE incorporates relatively low level concepts of what bugs are, such as incorrect clause instances. Some systems incorporate knowledge about various common kinds of bugs, which can lead to bugs being found more quickly and reported in a nicer way [Eisenstadt 85]. It is also important to investigate the different misunderstandings which lead to bugs [Bma 87].

NUDE is currently aimed only at detecting and locating bugs, but there is obvious merit in adding tools to help fix bugs. The techniques of [Shapiro 83] and [Dershowitz 87] can be used to fix bugs resulting in wrong and missing answers. Some bugs which result in looping or floundering are also mistakes in the logic, not just the control, and they may also be amenable to similar treatment. The algorithm used in *nac* is also useful for fixing infinite loop bugs and floundering bugs which are caused by user-defined control. Dataflow analysis such as that used for groundness analysis can also be useful.

Even without these extensions, the wide range of static checks provided by NUDE detect many errors without user intervention while the dynamic checks are an effective method for isolating errors in logical code. The testing mechanism and declarative debugger complement each other in the capture and use of knowledge about the desired program behaviour. By providing these features in an integrated environment, NUDE has proved to be useful for debugging non-trivial programs.

ACKNOWLEDGEMENTS

Giles Lean, Jeffrey Schultz and James Thom helped in the design and implementation of *nit* and *nude*. This research was supported by the Australian Commonwealth Department of Science and ARGS (now ARC).

REFERENCES

[Brna 87]
P. Brna, A. Bundy, H. Pain and L. Lynch, "Programming tools for Prolog environments", Research Report, Department of Artificial Intelligence, University of Ediburgh, 1987.

[Bruynooghe 82]
M. Bruynooghe, "Adding redundancy to obtain more reliable and more readable Prolog programs", *Proceedings of the First International Logic Programming Conference*, Marseille, France, September 1982, 129-133.

[Dart 88]
P. W. Dart and J. Zobel, "Transforming typed logic programs into well-typed logic programs", Technical Report 88/11, Department of Computer Science, University of Melbourne, Melbourne, Australia, May 1988.

[Dershowitz 87]
N. Dershowitz and Y. Lee, "Deductive debugging", *Proceedings of the Fourth IEEE Symposium on Logic Programming*, San Francisco, California, August 1987, 298-306.

[Drabent 88]
W. Drabent, S. Nadjm-Tehrani and J. Maluszynski, "The use of assertions in algorithmic debugging", *Proceedings of the 1988 International Conference on Fifth Generation Computer Systems*, Tokyo, Japan, December 1988, 573-581.

[Eisenstadt 85]
M. Eisenstadt, "Retrospective zooming: a knowledge based tracking and debugging methodology for logic programming", *Proceedings of the Ninth*

International Joint Conference on Artificial Intelligence, Los Angeles, California, September 1985, 717-719.

[Eisenstadt 88]
M. Eisenstadt and M. Brayshaw, "The Transparent Prolog Machine (TPM): an execution model and graphical debugger for logic programming", *Journal of Logic Programming 5*, 4 (December 1988).

[Lloyd 84a]
J. W. Lloyd and R. W. Topor, "Making Prolog more expressive", *Journal of Logic Programming 1*, 3 (October 1984), 225-240.

[Lloyd 84b]
J. W. Lloyd, *Foundations of logic programming*, Springer-Verlag, New York, 1984.

[Lloyd 87]
J. W. Lloyd, "Declarative error diagnosis", *New Generation Computing 5*, 2 (1987), 133-154.

[Mycroft 84]
A. Mycroft and R. A. O'Keefe, "A polymorphic type system for Prolog", *Artificial Intelligence 23* (1984), 295-307.

[Naish 85]
L. Naish, "Automating control of logic programs", *Journal of Logic Programming 2*, 3 (October 1985), 167-183.

[Naish 87]
L. Naish, "Specification = program + types", *Proceedings of 7th Conference on Foundations of Software Technology and Theoretical Computer Science*, Pune, India, December, 1987.

[Naish 88]
L. Naish, "Declarative diagnosis of missing answers", Technical Report 88/9, Department of Computer Science, University of Melbourne, Melbourne, Australia, May 1988.

[Shapiro 83]
E. Y. Shapiro, *Algorithmic program debugging*, MIT Press, Cambridge, Massachusetts, 1983.

[Thom 88]
J. Thom and J. Zobel, editors. "NU-Prolog reference manual, version 1.3", Technical Report 86/10, Department of Computer Science, University of Melbourne, Melbourne, Australia, 1988.

[Zobel 87]
J. Zobel, "Derivation of polymorphic types for Prolog programs", *Proceedings of the Fourth International Conference on Logic Programming*, Melbourne, Australia, May 1987, 816-838.

Program Transformations

DECIDABILITY RESULTS AND CHARACTERIZATION
OF STRATEGIES FOR THE DEVELOPMENT
OF LOGIC PROGRAMS

Alberto Pettorossi

University of Rome II
Via Orazio Raimondi
00173 Rome (Italy)

Maurizio Proietti

IAC - CNR
Viale del Policlinico 137
00161 Rome (Italy)

Abstract

We address the problem of applying the program transformation methodology to logic programs. We follow the 'rules + strategies' approach [4]. The rules are a slight variation of the familiar definition, unfolding, and folding rules. The strategies are realized by the invention of new predicates, and for making the efficiency improvement really significant (by propagating throughout the recursive structure of the entire computation the program enhancements) one has to find the recursive definitions of those predicates.

We show that the problem of deriving those recursive definitions is unsolvable, thus establishing some theoretical limitations to the mechanization of the transformation technique.

Some solvable subcases are then considered and for those cases we present an algorithm which allows us to invent the new predicates to be introduced and derive their recursive definitions, whenever possible.

1 The Transformation Technique and a Preliminary Example

The derivation of programs using the transformation technique is a valuable method for producing programs which are both correct and efficient [4].

Some problems occur in extending that technique introduced for functional programs [4] also to the case of logic programs and Prolog programs [1,6,12,14,15]. In those cases, in fact, particular care should be taken because of the following facts: i) logic programs compute relations, not functions, ii) in logic programs no difference is assumed between input and output parameters, and iii) the evaluation mechanism of logic programs is based on unification, not matching.

When transforming logic programs we consider that the semantics to be preserved is the least Herbrand model [11] and in all practical cases our choice is adequate.

In this paper we will study the case of logic programs (where the order of evaluation of the atoms in a clause and the order of the clauses are not significant), but the reader should realize that there is a way of extending our results to Prolog programs as well. By applying, in fact, the so-called Goal Inversion rule one may interchange the positions of the atoms in Prolog clauses, whenever necessary [13].

We will perform our program transformations by applying the following three correctness preserving *rules*: the definition rule, the unfolding rule, and the folding rule. They are slightly different from those considered in the literature [15].

Those rules are very flexible and powerful, but their application need to be directed by *strategies*, in order to guarantee the increase of efficiency. The strategies we will consider come from the following simple ideas for improving space or time performances:
- avoidance of repeated visits of input or intermediate data structures,
- avoidance of repeated execution of common subcomputations, and
- avoidance of construction of intermediate data structures which need not to
  be built (that is, we need only to know that they exist, not their value).

The application of strategies realizes efficiency improvements via the *introduction of new predicates* (which is, as we will see, an application of the definition rule given below). However, the desired enhancement of performances is really significant only if we get a *recursive definition* of the newly introduced predicates. In that case, in fact, that improvement is propagated throughout the entire recursive structure of the computation.

The above consideration is expressed in the transformation jargon as *need-for-folding*: after the introduction of a new predicate the derivation process should continue by looking for the explicit definition of that predicate.

It is often the case that the need-for-folding requires also the introduction of new *auxiliary* predicates. Their definition is *not* directly due to efficiency requirements, but indeed it comes from the fact that we want to obtain a recursive definition of the already introduced predicates.

Let us now introduce the transformation rules which we will use during our program derivations. We also present a preliminary example of program development, which will be our running example.

i) *the Definition Rule*. It consists in adding to the current program one clause, which is considered to be a *definition*, with a new head predicate defined in terms of already existing predicates. Notice that no recursive definitions are allowed, and each new predicate occurs as head of one clause only.

ii) *the Unfolding Rule*. It consists in performing a computation step by applying the SLD-resolution to a chosen clause with respect to a selected atom of its body. The chosen clause is replaced in the current program by *all* those which can be obtained by resolving it with any other clause (of the program at hand) whose head is unifiable with the selected atom.

iii) *the Folding Rule*. It consists in replacing an 'old clause': $H \leftarrow A_1,\ldots, A_n, A_{n+1},\ldots, A_r$ by a 'new clause': $H \leftarrow K\sigma, A_{n+1},\ldots, A_r$, using the *definition* (called 'bridge clause'): $K \leftarrow B_1,\ldots, B_n$, where σ is a substitution such that: $A_i = B_i \sigma$ for all $i = 1,\ldots, n$. This rule can be applied only if unfolding the new clause choosing the atom $K\sigma$ we obtain again the old clause. ∎

We will use the above rules in a suitably restricted way (as indicated in Definition 2.2). With those restrictions it can be shown that our rules preserve the least Herbrand model semantics.

Now let us consider a preliminary example of program derivation taken from [15]. That example motivates the introduction of some important concepts which we will define in the following Section. We will follow the development of [15], but while in [15] no suggestions are given for the invention of new predicates during the transformation process, we will indicate in the sequel how they can be generated in an automatic way.

Example 1. Suppose that we want to verify whether or not a sequence X is a common subsequence of the two sequences Y and Z. To do so we first verify that X is a subsequence of Y, and then we verify that X is a subsequence of Z. Here is the corresponding program, called CSUB.
1. csub(X,Y,Z) ← subseq(X,Y), subseq(X,Z).
2. subseq([],X).
3. subseq([A|X],[A|Y]) ← subseq(X,Y).
4. subseq(X,[A|Y]) ← subseq(X,Y).
where: i) a sequence is represented as a list of items, ii) subseq(X,Y) holds iff X is a subsequence of Y (the order of the elements should be preserved, but the elements selected by X need not to be consecutive in Y), and iii) csub(X,Y,Z) holds iff X is a common subsequence of Y and Z.
For instance, [2,4] is a subsequence of [1,2,3,4], but [4,2] is not.

The transformation process starts off by looking for the explicit recursive definition of the predicate csub, so that the duplicated visit of the list X is avoided. In that case, in fact, the double induction over X due to the two occurrences of the predicates subseq is transformed into a single induction. This will result in an improvement of the program performances.

For that purpose we will make some unfolding/folding steps from the initial clause 1, with the objective of eliminating all double occurrences of subseq in the derived clauses. That objective is called *need-for-folding*, and it is the driving force of our program derivation process.
It is easy to see that, by performing some unfolding steps, from clause 1 we can derive the following four clauses:
5. csub([],Y,Z).
6. csub([],Y,[A|Z]) ← subseq([],Z).
7. csub([A|X],[A|Y],Z) ← subseq(X,Y), subseq([A|X],Z).
8. csub(X,[A|Y],Z) ← subseq(X,Y), subseq(X,Z).
We can fold clause 8 using clause 1 as bridge clause and we get:
8.1 csub(X,[A|Y],Z) ← csub(X,Y,Z).

Unfortunately, in clause 7 we are not able to perform a folding step w.r.t. clause 1 (the atoms 'subseq(X,Y), subseq([A|X],Z)', in fact, do not match 'subseq(X,Y), subseq(X,Z)') and it can be easily realized that by unfolding steps we can never get a program version in which all double occurrences of subseq can be folded. Indeed, if we unfold in clause 7 either subseq(X,Y) or subseq([A|X],Z) we get, among other clauses, one whose body is again 'subseq(X,Y), subseq([A|X],Z)'.

Now, since unfoldings and foldings do not lead us to a recursive definition of csub, the only rule which may allow us to satisfy the need-for-folding is the Definition rule. Therefore, we introduce a new predicate which is exactly the body of clause 7, and thus it trivially allows folding. (The arguments of that new predicate are those which indeed allow folding, according to our rule above.). We have (as in [15]):
9. csub1(A,X,Y,Z) ← subseq(X,Y), subseq([A|X],Z).
Now we can fold clause 7 with the bridge clause 9 and we get:

7.1 csub([A|X],[A|Y],Z) ← csub1(A,X,Y,Z).

The derivation proceeds analogously to what we have done for csub, by looking for the explicit recursive definition of the newly introduced predicate csub1. After few unfolding and folding steps we have:

10. csub1(A,X,Y,[A|Z]) ← csub(X,Y,Z).

11. csub1(A,X,Y,[B|Z]) ← csub1(A,X,Y,Z).

The final program is made out of clauses 5, 6, 7.1, 8.1, 10 and 11 in which all double occurrences of the predicate subseq have been eliminated, and thus the need-for-folding has been satisfied. This program version is indeed faster the the original one and its correctness need *not* to be proved, because the least Herbrand model semantics is preserved by construction. ∎

Let us now consider the program derivation process in general. At each step of the derivation when the need-for-folding is not satisfied we are faced with the following two questions:

i) is there any sequence of unfolding/folding steps which may lead us to a situation in which the need-for-folding is satisfied?

ii) in case of a negative answer to question i), are there suitable new predicates whose introduction allows us to satisfy the need-for-folding?

Notice that in order to answer question i) we have to cope with the non-determinism of the unfoldings which is due to the selection of the atoms in the bodies of the clauses. Indeed, that selection may affect the satisfaction of the need-for-folding.

In Section 2 we will show that the problem related to question i) is unsolvable. In Section 3 we will show that there are some interesting classes of programs for which that problem is solvable, and for those classes we will present in Section 4 some algorithms for providing an answer to question ii) as well. We will also show how to use our results for transforming more general classes of programs.

2 The Foldability Problem

In the previous Section we have seen that given a program it is possible to improve the evaluation of a non-recursive predicate by deriving a recursive definition for it. We have informally called need-for-folding the objective of obtaining that recursive definition. In this Section we formalize the satisfaction of the need-for-folding as the positive solution to the so-called *Foldability Problem*. We show that it is an unsolvable problem, whereby showing an intrinsic limitation of the program transformation technique.

Let us first formalize the unfolding/folding process by considering a triple <C,Prog,F>, where C is a given clause (which is assumed to be a *definition*), Prog is a *program* (that is, a set of clauses necessary for performing unfolding steps), and F is a *folding set* (that is, a set of bridge clauses to be used for performing folding steps). It is often the case that C∈ F.

DEFINITION 2.1. A triple <C,Prog,F> is said to be a *transformation triple* iff the head predicate symbols of the set of clauses {C}∪F occur *only once* in {C}∪Prog∪F. ∎

Often a transformation triple will be simply called a triple.

Let us also formalize the selection of an atom during the unfolding process by considering an *Unfolding-Selection Rule*, or *U-Selection Rule*, for short.

DEFINITION 2.2. Let <C,Prog,F> be a transformation triple and S a U-Selection rule. A *UF-tree* (short for *Unfold/Fold tree*) for <C,Prog,F> via the rule S is a tree labelled by clauses and constructed as follows:

i) the root is labelled by the clause C;

ii) let M be a node (possibly the root) labelled by a clause of the form:
    'H ← A_1,...,A_h,..., A_k', such that no subset of the atoms of the body can be folded using a clause in F. Let A_h be the atom selected by the U-Selection rule S.
    For each clause 'A ←B_1,...,B_s' in Prog such that there exists a most general unifier σ of A and A_h, M has a son-node N labelled by the clause (H ← A_1,..., A_{h-1}, B_1, ..., B_s, A_{h+1},..., A_k) σ.

iii) Let M be a non-root node labelled by a clause of the form: 'H ← A_1,..., A_n, A_{n+1},..., A_r' such that A_1,..., A_n can be folded via a bridge clause in F of the form 'K ← B_1,..., B_n'.
    M has a son node N labelled by the new clause: 'H ← Kσ, A_{n+1},..., A_r' where σ is a substitution such that: $A_i = B_i$ σ for all i = 1,..., n. ∎

DEFINITION 2.3. Given a tree T we say that the subtree T1 of T is an *upper portion* of T iff i) if a node N is in T1 then every 'ancestor' of N in T is also in T1, and ii) if a node N is in T1 then every 'brother' of N in T is in T1 as well. ∎

With the above definitions it can be shown that the least Herbrand model of {C}∪Prog∪F is equal to the least Herbrand model of L∪Prog∪F, where L is the set of leaves of any upper portion of a UF-tree for <C,Prog,F> via any given U-Selection rule.

Example 2.1. Let us consider the program CSUB of the previous Section, and the transformation triple <C,Prog,F> where:
- C is clause 1, that is, csub(X,Y,Z) ← subseq(X,Y), subseq(X,Z);
- Prog is the set of clauses:
    2. subseq([],X).
    3. subseq([A|X],[A|Y]) ← subseq(X,Y).
    4. subseq(X,[A|Y]) ← subseq(X,Y).
- F is the set {C} ∪ {csub1(A,X,Y,Z) ← subseq(X,Y), subseq([A|X],Z).}
The tree T1 depicted in the next page is a UF-tree for <C,Prog,F>. The underlined atoms are the ones selected by the U-Selection rule. ❑

DEFINITION 2.4. A node of a UF-tree for <C,Prog,F> is said to be *closed* iff its label is a clause D such that for each subset {$p_1(t_1$,...,$t_k)$, ..., $p_n(u_1$,..., $u_k)$} of atoms in the body of D it does *not* exist a clause in F of the form: H ← p_1(...), ..., p_n(...). ∎

DEFINITION 2.5. A UF-tree T for <C,Prog,F> via the rule S is *closed* iff there exists an upper portion T1 of T such that each of its leaves either i) is closed or ii) has a labelling clause where the atom selected by S cannot be unfolded. ∎

UF-tree T1:

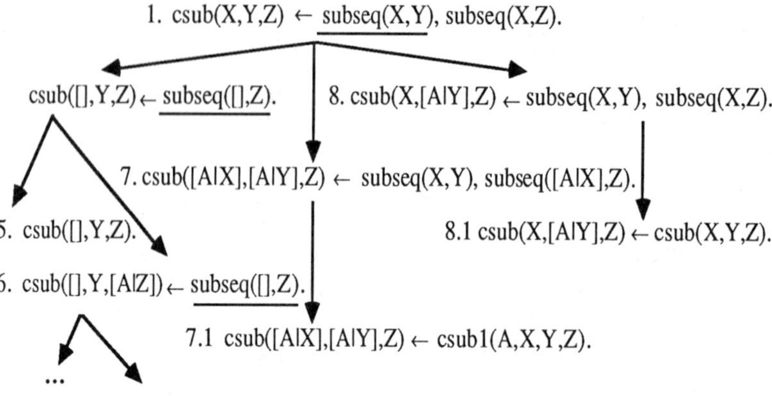

The above UF-tree T1 is closed.

Now we can formulate the FOLDABILITY PROBLEM as follows:
is it possible to determine whether or not given a transformation triple
τ=<C,Prog,F> there exist a U-Selection rule S and a *closed* UF-tree for τ
via S?

THEOREM 2.6. The Foldability Problem is partially solvable and it is not
solvable.

PROOF. i) There exists a non-deterministic algorithm which constructs a
finite upper portion of a UF-tree for any given transformation triple
<C,Prog,F> and it checks whether or not that tree is closed. ii) We reduce
the Word Problem of type 0 grammars to the Foldability Problem. Any
Turing Machine M can be encoded by a logic program ProgM such that: in
ProgM occurs one predicate symbol m only, m is unary, and the body of
each clause of ProgM has at most one atom [9]. We have that given an input
word w and a term w1 which encodes w, M halts accepting w iff ProgM ⊢
m(w1). Let us introduce a new constant c and consider the program ProgM1
derived from ProgM by adding the atom m(c) to the body of each unit
clause. There exists a closed UF-tree for <h←m(w1), ProgM1, {g←m(c)}>
(where h and g are fresh symbols) iff ProgM ⊢ m(w1). ∎

3 A Class of Programs for which Foldability is Decidable

In the pragmatics of the program transformation methodology the solution
of the Foldability Problem often reduces to the existence of a sequence of
unfolding steps such that in the bodies of the derived clauses some
arguments satisfy suitable constraints. For instance, in the Example 2.1,
the foldability w.r.t. clause 1 depends on the identity of the first arguments
of the two occurrences of subseq.

Therefore, in order to define a class of programs for which the
Foldability Problem is decidable we consider the notion of program
projections w.r.t. given arguments. Those projections generate the so-called
unary programs. In what follows we show that for a subclass of unary
programs the Foldability Problem is decidable. That result will be applied to

a class of programs whose projections are unary, and it will provide us with a method for constructing recursive definitions of predicates.

DEFINITION 3.1. *(Projections)*. Let us consider a set of pairs $\pi=\{<p_i,k_i> \mid i=1,\dots,m\}$ where each p_i is a predicate symbol, $p_i \neq p_j$ for $i \neq j$, and each k_i is at most the arity of p_i.
- The *projection* of a set of atoms R w.r.t. π is the *multiset* of atoms R_π constructed as follows: for each atom in R of the form $p_i(t_1,\dots)$ with p_i in π, the atom $p_i(t)$ where t is k_i-th argument of $p_i(t_1,\dots)$ is inserted in R_π. Notice that R_π may be empty even when R is not.
- Given a clause C of the form $H \leftarrow A_1, \dots, A_r$ the *projection* C_π of C w.r.t. π is the clause $K \leftarrow B_1, \dots, B_s$, where $\{B_1, \dots, B_s\}$ is the projection of $\{A_1, \dots, A_r\}$ w.r.t. π, and K is obtained from H by keeping the variables in $\{B_1, \dots, B_s\}$ only.
- The *projection* of a transformation triple <C,Prog,F> w.r.t. π is the triple $<C_\pi,Prog_\pi,F_\pi>$ where:
  - C_π is the projection of the clause C w.r.t. π;
  - for each clause in Prog of the form 'H $\leftarrow A_1, \dots, A_r$' such that the predicate symbol of H occurs in π, we insert in $Prog_\pi$ the clause '$K \leftarrow B_1,\dots,B_s$', where $\{K,B_1,\dots,B_s\}$ is the projection of $\{H,A_1,\dots,A_r\}$ w.r.t. π;
  - F_π is the set of projections w.r.t. π of the clauses in F. ∎

Notice that: i) all predicates in $Prog_\pi$ are unary, and ii) the transformation rules given above can easily be extended to the case of projected programs, where the bodies of clauses are multisets. (Those extended rules should be applied to *occurrences* of atoms, not *atoms*.)

Example 3.1. Let us consider the triple <C,Prog,F> of Example 2.1. Let π be the singleton $\{<subseq,1>\}$. The projection of that triple w.r.t. π is $<C_\pi,Prog_\pi,F_\pi>$, where C_π is: csub(X) $\leftarrow$ subseq(X), subseq(X).
  $Prog_\pi$ is: subseq([]).
        subseq([A|X]) $\leftarrow$ subseq(X).
        subseq(X) $\leftarrow$ subseq(X).
F_π is: $\{C_\pi\}\cup\{csub1(A,X) \leftarrow subseq(X), subseq([A|X])\}$. ❑

The following Theorem 3.3 establishes the relationship between the foldability of a given transformation triple and the one of its projection.
DEFINITION 3.2. A clause D_g is a *clause-generalization* (or *generalization* for short) of a clause D iff the body of D is an instance of the body of D_g and the head of D_g has a fresh predicate symbol and it has all variables of the body of D_g. ∎
For instance, we have that: genp(X1,X2,Z) $\leftarrow$ q(X1), r(X2,Z) is a generalization of p(X) $\leftarrow$ q(t(X)), r(X,Z).

THEOREM 3.3. Let us consider the transformation triple <C,Prog,F> and a set of pairs $\pi=\{<p_i,k_i> \mid i=1,\dots,m\}$, where every predicate symbol occurring in the body of a clause in $\{C\}\cup F$ is one of the p_i's, $p_i \neq p_j$ for $i \neq j$, and each k_i is at most the arity of p_i.
If there exists a closed UF-tree for the projection $<C_\pi,Prog_\pi,F_\pi>$ then there exists a closed UF-tree for <C,Prog,G>, where G is a folding set

such that i) the clauses in G are generalizations of the clauses in F, and ii) the bodies of G_π are equal to the bodies of F_π.

PROOF. Let G be a set of clauses determined as follows: for each clause D in F we insert in G the generalization D_g of D such that D_g has the most general body whose projection w.r.t. π is equal to the projection of the body of D w.r.t. π. Let T_π be a closed UF-tree for $<C_\pi,Prog_\pi,F_\pi>$. We can construct a UF-tree T for $<C,Prog,G>$ by performing (whenever possible) the unfolding and folding steps which correspond to those for its projection. T is closed because: (a) a new node in T can be produced by unfolding only if the corresponding node can be produced in T_π, and (b) the projection w.r.t. π of the body of a clause in T is an instance of the body of the corresponding clause in T_π. ∎

Theorem 3.3 gives us a sufficient condition for obtaining recursive definitions of new predicates introduced during program transformation, via the construction of closed UF-trees for the projected programs.

Example 3.2. Let us consider a triple $<C,Prog,F>$ defined as in the Examples 2.1 and 3.1, and the set $\pi=\{<subseq,1>\}$. A closed UF-tree for the projection $<C_\pi,Prog_\pi,F_\pi>$ is:

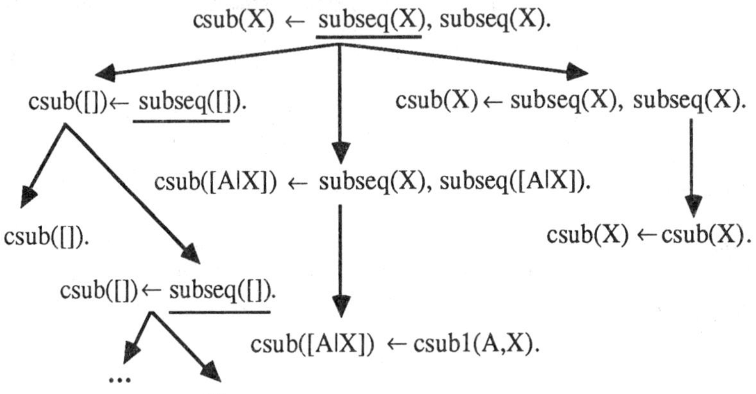

As indicated by the proof of Theorem 3.3, from the above closed UF-tree for $<C_\pi,Prog_\pi,F_\pi>$ we can construct the closed UF-tree T1 for $<C,Prog,F>$ of the Example 2.1.
Referring to the symbols used in the above Theorem 3.3 we have G=F. ☐

Unfortunately, even restricting ourselves to the class of projected triples $<C_\pi,Prog_\pi,F_\pi>$ the Foldability Problem remains unsolvable (indeed any Turing Machine can be encoded via a program involving unary predicates only). (see proof of Theorem 2.6).

Let us now study in some detail a subclass of the projected programs. For that subclass:
i)   we will state the decidability of termination (Theorem 3.6),
ii) we will give a U-Selection rule which constructs a closed UF-tree, if it exists, and
iii) we will give an algorithm for deciding whether or not a closed UF-tree

exists.

DEFINITION 3.4. i) A term is *linear* if each variable occurs in it at most once.
ii) A program is *unilinear* w.r.t. a predicate p iff i) there exists one predicate symbol p only, ii) p occurs at most once in the body of each clause, and iii) for each clause of the form: $p(t) \leftarrow p(u)$, t and u are linear terms and u is a subterm of t (denoted by $u \leq t$). ∎

Notice that often programs which are linear recursive and not mutually recursive, have unilinear programs as projections. The program $Prog_\pi$ in Example 3.1 is unilinear.

DEFINITION 3.5. Given an atom A and a program Prog, we say that the *derivation-tree* of <A, Prog> is *finite* iff all SLD-derivations of Prog∪{A} are finite. ∎

THEOREM 3.6. (*Decidability of the Finiteness Problem for Unilinear Programs*). Given a unilinear program Prog and an atom p(t), where t is a linear term, there is a decision procedure which determines whether or not the derivation-tree of <p(t), Prog> is finite.
PROOF. During the unfolding process of p(t), we can generate only a finite number, say k, of atoms modulo renaming of variables. Therefore, there exists an infinite SLD-derivation of Prog∪{p(t)} iff it is possible to unfold p(t) more than k times. ∎

Example 3.3. Let us consider subseq([a|X]) and $Prog_\pi$ where a is a constant and $Prog_\pi$ is the one of Example 3.1. Only the two atoms subseq([a|X]) and subseq(X) can be derived. We can unfold subseq([a|X]) more than twice using, for instance, the clause 'subseq(X) ← subseq(X).' Thus, the derivation-tree of <subseq([a|X]), $Prog_\pi$> is *not* finite. ❑

DEFINITION 3.7. Let $\mathcal{U}$ be the set of triples <C, P∪Q, F>, such that for each triple there exist two predicate symbols p and q and:
i) C is a clause of the form: 'H ← p(t), q(u)', where t and u are *linear* terms such that either $t \leq u$ or $u \leq t$,
ii) P and Q are *unilinear* programs w.r.t. p and q, respectively;
iii)F is {K ← p(X), q(X)}, where K is an atom and X is a variable. ∎

Since unilinear program are projected programs and for them we consider bodies of clauses to be multisets of atoms, in the above Definition 3.7 and always in the sequel we allow p(...) and q(...) to be different occurrences of the same atom.

Now we will show that the Foldability Problem for the triples in $\mathcal{U}$ is solvable. Let us first present a U-Selection rule, called *Synchronized Descent Rule (SDR* for short), which will be proved to be complete in the class $\mathcal{U}$, in the sense that it allows to obtain a closed UF-tree for any given triple <C,P∪Q,F> in $\mathcal{U}$, if it exists.

DEFINITION 3.8. Let us consider two unilinear programs P and Q w.r.t. the predicates p and q, respectively. The SDR rule is a partial function which selects for unfolding an atom in the body of a given clause N as follows:

if an atom A occurs in the body of N and the derivation-tree of $<A, P \cup Q>$ is finite <u>then</u>   A   <u>else</u> [<u>if</u> in the body of N the atoms p(t) and q(u) occur

<u>then</u> (<u>if</u> t ≤ u <u>then</u> q(u) <u>else</u> p(t))]   ∎

If P and Q are unilinear programs then for each atom A the finiteness of the derivation-tree of $<A,P \cup Q>$ is decidable.

THEOREM 3.9. (*Completeness of the U-Selection rule SDR*). Let us consider a triple $<C,P \cup Q,F>$ in $\mathcal{U}$. There exists a closed UF-tree for $<C,P \cup Q,F>$ via some U-Selection rule S iff there exists a closed UF-tree for $<C,P \cup Q,F>$ via SDR.

PROOF. By induction on the construction of the UF-tree. Let N be a node of a closed UF-tree for a triple in $\mathcal{U}$ via a given U-Selection S. Let its labelling clause be of the form: $H \leftarrow p(r),q(s)$. The interesting case is when the derivation-tree of $<q(s),P \cup Q>$ is not finite and s < r. In this case SDR immediately selects p(r) for unfolding. As a consequence of the Switching Lemma [11] it is enough to show that during the construction of the closed subtree rooted in N the rule S selects at least once the atom with predicate p. Indeed, if S never selects p, we get a clause of the form: $H\sigma \leftarrow p(r\sigma),q(s_1\sigma)$, where σ is the composition of the computed mgu's and $s_1\sigma < r\sigma$. That clause cannot be folded because p and q have different arguments.   ∎

LEMMA 3.10. Let us consider in $\mathcal{U}$ a triple τ of the form: $<H \leftarrow p(t),q(u), P \cup Q, \{K \leftarrow p(X), q(X)\}>$. The clauses of the UF-tree for τ via SDR have their bodies taken (modulo a renaming of variables) from a *finite* set. The elements of that set are of the form: either i) 'p(t_1), q(u_1)', or ii) 'p(t_2)', or iii) 'q(u_2)', or iv) Kσ (where t_1,t_2,u_1,u_2 are terms, and σ is a substitution).

PROOF. The proof of Theorem 3.6 shows that the elements of the form ii) and iii) are finite. The elements of the form iv) are finite if we know that the elements of the form i) are finite (because they derive from folding). For case i), let us consider in the UF-tree T for τ a clause of the form: $H1 \leftarrow p(r),q(s)$, such that it does *not* have an ancestor with an atom whose derivation-tree is finite. It can be proved by induction on the length of the path from the root to that clause that: $size(p(r)^\wedge q(s)) \leq max\{size(A) \mid A$ is a head in $P \cup Q$ or A=p(t) or A=q(u)\}+1$. Thus, in T we have a finite number of clauses which do not have an ancestor with an atom whose derivation-tree is finite.

For each clause in whose body there is an atom with finite derivation-tree, only a finite number of clauses can be derived.   ∎

PROCEDURE Tree-Closure. *Input*: $<C,P \cup Q,F>$ in $\mathcal{U}$. *Output*: Yes/No depending on the existence of a closed UF-tree for $<C,P \cup Q,F>$.

- Expand (via unfolding or folding steps) the UF-tree for $<C,P \cup Q,F>$ via SDR until for each node N either i) N is closed, or ii) the body of the labelling clause of N contains an atom for which an unfolding step *cannot* be performed, or iii) an ancestor of the node N has a labelling clause (called *recurrent* clause), whose body is equal to the body of the labelling clause of N itself, up to a renaming of variables, and both clauses are *not* foldable. Output 'Yes' iff case iii) never occurs (that is, the set of recurrent clauses is empty).   •

The above procedure is a decision procedure for the Foldability Problem restricted to the triples in $\mathcal{U}$ because i) the Completeness Theorem 3.9 ensures that it is a semidecision procedure, and ii) Lemma 3.10 ensures that it terminates. Thus, we have the following Theorem.

THEOREM 3.11.(*Decidability of the Foldability Problem for the triples in* $\mathcal{U}$)
It is possible to decide whether or not given a triple $\tau=$<C,P$\cup$Q,F> in $\mathcal{U}$, there exist a U-Selection rule S and a closed UF-tree for τ via S. ∎

Example 3.4 Let us consider the triple <C_π, $Prog_\pi$, $\{C_\pi\}$> in $\mathcal{U}$, where C_π and $Prog_\pi$ are the ones of Example 3.1. The procedure Tree-Closure tells us that a closed UF-tree for that triple does *not* exist. That procedure, in fact, constructs the following UF-tree:

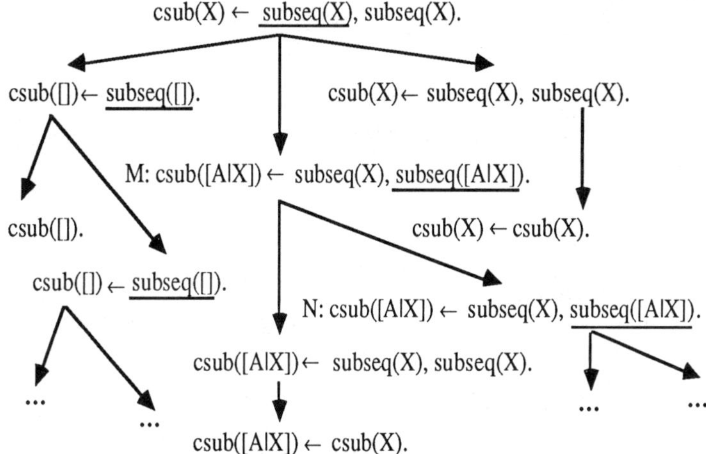

where the clause of the node M is a recurrent clause (see node N as well). ❑

Notice that Lemma 3.10 does *not* hold for UF-trees constructed by using an arbitrary U-Selection rule. For instance, if in the above Example 3.4 we choose for unfolding always the leftmost atom in the body of a clause, we obtain an *infinite* set of bodies of the form 'subseq(t), subseq(u)'.

4 Invention of New Predicates when Foldability Fails

In the previous Section we have shown that it is possible to decide whether or not there exists a closed UF-tree for any given triple in $\mathcal{U}$.
Let us now consider a triple $\tau=$<C,Prog,F> which is *not* in $\mathcal{U}$, and one of its suitable projections which is in $\mathcal{U}$. If by application of the Tree-Closure procedure we prove that there exists a closed UF-tree for the projection, we can obtain a closed UF-tree for the triple <C,Prog,G> where G is a generalization of the folding set F (that is, we can derive a recursive definition of the head predicate of C using auxiliary generalized predicates).

If a closed UF-tree does *not* exist for the projection (and unfortunately this is often the case in practice as the Example 3.4 shows) we may introduce auxiliary generalized predicates for performing the folding steps and closing the UF-tree for the projected triple and the given triple τ as well (see for instance the predicate csub1 in Example 1). For completing the program derivation process and satisfying the need-for-folding we are then left with the task of finding the recursive definitions of those generalized predicates (that is, finding closed UF-trees having those predicate as initial clauses).

The crucial problem of finding auxiliary predicates (also called *eureka steps*) during program transformation has been solved by our technique for the class of programs which have unilinear projections, as we now indicate. Let us first present a constructive method that given a triple in $\mathcal{U}$ finds a finite set of auxiliary predicates which allow us to obtain closed UF-trees and have closed UF-trees themselves.

We consider a triple $<C,P\cup Q,F>$ in $\mathcal{U}$. The procedure Tree-Closure constructs a UF-tree T and a finite (possibly empty) set R of recurrent clauses.

For each clause D in R we define a new clause NewD with the body of D and the head with a fresh predicate symbol with all variables of the body. Let NEWR be the set of the NewD's. It is easy to see that:

(†) $<C1,P\cup Q,F\cup NEWR>$ has a closed UF-tree for any C1 in $\{C\}\cup NEWR$.

Notice that it is possible to find a *trivial* set of clauses NEWR such that the above property (†) holds. For instance, if C has the form: $H \leftarrow p(t),q(u)$ such a trivial NEWR is $\{h(X,Y) \leftarrow p(X),q(Y)\}$. Obviously, we are *not* interested in those trivial sets, because in the derived programs they do not determine an increase of efficiency.

Let us now introduce a definition for avoiding trivial sets.
DEFINITION 4.1. Let us consider a triple $\tau = <C, P\cup Q, F>$ in $\mathcal{U}$. (Recall that C is a clause of the form: $H \leftarrow p(t),q(u)$). τ is *convergent* iff for each recurrent clause of the form: $K \leftarrow p(v),q(w)$ (with v and w terms) we have that $v \leq w$ or $w \leq v$. ∎

THEOREM 4.2. Let us consider a triple $<C, P\cup Q, F>$ in $\mathcal{U}$ and the set R of its recurrent clauses. There exists a folding set NEWR such that: i) for each clause C1 in $\{C\}\cup NEWR$ there is a closed UF-tree for $<C1, P\cup Q, F\cup NEWR>$ via the SDR U-Selection Rule, and ii) the bodies of the clauses of NEWR are equal to the bodies of the clauses of R.
PROOF. Use property (†). ∎
If the triple $<C,P\cup Q,F>$ is convergent then each clause of NEWR has the form: $H \leftarrow p(v),q(w)$, where $v \leq w$ or $w \leq v$, and trivial sets are avoided.

The following Corollary makes it algorithmic in many cases the invention of the auxiliary predicates during program transformation.
COROLLARY 4.3. Let us consider the triple $<C,Prog,F>$ and a set of pairs $\pi=\{<p_i,k_i> \mid i=1,\dots,m\}$ where every predicate symbol occurring in the body of a clause in $\{C\}\cup F$ is one of the p_i's, $p_i \neq p_j$ for $i \neq j$, and each k_i is at most the arity of p_i. Suppose that the projection $<C_\pi,Prog_\pi,F_\pi>$ is a triple in $\mathcal{U}$, and that R is the set of its recurrent clauses. It is possible to construct two folding sets G and INVR such that:
i) for each clause C1 in $\{C\}\cup INVR$ there is a closed UF-tree for

<C1,Prog,G∪INVR> via SDR, and
ii) the bodies of G_π are equal to the bodies of F_π, and the bodies of $INVR_\pi$ are equal to the bodies of R.

PROOF. By Theorem 4.2 there exists NEWR s.t. for each clause $C1_\pi$ in $\{C_\pi\}$∪NEWR there is a closed UF-treee for <$C1_\pi$,$Prog_\pi$,F_π∪NEWR>. The bodies of NEWR are equal to the bodies of the set R of the recurrent clauses. Therefore, each clause in NEWR has the form H ← p(t), q(u). Suppose that in Prog p and q have arities n and m, respectively. Let us construct the set INVR of clauses from NEWR as follows: for each clause D in NEWR we insert in INVR a clause InvD of the form: 'K ← $p(t_1,\ldots,t_n)$, $q(u_1,\ldots,u_m)$' such that: i) the body of InvD is the most general one whose projection is equal to the body of D, and ii) K has the same head predicate symbol of D and it contains all variables in $\{t_1,\ldots,t_n,u_1,\ldots,u_m\}$. We have: $INVR_\pi$=NEWR. (Thus, the bodies of $INVR_\pi$ are equal to the bodies of R.) Hence, we have that for each C1 in {C}∪INVR there is a closed UF-tree for <$C1_\pi$, $Prog_\pi$, F_π∪$INVR_\pi$> via SDR, and by Theorem 3.3 there exists a set G1 such that there is a closed UF-tree for <C1, Prog, G1> with the bodies of $G1_\pi$ equal to the bodies of F_π∪$INVR_\pi$. Thus, G=G1-INVR. ∎

Example 4.1. Let us consider the triple <C,Prog,{C}> where C and Prog are defined as in Example 3.1. Its projection <C_π,$Prog_\pi$,$\{C_\pi\}$> w.r.t. π={<subseq,1>} is a convergent triple in $\mathcal{U}$. Indeed the set R of recurrent clauses is {csub([A|X]) ← subseq(X), subseq([A|X])} (see Example 3.1). Therefore, NEWR = {csub1(A,X)←subseq(X),subseq([A|X])} and INVR = {csub1(A,X,Y,Z) ← subseq(X,Y), subseq([A|X],Z)}. The tree T1 of Example 3.1 is a closed UF-tree for <C,Prog,G∪INVR> where G={C} and the following tree is a closed UF-tree for <csub1(A,X,Y,Z)←subseq(X,Y), subseq([A|X],Z),Prog,G∪INVR>:

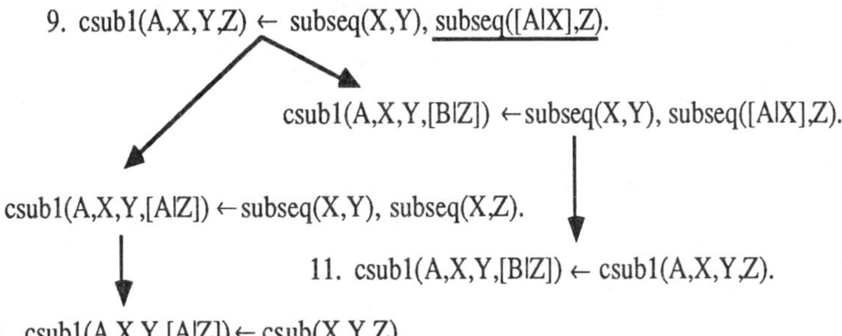

Let us finally present one more example of program derivation in which we apply the results of the above Corollary 4.3.

Example 4.2. Suppose we are given a word S in {0,1}*. We say that a subword W of S is a zero-subword if it is made of consecutive 0's and S=XWY where X is either empty or it ends by 1, and Y is either empty or it begins by 1. We are required to construct the list Z of all the zero-subwords and the list A of all the one-subwords of the given word S. The following program (where words are represented as lists) solves the problem :
1. zero-one(S,Z,A) ← zero(S,Z), one(S,A).

where the predicate zero-one(S,Z,A) holds iff Z is the list of all zero-subwords of S and A is the list of all one-subwords of S, respectively.

2. zero([],[]).	7. one([],[]).
3. zero([0],[[0]]).	8. one([1],[[1]]).
4. zero([1|S],Z) ← zero(S,Z).	9. one([0|S],A) ← one(S,A).
5. zero([0,0|S],[[0|Y]|Z]) ←	10. one([1,1|S],[[1|Y]|A]) ←
zero([0|S],[Y|Z]).	one([1|S],[Y|A]).
6. zero([0,1|S],[[0]|Z]) ← zero(S,Z).	11. one([1,0|S],[[1]|A]) ← one(S,A).

We consider the triple τ=<C,Prog,{C}> where C is clause 1 and Prog is the set of clauses {2,...,11}. We also consider the set π={<zero,1>, <one,1>} and the projection τ_π=<clause 1', ZERO'∪ONE', {clause 1'}> where clause 1' is zero-one(S) ← zero(S), one(S). ZERO' ∪ ONE' is the program {2',...,6'} ∪ {7',...,11'} with the clauses:

2'. zero([]).	7'. one([]).
3'. zero([0]).	8'. one([1]).
4'. zero([1|S]) ← zero(S).	9'. one([0|S]) ← one(S).
5'. zero([0,0|S]) ← zero([0|S]).	10'. one([1,1|S]) ← one([1|S]).
6'. zero([0,1|S]) ← zero(S).	11'. one([1,0|S]) ← one(S).

The triple τ_π is in $\mathcal{U}$. By applying the Tree-Closure procedure one can see that no closed UF-tree for τ_π exists, and the triple τ_π is convergent with the set {zero-one([1\|S]) ← zero(S), one([1\|S])} of recurrent clauses. The reader, in fact, may verify that a path in the UF-tree built by the Tree-Closure procedure consists of the following clauses:

(a) zero-one(S) ← zero(S), one(S).   (clause 1')

(b) zero-one([1\|S]) ← zero(S), one([1\|S]).   (by unfolding zero using 4')

(c) zero-one([1,0\|S]) ← zero([0\|S]), one(S).   (by unfolding one using 11' because S < [1\|S])

(d) zero-one([1,0,1\|S])←zero(S), one([1\|S]).   (by unfolding zero using 6' because S < [0\|S])

and the body of clause (b) is equal to the one of (d). By Theorem 4.2 we can construct the additional folding set NEWR={new-zero-one(S) ← zero(S), one([1\|S])}. Then, as indicated in the proof of Corollary 4.3, we construct the folding sets G={C} and INVR={new-zero-one(S,Z,A) ← zero(S,Z), one([1\|S],A)}. We have a closed UF-tree for <C,Prog,{C}∪INVR>, whose set of leaves L1 is made out of the clauses:

    zero-one([],[],[]).
    zero-one([0],[[0]],[]).
    zero-one([1\|S],Z,A) ← new-zero-one(S,Z,A).
    zero-one([0,0\|S],[[0\|Y]\|Z],A) ← zero-one([0\|S],[Y\|Z],A).
    zero-one([0,1\|S],[[0]\|Z],A) ← new-zero-one(S,Z,A).

A closed UF-tree for <new-zero-one(S,Z,A) ← zero(S,Z), one([1\|S],A), Prog, {C}∪INVR> has the following set L2 of leaves:

    new-zero-one([],[],[[1]]).
    new-zero-one([1\|S],Z,[[1\|Y]\|A]) ← zero-one([1\|S],Z,[Y\|A]).
    new-zero-one([0],[[0]],[[1]]).
    new-zero-one([0,0\|S],[[0\|Y]\|Z],[[1]\|A]) ← zero-one([0\|S],[Y\|Z],A).
    new-zero-one([0,1\|S],[[0]\|Z],[[1]\|A]) ← new-zero-one(S,Z,A).

The final program is L1 ∪ L2 is more efficient than the initial one because it visits the given list of 0's and 1's only once.   ❑

6 Conclusions

We have considered some theoretical questions concerning the programming methodology of deriving logic programs by transformations. We have shown that the need-for-folding which is a technique often used for deriving efficient programs, is in general associated to an unsolvable problem. We have then introduced and studied particular subclasses of programs for which that problem is solvable.

There is an algorithm which finds the recursively definable predicates which should be introduced as *eureka* steps during program development and ensure efficiency improvements in the derived programs.

7 References

[1]   Azibi, N., Costa, E.J. and Kodratoff, Y.: "Burstall-Darlington Program Transformation Method Applied to Logic Programming", Proc. Artificial Intelligence and Advanced Computer Technology Conference/Exhibition, Wiesbaden, 1986.

[2]   Boyer, R.S. and Moore, J.S.: "Proving Theorems about LISP Functions", JACM 22 (1) 1975, pp. 129-144.

[3]   Bruynooghe, M., De Schreye, D. and Krekels, B.: "Compiling Control", Departement of Computer Science, Katholieke Universiteit Leuven, 1987.

[4]   Burstall, R.M. and Darlington, J.: "A Transformation System for Developing Recursive Programs", JACM, Vol. 24,No. 1, January 1977, pp. 44-67.

[5]   Darlington, J.: "An Experimental Program Transformation and Synthesis System", Artificial Intelligence 16, 1981, pp. 1-46.

[6]   Debray, S.K.: "Optimizing Almost-Tail-Recursive Prolog Programs", Technical Report, S.U. of New York, Stony Brook, 1984.

[7]   van Emden, M.H. and Kowalski, R.: "The Semantics of Predicate Logic as a Programming Language", JACM, Vol. 23, No. 4, October 1976, pp. 733-742.

[8]   Hogger, C.J.: "Derivation of Logic Programs", JACM, No. 28, 2, 1981, pp. 372-392.

[9]   Itai, A. and Makowsky, J. A.: "Unification as a Complexity Measure for Logic Programming" J. Logic Programming, 4, 1987, pp.105-117.

[10] Kowalski, R.: "Logic for Problem Solving", North Holland, 1979.

[11] Lloyd, J.W.: "Foundations of Logic Programming", Springer-Verlag, Berlin, Heidelberg, New York, Tokio, 1987.

[12] Nakagawa, H.: "Prolog Program Transformations and Tree Manipulation Algorithms", J. Logic Programming 1985, 2, pp. 77-91.

[13] Proietti, M. and Pettorossi, A.: "Techniques for the Automatic Improvement of Logic Programs" Technical Report IASI-CNR R.231 (September 1988).

[14] Sterling, L. and Lakhotia, A.: "Composing Prolog Meta-Interpreters", Proc. 5-th Intern. Logic Programming Conference, Seattle, WA (USA), 1988.

[15] Tamaki, H. and Sato, T.: "Unfold/Fold Transformation of Logic Programs", Proc. 2nd International Logic Programming Conference, Uppsala, 1984.

Unfold/Fold Transformation of Stratified Programs

(Extended Abstract)[*]

Hirohisa SEKI

Institute for New Generation Computer Technology[†]
1-4-28, Mita, Minato-ku, Tokyo 108, JAPAN

Abstract

This paper describes several extensions of Tamaki-Sato's [15] unfold/fold transformation of definite programs. We first propose unfold/fold rules also preserving the finite failure set (by SLD-resolution) of a definite program, which the original rules proposed by Tamaki and Sato do not. Then, we show that our unfold/fold rules can be extended to rules for stratified programs, and prove that both the success set and the finite failure set (by SLDNF-resolution) of a stratified program are preserved. Preservation of equivalence of the perfect model semantics [10] is also discussed.

1   Introduction

Program transformation provides a powerful methodology for program development, especially for derivation of an efficient program preserving the same meaning as that of an original and possibly inefficient program. Thus, one of the most important properties of program transformation is preservation of equivalence (Maher [9] investigated various formulations of equivalence for logic programs).

Tamaki and Sato proposed an elegant framework for unfold/fold transformation of logic programs [15]. Their transformation rules preserve the equivalence of a definite program in the sense of the least Herbrand model. Kawamura and Kanamori [6] recently proved that Tamaki-Sato's transformation also preserves the *success set* of a program, that is, a transformed program has the same computed answer substitution as that of the original program for any goal. Thus, the transformation rules by Tamaki and Sato seem to be sufficient, at least as far as positive information inferred from a program is concerned.

---

[*]The full version of the paper is to appear in [11] and [12].

[†]*Current Address*: Central Research Laboratory, Mitsubishi Electric Corporation, 8-1-1, Tsukaguchi-Honmachi, Amagasaki, Hyogo, JAPAN 661

In general, however, their transformation does not always preserve the finite failure set (by SLD-resolution) of a definite program. The evaluation of a goal in a transformed program might not be terminating, even if the evaluation of that goal is finitely failed in the original program. Thus, when we are interested in negative information inferred from a program and Clark's Negation as Failure rule [3] is used, their transformation is not sufficient. Furthermore, when we consider an extension of their rules to a general logic program where the body of a clause may contain negative literals, the failure to preserve the finite failure of a program would lead to failure to preserve positive information inferred from the program.

In this paper, we propose unfold/fold rules which also preserve the finite failure set of a definite program. Then, we extend them to a stratified program and show that our transformation preserves both the success set and the finite failure set (by SLDNF-resolution) of a given stratified program. Preservation of equivalence of transformation in the perfect model semantics [10] is also discussed.

The organization of this paper is as follows. After summarizing preliminaries, section 2 gives transformation rules which preserve the finite failure set of a definite program. Section 3 extends them to stratified programs. Section 4 discusses transformation rules which preserve the perfect model semantics. Finally, a summary of this work and a discussion of related work are given in section 5.

Throughout this paper, we assume that the reader is familiar with the basic concept of logic programming, and the terminology follows that in [8]. As notation, variables are denoted by $X, Y, \cdots$, and atoms by $A, B, \cdots$. Multisets of atoms are denoted by $L, K, M, \cdots$, and $\theta, \sigma, \cdots$ are used for substitutions.

2   Unfold/fold Transformation

2.1   Preliminaries: Rules of Transformation

This section describes Tamaki-Sato's unfold/fold transformation for definite programs [15]. The following descriptions of transformation rules are borrowed mainly from [14] and [6].

Definition 2.1 Initial (Definite) Program

An initial (definite) program P_0 is a definite program satisfying the following conditions:

(I1) P_0 is divided into two disjoint sets of clauses, P_{new} and P_{old}. The predicates defined in P_{new} are called *new predicates*, while those defined in P_{old} are called *old predicates*.

(I2) The new predicates appear neither in P_{old} nor in the bodies of the clauses in P_{new}. □

Example 2.1 Let $P_0 = \{C_1, C_2, C_3, C_4, C_5, C_6, C_7\}$, where

$$
\begin{array}{lrcl}
C_1 : & p(0,0). & & \\
C_2 : & p(X,Y) & \leftarrow & eq(X,Y), p(X,Y). \\
C_3 : & q(0,0). & & \\
C_4 : & q(X,Y) & \leftarrow & plus1(X,Y), q(X,Y). \\
C_5 : & eq(X,X). & & \\
C_6 : & plus1(X, s(X)). & & \\
C_7 : & r(X,Y) & \leftarrow & p(X,Y), q(X,Y).
\end{array}
$$

and $P_{old} = \{C_1, C_2, C_3, C_4, C_5, C_6\}$, $P_{new} = \{C_7\}$. Thus, 'r' is a new predicate, while the other predicates are old predicates. □

We call an atom, A, a *new atom* (an *old atom*) when the predicate of A is a new predicate (an old predicate), respectively.

Definition 2.2 Unfolding

Let P_i be a program and C a clause in P_i of the form: $H \leftarrow A, L$. Suppose that $C_1, \cdots, C_k$ are all the clauses in P_i such that C_j is of the form: $A_j \leftarrow K_j$ and A_j is unifiable with A, by an mgu, say, θ_j, for each j $(1 \leq j \leq k)$.

Let C'_j $(1 \leq j \leq k)$ be the result of applying θ_j after replacing A in C with the body of C_j, namely, $C'_j = H\theta_j \leftarrow K_j\theta_j, L\theta_j$. Then, $P_{i+1} = (P_i - \{C\}) \cup \{C'_1, \cdots, C'_k\}$. C is called the *unfolded clause* and $C_1, \cdots, C_k$ are called the *unfolding clauses*. □

Example 2.2 (Continued from Example 2.1)

By unfolding C_7 at atom '$p(X,Y)$' in its body, program $P_1 = \{C_1, C_2, C_3, C_4, C_5, C_6, C_8, C_9\}$ is obtained, where

$$
\begin{array}{lrcl}
C_8 : & r(0,0) & \leftarrow & q(0,0). \\
C_9 : & r(X,Y) & \leftarrow & eq(X,Y), p(X,Y), q(X,Y).
\end{array}
$$
□

Definition 2.3 Folding

Let C be a clause in P_i of the form: $A \leftarrow K, L$ and D a clause in P_{new}[1] of the form: $B \leftarrow K'$. Suppose that there exists a substitution θ satisfying the following conditions:

(F1) $K'\theta = K$

(F2) Let $X_1, \cdots, X_j, \cdots, X_m$ be internal variables of D, namely, appearing only in the body K' of D but not in B. Then, each $X_j\theta$ appears neither in A nor in L, and, furthermore, $X_i\theta \neq X_j\theta$ if $i \neq j$.

---

[1] Note that D is not necessarily in P_i.

(F3) D is the only clause in P_{new} whose head is unifiable with $B\theta$.

(F4) Either the predicate of A is an old predicate, or C is the result of applying unfolding at least once to a clause in P_0.

Then, let C' be a clause of the form: $A \leftarrow B\theta, L$, and let P_{i+1} be $(P_i - \{C\}) \cup \{C'\}$. C is called the *folded* clause and D is called the *folding* clause. □

Example 2.3 (Continued from Example 2.2)

By folding the body of C_9 by C_7, program $P_2 = \{C_1, C_2, C_3, C_4, C_5, C_6, C_8, C_{10}\}$ is obtained, where

$$C_{10} : \quad r(X,Y) \quad \leftarrow \quad eq(X,Y), r(X,Y).$$

  □

2.1.1 Previous Results

Definition 2.4 Transformation Sequence

Let P_0 be an initial program and P_{i+1} ($i \geq 0$) a program obtained from P_i by applying either unfolding or folding. Then, the sequence of programs $P_0, P_1, \cdots, P_N$ is called a *transformation sequence starting from P_0*. □

For the above unfold/fold transformation, Tamaki and Sato proved the following result [15].

Theorem 2.1 [Tamaki-Sato 84] The least Herbrand model, M_{P_i}, of any program P_i in a transformation sequence starting from initial program P_0, is identical to that of P_0. □

Recently, Kawamura and Kanamori [6] showed that Tamaki-Sato's transformation also preserves *answer substitutions* for any goal.

Definition 2.5 Success Set

Let P be a (definite) program. The set of all the atom-substitution pairs (A, σ), such that there exists a successful SLD-derivation for $P \cup \{\leftarrow A\}$ with computed answer σ, is called the *success set* of P, and is denoted by $SS(P)$. □

Theorem 2.2 [Kawamura-Kanamori 88] The success set $SS(P_i)$ of any program P_i in a transformation sequence starting from initial program P_0, is identical to that of P_0. □

Example 2.4 (Continued from Examples 2.1 and 2.2)

Since $r(0,0) \in M(P_0)$ holds, $r(0,0)$ is also in $M(P_2)$ from Theorem 2.1. More precisely, $(r(X,Y), \sigma = \{X/0, Y/0\})$ is in $SS(P_0)$, thus, that pair is also in $SS(P_2)$, from Theorem 2.2. □

2.2 Modified Folding Rule and Preservation of FF

2.2.1 Modified Folding Rule

This paper also considers the finite failure set (by SLD-resolution) of a program.

Definition 2.6 Finite Failure (FF) Set

Let P be a (definite) program. The set of all atoms A such that there exists a finitely failed SLD-tree for $P \cup \{\leftarrow A\}$, is called the *(SLD) finite failure set* of P, and is denoted by $FF(P)$. $\qquad\square$

The *partial correctness* of the transformation *wrt FF* is easily shown.

Proposition 2.1 (Partial Correctness wrt FF) Let $P_0, \cdots, P_N$ be a transformation sequence. Then, $FF(P_N) \subseteq FF(P_0)$ for all $N \geq 0$.

Proof: Let G be a definite goal, and suppose that $P_N \cup G$ has a finitely failed SLD-tree. From the soundness of SLD-resolution [3], $comp(P_N) \vdash G$. It is easy to see that $comp(P_0) \vdash comp(P_N)$ holds[2]. Thus, G is also a logical consequence of $comp(P_0)$. Then, from the completeness of SLD-resolution [4], $P_0 \cup G$ has a finitely failed SLD-tree. $\qquad\square$

Tamaki-Sato's unfold/fold transformation, however, does *not* preserve the *total correctness wrt FF*. That is, $FF(P_0) \subseteq FF(P_i)$ for all i $(N \geq i > 0)$ does not hold in general.

Example 2.5 (Continued from Example 2.1, 2.2)

The failure set of the original program P_0 is *not* preserved. For example, $r(s(0), s(0)) \in FF(P_0)$, while $r(s(0), s(0))$ is not contained in $FF(P_2)$. In fact, any SLD-derivation for $P_2 \cup \{\leftarrow r(s(0), s(0))\}$ is *infinite*. Thus, $FF(P_0) \not\subseteq FF(P_2)$. $\qquad\square$

We now give a modified transformation rule which also preserves the total correctness wrt FF. In order to specify such a rule, we need several definitions.

Definition 2.7 Inherited Atom

Let $P_0, \cdots, P_N$ be a transformation sequence starting from P_0, and C a clause in P_i $(N \geq i \geq 0)$ whose head is a new atom. Then, an atom in the body of C is called an atom *inherited from P_0* if one of the following conditions is satisfied:

    (i) C is a clause in P_{new}. Then, each atom in the body of C is *inherited from P_0*.

---

[2] Note that the converse does not hold in general, that is, $comp(P_N) \not\vdash comp(P_0)$.

(ii) Let C be the result of unfolding in P_i. Suppose that C_+ in P_{i-1} is the unfolded clause of the form: $A \leftarrow B, B_1, \cdots, B_n$, and that C_- in P_{i-1} is one of the unfolding clauses of the form: $B' \leftarrow K$. Thus, C is of the form: $A\theta \leftarrow K\theta, B_1\theta, \cdots, B_n\theta$, where θ is an mgu of B and B'. Then, each atom $B_j\theta$ ($1 \leq j \leq n$) in C is *inherited from P_0* if B_j in C_+ is inherited from P_0.

(iii) Let C be the result of folding in P_i. Suppose that C_+ in P_{i-1} is the folded clause of the form: $A \leftarrow K, B_1, \cdots, B_n$, and that D in P_{new} is the folding clause of the form: $B \leftarrow K'$. Thus, C is of the form: $A \leftarrow B\theta, B_1, \cdots, B_n$, where θ is an mgu such that $K'\theta = K$. Then, each atom B_j ($1 \leq j \leq n$) in C is *inherited from P_0* if B_j in C_+ is inherited from P_0. $\qquad\square$

Intuitively, an inherited atom is (a possibly instantiated version of) an atom such that it was in the body of some clause in P_{new} and no unfolding has been applied to it.

Example 2.6 In Example 2.1, both '$p(X,Y)$' and '$q(X,Y)$' in the body of C_7 are inherited atoms. In the body of clause C_9 (Example 2.2), atom '$q(X,Y)$' is inherited from P_0, while neither '$eq(X,Y)$' nor '$p(X,Y)$' is inherited from P_0. $\qquad\square$

Now, we can define a *modified* folding rule.

Definition 2.8 (Modified) Folding

Let C and D be defined similarly in **Definition 2.3**, namely, C is a clause in P_i of the form: $A \leftarrow K, L$ and D is a clause in P_{new} of the form: $B \leftarrow K'$. Suppose that there exists a substitution θ satisfying the following conditions:

- (F1), (F2) and (F3) are the same as those defined in **Definition 2.3**.
- (F4') Either the predicate of A is an old predicate, or there is no atom in K which is inherited from P_0. $\qquad\square$

Example 2.7 (Continued from Example 2.2)

Consider clause C_9 in Example 2.2. As noted in Example 2.6, atom '$q(X,Y)$' in its body is inherited from P_0, thus the modified folding does not allow it to be folded by C_7.

Instead, by unfolding C_9 at atom '$q(X,Y)$' in its body, program $P_2^m = \{C_1, C_2, C_3, C_4, C_5, C_6, C_8, C_{11}, C_{12}\}$ is obtained, where

$$C_{11} : \quad r(0,0) \quad \leftarrow \quad eq(0,0), p(0,0).$$
$$C_{12} : \quad r(X,Y) \quad \leftarrow \quad eq(X,Y), p(X,Y), plus1(X,Y), q(X,Y).$$

Now, atom '$q(X,Y)$' in the body of C_{12} is not inherited from P_0, so that the modified folding is now applicable to C_{12}. That is, by folding the body of C_{12} by C_7, program $P_3^m = \{C_1, C_2, C_3, C_4, C_5, C_6, C_8, C_{11}, C_{13}\}$ is obtained, where

$$C_{13} : \quad r(X,Y) \quad \leftarrow \quad eq(X,Y), plus1(X,Y), r(X,Y). \qquad \square$$

Hereafter, except in section 4, by *folding* we mean the *modified* folding defined in Definition 2.8, and by a *transformation sequence*, we mean the one obtained by applying either unfolding or modified folding.

2.2.2 Preservation of FF for Definite Clauses

In this subsection, we show that the unfold/fold transformation (using modified folding) guarantees the total correctness wrt FF for definite programs. We need one more definition and a lemma.

Definition 2.9 P_{new}-expansion

Let A be an atom and let L be a sequence of atoms. L is called a P_{new}-*expansion of* A, denoted by $\overline{A}$, if the following conditions are satisfied:

- When A is an old atom, L is A itself.
- When A is a new atom, L is either A, or a sequence of atoms '$B_1\theta, \cdots, B_n\theta$' such that there exists a clause in P_{new} of the form: $A_0 \leftarrow B_1, \cdots, B_n$ and θ is an mgu of A and A_0.

Similarly, let M be a sequence of atoms of the form: $G_1, \cdots, G_k$. Then, L is called a P_{new}-*expansion of* M, denoted by $\overline{M}$, if $L=\overline{G_1}, \cdots, \overline{G_k}$. $\qquad \square$

Example 2.8 (Continued from Example 2.1)

Since $p(X,Y)$ is an old atom, a P_{new}-expansion of $p(X,Y)$ is itself. On the other hand, a P_{new}-expansion of $r(0,Y)$ is either itself, or a sequence of atoms '$p(0,Y), q(0,Y)$'. $\qquad \square$

Lemma 2.1 (P_0-**simulation of SLD-derivation in** P_N)

Let $P_0, \cdots, P_N$ be a transformation sequence. Let G be a goal, and suppose that there exists an SLD-derivation Dr for $P_N \cup \{G\}$, $G_0 = G, \cdots, G_k, \cdots$ using input clauses in P_N and substitutions $\theta_1, \cdots, \theta_k, \cdots$. Then, there exists an SLD-derivation Dr_0 for $P_0 \cup \{G\}$, $F_0 = G, \cdots, F_l, \cdots$ using input clauses in P_0 and substitutions $\sigma_1, \cdots, \sigma_l, \cdots$, satisfying the following conditions:

(i) For each k ($k \geq 0$), there exists some l (≥ 0) such that $F_l\sigma_1 \cdots \sigma_l$ is an P_{new}-expansion of $G_k\theta_1 \cdots \theta_k$, and

(ii) the restriction of $\sigma_1 \cdots \sigma_l$ to the variables in G is the same as that of $\theta_1 \cdots \theta_k$.

(iii) *(fairness)* Furthermore, if the SLD-derivation $G_0 = G, \cdots, G_k, \cdots$ is fair, then so is the SLD-derivation $F_0 = G, \cdots, F_l, \cdots$.

Dr_0 is called a P_0-*simulation of* Dr.

Notes on the proof: The proof is done by induction on both the length of a transformation sequence N and the length of SLD-derivation, k. In order to show the fairness in (iii), the folding condition (F4') is essential. Because of lack of space, we omit the proof (see [11]). $\square$

Example 2.9

Consider an SLD-derivation Dr_3 for $P_3^m \cup \{G_0 =\leftarrow r(s(0), s(0))\}$, where P_3^m was given in Example 2.7. See the right-hand side in Figure 1. Dr_3 has a P_0-simulation $F_0 = G_0, F_1, F_2, F_3$, which is shown in the left-hand side in the figure (underlined atoms mean selected atoms). Note that F_3 is a P_{new}-expansion of G_1. $\square$

$$
\begin{array}{ll}
F_0 :\leftarrow & r(s(0), s(0)) \\
& |\ C_7 \\
F_1 :\leftarrow & \underline{p(s(0), s(0))}, q(s(0), s(0)) \\
& |\ C_2 \\
F_2 :\leftarrow & eq(s(0), s(0)), p(s(0), s(0)), \\
& \quad \underline{q(s(0), s(0))} \\
& |\ C_4 \\
F_3 :\leftarrow & eq(s(0), s(0)), p(s(0), s(0)), \\
& \quad \underline{plus1(s(0), s(0))}, q(s(0), s(0)) \\
& | \\
& \text{fail}
\end{array}
\qquad
\begin{array}{ll}
G_0 :\leftarrow & r(s(0), s(0)) \\
& |\ C_{13} \\
G_1 :\leftarrow & eq(s(0), s(0)), \underline{plus1(s(0), s(0))}, \\
& \quad r(s(0), s(0)) \\
& | \\
& \text{fail}
\end{array}
$$

Figure 1: P_0-simulation (left) of an SLD-derivation for $P_3^m \cup \{\leftarrow r(s(0), s(0))\}$ (right)

Proposition 2.2 (Total Correctness wrt FF)

Let $P_0, \cdots, P_N$ be a transformation sequence. Then, $FF(P_0) \subseteq FF(P_N)$ for all $N \geq 0$.

Proof:

For simplicity of explanation, we assume here that G is a ground atom (a more general case is shown in **Proposition 3.3**). Suppose that an SLD-tree of $P_0 \cup \{\leftarrow G\}$ is finitely failed. Suppose further that $P_N \cup \{\leftarrow G\}$ has a *fair* SLD-tree which is not finitely failed. Obviously, no SLD-derivation $P_N \cup \{\leftarrow G\}$ ever succeeds; otherwise, a P_0-simulation of such a derivation would also succeed, which is a contradiction. Let BR be any non-failed infinite branch in the fair SLD-tree for $P_N \cup \{\leftarrow G\}$. From **Lemma 2.1**, there exists a fair SLD-derivation Dr_0 for $P_0 \cup \{\leftarrow G\}$ which is a P_0-simulation of BR. Thus, Dr_0 is a non-failed fair infinite derivation. From the result by Lassez and Maher [7], G is in the SLD finite failure set of P_0 iff every fair SLD-tree for $P_0 \cup \{\leftarrow G\}$ is finitely failed. Thus, Dr_0 should be finitely failed, which is a contradiction. $\qquad\square$

3　Unfold/Fold Transformation of Stratified Programs

3.1　Preliminaries

We now consider an extension of the unfold/fold transformation from definite programs to stratified programs.

Definition 3.1 Stratified Program [1]

A general logic program, P, is *stratified* if its predicates can be partitioned into levels so that, in every program clause, $p \leftarrow L_1, ..., L_n$, the level of every predicate in a positive literal is less than or equal to the level of p and the level of every predicate in a negative literal is less than the level of p. $\quad\square$

Throughout this paper, we assume that the levels of a stratified program are $1, ..., r$ for some integer r, where r is the *minimum* number satisfying the above definition. In this case, P is said to have the maximum level r and is denoted $P = \mathcal{P}^1 + ... + \mathcal{P}^r$, where $\mathcal{P}^i$ is a set of clauses whose head predicates have level i. Note that $\mathcal{P}^1$ is a set of definite clauses. When L is a literal whose predicate has level i, we denote it $level(L) = i$. Furthermore, the *stratum* [10] of a goal is defined as follows. For any positive atom A, let $stratum(A) = level(A)$ and $stratum(\neg A) = stratum(A) + 1$. Suppose that G is a goal of the form: $\leftarrow L_1, \cdots, L_n$, where $n \geq 0$ and L_i's are literals. Then, $stratum(G)$ is 0 if G is empty, and $max\{stratum(L_i) : 1 \leq i \leq n\}$, otherwise.

As in the previous section, we need to define an initial program, unfolding/folding and a transformation sequence for stratified programs. Although they are almost the same as the previous ones, we impose further restrictions on an initial stratified program.

Definition 3.2 Initial (Stratified) Program

An initial (stratified) program P_0 is a *stratified* program satisfying the following conditions:

- **(I1)** and **(I2)** are the same as those defined in **Definition 2.1**, and
- **(I3)** The definition of each new predicate consists of exactly one clause.
- **(I4)** Furthermore, the body of each clause in P_{new} contains no negative literal. $\qquad\square$

Condition (I3) above guarantees that a stratified program is also stratified after the unfold/fold transformation as shown below (Proposition 3.1), and most cases found in the literature seem to satisfy this condition. On the other hand, condition (I4) is due to the fact that we do not employ such "unfolding" as it is applicable to a *negative* literal in the body of a clause. Thus, if a clause C in P_{new} contained a negative atom '$\sim A$' in its body, then, after applying unfolding (possibly several times), C would be unfolded into a clause, say, C', where (a possibly instantiated version of) $\sim A$ in the body of C' would remain as an inherited atom from P_0. Thus, it would prevent us from applying the folding rule to C'. Needless to say, P_{old} is an arbitrary stratified program, and the body of a clause in P_{old} can thus contain negative literals.

Unfolding, (modified) folding and a transformation sequence are the same as those defined in Definition 2.2, Definition 2.8 and Definition 2.4, respectively. First, we have to confirm that our unfold/fold transformation preserves a stratification of an initial program.

Proposition 3.1 (Preservation of Stratification) Let $P_0, \cdots, P_N$ be a transformation sequence. Then, if P_0 is a stratified program, so is P_i ($N \geq i \geq 0$).

Proof: Let p be a new predicate, and let $C \in P_{new}$ be its definition of the form: $p \leftarrow L$. Then, we define the level of p by $level(p)=max\{level(B_j) \mid B_j \in L\}$. Then, the proposition is obvious from the definitions of unfolding and folding. $\square$

3.2   Partial Correctness of Transformation

The success set (SS) and the finite failure (FF) set of a stratified program are defined similarly to those of a definite program. That is, SS (FF) of a stratified program is defined by replacing "SLD-derivation (SLD-tree)" in Definition 2.5 (Definition 2.6) with "SLDNF-derivation (SLDNF-tree)" [8], respectively.

In this subsection, we show the partial correctness of our transformation wrt both SS and FF.

Proposition 3.2 (Partial Correctness wrt SS and FF)

Let $P_0, \cdots, P_N$ be a transformation sequence. Then,

(SS) : If $SS(P_i)=SS(P_0)$, then $SS(P_{i+1}) \subseteq SS(P_i)$ for $i=0, \cdots, N-1$.
(FF) : If $FF(P_i)=FF(P_0)$, then $FF(P_{i+1}) \subseteq FF(P_i)$ for $i=0, \cdots, N-1$.

Notes on the proof: We first note that we used the completeness of SLD-resolution for the proof wrt FF in Proposition 2.1. In this case, however, we cannot resort to the completeness of SLDNF-resolution, since we do not assume such conditions as allowedness and strictness ([1]) which guarantee its completeness ([2]). Thus, we show the above two properties (SS) and (FF) by a more direct proof, based on mutual induction on the stratum of a goal (see [11] for the complete proof). $\qquad\square$

3.3 Total Correctness of Transformation

3.3.1 Total Correctness wrt FF

We now show the total correctness of our unfold/fold transformation. We prove the total correctness wrt FF first. Due to the partial correctness wrt FF, it is easy to show that **Lemma 2.1** replacing "SLD-derivation" in it with "SLDNF-derivation" also holds for stratified programs. That is,

Lemma 3.1 (P_0-simulation of SLDNF-derivation in P_N)

Let $P_0, \cdots, P_N$ be a transformation sequence. Let G be a goal, and suppose that there exists an SLDNF-derivation Dr for $P_N \cup \{G\}$, $G_0 = G, \cdots, G_k, \cdots$ using input clauses in P_N and substitutions $\theta_1, \cdots, \theta_k, \cdots$. Then, there exists an SLDNF-derivation Dr_0 for $P_0 \cup \{G\}$, $F_0 = G, \cdots, F_l, \cdots$ using input clauses in P_0 and substitutions $\sigma_1, \cdots, \sigma_l, \cdots$, satisfying the following conditions:

(i) For each k ($k \geq 0$), there exists some l (≥ 0) such that $F_l \sigma_1 \cdots \sigma_l$ is a P_{new}-expansion of $G_k \theta_1 \cdots \theta_k$, and

(ii) the restriction of $\sigma_1 \cdots \sigma_l$ to the variables in G is the same as that of $\theta_1 \cdots \theta_k$.

(iii) *(fairness)* Furthermore, if the SLDNF-derivation $G_0 = G, \cdots, G_k, \cdots$ is fair, then so is the SLDNF-derivation $F_0 = G, \cdots, F_l, \cdots$.

Dr_0 is called a P_0-*simulation of* Dr. $\qquad\square$

Now we can show the total correctness wrt FF.

Proposition 3.3 (Total Correctness wrt FF)

Let $P_0, \cdots, P_N$ be a transformation sequence, where P_0 is an initial stratified program. Then, $FF(P_0) \subseteq FF(P_N)$ for all $N \geq 0$.

Outline of the proof: Suppose that an SLDNF-tree of $P_0 \cup \{\leftarrow A\}$ is finitely failed. Obviously, no SLDNF-derivation $P_0 \cup \{\leftarrow A\}$ ever succeeds. Furthermore, it does not flounder, from the proposition shown by Shepherdson [13], which says that, if a query Q flounders under a computation rule, then it cannot fail under *any* computation rule.

Suppose that $P_N \cup \{\leftarrow A\}$ has a *fair* SLDNF-tree which is *not* finitely failed. Let BR_N be any non-failed branch in that fair SLDNF-tree for $P_N \cup \{\leftarrow A\}$.

From **Lemma 3.1**, there exists a *fair* SLDNF-derivation BR_0 for $P_0 \cup \{\leftarrow A\}$ which is a P_0-simulation of BR_N. BR_0 neither succeeds nor flounders as noted above. Thus, BR_0 is a non-failed fair infinite derivation. Then, we can show that $comp(P_0) \cup \{\exists A\}$ has a model, using similar methods in the proofs of completeness of Negation as Failure rule by [8], [2], which is a contradiction. $\square$

3.3.2 Total Correctness wrt SS

Finally, we state the total correctness wrt SS.

Proposition 3.4 (Total Correctness wrt SS)

Let $P_0, \cdots, P_N$ be a transformation sequence, where P_0 is an initial stratified program. Then, $SS(P_0) \subseteq SS(P_N)$ for all $N \geq 0$.

Notes on the proof: The proof can be done along almost the same lines as those given by [15], [14] or [6], except for the handling of negative literals. However, it follows immediately from the total correctness wrt FF in **Proposition 3.3** (see [11] for the complete proof).

4 On Preservation of Perfect Model Semantics

The semantics we have considered is somewhat operational, in that the success set and the finite failure set of a stratified program are given by specific procedures such as SLD(NF)-resolution. In this section, we consider more declarative semantics, that is, the standard (minimal Herbrand) model M_P by Apt, Blair and Walker [1] and Van Gelder [16], or, more generally, the *perfect model semantics* for stratified programs introduced by Przymusinski [10].

It seems to be a more direct extension from Tamaki-Sato's original unfold/fold rules to consider transformation rules preserving the equivalence of M_P or the perfect model semantics, since their framework preserves the least Herbrand model for a definite program. Recall that, Tamaki-Sato's unfold/fold transformation does not preserve the finite failure set. However, from the viewpoint of the perfect model semantics, it poses no problems, since a goal: "$\leftarrow G$" which has neither a successful SLD-derivation nor a finite failed SLD-tree is simply considered to be false. Because of lack of space, we assume familiarity with the perfect model semantics (see [10]), and we state only the results (for details, see [12]).

Definition 4.1 Initial Program

An initial program P_0 is a *stratified* program satisfying the following conditions:

- (I1), (I2) and (I3) are the same as those defined in Definition 3.2. □

Thus, condition (I4) in Definition 3.2 is not necessary.

The unfolding rule and the folding rule are the same as those defined in Definition 2.2 and Definition 2.3, respectively. Note that we do not have to consider the modified folding rule. A transformation sequence is also defined similarly to Definition 2.4.

Then, we have the following proposition.

Theorem 4.1 (Preservation of Perfect Model Semantics)

The perfect model semantics of any program P_i in a transformation sequence starting from initial program P_0, is identical to that of P_0. □

Notes on the proof: First, we fix a pre-interpretation (e.g., [8]) J of a program P_0. Note that every perfect model M is *supported* (see [10]), that is, for every J-ground atom A in M there exists a J-ground instance of a clause from a program such that its head is equal to A, all positive premises belong to M and none of the negative premises belongs to M. From this property, we can consider a ground "proof tree" for any $A \in M$. Then, the proposition follows from the similar discussions in [15] and [14], where correctness proofs are based on the manipulation of ground finite proof trees. □

5 Conclusion

There have been several studies on equivalence-preserving transformation of logic programs. Tamaki and Sato's result [15] and its elaboration by Kawamura and Kanamori [6] are already described in section 2.1.1. Maher extensively studied various formulations of equivalence for definite programs [9]. In that paper, he considered a transformation system similar to that of Tamaki and Sato, and stated that his unfold/fold rules preserve logical equivalence of completions, while, as stated in section 2.2.1, those of Tamaki-Sato do not preserve it. Kanamori and Horiuchi [5] proposed a framework for transformation and synthesis based on generalized unfold/fold rules. Their system was shown to preserve the minimum Herbrand model semantics, but the finite failure set is not preserved in general.

Compared with previous work, the contributions of this paper will be summarized as follows :

1) The modified folding rule for a definite program was proposed.
   The unfolding rule together with the modified folding rule was shown to preserve the finite failure set (by SLD-resolution) of a program as well as the success set. This guarantees a safer use of Tamaki-Sato's transformation when negation as failure rule is used.

2) The unfold/fold rules for stratified programs were proposed.
The modified folding rule has made it possible to extend the applicability of unfold/fold transformation rules to a stratified program, so that they preserve both the success set and the finite failure set of a stratified program by SLDNF-resolution.

3) Preservation of equivalence of the perfect model semantics was discussed. We showed that unfold/fold rules by Tamaki and Sato can be extended to rules for a stratified program and preserve the equivalence of the perfect model semantics.

Acknowledgement

This work is based on the result by Tamaki and Sato, and the succeeding work by Kawamura and Kanamori. I would like to express deep gratitude to them for their stimulating work. The idea of modified folding arose from discussions with Kazunori Ueda and Tadashi Kanamori.

References

[1] K.R. Apt, H. Blair, and A. Walker. Towards A Theory of Declarative Knowledge. In J. Minker, editor, *Foundations of Deductive Databases and Logic Programming*, pages 89–148, Morgan Kaufmann, 1987. Los Altos, CA.

[2] L. Cavedon and J. W. Lloyd. *A Completeness Theorem For SLDNF-Resolution*. Technical Report CS-87-06, Computer Science Department. University Walk, Bristol, 1987.

[3] K.L. Clark. Negation as Failure. In H. Gallaire and J. Minker, editors, *Logic and Database*, pages 293–322, Plenum Press, 1978.

[4] J. Jaffar, J.-L. Lassez, and J. W. Lloyd. Completeness of the Negation as Failure Rule. In *IJCAI-83*, pages 500–506, Karlsruhe, 1983.

[5] T. Kanamori and K. Horiuchi. Construction of Logic Programs Based on Generalized Unfold/Fold Rules. In *Proceedings of the Fourth International Conference on Logic Programming*, pages 744–768, Melbourne, 1987.

[6] T. Kawamura and T. Kanamori. *Preservation of Stronger Equivalence in Unfold/Fold Logic Program Transformation*. ICOT Technical Report, ICOT, 1988. also in FGCS'88.

[7] J.-L. Lassez and M.J. Maher. Closures and Fairness in the Semantics of Programming Logic. *Theoretical Computer Science*, 29:167–184, 1984.

[8] J.W. Lloyd. *Foundations of Logic Programming*. Springer, 1987. Second, extended edition.

[9] M.J. Maher. Equivalences of Logic Programs. In *Proceedings of the Third International Conference on Logic Programming*, pages 410–424, London, 1986. also in Foundations of Deductive Databases and Logic Programming, (edited by Minker, J.), pp. 627-658, Morgan Kaufmann, 1987.

[10] T.C. Przymusinski. On the Declarative and Procedural Semantics of Logic Programs. submitted for publication. Its extended abstract appears in 5th International Conference Symposium on Logic Programming, Seattle, 1988.

[11] H. Seki. *Unfold/Fold Transformation of Stratied Programs*. ICOT Technical Report, ICOT, 1989. in preparation.

[12] H. Seki. *Unfold/Fold Transformation of Stratied Programs in the Perfect Model Semantics*. ICOT Technical Report, ICOT, 1989. in preparation.

[13] J.C. Shepherdson. Negation as Failure: A Comparison of Clark's Completed Data Base and Reiter's Closed World Assumption. *J. Logic Programming*, 1:51–79, 1984.

[14] H. Tamaki. *Program Transformation in Logic Programming*, pages 39–62. Kyoritsu Pub. Co., 1987. in Japanese.

[15] H. Tamaki and T. Sato. Unfold/Fold Transformation of Logic Programs. In *Proceedings of the Second International Logic Programming Conference*, pages 127–138, Uppsala, 1984.

[16] A. Van Gelder. Negation as Failure Using Tight Derivations for General Logic Programs. In *Proc. 1986 Symposium on Logic Programming*, pages 127–138, IEEE Computer Society, 1986.

Semantic Issues

Continuity, Consistency, and Completeness Properties for Logic Programs

Lawrence Cavedon

Australian AI Institute
1 Grattan St., Carlton
Victoria 3053, Australia

Abstract

We investigate various properties of the locally hierarchical, locally stratified and locally call-consistent programs, classes of programs defined via level mappings on ground atoms. We prove a continuity property for T_p, the operator acting on Herbrand interpretations, for the class of locally call-consistent programs and use this property to prove consistency of the completed program for this class. We then prove a general completeness result for a subclass (containing many programs that arise in practice) of the locally hierarchical programs. Finally, we use the continuity property to constructively define a standard model of a locally stratified program.

1. Introduction.

The classes of hierarchical, stratified and call-consistent programs can be generalized by imposing constraints on the dependencies between ground instances of atoms rather than predicate symbols, giving us, respectively, the *locally hierarchical, locally stratified* [12], and *locally call-consistent* [16] programs. We prove that various desirable properties possessed by the former set of classes also hold for the latter.

An initial important result of this paper is a continuity property for the mapping T_p associated with a locally call-consistent program. The continuity of T_p for P a definite program is fundamental to the proof of many important results for this class of programs. The result given below extends (for Herbrand interpretations) the continuity property of [5] for stratified programs and allows us to use powerful fixpoint properties to prove results for the locally hierarchical, locally stratified, and locally call-consistent programs. In particular, it is used to prove the consistency of the completed program [7,9], comp(P), for these classes of programs, resulting in a proof that greatly simplifies that of Sato [16], who proves the same result.

The hierarchical programs were originally introduced in [7] as demonstrative of a class of programs for which SLDNF-resolution [9] is complete. Unfortunately, the hierarchical condition prevents any recursion and, hence, is too strong for practical programming. We introduce a subclass of the locally hierarchical programs by imposing the condition that every atom is assigned a finite level and show that many programs written in practice satisfy this condition. In particular, this condition, called locally ω-hierarchical, seems to naturally capture much of the recursion that arises in practical programming. We prove that SLDNF-resolution is complete for the locally ω-hierarchical programs (under the condition of allowedness [11]), which we believe to be an important result in the theory of logic programming as a practical programming language.

Finally, we further demonstrate the use of our continuity result by constructively defining a *standard*, or canonical, model of a locally stratified program. This model generalizes that of [1] and [19], in which a standard model of a stratified program is defined. The standard model defined below proves to be the unique *perfect* [12] Herbrand model of a locally stratified program. We present soundness and completeness results for SLS-resolution [13] for locally stratified programs, with respect to our standard model.

2. Definitions.

In this section, we define the classes of programs with which the results of this paper are concerned. The terminology throughout follows that of [9]. In particular, U_P denotes the Herbrand universe and B_P the Herbrand base of a program P. We use letters of the Greek alphabet, e.g., $\alpha, \beta, \gamma,...$ to denote ordinals, with ω being the first limit ordinal greater than 0. We denote the empty set by $\varnothing$.

Definition A *program clause* is a clause of the form $A \leftarrow L_1,...,L_m$, where A is an atom and $L_1,...,L_m$ are literals. A *normal program* is a finite set of program clauses. A *normal goal* is a clause of the form $\leftarrow L_1,...,L_m$, where $L_1,...,L_m$ are literals.

We use the concept of a *level mapping* on ground atoms to define the following classes of programs. The *locally stratified* programs were introduced in [12] and the *locally call-consistent* programs in [16], where they are called *order-consistent*.

Definition An *atomic level mapping* of a normal program is a mapping from its Herbrand base to the countable ordinals. We refer to the value of a ground atom A under this mapping as the *level* of A and denote it by level(A).

Definition A normal program P is *locally hierarchical* if it has an atomic level mapping such that, for every ground instance $A \leftarrow B_1,...,B_n,\sim C_1,...,\sim C_m$ of a clause in P, we have level(B_i) < level(A), $1 \leq i \leq n$, and level(C_j) < level(A), $1 \leq j \leq m$.

Definition A normal program P is *locally stratified* if it has an atomic level mapping such that, for every ground instance $A \leftarrow B_1,...,B_n,\sim C_1,...,\sim C_m$ of a clause in P, we have level(B_i) $\leq$ level(A), $1 \leq i \leq n$, and level(C_j) < level(A), $1 \leq j \leq m$.

Before defining the next class of programs, we define the concept of dependency between atoms. The *dependency graph* of a program was introduced in [1]. We modify this concept to one in which nodes of the graph are ground atoms rather than predicate symbols.

Definition Let P be a normal program. The *atomic dependency graph* for P is the directed graph defined as follows:
(i) each node in the graph is a ground atom in B_P;
(ii) let A and B be ground atoms in B_P. There is an edge from A to B if there is a ground instance of a clause in P such that A is the head and B occurs in the body. The edge is marked *positive* (resp., *negative*) if B occurs in a positive (resp., negative) literal in the body of the clause instance. An edge may be both positive and negative.

Definition Let P be a normal program and let A, B be ground atoms in B_P. We say A *depends positively* (resp., *negatively*) *on* B if, in the atomic dependency graph for P, there is a path (possibly of length zero) from A to B containing an even (resp., odd) number of negative edges. We say A *depends on* B if A depends positively or negatively on B.

Allowing paths of length zero in the above definition ensures that every ground atom depends on itself positively. We now define the locally call-consistent programs. In [16], Sato identifies (via a more complicated definition) this same class of programs, which he there calls *order-consistent* programs. The definition below is equivalent to that of Sato.

Definition A normal program P is *locally call-consistent* if it has an atomic level mapping such that, for any atoms A, B in B_P, if A depends on B then level(A)$\geq$level(B), and if A depends both positively and negatively on B then level(A)>level(B).

As done with locally stratified programs [12], we can associate an ordering between ground atoms to each class of programs defined above, and show that the existence of the appropriate level mapping is equivalent to the corresponding ordering being well-founded.

Definition Let P be a normal program. We define the following relations on ground atoms in B_P:

(i) $A \gg_H B$ if there is a path of non-zero length in the atomic dependency graph for P from A to B;

(ii) $A \gg_S B$ if there is a path in the atomic dependency graph for P from A to B containing a negative edge;

(iii) $A \gg_C B$ if A depends both positively and negatively on B.

Proposition 1 Let P be a normal program.
(a) P is locally hierarchical if and only if $\gg_H$ is a well-founded partial ordering.
(b) P is locally stratified if and only if $\gg_S$ is a well-founded partial ordering.
(c) P is locally call-consistent if and only if $\gg_C$ is a well-founded partial ordering.

Proof The result for locally stratified programs can be found in [12]. The other two results follow analogously. $\square$

The above classes of programs generalize the classes of hierarchical, stratified and call-consistent programs as we would hope: every hierarchical program is locally hierarchical, every stratified program is locally stratified, and every call-consistent program is locally call-consistent. Furthermore, every locally hierarchical program is locally stratified, and every locally stratified program is locally call-consistent. Unfortunately, Cholak [6] shows that each of these classes of programs is undecidable.

3. Locally Call-Consistent Programs.

The monotonicity and continuity of the T_P mapping, defined below, have been fundamental to the proof of various important results for the definite programs. Monotonicity and continuity results for T_P have also been proved for the class of stratified programs by inductively considering each predicate symbol level separately [10][5]: a chain of operators is defined, one operator corresponding to each predicate symbol level, and each of these operators is shown to be monotonic and continuous on a complete lattice consisting of a subset of the interpretations for the program. In this section, we extend (for Herbrand interpretations) the continuity result of [5] to the locally call-consistent programs.

We define the operator T_P that maps the lattice of Herbrand interpretations to itself [9].

Definition Let P be a normal program and I a Herbrand interpretation for P. Then $T_P(I) = \{ A \in B_P : A \leftarrow L_1,...,L_m$ is a ground instance of a clause in P and $L_1 \wedge ... \wedge L_m$ is true in I $\}$.

The following well-known property relates models of comp(P) and fixpoints of T_P [9].

Proposition 2 Let P be a normal program and I a Herbrand interpretation for P. Let E be = assigned the identity relation and suppose $I \cup E$ is a model for the equality theory. Then $I \cup E$ is a model for comp(P) iff $T_P(I) = I$.

We now define a partial ordering on Herbrand interpretations under which the operator T_P is continuous. A similar ordering, with the partitioning performed on predicate symbols, was used by R. W. Topor [18] to prove a monotonicity result for T_P for P a call-consistent program. Note that the definition below (and all results of this paper) is independent of the chosen level mapping.

Definition Let P be a locally call-consistent, normal program. Consider any atomic level $\gamma \geq 0$ and partition the level γ ground atoms of B_P into disjoint sets S_γ^{+1} and S_γ^{-1} such that, for any level γ atoms A, B in B_P, if $A \in S_\gamma^i$ and A depends positively (resp., negatively) on B, then $B \in S_\gamma^i$ (resp., S_γ^{-i}), where $i \in \{+1,-1\}$. We define a partial ordering, $\leq_\gamma$, on Herbrand interpretations I_1, I_2 as follows:

$$I_1 \leq_\gamma I_2 \text{ if } (I_1 \cap S_\gamma^{+1}) \subseteq (I_2 \cap S_\gamma^{+1}) \text{ and } (I_1 \cap S_\gamma^{-1}) \supseteq (I_2 \cap S_\gamma^{-1}).$$

The partitioning described in the above definition is always possible for a locally call-consistent program since, at any given level γ, no atom of level γ depends on any other atom of level γ both positively and negatively. We drop the subscript γ from $\leq_\gamma$ when it is clear from the context.

As an example of this ordering, consider the following program P

$$A \leftarrow \sim B$$
$$B \leftarrow \sim A$$

and partition B_P into $S_0^{+1} = \{A\}$ and $S_0^{-1} = \{B\}$. The lattice of interpretations under the ordering $\leq_0$ is as follows:

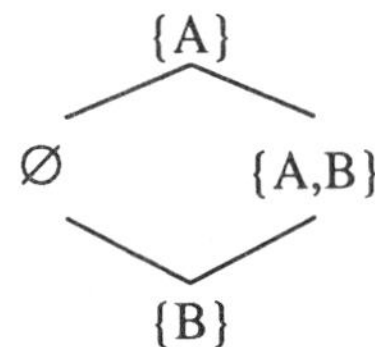

We now present a continuity property for locally call-consistent programs. This result is independent of the way the set of level γ atoms is partitioned to define the $\leq$ ordering.

Let P be a locally call-consistent program and, without loss of generality, assume P has atomic levels $0, 1, 2, ..., \omega, ...$ We denote by P^*_γ the set of ground instances of clauses in P such that the head of each clause instance has atomic level $\leq\gamma$.

Proposition 3 Let P be a locally call-consistent, normal program and consider P^*_γ, for any atomic level $\gamma\geq0$. Let $P^*_\beta = \bigcup_{\alpha<\gamma}P^*_\alpha$, and suppose M_β is a Herbrand interpretation for P such that M_β is a fixpoint of $T_{P^*_\beta}$. Consider the complete lattice

$$\Lambda = \{ M_\beta \cup S : S \subseteq \{ A : A \in B_P \text{ and level}(A)=\gamma \} \}$$

under the partial ordering $\leq$. Then

(i) Λ is a sublattice of the lattice of Herbrand interpretations of P, and $T_{P^*_\gamma}$ is well-defined and continuous on $(\Lambda, \leq)$, and

(ii) if I is an element of Λ and $I \leq T_{P^*_\gamma}(I)$, then $(T_{P^*_\gamma})^\omega(I)$ is a fixpoint of $T_{P^*_\gamma}$.

Proof See [4] $\square$

We refer to an interpretation I satisfying the condition $I \leq T_{P^*_\gamma}(I)$ as a *pre-fixpoint* of $T_{P^*_\gamma}$. The above result extends (for Herbrand interpretations) the monotonicity and continuity results of [10] and [5] from the class of stratified to the class of locally call-consistent programs. We can use this proposition to prove the consistency of comp(P) for locally call-consistent programs. This simplifies Sato's proof of the same result [16] (in proving his main consistency theorem, Sato actually proves a stronger result; i.e., that every 3-valued Herbrand model can be extended to a 2-valued Herbrand model).

Theorem 1 Let P be a locally call-consistent, normal program. Then comp(P) is consistent.

Proof The proof involves a model construction by transfinite induction on the atomic level of ground atoms. Consider any atomic level $\gamma\geq0$ and assume we have performed the required construction for each level $<\gamma$. If γ is the successor ordinal $\alpha+1$, then let $M_\beta = M_\alpha$, where M_α is the fixpoint (defined as below) of $T_{P^*_\alpha}$. If γ is a limit ordinal, then let $M_\beta = \bigcup_{\alpha<\gamma}M_\alpha$, where each M_α is the fixpoint of $T_{P^*_\alpha}$. For either case, it can be shown that M_β is a fixpoint of $T_{P^*_\beta}$, where $P^*_\beta = \bigcup_{\alpha<\gamma}P^*_\alpha$. Arbitrarily partition the level γ atoms of B_P as required in the definition of the $\leq$ ordering. $M_\beta \cup S_\gamma^{-1}$ is clearly a pre-fixpoint of $T_{P_\gamma^*}$ (under the ordering $\leq$ resulting from the chosen partition), and hence we can define the fixpoint $M_\gamma = (T_{P_\gamma^*})^\omega (M_\beta \cup S_\gamma^{-1})$.

It is clear that we can inductively define a fixpoint M_γ of $T_{P_\gamma^*}$ for each level $\gamma \geq 0$. Let M be the Herbrand interpretation $\bigcup_{\gamma \geq 0} M_\gamma$. It is straightforward to show that M is a fixpoint of T_P. Hence, M, together with = assigned the identity relation, is a model for comp(P). $\square$

Obvious corollaries to this result are the consistency of comp(P) for P a locally hierarchical or locally stratified program. The former of these is used to prove a completeness result in the following section.

4. Locally ω-Hierarchical Programs.

Locally hierarchical programs exhibit, within the context of Herbrand interpretations and models, analogues to some of the desirable properties possessed by hierarchical programs. In particular, if P is a hierarchical program, then there exists, for any pre-interpretation J of P, a single model based on J for comp(P), whereas if P is locally hierarchical, then it can be shown [4] that there exists a single Herbrand model for comp(P). Furthermore (as noted in [6]), if P is hierarchical, then every 3-valued model for comp(P) is 2-valued [8], whereas if P is locally hierarchical, then every 3-valued Herbrand model for comp(P) is 2-valued. Unfortunately, these desirable features do not extend to the completeness of SLDNF-resolution. If we consider the following locally hierarchical program P

$$p(a) \leftarrow q(a)$$
$$p(a) \leftarrow \neg q(a)$$
$$q(a) \leftarrow r(x)$$
$$r(f(x)) \leftarrow r(x)$$

then comp(P) $\models$ p(a) but $P \cup \{\leftarrow p(a)\}$ does not have an SLDNF-refutation.

The uncomputability demonstrated by the above example arises because the definition of an atomic level mapping allows an atom to be assigned a level greater than or equal to ω. For instance, q(a) and p(a) must each be assigned a transfinite level in the example above. In this section, we introduce a subclass of the locally hierarchical programs by restricting atoms to be assigned a level strictly less than ω. We show that this subclass possesses desirable computability properties (in particular, we prove a completeness result for SLDNF-resolution), while, unlike the hierarchical programs, still being general enough to include many programs written in practice.

Definition A normal program P is *locally ω-hierarchical* if it is locally hierarchical via an atomic level mapping that assigns each ground atom a level less than ω.

The following examples demonstrate the locally ω-hierarchical programs to be a very general class of programs. In particular, every hierarchical program is clearly locally ω-hierarchical. Some interesting non-hierarchical programs that are locally ω-hierarchical include many recursive list-processing programs, such as *member*, *append* and *reverse*. The *even* program

```
even(0) ←
even(s(x)) ← ~even(x)
```

is not call-consistent, yet is locally ω-hierarchical. The following "pure-Prolog" interpreter is locally ω-hierarchical if the database of clauses on which it operates is a locally ω-hierarchical program:

```
interp(true) ←
interp(x) ← clause((x ← y)), interp(y)
interp((x,y)) ← interp(x), interp(y)
interp((~x)) ← ~interp(x).
```

Unlike hierarchical programs, locally ω-hierarchical programs do not, in general, satisfy the *finite tree property* [7] (every SLDNF-tree for the program, with respect to any goal, is finite). For example, the *even* program is locally ω-hierarchical, but the SLDNF-tree associated with the goal ←even(x) contains an infinite branch. However, we are able to prove completeness of SLDNF-resolution for programs satisfying the following weaker condition.

Definition A normal program P is *atomically decidable* if, for every ground atom $A \in B_p$, $P \cup \{\leftarrow A\}$ has either an SLDNF-refutation or a finitely failed SLDNF-tree.

Obviously, the above condition is not a syntactic one and is clearly undecidable. Examples of classes of programs that are atomically decidable are the hierarchical programs and the *structured* programs [2]. The completeness of SLDNF-resolution for the hierarchical and structured programs ([7, 17] and [2] respectively) follows from the general completeness theorem below.

To prove the completeness of SLDNF-resolution for atomically decidable programs, we impose the following *allowedness* condition from [11] to ensure a program P and goal G do not flounder (we say $P \cup \{G\}$ *flounders* if some attempt to construct an SLDNF-derivation of $P \cup \{G\}$ results in a goal consisting of only non-ground negative literals).

Definition Let P be a normal program and G a normal goal. A program clause in P is *admissible* if every variable that occurs in the clause occurs either in the head or in a positive literal in the body of that clause. A program clause in P is *allowed* if every variable that occurs in the clause occurs in a positive literal in the body of that clause. G is *allowed* if every variable that occurs in G occurs in a positive literal in G.

P $\cup$ {G} is *allowed* if the following conditions are satisfied:
(a) every clause in P is admissible;
(b) every clause in the definition of a predicate symbol occurring in a positive literal in either G or the body of a clause in P is allowed;
(c) G is allowed.

The following completeness theorem, proved in [4], for atomically decidable programs is used to prove the completeness result for locally ω-hierarchical programs.

Theorem 2 Let P be a normal program such that P is atomically decidable and comp(P) is consistent, and let G be a normal goal such that P $\cup$ {G} is allowed. If θ is a correct answer for comp(P) $\cup$ {G}, then θ is a computed answer for P $\cup$ {G}.

We now show that any locally ω-hierarchical program P is atomically decidable, provided it does not flounder against any ground atomic goal. It is easily shown that this non-floundering condition is satisfied if P $\cup$ {G} is allowed, for some goal G.

Proposition 4 Let P be a locally ω-hierarchical, normal program and suppose there exists a normal goal G such that P $\cup$ {G} is allowed. Then P is atomically decidable.

Proof Let A be a ground atom in B_P. As mentioned above, P $\cup$ {G} being allowed, for some goal G, ensures that P $\cup$ {$\leftarrow$A} is non-floundered. We prove the proposition by induction on n, the atomic level of A. If n=0, then any clause in P that unifies with A must be a unit clause, and the result follows. Now suppose n>0 and assume the result holds for every k<n. Consider any computation of P $\cup$ {$\leftarrow$A}. Since any selected negative literal is ground and has atomic level less than n, we can apply the induction hypothesis to show that an SLDNF-tree for P $\cup$ {$\leftarrow$A} exists. It then easily follows that P $\cup$ {$\leftarrow$A} either succeeds or finitely fails if P^+ $\cup$ {$\leftarrow$A} either succeeds or finitely fails, where P^+ denotes the set of clauses formed by removing any negative literals from clauses in P. By theorems 8.3 and 13.6 of [9], the latter holds if and only if $A \notin T_{P^+}\downarrow\omega \setminus T_{P^+}\uparrow\omega$.

Let B be a ground atom in B_P. We show by induction on m, the atomic level of B, that $B \notin T_{P^+}\downarrow(m+1) \setminus T_{P^+}\uparrow(m+1)$. If m=0, then either there is a ground instance B$\leftarrow$ of a unit clause in P^+, and $B \in T_{P^+}\uparrow 1$, or B does not unify with any clause in P^+, and $B \notin T_{P^+}\downarrow 1$. Now suppose m>0 and the result holds for k<m. If $B \in T_{P^+}\downarrow(m+1)$, then there exists a

ground instance $B \leftarrow C_1,...,C_h$ of a clause in P^+ such that $\{C_1,...,C_h\} \subseteq T_{P^+}\!\downarrow m$. But each C_i has atomic level $<m$, hence, by the induction hypothesis, $\{C_1,...,C_h\} \subseteq T_{P^+}\!\uparrow m$, and $B \in T_{P^+}\!\uparrow(m+1)$.

So by the above, it follows that $A \notin T_{P^+}\!\downarrow\omega \setminus T_{P^+}\!\uparrow\omega$ and therefore $P^+ \cup \{\leftarrow A\}$ either succeeds or finitely fails, which implies $P \cup \{\leftarrow A\}$ either succeeds or finitely fails. Hence, P is atomically decidable. $\square$

Finally, we can prove the completeness of SLDNF-resolution for locally ω-hierarchical programs.

Theorem 3 Let P be a locally ω-hierarchical, normal program and G a normal goal such that $P \cup \{G\}$ is allowed. If θ is a correct answer for $comp(P) \cup \{G\}$, then θ is a computed answer for $P \cup \{G\}$.

Proof The result follows from theorems 1 and 2 and proposition 4. $\square$

We believe that this completeness result is a useful one. Unlike the hierarchical condition, which prevents any recursion, the locally ω-hierarchical condition seems to allow much of the recursion that arises in practice. In particular, programs defined "inductively" on some object, for example, the *append* program

    append(nil, x, x) ←
    append(x.y, u, x.v) ← append(y, u, v),

seem to naturally fit the condition that some value decreases with each recursive step (in the case of append, it is the length of the list in the first argument). Furthermore, for the recursion to terminate and the relation to be computable, we require less than ω steps to be performed. Hence, the locally ω-hierarchical condition seems to naturally capture much of the recursion that arises in practical programming. For this reason, we consider the above completeness result to be an important one in the theory of logic programming as a practical programming language.

The completeness result of this section cannot be extended to the locally stratified (or "ω-stratified") programs. Even for stratified programs, we need to impose a stronger allowedness condition, as well as a *strictness* condition [1] to prevent programs of the form

    p(a) ← q(x)
    p(a) ← ~q(x)
    q(f(x)) ← q(x).

[3] discusses these conditions (and the possibility of weakening them) in depth; they are used to prove completeness theorems in [5] for stratified programs and in [8] for call-consistent programs.

5. Locally Stratified Programs.

Recent attention has been directed towards defining a program's semantics by considering a particular model of the program as definitive of its intended semantics. [1] and [19] define a *standard model* of a stratified program via a recursive fixpoint definition. Przymusinski [12, 13] defines the *perfect model* semantics for a program, which is applicable to locally stratified programs and generalizes the semantics of [1, 19]. We further demonstrate an application of proposition 3 by using it to constructively define a standard model of a locally stratified program. This model generalizes the standard model of [1, 19].

As in section 3, we let P^*_γ denote the set of ground instances of clauses in P such that the head of the clause has atomic level $\leq \gamma$. If P is a locally stratified program and $\gamma \geq 0$ an atomic level, we can clearly partition the level γ ground atoms such that $S^{-1}_\gamma = \varnothing$. This reduces the $\leq_\gamma$ ordering (within the restricted lattice defined in proposition 3) to a simple subset ordering. We assume the set of ground atoms is partitioned in this way at each level in the following definition.

Definition Let P be a locally stratified, normal program. If γ is any atomic level, then assume we have performed the following construction for all levels $< \gamma$, and partition the level γ atoms such that $S^{-1}_\gamma = \varnothing$. Let

$$M^*_\gamma = (T_{P^*_\gamma})^\omega (M^*_{\gamma-1}) \quad \text{if } \gamma \text{ is a successor ordinal, or}$$

$$M^*_\gamma = (T_{P^*_\gamma})^\omega (\bigcup_{\alpha < \gamma} M^*_\alpha) \quad \text{if } \gamma \text{ is a limit ordinal.}$$

We define $M^*_P = \bigcup_{\gamma \geq 0} M^*_\gamma$.

Note that M^*_P is equivalent to the model constructed in the proof of theorem 5.8 in [12]. Hence, M^*_P coincides with the standard model of [1, 19] if P is stratified, and we also have the following result.

Proposition 5 Let P be a locally stratified, normal program. Then M^*_P is the unique perfect Herbrand model for P.

In [13], Przymusinski introduces *SLS-resolution*, a modification of SLDNF-resolution in which infinite derivations are regarded as failed. He proves the soundness and completeness of SLS-resolution with respect to the perfect model semantics, for stratified programs. We present the soundness and completeness of SLS-resolution for locally stratified programs, with respect to the model M^*_P. Note that, even though Przymusinski only defines SLS-resolution for stratified programs, SLS-resolution is clearly well-defined for locally stratified programs. A *selection rule* is any rule governing the order in which literals are selected in an SLS-derivation.

Theorem 4 Let P be a locally stratified, normal program and G a normal goal $\leftarrow L_1,...,L_n$.

(i) If θ is an SLS-computed answer for $P \cup \{G\}$, then $\forall((L_1 \wedge...\wedge L_n)\theta)$ is true in M_P^*.

(ii) If $P \cup \{G\}$ has a failed SLS-tree, then $\sim\exists(L_1 \wedge...\wedge L_n)$ is true in M_P^*.

Theorem 5 Let P be a locally stratified, normal program, R a selection rule, G a normal goal $\leftarrow L_1,...,L_n$ such that $P \cup \{G\}$ is not floundered via R, and θ a substitution.

(i) If $\forall((L_1 \wedge...\wedge L_n)\theta)$ is true in M_P^*, then there exists an SLS-computed answer α for $P \cup \{G\}$, via R, and a substitution γ such that $\theta = \alpha\gamma$.

(ii) If $\sim\exists(L_1 \wedge...\wedge L_n)$ is true in M_P^*, then the SLS-tree for $P \cup \{G\}$ via R is failed.

Proofs See [4]. The proofs make use of the continuity property of proposition 3 and resemble the proofs of the soundness and completeness of SLD-resolution in [9]. $\square$

In [20], van Gelder et al. define a standard model, called the *well-founded model*, which is more generally applicable than the standard model M_P^*. M_P^* coincides with the well-founded model for the class of locally stratified programs, but the latter is defined for a larger class of programs: every logic program has a unique well-founded model, which is 3-valued in the general case, but 2-valued for every locally stratified program (as well as some programs which are not locally stratified). Przymusinski [14] also investigates properties of the well-founded model and gives alternative characterizations of it. Ross [15] and Przymusinski [14] define a procedural semantics (a generalization of SLS-resolution) which they show to be sound and complete with respect to the well-founded model semantics. Although these results subsume those of this section, we believe we have succeeded in demonstrating the continuity property of proposition 3 to be a useful theoretical tool.

6. Acknowledgements.

The work described in this paper was performed at the University of Melbourne and was supported by a Commonwealth Postgraduate Research Award. Thanks to my supervisor Rodney Topor for invaluable comments and discussions, and to Kim Marriott, Harald Sondergaard and the referees for suggestions on presentation.

7. References.

[1] K. R. Apt, H. A. Blair and A. Walker, "Towards a Theory of Declarative Knowledge", in *Foundations of Deductive Databases and Logic Programming*, J. Minker (editor), Morgan Kaufman, Los Altos, 1988, 89-148.

[2] R. Barbuti and M. Martelli, "Completeness of the SLDNF-Resolution for a Class of Logic Programs", *Proceedings of the Third International Conference on Logic Programming*, London, 1986, 600-614. Published as *Lecture Notes in Computer Science 225*, Springer-Verlag.

[3] L. Cavedon, "On the Completeness of SLDNF-Resolution", M.Sc. Thesis, Technical Report 88/17, Department of Computer Science, University of Melbourne, 1988.

[4] L. Cavedon, "Properties of Logic Programs Defined via Atomic Level Mappings", Technical Report 88/33, Department of Computer Science, University of Melbourne, 1988.

[5] L. Cavedon and J. W. Lloyd, "A Completeness Theorem for SLDNF-Resolution", Technical Report 87/9, Department of Computer Science, University of Melbourne, 1987. To appear in *Journal of Logic Programming*.

[6] P. Cholak, "Post Correspondence Problem and Prolog Programs", manuscript, Department of Mathematics, University of Wisconsin, 1988.

[7] K. L. Clark, "Negation as Failure", in *Logic and Data Bases*, H. Gallaire and J. Minker (editor), Plenum Press, New York, 1978, 293-322.

[8] K. Kunen, "Signed Data Dependencies in Logic Programs", Technical Report #719, Computer Sciences Department, University of Wisconsin, 1987. To appear in *Journal of Logic Programming*.

[9] J. W. Lloyd, *Foundations of Logic Programming*, Springer-Verlag, New York, Second Edition, 1987.

[10] J. W. Lloyd, E. A. Sonenberg and R. W. Topor, "Integrity Constraint Checking in Stratified Databases", *Journal of Logic Programming 4*, 4 (1987), 331-344.

[11] J. W. Lloyd and R. W. Topor, "A Basis for Deductive Database Systems II", *Journal of Logic Programming 3*, 1 (1986), 55-67.

[12] T. C. Przymusinski, "On the Declarative Semantics of Deductive Databases and Logic Programs", in *Foundations of Deductive Databases and Logic Programming*, J. Minker (editor), Morgan

Kaufman, Los Altos, 1988, 193-216.

[13] T. C. Przymusinski, On the Declarative and Procedural Semantics of Logic Programs, To appear in *Journal of Automated Reasoning*. Also, extended abstract in *Proceedings of the Fifth International Conference Symposium on Logic Programming*, Seattle, 1988, 1080-1096, 1988.

[14] T. C. Przymusinski, Every Logic Program has a Natural Stratification and an Iterated Least Fixed Point Model, To appear in *Proceedings of the Eighth Symposium on Principles of Database Systems*, Philadelphia, 1989.

[15] K. Ross, A Procedural Semantics for Well-Founded Negation in Logic Programs, To appear in *Proceedings of the Eighth Symposium on Principles of Database Systems*, Philadelphia, 1989.

[16] T. Sato, "Completed Logic Programs and their Consistency", manuscript, Electrotechnical Laboratory, Ibaraki, Japan, 1988. To appear in *Journal of Logic Programming*.

[17] J. C. Shepherdson, "Negation as Failure: a Comparison of Clark's Completed Data Base and Reiter's Closed World Assumption", *Journal of Logic Programming 1*, 1 (1984), 51-79.

[18] R. W. Topor, "", personal communication, 1987.

[19] A. Van Gelder, "Negation as Failure using Tight Derivations for General Logic Programs", in *Foundations of Deductive Databases and Logic Programming*, J. Minker (editor), Morgan Kaufman, Los Altos, 1988, 149-176.

[20] A. Van Gelder, K. Ross and J. S. Schlipf, "Unfounded Sets and Well-Founded Semantics for General Logic Programs", *Proceedings of the Seventh Symposium on Principles of Database Systems*, Austin, 1988, 221-230.

A Deduction Procedure for First Order Programs

D. Lugiez *
Centre de Recherche en Informatique de Nancy
Nancy - FRANCE

Abstract

This paper presents a deduction process for a class of logic programs (including Horn clauses and general programs) called first order programs, which generalizes SLDNF resolution when it is restricted to general or definite programs. This deduction procedure may handle quantified goals as well as negative goals (and both). Our approach generalizes previous results concerning negation in logic programming and the transformation of first order programs into definite programs. Two basic assumptions are required: the *domain closure axiom* and the *complete definition* of predicates -usually provided through the notion of completed programs-. This deduction procedure called ENF deduction (for Extended Negation as Failure) is an extension of the disunification algorithm, studied by [Com88] and [Mah88], which is a decision procedure for first order formula constructed on the equality predicate "=". We show how this algorithm generalizes to formulas involving other predicates than the equality predicate, and how the main results of disunification are modified by this extension. It defines a deduction procedure, called ENF deduction (for extended Negation as Failure) which generalizes SLDNF resolution since any goal provable by SLDNF resolution is provable by ENF deduction. Therefore the completeness results holding for SLDNF resolution still hold for ENF deduction. Our results improve previous results of [BMPT88] about the negation in logic programming, and [ST88] about the transformation of first order programs. In particular our approach can be successfully used for the transformation of first order logic programs into Horn clauses.

Introduction

Logic programming is usually restricted to Horn clauses, and its extension to general programs, i.e. programs with negative literals in the body of clauses causes some trouble. The extension to more general forms, i.e

---

*author's address: CRIN, BP 239, 54506 Vandoeuvre les Nancy Cedex, FRANCE.
e-mail lugiez@crin.crin.fr

when the body of the clause (which does not deserve the name of clause any longer) contains universally quantified literals, is even more worrisome. However, when writing specifications or prototyping some software, it is often easier to write definition of predicates involving quantification and negation, as in the following example where one defines the lists of natural numbers consisting of 0's and 1's. This can be expressed by: $zerone(l) \Leftrightarrow (\forall x \in l, x = 0 \lor x = 1)$. The usual logic programming systems cannot deal with such definition, but ENF deduction, the procedure described in this paper can. Moreover, it is possible to use the set of transformation rules of ENF deduction to transform automatically the above definition into the nice recursive logic program:

$$zerone(l) \Leftarrow l = nil$$
$$zerone(l) \Leftarrow l = cons(0, L) \land zerone(L)$$
$$zerone(l) \Leftarrow l = cons(1, L) \land zerone(L)$$

To provide a semantic base to our work, we assume two main hypothesis:

The Domain Closure axiom: we consider only those models where the objects are built from constants, variables and (a finite number of) function symbols.

Completed Programs: the predicates defined by the program P are intended to be completely defined. The completion of P, is denoted by $comp(P)$.

The first hypothesis restricts the class of models to models where a complete set of solutions can be computed for sets of equations. The second hypothesis provides the semantics for the Negation as Failure rule [Cla78],[Rei78].

Our deduction process relies on replacement and simplification, avoiding backtracking. Replacement is achieved by selecting an atom and replacing it by its definition, and simplification is achieved a set of simplification rules (a straightforward generalization of the rules given in [CL88], [Mah88]) Quantified variables and non ground negative literals are allowed, which can not be allowed by SLDNF resolution.

The first section describes how the results of [Com88], [Mah88], concerning the decidability of the equality predicate, can be generalized. The next section recalls the basic results about completed programs and describes ENF deduction. The main results is that it is sound and that it strictly extends SLDNF resolution (every solution computable with SLDNF resolution is computable by ENF deduction). Then, some refinements about definite and general programs are described. Finally, we show how the transformation rules can be used to derive definite programs from first order programs (improving previous results concerning this topic and the problem of negation). Usually, proofs are omitted and are found in [Lug88].

1 Simplification of First Order Formulas

This section is devoted to the presentation of a set of transformation rules for first order formulas. Firstly, we recall the results of [CL88] and [Mah88]: there exists an algorithm (described by a set of transformation rules and a related control) to decide the validity of first-order formulas built on the equality predicate. Then we give the extension of these results to any first order formula, which allow to transform a first order formula into a more tractable one (but the validity of the simplified formula is no longer decidable and the simplified form is more complex than in the previous case).

1.1 The Framework

The reader is assumed to be familiar to the notions and definitions of first order logic, see [Llo87] for example.

The Herbrand univers will be denoted by $T_\Sigma(X)$ where Σ is a *finite* set of functions symbols. A ground term is a term without variable and a linear term is a term in which a variable may occur only once. For simplicity a t-uple of variables $(x_1, \ldots, x_n)$ is denoted by $\overline{x}$, and a t-uple of terms $t_1, \ldots, t_m$ is denoted by $\overline{t}$. When $\overline{s}$ and $\overline{t}$ have the same length, the notation $\overline{s} = \overline{t}$ is a shorthand for $s_1 = t_1 \wedge \ldots \wedge s_n = t_n$, and $\overline{s} \neq \overline{t}$ is another one for $s_1 \neq t_1 \vee \ldots \vee s_n \neq t_n$.

A substitution is a morphism of $T_\Sigma(X)$ such that $x\sigma = x$ except for the domain of σ, $Dom(\sigma)$, a finite set of variables. The application of σ to the term t is denoted by $t\sigma$.

From now, we consider models where the Domain Closure Axiom holds (in short DCA).

Domain Closure Axiom:

$\forall x \in T, x = c_1 \vee \ldots \vee c_k \vee (\exists \overline{y}_1, x = f_1(\overline{y})) \vee \ldots \vee (\exists \overline{y}_r, x = f_r(\overline{y}_r))$ if $\Sigma = \{c_1, \ldots, c_k, f_1, \ldots, f_r\}$ where the c_i are the functions of arity 0

1.2 Decidability of First Order Formula with Equality

In this section, we consider formulas constructed with the equality predicate, and, given a formula $\mathcal{F}$, we try to find the substitutions σ such that $Dom(\sigma)$ is included in the the set of the free variables of $\mathcal{F}$ and such that $\mathcal{F}\sigma$ evaluates to true. The main result is that this problem is decidable.

For a complete and (very) clean presentation of the algorithm, the reader is strongly advised to consult these papers. This section will provide only a brief look at their results.

1.3   The transformation rules

First, we introduce the notion of solved form. $\top$ (resp $\perp$) are notation for formula which are identical to *true* (resp *false*).

Definition 1 *A formula is in solved form iff it is* $\top$, $\perp$, *or it has the form* $\exists \overline{z}, \; x_1 = s_1 \wedge \ldots \wedge x_n = s_n \wedge x'_1 \neq u_1 \wedge \ldots \wedge x'_m \neq u_m$ *where:*

- x_i *are variables which occur once*
- *for* $1 \leq i \leq m, x'_i$ *is a variable distinct from* u'_i

The main result concerning solved form is that the validity of a solved form is decidable.

Now, we give some inference rules which are used to transform formula into solved form. The main inference rules are given, but less interesting ones are omitted. In particular, all the usual rules about the Boolean calculus are assumed. For a complete and precise study one is referred to [CL88]. The application of the rules is illustrated in section 1.4. In the following a parameter is a universally quantified variable.

- Elimination of parameters: EP

  (EP) $\forall y_1, \ldots, y_i, \ldots, y_k, \; \mathcal{P} \rightarrow \forall y_1, \ldots, y_{i-1}, y_{i+1}, \ldots, y_k, \; \mathcal{P}$ if $y_i \notin Var(\mathcal{P})$.

- Universality of parameters

  $(U1)$ $\forall y_1, \ldots, y_k, \mathcal{P} \wedge y \neq t \rightarrow \perp$ if $y \in \{y_1, \ldots, y_k\}$

  $(U2)$ $\forall y_1, \ldots, y_k, \; \mathcal{P} \wedge (y \neq t \vee D) \rightarrow \forall y_1, \ldots, y_k, \; \mathcal{P} \wedge D(y \leftarrow t)$ if $y \in \{y_1, \ldots, y_k\}$

- Clash: C

  $(C1)$ $f(t_1, \ldots, t_n) = g(u_1, \ldots, u_m) \rightarrow \perp$ if $f \neq g$.

  $(C2)$ $f(t_1, \ldots, t_n) \neq g(u_1, \ldots, u_m) \rightarrow \top$ if $f \neq g$.

- Decomposition: D

  $(D1)$ $f(t_1, \ldots, t_m) = f(u_1, \ldots, u_m) \rightarrow t_1 = u_1 \wedge \ldots \wedge t_m = u_m$

  $(D1)$ $f(t_1, \ldots, t_m) \neq f(u_1, \ldots, u_m) \rightarrow t_1 \neq u_1 \vee \ldots \vee t_m \neq u_m$

- Explosion: E

  (E) $\forall \overline{y}, \mathcal{P} \rightarrow \forall \overline{y}, \mathcal{P} \wedge s = f(z_1, \ldots, z_d)$ where the z_i are fresh variables.

The rules which are not given are the *Merging* rules, *Occur check* rules, *Replacement* rule, one *universality of parameter* rule and the rule for the *Elimination of disjunctions*. The set of rules is denoted by (SR), and the result of their application to a formula $\mathcal{F}$ with a suitable strategy, is denoted by $Solved(\mathcal{F})$.

To get a complete set of inference rules for any first order formula built on "=", one adds the next rule:

$Solved(\exists\overline{x}, \forall\overline{y}, \neg P) = \exists\overline{z}, Q \rightarrow Solved(\forall x, \exists y, P) = Solve(\forall\overline{z}, \neg Q)$
if P and Q are two systems

The main theorem is the following one, from [Com88].

Proposition 1 *The above set of inference rules, together with an appropriate control transforms any first order formula $\mathcal{F}$ involving the predicate $=$ into a finite set of solved forms Q_i such that:*

- *The transformation is performed in a finite number of steps.*
- *The set of solution of $\mathcal{F}$ is equal to the union of the set of the solutions of the Q_i.*
- *The Q_i are in solved form.*
- *No rule is applicable to any of the Q_i.*

The corresponding algorithm is called the *disunification algorithm*.

1.4 Extension to other Predicates

The above results do not generalize fairly to formulas involving other predicate symbols because the universally quantified variables cannot be eliminated in all cases. However, the main result is that the above set of rule is sound for first order formula, and it can be slightly modified into a extended set (ESR) such that the following proposition holds:

Proposition 2 *The set of inference rules, with an appropriate control, transforms any first order formula $\mathcal{F}$ into a set of formula $\mathcal{F}'$ such that:*

- *the set of solutions of $\mathcal{F}$ is equal to the union of the set of solutions of the $\mathcal{F}'$.*
- *each quantified variable of $\mathcal{F}$, occurring in an equality (or negation of an equality) and in the scope of an universal quantifier does not appear in $\mathcal{F}'$, but each quantified variable not occurring in an equality remains in $\mathcal{F}$.*
- *All literal of $\mathcal{F}$ but those involving $=$, are instances of literals of $\mathcal{F}$*

Proof. (sketch) The first step is to show that the rules of (ESR) are sound, then a careful study of the application of the rules shows that the resulting formula satisfy the above properties.

Example 1

This example shows how to define the negation of the predicate *even* over the integers (constructed from 0 and s), given the definition of the predicate *even*:

$even(x) \Leftrightarrow ((x = 0) \vee (\exists y, x = s(y) \wedge \neg even(y)))$

To define $\neg even(x)$ one takes the negation of the right-hand-side which gives

$((x \neq 0) \wedge (\forall y, x \neq s(y) \vee even(y)))$

First, one explodes x into 0 and $s(x')$. The problem obtained by the explosion $x = 0$ results in $\perp$ because of the disequation $x \neq 0$. The other one gives (after the replacement of each occurrence of x by $s(x')$)

$(x = s(x') \wedge s(x') \neq 0 \wedge (\forall y, s(x') \neq s(y) \vee even(y)))$

the first inequation simplifies into $\top$ and one may simplify by s in the quantified part

$(x = s(x') \wedge (\forall y, x' \neq y \vee even(y)))$

Finally the elimination of parameters yields

$x = s(x') \wedge even(x')$

which corresponds to the definition of $\neg even$ by:

$\neg even(s(x)) \Leftarrow even(x)$

$\square$

2   ENF Deduction

SLDNF resolution relies on the notion of *completed programs* for its semantics foundation. Our method also relies on completed programs and is a deduction procedure which transforms the initial goal until a solution is found. Backtrack is avoided and positive or negative goals, existential or universal quantification of some variables are allowed and it can deal with first order programs. Moreover any goal refutable by SLDNF resolution is provable by ENF deduction, which means that ENF deduction strictly enhances SLDNF resolution.

2.1   Definitions

Definition 2

- *A first order program clause is a formula $L \Leftarrow (\forall \overline{y}_1, L_1) \wedge \ldots \wedge (\forall \overline{y}_n, L_n)$ where L is a positive literal, the L_i are literal (positive or negative) and $\overline{y}_i$ a subset (possibly empty) of the variables of L_i.*
  L is the head of the clause and $(\forall \overline{y}_1, L_1) \wedge \ldots \wedge (\forall \overline{y}_n, L_n)$ is the body. If no quantified literal occurs in the body, the clause is a general program clause, moreover if all the literals are positive, the clause is a Horn clause.

- *A first order program is a set of first order program clauses*

- *A definite program is a finite set of Horn clauses.*

- *A general program is a finite set of general program clauses.*

The clause $p(\bar{t}_i) \Leftarrow F_{i,1} \wedge \ldots \wedge F_{i,m_i}$ may be transformed into $p(\bar{x}) \Leftarrow \exists \bar{y}, (\bar{x} = \bar{t}_i \wedge F_{i,1} \wedge \ldots \wedge F_{i,m_i})$

The transformation is performed on each clause whose head contains the symbol predicate p, yielding a set:

$$p(\bar{x}) \Leftarrow \exists \bar{y}, (\bar{x} = \bar{t}_1 \wedge F_{1,1} \wedge \ldots \wedge F_{1,m_1})$$

$$\ldots$$

$$p(\bar{x}) \Leftarrow \exists \bar{y}, (\bar{x} = \bar{t}_p \wedge F_{p,1} \wedge \ldots \wedge F_{p,m_p})$$

and $def(p)$, the *definition* of p is the union of the right-hand-sides of these clauses i.e:

$$\exists \bar{y}, \bigvee_i (x = \bar{t}_i \wedge F_{i,1} \wedge \ldots \wedge F_{i,m_i})$$

Definition 3 *The completed program $comp(P)$ associated to a given program P is the set:*

$\{ p(\bar{x}) \Leftrightarrow \exists \bar{y}, \bigvee_i (x = \bar{t}_i \wedge F_{i,1} \wedge \ldots \wedge F_{i,m_i}) $ *for each predicate symbol appearing in the head of a clause of P}.*

When we consider definite or general programs, this is the classical definition of completed programs.

2.2 Completed Programs and Negation

The classical results [Llo87] on completed programs and SLDNF resolution are:

Proposition 3 *Let G be a ground literal and P be a definite program.*

(soundness) *if the goal clause $\Leftarrow G$ has a finitely failed SLD tree, then G is a logical consequence of $comp(P)$.*

(completeness for Horn clauses) *if $\neg G$ is a logical consequence of comp(P), then the goal clause $\Leftarrow G$ has a finitely failed tree.*

For general programs, the completeness result does not hold. Moreover SLDNF resolution cannot deal with non ground negative goals, otherwise it may be unsound as shown by the following example:

Let $\Sigma = \{0, s\}$ and the program be:

$$p(x) \Leftarrow \neg q(x)$$

$$q(0) \Leftarrow$$

the goal $\Leftarrow p(x)$ would return "failure" while $p(s(x))$ holds. ENF deduction deals successfully with such cases.

2.3 ENF Deduction Procedure

This section is devoted to the inference rules which define ENF deduction. $\mathcal{F}$ is a given formula, and we are looking for the substitutions σ such that $\mathcal{F}\sigma$ is valid. Actually, we will not return substitutions but a conjunction of equations and disequations from which the substitutions solutions can be easily derived. Of course, such a conjunction may represent a infinite set of distincts substitutions (e.g. $x \neq y$).

We suppose that we are given a selection function SL which selects a position and the literal occurring at this position in a first order formula. The result of applying the selection function to the formula $\mathcal{F}$ is denoted by $SL(\mathcal{F}) = (o, l)$ where o is a position in $\mathcal{F}$, and l is the literal of $\mathcal{F}$ at position o.

The substitution in $\mathcal{F}$, of the literal occurring at position o, by a formula G is denoted by $\mathcal{F}_{[o \leftarrow G]}$.

In what follows $p(\bar{t})$ always denotes a positive literal, $\mathcal{D}ef(p)$ denotes the definition of p, i.e a formula such as $\exists \bar{y}, \bigvee_i (\, x = \bar{t}_i \wedge q_{i,1} \wedge \ldots \wedge q_{i,m_i})$.

$\mathcal{F}$ is the formula to prove, $Solution$ denotes the set of computed solutions, $Solve(\mathcal{F})$ denotes the result of the disunification algorithm applied to the formula $\mathcal{F}$.

The inference rules are:

- Replacement: R

$$\mathcal{F}, SL(\mathcal{F}) = (o, p(\bar{t})) \rightarrow \mathcal{F}_{[o \leftarrow (\exists \bar{z}, (\bar{x} = \bar{t} \wedge \mathcal{D}ef(p))]}$$
$$with \; \bar{z} = \bar{x} \cup Var(\mathcal{D}ef(p)) \; a \; set \; of \; new \; variables$$

- Simplification: SIMP

$$\mathcal{F} \rightarrow Solve(\mathcal{F})$$

- Solutions: SOL

$$\mathcal{F} = E \vee \mathcal{F}', \rightarrow \mathcal{F}', Solution \cup \{E\}$$
$$if \; E = (\bar{x} = t_1 \wedge \ldots \wedge x_n = t_n \wedge x'_1 \neq u_1 \wedge \ldots \wedge x'_m \neq u_m) \; in \; solved \; form$$

Moreover the classical boolean computation rules are assumed and the strategy given is $(Sol) \geq (SIMP) \geq (R)$. By definition an ENF derivation is a sequence of application of the above inference rules.

This procedure is a brute-force one and many refinements are currently investigated to get a more efficient one.

2.4 General Results

Basic results concerning ENF deduction are stated, the first one is that ENF deduction is sound and the second one precises the relationship with SLDNF resolution.

Proposition 4 *ENF deduction is sound.*

The proof is straightforward since any rule used in ENF deduction is sound.

Proposition 5 *Let l be a literal, if the goal $\Leftarrow l$ has a SLDNF refutation, then there is an ENF derivation $l \rightarrow \top$*

This proposition gives, as byproduct, that each completeness result established for SLDNF resolution holds also for ENF resolution. But ENF resolution is more powerful since it deals with non-ground negative goals and universally quantified formula.

Proof In fact we prove by induction on n the following property: if a literal l has a SLDNF refutation of length n or a finitely failed tree of height n, then there is a ENF derivation $l \rightarrow \top$ or $l \rightarrow \bot$. We recall that if the set of solution of $\forall \overline{y}, x \neq t$ where $\overline{y} = Var(t)$ is the set of substitutions θ such that $x\theta$ and $t\theta$ are not unifiables.

If l is positive, we write $l = p(\overline{s})$, otherwise we write $l = \neg p(\overline{s})$. The clauses defining p are $p(\overline{s}_i) \Leftarrow Q_i$ with Q_i a conjunction of literals, and the definition of p is $\vee(\exists \overline{y}_i, \overline{x} = \overline{s}_i \wedge Q_i)$.

1. $n = 0$

   - l is positive and has a SLDNF refutation of length 0. This means that l unifies with the left-hand side of some clause $p(s_{i_0}) \Leftarrow$. Therefore there is an ENF derivation $l \rightarrow \top$.

   - l is negative and $\neg l = p(\overline{s})$ has a finitely failed SLD tree of height 0. This means that the positive goal $p(\overline{s})$ does not unify with any left-hand side of clause, i.e that $\overline{s}$ is a solution of $\forall \overline{z}, x \neq s_1 \wedge \ldots x \neq s_m$ with $\overline{z} = \cup_i Var(s_i)$. Therefore there is a ENF derivation $\neg p(\overline{s}) \rightarrow \top$.

2. Let us suppose that the property is true for n=0,..,m

   - l is positive and has a SLDNF refutation of length p. Let $G_0 \Leftarrow l, \ldots, G_n = \square$ be a SLDNF refutation of l of length $m + 1$. We have that $G_1 = \Leftarrow Q_i \theta$ where $p(\overline{s}_i) \Leftarrow Q_i$ with Q_i is a conjunction of literals, is a clause of the program and $\theta = m.g.u.(p(\overline{s}), p(\overline{s}_i))$. Therefore there is an ENF derivation $l \rightarrow G_1 \vee F'$. Moreover each literal in G_1 has either a SLDNF refutation of length less or equal m or a SLDNF finitely failed tree of height less or equal m, therefore there is a ENF derivation $G_1 \rightarrow \top$

   - l is negative and $\neg l = p(\overline{s})$ has a finitely failed tree of height p. Let $G_1, G_2, \ldots, G_l$ be the successors of $\Leftarrow p(\overline{s})$ in the tree.

Then there is an ENF derivation $p(\bar{s}) \rightarrow G_1 \vee \ldots \vee G_l$ Since each G_i has a finitely failed SLDNF tree, then there is for each G_i an ENF derivation $G_i \rightarrow \bot$, and therefore there is an ENF derivation $l \rightarrow \bot$.

$\square$

3 ENF Deduction for Logic Programs

3.1 ENF Deduction for Horn Clauses

First, we give the general form of the formulas involved in ENF deduction when it deals with Horn clauses. Then, an example shows how ENF deduction works in the case of Horn clause.

Proposition 6 *Let P be a definite program, let p be a positive literal and $\mathcal{F}$ the result of a ENF derivation from p, ending by an application of (SIMP), then, in $\mathcal{F}$, only a existential quantifier may occur in the scope of an universal quantifier.*

This proposition states that the level of quantification involved in ENF deduction is limited when we are dealing with Horn clauses. Unfortunately, complex universally quantified disjunction of conjunctions of literal may occur. The behavior of ENF deduction is illustrated by the following example which causes troubles to SLDNF resolution as well as to other methods.

Example 2 : Let $\Sigma = \{0, s\}$ and P be the program:

$r(s(s(x))) \Leftarrow r(x)$

$p(x) \Leftarrow q(x, y)$

$p(x) \Leftarrow r(x)$

$q(0, 0) \Leftarrow$

and let the goal be $\neg p(x)$

The definition of p, q and r are: $p(x) \Leftrightarrow (\exists y, \, q(x, y) \vee r(x)$, $q(x, y) \Leftrightarrow x = 0 \wedge y = 0$ and $r(x) \Leftrightarrow (\exists y, \, x = s(s(y)) \wedge r(y)$

The resolution steps are:

$\neg p(x) \rightarrow \neg((\exists y, \, q(x, y)) \vee r(x))$ by (R)

$\neg((\exists y, \, q(x, y)) \vee r(x)) \rightarrow \neg((\exists y, \, x = 0 \wedge y = 0) \vee (\exists z, \, x = s(s(z)) \wedge r(z)))$ by selecting the position of q and (R)

The negation is eliminated yielding:

$\neg((\exists y, \, x = 0 \wedge y = 0) \vee (\exists z, \, x = s(s(z)) \wedge r(z))) \rightarrow (\forall y, x \neq 0 \vee y \neq 0) \wedge (\forall z, x \neq s(s(z)) \vee \neg r(z))$

and the disunification algorithm is applied to:

$(\forall y, x \neq 0 \vee y \neq 0) \wedge (\forall z, x \neq s(s(z)) \vee \neg r(z))$

The first part is solved into $x = s(x')$ and the second one into $x = 0$ or $x = s(0)$ or $x = s(s(x')) \wedge \neg r(x')$.

Therefore, one has the derivation:

$(\forall y, x \neq 0 \lor y \neq 0) \land (\forall z, x \neq s(s(z)) \lor \neg r(z)) \to x = s(0) \lor (x = s(s(x')) \land \neg r(x'))$ by (SIMP)

Then, one gets:

$x = s(0) \lor (x = s(s(x')) \land \neg r(x')) \to (x = s(s(x')) \land \neg r(x')), Solution = \{x = s(0)\}$ by (SOL)

The iteration of the process will result in an infinite computation of $Solution = \{x = s(0), x = s(s(0)), \ldots\}$

$\square$

This example shows that it is possible to deal with non-ground negative goals and universally quantified goals. Now we give the completeness result implied by proposition 5.

Proposition 7 *Let P be a definite program, let L be a literal, if L is a logical consequence of $comp(P)$, then there exists an ENF deduction $L \to \top$.*

3.2 ENF Deduction for General Programs

The procedure is the same as for definite programs, but when a clause contains a variable not occurring in its head, the level of quantification involved may grow rapidly since negative literal may occur recursively, which leads to an extra and costly processing. The next example illustrates how ENF deduction works when dealing with general programs.

Moreover we add another simplification rule to eliminate tautologies, which is useless in the case of Horn clauses.

- Elimination of tautologies: ET $p(\bar{t}) \lor \neg p(\bar{t}) \to \top$

There are no differences with the case of Horn clauses, except for the complexity of the formula involved in the process.

Completeness results have been established for some classes of general programs, and because of the proposition of section 2, these results holds for ENF deduction. In particular, ENF deduction is complete for hierarchical programs and strict stratified programs (if the *dependence* relation meets some additional requirement) see [ABW87], [CL87] for the completeness of SLDNF resolution in these cases. Moreover Kunen has proved that the completeness result holds for strict programs [Kun87], which means that ENF deduction is complete for these classes of logic programs. Moreover we conjecture that ENF is complete when the completion of the program is consistent.

4 Application to Program Transformation

4.1 Sketch of the Method

In [ST88], a first order compiler which transforms a set of first order programs (i.e logic program with universal quantification) into a definite program is presented. The main idea is to introduce new predicates and new function symbols with a fold/unfold mechanism, but some universally quantified disequations remain.

Meanwhile, a transformational approach has been proposed to solve the problem of negation in [BMPT88]. It consists in defining new predicates which are intended to represent the negation of the predicates defined in the original program.

Both methods present unsolved problems: in Barbuti's method, there remains universally quantified literals called $n.a.f$ literal, while Sato and Tamaki's approach is left with universally quantified equations (ou disequations). The rules presented in this paper give a solution to both problems. Since Barbuti's method can be seen as a sub-case of Sato and Tamaki's one, we will focus on Sato and Tamaki's algorithm.

The algorithm is a fold-unfold transformation which transforms a first order program into a set of Horn clauses such that the set of solutions of each program is the same (but it does not means that the two programs are logically equivalent). This method requires the introduction of new predicate and function symbols, but the use of our transformation rules allows to get rid of new function symbols as well as of the universally quantified disequations. Only new predicate symbols, (corresponding to universally quantified disjunction of conjunctions) are required. We limit ourselves to a (very) short sketch of the modified method.

Let $\mathcal{P}$ is a first order program to be transformed into a set of Horn clauses $\mathcal{H}$. The predicates of $|calP$ are divided into two sets: HP the set of predicates defined by a set of Horn clauses, and NHP the set of predicates not defied by Horn clauses. The method will empty the set NHP and $\mathcal{H}$ will be the set of the definitions of the elements of HP.

The transformation is sketched as follows:

- Let $p \in NHP$. For each universally quantified formula u_i occurring in $def(p)$ introduce a new predicate name p_i.

- For each new predicate p_i, unfold the literals occurring in u_i and simplify the result with the (SIMP) rule. This result is the definition of p_i.

- $HP \leftarrow HP \cup \{p\} \cup \{p_i\}$ if p_i is defined by a set of Horn clauses.

  $NHP \leftarrow (NHP - \{p\}) \cup \{p_i\}$ if p_i is not defined by a set of Horn clauses.

This process will not terminate, and we need some more control rules for termination which state that a new predicatemust not be unfolded. One of these rules relies on the next proposition:

Proposition 8 *Let l be a positive literal, let θ be a substitution with $Dom(\theta)$ $\subseteq \overline{y}$, if σ is an idempotent substitution solution of $\forall \overline{y}, l$, then σ is a idempotent solution of $\forall \overline{z}, l$ with $\overline{z} = Var(y\theta)$.*

We show on an example how this transformation works with our approach.

4.2 An Example

The following example is a slight adaptation of an example given in [ST88] and illustrates how the disunification works on the transformation of program clauses into Horn clauses.

To have a more realistic example, we will consider the many-sorted algebra $T_{\Sigma,S}(X)$ with two sorts:

- N the sort of the integers, constructed from $0 :\to N$ and $s : N \to N$.

- $\mathcal{L}$ the sort of lists, constructed from $nil :\to \mathcal{L}$ and $cons : (N, \mathcal{L}) \to \mathcal{L}$

x is of sort integer is denoted by $x : N$ and l is of sort list is denoted by $l : \mathcal{L}$

Since we are dealing with many sorted algebra, the inference rule must respect the sorts. The most important change concerns the explosion rule, i.e a list is exploded into nil, or $\exists x : N, l' : \mathcal{L}, cons(x, l')$ and an integer is exploded into 0 or $\exists x', s(x')$.

This program defines the membership predicate and the predicate $zerone(l)$ which states that the elements of the list l are either 0 or $s(0)$.

$zerone(l) \Leftarrow (\forall x, member(x, l) \Rightarrow (x = 0 \lor x = s(0)))$
$member(x, cons(x, l)) \Leftarrow$
$member(x, cons(x', l')) \Leftarrow member(x, l')$
The definition of $zerone$ is:

$$zerone(l) \Leftrightarrow (\forall x, member(x, l) \Rightarrow (x = 0 \lor x = s(0)))$$

which is equivalent to (transform the implication into a disjunction)

$$zerone(l) \Leftrightarrow (\forall x, (\neg member(x, l) \lor x = 0 \lor x = s(0)))$$

and the definition of $member$ is:

$$member(x, l) \Leftrightarrow ((\exists l', l = cons(x, l')) \lor (\exists x', l', l = cons(x', l') \land member(x, l')))$$

The disunification algorithm is applied to the definition of *zerone* in order to get a simplified definition and one gets:

$$zerone(l) \;\Leftrightarrow\; (\forall z, \neg member(s(s(z)), l))$$

This definition expresses the fact *zerone(l)* is equivalent to: "every integer different from 0 and $s(0)$ does not belong to l". The problem is then to define by a set of definite clauses, the new predicate $Q(l)$ whose definition is $\forall z, \neg member(s(s(z)), l)$. The literal occurring in the definition is replaced according to the definition of *member*

$$Q(l) \;\Leftrightarrow\; (\forall z, \neg(\exists x', l', (l = cons(s(s(z)), l')$$

$$\vee(l = cons(x', l') \wedge member(s(s(z)), l')))))$$

The negation is eliminated and one gets:

$$Q(l) \;\Leftrightarrow\; (\forall z, x', l', (l \neg cons(s(s(z)), l') \wedge (l \neq cons(x', l') \vee \neg member(s(s(z)), l')))$$

The simplification rule is applied, yielding:

$$Q(l) \;\Leftrightarrow\; (\exists L, (l = nil \vee (l = cons(0, L) \wedge (\forall z, \neg member(s(s(z)), L)))$$

$$\vee(l = cons(s(0), L) \wedge (\forall z, \neg member(s(s(z)), L)))))$$

There remain some universally quantified literals which are built with the same predicate symbol *member* than Q and which are quantified in the same occurrences. Therefore they are replaced by $Q(L)$. Moreover since $Q(l)$ is nothing but an alias for *zerone(l)* one can replace Q par *zerone*. The final program becomes:

$zerone(l) \Leftarrow l = nil$
$zerone(l) \Leftarrow (l = cons(0, L) \wedge zerone(L))$
$zerone(l) \Leftarrow (l = cons(s(0), L) \wedge zerone(L))$

which is equivalent to the initial definition (and simpler than the corresponding result of [ST88]).

$\square$

Conclusion

The bases of ENF deduction have been presented, as well as its the main results about it. It appears to be a very powerful tool for logic programming, automated theorem proving and program transformation. Two main research topics are currently investigated:

- the refinements required for a efficient implementation.

- the extension to other domains (although there is no hope to have a general algorithm since solving formulas in a equational theory is even not semi-decidable)

References

[ABW87]   K. R. Apt, H. A. Blair, and A. Walker. Towards a theory of declarative knowledge. In J. Minker, editor, *Foundations of Deductive Databases and Logic Programming*, Morgan Kaufmann, 1987. Available as LITP Research Report 86-10.

[BMPT88]   R. Barbuti, P. Mancarella, D. Pedreschi, and F. Turini. A transformational approach to negation in logic programming. *submitted to Journal of Logic Programming*, 1988.

[CL87]   C. Cavedon, J. W. Lloyd. *A Completeness Result in SLDNF Resolution.* to appear.

[CL88]   H. Comon and P. Lescanne. *Equational Problems and Disunification.* Research Report Lifia 82 Imag 727, Univ. Grenoble, May 1988. To appear in J. Symbolic Computation.

[Cla78]   K. L. Clark. Negation as failure. In H. Gallaire and J. Minker, editors, *Logic and Data Bases*, Plenum, New York, 1978.

[Col84]   A. Colmerauer. Equations and inequations on finite and infinite trees. In *FGCS'84 Proceedings*, pages 85–99, November 1984.

[Com88]   H. Comon. *Unification et Disunification: Théorie et Applications.* Thèse de Doctorat, I.N.P. de Grenoble, France, 1988.

[JL86]   J. Jaffar and J. L. Lassez. *Constraint Logic Programming* Tech. Report, Departement of Computer Science, Univ. Monash June 1986.

[Kun87]   K. Kunen. *Signed Data Dependencies in Logic programs.* Tech. Report 719, Univ. Wisconsin, Madison, October 1987.

[Llo87]   J. W. Lloyd. *Foundations of Logic Programming.* Springer-Verlag, second edition, 1987.

[Lug88]   D. Lugiez. *Disunification and Logic Programming.* Research Report Lifia 74, Univ. Grenoble, 1988.

[Mah88]   M. J. Maher. Complete axiomatization of the algebra of finite, rational and infinite trees. January 1988. Draft Paper.

[Rei78]   R. Reiter. On closed world data bases. In H. Gallaire and J. Minker, editors, *Logic and Data Bases*, Plenum, New York, 1978.

[ST88]   T. Sato and H. Tamaki. Deterministic transformation and deterministic synthesis. In *Programming of Future Generation Computers*, North-Holland, 1988.

THE RELATIONSHIP BETWEEN LOGIC PROGRAM SEMANTICS AND NON-MONOTONIC REASONING

Wiktor Marek
Department of Computer Science
University of Kentucky
Lexington, KY 40506-0027.

V.S. Subrahmanian
Computer & Information Science
Syracuse University
Syracuse, NY 13244-1240.

Abstract

We investigate the relationship between various alternative semantics for logic programming, viz. the stable model semantics of Gelfond and Lifschitz [6], the supported model semantics as developed by Apt, Blair and Walker [2], autoepistemic translations of general logic programs and default translations (due to Przymusinska) of general logic programs [24].

1   Introduction

Several techniques have been proposed to handle negative information in deductive databases and logic programs. These include, in the AI community, the methods of circumscription [19,20], default logics [24,27], and autoepistemic logics [21,16].

In the logic programming community, the general idea has been to identify one or more models of the *completion* (cf. Clark [4]) of a program as being the intended meaning(s) of the program. These techniques led to the notion of *stratification* [2,26] in which a so-called *standard* (or canonical) model of the program completion was constructed and it was claimed that this model was the intended model of the program. This approach was extended by Przymusiński [22] who defined a class of programs called locally stratified programs. Recently, Gelfond and Lifschitz [6] proposed a stable model semantics for logic programs and showed that the stable model semantics extends the locally stratified semantics.

However, it was soon realized by various researchers that a close investigation of the relationship between these varying formalisms is needed. This is because the number of such schemes for handling negative information is rapidly increasing – before allowing such an increase, one needs to examine the relationships between different schemes to understand exactly what the differences are, and to determine where the strengths and/or weaknesses of a particular scheme lie. At this point we are aware of investigations of the following relationships

1. between circumscription and Clark's completion [9,24]

2. between circumscription and the closed world assumption [8,12]

3. between autoepistemic logic and circumscription [7]

4. between default logic and circumscription [10]

5. between the Clark Completion and the Closed World Assumption [13, 25]

6. between autoepistemic logic and default reasoning [11,17].

In this paper, we study the connection between the supported model semantics for logic programming as developed by Apt, Blair and Walker [2], and non-monotonic logic based semantics for logic programming. The latter consists of translating general logic programs into either auto-epistemic theories or default logic theories (cf. such translational semantics are attributed by Apt and Blair[1] to Halina Przymusinska). We show that there is a close correspondence between the semantics of logic programs under these differing semantical characterizations.

2 Supported Models and Stable Models

We assume that the reader is familiar with the usual notions of term, atom, etc. Unless explicitly stated otherwise, the languages we consider contain function symbols.

Definition 1 *If A is an atom and $L_1, \ldots, L_n$ are literals (i.e. atoms or negated atoms), then*

$$A \leftarrow L_1 \,\&\, \cdots \,\&\, L_n$$

is a clause. *A is called the* head *of the above clause, and $L_1 \,\&\, \cdots \,\&\, L_n$ is called the* body *of the above clause.*

Definition 2 *A general logic program is a finite set of clauses.*

For the sake of notational simplicity, we will assume that the body of any clause is written as:

$$B_1 \ \& \cdots \& \ B_m \ \& \ \neg D_1 \ \& \cdots \& \ \neg D_k$$

where the B_i's and D_j's are all atomic. Thus, in the body of any clause, the negative atoms occur to after the positive atoms. As conjunction is commutative in nature, there is no loss of generality in making this assumption.

We may, in fact, assume that a general logic program P is a possibly infinite set of ground clauses. This is the same simplifying assumption made by Gelfond and Lifschitz [6]. *Unless explicitly mentioned otherwise, throughout this paper, we assume that P is a possibly infinite set of ground clauses.* The completion of P is defined in the same way as in Lloyd [13] except that one may now have infinitary disjunctions occurring in the completion. As usual, we restrict our interest to Herbrand models only and consider an interpretation to be a subset of the Herbrand Base B_P of the program P. The following definition is due to Apt, Blair and Walker[2].

Definition 3 *A model M of P is supported iff for all $A \in M$, there is a clause in P of the form*

$$A \leftarrow B_1 \& \ldots \& B_k \& \neg D_1 \& \ldots \& \neg D_m$$

such that $M \models B_1 \& \ldots \& B_k \& \neg D_1 \& \ldots \& \neg D_m$.

Intuitively, a supported model needs some definite "reason" based on the program clauses for assigning the truth value **true** to an atom.

Proposition 1 (Apt, Blair, Walker) *M is a supported model of P iff M is a fixed point of T_P.* $\qquad\square$

Proposition 2 *I is an Herbrand model of $comp(P)$ iff $T_P(I) = I$.* $\qquad\square$

Definition 4 *Suppose P is a general logic program and $M \subseteq B_P$ is an interpretation. The Gelfond-Lifschitz transform, $G(M, P)$, of P is the logic program obtained as follows:*

1. *Every negation-free clause in P is in $G(M, P)$.*

2. *If $A \leftarrow B_1 \& \ldots \& B_k \& \neg D_1 \& \ldots \& \neg D_m$ is a clause in P such that for all $1 \leq j \leq m$, $D_j \notin M$, then $A \leftarrow B_1 \& \ldots \& B_k$ is in $G(M, P)$.*

3. *Nothing else is in $G(M, P)$*

Definition 5 *Suppose P is a general logic program and $M \subseteq B_P$ is an interpretation. M is said to be* stable *iff $M = T_{G(M,P)} \uparrow \omega$.*

Example 1 *Let $M = \{p, r\}$. A logic program P and its Gelfond-Lifschitz transform $G(M, P)$ are shown below:*

P	$G(M, P)$
$p \leftarrow \neg q$	$p \leftarrow$
$q \leftarrow \neg r$	
$r \leftarrow$	$r \leftarrow$

The least model of $G(M, P)$ is $\{p, r\}$ which is identical to M. Hence, M is stable.

Theorem 1 *Every stable model of P is supported.* $\square$

Corollary 1 *1. If M is a stable model of P, then M is a model of $comp(P)$.*

2. Suppose A is a ground atom. If A is false in all Herbrand models of $comp(P)$, then A is false in all stable models of P. $\square$

Stable models of logic programs are closely related to the Default Logic of [24]. Recall that a default is a triple $d = < p(d), j(d), c(d) >$ where $p(d)$ is a formula called the *prerequisite* of d, $j(d)$ is a finite list of formulas of L, $j(d) = \beta_1, \ldots, \beta_k$, is called the *justification* of d, and $c(d)$ is again a formula of L called the *conclusion* of d. Traditionally, we write:

$$d = \frac{p(d) \ : \ \beta_1, \ldots, \beta_k}{c(d)}$$

Given a program P, we assign to it a default theory (D_P, W_P) constructed as follows. If $(A \leftarrow B_1 \& \ldots \& B_k)$ is a negation-free clause in P, then the formula $(B_1 \& \ldots \& B_k \Rightarrow A)$ belongs to W_P. Nothing else is in W_P. Clauses containing negations in the body are interpreted as default rules:

$$A \leftarrow B_1 \& \ldots \& B_k \& \neg D_1 \& \ldots \& \neg D_m$$

is transformed to:

$$\frac{B_1 \& \ldots \& B_k \ : \ \neg D_1, \ldots, \neg D_m}{A}$$

which belongs to D_P.

Example 2 *If P is the general logic program:*

$p \leftarrow q$

$q \leftarrow r \,\&\, \neg w$

$w \leftarrow$

$r \leftarrow w \,\&\, \neg p$

Then the default theory (W_P, D_P) associated with P is: $W_P = \{p \leftarrow q, \, w \leftarrow \}$. D_P consists of the following two default rules:

$$\frac{r \;:\; \neg w}{q} \,, \quad \frac{w \;:\; \neg p}{r}$$

Given a theory S included in L and a fixed default theory (D, W), let *Reiter's* operator R_S be defined as follows:

$$R_S(T) = Cn\left(S \cup \{c(d) : d \in D \,\&\, p(d) \in T \,\&\, \forall_{\beta \in j(d)} \neg\beta \notin S\}\right)$$

The operator R_S is monotone and finitary and so it can be easily shown that it possesses a least fixed point above any set T of formulas. Let F_W^S be the least fixed point of R_S above W. S is called an *extension* of (D, W) if this least fixed point is precisely S, i.e. $F_W^S = S$.

We quote the following result from [17]:

Theorem 2 *M is a stable model of a logic program P if and only if M is a maximal set of atoms such that $Cn(W_P \cup M)$ is an extension of (W_P, D_P).*
$\square$

In this fashion we get a close connection between the class of stable models of a program and a classical mode of non-monotonic reasoning. In section 3 we shall establish yet another interpretation of logic programs in autoepistemic logic and with the help of it in default logic which ties up supported models with different aspects of default logic.

Lemma 1 *Let M be a supported model of P. Then $T_{G(M,P)} \uparrow \omega \subseteq M$.* $\square$

Unfortunately, the reverse inclusion does not hold, i.e. there are supported models that are not stable.

Example 3 *Let P be the program $\{p \leftarrow p\}$. Then $M = \{p\}$ is a supported model of P, but M is not a stable model of P. This is because $G(M, P)$ is P itself, and the least model of P is $\emptyset$. Hence, M is not stable.*

We know, by the theorems above, that if P has a stable model, then $comp(P)$ is consistent. Unfortunately, there are simple programs having consistent completions but possessing no stable models. (Gelfond and Lifschitz present an example of a program having no stable models, but their program has an inconsistent completion).

Example 4 *Let P be the program:*

$$p \leftarrow \neg p$$

$$p \leftarrow q$$

$$q \leftarrow q$$

It can easily be verified that this program has no stable model; however, $comp(P)$ is consistent (the interpretation $\{p,q\}$ is a model of $comp(P)$ and indeed, this is the only Herbrand model of $comp(P)$.)

Example 5 *Let P be the program:*

$$p \leftarrow \neg q$$

$$q \leftarrow \neg p$$

The $M_1 = \{p\}$ and $M_2 = \{q\}$ are stable models of P, but $M_1 \cap M_2 = \emptyset$ is not a stable model of P. Similarly, $M_1 \cup M_2 = \{p,q\}$ is not stable either. Indeed, it is easy to verify that there is no interpretation M such that $M \supseteq M_1$ and $M \supseteq M_2$ such that M is a stable model of P. Similarly, there is no interpretation M' such that $M' \subseteq M_1$ and $M' \subseteq M_2$ such that M' is a stable model of P.

Proposition 3 (Gelfond and Lifschitz [6]) *Let P be any general logic program. Then each stable model of P is a minimal model of P; hence the set $st(P)$ of stable models of P forms an anti-chain.* $\square$

Theorem 3 (Gelfond and Lifschitz) *Suppose P is a locally stratified program. Then:*

1. *P has a unique stable model, denoted $\mathcal{S}_P$ and*

2. *$\mathcal{S}_P$ is exactly the model $\mathfrak{N}_P$ constructed by the transfinite iteration procedure of Przymusiński.* $\square$

Proposition 4 *Let P be a general logic program and M a recursively enumerable subset of the Herbrand Base B_P of P. Then*

606

1. *the problem* Is M *a stable model for* P *?* *is* Π_2^0*-hard. Moreover, it is in* Π_3^0.

2. *is* $P' = G(M, P)$ *?* *is* Π_2^0*-hard. Moreover, it is in* Π_3^0.

Proof Outline. We outline the proof of (1) above. The proof for (2) proceeds along similar lines.

First we show that (1) is Π_2^0-hard. This is shown by demonstrating a reducibility to the well known Π_2^0-complete problem "Given r.e. sets S_1, S_2, is $S_1 = S_2$?" Let Q be a *pure* logic program having success set S_1. Then $G(S_1, Q) = G(S_2, Q) = Q$. Clearly, $S_1 = S_2$

iff $T_Q \uparrow \omega = S_2$
iff $T_{G(S_1, Q)} \uparrow \omega = S_2$
iff $T_{G(S_2, Q)} \uparrow \omega = S_2$
iff S_2 is a stable model of Q.

It follows that the problem $S_1 = S_2$ can now be solved by an oracle query asking if S_2 is a stable model of Q. Hence (1) is Π_2^0-hard.

We now show that (1) is in Π_3^0. As M is r.e. and as P is recursive, it is easy to see that the problem of whether a ground clause is in $G(M, P)$ is Σ_2^0. Thus, $G(M, P)$ is a Σ_2^0 set of clauses. Let $F[x]$ be a Σ_2^0 formula containing free variable x that *defines* $G(M, P)$. It is easy to show that $T_{G(M,P)} \uparrow \omega$ is r.e. relative to $G(M, P)$. Thus, $T_{G(M,P)} \uparrow \omega$ is in Σ_2^0. Let $G[x]$ be a Σ_2^0 formula containing free variable x that *defines* $T_{G(M,P)} \uparrow \omega$. Then M is a stable model of P iff $M = T_{G(M,P)} \uparrow \omega$ iff $(\forall x)(F[x] \Leftrightarrow G[x])$ which is a Π_3^0 formula.

To see (2) we notice that comparing recursive set (P') and a Δ_2^0 set is expressible as a Π_2^0 sentence. $\qquad\square$

Lemma 2 *Suppose* P_1, P_2 *are general logic programs such that no predicate symbol occurring in* P_1 *occurs in* P_2 *and vice-versa. Then, if* M_1, M_2 *are stable models of* P_1, P_2 *respectively,* $M_1 \cup M_2$ *is a stable model of* $P_1 \cup P_2$. $\square$

Theorem 4 *Let* $n > 0$ *be an arbitrary positive integer. Then there exists a logic program* P *having at least* n *stable models.* $\qquad\square$

The above Theorem proves that there is no upper bound on the number of stable models a logic program might have. The results hold even if we restrict programs to be function symbol free. (The programs constructed in the proof of the preceding theorem are function-free, cf. [15]).

Example 6 *Given a general logic program* P, *comp*(P) *may have a unique Herbrand model, but* P *may not possess any stable model. For example, let*

P be the general logic program of Example 4. Then comp(P) is consistent (the interpretation {p, q} is a Herbrand model of comp(P)), but P has no stable model (this is a simple matter of checking that the only fixed-point of T_P, viz. {p, q} is not stable).

As usual, we denote strict inclusion with the symbol $\subset$.

Definition 6 *Let P be a general logic program. A model M of comp(P) is comp-minimal iff there is no model M' of comp(P) such that $M' \subset M$.*

Definition 7 *A supported model M of a general logic program P is supp-minimal iff no $M' \subset M$ is a supported model of P.*

Definition 8 *Suppose P is a general logic program, and $A \in B_P$ is a ground atom.*

1. *we say A is* stably valid *w.r.t. P (denoted $P \mapsto_{st} A$) iff A is true in all stable models of P*

2. *A is* minimally supportedly valid *w.r.t. P (denoted $P \mapsto_{ms} A$) iff A is true in all supp-minimal supported models of P*

Theorem 5 *Let P be a general logic program and $A \in B_P$ is a ground atom. Then:*

1. *if $P \mapsto_{ms} A$ then $P \mapsto_{st} A$.*

2. *if $P \mapsto_{st} \neg A$ then $P \mapsto_{ms} \neg A$.* □

Theorem 6 *Suppose P is a general logic program. If $A \in T_{G(B_P, P)} \uparrow \omega$, then $P \mapsto_{st} A$.* □

Theorem 7 *Suppose P is a general logic program and $A \in B_P$. If $A \notin T_{G(\emptyset, P)} \downarrow \omega$, then $P \mapsto_{st} \neg A$.* □

Theorem 5 establishes a close connection between the set of ground atoms and negations of ground atoms that are stably valid and minimally supportedly valid w.r.t. a given program P. As we shall see below, the set of atoms that are stably valid is highly undecidable. Theorem 6 defines for us a set of ground atoms that is included in the set of stably valid ground atoms.

Proposition 5 (Apt and Blair [1, Theorem 22]) *Then for each $n > 0$, there a program P such that the standard model of P constructed by the transfinite iteration procedure of Apt, Blair and Walker [2] is a Σ^0_n-complete subset of the Herbrand Base of P.* $\square$

Corollary 2 *For each $n > 0$, there is a logic program P such that*

1. *the set $\mathcal{S}(P) = \{A \in B_P \mid P \mapsto_{st} A\}$ is a Σ^0_n-complete subset of B_P.*

2. *the set $\mathcal{F}(P) = \{A \in B_P \mid P \mapsto_{st} \neg A\}$ is a Π^0_n-complete subset of B_P.*
$\square$

Theorem 8 *If M is a stable model of P, then M is a comp-minimal model of $comp(P)$, i.e. M is a minimal fixed-point of T_P.* $\square$

The contents of this section establish an intricate relationship between stable models of logic programs and supported models of logic programs. Stable models derive their motivation from the so-called *stable theories* of auto-epistemic logic. We discuss the connections of supported model semantics and auto-epistemic logics below.

3   Autoepistemic Translation of a Logic Program

In this section we investigate the relationship between supported models of a general logic program and the logic of an ideally introspective agent. We show that under the epistemic translation **ET** (to be introduced below) of logic programs there is a one to one correspondence between the supported models and the so-called autoepistemic expansions of translations (cf [21]).

Autoepistemic logic was proposed by Moore [21] as a formalism for a reasoning agent to be able to reflect upon her/his own knowledge. We observe that Gelfond [5] has also defined a translation of logic programs into autoepistemic theories, but as will shortly become apparent, our transformation is somewhat different and leads to some interesting connections between supported models of logic programs and expansions of autoepistemic theories. We briefly review the basic results pertaining to autoepistemic logic, as proved in [14,11] and [16].

Let L denote a *propositional* language whose logical symbols are the usual symbols of propositional logic. Cn is the consequence operation of the propositional logic, sometimes called tautological consequence. L can be extended to a modal language, L_K, by introducing a unary connective K. Every formula ϕ of L is in L_K, and if ψ is a formula of L_K, then $K\psi$ is a formula of L_K. Intuitively, if ψ is a formula, then $K\psi$ means "ψ is known to be true". When discussing L_K, the consequence operation Cn acts on the theories in the modal language as well, except that here every expression $K\phi$ is treated as an atom.

Given the language of modal logic L_K, a theory $T \subseteq L_K$ is called *stable* if it satisfies the following conditions:

(St 1) T is closed under propositional consequence

(St 2) $\phi \in T \Rightarrow K\phi \in T$

(St 3) $\phi \notin T \Rightarrow \neg K\phi \in T$

Given a theory $I \subseteq L_K$ (think about I as *initial assumptions* of an agent), a theory $T \subseteq L_K$ is called an *expansion* of I ([21]) if it satisfies the following condition:

$$(*) \quad T = Cn(I \cup \{K\phi : \phi \in T\} \cup \{\neg K\phi : \phi \notin T\}).$$

Hence, as is often the case both in logic programming and in AI, expansion is defined via a fixed point of an operator. Not every theory I possesses an expansion and if one exists, it need not be unique. The operator whose fixed points are expansions is by no means monotone. One notices that every expansion of I is a stable theory in L_K. In [14,11] it was proved that every $I \subseteq L$ (i.e. without occurence of K) possesses a unique expansion. This unique expansion, called below $\mathbf{Exp}(I)$ possesses the property that $\mathbf{Exp}(I) \cap L = Cn(I)$.

In order to investigate expansions we need a criterion from [16] which establishes both a normal form for expansions and a necessary and sufficient conditions for existence of expansions. To this end, notice first that theories with identical propositional consequences have precisely same expansions (this follows easily from the definition of expansion). Consequently, every theory I can be represented by a collection of implications of form:

$$(**) \quad (K\phi_1 \& \ldots \& K\phi_m \& \neg K\psi_1 \& \ldots \& \neg K\psi_n) \Rightarrow o$$

where $o \in L$. Hence assume that I consists of implications of form $(**)$. To simplify notation we write such formula as $E \Rightarrow o$ where E is:

$$K\phi_1 \& \ldots \& K\phi_m \& \neg K\psi_1 \& \ldots \& \neg K\psi_n$$

is called the *epistemic justification* of o and o is called the *objective* part of the implication.

Hence, let $I = \{\phi_i : 1 \leq i \leq k\}, \phi_i = E_i \Rightarrow o_i$. We have ([16])

Theorem 9   *1. Every expansion of I is of form $\mathbf{Exp}(\{o_i : i \in J\})$ for a suitably chosen $J \subseteq \{1, \ldots, k\}$.*

2. *If T is an expansion of I, then for some set $J \subseteq \{1, \ldots, k\}$, $T = \mathbf{Exp}(\{o_i : i \in J\})$ and $I \subseteq T$ and for all $i \in J$, $E_i \in T$.*

3. *If $I \subseteq T = \mathbf{Exp}(\{o_i : i \in J\})$ and for all $i \in J$, $E_i \in T$, then T is an expansion of I.* $\Box$

A word of caution is in place here. In general, a given theory T does not uniquely determine a set J such that $T = \mathbf{Exp}(\{o_i : i \in J\})$. $T \supseteq I$ is an expansion of I if and only if there exists at least one set J such that $T = \mathbf{Exp}(\{o_i : i \in J\})$ and for all $i \in J$, $E_i \in T$.

Before we introduce the translation and prove the results connecting supported models and expansions of translation, we need to introduce one more property of stable sets (and hence expansions as well).

Theorem 10 *([16]). Let the formula ϕ have the property that for every atom a, every occurrence of a appears within the scope of modal operator K. Then, for every stable theory T, $\phi \in T$ or $(\neg\phi) \in T$.* $\Box$

We introduce now the notion of epistemic translation of a logic program. This translation is different from that of Gelfond (cf [5]) and in fact relates to the notion of supported model and not to that of stable model. We assume now that P is a finite set of ground clauses.

Definition 9 *Suppose P is a logic program, and $A \in B_P$. Denote by $\Re(P, A)$ the set of clauses in P having A as the head. Thus,*

$$P = \bigcup_{A \in B_P} \Re(P, A)$$

Let $\Re(P, A) = \{C_1, C_2, \ldots\}$, where each C_i is of the form:

$$A \leftarrow B_1^i \,\&\, \cdots \,\&\, B_{m_i}^i \,\&\, \neg D_1^i \,\&\, \cdots \,\&\, \neg D_{n_i}^i$$

Then the epistemic translation $\mathbf{ET}(P, A)$ of P w.r.t. A is the set of clauses:

$$\{\mathbf{K}B_1^1 \,\&\, \cdots \,\&\, \mathbf{K}B_{m_1}^1 \,\&\, \neg\mathbf{K}D_1^1 \,\&\, \cdots \,\&\, \neg\mathbf{K}D_{n_1}^1 \rightarrow A$$

$$\cdots$$

$$\mathbf{K}B_1^i \,\&\, \cdots \,\&\, \mathbf{K}B_{m_i}^i \,\&\, \neg\mathbf{K}D_1^i \,\&\, \cdots \,\&\, \neg\mathbf{K}D_{n_i}^i \rightarrow A\}$$

together with the sentence:

$$\bigwedge_{i \geq 1} \left(\neg \left(\mathbf{K}B_1^i \,\&\, \cdots \,\&\, \mathbf{K}B_{m_i}^i \,\&\, \neg \mathbf{K}D_1^i \,\&\, \cdots \,\&\, \neg \mathbf{K}D_{n_i}^i \right) \right) \to \neg A$$

The epistemic translation $\mathbf{ET}(P)$ *of the logic program P is*

$$\mathbf{ET}(P) = \bigcup_{A \in B_P} \mathbf{ET}(P, A)$$

As usual, in the above translation, we replace all occurrences of formulas of the form $\neg \neg F$ by F.

Example 7 *A logic program P and its epistemic translation $\mathbf{ET}(P)$ are shown below:*

$P:$	$\mathbf{ET}(P):$
$p \leftarrow q$	$\mathbf{K}q \to p$
$p \leftarrow \neg q$	$\neg \mathbf{K}q \to p$
	$\neg(\mathbf{K}q \,\&\, \neg \mathbf{K}q) \to \neg p$
$q \leftarrow q$	$\mathbf{K}q \to q$
	$\neg \mathbf{K}q \to \neg q$

Theorem 11 *Suppose P is a general logic program and M is a supported model of P. Then $\mathbf{Exp}(Th(M))$ is an expansion of $\mathbf{ET}(P)$.*

Proof. Notice first that the formulas of the translation have the form: $E \Rightarrow p$ or $E \Rightarrow \neg p$ for epistemic formulas E (in fact E's are epistemic justifications for p and $\neg p$). Moreover in the latter case, the formula E is unique (up to reordering of the individual conjuncts).

Since $Th(M) = Cn(M \cup \{\neg p : p \in B_P - M\})$, we would have a proof of the theorem if the following three items are proved:

(a) $\mathbf{ET}(P) \subseteq \mathbf{Exp}(Th(M))$

(b) Whenever $p \in M$ there exists a formula $E \Rightarrow p$ in $\mathbf{ET}(P)$ such that E belongs to $\mathbf{Exp}(Th(M))$.

(c) Whenever $p \in B_P - M$, the unique E such that $E \Rightarrow \neg p \in \mathbf{ET}(P)$ belongs to $\mathbf{Exp}(Th(M))$.

(a) *Case 1.* $\phi = E \Rightarrow p$.
I. If $p \in M$ then $p \in \mathbf{Exp}(Th(M))$, hence $\phi \in \mathbf{Exp}(Th(M))$.

II. If $p \notin M$ then, since M is a supported model all the the bodies of clauses of P having p as the head must be false in M. It is easy to check that the epistemic translation of such a body does not belong to $\mathbf{Exp}(Th(M))$ and consequently, using theorem 10 we find that its negation does belong to $\mathbf{Exp}(Th(M))$. Since the latter is closed under consequence, $E \Rightarrow p \in \mathbf{Exp}(Th(M))$.

Case 2. $\phi = E \Rightarrow \neg p$.
I. If $p \notin M$ then $\neg p \in Th(M)$, hence $E \Rightarrow \neg p \in \mathbf{Exp}(Th(M))$.
II. If $p \in M$ we reason similarly to the case 1.II. Since M is a supported model, at least one of epistemic justifications for p belongs to $\mathbf{Exp}(Th(M))$. Since the unique epistemic justification of $\neg p$ is the conjunction of negations of epistemic justifications for p, it is easy to see that the negation of the epistemic justification of $\neg p$ belongs to $\mathbf{Exp}(Th(M))$. Hence $E \Rightarrow \neg p \in \mathbf{Exp}(Th(M))$.

(b) Let $p \in M$. We need to prove that p possesses at least one epistemic justification in $\mathbf{Exp}(Th(M))$. This, however, follows directly from the fact that M is a supported model of P.

(c) Let $p \notin M$. Since M is a supported model, all the bodies of clauses of P having p as the head must be false in M. Hence their epistemic translations do not belong to $\mathbf{Exp}(Th(M))$. Consequently negations for all the epistemic justifications of p do belong to $\mathbf{Exp}(Th(M))$. Hence their conjunction (which is the epistemic justification of $\neg p$ belongs to $\mathbf{Exp}(Th(M))$.
This completes the proof of the theorem. $\qquad\square$

Theorem 12 *Suppose P is a general logic program. If T is an expansion of $\mathbf{ET}(P)$, then T is of the form $\mathbf{Exp}(Th(M))$ for a unique supported Herbrand model M of P.*

Proof. It is quite clear what M should be, namely let:

$$M = \{p \in B_P : p \in T\}$$

We need to prove three items:

(a) M is a model of P

(b) M is supported

(c) $T = \mathbf{Exp}(Th(M))$.

(a) If $C = A \leftarrow B_1 \& \ldots B_m \& \neg D_1 \& \ldots \& D_m$ is a clause of P, then, if $A \in M$, then M models C. If $A \notin M$, then since $\mathbf{ET}(P) \subseteq T$, A cannot possess an epistemic justification in T. Consider such justification:

$$E = KB_1 \& \ldots \& KB_m \& \neg KD_1 \& \ldots \& \neg KD_n$$

Since E does not belong to T, and as T is an expansion,

$$\neg KB_1 \vee \ldots \vee \neg KB_m \vee KD_1 \vee \ldots \vee KD_n$$

does belong to T. Since T is stable and consistent:

$$B_1 \notin T \vee \ldots \vee B_m \notin T \vee D_1 \in T \vee \ldots \vee D_n \in T$$

This means, according to the definition of M, that M does not satisfy $B_1 \& \ldots B_m \& \neg D_1 \& \ldots \& D_m$. Hence $M \models C$.

(b) We need to show that, whenever $A \in M$, there is a clause $A \leftarrow B_1 \& \ldots \& B_m \& \neg D_1 \& \ldots \& D_m$ of P, such that $M \models B_1 \& \ldots B_m \& \neg D_1 \& \ldots \& D_m$ of P.

Otherwise, for every epistemic justification E of A, $E \notin T$, but then the conjunction of the negations of justifications does belong to T. Since $\mathbf{ET}(P) \subseteq T$, and the justification of $\neg A$ is in T, $\neg A \in T$. This, however, is a contradiction since for all $A \in B_P$, $A \in M$ iff $A \in T$.

(c) Finally, we show that $T = \mathbf{Exp}(Th(M))$. Let us notice that the reasoning of point (b) shows that for every atom $A \in B_P$, $A \in T$ or $\neg A \in T$. This, in particular, implies that $T \cap L$ is a complete theory. Now, $Th(M)$ is also a complete theory and $T \cap L$ and $Th(M)$ contain precisely same atoms. Hence $Th(M) = T \cap L$ and since $T = \mathbf{Exp}(T \cap L)$, the proof is complete. $\quad \square$.

In section 2 we noticed a connection between stable models and extensions of default translation of logic program. Our results of this section provide us with yet another connection with default logic, this time, however, with different structures.

In [18] the connection between autoepistemic logic and default logic was studied in detail and the class of objects in default logic corresponding to autoepistemic expansions was fully identified. These objects, called in [18] *weak extensions* are defined as follows:

Definition 10 *Let (D, W) be a default theory. A theory $T \subseteq L$ is called a weak extension of (D, W) if and only if T satisfies the following fixed point equation:*

$$T = Cn(W \cup \{c(d) : d \in D \& p(d) \in T \& \forall_{\beta \in j(d)} \neg \beta \notin T\})$$

Extensions of default are weak extensions but the converse implication does not need to hold. By *Konolige's translation* of a default theory (D, W) we mean the theory

$$T_{D,W} = W \cup \{Kp(d) \& \bigwedge \{\neg K \neg \beta : \beta \in j(d) \Rightarrow c(d)\} : d \in D\}$$

Let us quote now two results of [18] which are immediately seen to be relevant to our considerations.

Theorem 13 *A theory $S \subseteq L$ is a weak extension of a default theory (D, W) if and only if $\mathbf{Exp}(S)$ is an autoepistemic expansion of $T_{D,W}$.* $\qquad\square$

Theorem 14 *For every theory $I \subseteq L_K$ there exists a default theory (D, W) such that the expansions of T are precisely the same as the weak extensions of $T_{D,W}$. Hence the expressive power of autoepistemic logic is precisely the same as that of default logic with* weak *expansions.* $\qquad\square$

Combining these results and Theorem 12 together, we get:

Corollary 3 *For every general logic program P there exists a default theory (D, W) such that for every subset M of B_P: M is a supported model for P if and only if $Th(M)$ is a weak extension of (D, W).* $\qquad\square$

4   Conclusions

It is always surprising when constructions from seemingly unrelated domains turn out to be closely connected. Our results as well as other results mentioned in section 2 point to the existence of the same basic principles behind various modes of reasoning considered by the Artificial Intelligence community and by various interpretations of negation considered by the Logic Programming community. We can only hope that a single, unifying, approach will eventually emerge.

The primary aim of this paper is to clarify the various relationships between stable models of logic programs, supported models of logic programs, the default semantics for logic programs and the autoepistemic semantics for logic programs. The first two of these claim that the meaning of a program is just the set of models of the program possessing certain properties. On the other hand, the last two claim that the program's meaning is exactly that of an (appropriately defined) translation of the program into a different logic (viz. default logic and autoepistemic logic). In this paper, we have studied:

1. the connection between stable and supported models (Section 2).

2. the relationship between supported models and default logics (Corollary 3).

3. the relationship between supported models of a program and expansions of the program's autoepistemic translation (Theorems 11 and 12).

Thus, these results demonstrate the intricate, yet intimate, relationship between differing formalisms for negation in logic programming. We strongly believe that a thorough study of the inter-relationsips between varying formalisms for treating negation in logic programming and in AI are necessary, as there are far too many such formalisms today.

Acknowledgements. Wiktor Marek's work was supported by National Science Foundation grant RII 8610671 and the Commonwealth of Kentucky EPSCoR program. V.S. Subrahmanian's work was funded by U.S. Air Force Contract F30602-85-C-0008. The suggestions of the anonymous referees helped improve the presentation. We are indebted to Howard Blair for useful discussions on Proposition 4.

References

[1] K. R. Apt, H. A. Blair. (1988) *Arithmetic Complexity of the Perfect Models of Stratified Logic Programs*, Proc. 5th Intl. Conf./Symp. on Logic Programming, MIT Press.

[2] K. R. Apt, H.A. Blair, A. Walker. (1988) *Towards a Theory of Declarative Knowledge*, in: Jack Minker, ed. "Foundations of Deductive Databases and Logic Programming" , Morgan Kaufmann, pp. 89–148.

[3] H. A. Blair. (1986) *Decidability in the Herbrand Base*, Proc. of the Workshop on Foundations of Deductive Databases and Logic Programming, ed. Jack Minker, Washington DC.

[4] K. L. Clark. (1978) *Negation as Failure*, in: H. Gallaire and J. Minker, eds. "Logic and Databases" , Plenum Press.

[5] M. Gelfond. (1987) *Stratified autoepistemic theories*, unpublished note.

[6] M. Gelfond, V. Lifschitz. (1988) *The Stable Model Semantics for Logic Programming*, in Proc. of the 5th Intl. Conf./Symp. on Logic Programming, MIT Press.

[7] M. Gelfond, H. Przymusińska. (1986) *On the Relationship between Autoepistemic Logic and Parallel Circumscription*, Proc. of the Intl. Symp. on Methodologies for Intelligent Systems, pp. 256–262.

[8] M. Gelfond, H. Przymusińska, T. Przymusiński. (1986) *The Extended Closed World Assumption and its Relationship to Parallel Circumscription*, Proc. Symp. on Principles of Database Systems, pp. 133–139.

[9] M. Gelfond, H. Przymusińska, T. Przymusiński. (1988) *On the Relationship between Circumscription and Negation as Failure*, ISMIS'88.

[10] T. Imielinski. (1986) *Results on Translating Defaults to Circumscription*, Artificial Intelligence 32, pp. 131–146.

[11] K. Konolige. (1988) *On the Relation between Default and Autoepistemic Logic*, Artificial Intelligence 35, pp. 343–382.

[12] V. Lifschitz. (1985) *Closed World Databases and Circumscription*, Artificial Intelligence 27, pp. 229–235.

[13] J. W. Lloyd. (1984) *Foundations of Logic Programming.* Springer Verlag.

[14] W. Marek. (1986) *Stable theories in autoepistemic logic*, to appear in: Fundamenta Informaticae.

[15] W. Marek and V. S. Subrahmanian. (1988) *The Relationship Between Stable, Supported, Default and Auteo-Epistemic Semantics for General Logic Programs*, submitted.

[16] W. Marek, M. Truszczynski. (1988) *Autoepistemic Logic*, submitted to a technical journal.

[17] W. Marek, M. Truszczynski. (1988) *Stable semantics for logic programs and default theories*, TR 127-88, Department of Computer Science, University of Kentucky.

[18] W. Marek, M. Truszczynski. (1988) *Note on relationship of autoepistemic logic and default logic*, unpublished note.

[19] J. McCarthy. (1980) *Circumscription – A Form of Non-Monotonic Reasoning*, Artificial Intelligence 13, pp. 27–39.

[20] J. McCarthy (1986) *Applications of Circumscription to Formalizing Common-Sense Knowledge*, Artificial Intelligence 28, pp. 89–116.

[21] R. C. Moore. (1985) *Semantical Considerations on Non-Monotonic Logic*, Artificial Intelligence 25, pp. 75–94.

[22] T. Przymusiński. (1988) *On the Declarative and Procedural Semantics of Stratified Deductive Databases*, in: J. Minker, ed. "Foundations of Deductive Databases and Logic Programming ", Morgan Kaufmann, pp. 193–216.

[23] T. Przymusiński. (1988) *On the Relationship between Logic Programming and Non-Monotonic Reasoning*, in: Proc. AAAI 1988.

[24] R. Reiter. (1980) *A Logic for Default Reasoning*, Artificial Intelligence 13, pp. 81–132.

[25] J. C. Shepherdson. (1984) *Negation as Failure: A Comparison of Clark's Completed Database and Reiter's Closed World Assumption*, J. of Logic Programming 1, pp. 51–79.

[26] A. Van Gelder. (1988) *Negation as Failure Using Tight Derivations for General Logic Programs*, in: J. Minker, ed. "Foundations of Deductive Databases and Logic Programming " , Morgan Kaufmann, pp. 149–176.

[27] W. W. Zadrożny. (1987) *A Theory of Default Reasoning*, Proc. AAAI 1987, pp. 385–390.

Semantics of Concurrency

Semantic models for a version of PARLOG

Frank S. de Boer[1]**, Joost N. Kok**[2]**,
Catuscia Palamidessi**[3] **and Jan J.M.M. Rutten**[1]

[1]Centre for Mathematics and Computer Science,
P.O. Box 4079, 1009 AB Amsterdam, The Netherlands

[2]Department of Computer Science, University of Utrecht,
P.O. Box 80089, 3508 TB Utrecht, The Netherlands

[3]Dipartimento di Informatica, Università di Pisa,
Corso Italia 40, 56100 Pisa, Italy

Abstract. This paper gives four semantics for PARLOG: two operational semantics based on a transition system, a declarative semantics and a denotational semantics. One operational and the declarative semantics model the success set of a PARLOG program, that is, the set of computed answer substitutions corresponding to all successfully terminating computations. The other operational and the denotational semantics model also deadlock and infinite computations. For the declarative and the denotational semantics we extend standard notions like unification in order to cope with the synchronization mechanism of PARLOG. The basic mathematical structure for the declarative semantics is the set of finite streams of substitutions. In the denotational semantics we use tree-like structures that are labelled with streams of substitutions. We look at the relations between the different models: First we relate the two operational semantics and next we show the relation of the declarative and denotational semantics with their operational counterparts. We treat a version of PARLOG because we do not cover all aspects of the language.

Key words and phrases: operational semantics, denotational semantics, declarative semantics, parallelism, concurrent logic languages, correctness, complete metric spaces.

1   Introduction.

The language PARLOG [9,10,17], as well as most of the concurrent logic languages, is based on the Horn Clause Logic (HCL) plus some mechanisms for expressing concurrency. One of the main drawbacks of this approach is that these new mechanisms heavily affect the clean declarative understanding of HCL. Indeed, although many operational semantics have been investigated ([26,27,28,3,16,4]), a satisfactory declarative one is still to be defined. PARLOG belongs to a class of concurrent logic languages whose main features are:

- the *input-constraints*, on which the mechanism of synchronization between AND-processes is based, and

Part of this work was carried out in the context of ESPRIT 415: Parallel Architectures and Languages for Advanced Information Processing – a VLSI-directed approach.

- the presence of *commit*, that realizes the *don't know nondeterminism*, controlled by guards.

Other languages in this class are Guarded Horn Clauses [32,33], Concurrent Prolog [29,30], and their flat versions. These mechanisms affect the semantics of the pure underlying language in several ways [31]:

- the *success set* is reduced by the input-constraints,

- the *finite failure set* is enlarged by the commit, and modified (i.e., either reduced or enlarged) by the input-constraints,

- the *infinite failure set* is modified both by the commit and the input-constraints.

In this paper we address the problem of characterizing these new sets, for PARLOG, first in a declarative and then in a compositional way (i.e., by giving the meaning of a composite goal in terms of the meaning of its conjuncts). We deal with a version of PARLOG. For example, we do not consider unification related primitives, OR-parallel aspects and local deadlock in deep guards.

First, we describe these sets by a formal operational semantics based on a transition relation (in the style of [18], see also [27,16,4] for similar approaches). The operational meaning is given in terms of sets of *words* (or *streams*) of substitutions, that correspond to the answers computed during the derivation.

Next, we characterize declaratively the new success set, as the least fixpoint of an *immediate consequence* operator on interpretations. (The full model-theoretic semantics is still under investigation.) Our approach can be considered an evolution of the one developed in [21] and [22]. The basic idea there is to model the ability of a process to produce and to consume data structures. This is done by introducing annotations on data structures (terms) and by extending the Herbrand universe with variables (see also [15] and [14]). However, the declarative semantics presented in those papers is not able to fully characterize the behaviour of concurrent logic languages. The main problem has to do with the situation of *deadlock* that arises when two processes are obliged to wait for each other for bindings. Consider, for example, the goal $\leftarrow p(x, y), q(x, y)$ and the programs

$$P_1 = \{p(a, b) \leftarrow |., \quad q(a, b) \leftarrow |.\},$$

$$P_2 = \{p(z, b) \leftarrow |r(z)., \quad r(a) \leftarrow |., \quad q(a, b) \leftarrow |.\},$$

and assume that in both cases the first argument of p and the second argument of q are input-constrained (expressed in PARLOG by the declaration modes $D_1 = \{p(?, \hat{\ }), q(\hat{\ }, ?)\}$, and $D_2 = \{p(?, \hat{\ }), q(\hat{\ }, ?), r(?)\}$, respectively). According to the operational semantics, the computation of the goal cannot succeed in P_1 (it results in a deadlock), whilst in P_2 always can. Now it is the case that the approach presented in [21] and [22] is not able to distinguish between the two situations. Indeed, $r(a^+, b^+)$ (r producing a and b) happens there to be *true* in the models (and in the least fixpoint interpretation) of both the programs. So, a full completeness result (between the declarative and the operational semantics) could not be obtained. For a detailed discussion of this problem see also [23].

Our solution to this problem consists in enriching the interpretations with streams of substitutions. Due to the presence of guards, whose evaluation has to be interpreted as an atomic action (internal action), the streams of the operational semantics offer too little structure, and we have to add some delimiters to represent *critical sections*. We call these new structures *sequences*. This allows us to characterize declaratively (and, therefore, compositionally) the bindings obtained at different stages in the computation. In this way we obtain a full equivalence result. An other basic difference with respect to the previous approach is to annotate the variables instead of the data constructors. This allows us to extend the unification theory ([11,20]) in order to deal with input-constraints in a formal way. We also give an extended algorithm for the computation of the (extended) most general unifier. Moreover, we introduce the notion of parallel composition of substitutions, that allows us to model the combination of the substitutions computed by and-parallel processes.

Other compositional models for the success set are presented in [26] and [24]. Both these approaches are based on streams of input/output *simple* substitutions, where *simple* means that the bindings are of the form x/y or $x/f(x_1, ..., x_n)$. This restriction introduces additional complications for modeling the full unification mechanism. Thanks to our extended unification theory, we deal directly with (general) substitutions, and the correspondence with the operational semantics is therefore simpler and more intuitive.

Finally we consider the problem of characterizing the finite failures and the infinite computations in a compositional way. It turns out that the streams of the declarative semantics offer again too little structure, but also the sequences introduced in the declarative semantics are not powerfull enough. Indeed, in order to model the failure set, we need not only to distinguish between external and internal computation steps, but also between different points of nondeterministic choice.

To justify this, let's illustrate how the absence of nondeterminism informations (branching informations) causes our operational semantics to be *not* compositional. Consider the programs

$$P_1 = \{p(x) \leftarrow |q(x).,\ \ p(x) \leftarrow |r(x).,\ \ q(a) \leftarrow |.\ \ r(b) \leftarrow |.\ \ s(a) \leftarrow |.\},$$

$$P_2 = \{p(x) \leftarrow |q(x).,\ \ q(a) \leftarrow |.\ \ q(b) \leftarrow |.\ \ s(a) \leftarrow |.\},$$

with mode declarations $D_1 = \{p(?), q(?), r(?), s(\hat{})\}$, and $D_2 = \{p(?), q(?), s(\hat{})\}$, respectively. Consider the goal $\leftarrow p(y)$. Operationally, in both P_1 and P_2 it will suspend waiting for a binding on y (either a or b). However, if we extend the goal with an atom $s(x)$, thus yielding the goal $\leftarrow p(y), s(y)$, then we get *different* operational meanings. In P_1 the goal can fail (due to the choice of the wrong clause for $p(y)$), whereas in P_2 it cannot.

A possible way to provide these branching informations is to use tree-like structures. However, it still remains an open question what exactly is the minimal information needed to obtain a compositional semantics. This question is related to the problem of *full abstractness*. A fully abstract denotational semantics for Flat-Concurrent Prolog is described in [16]. Their approach is based on *suspension sets*, which are a more abstract structure than the three-like one. However, it is not clear how their result can be extended to the general case of non-flat guards. The same applies to the declarative approach taken in [13] to characterize the finite failures.

In our approach we code the branching informations by using trees labelled with streams of substitutions. We see them as elements of complete metric spaces, satisfying so-called reflexive domain equations ([8], [2]). We use a *denotational* style: for every operator in the language we define a semantic operator that can be seen as a function on these spaces. The meaning of a goal can then be given by a semantic operator that results to be the *unique* fixpoint of a *contraction* on the functional metric spaces ([8], [2]). The relation of this denotational semantics with respect to the operational one is obtained via an *abstraction operator*, that identifies some denotations. The correctness of the denotational semantics is then stated as the equality between the result of this abstraction and the operational semantics.

Due to space limitations we only give proofs in outline form. Full proofs can be found in [25] (for the declarative part) and in [6] (for the denotational part).

The definition of PARLOG has been changed with respect to the previous versions. We consider the one described in [17].

2 The language PARLOG

To describe the syntax of the language PARLOG we introduce the following sets:

- The set of atoms, with typical elements A, B, H, we denote by *Atom*.

- The set of conjunctions, with typical elements $\bar{A}, \bar{B}, \bar{G}$, we denote by *Conj*.

- The set of goals, with typical elements $\leftarrow \bar{A}, \leftarrow \bar{B}, \leftarrow \bar{G}$, we denote by *Goal*.

- The set of clauses, with typical element C, we denote by *Clause*.

- The set of programs, with typical element W, we denote by *Prog*.

Conjunctions are of the form: $\bar{A} = A_1, \ldots, A_n$. A special element in *Conj* is *true*, denoting the empty conjunct. With $\square$ we denote the goal $\leftarrow true$. A clause is of the form $C = H \leftarrow \bar{G}|\bar{B}$, where H, $\bar{G}$ and $\bar{B}$ are called the head, the guard, and the body of the clause, respectively. The symbol $|$ is called the commit operator. We do not consider operators (like ;) that impose any ordering on clauses. Every program W consists of a finite set of clauses together with a so-called *mode declaration*, which specifies for every predicate which of its arguments are *input* and *output*. They are indicated by the symbols ? and ^ respectively. So, for instance, the declaration $p(?, ?, \hat{})$ specifies that the first two arguments of p are *input* and the third one is *output*.

An atom A in a goal is seen as an (AND-) process. Its computation proceeds by looking for a *candidate clause* in W. A clause is candidate if its head H *input-unifies* with A (i.e. the input arguments unify) and the computation of the guard succeeds, both without binding the (variables in the) input arguments of A. If there are candidate clauses, then the computation of A *commits* to one of them (i.e. no backtraking will take place), the *output-unification* is performed and A is replaced by the body of the clause. If no clauses are candidate but there are *suspended* clauses (i.e. clauses in which the input unification would succeed and bind the input-arguments), then the computation of A *suspends*, and will be resumed when its (input) arguments get bound by other processes in the goal. If a guard would succeed by binding the input-arguments (of A), then an *error* is generated (*unsafe guard*). If none of this cases applies, then the process A and the whole goal *fail*. Of course, a failure occurs also when all the processes in the goal get suspended (*deadlock*).

To simplify the discussion, we do not deal with the *error* case. More precisely, we include this case into the suspension case. So, we consider a suspension mechanism similar to the one of GHC, namely: *a clause suspends if either the input-unification or the goal evaluation would instantiate the input-arguments of A.*

3 Operational semantics.

For the rest of the paper let W denote a fixed program. The set of variables occurring in a conjunction $\bar{A}$ is indicated by $\mathcal{V}(\bar{A})$. We postulate a function *invar* that gives for every atom A the set of variables occurring in those arguments of A that are specified as input by the mode declaration of W. Given a set of variables V, W_V denotes the program whose clauses are *variants* (see [20]), with respect to V, of the clauses of W.

We introduce the set of substitutions $(\vartheta, \gamma \in)$ *Subst*. ϵ is the *empty substitution*. For V a finite set of variables, we use $\vartheta_{|V}$ to denote the restriction of ϑ to V. Further we have the familiar notion of *mgu*, which is a partial function from pairs of atoms to substitutions. We introduce the notions of *input* and *output* mgu's: Consider two atoms $A = p(t_1, ..., t_n)$ and $A' = p(t'_1, ..., t'_n)$. Assume that the declaration-mode of p has the symbol ? (input-mode) on the arguments $i_1, ..., i_k$. Then, $mgu_i(A, A')$ denotes $mgu(\{\{t_{i_1}, t'_{i_1}\}, ... \{t_{i_k}, t'_{i_k}\}\})$. In a similar way we define $mgu_o(A, A')$ to be the *mgu* of the output arguments.

The operational semantics will be based on the following *transition relation*:

Definition 3.1 (Transition relation)
Let $\to \subseteq (Goal \times Subst) \times (Goal \times Subst)$ be the smallest relation satisfying

1. If $\exists H \leftarrow \bar{G}|\bar{B} \in W_{\mathcal{V}(A)}, \exists mgu_i(A\vartheta, H)$
   $[<\leftarrow \bar{G}, mgu_i(A\vartheta, H) > \overset{*}{\to} < \square, \vartheta' >, \text{ and } \vartheta'|_{invar(A\vartheta)} = \epsilon],$
   then $<\leftarrow A, \vartheta > \to <\leftarrow outunif(A\vartheta, H\vartheta'), \bar{B}, \vartheta\vartheta' >$

2. If $\exists mgu_o(A\vartheta, H\vartheta'),$
   then $<\leftarrow outunif(A\vartheta, H\vartheta'), \bar{B}, \vartheta' > \to <\leftarrow \bar{B}, \vartheta' mgu_o(A\vartheta, H\vartheta') > .$

3. If $<\leftarrow \bar{A}, \vartheta > \to <\leftarrow \bar{A}', \vartheta' > \mid < \square, \vartheta' >$
   then $<\leftarrow \bar{A}, \bar{B}, \vartheta > \to <\leftarrow \bar{A}', \bar{B}, \vartheta' > \mid <\leftarrow \bar{B}, \vartheta' >$
          $<\leftarrow \bar{B}, \bar{A}, \vartheta > \to <\leftarrow \bar{B}, \bar{A}', \vartheta' > \mid <\leftarrow \bar{B}, \vartheta' >$

                                                                    $\diamond$

In these transitions, ϑ represents the substitution that has been computed until that moment. In 1., it is stated that we can resolve $\leftarrow A$ if we can find a (renamed) clause in our program with a head H that can be input-unified with A; moreover, the refutation of the guard $\bar{G}$ of that clause must terminate successfully and the total substitution ϑ' must not instantiate any input variables of $A\vartheta$. The transition 2. represents the first action performed after the commitment, namely the output-unification. A conjunction, in 3., is evaluated by the parallel execution of its conjuncts, modelled here by interleaving. In the following definition we give the operational semantics.

Definition 3.2 (Operational semantics)
We define

$$\mathcal{O}_1 : Goal \to M_1, \quad \text{with } M_1 = \mathcal{P}(Subst)$$
$$\mathcal{O}_2 : Goal \to M_2, \quad \text{with } M_2 = \mathcal{P}(Subst_\delta^\infty).$$

(Here $Subst_\delta^\infty = Subst^+ \cup Subst^\omega \cup Subst^*.\{\delta\}$, with typical element $\vartheta_1 \cdots \vartheta_n \cdots$; the symbol δ denotes failure; $\mathcal{P}(X)$ is the set of all the subsets of X.)

We put $\mathcal{O}_i[\![\leftarrow true]\!] = \{\epsilon\}$, and

$$\mathcal{O}_1[\![\leftarrow \bar{A}]\!] = \{\vartheta_{|\mathcal{V}(\bar{A})} \mid <\leftarrow \bar{A}, \epsilon > \overset{*}{\to} < \square, \vartheta >\};$$

$$\mathcal{O}_2[\![\leftarrow \bar{A}]\!] = \{(\vartheta_1 \cdots \vartheta_n)_{|\mathcal{V}(\bar{A})} \in Subst^+ \mid$$
$$<\leftarrow \bar{A}, \epsilon > \to <\leftarrow \bar{A}_1, \vartheta_1 > \to \cdots \to < \square, \vartheta_n >\}$$
$$\cup \ \{(\vartheta_1 \cdots \vartheta_n)_{|\mathcal{V}(\bar{A})}.\delta \in Subst^*.\{\delta\} \mid$$
$$<\leftarrow \bar{A}, \epsilon > \to \cdots \to <\leftarrow \bar{A}_n, \vartheta_n > \not\to \wedge \leftarrow \bar{A}_n \neq \square\}$$
$$\cup \ \{(\vartheta_1 \cdots)_{|\mathcal{V}(\bar{A})} \in Subst^\omega \mid <\leftarrow \bar{A}, \epsilon > \to <\leftarrow \bar{A}_1, \vartheta_1 > \to \cdots\}.$$

                                                                    $\diamond$

The *success set* for $\leftarrow \bar{A}$ is given by $\mathcal{O}_1[\![\leftarrow \bar{A}]\!]$: it contains all computed answer substitutions corresponding to all successfully terminating computations. The set $\mathcal{O}_2[\![\leftarrow \bar{A}]\!]$ takes in addition into account all failing and infinite computations, represented by elements of $Subst^* \cdot \{\delta\}$ and $Subst^\omega$, respectively. The relation between $\mathcal{O}_1$ and $\mathcal{O}_2$ is obvious: If we set

$$last(X) = \{\vartheta \mid \exists s \in Subst^*(s.\vartheta \in X)\}$$

then we have: $\mathcal{O}_1 = last \circ \mathcal{O}_2$.

In the following sections, $\mathcal{O}_1$ and $\mathcal{O}_2$ will be related to a declarative and a denotational semantics, respectively.

4 Declarative semantics.

In this section we define the declarative (fixpoint) semantics of PARLOG. We make use of an extended notion of Herbrand base and interpretations, enriched with variables (that allows to model the notion of *computed substitution*, [22],[15],[14]), and with *annotations* (that allows to model the synchronization mechanism of concurrent logic languages, see [21] and [22] for similar approaches). We extend the standard notions of the unification theory ([11], [20]) in a formal framework. Moreover, we introduce the notion of *parallel composition*, that allows to formalize the combination (plus consistency check) of the substitutions computed by subgoals run in parallel. Finally, we introduce the notion of *sequences of substitutions*, that allows to overcome the difficulties presented in [22] about the situations of deadlock. A similar construction has been made for defining the declarative semantics of GHC ([5], [25]). For the proofs we refer to [25].

4.1 Annotated variables.

In order to model the synchronization mechanism of PARLOG we introduce the notion of *annotated variable*. The annotation can occur on a variable in the goal, and it means that such a variable is in an input-argument and therefore cannot be bound, during the derivation step, before commitment. In other words, such a variable can receive bindings from the execution of other atoms in the goals, but cannot produce bindings by the execution of the atom in which it occurs (before commitment).

We will denote the set of variables, with typical elements $x, y, \ldots$, by Var, and the set of the annotated variables, with typical elements $x^-, y^-, \ldots$, by Var^-. We can consider "$-$" as a bijective mapping $^- : Var \to Var^-$. The set of terms $Term$ is extended on the new set of variables $Var \cup Var^-$. The set of variables occurring in the term t is denoted by $\mathcal{V}(t)$. For $V \subseteq Var$, $t^{|V^-}$ is the term obtained by replacing in t every variable $x \in V$ by x^-. The term $t^{|Var^-}$ will be simply denoted by t^-.

A substitution ϑ is now a mapping $\vartheta : Var \cup Var^- \to Term$, such that only a finite number of variables are mapped into terms different from themselves. In order to model the difference between producing and receiving a binding we introduce an asymmetry in the definition of the application of a substitution ϑ to a term (or atom, or formula) t:

$$t\vartheta = \begin{cases} \vartheta(x) & \text{if } t = x \in Var \\ \vartheta(x^-) & \text{if } t = x^- \in Var^- \text{ and } \vartheta(x^-) \neq x^- \\ \vartheta(x)^- & \text{if } t = x^- \in Var^- \text{ and } \vartheta(x^-) = x^- \\ f(t_1\vartheta, \ldots, t_n\vartheta) & \text{if } t = f(t_1, \ldots, t_n) \end{cases}$$

The reason why the application of ϑ to x^- can result in $\vartheta(x)^-$ (instead of $\vartheta(x)$) is related to the peculiarity of the input-mode constraint of PARLOG. In fact, it does not apply to a specific variable (as in CP), but to the arguments of the atom. Therefore, when an annotated variable is bound to a term t, all the variables occurring in t get under the influence of the input-mode constraint, and therefore they have to inherit the annotation.

We factorize the set of substitution with respect to the equivalence relation $\vartheta_1 \equiv \vartheta_2$ *iff* $\forall x \in Var \cup Var^-[x\vartheta_1 = x\vartheta_2]$. From now on, a substitution ϑ will indicate its equivalence class.

Example 4.1 Consider the atom $A = p(f(x, y), x, y)$. We annotate the variables in A so to get $A^- = p(f(x^-, y^-), x^-, y^-)$. Consider now the substitution $\vartheta = \{x/g(z), y/h(w), y^-/h(a)\}$. We have: $A^-\vartheta = p(f(g(z^-), h(a)), g(z^-), h(a)))$. $\diamond$

The notion of composition $\vartheta_1\vartheta_2$, of two substitutions, ϑ_1 and ϑ_2 is extended as follows

$$\forall x \in Var \cup Var^-[x(\vartheta_1\vartheta_2) = (x\vartheta_1)\vartheta_2].$$

The composition is associative and the empty substitution ϵ is the neutral element. ϑ is called *idempotent* iff $\vartheta\vartheta = \vartheta$. Given a set of sets of terms M, we define ϑ to be an unifier for M iff

$$\forall S \in M : \forall t_1, t_2 \in S\ [t_1\vartheta = t_2\vartheta \text{ and } t_1^-\vartheta = t_2^-\vartheta].$$

The ordering on substitutions is the standard one, namely: $\vartheta_1 \leq \vartheta_2$ *iff* $\exists \vartheta_3\ [\vartheta_1\vartheta_3 = \vartheta_2]$ (ϑ_1 *is more general than* ϑ_2). The set of mgu's (most general unifiers) of a set of sets of terms M is denoted by $mgu(M)$.

We give an extended version of the unification algorithm, based on the one presented in [1], that works on finite sets of pairs. Given a finite set of finite sets of terms M, consider the (finite) set of pairs

$$M_{pairs} = \bigcup_{S \in M} \{< t, u >|\ t, u \in S\}.$$

We define the unifiers of a set $\{< t_1, u_1 >, \ldots, < t_n, u_n >\}$ as the ones of $\{\{t_1, u_1\}, \ldots, \{t_n, u_n\}\}$. Of course, M and M_{pairs} are equivalent (i.e. they have the same unifiers). A set of pairs is called *solved* if it is of the form

$$\{< x_1, t_1 >, \ldots, < x_n, t_n >\}$$

where all the x_i's are distinct elements of $Var \cup Var^-$, $x_i \notin \mathcal{V}(t_1, \ldots, t_n)$, and, if $x_i \in Var$ and $t_i \neq x_i^-$, then $x_i^- \notin \mathcal{V}(x_1, \ldots, x_n, t_1, \ldots, t_n)$. For P solved, define $\gamma_P = \{x_1/t_1, \ldots, x_n/t_n\}$, and $\delta_P = \gamma_P\gamma_P$.

The following algorithm transforms a set of pairs into an equivalent one which is solved, or halts with failure if the set has no unifiers.

Definition 4.2 (Extended unification algorithm)

- Let P, P' be sets of pairs. Define $P \Rightarrow P'$ if P' is obtained from P by choosing in P a pair of the form below and by performing the corresponding action

    1. $< f(t_1, ..., t_n), f(u_1, ..., u_n) >$ replace by the pairs
                                                                       $< t_1, u_1 >, ..., < t_n, u_n >$

2. $< f(t_1, ..., t_n), g(u_1, ..., u_n) >$, where $f \neq g$ halt with failure

3. $< x, x >$ where $x \in Var \cup Var^-$ delete the pair

4. $< t, x >$ where $x \in Var \cup Var^-$,   replace by the pair $< x, t >$
          $t \notin Var \cup Var^-$

5. $< x, t >$ where $x \in Var$, $x \neq t$, $x^- \neq t$,   if $x \in \mathcal{V}(t)$ or $x^- \in \mathcal{V}(t)$
          x or x^- occurs in other pairs   then halt with failure
                                       else apply the substitution
                                       $\{x/t\}$ to all the other pairs

6. $< x, x^- >$ where $x \in Var$,   apply the substitution
          and x occurs in other pairs $\{x/x^-\}$ to all the other pairs

7. $< x^-, t >$ where $x^- \in Var^-$, $x^- \neq t$ if $x^- \in \mathcal{V}(t)$
          and x^- occurs in other pairs   then halt with failure
                                         else apply the substitution
                                       $\{x^-/t\}$ to all the other pairs.

We will write $P \Rightarrow \textit{fail}$ if a failure is detected (steps 2, 5 or 7).

- Let $\Rightarrow^*$ be the reflexive-transitive closure of the relation $\Rightarrow$, and let P_{sol} be the set $P_{sol} = \{P' \mid symm(P) \Rightarrow^* P', \text{ and } P' \text{ is solved}\}$, where

$$symm(\{< t_1, u_1 >, \ldots, < t_n, u_n >\}) = \{< t_1, u_1 >, \ldots, < t_n, u_n >\}$$
$$\cup \ \{< t_1^-, u_1^- >, \ldots, < t_n^-, u_n^- >\}.$$

The set of substitutions determined by the algorithm is

$$\Delta(P) = \{\delta_{P'} \mid P' \in P_{sol}\}. \qquad\qquad \diamond$$

The following proposition shows that the set of the idempotent most general unifiers of M is finite and can be computed in finite time by the extended unification algorithm.

Proposition 4.3   Let P be a finite set of pairs, and M be a finite set of finite sets of terms.

1. **(finiteness)** The relation $\Rightarrow$ is *finitely-branching* and *noetherian* (i.e. *terminating*).

2. **(solved form)** If P is in *normal form* (i.e. there exist no P' such that $P \Rightarrow P'$), then P is in solved form.

3. **(soundness)** $\Delta(P) \subseteq mgu(P)$

4. **(completeness)** $mgu(M) \subseteq \Delta(M_{pairs})$.

5. $P \Rightarrow^* \textit{fail}$ iff P is not unifiable. $\diamond$

4.2   Parallel composition on substitutions.

In this section we introduce the notion of *parallel composition* on substitutions and on sets of substitutions, both denoted by $\hat{\circ}$. Intuitively, the parallel composition is meant to be the formalization of one of the basic operations performed by the *parallel execution model* of logic programs. When two atoms A_1 and A_2 (in the same goal) are run in parallel, the associated computed answer substitutions ϑ_1 and ϑ_2 have to be combined, afterwards, in order to get the final result. This operation can be performed in the following way: Consider the set of all the pairs corresponding to the bindings of both ϑ_1 and ϑ_2. Then, compute the most general unifier of such a set. Note that the *consistency check* corresponds to a verification that such a set is unifiable.

Definition 4.4 In the following, $\mathcal{S}(\vartheta)$ is the set of sets $\{\{x,t\} \mid x/t \in \vartheta\}$. Θ_1, Θ_2 are sets of substitutions.

1. $\vartheta_1 \hat{\circ} \vartheta_2 = mgu(\mathcal{S}(\vartheta_1) \cup \mathcal{S}(\vartheta_2))$.

2. $\Theta_1 \hat{\circ} \Theta_2 = \displaystyle\bigcup_{\vartheta_1 \in \Theta_1, \vartheta_2 \in \Theta_2} \vartheta_1 \hat{\circ} \vartheta_2$.

We will denote the sets $\{\vartheta\} \hat{\circ} \Theta$ and $\Theta \hat{\circ} \{\vartheta\}$ by $\vartheta \hat{\circ} \Theta$ and $\Theta \hat{\circ} \vartheta$ respectively.   ◇

Example 4.5

1. Consider the program $\{p(f(a)) \leftarrow |., q(f(a)) \leftarrow |.\}$, with declaration-mode $\{p(?), q(\hat{\ })\}$, and consider the goal $\leftarrow p(x), q(x)$. We annotate the variable x, in $p(x)$, in order to express the input-mode constraint. We have
   $mgu(p(x^-), p(f(a))) = \{\vartheta_1\}$, where $\vartheta_1 = \{x^-/f(a)\}$, and
   $mgu(q(x), q(f(a))) = \{\vartheta_2\}$, where $\vartheta_2 = \{x/f(a)\}$.
   Now observe that $\vartheta_1 \in mgu(\mathcal{S}(\vartheta_1))$, $\vartheta_2 \in mgu(\mathcal{S}(\vartheta_2))$ and $\vartheta_1 \leq \vartheta_2$, therefore $\vartheta_2 \in \vartheta_1 \hat{\circ} \vartheta_2$.

2. Consider now the same program and goal as before, but let the declaration mode be $\{p(?), q(?)\}$. We have $mgu(p(x^-), p(f(a))) = mgu(q(x^-), q(f(a))) = \{\vartheta_1\}$, and $\vartheta_1 \in \vartheta_1 \hat{\circ} \vartheta_1$, whilst $\vartheta_2 \notin \vartheta_1 \hat{\circ} \vartheta_1$.

In 1. the goal can be refuted by a suitable ordering on the execution of the atoms ($q(x)$ before $p(x)$). This corresponds to get a substitution (ϑ_2), that does not bind any annotated (i.e. input-constrained) variable. This is not the case in 2., and indeed no refutation are possible.   ◇

4.3   Sequences of substitutions.

As shown in [15], and [14], the computed bindings in HCL can be declaratively modeled by using a not ground Herbrand Base, or equivalently, a set of couples atom-substitution. However, when the input-constraints are present, it is not sufficient to consider only a substitution. In fact, as shown in [21] and [22], a *flat* representation of the computed bindings is not powerful enough to model the *effects* of the possible interleavings in the executions of the atoms in a goal. Namely, the possibility for atoms to provide each other the bindings necessary for going on in the respective computations. In a sense, we have to *register* the whole history of the execution of the atom, and therefore we have to deal with *sequences of substitutions*. Since we only model declaratively the success set, we need to consider only finite sequences. Anyway, the set $Subst^+$ used for the operational semantics is still a too weak structure. Indeed, to represent the *critical sections* given by the input-unification and the guard evaluation, we need to separate a subsequence from the rest.

Definition 4.6 The finite sequences of substitutions, with typical element s, are defined by the following (abstract) syntax

$$s ::= \vartheta \mid [s] \mid s_1.s_2$$
  ◇

The role of the squared brackets, is to delimitate the *critical sections*. Their meaning will be clarified by the definition of the *interleaving operator*. We introduce the following notations. If S and S' are sets of sequences, then $S.S' \stackrel{def}{=} \{s.s' \mid s \in S, s' \in S'\}$ and $[S] \stackrel{def}{=} \{[s] \mid s \in S\}$. If $s = \vartheta'.s'$, then $\vartheta \hat{\circ} s \stackrel{def}{=} (\vartheta \hat{\circ} \vartheta').s'$ and $\vartheta \hat{\circ} [s] \stackrel{def}{=} [(\vartheta \hat{\circ} \vartheta').s']$. For Θ a set of substitution we have $\Theta \hat{\circ} s \stackrel{def}{=} \bigcup_{\vartheta \in \Theta} \vartheta \hat{\circ} s$.

Definition 4.7 (Interleaving operator).

1. $s_1 \parallel s_2 = \quad \{\vartheta.s \mid \exists s' : \vartheta.s' = s_1, s \in s' \parallel s_2\}$
   $\cup \quad \{\vartheta.s \mid \exists s' : \vartheta.s' = s_2, s \in s' \parallel s_1\}$
   $\cup \quad \{[s'].s \mid \exists s'' : [s'].s'' = s_1, s \in s'' \parallel s_2\}$
   $\cup \quad \{[s'].s \mid \exists s'' : [s'].s'' = s_2, s \in s'' \parallel s_1\}$

2. $S_1 \parallel S_2 = \bigcup_{s_1 \in S_1, s_2 \in S_2} s_1 \parallel s_2.$ $\qquad\qquad\diamond$

The following definition introduces the notion of *result* $\mathcal{R}$ of a sequence s (or a set of sequences S) of substitutions. Roughly, such a result is obtained by performing the parallel composition of each element of the sequence with the next one, and by checking, each time, that the partial result does not map annotated variables.

Definition 4.8

1. $\mathcal{E}(\Theta) = \{\vartheta \in \Theta \mid \vartheta_{|Var^-} = \epsilon\}$
2. $\mathcal{R}(\vartheta) = \mathcal{E}(\{\vartheta\})$
3. $\mathcal{R}([s]) = disann(\mathcal{R}(s))$
4. $\mathcal{R}(s_1.s_2) = \mathcal{R}(\mathcal{R}(s_1) \hat{\circ} s_2)$
5. $\mathcal{R}(S) = \bigcup_{s \in S} \mathcal{R}(s).$

where $disann(s)$ removes all the annotations in s. Thus, rule 3. specifies that, after a critical section, the input-constraints are released. $\mathcal{E}(\Theta)$ is a *filter* that eliminates from Θ all the substitutions mapping annotated variables. $\qquad\diamond$

4.4 Least fixpoint semantics.

In this section we introduce the notion of interpretation, and we define a continuous mapping (associated to the program) on interpretations. The least fixpoint of this mapping will be used to define the fixpoint semantics. Such a mapping is the extension of the *immediate consequence* operator for HCL ([12],[1]).

The *Herbrand base with variables* $\mathcal{B}$ associated to the program W is the set of all the possible atoms that can be obtained by applying the predicates of W to the elements of *Term*. An interpretation I of W is a set of pairs of the form $< A, s >$, where A is an atom in $\mathcal{B}$ and s is a sequence of substitutions on *Var* and *Term*. $< A, s > \in I$ can be read declaratively as A *is true in* I *under the sequence s*. We remark the symilarity with the temporal logic, although we do not investigate this relation here. $\mathcal{I}$ will denote the set of all the interpretations of W.

$\mathcal{I}$ is a complete lattice with respect to the set-inclusion, where the empty set $\emptyset$ is the minimum element, and the *set union* $\cup$ and the *set intersection* $\cap$ are the *sup* and *inf* operations, respectively.

The following definition, that will be used in the least fixpoint construction, is mainly introduced for technical reasons.

Definition 4.9 Let $s_1, \ldots, s_h$ be sequences of substitutions, and let $A_1, \ldots, A_k$ ($h \leq k$) be atoms. $s_1, \ldots, s_h$ are *locally independent* on $A_1, \ldots, A_k$ iff

$$\forall s_i, \forall \vartheta \text{ in } s_i : (\mathcal{D}(\vartheta) \cup \mathcal{C}(\vartheta)) \cap \mathcal{V}(A_1, \ldots, A_k) \subseteq \mathcal{V}(A_i).$$

where $\mathcal{D}(\vartheta)$ and $\mathcal{C}(\vartheta)$ are the standard *domain* and *codomain* of ϑ. $\diamond$

In the following, we use the notation $\bar{s}$ to denote a sequence of sequences of substitutions $s_1, \ldots, s_n$. Moreover, if $\bar{s} = s_1, \ldots, s_n$ and $\bar{A} = A_1, \ldots, A_n$, then $< \bar{A}, \bar{s} >$ stands for $< A_1, s_1 >, \ldots, < A_n, s_n >$, and $\| (\bar{s})$ stands for $s_1 \| \cdots \| s_n$.

Definition 4.10 The mapping $T : \mathcal{I} \to \mathcal{I}$, associated to W, is defined as follows:

$$
\begin{aligned}
T(I) = \quad &\{< A, s >| \quad \exists H \leftarrow \bar{G}|\bar{B} \in W_{\mathcal{V}(A)}, \\
&\exists \bar{s}', \bar{s}'' \text{ locally independent on } \bar{G}, \bar{B}, A, \\
&< \bar{G}, \bar{s}' >, < \bar{B}, \bar{s}'' >\in I : \\
&s \in [mgu_i(A^-, H).(\| (\bar{s}'))].mgu_o(A, H).(\| (\bar{s}''))\}
\end{aligned}
$$

$\diamond$

A possible sequence for A results from the critical section containing the mgu_i with the head of a clause, and a sequence resulting from the guard. The input variables in A are annotated. The whole is followed by the mgu_o and a sequence resulting from the body.

Proposition 4.11 T is continuous. Then, its least fixpoint $lfp(T)$ exists, and $lfp(T) = \bigcup_{n \geq 0} T^n(\emptyset)$ holds. $\diamond$

We define the least fixpoint semantics associated to W as the set $\mathcal{F}(W) = lfp(T)$.

Theorem 4.12 (Equivalence of declarative and operational semantics)

$$
\begin{aligned}
\mathcal{O}_1(\leftarrow \bar{A}) = \\
\{\vartheta \mid \exists \bar{s} \text{ locally independent on } \bar{A} : < \bar{A}, \bar{s} >\in \mathcal{F}(W) \text{ and } \vartheta \in \mathcal{R}(\| (\bar{s}))_{|\mathcal{V}(\bar{A})}\}
\end{aligned}
$$

$\diamond$

Example 4.13

1. Consider the program $\{p(y) \leftarrow q(y)|., \quad q(a) \leftarrow |.\}$, with declaration-mode $\{p(?), q(\hat{\ })\}$, and consider the goal $\leftarrow p(x)$. The possible s's such that $< p(x), s >\in lfp(T)$, are those of the form $s = [\{y/x^-\}.\{y/a\}]$. We have: $\mathcal{R}(s) = disann(\mathcal{E}(\{y/x^-\} \hat{o} \{y/a\})) = disann(\mathcal{E}(\{\{x^-/a, y/a\}\})) = \emptyset$, and indeed no refutations are possible.

2. Consider now the program $\{p(y) \leftarrow |q(y)., \quad q(a) \leftarrow |.\}$, with the same declaration mode. The possible s's are of the form $s = [\{y/x^-\}].\{y/a\}$. We have: $\mathcal{R}(s) = \mathcal{R}(disann(\mathcal{E}(\{y/x^-\})) \hat{o} \{y/a\}) = \mathcal{R}(\{y/x\} \hat{o} \{y/a\}) = \{\{x/a, y/a\}\}$, and we notice that indeed there exists a refutation for $\leftarrow p(x)$ giving the answer $\{x/a\}$. $\diamond$

Now we consider again the example showed in the introduction (*deadlock* situation), which illustrates the necessity to use streams-like structures.

Example 4.14

1. Consider the program $\{p(a, b) \leftarrow |., \quad q(a, b) \leftarrow |.\}$, with declaration-mode $\{p(?, \hat{\ }), q(\hat{\ }, ?)\}$, and consider the goal $\leftarrow p(x, y), q(x, y)$. We have $< p(x, y), s_1 >, < q(x, y), s_2 >\in lfp(T)$, for $s_1 = [\{x^-/a\}].\{y/b\}$ and $s_2 = [\{y^-/b\}].\{x/a\}$. For all the possible interleavings $s \in s_1 \| s_2$, we get $\mathcal{R}(s) = \emptyset$. Indeed, no refutations are possible (*deadlock*).

2. Consider now the program $\{p(z,b) \leftarrow |r(z)., \quad r(a) \leftarrow |., \quad q(a,b) \leftarrow |.\}$, with the same declaration-mode for p and q, and with $r(?)$. We have
$$< p(x,y), s_1 >, < q(x,y), s_2 > \in \mathit{lfp}(T), \text{ for } s_1 = [\{z/x^-\}].\{y/b\}.[\{z^-/a\}] \text{ and}$$
$s_2 = [\{y^-/b\}].\{x/a\}$. We have
$s = [\{z/x^-\}].\{y/b\}.[\{y^-/b\}].\{x/a\}.[\{z^-/a\}] \in s_1 \parallel s_2$ and $\{x/a, y/b, z/a\} \in$
$\mathcal{R}(s)$. Indeed, there exists a refutation of the goal $\leftarrow p(x,y), q(x,y)$ giving the
answer $\{x/a, y/b\}$. $\diamond$

5   Denotational semantics.

In this section, we give an overview of the definition of a denotational model for PAR-LOG. We refer to [6] for a more elaborate explanation and detailed formal definitions. Denotational semantics for flat versions of concurrent logic languages can be given with standard techniques. It is more difficult to assign a denotational semantics to concurrent logic languages with deep guards. Our denotational semantics does not deal with local deadlock in guards. Namely, we assume that if one of the guards has a successful computation then there will be no deadlock (cf the operational semantics).

To define our denotational model we first introduce two semantic universes $(p \in)$ P and $(q \in)$ Q; they are complete metric spaces satisfying the following two *reflexive domain* equations:

$$P \cong \mathcal{P}_{\mathrm{co}}(Q) \text{ and } Q \cong \mathit{Subst} \cup (\mathit{Subst} \times Q) \cup (\mathit{Subst} \times P).$$

(Here $\mathcal{P}_{\mathrm{co}}(Q)$ is the set of all *compact* subsets of Q; the symbol $\cong$ is interpreted "is isometric with".) In [8] and [2] it is described how to solve such equations; in [4] similar semantic universes are used. The elements p and q, called *processes*, are tree-like structures. The difference between $< \vartheta, p >$ and $< \vartheta, q >$ can be best explained by pointing out the different role played by the comma in both pairs: In $< \vartheta, p >$ it indicates an interleaving point whereas in $< \vartheta, q >$ it does not. Thus, $< \vartheta, q >$ represents an internal computation step, which will be used to model the computation of a guard. Formally, this difference appears explicitly in the definition of the semantic operator for interleaving (of processes) $\tilde{\parallel}$.

Example 5.1 A typical example of a process p would be $p = \{q_1, q_2\}$,
with $q_1 = \{< \vartheta_1, < \vartheta_2, \vartheta_3 >>\}$, $q_2 = \{< \vartheta_4, \bar{p} >\}$, and $\bar{p} = \{< \vartheta_5, \vartheta_6 >, \vartheta_7\}$, which
can graphically be represented by

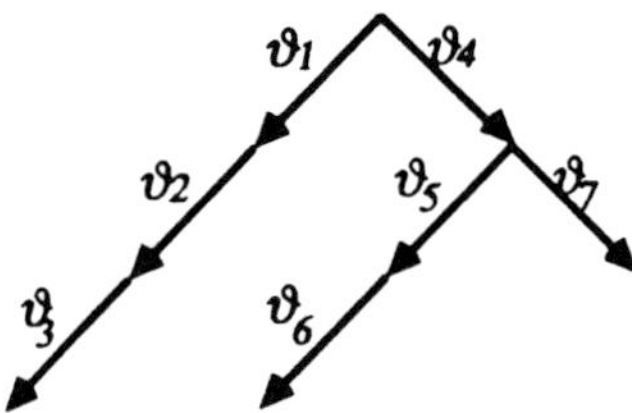

$\diamond$

In using reflexive domains with processes as elements, we follow the scheme that was used for imperative languages in [8]. Processes contain branching information, which here is used to distinguish between a failure possibility stemming from a failing guard computation and a failure resulting from the absence of a suitable candidate clause. (As it was already observed in the introduction, it is still to be investigated what kind of branching information we need in order to obtain a full abstract model.)

We introduce three semantic operators:

$$\tilde{;}, \tilde{\|} : P \times P \to P \quad \text{and} \quad str : P \to P.$$

The operator $\tilde{;}$ for sequential composition is defined as usual. Namely

$$p_1 \tilde{;} p_2 = \{q \tilde{;} p_2 \mid q \in p_1\}$$

where

$$\vartheta \tilde{;} p_2 = < \vartheta, p_2 >, \quad < \vartheta, q > \tilde{;} p_2 = < \vartheta, q \tilde{;} p_2 > \quad \text{and} \quad < \vartheta, p > \tilde{;} p_2 = < \vartheta, p \tilde{;} p_2 > .$$

The operator $\tilde{\|}$ for interleaving is defined by

$$p_1 \tilde{\|} p_2 = \{q \, \underline{\|} \, p_2 \mid q \in p_1\} \cup \{q \, \underline{\|} \, p_1 \mid q \in p_2\}.$$

Here $\underline{\|}$ is the *left-merge* operator, which always starts with a step of the left component. It is defined by $\vartheta \, \underline{\|} \, p = < \vartheta, p >$ and

$$< \vartheta, q > \underline{\|} \, p = < \vartheta, q \, \underline{\|} \, p >, \quad < \vartheta, \bar{p} > \underline{\|} \, p = < \vartheta, \bar{p} \tilde{\|} p > .$$

Note that in the first case we stay in the "left-merge mode", whereas in the latter, where we have an interleaving point, the left-merge is changed into the normal merge again. We also observe that this definition is recursive; it can be justified by giving it as the unique fixed point of a suitable defined contraction. (The same applies to the recursive definitions of $\mathcal{D}$ and *yield*, below.) See [19] and [7] for many examples of this style of definition.

Finally, in $str(p)$ all the streams in p are collected; in other words, this operator removes all the interleaving points:

$$str(p) = \cup\{\widehat{str}(q) \mid q \in p\}$$

where

$$\widehat{str}(\vartheta) = \{\vartheta\}, \quad \widehat{str}(< \vartheta, q >) = \{< \vartheta, q' > : q' \in \widehat{str}(q)\} \quad \text{and}$$

$$\widehat{str}(< \vartheta, p >) = \{< \vartheta, q' > \mid q' \in \widehat{str}(p)\}.$$

Example 5.2 The streams of the process p given in example 5.1 are:

$$str(p) = \{< \vartheta_1, < \vartheta_2, \vartheta_3 >>, < \vartheta_4, < \vartheta_5, \vartheta_6 >>, < \vartheta_4, \vartheta_7 >\},$$

or, graphically,

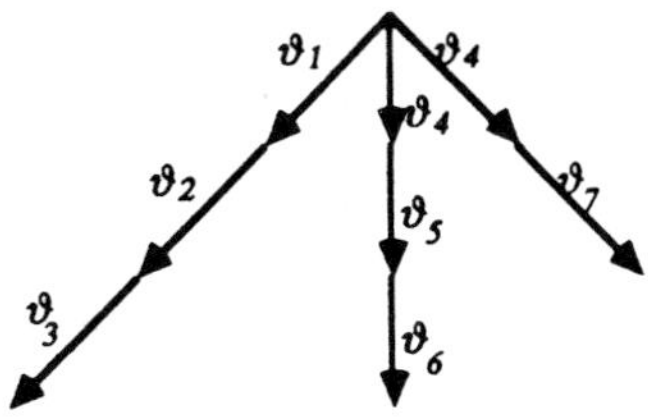

Definition 5.3 (Denotational semantics)
The function $\mathcal{D} : Goal \to P$ is given by the following three clauses:

1. $\mathcal{D}[\![\leftarrow true]\!] = \{\epsilon\}$,

2. $\mathcal{D}[\leftarrow A] = \bigcup \{str(mgu_i(A^-, H); \mathcal{D}[\leftarrow \bar{G}]); mgu_o(A^-, H); \mathcal{D}[\leftarrow \bar{B}] \mid$
$$H \leftarrow \bar{G}|\bar{B} \in W_{\mathcal{V}(A)}\},$$

3. $\mathcal{D}[\leftarrow \bar{A}, \bar{B}] = \mathcal{D}[\leftarrow \bar{A}]\tilde{\|}\mathcal{D}[\leftarrow \bar{B}]$.

(these equations define a contraction, and $\mathcal{D}$ is defined as the unique fixpoint of this contraction.) $\diamond$

In 2., the meaning of the resolution of an atom A is given as the union over all the clauses in the program W that have a head H that can be unified with A. This unification is given, similarly to the declarative semantics, in two parts: First the input variables are annotated (in A^-) and unified with H; next, after the guard evaluation, the output variables are unified. This ordering is important, since it will be used by the operator it yield, which is defined below with the help of the function $\mathcal{R}_{Var}$ (given in definition 4.8). Notice that this unification together with the computation of the guard is considered to be an atomic action, which is formally expressed by the use of the function str.

We conclude with the formulation of the correctness of $\mathcal{D}$ with respect $\mathcal{O}_2$. To this end, we introduce a function $yield : P \rightarrow (Subst \rightarrow M_2)$; it is given by

$$yield(p)(\vartheta) = \quad \bigcup_\delta \{\vartheta' \mid \, < \vartheta_1, < \vartheta_2, \cdots, < \vartheta_{n-1}, \vartheta_n > \cdots >> \in p\} \cup$$
$$\bigcup_\delta \{\vartheta'.yield(p')(\vartheta') \mid \, < \vartheta_1, < \vartheta_2, \cdots, < \vartheta_n, p' > \cdots >> \in p\},$$

where $\vartheta' \in \mathcal{R}_{Var}(\vartheta.\vartheta_1.\cdots.\vartheta_n)$. (We have: $\bigcup_\delta = \bigcup X \setminus \{\delta\}$ if this is non-empty, and $\{\delta\}$, otherwise.) The correctness result now can be formulated as follows:

Theorem 5.4

$$\mathcal{O}_2[\leftarrow \bar{A}] = \{(\vartheta_1.\cdots.\vartheta_n.\cdots)_{|\mathcal{V}(\bar{A})} \mid \vartheta_1.\cdots.\vartheta_n.\cdots \in yield(\mathcal{D}[\leftarrow \bar{A}])(\epsilon)\}. \qquad \diamond$$

6 Conclusions and future work.

We have defined a declarative semantics that models the success set of PARLOG and a denotational semantics that models also the finite failures and the infinite computations. Similar approaches can be taken for GHC (see [5,25]) and for Concurrent Prolog.

If we compare the denotational semantics given here to the ones given in [4] and [5], we observe that this one is more abstract, i.e., it makes less distinctions. Moreover, this one is in some sense closer to the declarative model. In fact, the restrictions on unifications imposed by the mode declarations are formalized in the same way by the denotational and the declarative model.

Still, the denotational model is not fully abstract and the construction of such a model remains a topic for further research. Another topic to be investigated is the relation between the denotational and the declarative semantics. In this paper both models are related via their corresponding operational semantics, and no direct comparison is done.

References

[1] K.R. Apt. *Introduction to logic programming*. Technical Report CS-R8741, Centre for Mathematics and Computer Science, Amsterdam, 1987. To appear as a chapter in Handbook of Theoretical Computer Science, North-Holland.

[2] P. America and J.J.M.M. Rutten. *Solving reflexive domain equations in a category of complete metric spaces.* Proc. of the third workshop on mathematical foundations of programming language semantics, LNCS 298, 1988, pp. 254-288.

[3] L. Beckman, *Towards a Formal Semantics for Concurrent Logic Programming Languages*, Proc. of the Third International Conference on Logic Programming, LNCS 225, 1986, pp. 335-349.

[4] J.W. Bakker and J.N. Kok. *Uniform abstraction, atomicity and contractions in the comparative semantics of concurrent prolog.* Technical Report CS 88.., Centre for Mathematics and Computer Science, Amsterdam, 1988. Extended abstract in Proc. of FGCS 1988. To appear in TCS.

[5] F.S. de Boer, J.N. Kok, C. Palamidessi, and J.J.M.M. Rutten. *Control flow versus logic: a denotational and a declarative model for Guarded Horn Clauses.* Technical Report, Centre for Mathematics and Computer Science, 1988. To appear in Proc. MFCS 1989.

[6] F.S. de Boer, J.N. Kok, C. Palamidessi, and J.J.M.M. Rutten. *Semantics models for PARLOG.* Technical Report, Centre for Mathematics and Computer Science, 1988.

[7] J.W. de Bakker and J.-J.Ch. Meyer. *Metric semantics for concurrency.* BIT, 28,1988, pp. 504-529..

[8] J.W. de Bakker and J.I. Zucker. *Processes and the denotational semantics of concurrency.* Information and Control 54, 1982, pp. 70-120.

[9] K.L. Clark, S. Gregory, *Notes on the implementation of PARLOG,* Journal of Logic Programming 2(1), 1985, 17-42.

[10] K.L. Clark, S. Gregory, *PARLOG: Parallel programming in logic,* ACM Trans. Program. Lang. Syst. Vol. 8, 1, 1986, 1-49. Res. Report DOC 84/4, Dept. of Computing, Imperial College, London,1984.

[11] E. Eder. *Properties of substitutions and unifications.* Journal Symbolic Computation 1, 1985, pp. 31-46.

[12] M.H. van Emden and R.A. Kowalski. *The semantics of predicate logic as a programming language.* Journal of the ACM 23(4), 1976, pp. 733-742.

[13] M. Falaschi, G. Levi, *Finite Failures and Partial Computations in Concurrent Logic Languages*, Proc. of FGCS 1988, pp. 364-373.

[14] M. Falaschi, G. Levi, M. Martelli, and C. Palamidessi. *Declarative modeling of the operational behaviour of logic languages.* To appear on TCS.

[15] M. Falaschi, G. Levi, M. Martelli, and C. Palamidessi. *A new declarative semantics for logic languages.* In Proceedings Conf. and Symp. on Logic Programming, 1988, pp. 993-1005.

[16] R. Gerth, M. Codish, Y. Lichtenstein, and E. Shapiro. *Fully abstract denotational semantics for concurrent prolog.* In Proc. Logic In Computer Science, 1988, pp. 320-335.

[17] S. Gregory. *Parallel logic programming in PARLOG.* International Series in Logic Programming, Addison-Wesley, 1987.

[18] M. Hennessy and G.D. Plotkin. *Full abstraction for a simple parallel programming language.* In J. Becvar, editor, Proceedings 8th MFCS, Lecture Notes in Computer Science 74, Springer Verlag, 1979, pp. 108-120.

[19] J.N. Kok and J.J.M.M. Rutten. *Contractions in comparing concurrency semantics.* In Proceedings 15th ICALP, Tampere, LNCS 317, 1988, 317-332.

[20] J.-L. Lassez, M.J. Maher, and K. Marriot. *Unification revisited.* In J. Minker, editor, Foundations of deductive databases and logic programming, Morgan Kaufmann, Los Altos, 1988.

[21] G. Levi and C. Palamidessi. *The declarative semantics of logical read-only variables.* In Proc. Symp. on Logic Programming, IEEE Comp. Society Press, 1985, pp. 128- 137.

[22] G. Levi and C. Palamidessi. *An approach to the declarative semantics of synchronization in logic languages.* In Proc. 4th Int. Conf. on Logic Programming, 1987, 877-893.

[23] G. Levi. *Models, unfolding rules and fixed point semantics.* Proc. Conf. and Symp. on Logic Programming, 1988, pp. 1649-1665.

[24] M. Murakami. *A New Declarative Semantics of Parallel Logic Programs with Perpetual Processes.* Proc. of FGCS, 1988, pp. 374-381.

[25] C. Palamidessi. *A fixpoint semantics for Guarded Horn Clauses.* Technical Report CS-R8833, Centre for Mathematics and Computer Science, Amsterdam, 1988.

[26] V.A. Saraswat: *Partial Correctness Semantics for CP($\emptyset, |, \&$).* Proc. of the Conf. on Foundations of Software Computing and Theoretical Computer Science, LNCS 206, 1985, 347-368.

[27] V.A. Saraswat: *The concurrent logic programming language CP: definition and operational semantics,* in: Conference Record of the Fourteenth Annual ACM Symp. on Principles of Programming Languages, Munich, 1987, pp. 49-62.

[28] V.A. Saraswat. *GHC: operational semantics, problems and relationship with* $cp(\downarrow, |)$. In IEEE international symposium on logic programming, 1987, pp. 347-358.

[29] E.Y. Shapiro. *A subset of concurrent prolog and its interpreter.* Tech. Report TR-003, ICOT, Tokyo, 1983.

[30] E.Y. Shapiro. *Concurrent Prolog: Collected Papers.* Vol. 1-2 MTI press, 1988.

[31] A. Takeuchi and K. Furukawa. *Parallel Logic Programming Languages.* Proc. Conf. on Logic Programming, LNCS 225, London, 1986, 242-254.

[32] K. Ueda. *Guarded Horn Clauses.* Technical Report TR-103, ICOT, Tokyo, 1985. Revised in 1986. A revised version is in Proc. Logic Programming 1985, pp. 168-179. Also in E.Y. Shapiro, editor, *Concurrent Prolog, Collected Papers.*, chapter 4.

[33] K. Ueda. *Guarded Horn Clauses, A Parallel Logic Programming Language with the Concept of a Guard.* Technical Report TR-208, ICOT, Tokyo, 1986. Revised in 1987. Also in Proc. Programming of Future Generation Computers, North Holland, 1988, pp. 441-456.

Model-Theoretic, Fixpoint and Operational Semantics for a Distributed Logic Language

Antonio Brogi & Roberto Gorrieri
Dipartimento di Informatica - Università di Pisa
Corso Italia,40 — I-56100 Pisa, Italy

ABSTRACT

This paper addresses the problem of semantically denoting a model of concurrency in logic languages based on a form of AND parallelism and on cooperation via an explicit communication mechanism. A declarative (model-theoretic and fixpoint) and a distributed operational semantics for a version of Delta Prolog are defined. The equivalence between the three presented semantics is proved.

1. INTRODUCTION

In the process interpretation of HCL [29], a goal $\leftarrow A_1, A_2 \dots, A_n$ is viewed as a net of n processes communicating via shared variables and the clauses of the program correspond to the alternative definitions of the processes. The concurrent computation exploits a *nondeterministic choice* between several alternatives (clause selection phase) and a reconfiguration of the net is the result of applying a clause to a goal. However, such a simple communication mechanism (shared variables) is not expressive enough to model real problems, where communication and concurrency are to be explicitly controlled. Most of the concurrency oriented extensions of logic languages restrict the possible modes of the unification mechanism by introducing a distinction between the producers and the consumers of the values of a logical variable. The resulting model is a subcase of AND-parallelism, called STREAM parallelism. The most famous representatives of this class of languages are PARLOG [7], Concurrent Prolog [29] and GHC [30].

At the *linguistic* level, these languages naturally define an intrinsically centralized abstract machine where communication is performed *via* shared variables. In fact, the problem of managing global environments has led to define models of computations which are targeted for execution on shared memory architectures [19]. Moreover, the operational semantics for these languages are based on interleaving models [28], where concurrency is expressed by nondeterminism. In order to exploit the implicit parallelism of STREAM languages, we have to move towards the *implementation* level, possibly resorting to sophisticated compilative techniques, e.g. abstract interpretation [1].

In this paper we study a form of distributed logic defined *at the language level*, where explicit operators for controlling parallelism and concurrency are included into the language. A possible solution leads to a message passing model of computation by extending HCL with the introduction of the classical primitives for message passing (send/receive) [22] and of explicit operators like fork and join [8,22].
We study a distributed logic language defined by abstracting the main features of Delta Prolog [2,25,26] and of the underlying Distributed Logic [22]. The language is here improperly referred as Delta Prolog by affinity. The target of our semantical definition is to model the peculiar aspects of control operators for concurrency. Therefore we do not deal with clause order, as it is specified in the original proposal of Distributed Logic.

Extra-logical primitives allow to control concurrency but, at the same time, they decrease the logical flavor of concurrent logic languages. Phenomena such as synchronization, communication, deadlock and process creation may be more advantageously modeled using techniques stemming from imperative and functional concurrent languages, emphasizing *control* rather than *logic*. In fact, denotational and interleaving operational semantics have been recently defined [3,4,15,28]. Orthogonally, only recently some remarkable results have been achieved in order to define a declarative semantics for concurrent logic languages [14,17,18,24], even if a completely satisfactory general treatment of this issue has not been reached yet.

A declarative (model theoretic and fixpoint) semantics is defined here in a simple and direct way for Delta Prolog, fully reinstating it in the class of logic languages. We extend the declarative approach of [13], where interpretations containing (possibly) non ground atoms are introduced. The presence of variables in the Herbrand Model allows to model universally quantified variables. This approach is very adequate for the declarative description of the operational behaviour of logic languages and thus for relating different kinds of semantics.
One of the main problems for declaratively modeling Delta Prolog is the logical meaning of communication predicates. We will consider a proper subset of the Herbrand base, containing program-defined predicate atoms only, and relate the truth and the falsity of a goal with the *"history"* of the communications performed by independent processes, as proposed in [23].

A truly distributed operational semantics for Delta Prolog is recalled from [5] where it has been originally presented. Differently from those semantics based on intrinsically sequential interleaving models, we describe a concurrent system as a set of sequential processes, possibly located in different places, which cooperate in accomplishing a task. Thus, neither a global state nor a global clock must be assumed. Our operational semantics suggests a naive implementation of a Delta Prolog program on several processors, where each processor has a copy of the program and solves a goal by exchanging information with other goals.

Finally, the major result of this paper is the equivalence (consistency and completeness) between the declarative (model theoretic and fixpoint) and operational semantics.

An outline of the paper follows. Section 2 introduces the abstract syntax for the language and some other preliminaries. Section 3 presents the declarative semantics, while the operational semantics is given in Section 4. The equivalence of the two semantics is proved in Section 5.

2. PRELIMINARIES

Delta Prolog is an extension of HCL with some operators on goals which resemble those of other concurrent languages such as CCS [21] and CSP [16]. In Delta Prolog (DP for short) a neat syntactical distinction is introduced between sequential ";" and parallel composition "||" of goals. The meaning of the operator "," can not be immediately turned to either one. It is not a sequential composition operator since the success set does not depend on the order, if any, atoms in a goal are to be reduced (i.e. on the computation rule) nor it is a parallel operator since atoms can not be independently derived in parallel (because of shared variables).

In the following, we use classical notations of logic programming languages [20,13]. The language alphabet is $\langle D, V, P \cup C \rangle$, where D is a family indexed on $\mathbf{N}$ (natural numbers) of data constructor (D_0 is the set of constants), V represents the set of variable symbols, P the set of all program-defined predicate symbols, and C the set of (unary, postfixed) communication predicate symbols $\{ ?e, !e \mid e \in D_0 \}$. The DP-Herbrand universe U_{DP} is U_V, i.e. $T_{D(V)/\approx}$ (the free D-algebra on V modulo variance). Let A represent a program-defined atomic formula.

Definition 2.1. *(Delta Prolog Syntax)*
The abstract syntax is given by the following BNF-like grammar:

$$P ::= A \leftarrow \mid A \leftarrow G \mid P \oplus P$$
$$G ::= A \mid G_e \mid G_c \mid G;G \mid G\|G$$
$$G_e ::= U?e \mid U!e$$
$$G_c ::= G_e;G \mid G_c \therefore G_c$$

We denote by:

Pr the set of *programs*, ranged over by p, P (possibly indexed)

G the set of *goals*, ranged over by g, G (possibly indexed)

G_e the set of *event goals*, ranged over by g_e, G_e (possibly indexed)

G_c the set of *choice goals*, ranged over by g_c, G_c (possibly indexed)

A goal g is a *parallel goal* iff it has either form:

$\quad$ g = g$_1$ ‖ g$_2$ $\hspace{4cm}$ g = g';g''$\quad$ where g' is a parallel goal.

Otherwise g is a *sequential goal*. $\hspace{8cm}$ ◆

Let us give an informal overview of the DP syntax and semantics. A program is a set of clauses ($\oplus$ denotes union of clauses). There are two types of events goals with the form, respectively: U?e and U!e, where U is a term (the message), e is the event name (the communication channel) and "!" and "?" specify the communication mode (send/receive). In order to solve an event goal U?e, a complementary event goal U'!e has to be simultaneously solved. Moreover, both goal solve if and only if U and U' unify and, after the unification is performed, they become ground [2]. Every communication is due to the simultaneous execution of exactly two complementary event goals, thus only symmetric, synchronous communications are allowed.

When dealing with a choice goal, only one goal is chosen for the rest of the derivation. If both goals could be reduced, one of them is nondeterministically selected. Finally, in order to solve a goal g$_1$ ‖ g$_2$, g$_1$ and g$_2$ are to be solved in parallel. In contrast with the fact that DP is based on a message-passing model of computation, it allows variable sharing by parallel goals and the compatibility of the independently computed substitutions is checked at *join* time only. In [24] an explicit operator on substitutions is introduced in order to define this notion of compatibility: the *parallel composition* of substitutions. Given two substitutions ϑ_1 and ϑ_2, $\vartheta_1 \Diamond \vartheta_2 = \vartheta$ where ϑ is the minimal substitution satisfying $\vartheta_1, \vartheta_2 \leq \vartheta$ ($\vartheta_1 \leq \vartheta_2$ iff $\exists \gamma$ s.t. $\vartheta_1 \gamma = \vartheta_2$). There, it is shown that $\vartheta_1 \Diamond \vartheta_2 = \text{mgu}(S(\vartheta_1) \cup S(\vartheta_2))$, where $S(\vartheta_i)$ represents the set of equations x=t for each bindings x/t in ϑ_i. Thanks to a result in [11], $\vartheta_1 \Diamond \vartheta_2 = \text{mgu}(S(\vartheta_1) \cup S(\vartheta_2)) = \vartheta_1 \, \text{mgu}(S(\vartheta_2)\vartheta_1) = \vartheta_2 \, \text{mgu}(S(\vartheta_1)\vartheta_2)$.

Substitution σ is a *substitution unifier* (SU for short) of ϑ_1 and ϑ_2 iff $\vartheta_1\sigma = \vartheta_2\sigma = \vartheta_1 \Diamond \vartheta_2$. If $\vartheta_1 \Diamond \vartheta_2$ is defined, then a SU σ always exists. In fact, the two sets $S(\vartheta_1)\vartheta_2$ and $S(\vartheta_2)\vartheta_1$ denote the same set of equations, where for each equation t=t' in the former set, t'=t appears in the latter, and viceversa. Up to variable renaming, a substitution unifier is unique: so we usually call it *the* SU.

3. DECLARATIVE SEMANTICS

Before introducing a declarative semantics for DP, let us make some considerations about the correspondence between the declarative (model-theoretic and fixpoint) and the operational semantics of logic languages. The equivalence of these two different kinds of semantics has been proved by considering grounds atoms only. The correspondence is sound and complete: the minimal Herbrand model M of a program P is equal to its success set [12]. Anyway, the classical notion of success set:

$$SS = \{p(t_1,\ldots,t_n) \mid p(t_1,\ldots,t_n) \in B \text{ and } \exists \vartheta \text{ s.t. } \leftarrow p(t_1,\ldots,t_n) \longrightarrow^* \Box \}$$

hides one of the fundamental aspects of logic programs: the ability to compute substitutions. A more adequate definition could be:

$$SS' = \{ \langle p(t_1,\ldots,t_n), \vartheta' \rangle \mid p(t_1,\ldots,t_n) \in B_V, \exists \vartheta \text{ such that}$$

$$\leftarrow p(t_1,\ldots,t_n) \longrightarrow^* \Box \text{ and } \vartheta_{|p(t_1,\ldots,t_n)} = \vartheta' \},$$

but, in this case, the equivalence with the minimal model is lost. Paper [13] introduces a new interesting approach to the definition of declarative semantics based on interpretations containing (possibly) non ground atoms. That semantics fully characterizes set SS', by establishing a tight correspondence between the operational and the declarative semantics.
Our purpose is to extend their results in order to cope with the extra logical operators of Delta Prolog.

3.1. DP-interpretations and DP-models

The first step for the definition of a declarative semantics for a DP program P is to understand the logical meaning of event goals. They are not normal user-defined predicates since they can not be redefined in a program, i.e. they can not appear in the left-hand side of a clause. From this point of view, event goals could seem similar to built-in predicates. However, they can not be considered built-ins since the logical meaning of a communication predicate does not depend on the values of its arguments only, but rather on the (possible) presence of a matching complementary event. Such predicates are not true or false by their own. By the way, their existence as syntactical entities strongly suggests to include them into the Herbrand base. This way, the Herbrand base should contain atoms for which it is not possible to assign a well defined logical meaning. In this sense it is not clear what an interpretation should be. Our proposal considers a proper subset of the Herbrand base, containing program-defined predicate atoms only, and relates the truth and the falsity of a goal with the *history* of the communications performed by independent processes.
A goal can be true for some histories and false for others. This means that event histories are to be taken into account as a part of the model. In our declarative semantics, event histories are modeled by finite sequences of events, called *traces*. For the sake of simplicity, we consider ground communication events, thus only pure synchronizations are dealt with.

The DP-Herbrand universe U_{DP} is U_V, i.e. $T_{D(V)/\approx}$ (the free D-algebra on V modulo variance), while the DP-Herbrand base B_{DP} is a proper subset of B_V, composed of all program-defined predicate symbols (predicates belonging to P) applied to terms. Let E denote the set of all communication predicate symbols applied to ground terms, i.e. $B \backslash B_{DP}$, ranged over by e with abuse of notation. Let e^- denote the complementary event of e. A trace is a list of elements from E, and the set of all the traces is denoted by T. We define two operators on *ground* traces: concatenation and merging.

Definition 3.1. (*Trace Concatenation*)
Given t_1, $t_2 \in T$, the concatenation t of t_1 and t_2 is the juxtaposition of the elements of the two lists: $t = t_1 t_2$. The identity is the empty trace λ. ◆

Definition 3.2. (*Trace Merging*)
Given t_1, $t_2 \in T$, the merging t of t_1 and t_2, $t = t_1 \otimes t_2$ is defined as follows:

$$t \otimes \lambda = \lambda \otimes t = t \qquad\qquad (et_1) \otimes (e^- t_2) = (t_1 \otimes t_2)$$
$$(et_1) \otimes (t_2) = e(t_1 \otimes t_2) \qquad\qquad (t_1) \otimes (et_2) = e(t_1 \otimes t_2) \qquad ◆$$

The definition of merging is intrinsically nondeterministic. For instance, given $t_1 = [U?e, U'?e']$ and $t_2 = [U!e]$, $t_1 \otimes t_2$ is anyone of the following four traces: $[U?e, U'?e', U!e]$, $[U!e, U?e, U'?e']$, $[U?e, U!e, U'?e']$, $[U'?e']$.

Let us now introduce the definitions of interpretation domain, interpretation and truth for a Delta Prolog program P.

Definition 3.3. (*Interpretation Domain*)
The domain H of DP-interpretations is defined as:
$$H = \{ \langle A, t \rangle \mid A \in B_{DP} \text{ and } t \in T \}. \qquad ◆$$

Definition 3.4. (*DP Interpretations*)
A DP-interpretation I is any subset of H. ◆

Definition 3.5. (*DP-Truth*)
Let I be a DP-interpretation. Then:
- a unit clause $A \leftarrow$ is DP-true in I iff $\langle A, \lambda \rangle \in I$,
- $A \leftarrow G$ is DP-true in I iff $\forall G'$ s.t. s-mgu$_I$(G, G')=$\langle \vartheta, t \rangle$ then $\langle A\vartheta, t \rangle \in I$
- a goal G is DP-true with a trace t in I iff $\exists G'$ s.t. r-mgu$_I$(G, G')= $\langle \vartheta, t \rangle$

where relation s-mgu$_I$ is defined as follows:

- s-mgu$_I$(A, A') = $\langle \vartheta, t \rangle$ *if* $\langle A', t \rangle \in I$, ϑ = mgu (A, A'), A and A' do not share any variable,
- s-mgu$_I$(U!e, U!e) = $\langle \varepsilon, [U!e] \rangle$ *if* U is a ground term,
- s-mgu$_I$(U?e, U?e) = $\langle \varepsilon, [U?e] \rangle$ *if* U is a ground term,
- s-mgu$_I$((G_1;G_2), (G_1';G_2')) = $\langle \vartheta_1\vartheta_2, t_1 t_2 \rangle$ *if*
  s-mgu$_I$(G_1, G_1') = $\langle \vartheta_1, t_1 \rangle$ and s-mgu$_I$($G_2\vartheta_1$, $G_2'\vartheta_1$) = $\langle \vartheta_2, t_2 \rangle$
- s-mgu$_I$($G_1 \therefore G_2$, $G_1' \therefore G_2$) = $\langle \vartheta_1, t_1 \rangle$ *if* s-mgu$_I$(G_1,G_1') = $\langle \vartheta_1, t_1 \rangle$
- s-mgu$_I$($G_1 \therefore G_2$, $G_1 \therefore G_2'$) = $\langle \vartheta_2, t_2 \rangle$ *if* s-mgu$_I$(G_2,G_2') = $\langle \vartheta_2, t_2 \rangle$

- s-mgu$_I$(G$_1$‖G$_2$, G$_1$'‖G$_2$')= ‹ϑ, t›   *if*
  s-mgu$_I$(G$_1$,G$_1$') = ‹ϑ_1, t$_1$›   and   s-mgu$_I$(G$_2$,G$_2$') = ‹ϑ_2, t$_2$›,
  t = t$_1 \otimes$t$_2$.   and $\vartheta_1 \diamond \vartheta_2 = \vartheta$

and r-mgu is defined like s-mgu except for the case of atomic goals, where:

- r-mgu$_I$(A, A') = ‹ϑ, t› *if* ‹A', t› $\in$ I, ϑ = mgu (A, A'), A and A' do not share any variable, and A'$\leq$A.   ◆

Relations s-mgu and r-mgu are parametric with respect to the DP-interpretation I. By structural induction they relate the truth of a complex goal G to the truth of its atomic components. These relations compute a substitution ϑ and a trace t which have an operational counterpart, as stated in Theorem 5.1: $\vartheta_{|G}$ is the computed answer substitution of a computation generating trace t. In the case of atoms, we check whether there is a unifying atom in the interpretation. A communication event is considered always true with empty substitution by taking itself as a trace. The goal constructors build substitution ϑ and trace t in a compositional way. The case of sequential composition is straightforward. When considering a choice goal, one of the two alternatives is chosen and the other has to be ignored by taking it unmodified. For the parallel goal, the merging of the two traces t$_1$ and t$_2$ generates a trace t and the resulting substitution ϑ is the parallel composition of the two substitutions ϑ_1 and ϑ_2.
Finally, observe that relation r-mgu is defined a bit differently from s-mgu for the case of atoms since an atom A is true if and only if there is an atom A' in the interpretation which is less defined than A.

Definition 3.6. *(DP Model)*
Let I be a DP-interpretation (of a program P). I is a DP-model of P iff every clause of P is DP-true in I.   ◆

Definition 3.7. *(Partial Ordering on DP-interpretation)*
Let I, I' be DP-interpretations. I $\leq_{DP}$ I' iff I $\subseteq$ I'.   ◆

The proofs of the following propositions are almost standard and are omitted for the sake of brevity.

Proposition 3.8.
If I $\leq_{DP}$ I' then $\forall$ G DP-true in I with trace t, G is DP-true in I' with t.

Proposition 3.9.
The class of DP-interpretations is a complete lattice w.r.t. $\leq_{DP}$.

It is worth observing that $\varnothing$ and H are the bottom and the top element of the complete lattice, respectively.

Proposition 3.10.
If L is a non empty set of DP-models of a program P, then glb(L)=$\cap L$ is a

DP-model of P.

Proposition 3.11.

Given a program P,

   i) the class of DP-model is a complete lattice and

  ii) there exists a minimal DP-model M_{DP}.

3.2. DP-transformation and DP-fixpoint Semantics

The declarative semantics of a program is generally given in terms of the least fixpoint of a continuous transformation associated to it. In logic programming, the fixpoint of this transformation is the proof of the effectiveness of the minimal model.

We define a functional T_{DP} for Delta Prolog programs and state that it is monotonic and continuous. Then, we state the equivalence between the model-theoretic and the fixpoint semantics.

Definition 3.12.

Let P be a Delta Prolog program. The mapping $T_{DP} : 2^H \to 2^H$ on the set of DP-interpretations is defined as follows:

$$T_{DP}(I) = \{\langle A', t\rangle \mid \exists\ A \leftarrow G\ \text{in P, s-mgu}_I(G, G') = \langle \vartheta, t\rangle\ \text{and}\ A' = A\vartheta\} \cup$$
$$\{\langle A, \lambda\rangle \mid \exists\ A \leftarrow\ \text{in P}\}. \qquad\qquad\blacklozenge$$

Proposition 3.13.

Transformation T_{DP} is monotonic and continuous.

Proposition 3.14.

Functional T_{DP} has least fixpoint $\text{lfp}(T_{DP})$ and $\text{lfp}(T_{DP}) = \cup_{n \in \omega} T_{DP}{}^n(\varnothing)$.

Proposition 3.15.

Given a program P, a DP-interpretation I is a DP-model iff $T_{DP}(I) \subseteq I$
$(T_{DP}(I) \leq_{DP} I)$.

Theorem 3.16. *(Equivalence between Model-Theoretic and Fixpoint)*

For every Delta Prolog program P, $M_{DP} = \text{lfp}(T_{DP}(I)) = \cup_{n \in \omega} T_{DP}{}^n(\varnothing)$.

4. OPERATIONAL SEMANTICS

Here we present an operational semantics for Delta Prolog essentially taken from [5] where the interested reader can find more details. We define the operational semantics by means of a hierarchy of two abstract machines in the Structural Operational Semantics style [27]. The lower level machine, defined as a transition system, describes the evolution of the sequential goals. Then, the evolution of the whole system is represented by a rewriting system. Given a parallel goal, we single out its sequential components, named sequential processes, which are possibly located in different places. A state of the rewriting system is represented by a set of sequential processes and the rewriting rules describe process interactions. This constructive technique has been inspired by papers [9,10].

Definition 4.1. *(Labelled Transition System)*
A *labelled transition system* is a triple $\langle \Gamma, \Lambda, \rightarrow \rangle$, where Γ is a set of configurations, Λ a set of labels and $\rightarrow \subseteq \Gamma \times \Lambda \times \Gamma$ is the transition relation. A configuration γ is called *stuck* iff $\forall \lambda \in \Lambda$, $\forall \gamma' \in \Gamma$: $\langle \gamma, \lambda, \gamma' \rangle \notin \rightarrow$. ♦

Labelled transition systems are essentially infinite state automata. We define the sets of labels and configurations for sequential goals. We do not include the program into the configurations and just leave it as an implicit parameter since it does never change during the refutation of the goal.

Definition 4.2. *(Labels and Configurations)*
Let g be a goal, A an atom, ϑ a substitution, $\square$ the empty goal, U a ground term and *failure* a special symbol. The sets of *labels* Λ_G and *configurations* Γ_G for sequential goals are:
$$\Lambda_G = \{\vartheta\} \cup \{U!e\} \cup \{U?e\} \qquad \Gamma_G = \langle g, \vartheta \rangle \cup \langle \square, \vartheta \rangle \cup \langle failure \rangle \qquad ♦$$

A configuration $\langle g, \vartheta \rangle$ stands for a goal g to be reduced and the substitution ϑ represents the history of the whole derivation from the initial goal to g. Every transition is labelled with the substitution computed in that step of derivation or with an event goal. When a sequential goal communicates, it assumes the existence of a partner for the communication. The existence of such a partner will be checked only at composition time and thus we have to store the name, the communication mode (! or ?) and the (ground) message U of a not yet matched event goal. Configuration $\langle \square, \vartheta \rangle$ stands for the special stuck configuration "nothing to do". When the goal A is unable to make further progress because an unifiable clause is missing, the configuration $\langle failure \rangle$ is reached. This way, we directly see the case of failure and distinguish it from deadlock.

4.1. Transitions for Sequential Goals

The (possibly infinite) set of transitions is generated by means of an inference system defined in a syntax driven style (Plotkin's SOS).
In the following definitions we use:
$$\gamma_0 \longrightarrow \gamma_1 / \ldots / \gamma_n \qquad \textbf{implies} \qquad \gamma'_0 \longrightarrow \gamma'_1 / \ldots / \gamma'_n$$
as an abbreviation for the n rules:
$$\gamma_0 \longrightarrow \gamma_i \qquad \textbf{implies} \qquad \gamma'_0 \longrightarrow \gamma'_i \qquad \text{for } i = 1, \ldots, n.$$

Definition 4.3.
The *sequential goal derivation relation* over configurations, written as:
$$\gamma_G = \lambda_G \Rightarrow \gamma'_G$$
is defined as the least relation satisfying the following inference rules.

Atom)

$\exists\, A_2 \leftarrow g \in P$ s.t. $\sigma = mgu(A_1, A_2)$ **implies** $\langle A_1, \vartheta \rangle =\!\sigma\!\Rightarrow \langle g\sigma, \vartheta\sigma \rangle$

$\exists\, A_2 \leftarrow\, \in P$ s.t. $\sigma = mgu(A_1, A_2)$ **implies** $\langle A_1, \vartheta \rangle =\!\sigma\!\Rightarrow \langle \square, \vartheta\sigma \rangle$

No clause unifies with A_1 **implies** $\langle A_1, \vartheta \rangle =\!\varepsilon\!\Rightarrow \langle failure \rangle$

Seq)

$\langle g, \delta \rangle =\!\lambda_G\!\Rightarrow \langle \square, \delta\vartheta \rangle\ /\ \langle g', \delta\vartheta \rangle\ /\ \langle failure \rangle$

    implies $\langle g;g'', \delta \rangle =\!\lambda_G\!\Rightarrow \langle g''\vartheta, \delta\vartheta \rangle\ /\ \langle g';(g''\vartheta), \delta\vartheta \rangle\ /\ \langle failure \rangle$

Event)

U is a ground term   **implies** $\langle U!e, \vartheta \rangle =\!U!e\!\Rightarrow \langle \square, \vartheta \rangle$

                    and $\langle U?e, \vartheta \rangle =\!U?e\!\Rightarrow \langle \square, \vartheta \rangle$

Choice)

$\langle g_c, \delta \rangle =\!\lambda_G\!\Rightarrow \langle \square, \delta\vartheta \rangle\ /\ \langle g, \delta\vartheta \rangle$

    implies $\langle g_c \therefore g_c', \delta \rangle =\!\lambda_G\!\Rightarrow \langle \square, \delta\vartheta \rangle\ /\ \langle g, \delta\vartheta \rangle$

        and $\langle g_c' \therefore g_c, \delta \rangle =\!\lambda_G\!\Rightarrow \langle \square, \delta\vartheta \rangle\ /\ \langle g, \delta\vartheta \rangle$ $\blacklozenge$

Atom) This rule simply states that an atom A_1 can be rewritten if there is a clause whose head unifies with it. If an unifiable clause is missing, the configuration $\langle failure \rangle$ is reached. **Seq)** The left component of a sequential goal has to be solved first and the computed substitution has to be applied to the right component, too. On the other side, if the derivation of the left goal leads to a failure, the whole goal fails. **Event)** In order to solve an event goal $U_1?e$, a complementary event goal $U_2!e$ has to be simultaneously solved. Since we deal with ground event goals only, U_1 and U_2 must be the same term. A sequential goal performs an open communication supposing the existence of its partner. The process interaction will be described by rule Sync) in the rewriting systems for parallel goals. **Choice)** If a goal g_c can be reduced somehow, the choice goal discards the alternative and follows the derivation of g_c.

Finally, note that all the configurations whose left component is a parallel goal are stuck in the transition system for sequential goals.

4.2. The Rewriting Derivation Relation for Parallel Goals

We now decompose a parallel goal into those subgoals representing its *sequential processes*, in the style of [9,10]. For instance, from goal $g\|g'$ we obtain two subgoals $g\|id$ and $id\|g'$ (tag "lid" records that subterm g is in the left context of a parallel composition and symmetrically tag "idl"). The evolution of a set of sequential processes I, included in a state, is represented by a rewriting rule of the form $I\!-\!\lambda\!\rightarrow I'$. The intended dynamic meaning of such a rewriting rule is that the set I occurring in the current state can be replaced, after showing an event (labelled by) λ, by the set of processes I'. We call these states *distributed*, since their components can be allocated in different places and can proceed on their own without requiring any centralized control, even when they synchronize.

4.2.1. Splitting a Parallel Goal

Definition 4.4. *(Sequential Processes)*
We give the syntax of *sequential processes*.

 SP::= ‹ $\Box$, ϑ› / ‹g, ϑ› / ‹failure› /‹SPlid, g'› / ‹idlSP, g'›

where $\Box$ is the empty goal, g is a sequential goal, ϑ is a substitution, g' is a goal, failure is a special configuration and tags lid and idl record the context in which a sequential process is set. The set of sequential processes SP is ranged over by sp, and its subsets are named I, J (possibly indexed).   ♦

Intuitively speaking, a sequential process is a sequential goal together with a substitution and an access path defining its location within the syntactical structure of the parallel goal. If the access path is not empty, the second component of the pair is a goal representing a continuation (what its ancestor has to do next).

Now we describe how to map any pair ‹goal, substitution› into a (finite) set of sequential processes.

Definition 4.5. *(From Goals to Sets of Sequential Processes)*
Function **dec** : Γ_G —> $fin(2^{SP})$ is defined by structural induction on goals.
Sequential Goal)

    dec(‹$\Box$,ϑ›) = {‹$\Box$,ϑ›}   dec(‹failure›) = {‹failure›}

    g is a sequential goal   **implies**   dec(‹g,ϑ›) = {‹g,ϑ›}

The following rules apply only to parallel goals.
Sequential Composition)

    ‹sp, g'› $\in$ dec(‹g, ϑ›)   **implies**   ‹sp, g';g''› $\in$ dec(‹g;g'', ϑ›)

    ‹sp, $\Box$› $\in$ dec(‹g, ϑ›)   **implies**   ‹sp, g'› $\in$ dec(‹g;g', ϑ›)

Parallel Composition)

    sp $\in$ dec(‹g, ϑ›)   **implies**   ‹splid, $\Box$› $\in$ dec(‹g∥g', ϑ›)

                                    and   ‹idlsp, $\Box$› $\in$ dec(‹g'∥g, ϑ›) ♦

The configurations for the empty goal, failure and for a sequential goal are singleton sets of sequential processes. The *Sequential Composition* rule simply states that the decomposition recursively splits only the left component and that the right component contributes to the continuation. Finally, the sequential processes derived from a parallel goal are exactly those derived by its two components, enriched by tags lid or idl, and with the empty goal as continuation, since nothing has to be done once the parallel goal is resolved.

Notation: We sometimes denote the set {‹i,g› | i$\in$ I} by the pair ‹I,g›.

4.2.2. Rewriting Rules for Parallel Goals

Definition 4.6. *(Labels)*

The set Λ_D of *labels* is the set $\{\vartheta\} \cup \{U!e\} \cup \{U?e\}$. ◆

In the following definition ǥ stands for a goal g or for the empty goal □.

Definition 4.7. *(Rewriting Derivation Relation for Parallel Goals)*

The *parallel goal derivation relation* $I_1 -\lambda_D-> I_2$ is defined as the least relation satisfying the following axioms and inference rules.

Join)

$\quad$ ϑ_1 and ϑ_2 are *compatible* with *SU* σ

$\quad$ **implies** $\qquad \{sp_1, sp_2\} -\sigma-> dec(‹(g)\vartheta_1 \clubsuit \vartheta_2, \vartheta_1 \clubsuit \vartheta_2›)$

$\qquad\qquad\qquad\qquad$ **where** $sp_1 = ‹‹□,\vartheta_1›|id, ǥ›$ and $sp_2 = ‹id|‹□,\vartheta_2›, ǥ›$

$\quad$ $sp_1 = ‹‹failure›|id, ǥ›$ *and* $sp_2 = ‹id|‹□,\vartheta_2›, ǥ›$ $\qquad$ **or**

$\quad$ $sp_1 = ‹id|‹failure›, ǥ›$ *and* $sp_2 = ‹‹□,\vartheta_2›|id, ǥ›$ $\qquad$ **or**

$\quad$ $sp_1 = ‹‹failure›|id, ǥ›$ *and* $sp_2 = ‹id|‹failure›, ǥ›$

$\quad$ **implies** $\qquad \{sp_1, sp_2\} -\varepsilon-> \{‹failure›\}$

Act)

$\quad$ $‹g,\vartheta› =\lambda_G\Rightarrow ‹g',\vartheta'› / ‹□,\vartheta'› / ‹failure›$

$\quad$ **implies** $\qquad \{‹g,\vartheta›\} -\lambda_G-> dec(‹g',\vartheta'›) / \{‹□,\vartheta'›\} / \{‹failure›\}$

Async)

$\quad$ $I_1 -\lambda_D-> I_2$ $\qquad$ **implies** $\quad ‹I_1|id, ǥ› -\lambda_D-> ‹I_2|id, ǥ›$

$\qquad\qquad\qquad\qquad$ **and** $\qquad ‹id|I_1, ǥ› -\lambda_D-> ‹id|I_2, ǥ›$

Sync)

$\quad$ $I_1-\lambda_1->I'_1$ **and** $I_2 -\lambda_2->I'_2$ **and** $\lambda_1 = U!e$ **and** $\lambda_2 = U?e$

$\quad$ **implies** $\qquad ‹I_1|id\cup id|I_2, ǥ› -\varepsilon-> ‹I'_1|id \cup id|I'_2, ǥ›$

$\quad$ **and** $\qquad\quad ‹I_2|id\cup id|I_1, ǥ› -\varepsilon-> ‹I'_2|id \cup id|I'_1, ǥ›$ ◆

Join) As soon as both components of a parallel goal terminate, the continuation of the parallel goal is enabled and its substitution is updated. If ϑ_1 and ϑ_2 are not compatible then the set $\{sp_1, sp_2\}$ represents a deadlocked state. If one of (or both) the components has failed then the whole system fails. **Act)** This is an *import* rule for sequential goals. Everything a sequential goal can perform in the transition system for sequential goals can also be performed by the corresponding singleton set in the transition system for parallel goals. **Async)** From the premise that a set J of sequential processes performs an action, we can infer that the same set is able to perform that action in any context. **Sync)** The communication mechanism is handshake. A communication takes place if and only if the message in the two event goals is the same ground term.

It is worth observing that our rewriting system is asynchronous. Actually, the derivations of a system are independent of those sequential processes which are concurrent with the rewritten ones, but inactive. In other words, every rule is context-independent.

4.3 The Semantics of a Delta Prolog System

Given a program P, a initial goal G and its rewriting system $S_{P,G}$, we introduce the notion of computation and study what to observe from it.

Definition 4.8.

Given a system $S_{P,G}$ the (possibly infinite) sequence of states and rewriting rules:

$\xi = \{S_0\ I_1\ -\lambda_1 \to\ I'_1\ S_1\ I_2\ -\lambda_2 \to\ I'_2\ S_2 \ldots\}$ is a *computation* iff

i) $\quad \bullet \quad S_0 = dec(\langle G, \varepsilon \rangle)$

$\quad \bullet \quad I_i\ -\lambda_i \to\ I'_i$ belongs to the parallel goal derivation relation, $i > 0$

ii) $\bullet\ I_i \subseteq S_{i-1}$ $\qquad \bullet\ S_i = (S_{i-1} \setminus I_i) \cup I'_i,\ i \geq 0$.

Given a finite computation ξ, its final state is denoted by $last(\xi)$. A finite computation ξ is *terminal* iff $\forall I \subseteq last(\xi)$ no rewriting rule $I\ -\lambda \to\ I'$ belongs to the parallel goal derivation relation. A terminal computation is *successful* iff the final state is $\{\langle \Box, \vartheta \rangle\}$. $\qquad\qquad\qquad \blacklozenge$

The operational semantics captures more than the set of all the correct answer substitutions. In fact, the last state of a terminal computation may be:

- the singleton $\{\langle \Box, \vartheta \rangle\}$, i.e. correct answer substitution ϑ
- the singleton $\{\langle failure \rangle\}$, i.e. a failure occurs since an atom goal can not unify with any clause
- a non singleton set I, which stands for a deadlock possibly due to (possibly more than) one of the following reasons:
  - the non-existence of a compatible substitution (termination of a parallel goal)
  - the inability to unify terms in a matching pair of event goals
  - the possible partner for communication is terminated or failed.

Summing up, we can say that the operational semantics of a Delta Prolog system $S_{P,G}$ is:

$$\llbracket S_{P,G} \rrbracket_\mathbf{O} \quad = \quad \{\vartheta \mid \xi \text{ is terminal and } last(\xi) = \{\langle \Box, \vartheta \rangle\}\}$$
$$\cup\ \{fail \mid \xi \text{ is terminal and } last(\xi) = \{\langle failure \rangle\}\}$$
$$\cup\ \{\Delta \mid \xi \text{ is terminal and } |last(\xi)| \geq 2\}$$
$$\cup\ \{\infty \mid \xi \text{ is infinite}\}.$$

We could be dissatisfied for this *final state* semantics since it is not adequate w.r.t. infinite computations (perpetual processes) in the sense that relevant features of behaviours are not dealt with. A better description of system $S_{P,G}$ should take into account all the actions performed (thus we know what the system is doing) and their causal relations, i.e. every computation is observed as the partial ordering of events its generates. This way, important properties, such as safety and liveness properties, can be observed. We do not linger on this subject since the interested reader can find more details in [9,5].

5. EQUIVALENCE BETWEEN THE DECLARATIVE AND THE OPERATIONAL SEMANTICS

The main result of the paper, i.e. the equivalence between the declarative and the operational semantics, is presented in this section. All the proofs - here omitted because of space limitation - can be found in [6]. For the sake of brevity, given a DP system $S_{P,G}$, we denote a successful computation $\xi = \{ dec(\langle G, \varepsilon \rangle)\ I_1 - \lambda_1 -> I'_1\ S_1\ \dots S_{n-1}\ I_n - \lambda_n -> I'_n\ \{ \langle \Box, \vartheta \rangle \} \}$ by $dec(\langle G, \varepsilon \rangle) - t -> * \{ \langle \Box, \vartheta \rangle \}$, with t the substring of $\lambda_1 \lambda_2 \dots \lambda_n$ where only communication labels are taken.

Theorem 5.1. *(Soundness)*

Given a DP system $S_{P,G}$ let us assume $dec(\langle G, \varepsilon \rangle) - t -> * \{ \langle \Box, \vartheta \rangle \}$.

Then $\exists$ G' such that $s\text{-mgu}_{M_{DP}}(G, G') = \langle \vartheta', t \rangle$ and $\vartheta_{|G} = \vartheta'_{|G}$.

Outline of the proof.

By induction on the length of the computation and by structural induction on the goal. The induction is proved by means of inference rules. Next we show just a couple of them. The Unit rule represents the base of the induction on the length of the computation:

A'← is a variant of a unit clause in P   **implies**

if $dec(\langle A, \varepsilon \rangle) - \theta -> \{ \langle \Box, \theta \rangle \}$ *then* $s\text{-mgu}(A, A') = \langle \theta', \lambda \rangle$ and $\theta_{|A} = \theta'_{|A}$

As an example of inference rule on the syntactical structure of the goal, let us show the rule for sequential composition.

if $dec(\langle G_1, \varepsilon \rangle) - t_1 -> * \{ \langle \Box, \theta_1 \rangle \}$ *then* $s\text{-mgu}(G_1, G'_1) = \langle \theta'_1, t_1 \rangle$ and $\theta_{1|G_1} = \theta'_{1|G_1}$

and

if $dec(\langle G_2 \theta_1, \varepsilon \rangle) - t_2 -> * \{ \langle \Box, \theta_2 \rangle \}$ *then* $s\text{-mgu}(G_2 \theta_1, G'_2) = \langle \theta'_2, t_2 \rangle$ and $\theta_{2|G_2 \theta_1} = \theta'_{2|G_2 \theta_1}$

implies

if $dec(\langle G_1; G_2, \varepsilon \rangle) - t_1 t_2 -> * \{ \langle \Box, \theta \rangle \}$ *then* $s\text{-mgu}(G_1; G_2, G'_1; G'_2) = \langle \theta', t_1 t_2 \rangle$ and $\theta_{|G_1; G_2} = \theta'_{|G_1; G_2}$ ♦

Theorem 5.2. *(Completeness)*

Given a DP system $S_{P,G}$, if $\exists$ G' such that $s\text{-mgu}_{M_{DP}}(G, G') = \langle \vartheta, t \rangle$, then there exists a computation $dec(\langle G, \varepsilon \rangle) - t -> * \{ \langle \Box, \vartheta \rangle \}$ such that $\vartheta_{|G} = \vartheta'_{|G}$.

Outline of the proof.

The proof is by structural induction on G and, for the case of atomic goals, the induction relies on the proof of the membership of G' to the minimal model. The inference rules are similar to those of the precedent proof (theorem 5.1) by reversing the arguments. ♦

Acknowledgments

We would like to thank Catuscia Palamidessi for many helpful suggestions and encouragement. We also thank Pierpaolo Degano and Dino Pedreschi for stimulating remarks and discussions on concurrency and logic languages, and the anonymous referees for their comments.

REFERENCES

[1]   S. Abramsky, C. Hankin (eds.), *Abstract Interpretation of Declarative Languages*, Ellis-Horwood, 1987.

[2]   J.N. Aparicio, J.C. Cunha, L.F. Monteiro, L.M. Pereira, "The Specification of Delta Prolog", Draft manuscript, June 1987.

[3]   J.W. de Bakker, J.N. Kok, "Uniform Abstraction, Atomicity and Contractions in the Comparative Semantics of Concurrent Prolog", in *Proc. of Int. Conf. on Fifth Generation Computer Systems* Tokyo, 1988.

[4]   L. Beckmann, "Towards a formal semantics for concurrent logic programming languages", in *Proc. 3rd ICLP*, Imperial College, London, 1986.

[5]   A. Brogi, R. Gorrieri, "A Distributed, Net Oriented Semantics for Delta Prolog", *Proc. TAPSOFT - CAAP '89*, Barcelona, LNCS 351, pp.162-177, 1989.

[6]   A. Brogi, R. Gorrieri, "Model Theoretic, Fixpoint and Operational Semantics for a Distributed Logic Language", Internal Report , Dip. di Informatica, March 1989.

[7]   K.L. Clark, S. Gregory, "PARLOG: A Parallel Logic Programming Language", *ACM Trans. on Prog. Lang. and Syst.* 8,1, pp. 1-49, Jan. 86.

[8]   P. Degano, S. Diomedi, "A first order semantics of a connective suitable to express concurrency", in *Proc. 2nd Logic Programming Workshop*, Albufeira (Portugal), pp. 506-517, 1983.

[9]   P. Degano, U. Montanari, "Concurrent Histories: A Basis for Observing Distributed Systems", *J.CSS* 34, pp. 442-461, 1987.

[10] P. Degano, R. Gorrieri, S. Marchetti, "An Exercise in Concurrency: A CSP Process as a Condition/Event System", in *Advances in Petri Nets 1988* (G. Rozenberg, ed.) *LNCS 340*, pp.85-105, Springer 1988.

[11] E. Eder, "Properties of Substitutions and Unifications", *J. Symbolic Computation*, 1, pp. 31-46, 1985.

[12] M. van Emden, R.A. Kowalski, "The Semantics of Predicate Logic as a Programming Language", *J. ACM*, 23, pp. 733-742, 1976.

[13] M. Falaschi, G. Levi, M. Martelli, C. Palamidessi, "Declarative Modeling of the Operational Behaviour of Logic Languages", *Proc. 5th ICLP*, pp. 993-1005, 1988

[14] M. Falaschi, G. Levi, "Finite Failure and Partial Computations in Committed Choice Logic Languages", *Proc. of FGCS, Tokyo, December 1988*.

[15] R. Gerth, M. Codish, Y. Lichtenstein, E.Y. Shapiro, "Fully Abstract Denotational Semantics for Concurrent Prolog", *Proc. Logic in Computer Science 1988*.

[16] C.A.R. Hoare, "Communicating Sequential Processes", *C. ACM* 21, 8, pp. 666-677, 1978.

[17] G. Levi, C. Palamidessi, "The Declarative Semantics of Read-Only Variables", *Proc. Symposium on Logic Programming*, IEEE Computer Society Press, pp. 128-137, 1985.

[18] G. Levi, C. Palamidessi, "An Approach to the declarative semantics of synchronization languages", *Proc. 4th ICLP*, pp.877-893, 1987.

[19] J. Levy, "Shared Memory Execution of Committed-choice Languages",*Proc. 3rd ICLP*, pp.298-312, 1986.

[20] J.W. Lloyd, *Foundations of Logic Programming*, Springer 1987.

[21] R. Milner, "A Calculus of Communicating Systems", *LNCS* 92, Springer, 1980.

[22] L. Monteiro, "A proposal for distributed programming in logic", *Implementations of Prolog - Ellis Horwood, 1984*.

[23] L. Monteiro, "Distributed Logic: A Theory of Distributed Programming in Logic", *Technical Report*, Departamento de Informatica, Universidade Nova de Lisboa, 1986.

[24] C. Palamidessi, "A Fixpoint Semantics for Guarded Horn Clauses", *Report CS-R8833*, CWI, Amsterdam, September 1988.

[25] L.M. Pereira, R. Nasr, "Delta Prolog: a distributed logic programming language", *Proc. of FGCS, Tokyo, November 1984*.

[26] L.M. Pereira, L. Monteiro, J.C.. Cunha, J.N. Aparicio, "Delta Prolog: a distributed backtracking extension with events", *Proc. of 3rd ICLP*, July 1986.

[27] G.D. Plotkin, "A Structural Approach to Operational Semantics", T. R. DAIMI FN-19, CS Department, University of Aarhus, 1981.

[28] V.A. Saraswat, "The Concurrent Language CP: Definition and Operational Semantics", *Proc. of the 14th Symposium on Principles of Programming Languages, ACM*, pp. 49-62, January 1987.

[29] E.Y. Shapiro, "A Subset of Concurrent Prolog and its interpreter", *Technical Report 003 ICOT*, Tokyo, 1983.

[30] K. Ueda, *Guarded Horn Clauses*, Ph.D. Thesis, University of Tokyo, 1986 (also as Technical Report TR-103, ICOT 1986).

Invited Talks

NON-MONOTONIC FORMALISMS
AND LOGIC PROGRAMMING

Teodor C. Przymusinski
The University of Texas at El Paso
teodor%utep.uucp@cs.utexas.edu

> "It seems to me, that work in databases, logic programming, deductive databases, artificial intelligence and expert systems will move closer towards one another. Formalisms and techniques developed in each one of those areas will assist the others. Science builds on theories." — J. Minker, 1987

1 Introduction

In order to provide intelligent machines with the necessary declarative knowledge, a language has to be chosen in which this knowledge can be represented. In 1960, McCarthy first proposed to use logic as a language for knowledge representation in AI. The 'logical approach' to knowledge representation proved to be very fruitful and, among other significant contributions, resulted in the creation and successful development of three basic research areas: *logic programming*, *deductive databases* and *non-monotonic reasoning*.

The three areas play an increasingly important role in artificial intelligence and in the whole field of computer science and are closely related. The purpose of this paper is to discuss recent research developments, which greatly clarify the nature of this relationship and show that it is significantly closer than it was perceived in the past.

We begin with a brief general discussion of declarative knowledge and the role of logic in artificial intelligence[1].

2 Declarative Knowledge

The purpose of *declarative knowledge* is to provide intelligent machines with a mathematically precise definition of the knowledge that they possess, in a manner, which is independent of procedural considerations, context-free, and easy to manipulate, exchange and reason about.

The importance of declarative representation of knowledge in AI has been stressed by many researchers. In their fundamental paper McCarthy and Hayes [MH69] wrote:

---

[1] This part of the paper closely follows [Prz88a].

"A computer program capable of acting intelligently in the world must have a general representation of the world in terms of which its inputs are interpreted"

and in [McC87] McCarthy adds:

"Expressing information in declarative sentences is far more modular than expressing it in segments of computer program or in tables. Sentences can be true in much wider context than specific programs can be used. The supplier of a fact does not have to understand much how the receiver functions or how or whether the receiver will use it. The same fact can be used for many purposes, because the logical consequences of collections of facts can be available".

Nillson made a similar point of view a central thesis of his recent paper [Nil87]:

"Thus my thesis: 'General intelligence depends on context-free, declarative knowledge and on the means to manipulate it'. [...] The sharpest boundary exists between us and the 'proceduralists' who claim that intelligence consists of having numerous special procedures for dealing with all of the situations that might confront an agent. We admit that these procedures may in fact be said to possess knowledge, but such knowledge is tied to the special situations for which the procedures are designed; it is not portable. In our view, an agent built in this way is a collection of niche intelligencies. Such agents may in fact function well in many situations, but we fail to see how they will be able to transport knowledge from one situation to another."

Even some of the researchers who advocate a more procedural approach to knowledge representation, still see an important role for declarative semantics. McDermott writes in [McD87]:

"One can accept my conclusions about the futility of formalizing knowledge without a program, and yet still, as I do, have a strong intuition that it is better for a notation to have a denotational semantics than not to. One reason for this might be that at least a sound semantics helps ensure that the deductive inferences done by a program will be right..."

3 Logic in Artificial Intelligence

In order to provide intelligent machines with declarative knowledge, a language has to be chosen in which this knowledge can be represented. McCarthy [McC60] first proposed to use logic as a language for knowledge representation in AI. Later these ideas were amplified and put to work in his joint paper with Hayes [MH69]. Presently, the so called 'logical approach' to knowledge representation plays an increasingly important role in artificial intelligence. As Reiter put it in [Rei84]:

"Logic provides a rigorous specification of meaning."

He added in [Rei86]:

"Because an agent must reason about something (its knowledge, its
beliefs) any consideration of the nature of reasoning requires a concom-
mitant concern with how the agent represents its beliefs. The stance
adopted by AI research on non-monotonic reasoning is in agreement
with the dominant view in AI on knowledge representation; the 'knowledge content' of a reasoning program ought to be represented by data
structures interpretable as logical formulas of some kind."

3.1   Logic Programming

One of the unquestionable successes of the logical approach to knowledge representation was the introduction of logic programming and the rapid proliferation of
logic programming languages – especially Prolog. Logic programming was introduced in the early 1970's by Colmerauer [CKRP73] and Kowalski [Kow74] and the
first Prolog interpreter was implemented by Roussel in 1972 [Rou75]. The emergence of logic programming was made possible by the earlier fundamental discovery
by Robinson of the resolution principle [Rob65] and subsequent development of efficient resolution refutation strategies, that could serve as inference engines for logic
programming systems.

Logic programming is based on the idea of declarative programming stemming
from Kowalski's principle of separation of logic and control [Kow74, Kow79]. Ideally, a programmer should be only concerned with the declarative meaning of his
program, while the procedural aspects of program's execution are handled automatically. As Kunen puts it [Kun87]:

"The user should be able to understand the semantics just by 'logic'; not
by a detailed understanding of the implementation of the interpreter.
It is really this key fact that separates logic programming from more
conventional procedural forms of programming."

Unfortunately, this ideal has not yet been fulfilled. One of the reasons is the lack
of clarity as to what should be the proper declarative semantics of logic programs
and, in particular, what should be the meaning of negation in logic programming.
Without proper declarative semantics the user needs an intimate knowledge of procedural aspects in order to write correct programs.

3.2   Deductive Databases

Introduction and subsequent development, at the beginning of 1980's, of the theory
and formal foundations of deductive databases has undoubtedly been another successful application of the logical approach to knowledge representation (see Minker
[Min89] for a historical survey). In their classic paper on logic and databases Gallaire, Minker and Nicolas wrote [GMN84]:

"Logic, we believe, provides a firm theoretical basis upon which one can
pursue database theory in general."

However, Reiter, who was the first to propose, in 1984, a theoretical basis for
deductive databases, stressed the need for proper declarative semantics of negation
[Rei84]:

"Any algorithm for extended conceptual modelling must provide for the
representation of negative information and its use in query evaluation,
although this problem is rarely addressed in the literature."

It has quickly become clear that logic programming and deductive databases are closely related [LT85, LT86] and that they are based on very similar theoretical foundations.

3.3 Non-monotonic Reasoning

In the middle of 1970's, Minsky [Min75] and McCarthy [McC77] pointed out that pure classical logic is inadequate to represent the common sense nature of human reasoning. This difficulty is caused primarily by the non-monotonic character of human reasoning. Using McCarthy's words [McC87]:

> "While much human reasoning corresponds to that of traditional logic, some important human common sense reasoning seems not to be monotonic. We reach conclusions from certain premisses that we would not reach if certain other sentences were included in our premisses. For example, learning that I own a car, you conclude that it is appropriate on a certain occasion to ask me for a ride, but when you learn a further fact that the car is in the garage being fixed you no longer draw this conclusion."

Non-monotonicity of human reasoning is caused by the fact that our knowledge about the world is almost always incomplete and therefore we are forced to reason in the absence of complete information and as a result we often have to revise our conclusions, when new information becomes available.

Once the need for non-monotonic reasoning in AI had been recognized, work has begun on finding formal foundations of non-monotonic reasoning. Several formalizations of non-monotonic reasoning have been proposed, among which the best known are McCarthy's circumscription [McC80, McC86], Reiter's default theory [Rei80], Moore's autoepistemic logic [Moo85] (reconstruction of non-monotonic logics of McDermott and Doyle [MD80, McD82]) and Reiter's closed world assumption [Rei78] (and its extensions, e.g. Minker's GCWA [Min82]).

All of these formalizations are obtained by augmenting a classical first order logic with some mechanism, which − by allowing defeasible conclusions − permits us to reason in the absence of complete knowledge. Formalizations of non-monotonic reasoning provide yet another example of a successful application of logic to knowledge representation. As Reiter put it in [Rei86]:

> "Nonmonotonicity appears to be the rule, rather than the exception, in much of what passes for human common sense reasoning. The formal study of such reasoning patterns and their applications has made impressive, and rapidly accelerating progress. Nevertheless, much remains to be done. [...] The ultimate quest, of course, is to discover a single theory embracing all the seemingly disparate settings in AI where non-monotonic reasoning arises."

4 Non-monotonic Reasoning vs. Logic Programming and Deductive Databases

Non-monotonic reasoning, logic programming and deductive databases are areas of crucial and growing significance to Artificial Intelligence and to the whole field of computer science. It is therefore important to achieve a better understanding of the relationship existing between these three fields.

There is no doubt that the three areas are related. Logic programming and database systems implement negation using various non-monotonic negation operators, such as the negation as failure mechanism of Prolog. The non-monotonic character of those operators closely relates logic programming and deductive databases to non-monotonic reasoning. Conversely, because of non-monotonic character of such procedural operators, they can often be used to implement other non-monotonic formalisms [Rei86], thus opening the possibility for using logic programming and deductive databases as inference engines for non-monotonic reasoning.

In spite of the close relationship between non-monotonic reasoning, on the one hand, and logic programming and deductive databases, on the other, in the past these research areas have been developing largely independently of one another and the exact nature of their relationship has not been closely investigated or understood. As Reiter recently commented in [Rei86]:

> "AI researchers have routinely been implementing nonmonotonic reasoning systems for some time, usually without consciously focusing on the underlying reasoning patterns on which their programs rely."

The nature of this relationship becomes much clearer when we view a logic program or a deductive database P as a triple:

$$\overline{P} = <P, SEM(P), IC>$$

where P is the theory itself, usually consisting of a finite set of universally quantified clauses, SEM(P) is the declarative semantics of P, i.e. the intended meaning of P, most often represented as a (finite or infinite) set of closed formulae and IC represents the so called integrity constraints, a usually finite set of closed formulae, which are supposed to be satisfied by the semantics SEM(P). A closed formula (sentence) F is valid in $\overline{P}$ if and only if it is logically implied by the semantics, i.e., if:

$$SEM(P) \models F.$$

In particular, as a necessary condition, we require any semantics SEM(P) to satisfy all formulae from P and IC, i.e., we assume:

$$SEM(P) \models P \wedge IC.$$

We will not comment here on the intricate nature of the distinction between the theory P and integrity constraints IC.

For example, if P is any (pure) logic program, then we could define the integrity constraints IC to consist of Clark's Equality Axioms (see [Llo84, Kun87, Prz88b]) and the semantics SEM(P) of P may be defined as Clark's completion of the program (Clark's semantics [Cla79]) or – alternatively – as the set of all sentences true in all perfect models of P (perfect model semantics [Prz88b]).

Finding a suitable declarative or intended semantics is one of the most important and difficult problems in logic programming and deductive databases. The importance of this problem stems from the declarative character of logic programs and deductive databases, whereas its difficulty can be largely attributed to the fact that there does not exist a precisely defined set of conditions that a 'proper' semantics should satisfy. While all researchers seem to agree that a suitable semantics SEM(P) must reflect the intended meaning of a program or a database and also be suitable for mechanical computation, there is no agreement as to which semantics best satisfy these criteria.

One thing, however, appears to be clear. Logic programs and deductive databases must be as easy to write and comprehend as possible, free from excessive amounts of explicit negative information and as close to natural discourse as possible. In other words, the declarative semantics of a program or a database must be determined more by its *commonsense meaning* than by its purely logical contents. For example, given the information that 1 is a natural number and that $n + 1$ is a natural number if so is n, we should be able to derive a non-monotonic or commonsense conclusion that neither 0 nor *Mickey Mouse* is a natural number, even though those facts do not logically follow from our assumptions.

The intended semantics must therefore be *non-monotonic*, i.e., SEM(P) cannot monotonically increase with the theory P. For example, after learning (adding to P) the fact that 0 is also a natural number, we have to withdraw the previously reached conclusion. Consequently, the problem of finding a suitable semantics for logic programs and deductive databases can be viewed as the *problem of finding a suitable non-monotonic formalization of the type of reasoning used in logic programs and deductive databases.* ¿From this point of view, the problem of a suitable semantics for negation is just a special case of the more general problem of the intended semantics of a program or a database.

5 Perfect Model Semantics
Attractive Alternative to Clark's Semantics

One possible explanation of the fact that, in spite of their close relationship described above, non-monotonic reasoning and logic programming in the past have been developing largely in parallel rather than in tandem, is the fact that, traditionally (see [Llo84]), the declarative semantics of logic programs has been based on the non-monotonic formalism called Clark's predicate completion [Cla79]. Clark's formalism, although very elegant and natural is not sufficiently general to be applied beyond the realm of logic programming and therefore does not play a major role in formalizing general non-monotonic reasoning in AI. More importantly, Clark's semantics is considered by many researchers to be too weak and to have various unintuitive features and drawbacks, frequently discussed in recent literature (see e.g. [She87, She84, Prz88b, VGRS88]).

The situation has changed recently, following the introduction by Apt, Blair and Walker [ABW87] and by Van Gelder [VG87] (see also [CH85, Naq86]) of the class of *stratified logic programs*, later extended by Przymusinski [Prz87, Prz88b] to the class of (locally) stratified disjunctive databases, and the development of a new elegant and easily intelligible semantics for stratified programs and databases, called the *perfect model semantics* [Prz87, Prz88b, ABW87, VG87][2].

5.1 Natural Features of the Perfect Model Semantics

Perfect model semantics provides an attractive alternative to Clark's semantics, while eliminating many of its drawbacks. Its basic features include the following:

- Perfect models can be equivalently defined in several different ways, namely, as:

---

[2] In fact, the perfect model semantics is defined for a much broader class of theories.

- Iterated least models of a program [ABW87, VG87].

- Iterated least fixed points of a natural consequence operator [ABW87].

- Preferred models of the program w.r.t. a natural priority relation [Prz87, Prz88b].

- Perfect model semantics extends the least model semantics of positive programs or databases. More precisely, for a positive program P, perfect models of P coincide with minimal models of P and the unique perfect *Herbrand* model of P coincides with the least model of P [Prz88b]. Clark's semantics of positive programs is essentially different from the least model semantics.

- The perfect model semantics is more powerful than Clark's semantics, at the same time eliminating various unintuitive features of the latter, which have been extensively discussed in recent literature (see e.g. [She87, She84, Prz88b, VGRS88]). In particular, the perfect model semantics is sufficiently expressive to naturally represent transitive closures, while Clark's semantics lacks this capability [Kun88].

- Perfect model semantics admits a natural sound and complete procedural mechanism, called *SLS-resolution* (SL-resolution for Stratified programs), [Prz88b], which extends SLD-resolution (SL-resolution for Definite (positive) programs).

- The perfect model semantics is actually used in two large experimental deductive database systems, namely in the LDL system, implemented at MCC [Zan88], and in NAIL!, which is currently under development at Stanford [MUG86].

5.2 Equivalence to Non-Monotonic Formalisms

The perfect model semantics has one more very important property. It has been shown (see [Prz88a] for an overview) that for stratified programs the perfect model semantics is *equivalent* to natural forms of *all four* major formalizations of non-monotonic reasoning in AI:

- McCarthy's circumscription [Prz88b, Lif87];

- Reiter's default theory [BF87];

- Moore's autoepistemic logic [Gel87];

- Reiter's CWA [GPP89].

5.3 Significance

These results shed a new light on the semantics of logic programs and deductive databases and establish a close link between non-monotonic reasoning, on the one hand, and logic programming and deductive databases, on the other. They are, therefore, of significant importance to all three areas:

- The introduction of the class of stratified programs and perfect model semantics constitutes and important step towards the solution of the problem of declarative semantics for logic programs and deductive databases.

- The class of stratified logic programs has been shown to be a relatively large class of theories in in which natural forms of all four major non-monotonic formalisms coincide. This should contribute to a better understanding of relations existing between various formalizations of non-monotonic reasoning and, hopefully, to the eventual discovery of deeper underlying principles of non-monotonic reasoning.

- The discovery of the equivalence between the perfect model semantics and non-monotonic formalisms paves the way for using *efficient computation methods*, developed for logic programs and deductive databases, as inference engines for non-monotonic reasoning. This fact is very significant, not only because the class of logic programs is sufficiently large to allow formalizations of many important problems in non-monotonic reasoning, as well as providing fertile testing grounds for new formalizations, but also because it has been demonstrated [GL88a] that it is often possible to translate (compile) non-monotonic theories, which are originally *not* represented as logic programs, into logic programs.

Clearly, the problem of finding efficient inference mechanisms, capable to model human common-sense reasoning and to reason in the absence of complete information, is one of the major research and implementation problems in AI.

6   Extensions

Perfect model semantics has an important drawback. It is defined only for a restricted class of programs, which includes the class of (locally) stratified programs. Several researchers observed that there exist natural programs with clearly defined intended semantics, which are not (locally) stratified and, in fact, do not have perfect models [GL88b, VGRS88]. As a result, four different, although closely related, model-theoretic extensions of the perfect model semantics have been proposed:

Stable models [GL88b] are based on Moore's Autoepistemic Logic and are defined for those programs, which admit a suitable unique stable autoepistemic expansion.

Default models [BF88] are based on Reiter's Default Theory and, although introduced independently, they coincide with stable models.

Weakly perfect models [PP88] are based on McCarthy's Circumscription or on Reiter's CWA and are defined for a fairly broad class of programs, which includes the the class of *weakly stratified* programs.

Well-founded models [VGRS88] are 3-valued models defined for arbitrary logic programs and deductive databases. Initially, their relationship to non-monotonic formalisms was not clear.

All four semantics coincide in the class of *weakly stratified* programs [PP88] and, for (locally) stratified programs, all of them coincide with the perfect model semantics.

7 Well-Founded Semantics — A Natural Extension of the Perfect Model Semantics

Originally, it appeared that in view of the existence of four natural, but distinct, extensions of the perfect model semantics, we will not be able to single out a unique semantics, which would be defined for a sufficiently broad class of programs and databases and yet would enjoy all, or at least most, of the natural properties of the perfect model semantics.

Well-founded semantics [VGRS88] proved these worries totally un-founded! In [Prz89a, Prz89b] Przymusinski showed that the well-founded semantics has properties entirely analogous to the properties of the perfect model semantics and also leads to a natural notion of stratification of an *arbitrary* logic program.

We begin by recalling, after [Prz89a], a new and, in our opinion, more intuitive definition of the well-founded model M_P of a program P, than the one originally presented in [VGRS88]. As opposed to the original definition, our definition is constructive[3] and it defines the well-founded model as an *iterated least fixed point* of a natural operator. However, before defining well-founded models, we first have to discuss 3-valued interpretations and models.

7.1 Three-Valued Models

We will restrict our considerations to Herbrand models, but our definitions can be easily extended to the non-Herbrand case. We first define the language $\mathcal{L}$ of 3-valued first order logic.

The *alphabet* of $\mathcal{L}$ consists of (finite or countably infinite) sets of constant, predicate and function symbols, a countably infinite set of variable symbols, the connectives $\neg, \wedge,$ and $\rightarrow$, the universal quantifier $\forall$, and the usual punctuation symbols. The *language* $\mathcal{L}$ consists of all the well-formed first order formulae obtained using the alphabet. The *Herbrand base* $H_{\mathcal{L}}$ of $\mathcal{L}$ is the set of all ground atoms in $\mathcal{L}$.

By a *3-valued interpretation* I of the language $\mathcal{L}$ we mean a pair $< T; F >$, where T and F are subsets of the Herbrand base $H_{\mathcal{L}}$ of $\mathcal{L}$. Intuitively, the set T contains all ground atoms true in I, the set F contains all ground atoms false in I and the truth value of the remaining atoms in $U = H_{\mathcal{L}} - (T \cup F)$ is undefined. If there are no undefined atoms, then the interpretation is 2-valued. If A is a ground atom from $H_{\mathcal{L}}$ then we write $val_I(A) = \mathbf{t}$ (resp. $val_I(A) = \mathbf{f}$; resp. $val_I(A) = \mathbf{u}$) if A is true (resp. false; resp. undefined) in I. We call $val_I(A)$ the *truth value* of A in I.

If $I_s =< T_s, F_s >$, for $s \in S$, are interpretations, then by their *intersection* we mean the interpretation $I =< \bigcap_{s \in S} T_s, \bigcap_{s \in S} F_s >$. Clearly, A is true (false) in I iff it is true (false) in all interpretations I_s.

Using the truth values of ground atoms we recursively extend the truth valuation val_I to the set of all sentences, namely, for any sentences S and V we define:

$$val_I(\neg S) = \neg val_I(S),$$

where $\neg \mathbf{t} = \mathbf{f}$, $\neg \mathbf{f} = \mathbf{t}$ and $\neg \mathbf{u} = \mathbf{u}$,

$$val_I(S \wedge V) = min\{val_I(S), val_I(V)\},$$

$$val_I(S \rightarrow V) = \begin{cases} \mathbf{t}, & \text{if } val_I(V) \geq val_I(S) \\ \mathbf{f}, & \text{otherwise.} \end{cases}$$

---

[3] Independently, [VG89] proposed a different constructive definition of the well-founded model.

For any formula $S(x)$ with one unbounded variable x we define:

$$val_I(\forall x\ S(x)) = min\{val_I(S(A)) : A \in H_\mathcal{L}\},$$

where the ordering of truth values is given by $\mathbf{t} > \mathbf{u} > \mathbf{f}$ and the minimum of an empty set of values is defined as $\mathbf{t}$.

Definition 7.1 ([Prz89a]) *A 3-valued interpretation I of $\mathcal{L}$ is a 3-valued model of a theory P if $val_I(S) = \mathbf{t}$, for all sentences S in P. If M is 2-valued then it is called a 2-valued model of P.*

In the sequel, by a model we will mean a 3-valued model. By a *logic program* or a *deductive database* (see [Llo84]) we mean a theory consisting of universally quantified clauses of the form

$$A \leftarrow B_1, \ldots, B_m, \neg C_1, \ldots, \neg C_n.$$

where A, B_i's and C_i's are atoms. (Following a standard convention, commas are used instead of $\wedge$'s.) Observe, that an interpretation M is a model of a program P if and only if for every ground instance

$$A \leftarrow K_1, \ldots, K_m$$

of a program clause we have

$$val_M(A) \geq val_M(K_1 \wedge \ldots \wedge K_m),$$

i.e., if and only if

$$val_M(A) \geq min\{val_M(K_i) : i \leq m\}.$$

7.2   Iterated Fixed Point Definition of Well-founded Models

Suppose that P is a program and I is its fixed interpretation. We will assume that P has been fully instantiated and thus consists exclusively of ground clauses. We first introduce two operators $\mathcal{T}_I$ and $\mathcal{F}_I$. The operator $\mathcal{T}_I$ (resp. $\mathcal{F}_I$) assigns to every set T (resp. F) of ground atoms a new set $\mathcal{T}_I(T)$ (resp. $\mathcal{F}_I(F)$) of ground atoms. Intuitively, I represents facts currently known to be true or false and $\mathcal{T}_I(T)$ (resp. $\mathcal{F}_I(F)$) contains *new* facts (i.e. facts *not* contained in I), whose truth (resp. falsity) can be immediately derived from the program P assuming that all facts in I hold and assuming that all facts in T are true (resp. all facts in F are false).

Definition 7.2 ([Prz89a]) *For sets T and F of ground atoms we define:*
   $\mathcal{T}_I(T) = \{A\colon$ *there is a clause* $A \leftarrow L_1, \ldots, L_m$ *in P such that for every* $i \leq m$ *either* L_i *is true in I or* $L_i \in T\};$
   $\mathcal{F}_I(F) = \{A\colon$ *for every clause* $A \leftarrow L_1, \ldots, L_m$ *in P there exists an* $i \leq m$ *such that either* L_i *is false in I or* $L_i \in F\}.\Diamond$

Proposition 7.1 ([Prz89a]) *The operators $\mathcal{T}_I$ and $\mathcal{F}_I$ are monotonic.*

We will now define two subsets T_I and F_I of the Herbrand base obtained by iterating the operators $\mathcal{T}_I$ and $\mathcal{F}_I$.

Definition 7.3 ([Prz89a]) *Let $I = <T;F>$ be an interpretation. Define:*

$$T_I^{\uparrow 0} = \emptyset \quad and \quad F_I^{\downarrow 0} = H_P;$$

$$T_I^{\uparrow n+1} = T_I(T_I^{\uparrow n}) \quad and \quad F_I^{\downarrow n+1} = \mathcal{F}_I(F_I^{\downarrow n});$$

$$T_I = \bigcup_{n<\omega} T_I^{\uparrow n} \quad and \quad F_I = \bigcap_{n<\omega} F_I^{\downarrow n}.\lozenge$$

Proposition 7.2 ([Prz89a]) *The transfinite sequence $\{T_I^{\uparrow n}\}$ is monotonically increasing and the transfinite sequence $\{F_I^{\downarrow n}\}$ is monotonically decreasing.*

The set T_I is the least fixed point of the operator T_I and the set F_I is the least fixed point of the operator $\mathcal{F}_I$ (under the ordering by reverse inclusion).

Intuitively, the least fixed point T_I contains new atomic facts which can be derived from P knowing I and the least fixed point F_I contains new atomic facts which can be assumed false about P knowing I.

Definition 7.4 ([Prz89a]) *Let $\mathcal{I}$ be the operator assigning to every interpretation I of P a new interpretation $\mathcal{I}(I)$ defined by:*

$$\mathcal{I}(I) = I \cup <T_I;F_I> .\lozenge$$

The operator $\mathcal{I}$ extends the interpretation I to $\mathcal{I}(I)$ by adding to I new atomic facts T_I which can be derived from P knowing I and negations of new atomic facts F_I which can be assumed false about P knowing I.

Proposition 7.3 ([Prz89a]) *The operator $\mathcal{I}$ is monotonic.*

We now define the model M_P of the program P.

Definition 7.5 ([Prz89a]) *Let:*

$$M_0 = <\emptyset,\emptyset>;$$

$$M_{\alpha+1} = \mathcal{I}(M_\alpha), \quad i.e. \quad M_{\alpha+1} = M_\alpha \cup <T_{M_\alpha};F_{M_\alpha}>;$$

$$M_\alpha = \bigcup_{\beta<\alpha} M_\beta, \quad for\ limit\ \alpha\ .$$

Since the transfinite sequence $\{M_\alpha\}$ of interpretations is clearly monotonically increasing there exists the smallest countable ordinal δ such that M_δ is a fixed point of the operator $\mathcal{I}$, i.e. such that

$$M_\delta = \mathcal{I}(M_\delta) = M_{\delta+1}.$$

In other words, there exists the first such δ that both sets T_{M_δ} and F_{M_δ} are empty. We call $\delta = \delta(P)$ the **depth** *of the program P. We denote the fixed point interpretation M_δ by $M_P.\lozenge$*

It turns out that the interpretation M_P is in fact a model of P and has other important properties.

Theorem 7.1 ([Prz89a]) *The interpretation M_P is a minimal 3-valued model of P. It is also the least fixed point of the operator $\mathcal{I}$.*

The model M_P is therefore the least fixed point of the operator $\mathcal{I}$, which itself is defined using least fixed points of the operators $\mathcal{T}_I$ and $\mathcal{F}_I$. The model M_P is therefore an *iterated least fixed point model* of P.

Theorem 7.2 ([Prz89a]) *The model M_P coincides with the well-founded model of the program P as defined in [VGRS88].*

In [Prz89a] the iterated least fixed point definition of the well-founded model has been used to introduce the concept of a *dynamic stratification* $\{S_\alpha : 0 \leq \alpha \leq \delta\}$ of an *arbitrary* logic program P. The dynamic stratification $\{S_\alpha : 0 \leq \alpha \leq \delta\}$ of P is a decomposition of the set of all ground atoms in $H_{\mathcal{L}}$ into disjoint strata S_α and has properties analogous to properties of standard stratification.

A particularly important class of logic programs consists of those programs which have a *2-valued* well-founded model.

Definition 7.6 ([Prz89a]) *We call a logic program P saturated if its well-founded model M_P is 2-valued.*

We have demonstrated in [Prz89a] that saturated programs can be viewed as 'stratified programs in disguise', i.e., programs which, in spite of not necessarily being (locally) stratified, have all the essential properties of stratified programs. For saturated logic programs, the well-founded semantics, the stable model semantics [GL88b] and the default semantics [BF88] coincide [VGRS88].

7.3 Natural Features of the Well-Founded Semantics

Well-founded semantics possesses most of the natural features of the perfect model semantics:

- Well-founded models can be equivalently defined in several different ways, namely, as:

    - Iterated least models of a program [Prz89a].
    - Iterated least fixed points of a natural consequence operator [Prz89a].
    - Preferred models of the program w.r.t. a suitable priority relation [Prz89a].

- Well-founded model semantics extends the perfect model semantics of stratified programs [VGRS88].

- The well-founded model semantics is more powerful than Clark's semantics [VGRS88, Prz89a]. More precisely, if Clark's completion COMP(P) of the program P is consistent and if a sentence F is implied by COMP(P) then F is also implied by the well-founded semantics. Analogous results apply to 3-valued extensions of Clark's semantics defined in [Fit85, Kun87]. At the same time the well-founded semantics eliminates various unintuitive features of Clark's semantics.

- Well-founded semantics admits a natural sound and complete procedural mechanism. Namely, in [Prz89a] and, independently, in [Ros89], SLS-resolution has been extended from the class of stratified programs to the class of *all* logic programs and shown to be sound and complete (for non-floundering queries) with respect to the well-founded semantics.

The only essential difference between the extended SLS-resolution and the standard one is its ability to handle undefined answers. Although the program's dependency graph may contain negative cycles, indicating *potential* negative recursion, no *actual* negative recursion is allowed in the the extended SLS-resolution proof tree.

7.4 Equivalence of Well-Founded Semantics to 3-Valued Non-Monotonic Formalisms

Initially, the relationship of the well-founded semantics to non-monotonic formalisms was unclear. Moreover, it seemed that it will not be possible to extend the result stating the equivalence of the perfect model semantics to suitable forms of all four major non-monotonic formalisms to much broader classes of programs. The reason appeared to be the fact that the four proposed extensions of the perfect model semantics – the *stable model semantics* [GL88b] (based on autoepistemic logic), the *default semantics* [BF88] (based on default logic), the *weakly perfect model semantics* [PP88] (based on circumscription or on CWA) and the well-founded semantics [VGRS88] – turned out to lead to different results.

Nevertheless, Przymusinski has shown [Prz89b] that the well-founded semantics is in fact also equivalent to suitable forms of all four major non-monotonic formalisms. However, in order to achieve this equivalence, *3-valued extensions of non-monotonic formalisms* are needed, which is natural in view of the fact that the well-founded semantics is, in general, 3-valued. Accordingly, in [Prz89b] 3-valued extensions of all four non-monotonic formalisms were defined and the following result has been proven:

Theorem 7.3 ([Prz89b]) *For arbitrary logic programs, the well-founded semantics is equivalent to natural forms of 3-valued extensions of all four major formalizations of non-monotonic reasoning:*

- *McCarthy's circumscription;*

- *Reiter's default theory;*

- *Moore's autoepistemic logic;*

- *Reiter's closed world assumption.*

In [Bry89] logic programs were investigated from the point of view of *constructivistic logic*. Bry proposed a natural semantics for constructively consistent logic programs, extended the Magic Sets query processing method and showed its completeness with respect to his semantics. One can prove that Bry's semantics also coincides with the well-founded semantics, thus providing yet another, constructivistic, argument in favor of the well-founded semantics, and showing that, in addition to the top-down SLS-resolution, also the bottom-up Magic Sets method can be used to compute the well-founded semantics.

In the next two subsections, we will illustrate the equivalence of the well founded semantics to non-monotonic formalisms by briefly discussing circumscription and autoepistemic logic. Readers not familiar with the two formalisms may wish to skip this material.

7.5 Equivalence to Three-Valued Circumscription

The only difference between the (model theoretic) definition of standard (2-valued) circumscription – defined in [McC80, McC86, Lif85, Lif86] – and the definition of 3-valued circumscription given in [Prz89b] consists in the fact that the former uses only 2-valued minimal models while the latter uses all 3-valued models.

Suppose that P is a theory over the language $\mathcal{L}$ and suppose that R and Z are two disjoint subsets of the Herbrand base $H_{\mathcal{L}}$ of $\mathcal{L}$. Atoms in R are called *minimized atoms* and atoms in Z are called *variable atoms*. Atoms which are neither in R nor in Z are called *parameters*. We now define 3-valued (R,Z)-minimal models of P.

Definition 7.7 ([Prz89b]) *We will say that a model $M = <T; F>$ is less than a model $M' = <T'; F'>$ modulo (R,Z) if both models coincide on parameters, if $T \cap R \subseteq T' \cap R$ and $F \cap R \supseteq F' \cap R$ and if at least one of these inclusions is strict. In other words, $M < M'$ mod (R,Z) if both models coincide on parameters, differ on the set R of minimized atoms and if M has no more true facts about R than M' and M has no less false facts about R than N'. A model M is an (R,Z)-minimal model of P if there is no model M' less than M modulo (R,Z).*

Thus (R,Z)-minimal models keep truth values of parameters fixed, minimize the set of true atoms in R, maximize the set of false atoms in R and vary atoms in Z. Naturally, in case of 2-valued models, minimization of the set of true atoms automatically implies maximization of the set of false atoms, thus in this case the above definition coincides with the standard definition. We now give a model-theoretic definition of 3-valued parallel circumscription.

Definition 7.8 ([Prz89b]) *A structure M is called a model of* 3-valued parallel circumscription CIRC3(P;R;Z) of P, *with atoms in R minimized and atoms in Z varied, if and only if M is a 3-valued (R,Z)-minimal model of P.*

We now turn to 3-valued prioritized circumscription. Suppose that $\{S_\alpha\}_{0 \leq \alpha < \delta}$ are disjoint subsets of the Herbrand base $H_{\mathcal{L}}$ of $\mathcal{L}$ and suppose that Z is a subset of $H_{\mathcal{L}}$ disjoint from all the sets S_α. The collection $\{S_\alpha\}$ can be thought of as assigning different *priorities* for minimization to the elements of the Herbrand base, with the highest priority given to the atoms in S_0, the next highest to the atoms in S_1, etc. Elements of Z will be called, as before, variable atoms.

Definition 7.9 ([Prz89b]) *A structure M is called a model of* 3-valued prioritized circumscription $CIRC3(P; S_0 > S_1 > \ldots; Z)$ of P, *with respect to priorities $S_0 > S_1 > \ldots$ and with variables Z if and only if for every $\alpha < \delta$, M is an $(S_\alpha, \bigcup_{\beta > \alpha} S_\beta \cup Z)$-minimal model of P.*
If $Z = \emptyset$ then $CIRC3(P; S_0 > S_1 > \ldots; Z)$ will be simply denoted by $CIRC3(P; S_0 > S_1 \ldots)$.

It is easy to see that parallel circumscription is a special case of prioritized circumscription. Now we can state the main result:

Theorem 7.4 ([Prz89b]) (Equivalence of well-founded and circumscriptive semantics) *Suppose that P is a logic program and $\{S_\alpha\}_{\alpha \leq \delta}$ is its dynamic stratification (see [Prz89a]). Then, the well-founded model M_P of P coincides with the intersection of all models of prioritized circumscription $CIRC3(P; S_0 > S_1 > \ldots > S_\delta)$.*

Observe that the dynamic stratification of the program P, and thus the circumscription policy used with the theory P, is automatically determined by the syntactic form of the program.

7.6 Equivalence to Three-Valued Autoepistemic Logic

In order to show the equivalence between the well-founded semantics of logic programs and the 3-valued autoepistemic semantics, we need to translate logic programs into autoepistemic theories, which we will call *autoepistemic logic programs.* We will denote by **L** the autoepistemic *belief symbol* [Moo85], also called the *belief operator.*

Definition 7.10 *[Gel87] Let P be a logic program.* The autoepistemic translation $\hat{P}$ *of P consists of all clauses of the form*

$$A \leftarrow B_1, \ldots, B_m, \neg \mathbf{L}C_1, \ldots, \neg \mathbf{L}C_n,$$

for all possible ground instances

$$A \leftarrow B_1, \ldots, B_m, \neg C_1, \ldots, \neg C_n$$

of clauses from P.

For a definition of 3-valued autoepistemic logic the reader is referred to [Prz89b]. Here we only state the main result:

Theorem 7.5 ([Prz89b]) (Equivalence of well-founded and autoepistemic semantics) *Suppose that P is a logic program, M_P is its well-founded Herbrand model and $\hat{P}$ is the autoepistemic translation of P. Then for any ground atom A the following holds:*

- *A is true in M_P iff A is believed in $\hat{P}$;*

- *A is false in M_P iff A is disbelieved in $\hat{P}$;*

- *A is undefined in M_P iff A is undefined in $\hat{P}$.*

Observe, that – as opposed to circumscription – no explicit 'prioritization' of ground atoms was necessary to obtain the equivalence of the two semantics. As a byproduct of the main theorem the following important result can be proved:

Theorem 7.6 ([Prz89b]) *Every autoepistemic logic program has at least one 3-valued autoepistemic extension.*

Analogous result is false for 2-valued autoepistemic extensions.

8 Conclusion

The results presented in this paper shed a new light on the semantics of logic programs and deductive databases and establish a close link between non-monotonic reasoning, on the one hand, and logic programming and deductive databases, on the other.

The introduction of the well-founded semantics constitutes and important step towards the solution of the problem of declarative semantics for logic programs and deductive databases. The equivalence of the well-founded semantics to non-monotonic formalisms establishes the class of *all* logic programs as a large class of theories in in which natural forms of all four major non-monotonic formalisms coincide, thus contributing to a better understanding of relations existing between various formalizations of non-monotonic reasoning and, hopefully, to the eventual discovery of deeper underlying principles of non-monotonic reasoning. It also paves the way for applying logic programming and deductive databases as inference engines for non-monotonic reasoning.

As a result of these developments, a fairly clear picture emerges, showing the existence of *two essentially different 2-valued semantics* of logic programs which are closely related to non-monotonic formalisms. One of them is the *stable model semantics* [GL88b], which coincides with the *default model semantics* [BF88] and is based on autoepistemic logic or default theory. The other is the *weakly perfect model semantics* [PP88], based on circumscription or CWA. On the other hand, there is a *unique 3-valued semantics*, namely the *well-founded semantics* [VGRS88], which is equivalent to suitable forms of all 3-valued non-monotonic formalisms.

The well-founded semantics is defined for all logic programs, whereas the 2-valued semantics are restricted to more narrow domains. All three semantics extend the *perfect model semantics* of stratified programs and coincide in the class of *weakly stratified programs* [PP88].

References

[ABW87] K. Apt, H. Blair, and A. Walker. Towards a theory of declarative knowledge. In J. Minker, editor, *Foundations of Deductive Databases and Logic Programming*, pages 89–142, Morgan Kaufmann, Los Altos, CA., 1987.

[BF87] N. Bidoit and C. Froidevaux. Minimalism subsumes default logic and circumscription in stratified logic programming. In *Proceedings of the Symposium on Principles of Database Systems*, ACM SIGACT-SIGMOD, 1987.

[BF88] N. Bidoit and C. Froidevaux. General logical databases and programs: default logic semantics and stratification. *Journal of Information and Computation*, 1988. (in print).

[Bry89] F. Bry. Logic programming as constructivism: a formalization and its application to databases. In *Proceedings of the Symposium on Principles of Database Systems*, ACM SIGACT-SIGMOD, 1989. (in print).

[CH85] A. Chandra and D. Harel. Horn clause queries and generalizations. *Journal of Logic Programming*, 1:1–15, 1985.

[CKRP73] A. Colmerauer, H. Kanoui, P. Roussel, and R. Passero. *Un Systeme de Communication Homme-Machine en Francais*. Research report, Groupe de Recherche en Intelligence Artificielle, Universite d'Aix-Marseille, 1973.

[Cla79] K.L. Clark. *Predicate Logic as a Computational Mechanism*. Research report 79/59, Dept. of Computing, Imperial College, 1979.

[Fit85] M. Fitting. A Kripke-Kleene semantics for logic programs. *Journal of Logic Programming*, 2(4):295–312, 1985.

[Gel87] M. Gelfond. On stratified autoepistemic theories. In *Proceedings AAAI-87*, pages 207–211, American Association for Artificial Intelligence, Morgan Kaufmann, Los Altos, CA, 1987.

[GL88a]   M. Gelfond and V. Lifschitz. Compiling circumscriptive theories into logic programs. In *Proceedings of the Second Workshop on Non-monotonic Reasoning, Munich, July 1988*, 1988. to appear.

[GL88b]   M. Gelfond and V. Lifschitz. The stable model semantics for logic programming. In R. Kowalski and K. Bowen, editors, *Proceedings of the Fifth Logic Programming Symposium*, pages 1070–1080, Association for Logic Programming, MIT Press, Cambridge, Mass., 1988.

[GMN84]   H. Gallaire, J. Minker, and J. Nicolas. Logic and databases: a deductive approach. *ACM Computing Surveys*, 16:153–185, 1984.

[GPP89]   M. Gelfond, H. Przymusinska, and T. Przymusinski. On the relationship between circumscription and negation as failure. *Journal of Artificial Intelligence*, 38:75–94, 1989.

[Kow74]   R. Kowalski. Predicate logic as a programming language. In *Proceedings of IFIP-74*, pages 569–574, 1974.

[Kow79]   R. Kowalski. Algorithm = logic + control. *Communications of the ACM*, 22:424–436, 1979.

[Kun87]   K. Kunen. Negation in logic programming. *Journal of Logic Programming*, 4(4):289–308, 1987.

[Kun88]   K. Kunen. Some remarks on the completed database. In R. Kowalski and K. Bowen, editors, *Proceedings of the Fifth Logic Programming Symposium*, pages 978–992, Association for Logic Programming, MIT Press, Cambridge, Mass., 1988.

[Lif85]   V. Lifschitz. Computing circumscription. In *Proceedings IJCAI-85*, pages 121–127, American Association for Artificial Intelligence, Morgan Kaufmann, Los Altos, CA, 1985.

[Lif86]   V. Lifschitz. On the satisfiability of circumscription. *Journal of Artificial Intelligence*, 28:17–27, 1986.

[Lif87]   V. Lifschitz. On the declarative semantics of logic programs with negation. In J. Minker, editor, *Foundations of Deductive Databases and Logic Programming*, pages 177–192, Morgan Kaufmann, Los Altos, CA., 1987.

[Llo84]   J.W. Lloyd. *Foundations of Logic Programming*. Springer Verlag, New York, N.Y., first edition, 1984.

[LT85]   J.W. Lloyd and R.W. Topor. A basis for deductive database systems. *Journal of Logic Programming*, 2:93–109, 1985.

[LT86]   J.W. Lloyd and R.W. Topor. A basis for deductive database systems ii. *Journal of Logic Programming*, 3:55–67, 1986.

[McC60]   J. McCarthy. Programs with common sense. In *Proceedings of the Teddington Conference on the Mechanisation of Thought Processes*, pages 77–84, Her Majesty's Stationary Office, London, 1960.

[McC77]   J. McCarthy. Epistemological problems in artificial intelligence. In *Proceedings of IJCAI-77*, pages 1038–1044, American Association for Artificial Intelligence, Morgan Kaufmann, Los Altos, CA, 1977.

[McC80]   J. McCarthy. Circumscription – a form of non-monotonic reasoning. *Journal of Artificial Intelligence*, 13:27–39, 1980.

[McC86]   J. McCarthy. Applications of circumscription to formalizing common sense knowledge. *Journal of Artificial Intelligence*, 28:89–116, 1986.

[McC87]   J. McCarthy. *Mathematical Logic in Artificial Intelligence*. Research report, Stanford University, 1987.

[McD82]   D. McDermott. Non-monotonic logic ii. *Journal of the ACM*, 29(1):33–57, 1982.

[McD87]   D. McDermott. A critique of pure reason. *Computational Intelligence*, 1987.

[MD80]   D. McDermott and J. Doyle. Non-monotonic logic i. *Journal of Artificial Intelligence*, 13:41–72, 1980.

[MH69]   J. McCarthy and P. Hayes. Some philosophical problems from the standpoint of artificial intelligence. *Machine Intelligence*, 4:463–502, 1969.

[Min75]   M. Minsky. A framework for representing knowledge. In P. Winston, editor, *The Psychology of Computer Vision*, MIT Press, New York, 1975.

[Min82]   J. Minker. On indefinite data bases and the closed world assumption. In *Proc. 6-th Conference on Automated Deduction*, pages 292–308, Springer Verlag, New York, 1982.

[Min89]   J. Minker. Perspectives in deductive databases. *Journal of Logic Programming*, 1989. (In print.).

[Moo85]   R.C. Moore. Semantic considerations on non-monotonic logic. *Journal of Artificial Intelligence*, 25:75–94, 1985.

[MUG86]   K. Morris, J.D. Ullman, and A. Van Gelder. Design overview of the nail! system. In *Proceedings of the Third International Conference on Logic Programming, London, July 1986*, Association for Logic Programming, Springer Verlag, 1986.

[Naq86]   S.A. Naqvi. A logic for negation in database systems. In J. Minker, editor, *Proceedings of the Workshop on Foundations of Deductive Databases and Logic Programming, Washington, D.C.*, pages 378–387, August 1986.

[Nil87]   N.J. Nilsson. Logic and artificial intelligence. In *MIT Workshop on Foundations of AI*, 1987.

[PP88]   H. Przymusinska and T. Przymusinski. Weakly perfect model semantics for logic programs. In R. Kowalski and K. Bowen, editors, *Proceedings of the Fifth Logic Programming Symposium*, pages 1106–1122, Association for Logic Programming, MIT Press, Cambridge, Mass., 1988.

[Prz87]   T. Przymusinski. On the declarative semantics of stratified deductive databases and logic programs. In J. Minker, editor, *Foundations of Deductive Databases and Logic Programming*, pages 193–216, Morgan Kaufmann, Los Altos, CA., 1987.

[Prz88a] T. Przymusinski. Non-monotonic reasoning vs. logic programming: a new perspective. In D. Partridge and Y. Wilks, editors, *Formal Foundations of Artificial Intelligence*, Cambridge University Press, London, 1988. In print. (Extended abstract appeared in: T. Przymusinski. On the relationship between non-monotonic reasoning and logic programming. In *Proceedings AAAI-88*, pages 444–448, American Association for Artificial Intelligence, Morgan Kaufmann, Los Altos, CA, 1988.).

[Prz88b] T. Przymusinski. On the declarative and procedural semantics of logic programs. *Journal of Automated Reasoning*, 4, 1988. In print. (Extended abstract appeared in: T. Przymusinski. Perfect model semantics. In R. Kowalski and K. Bowen, editors, *Proceedings of the Fifth Logic Programming Symposium*, pages 1081–1096, Association for Logic Programming, MIT Press, Cambridge, Mass., 1988.).

[Prz89a] T. Przymusinski. Every logic program has a natural stratification and an iterated fixed point model. In *Proceedings of the Eighth Symposium on Principles of Database Systems*, ACM SIGACT-SIGMOD, 1989. (In print).

[Prz89b] T. Przymusinski. Three-valued non-monotonic formalisms and logic programming. In *Proceedings of the First International Conference on Principles of Knowledge Representation and Reasoning (KR'89)*, Toronto, Canada, 1989. (In print).

[Rei78] R. Reiter. On closed-world data bases. In H. Gallaire and J. Minker, editors, *Logic and Data Bases*, pages 55–76, Plenum Press, New York, 1978.

[Rei80] R. Reiter. A logic for default theory. *Journal of Artificial Intelligence*, 13:81–132, 1980.

[Rei84] R. Reiter. Towards a logical reconstruction of relational database theory. In M. Brodie and J. Mylopoulos, editors, *On Conceptual Modelling*, pages 191–233, Springer Verlag, New York, 1984.

[Rei86] R. Reiter. Nonmonotonic reasoning. *Annual Reviews of Computer Science*, 1986.

[Rob65] J. Robinson. A machine-oriented logic based on the resolution principle. *Journal of the ACM*, 12:23–41, 1965.

[Ros89] K. Ross. A procedural semantics for well founded negation in logic programs. In *Proceedings of the Eighth Symposium on Principles of Database Systems*, ACM SIGACT-SIGMOD, 1989. (In print).

[Rou75] P. Roussel. *PROLOG, Manuel de Reference et d'Utilisation*. Research report, Group d'Intelligence Artificielle, U.E.R. de Marseille, France, 1975.

[She84] J. Shepherdson. Negation as finite failure: a comparison of clark's completed data bases and reiter's closed world assumption. *Journal of Logic Programming*, 1:51–79, 1984.

[She87]   J.C. Shepherdson. Negation in logic programming. In J. Minker, editor, *Foundations of Deductive Databases and Logic Programming*, pages 19–88, Morgan Kaufmann, Los Altos, CA., 1987.

[VG87]   A. Van Gelder. Negation as failure using tight derivations for general logic programs. In J. Minker, editor, *Foundations of Deductive Databases and Logic Programming*, pages 149–176, Morgan Kaufmann, Los Altos, CA., 1987.

[VG89]   A. Van Gelder. The alternating fixpoint of logic programs with negation. In *Proceedings of the Symposium on Principles of Database Systems*, ACM SIGACT-SIGMOD, 1989. (to appear).

[VGRS88]   A. Van Gelder, K. Ross, and Schlipf. Unfounded sets and well-founded semantics for general logic programs. In *Proceedings of the Symposium on Principles of Database Systems*, ACM SIGACT-SIGMOD, 1988.

[Zan88]   C. Zaniolo. Design and implementation of logic-based language for data intensive applications. In R. Kowalski and K. Bowen, editors, *Proceedings of the Fifth Logic Programming Symposium*, pages 1666–1688, Association for Logic Programming, MIT Press, Cambridge, Mass., 1988.

A Logical Database Query Language
with Object Identity and Strong Typing

Paris Kanellakis
Serge Abiteboul

INRIA
Rocquencourt, BP 105
78153, Le Chesnay Cedex, France
paris@bdblues.altair.fr, abitebou@inria.inria.fr

Abstract

We clarify some of the foundations of object-oriented databases. We show that, while these do involve an excursion into new realms, they are wholly compatible with the classical theory of logic and databases. In particular, we demonstrate that the concept of object identity is a powerful programming primitive for database query languages: by having it as the centerpiece of a data model with a rich type system and a complete query language, called Identity Query Language (IQL). Our structural and operational framework generalizes most of the previous work on complex-object databases and on logical database query languages. Programs in IQL consist of logical rules, that are strongly typed. Also, because we allow union types, we can easily add type inheritance to the model. In this invited lecture, our exposition is by an extended set of examples and we refer to [5] for the many important technical details.

1   Introduction

We demonstrate the power of *object identities* (oid's) as a database query language primitive. We develop an object-based data model, whose structural part generalizes most of the known complex-object data models: cyclicity is allowed in both its schemas and instances. The conceptual contribution, which we explain here by detailed examples, is the *Identity Query Language* (IQL). This operational part of the data model uses oid's for three critical purposes: (1) to represent data-structures with sharing and cycles, (2) to manipulate sets and (3) to express any computable database query.

IQL is both a mathematical model of computation with types

and a useful high level query language. Like pure Prolog, it can be used to manipulate unbounded structured terms in full generality. Unlike pure Prolog, it is typed, it has negation, it is a good candidate for conventional database optimizations, and its semantics are not complicated by depth-first search strategies. Also, the object-based data model can be extended to incorporate type inheritance, without changes to IQL. For those interested in the object-based vs valued-based issue, we would like to note that: there is an analogous value-based data model whose structural part is founded on regular infinite trees and whose operational part is IQL (see [5]).

The main motivation of our work was the study of object-oriented database systems. It is quite probable that these will be the next generation of commercial database systems (see [10]). They are currently the focus of a great deal of experimentation and research, e.g., [39,45,13,22,16,12]. These recent developments in databases are largely based on concepts and software tools from object-oriented programming, e.g., [23,10,29]. More generally, the integration of programming languages and database systems is an important research and development activity, for a detailed exposition of the state-of-the-art see [9].

Unfortunately, much of the terminology currently used in object-oriented database systems is overloaded and experts disagree on the precise meaning of concepts such as: "object-identity, types, inheritance, methods and encapsulation etc." Consequently, there has been very little progress on understanding the "principles of object-oriented databases". This is in marked contrast with the previous generation of database systems, where the relational model of [18] provided the basis for many successful implementation efforts and, at the same time, for the development of an elegant and relevant theory [43,27].

Here, we examine "oid's and types" in some detail. Oid's have been part of many data models, for example they are called *surrogates* in [19], *l-values* in [34], or *object identifiers* in [3]. They have recently been highlighted as an essential part of object-oriented database systems [28]. A variety of reasons have been given for their use, e.g., structure sharing, updates [3] or the encoding of cyclicity [34]. As mentioned above we make a more general use of oid's. At an intuitive level, oid's are "typed pointers" and IQL is based on a *controlled use of indirection*.

677

The types are an element of the structural part of our *object-based model*. This part is really a synthesis of elements that existed in the literature. It generalizes the relational data model [18], most complex-object data models, e.g., [1,41,26,31,40,44], and the logical data model (LDM) [34,32]. It can be viewed as the common upper bound of the models used in [34,1]. The pleasant surprise is that little mathematical simplicity had to be traded-off in order to achieve this synthesis.

The operational part of the data model, the language IQL, is also surprisingly simple both in syntax and semantics. It has three basic properties: (1) it is a rule-based, (2) it can be statically type checked, and (3) it is complete, in the sense that it expresses exactly all database transformations with certain desirable properties. Let us comment on these three points: (1) highlights the logical and declarative nature of the programming paradigm used, (2) illustrates what is controlled about the use of pointers, and (3) involves generalizing the basic theorem of [17] from the relational model to a data model with first-order and recursive types.

As in the relational model, there is a clear separation of the notions of instance and schema. As a consequence, the typing of IQL is similar to that of query languages in [34,1,2] and corresponds to strong typing in programming languages. A number of recent language proposals in this area do not have these properties. For example, in [11,38,35] there is no instance-schema separation and the query languages can be viewed as untyped variations of Prolog.

One motivation for our work was the study of the formal aspects of the O_2 system, [12,37,36]. O_2 is a multilanguage object-oriented database system, whose types resemble those of our model. The operational part of O_2 is based on general purpose programming languages, such as C or *Basic*, enriched with language independent statements for database objects. Features of IQL, such as strong typing, relations as temporaries, oid-invention, assign-to-oid and value-of-oid, have been incorporated in this language independent formalism.

In Sections 2 and 3, we give brief overviews (by example) of the structural and operational parts of our data model. In Section 4, we comment on extensions of the framework for incorporating type inheritance. In Section 5, we comment on a value-based alternative. Finally in Section 6, we summarize the key ideas, that we believe are independent of the chosen programming paradigm (e.g., logical or functional).

2   The Structural Part

First the basic building blocks: these we call *o-values*, i.e., values containing oid's. Oid's and constants (such as strings) are o-values, but so are finite trees built-out of constants and oid's via finite tuple or set constructors.

An *instance* consists of "data" in the form of: (1) *finite sets of o-values* and (2) a *partial function ν* from oid's to o-values; this mapping is the essence of the data model.

We allow ν to be partial; this is in order to model *incomplete information* and will be very useful in the operational part of the model.

A *schema* contains the information on the structure of the data allowed in an instance. In popular terminology, it contains the names and types of "persistent data". We have chosen to include two forms of information: (1) *relation names R* for naming *relations*, finite sets of o-values of the same type $\mathbf{T}(R)$, and (2) *class names P* for naming *classes*, finite sets of oid's, where these oid's are mapped through ν to o-values of the same type $\mathbf{T}(P)$. An important assumption is that the classes of any legal instance are pairwise disjoint sets of oid's.

Our types $\mathbf{T}$ include: *base types, tuple types, finite set types, union types and recursive types.* The type language and interpretation is somewhat nonstandard for the recursive case (i.e., without a μ constructor). The subtle point is that: the recursion is captured by having the types $\mathbf{T}(R)$ and $\mathbf{T}(P)$ refer to base domains or class names. (The mathematical analog is the theory of non-well founded sets of Aczel).

Example 2.1 (From *Genesis* 4 and 5.) Schema S has class names *1st-generation, 2nd-generation* and relation names *founded-lineage, ancestor-of-celebrity.* Their types are defined as follows:

$\mathbf{T}(\textit{1st-generation}) =$
[name: *string*, spouse: *1st-generation*, children: {*2nd-generation*}]
$\mathbf{T}(\textit{2nd-generation}) =$ [name: *string*, occupations: {*string*}]

$\mathbf{T}(\textit{founded-lineage}) = \textit{2nd-generation}$
$\mathbf{T}(\textit{ancestor-of-celebrity}) =$
[anc: *2nd-generation*, desc: (*string* $\vee$ [spouse: *string*])]

Note that the types refer to base domain, e.g., *string*, and to class names, e.g., *1st-generation*, but not to relation names. Also, note the cyclicity in the type associated with *1st-generation* and the presence of union types.

Now let us come to an instance I of S. To each relation name R, the instance associates a finite set $\rho(R)$ of o-values of the right type. So, strictly speaking, the type of $\rho(R)$ is $\{\mathbf{T}(R)\}$. To each class name P, the instance associates a finite set $\pi(P)$ of oid's. Classes are assigned disjoint sets of oid's. The partial function ν assigns o-values to the oid's of the instance. Each one of these oid's has a value of the right type or is undefined. So, again strictly speaking, the type of $\pi(P)$ is $\{P\}$ and the type of $\nu(\pi(P))$ is $\{\mathbf{T}(P)\}$.

In instance I, we denote the oid's as *adam, eve, cain, abel, seth, other*. Note that *adam* is distinct from string Adam. I is cyclic, see this by following the ν mapping of the oid's.

$\pi(\textit{1st-generation}) = \{\ adam,\ eve\ \}$,
$\pi(\textit{2nd-generation}) = \{\ cain,\ abel,\ seth,\ other\ \}$,

$\rho(\textit{founded-lineage}) = \{\ cain,\ seth,\ other\ \}$,
$\rho(\textit{ancestor-of-celebrity}) =$
$\{$ [anc: *seth*, desc: Noah], [anc: *cain*, desc: [spouse: Ada]] $\}$,

$\nu(adam) =$
[name: Adam, spouse: *eve*, children: $\{$ *cain, abel, seth, other* $\}$],
$\nu(eve) =$
[name: Eve, spouse: *adam*, children: $\{$ *cain, abel, seth, other* $\}$]
$\nu(cain) =$
[name: Cain, occupations: $\{$ Farmer, Nomad, Artisan $\}$],
$\nu(abel) =$ [name: Abel, occupations: $\{$ Shepherd $\}$],
$\nu(seth) =$ [name: Seth, occupations: $\{\ \}$]
$\nu(other)$ is undefined. (*Genesis* is rather vague on this point). $\square$

The dichotomy between relations and classes is the only design decision that slightly complicates the structural part. Its justification is that it greatly simplifies the operational part. Since relations are sets of o-values, duplicates are eliminated from them at a logical level. Thus, it is possible to program directly in popular rule-based formalisms, e.g., Datalog (that is pure Prolog without function symbols). Relations can name subsets of classes and function as useful temporaries. Also, this distinction allows a direct generalization of both [34] and [1].

3   The Operational Part

The design of IQL was greatly influenced by both the COL language of [2], for the manipulation of sets, and the detDL language of [7], for the invention of new oid's. The focus was on adding the minimum to Datalog rules in order to obtain an object-based language, that can express all computable queries.

In summary, IQL is inflationary Datalog with negation [7,30], *combined with set/tuple types, invention of new oid's, and a weak form of assignment.*

Inflationary semantics has been chosen because of its simplicity and its generality as a control flow mechanism. Other (perhaps more practical) alternatives are possible.

The flexibility of a type system, such as the one used here, allows multiple representations of the same information. For example, a directed graph may be represented as a binary relation whose tuples are the arcs of the graph or as a class whose type is recursive. In the second representation each node has an oid, a name, and a set of descendant nodes. IQL allows converting the first representation into the second and vice-versa. Thus, it is possible *to go from acyclic to cyclic schemas.* IQL is the first database language with this property. The following example illustrates most of the features of IQL on this very transformation.

Example 3.1 Let the input schema be just a relation R with $\mathbf{T}(R)$ = $[A_1{:}D, A_2{:}D]$ and the output schema be a class P with $\mathbf{T}(P)$ = $[A_1{:}D, A_2{:}\{P\}]$. The input instance I represents a directed graph G with nodes in D. The desired query is to transform the input instance I into an output instance J representing the same graph. Note that in this new representation every node is associated with an oid, whose value is the pair with the node name for first component, and the set of successors for second component. Note also that the individual oid's used in the output do not matter only their interrelationships do. Let us examine the computation in IQL in four stages:

During the first stage, we produce (in standard Datalog fashion) the set of node names. We use a relation R_0 with $\mathbf{T}(R_0) = [A_1 : D]$. As a shorthand, we do not list the attributes $A_1, A_2, A_3, \ldots$ in the rules, but think of them as first argument of relation, second argument of relation etc. The following rules are used:

$$R_0(x) \leftarrow R(x, y)$$

$R_0(x) \leftarrow R(y, x)$

In the second stage, we produce two oid's per node using a semantics in the style of detDL [7]. We use a relation R' with $\mathbf{T}(R')$ $=[A_1 : D, A_2 : P, A_3 : P']$ whose tuples contain oid's from class P and from another class P'. Class P' is a class with $\mathbf{T}(P') =\{P\}$, i.e., it's oid's have values that are sets of oid's from P. The following rule invents two oid's for each node, one of which will go into class P and the other into class P'.

$R'(x, p, p') \leftarrow R_o(x)$

Note how the variables p, p' in the head are not in the body. When the new oid's are invented they are placed in the proper classes and they are automatically assigned default values: p is undefined and p' is the empty set (because of the set valued type of P').

In the third stage, we nest the oid's representing nodes in P into sets of successors of a node. This nesting of elements q is done by using the oid's p' of P' as temporary names. Each p' is set valued and its value, noted $\widehat{p'}$, is a set in which the corresponding q's are collected. This dereferencing and assignment to objects in P' simulates the effect of a COL data-function [2] or a grouping in LDL [14].

$\widehat{p'}(q) \leftarrow R'(x, p, p'), R'(y, q, q'), R(x, y)$

In the final stage, the nodes of P have been grouped into P', and the connection in R' between x, p, p' is used to produce the desired result. Note that the value of some node p is a tuple with the name of the node as first component, and a set of P-oid's as a second component. This weak form of assignment is performed only when $\hat{p}$ was undefined (see [4]). No further changes are made to $\hat{p}$.

$\hat{p} = [x, \widehat{p'}] \leftarrow R'(x, p, p')$

We have presented the program in four separate stages. We need not separate the stages. It is possible through standard techniques (using negation) to slightly modify the rules above and think of them as operating in parallel with inflationary semantics. A useful construct, definable in IQL, is that of sequential composition (;). In fact, only the last rule need to be modified by separating it with a (;) from the rest of the rules. $\square$

As illustrated by this example, IQL allows the creation of objects and the sharing of objects. It is somewhat surprising that this graph example uses most of the features of IQL such as: Datalog rules, set manipulation, invention of oid's (here bounded by a polynomial in the size of the input), composition, and weak assignment to non-set oid's. Now let us illustrate how various rule-based formalisms are embedded in IQL.

We accept $R(t_1,\ldots,t_k)$ as a notation for $R([A_1{:}t_1,\ldots,A_k{:}t_k])$, when some implicit ordering on the attributes is understood. Each *Datalog* program can be viewed as a valid IQL program on a relational schema, and its Datalog and IQL semantics are identical. The same applies to *Datalog with negation and inflationary semantics.*

Continuing with relational schemas, other relational languages can be viewed as IQL sublanguages, for example *detDL* [7]. The differences between detDL and IQL restricted to relations are: slightly different semantics for evaluation and invented constants in detDL versus invented oid's in IQL. However, it is very simple to simulate detDL in IQL.

It is shown in [7] that control mechanisms such as *composition,* *if-then-else,* and *while-statements* can be simulated in detDL (using negation and inflationary semantics). These mechanisms can now be used as shorthands. In particular, we use ";" to denote composition. The transformation expressed by an IQL program $\Gamma_1;\Gamma_2$ is the composition of the transformations expressed by Γ_1 and Γ_2. Using composition, *relational calculus* queries and *Datalog with stratified negation* are expressible in IQL almost verbatim.

Now consider complex-objects. The most famous operations on complex-objects are *nest* and *unnest.* Nest/unnest in IQL resembles the expression of these operations in the language *COL* [2]. The next example shows the IQL realization. For better clarity, we use capital letters, e.g., X,Y, for set variables.

Example 3.2 Let $(\mathbf{R},\mathbf{P},\mathbf{T})$ be a schema, R_1, R_2, $R_3 \in \mathbf{R}$,

$$\mathbf{T}(R_1)= \mathbf{T}(R_3)= [A_1{:}D,A_2{:}\{D\}], \text{ and } \mathbf{T}(R_2)= [A_1{:}D,A_2{:}D]$$

We want to unnest R_1 into R_2, and then nest R_2 into R_3. For unnesting, use the single rule:

$\quad R_2(x,y) \leftarrow R_1(x,Y), Y(y).$

For nesting, use an auxiliary class P associated with $\mathbf{T}(P) = \{D\}$, and auxiliary relations R_4, R_5 associated with $\mathbf{T}(R_4) = D$, $\mathbf{T}(R_5) = [A_1{:}D,A_2{:}P]$.

Nesting is realized with $\Gamma_1;\Gamma_2$ where Γ_1 is:

$\quad R_4(x) \leftarrow R_2(x,y)$
$\quad R_5(x,z) \leftarrow R_4(x)$
$\quad \widehat{z}(y) \leftarrow R_2(x,y), R_5(x,z)$

and Γ_2:

$\quad R_3(x,\widehat{z}) \leftarrow R_5(x,z)$

Γ_1 creates one oid z per x in the A_1-column of R_2. The value of the oid z is the set of values paired to its x in the A_2-column of R_2. The program Γ_2 starts after Γ_1 completes and constructs the result. Note how attributes were omitted from the rules, without any ambiguity. $\square$

One can show that each COL query can be computed using an IQL program. The proof is easy given the above programs for nest/unnest. As a consequence, all *algebraic operations on complex objects* of [41, 26,40,1], and the calculus queries of [1,31] are expressible in IQL. Also, it is easy to show that all calculus and algebra queries in LDM can be simulated in IQL.

One important operation found in the algebra for LDM and the algebra for complex-objects of [1] is *powerset*. This operation is expensive: it is exponential in the input size. Indeed, in [5], we emphasize sublanguages of IQL that cannot express the powerset, but can express important classes of queries evaluable in time polynomial in the input instance size. The powerset operation is considered in the next example. This example provides all the necessary guidelines for the "range" restrictions that are imposed on IQL in [5] in order to obtain efficiently evaluable sublanguages.

Example 3.3 First suppose that the input consists of a single relation R of type D and the output, of a single relation R_1 of type $\{D\}$. The powerset of R is computed in R_1 by:

$$R_1(X) \leftarrow X = X$$

where X is a variable of type $\{D\}$. Indeed, since R is the single input relation, by the definition of valuation (given I), the variable X will range only over the subsets of R, and R_1 will contain the powerset of R.

The obvious problem is that the variable X is not *range-restricted* in the program. However, the powerset can also be computed in a range-restricted manner using oid's. Let R and R_1 be the input and output as above. We also use a class P with type $\{D\}$, and an auxiliary relation R_2 with type $[A_1{:}\{D\}, A_2{:}\{D\}, A_3{:}P]$.

The powerset program consists of the rules:

$$R_1(\{\}) \leftarrow$$
$$R_1(\{x\}) \leftarrow R(x)$$
$$R_2(X,Y,z) \leftarrow R_1(X), R_1(Y)$$
$$\hat{z}(x) \leftarrow R_2(X,Y,z), X(x)$$
$$\hat{z}(y) \leftarrow R_2(X,Y,z), Y(y)$$

$R_1(\widehat{z}) \leftarrow P(z).$

One can check that this computes the powerset in a constructive way. Suppose that relation R is $\{d_1, d_2, d_3\}$. Then $\{\}$, $\{d_1\}$, $\{d_2\}$, $\{d_3\}$ are first obtained then $\{d_1, d_2\}$, $\{d_2, d_3\}$, etc. In this computation some subsets are obviously derived more than once.

Note that in this second way of computing the powerset, invention of oid's occurs in a "loop". Such recursion with invention of oid's may clearly be the cause of nonterminating computations. For instance, let R_3 be a relation with $\mathbf{T}(R_3) = [A_1{:}P, A_2{:}P]$. Then the rule

$R_3(y,z) \leftarrow R_3(x,y)$

may cause the nontermination of the computation. $\square$

The union of types is treated in IQL in a special fashion. This is based on allowing the use of a less constrained typing condition in the rule bodies, (i.e., allowing a certain form of *coercion*). The following is an example involving union types.

Example 3.4 Consider the two schemas:

S has one class P with $\mathbf{T}(P) = P \vee [A_1 : P, A_2 : P]$. S' has one class P' with $\mathbf{T}'(P') = [A_1 : \{P'\}, A_2 : \{[A_1 : P', A_2 : P']\}]$.

We use one temporary relation R with $\mathbf{T}(R) = [A_1 : P, A_2 : P']$ and omit the attributes, when there is no ambiguity.

The first program encodes an instance with union types into an instance without union types. Applying the second program on the output of the first produces an instance identical (up-to renaming of the oid's) with the input of the first program. Thus, no information is lost when using the first program.

S instances can be "losslessly" transformed to S' instances using the rules:

$R(x, x') \leftarrow P(x)$
$\widehat{x}' = [\{y'\}, \emptyset] \leftarrow R(x, x'), R(y, y'), y = \widehat{x}$
$\widehat{x}' = [\emptyset, \{[y', z']\}] \leftarrow R(x, x'), R(y, y'), R(z, z'), [y, z] = \widehat{x}.$

An "inverse" mapping from S' to S can be realized using the rules:

$R(x, x') \leftarrow P'(x')$
$\widehat{x} = w \leftarrow R(x, x'), R(y, y'), y = w, \widehat{x}' = [\{y'\}, \emptyset]$
$\widehat{x} = w \leftarrow R(x, x'), R(y, y'), R(z, z'), [y, z] = w, \widehat{x}' = [\emptyset, \{[y', z']\}].$

Note the use of coercions in the bodies. For instance, in the the first program, $\widehat{x}$ is of type $P \vee [A_1{:}P, A_2{:}P]$, whereas y, z are of type P.

In the second program, w has type $P \vee [A_1{:}P,A_2{:}P]$, different from the types of y and $[y, z]$. We use w in order to have typed heads. $\square$

An important primitive in the language is the invention of oid's. This serves a triple goal: (1) objects may be part of the result and oid's must be assigned to them, (2) invented oid's are used for set manipulation, (3) they are also used to obtain completeness in the sense of [17]. The reason we use (1) is to code sharing of structures and cyclic structures. Regarding (2), the rule-based language does not need to have any mechanism such as *grouping* in LDL [14], *data-functions* in COL [2], or *universal quantification* [33]. Thus, one of our contributions is to show that: *the manipulation and creation of sets can be realized only using invented oid's.* For (3), the notion of completeness of [17] is adapted to our context.

Intuitively, the language must capture all transformations that are recursively enumerable and that preserve some isomorphism properties [17,24]. Completeness results have been shown for the relational [17,6,7] and for many complex-object data models [21,8,25]. Our notion of completeness is more general than the notion used in [17,7]. However, on relational schemas, the two notions coincide. The originality of our extension comes from the presence of oid's: two instances are viewed as identical if they are isomorphic up-to renaming of oid's. A basic contribution of [5] is a completeness result for IQL.

Theorem: *For disjoint input and output schemas, all database transformations are expressible in IQL, up to copy elimination.*

In many cases we can express copy elimination in IQL, but it is open if this technical restriction is necessary. Disjoint input-output schemas are sufficient for the study of queries and updates, such as insertions. To obtain completeness for non-disjoint schemas, we need to add non-inflationary features to IQL. These are based on the study of deletions in [7].

IQL can be specilized using a number of syntactic "range restrictions". This specialization allows us to discover as "range restricted" IQL sublanguages most of the popular rule-based formalisms. Also in [5], we show that these restrictions can be used to guarantee efficient query evaluation, i.e., with PTIME *data-complexity.*

The subsequent sections of our paper deal with two issues which, we believe are orthogonal to the structural and the operational parts of our object-based model. The first is type inheritance and the second is the relationship of object-based with value-based.

4   Type Inheritance and Union Types

In all the development of IQL, we make crucial use of a technical condition, the pairwise disjointness of the various classes of an instance. This condition guarantees the soundness and the static typability of IQL programs. However, the removal of this condition is necessary if one is to study *type inheritance* as proposed in [15].

With inheritance, the disjointness condition on the classes is replaced by a less restricted condition that, we argue, is natural. This is that oid assignments to classes are *inherited: objects are created in one class and automatically belong to all of its superclasses.* The type inheritance ala [15] is possible using this assumption and a slight modification of the type semantics.

Thus, in [5], we argue that type inheritance has simple semantics. The use of the union type constructor is critical in this development. What we essentially observe is that: *the union type is a more general mechanism for sharing structure than type inheritance.* As a result, IQL can be used, at no cost of expressive power, to deal with schemas with inheritance. Our approach is intended to show the existence, in the presence of inheritance, of a statically typable and complete database query language. This is interesting, because it is not obvious that static typing, inheritance and completeness are all compatible notions.

Also, our definition of type inheritance allows the precise formulation of a number of important, new database query language problems. What happens to static typing, inheritance and completeness if union types are not provided? Practical languages make direct use of inheritance, by allowing some forms of value coercions. What is a good coercion strategy, that does not trade-off static typing or completeness?

5   Value-Based vs Object-Based

Oid's can be viewed as a syntactic trick to avoid manipulating recursive objects. The same is true for the use of class names in the type syntax. Even with these devices, recursive structures stay in the background in a fundamental way. Intuitively, repeated applications on oid's of the ν mapping of an instance yield *pure values*, that are regular infinite trees.

Object-based systems often allow features such as *equality-by-value*, which is a precise way of addressing the underlying infinite objects. In [5], we illustrate a natural connection with a *value-based model* founded on regular infinite trees [20]. Our analysis allows us to show that IQL can serve as a language for this model as well. Object identities, in this context, loose all semantic denotation to become purely, primitives of the language. This is a nontrivial link between value-based and object-based [42].

A value-based point of view can be used to understand *pure-values* (no oid's), *pure types* (no class names in the type syntax) and *equality-by-value* (as a coercion mechanism for realizing inheritance).

6   Some Design Principles

The language IQL is based on a logic programming paradigm. We believe that any statically typable language, based on a different paradigm but expressing the same database transformations, would have many fundamental similarities with IQL. In particular, the following features appear as central.

Types: The concrete types used here are present in most object-oriented databases. Their type constructors largely determine what terms must be available in the language. Typing the language serves *both* for correctness and for efficiency. Efficiency is the main justification for the separation of database schema and instance, as well as for the requirement of static type checking.

Basic query and update capabilities: The means must be there to easily extract information from the database and modify its state. It should be easy to express common queries, e.g., sets of conjunctive queries on complex-objects. It should be possible to both: find the *value-of-oid*'s and to *assign-values* to oid's. Weak forms of assignment suffice for queries and insertions, but deletions introduce a certain amount of complexity.

Flow of control capabilities: The means must be available for realizing sequential composition and looping. In rules, this can be provided by inflationary semantics and negation (but there are also more practical alternatives like stratification together with looping).

Cyclicity and oid's: There is some subtlety in the use of oid's to code and manipulate cyclic structures, since these are represented in an acyclic manner by o-values. To deal with cyclicity, controlled use of typed pointers should be a key component of the language.

Invention of oid's: A primitive for oid invention must be in the language. We believe that this is necessary, if unbounded structures are to be constructed. Invention is a powerful mechanism; it is crucial if arbitrary computations are to be simulated and it should be carefully restricted. Also, oid invention can be very useful for manipulating set types.

Relations vs classes: This dichotomy is essential for being able to express simple queries in a simple manner. We think that without this (in some sense) redundancy, the language will have difficulties in maintaining temporary results, eliminating duplicates, and it will use indirection excessively.

Incomplete information: Incomplete information is important for a variety of database applications. The (benign) form of incomplete information that we use seems fundamental if complex cyclic structures have to be created in stages.

Type inheritance and coercions: For union types, our language employs coercion and inheritance is handled indirectly, through union types. If a language is to use inheritance directly, it will need sophisticated coercion strategies. Finally, inheritance and union types need not be the only means to specify structure sharing. One might use other forms of polymorphism, e.g., parametric types, abstraction over types.

We have investigated *object-identity, types* and *type inheritance.* There are other aspects of object-oriented database systems that our mathematical model cannot capture. For example, O_2 emphasizes programming in a modular fashion, by having *methods* attached to classes and by accessing data only through these methods (*encapsulation*). Moreover, sharing of programs is possible via *method inheritance.* We view these *abstract data type* issues as largely orthogonal to the *concrete data types* studied here. Our design principles above are meant to address one question: "what should be the computational capabilities of a query language for an object-oriented database?"

Acknowledgements: P. Kanellakis would like to acknowledge the support of INRIA / GIP Altaïr, where he is spending a one year leave from Brown University. His work has also been supported by: NSF grant IRI-8617344 and an Alfred P. Sloan Fellowship. The work of S. Abiteboul was supported by the PRC BD3.

References

[1] S. Abiteboul and C. Beeri. On the Power of Languages for the Manipulation of Complex Objects, INRIA Technical Report, No

846, 1988.

[2] S. Abiteboul and S. Grumbach. COL: a Logic-based Language for Complex Objects. In *Proc. EDBT*, 271–293, 1988.

[3] S. Abiteboul and R. Hull. IFO: A Formal Semantic Database Model. *ACM TODS*, 12:525–565, 1987.

[4] S. Abiteboul and R. Hull. Data-functions, Datalog and Negation. In *Proc. ACM SIGMOD*, 143–153, 1988.

[5] S. Abiteboul and P. Kanellakis. *Object Identity as a Query Language Primitive* INRIA Techical Report, March 1989. A preliminary version to appear in *Proc. ACM SIGMOD 89*.

[6] S. Abiteboul and V. Vianu. A Transaction Language Complete for Database Update and Specification, to appear in *JCSS*. In *Proc. ACM PODS*, 260–268, 1987.

[7] S. Abiteboul, V. Vianu. Procedural and Declarative Database Update Language. In *Proc. ACM PODS*, 240–250, 1988.

[8] S. Abiteboul and C. Beeri and M. Gyssens and D. van Gucht, An Introduction to the Completeness of Languages for Complex Objects and Nested Relations. To appear in Nested Relations and Complex Objects *Springer-Verlag*).

[9] M. Atkinson and P. Buneman. Types and Persistence in Database Programming Languages. *ACM Computing Surveys*, June 1987.

[10] F. Bancilhon. Object-Oriented Database Systems. In *Proc. ACM PODS*, 152–162, 1988.

[11] F. Bancilhon and S. Khoshafian. A Calculus for Complex Objects. In *Proc. ACM PODS*, 53–60, 1986.

[12] F. Bancilhon, G. Barbedette, V. Benzaken, C. Delobel, S. Gamerman, C. Lecluse, P. Pfeffer, P. Richard, and F. Velez. The Design and Implementation of O_2, an Object-Oriented Database System. In *Proc. OODBS2 Workshop*, Badmunster RFA, 1988.

[13] J. Banerjee, H.-T. Chou, J.F. Garza, W. Kim, D. Woelk, and N. Ballou. Data Model Issues for Object-Oriented Applications. *ACM TOIS*, 5:1:3–26, 1987.

[14] C. Beeri and al. Sets and Negation in a Logic Database Language (LDL1). In *Proc. ACM PODS*, 21–37, 1987.

[15] L. Cardelli. A Semantics of Multiple Inheritance. *Information and Computation*, 76:138–164, 1988.

[16] M.J. Carey, D.J. Dewitt, and S.L. Vandenberg. A Data Model and Query Language for EXODUS. In *Proc. ACM SIGMOD*, 413–423, 1988.

[17] A. Chandra and D. Harel. Computable Queries for Relational Data Bases. *JCSS*, 21:2:156–178, 1980.

[18] E.F. Codd. A Relational Model of Data for Large Shared Data Banks. *CACM*, 13:6:377–387, 1970.

[19] T. Codd. Extending the Database Relational Model to Capture more Meaning. *ACM TODS*, 4:4:397–434, 1979.

[20] B. Courcelle. Fundamental Properties of Infinite Trees. *TCS*, 25, 95–169, 1983.

[21] E. Dahlaus and J. Makowski. Computable Directory Queries. In *Proc. CAAP*, 1986. LNCS 214, Springer-Verlag.

[22] D. Fishman et al. Iris: an Object-Oriented Database Management System. *ACM TOIS*, 5:1:46–69, 1987.

[23] A. Goldberg and D. Robson. *Smalltalk 80, the Language and Implementation*. Addison-Wesley, 1983.

[24] R. Hull. Relative Information Capacity of Simple Relational Schemata. *Siam J. of Computing*, 15:3, 1986.

[25] R. Hull and J. Su. Untyped Sets, Invention and Computable Queries. In *Proc. ACM PODS* 1989. To appear.

[26] B. Jaeschke and H.J. Schek. Remarks on the Algebra of Non-first-normal-form Relations. In *Proc. ACM PODS*, 124–138, 1982.

[27] P. Kanellakis. *Elements of Relational Database Theory*. Brown U. Technical Report, 1988. To appear as a chapter in the Handbook of Theoretical Computer Science.

[28] S. Khoshafian and G. Copeland. Object Identity. In *Proc. OOP-SALA*, 1986.

[29] W. Kim. *A Foundation for Object-Oriented Databases*. Technical Report, MCC, 1988.

[30] P.G. Kolaitis and C.H. Papadimitriou. Why not Negation by Fixpoint? In *Proc. ACM PODS*, 231–239, 1988.

[31] H.F. Korth, M.A. Roth, and A. Silberschatz. *Extended Algebra and Calculus for not 1NF Relational Databases*. U. Texas Austin Technical Report, 1985.

[32] G.M. Kuper. *The Logical Data Model: a New Approach to Database Logic*. Stanford U., PhD thesis, 1985.

[33] G.M. Kuper. Logic Programming with Sets. In *Proc. ACM PODS*, 11-20, 1987.

[34] G.M. Kuper and M.Y. Vardi. A New Approach to Database Logic. In *Proc. ACM PODS*, 86–96, 1984.

[35] M. Kifer and J. Wu. A Logic for Object-Oriented Logic Programming (Maier's O-logic: Revisited). In *Proc. ACM PODS*, 1989. To appear.

[36] C. Lecluse and P. Richard. Modeling Complex Structures in Object-Oriented Databases. In *Proc. ACM PODS*, 1989. To appear.

[37] C. Lecluse, P. Richard, and F. Velez. O_2, an Object-Oriented Data Model. In *Proc. ACM SIGMOD*, 424-434, 1988.

[38] D. Maier. A Logic for Objects. In *Proc. of Workshop on Foundations of Deductive Databases and Logic Programming*, Washington USA, 1986.

[39] D. Maier, A. Otis, and A. Purdy. Development of an Object-Oriented Dbms. *Quarterly Bulletin of IEEE on Database Engineering*, 8, 1985.

[40] H. Schek and M. Scholl. The Relational Model with Relation-valued Attributes. *Information Systems*, 1986.

[41] S.J. Thomas and P.C. Fischer. Nested Relational Structures. In *Advances in Computing Research, Vol. 3, the Theory of Databases*, JAI press, 269–308, 1986.

[42] J.D. Ullman. Database Theory - Past and Future. In *Proc. ACM PODS*, 1–10, 1987.

[43] J.D. Ullman. *Principles of Database and Knowledge-Base Systems, Volume I.* Computer Science Press, 1988.

[44] J. Verso. *Verso: a Database Machine Based on non-1NF Relations.* INRIA Technical Report, 1986. (Verso is a pen name for the Verso team). To appear in Nested Relations and Complex Objects *Springer-Verlag.*

[45] S. Zdonik. Object Management Systems for Design Environments. *Quarterly Bulletin of IEEE on Database Engineering,* 8, 1985.